Productivity and Efficiency Analysis

Christopher J. O'Donnell

Productivity and Efficiency Analysis

An Economic Approach to Measuring and Explaining Managerial Performance

Springer

Christopher J. O'Donnell
University of Queensland
Brisbane, QLD, Australia

Additional material to this book can be downloaded from http://extras.springer.com.

ISBN 978-981-13-2982-1 ISBN 978-981-13-2984-5 (eBook)
https://doi.org/10.1007/978-981-13-2984-5

Library of Congress Control Number: 2018958930

This Springer imprint is published by the registered company Springer Nature Singapore Pte Ltd.
The registered company address is: 152 Beach Road, #21-01/04 Gateway East, Singapore 189721, Singapore

To the memory of my parents, Brian James and Arkley Jean.

Preface

This book provides a coherent description of the main economic concepts and statistical methods used to analyse managerial performance. It is primarily aimed at researchers, statisticians, accountants and economists working in regulatory authorities, government departments and private firms. The target audience also includes graduate students and academics. All readers are expected to have completed introductory university courses in economics, mathematics and statistics.

The book contains nine chapters. Chapter 1 provides a summary of the main ideas presented later in the book. Among other things, it explains exactly what is meant by the terms 'production technology', 'production environment', 'productivity' and 'efficiency'. Chapter 2 discusses various sets and functions that can be used to represent the input–output combinations that are possible using different technologies in different environments. The focus is on distance, revenue, cost and profit functions. Chapter 3 explains how to measure productivity change. In this book, measures of productivity change are defined as measures of output quantity change divided by measures of input quantity change. To explain changes in outputs and inputs, and therefore changes in productivity, we need to know something about managerial behaviour. Chapter 4 explains that firm managers tend to behave differently depending on what they value, and on what they can and cannot choose. It then discusses some of the simplest optimisation problems faced by managers (e.g. profit maximisation). Chapter 5 defines various measures of efficiency. Measures of efficiency can be viewed as *ex post* measures of how well managers have solved different optimisation problems. Estimating and predicting levels of efficiency involves estimating production frontiers. Chapter 6 explains how to estimate the parameters of piecewise frontiers. The focus of this chapter is on data envelopment analysis (DEA) estimators. Chapter 7 explains how to estimate the parameters of deterministic frontiers. Here, the focus is on least squares (LS) estimators. Chapter 8 explains how to estimate the parameters of stochastic frontiers. Here, the focus is on maximum likelihood (ML) estimators. Finally, Chap. 9 provides a practical step-by-step guide to analysing managerial performance. It also considers government policies that can be used to target the main drivers of performance.

There is enough material in Chap. 1 for a one- or two-day introductory course on productivity and efficiency analysis. There is enough material in the remaining chapters to build courses that can run over one or two semesters. Approximately eight hours of lectures and four hours in the computer laboratory should be enough to cover most of the material in Chaps. 2–5. Approximately twenty hours of lectures and another fifteen hours in the computer laboratoty should be enough to cover most of the material in Chaps. 6–8. A one-hour lecture and another hour in the computer laboratory is enough to cover the material in Chap. 9. These time estimates assume that students have little or no experience with computer programming. The empirical results reported in this book were obtained by running R Version 3.3.3 (2017-03-06) on a MacBookPro with an OS X 10.10.5 (Yosemite) operating system. The datasets and computer codes are available at http://extras.springer.com/2018. Slightly different results may be obtained by running different software packages (including more recent versions of R) on computers with different operating systems.

Parts of the book are somewhat repetitive. Some readers may find this annoying. However, it should help other readers see patterns in, and make connections between, seemingly unrelated concepts and techniques. It should also help some readers commit new material to memory. It also means that most chapters are reasonably self-contained, which should make the book more useful as a reference text.

Finally, some acknowledgements are due. Many of the definitions and concepts presented in the book were first developed while I was on sabbatical at the Universitat Autónoma de Barcelona in 2008. I would like to thank Emili Grifell-Tatjé for hosting me during that visit, and also the Generalitat de Catalunya for providing financial support. In the last decade, I have been refining the main ideas and bringing them together in the form of this book. During this time, I have received enormous encouragement from my wife, Adrienne, and my children, Benjamin, Lachlan, Joshua and Courtney; I cannot thank them enough for their patience and unwavering support. On an academic level, I am grateful for constructive comments provided by staff, students and academic visitors to the School of Economics at the University of Queensland. I am also grateful for feedback received during short courses delivered at the Australian Department of Health and Ageing (DoHA), the Australian Consumer and Competition Commission (ACCC), the Independent Hospital Pricing Authority (IHPA), the Victorian Department of Education and Early Childhood Development (DEECD), the University of Queensland, the University of Waikato, and the Australian Defence Force Academy (ADFA). Individuals who deserve special mention include (in alphabetical order) Julian Alston, Boris Bravo-Ureta, Cinzia Daraio, Rolf Färe, Finn Førsund, Bill Greene, Kristiaan Kerstens, Chris Parmeter, Antonio Peyrache, Victor Podinovski, Marshall Reinsdorf and Peter Schmidt. None of these individuals are in any way responsible for any errors in the book.

Brisbane, Australia
August 2018

Christopher J. O'Donnell

Contents

Acronyms

ADF	Augmented Dickey-Fuller
AR	Autoregressive
ARMA	Autoregressive moving average
BOD	Benefit-of-the-doubt
BP	Breusch-Pagan
CCD	Caves-Christensen-Diewert
CDF	Cumulative distribution function
CE	Cost efficiency
CES	Constant elasticity of substitution
CF	Chained Fisher
CGM	Chained generalised Malmquist
CLS	Corrected least squares
CNLS	Corrected nonlinear least squares
COLS	Corrected ordinary least squares
CRLS	Corrected restricted least squares
CRS	Constant returns to scale
CT	Chained Törnqvist
CTSLS	Corrected two-stage least squares
DEA	Data envelopment analysis
DF	Dickey-Fuller
DFA	Deterministic frontier analysis
DFM	Deterministic frontier model
DGP	Data generating process
DMU	Decision-making unit
DRS	Decreasing returns to scale
DW	Durbin-Watson
EKS	Elteto-Koves-Szulc
ETI	Environment and technology index
FDH	Free disposal hull
FGLS	Feasible generalised least squares

FP	Färe-Primont
GA	Growth accounting
GM	Generalised Malmquist
GY	Geometric Young
HM	Hicks-Moorsteen
HN	Hicks neutral
HPDI	Highest posterior density interval
IAE	Input-oriented allocative efficiency
IBOD	Implicit benefit-of-the-doubt
ICCD	Implicit Caves-Christensen-Diewert
ICT	Implicit chained Törnqvist
ID	Implicit dual
IEI	Input-oriented environment index
IETSMEI	Input-oriented environment, technology, and scale and mix efficiency index
IGY	Implicit geometric Young
IHIN	Implicit Hicks input neutral
IHON	Implicit Hicks output neutral
IL	Implicit Lowe
IM	Input-oriented Malmquist
IME	Input-oriented mix efficiency
IMEI	Input-oriented mix efficiency index
IMR	Input-oriented metatechnology ratio
IRRI	International Rice Research Institute
IRS	Increasing returns to scale
ISAE	Input-oriented scale and allocative efficiency
ISE	Input-oriented scale efficiency
ISEI	Input-oriented scale efficiency index
ISME	Input-oriented scale and mix efficiency
ISMEI	Input-oriented scale and mix efficiency index
IT	Implicit Törnqvist
ITE	Input-oriented technical efficiency
ITEI	Input-oriented technical efficiency index
ITI	Input-oriented technology index
ITME	Input-oriented technical and mix efficiency
IV	Instrumental variables
KPSS	Kwaitowski-Phillips-Schmidt-Shin
KS	Kolmogorov-Smirnov
LLF	Log-likelihood function
LP	Linear programming
LR	Likelihood ratio
LS	Least squares
MC	Marginal cost
MCMC	Markov chain Monte Carlo
MFP	Multifactor productivity

MGF	Moment generating function
MGM	Multilateral generalised Malmquist
MI	Marginal input
ML	Maximum likelihood
MNLS	Modified nonlinear least squares
MOLS	Modified ordinary least squares
MP	Marginal product
MR	Marginal revenue
MRLS	Modified restricted least squares
MRS	Marginal rate of substitution
MRT	Marginal rate of transformation
MRTS	Marginal rate of technical substitution
NDRS	Nondecreasing returns to scale
NIRS	Nonincreasing returns to scale
NLS	Nonlinear least squares
NO	Net output
NTC	No technical change
OAE	Output-oriented allocative efficiency
OEI	Output-oriented environment index
OETSMEI	Output-oriented environment, technology, and scale and mix efficiency index
OLS	Ordinary least squares
OM	Output-oriented Malmquist
OME	Output-oriented mix efficiency
OMEI	Output-oriented mix efficiency index
OMR	Output-oriented metatechnology ratio
OSAE	Output-oriented scale and allocative efficiency
OSE	Output-oriented scale efficiency
OSEI	Output-oriented scale efficiency index
OSME	Output-oriented scale and mix efficiency
OSMEI	Output-oriented scale and mix efficiency index
OTE	Output-oriented technical efficiency
OTEI	Output-oriented technical efficiency index
OTI	Output-oriented technology index
OTME	Output-oriented technical and mix efficiency
PDF	Probability density function
PE	Profit efficiency
PFA	Piecewise frontier analysis
PFM	Piecewise frontier model
PFP	Partial factor productivity
PP	Phillips-Perron
QR	Quantile regression
R&D	Research and development
RE	Revenue efficiency
RISE	Residual input-oriented scale efficiency

RISEI	Residual input-oriented scale efficiency index
RITE	Residual input-oriented technical efficiency
RLS	Restricted least squares
RME	Residual mix efficiency
RMEI	Residual mix efficiency index
RML	Restricted maximum likelihood
ROSE	Residual output-oriented scale efficiency
ROSEI	Residual output-oriented scale efficiency index
ROTE	Residual output-oriented technical efficiency
RTD	Return-to-the-dollar
SFA	Stochastic frontier analysis
SFM	Stochastic frontier model
SNI	Statistical noise index
SSE	Sum of squared errors
SUR	Seemingly unrelated regression
TFE	True fixed effects
TFP	Total factor productivity
TFPI	Total factor productivity index
TRE	True random effects
TSDEA	Two-stage data envelopment analysis
TSE	Technical and scale efficiency
TSEI	Technical and scale efficiency index
TSLS	Two-stage least squares
TSME	Technical, scale and mix efficiency
TSMEI	Technical, scale and mix efficiency index
TT	Terms of trade
TTI	Terms of trade index
VAR	Vector autoregressive
VRS	Variable returns to scale

Notation

$\odot$	Element-wise (or Hadamard, or Schur) product
$\oslash$	Element-wise division
$\imath$	A vector of ones
$\propto$	Proportional to
$a < b$	Every element of a is strictly less than every element of b
$a \leqq b$	Every element of a is less than or equal to every element of b
$a \leq b$	$a \leqq b$ but $a \neq b$
$a > b$	Every element of a is strictly greater than every element of b
$a \geqq b$	Every element of a is greater than or equal to every element of b
$a \geq b$	$a \geqq b$ but $a \neq b$
$A \subseteq B$	(subset) every element of A is also an element of B
$A \subset B$	(proper subset) $A \subseteq B$ but $A \neq B$
$A \supseteq B$	(superset) every element of B is also an element of A
$A \supset B$	(proper superset) $A \supseteq B$ but $A \neq B$
$EXP(b)$	Exponential distribution with scale parameter b
$G(a,b)$	Gamma distribution with shape parameter a and scale parameter b
$N(a,B)$	Normal distribution with mean vector a and covariance matrix B
$N^+(a,B)$	$N(a,B)$ distribution that has been truncated to the interval (0, ∞)
$f_G(x\|1,1/b)$	Probability density function of $X \sim EXP(b)$
$f_G(x\|a,1/b)$	Probability density function of $X \sim G(a,b)$
$f_N(x\|a,B)$	Probability density function of $X \sim N(a,B)$
$\mathbb{R}$	The set of all real numbers (does not include $-\infty$ or ∞)
$\mathbb{R}^k$	The set of all k-tuples of real numbers
$\mathbb{R}^k_+$	The set of all k-tuples of real, nonnegative numbers
$\mathbb{R}^k_{++}$	The set of all k-tuples of real, positive numbers

Chapter 1
Overview

This book describes a coherent framework for analysing managerial performance. The focus is on measures of performance that are useful for policy makers. The title of the book reflects the fact that most, if not all, of these measures can be viewed as measures of productivity and/or efficiency. This chapter provides an overview of the main concepts and analytical methods described later in the book.

1.1 Basic Concepts and Terminology

The first step in analysing managerial performance is to identify the manager(s). A manager is a person or other accountable body responsible for controlling (or administering) a firm. In this book, the term 'firm' refers to a production unit (e.g., a school, an assembly line, or an economy). Firm managers are decision makers. For this reason, firms are often[1] referred to as decision-making units (DMUs).

Assessments of managerial performance often depend on the way different variables involved in production processes are classified. In this book, all of the possibly millions of variables that are *physically* involved in production processes are classified into those that are controlled by managers and those that are not. Those that are controlled by managers are then further classified into inputs (i.e., products and services that go *in* to production processes) and outputs (i.e., products and services that come *out* of production processes). Those that are *never* controlled by managers are referred to as environmental variables (e.g., rainfall in crop production). Classifying variables in this way means that managers will not be held responsible for the effects of variables they do not control. For example, farm managers will not be labelled as inefficient when relatively low crop yields are due to low rainfall,

[1] See, for example, Charnes et al. (1981), Cooper et al. (2004) and Färe and Grosskopf (2010).

C. J. O'Donnell, *Productivity and Efficiency Analysis*,
https://doi.org/10.1007/978-981-13-2984-5_1

and truckers will not be labelled as inefficient when delivery delays are due to poor roads. Unless explicitly stated otherwise, the term ‘environmental variable’ is used in this book to refer to a characteristic of a *production* environment. Characteristics of production environments are variables that are *physically* involved in production processes. They should not be confused with characteristics of market environments (e.g., the degree of competition in output markets) or institutional environments (e.g., laws that prevent the use of child labour). Characteristics of market and institutional environments do not generally affect the input-output combinations that are physically possible (i.e., they do not affect the physics). However, as we shall see, they often affect the input-output combinations that managers choose.

One of the most important concepts in efficiency and productivity analysis is the concept of a production technology. In this book, a production technology (or simply ‘technology’) is defined as a technique, method or system for transforming inputs into outputs (e.g., a technique for transforming seeds and other inputs into vegetables). For most practical purposes, it is convenient to think of a technology as a book of instructions, or recipe. The set of technologies that exist in a given period is called a ‘technology set’ (e.g., the set of sustainable, hydroponic, organic, multilayer and vertical-farming techniques for growing vegetables). If we think of a technology as a book of instructions, or recipe, then we can think of a technology set as a library. Measures of ‘technical efficiency’ are viewed as measures of how well technologies are chosen and used (i.e., how well managers ‘choose books/recipes from the library’ and ‘follow the instructions’). The term ‘technical progress’ refers to the discovery of new technologies. Investigative activities aimed at discovering new technologies are referred to as ‘research and development’ (R&D) activities. The term ‘technical regress’ refers to the loss of existing technologies. An important assumption that is maintained throughout the book is that there is no technical regress (i.e., as a society, we do not forget the techniques, methods and systems we know).

The input-output combinations that are possible using different technologies can usually be represented by distance, revenue, cost and/or profit functions. The existence of these functions has few, if any, implications for managerial behaviour. The existence of a cost function, for example, does not imply that managers will aim to minimise costs. Rather, different managers will tend to behave differently depending on what they value, and on what they can and cannot choose. For example, if managers value goods and services at market prices, then, if possible, they will tend to choose inputs and outputs to maximise profits. On the other hand, if managers value products and services differently to the market, then they may instead choose inputs and outputs to maximise measures of productivity. In this book, measures of productivity are defined as measures of output quantity divided by measures of input quantity. Government and community interest in productivity stems from the fact that productivity change is often associated with changes in social welfare; according to Kendrick (1961, p. 3), for example, “[t]he story of productivity, the ratio of output to input, is at heart the record of man’s efforts to raise himself from poverty”.

Decision makers are often interested in measuring levels of efficiency. Measures of efficiency can be viewed *ex post* measures of how well firm managers have solved different optimisation problems. For example, measures of output-oriented technical efficiency can be viewed as measures of how well managers have maximised outputs when inputs and output mixes have been predetermined. On the other hand, measures of profit efficiency can be viewed as measures of how well managers have maximised profits when inputs and outputs have been chosen freely.

Many decision makers are also interested in measuring productivity. This involves assigning numbers to baskets of inputs and outputs. Measurement theory says that so-called index numbers must be assigned in such a way that the relationships between the numbers reflect the relationships between the baskets. For example, if we are measuring changes in output quantities, and if basket A contains exactly twice as much of every output as basket B, then the index number assigned to basket A should be exactly twice as big as the number assigned to basket B. Index numbers that are consistent with measurement theory can be computed using various additive, multiplicative, primal and dual indices (i.e., formulas). Most of the indices currently used in the productivity and efficiency literature yield numbers that are *not* consistent with measurement theory.

Measuring changes in productivity is one thing. Explaining changes in productivity is another. In this book, changes in productivity are explained using a combination of economic theory, measurement theory and statistical methods. Using this so-called econometric approach, changes in productivity can be attributed to four main factors: (a) technical progress (i.e., the discovery of new technologies), (b) environmental change (i.e., changes in variables that are physically involved in production processes but *never* controlled by managers), (c) technical efficiency change (i.e., changes in how well technologies are chosen and used) and (d) scale and mix efficiency change (i.e., changes in economies of scale and substitution). In practice, estimating these different components involves estimating changes in the limits to production (i.e., changes in production frontiers). As we shall see, the choice of estimator depends partly on what is known, or assumed, about production technologies.

1.2 Production Technologies

It is common to make assumptions about technologies by way of assumptions about what they can and cannot produce. For example, it is common to assume that, with a given set of technologies,

- A1 it is possible to produce zero output (i.e., inactivity is possible);
- A2 there is a limit to what can be produced using a finite amount of inputs (i.e., output sets are bounded);
- A3 a positive amount of at least one input is needed in order to produce a strictly positive amount of any output (i.e., inputs are weakly essential; there is 'no free lunch');
- A4 the set of outputs that can be produced using given inputs contains all the points on its boundary (i.e., output sets are closed);

A5 the set of inputs that can produce given outputs contains all the points on its boundary (i.e., input sets are closed);
A6 if particular inputs can be used to produce a given output vector, then they can also be used to produce a scalar contraction of that output vector (i.e., outputs are weakly disposable); and
A7 if particular outputs can be produced using a given input vector, then they can also be produced using a scalar magnification of that input vector (i.e., inputs are weakly disposable).

Assumptions A1–A7 are maintained throughout this book. Other assumptions that are made from time to time include the following:

A6s if given inputs can be used to produce particular outputs, then they can also be used to produce fewer outputs (i.e., outputs are strongly disposable);
A7s if given outputs can be produced using particular inputs, then they can also be produced using more inputs (i.e., inputs are strongly disposable);
A8s if a given output-input combination is possible in a particular production environment, then it is also possible in a better production environment (i.e., environmental variables are strongly disposable).

The word 'strong' is used in A6s and A7s to reflect the fact that A6s implies A6 and A7s implies A7 (symbolically, A6s $\Rightarrow$ A6 and A7s $\Rightarrow$ A7). The input-output combinations that are possible using different sets of technologies can be represented by output sets, input sets and production possibilities sets. If A2, A6 and A7 are true, then they can also be represented by output and input distance functions.

1.2.1 Output Sets

An output set is a set containing all outputs that can be produced using given inputs. In this book, the focus is on *period-and-environment-specific* output sets. A period-and-environment-specific output set is a set containing all outputs that can be produced using given inputs *in a given period in a given production environment*. For a precise definition, let $x = (x_1, \ldots, x_M)'$, $q = (q_1, \ldots, q_N)'$ and $z = (z_1, \ldots, z_J)'$ denote vectors of nonnegative inputs, outputs and environmental variables (respectively). In mathematical terms, the set of outputs that can be produced using the input vector x in period t in a production environment characterised by z is

$$P^t(x, z) = \{q : x \text{ can produce } q \text{ in period } t \text{ in environment } z\}. \tag{1.1}$$

To illustrate, Table 1.1 reports artificial (or 'toy') data on $I = 5$ firms over $T = 5$ time periods. Each firm has used two inputs to produce two outputs in one of two production environments. Figure 1.1 depicts the set of outputs that could have been produced using the input vector $\iota = (1, 1)'$ in period 1 in environment 1. The dots in this figure mark the observed output combinations of the two firms that used this

Table 1.1 Toy data

Row	Firm	Period	q_1	q_2	x_1	x_2	z
A	1	1	1	1	1	1	1
B	2	1	1	1	0.56	0.56	1
C	3	1	2.37	2.37	1	1	1
D	4	1	2.11	2.11	1.05	0.7	1
E	5	1	1.81	3.62	1.05	0.7	1
F	1	2	1	1	0.996	0.316	2
G	2	2	1.777	3.503	1.472	0.546	2
H	3	2	0.96	0.94	0.017	0.346	1
I	4	2	5.82	0.001	4.545	0.01	2
J	5	2	6.685	0.001	4.45	0.001	1
K	1	3	1.381	4.732	1	1	1
L	2	3	0.566	4.818	1	1	1
M	3	3	1	3	1.354	1	1
N	4	3	0.7	0.7	0.33	0.16	1
O	5	3	2	2	1	1	2
P	1	4	1	1	0.657	0.479	1
R	2	4	1	3	1	1	1
S	3	4	1	1	1.933	0.283	2
T	4	4	1.925	3.722	1	1	2
U	5	4	1	1	1	0.31	1
V	1	5	1	5.166	1	1	1
W	2	5	2	2	0.919	0.919	2
X	3	5	1	1	1.464	0.215	2
Y	4	5	1	1	0.74	0.74	1
Z	5	5	1.81	3.62	2.1	1.4	1

input vector in this period in this environment (in this book, letters in figures generally correspond to rows in tables). The set $P^1(\iota, 1)$ is the area bounded by the two axes and the curve passing through point C.

1.2.2 *Input Sets*

An input set is a set containing all inputs that can produce given outputs. Again, this book focuses on *period-and-environment-specific* input sets. A period-and-environment-specific input set is a set containing all inputs that can produce given outputs *in a given period in a given production environment*. For example, the set of inputs that can produce the output vector q in period t in an environment characterised

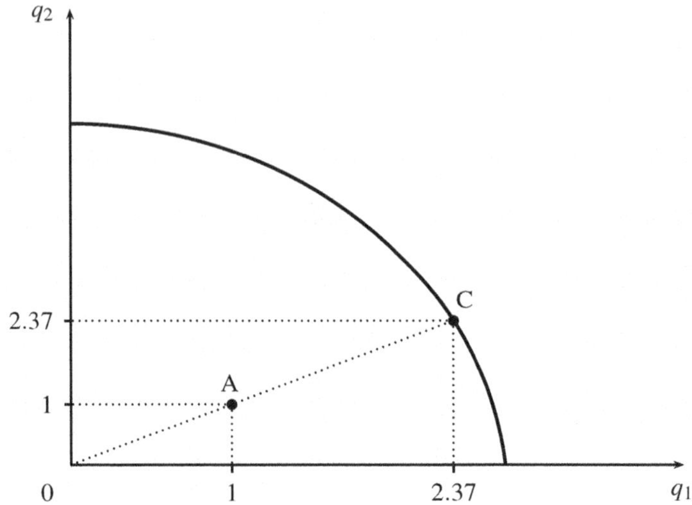

Fig. 1.1 The outputs that could have been produced using one unit of each input in period 1 in environment 1. The set $P^1(\iota, 1)$ is the area bounded by the two axes and the curve passing through point C

by z is

$$L^t(q, z) = \{x : x \text{ can produce } q \text{ in period } t \text{ in environment } z\}. \tag{1.2}$$

To illustrate, reconsider the toy data in Table 1.1. Figure 1.2 depicts the set of inputs that could have produced one unit of each output in period 1 in environment 1. The dots in this figure mark the observed input combinations of the two firms that produced these outputs in this period in this environment. The set $L^1(\iota, 1)$ comprises all points on and above the curve passing through point B.

1.2.3 Production Possibilities Sets

A production possibilities set is a set containing all input-output combinations that are physically possible. In this book, the focus is on two specific types of production possibilities set: *period-and-environment-specific* production possibilities sets and period-environment-*and-mix-specific* production possibilities sets.

A *period-and-environment-specific* production possibilities set is a set containing all input-output combinations that are physically possible *in a given period in a given production environment*. For example, the set of input-output combinations that are physically possible in period t in a production environment characterised by z is

$$T^t(z) = \{(x, q) : x \text{ can produce } q \text{ in period } t \text{ in environment } z\}. \tag{1.3}$$

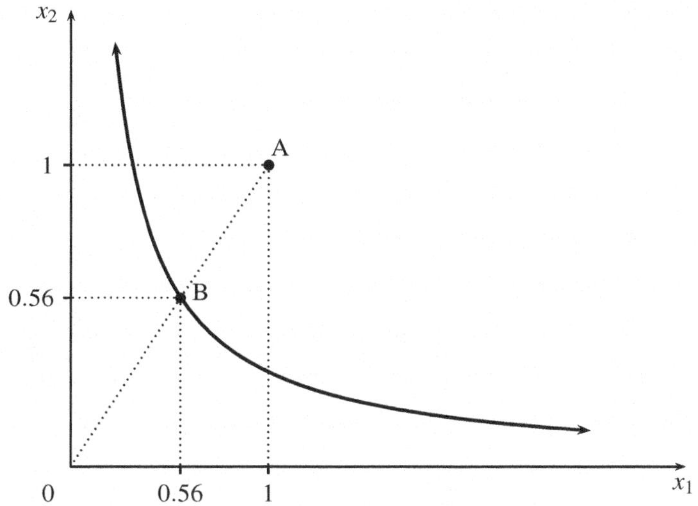

Fig. 1.2 The inputs that could have produced one unit of each output in period 1 in environment 1. The set $L^1(\iota, 1)$ comprises all points on and above the frontier passing through point B

If there are more than two outputs and inputs, then the only way to represent this set in a two-dimensional figure is to map many variables into just two variables. Throughout this book, outputs are mapped into scalar-valued measures of total output and inputs are mapped into scalar-valued measures of total input. In the case of outputs, the measure of total (or aggregate) output associated with the vector q is given by $Q(q)$, where $Q(.)$ is any nonnegative, nondecreasing, linearly-homogeneous, scalar-valued aggregator function. In the case of inputs, the measure of total (or aggregate) input associated with the vector x is given by $X(x)$, where, again, $X(.)$ is any nonnegative, nondecreasing, linearly-homogeneous, scalar-valued aggregator function.

For a simple illustration, reconsider the toy data in Table 1.1, and let $Q(q) = 0.484q_1 + 0.516q_2$ and $X(x) = 0.23x_1 + 0.77x_2$. The associated aggregate outputs and inputs are reported in Table 1.2. Figure 1.3 plots the aggregate outputs and inputs of the five firms that operated in period 1 in environment 1. In this figure, the set $T^1(1)$ is represented by the area bounded by the horizontal axis and the curve passing through point E.

A period-environment-*and-mix-specific* production possibilities set is a set containing all input-output combinations that are physically possible *when using a scalar multiple of a given input vector to produce a scalar multiple of a given output vector* in a given period in a given production environment. For example, the set of input-output combinations that are possible when using a scalar multiple of $\bar{x}$ to produce a scalar multiple of $\bar{q}$ in period t in an environment characterised by z is

$$T^t(\bar{x}, \bar{q}, z) = \{(x, q) : x \propto \bar{x}, \; q \propto \bar{q}, \; (x, q) \in T^t(z)\}. \tag{1.4}$$

Table 1.2 Aggregate outputs and inputs[a]

Row	Firm	Period	$Q(q)$	$X(x)$
A	1	1	1	1
B	2	1	1	0.56
C	3	1	2.37	1
D	4	1	2.11	0.7805
E	5	1	2.744	0.7805
F	1	2	1	0.472
G	2	2	2.668	0.759
H	3	2	0.950	0.270
I	4	2	2.817	1.053
J	5	2	3.236	1.024
K	1	3	3.110	1
L	2	3	2.76	1
M	3	3	2.032	1.081
N	4	3	0.7	0.199
O	5	3	2	1
P	1	4	1	0.520
R	2	4	2.032	1
S	3	4	1	0.663
T	4	4	2.852	1
U	5	4	1	0.469
V	1	5	3.150	1
W	2	5	2	0.919
X	3	5	1	0.502
Y	4	5	1	0.74
Z	5	5	2.744	1.561

[a]Numbers reported to less than three decimal places are exact in the sense that they have not been rounded. Some of the other numbers may have been rounded

To illustrate, reconsider the toy data in Tables 1.1 and 1.2. Figure 1.4 plots the aggregate outputs and inputs of the three firms that used a scalar multiple of ι to produce a scalar multiple of ι in period 1 in environment 1. In this figure, the set $T^1(\iota, \iota, 1)$ is represented by the area bounded by the horizontal axis and the curve passing through points B and C.

1.2.4 Output Distance Functions

Set representations of technologies can be difficult to work with mathematically. In practice, it is common to work with distance functions. An output distance function

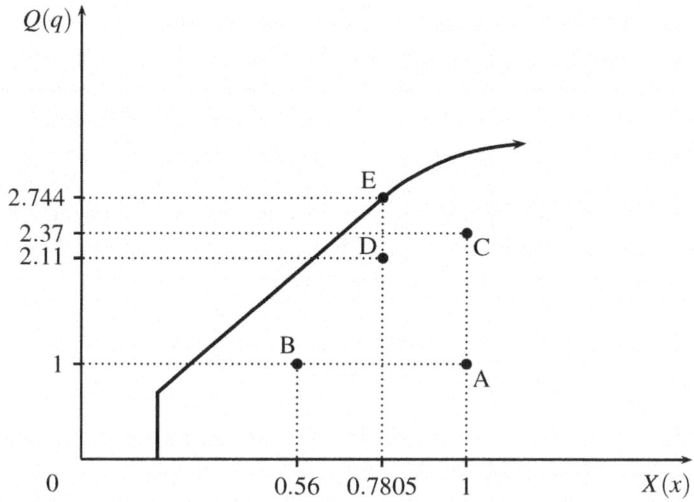

Fig. 1.3 The input-output combinations that were possible in period 1 in environment 1. The set $T^1(1)$ is the area bounded by the horizontal axis and the curve passing through point E

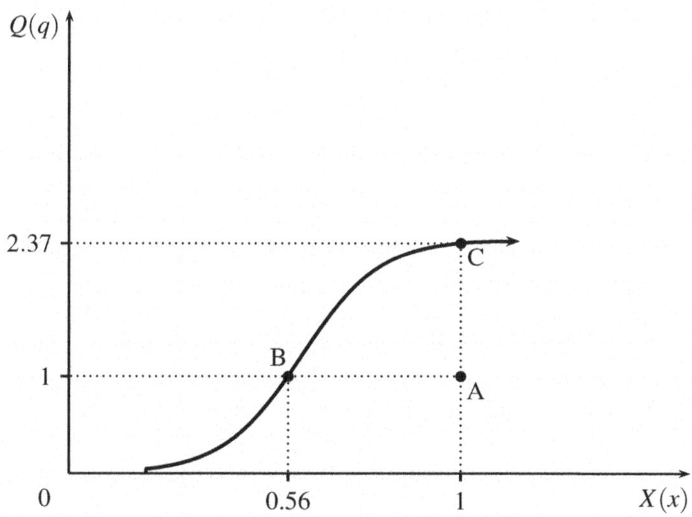

Fig. 1.4 The input-output combinations that were possible when using a scalar multiple of ι to produce a scalar multiple of ι in period 1 in environment 1. The set $T^1(\iota, \iota, 1)$ is the area bounded by the horizontal axis and the curve passing through points B and C

gives the reciprocal of the largest factor by which it is possible to scale up a given output vector when using a given input vector. For example, if it is technically possible to use given inputs to produce four times as much of every output, then the output distance function takes the value $1/4 = 0.25$. Again, this book focuses on *period-and-environment-specific* output distance functions. A period-and-environment-specific output distance function gives the reciprocal of the largest factor by which it is possible to scale up a given output vector when using a given input vector *in a given period in a given production environment*. For example, the reciprocal of the largest factor by which it is possible to scale up q when using x in period t in environment z is

$$D_O^t(x, q, z) = \inf\{\rho > 0 : q/\rho \in P^t(x, z)\}. \tag{1.5}$$

For a numerical example, reconsider the toy data reported in Table 1.1. The outputs of firm 1 in period 1 (hereafter firm A) were previously mapped to point A in Fig. 1.1. That figure reveals that it would have been technically possible to hold the inputs of the firm fixed and scale up its outputs by a factor of no more than 2.37. Thus, in the case of firm A, the output distance function takes the value $D_O^1(\iota, \iota, 1) = 1/2.37 = 0.422$.

1.2.5 Input Distance Functions

An input distance function gives the reciprocal of the smallest fraction of a given input vector that can produce a given output vector. For example, if it is technically possible to produce a given output vector using as little as one-half of a given input vector, then the input distance function takes the value $1/0.5 = 2$. Again, this book focuses on *period-and-environment-specific* input distance functions. A period-and-environment-specific input distance function gives the reciprocal of the smallest fraction of a given input vector that can produce a given output vector *in a given period in a given production environment*. For example, the reciprocal of the smallest fraction of x that can produce q in period t in environment z is

$$D_I^t(x, q, z) = \sup\{\theta > 0 : x/\theta \in L^t(q, z)\}. \tag{1.6}$$

For a numerical example, reconsider the toy data in Table 1.1. The inputs of firm 1 in period 1 (i.e., firm A) were previously mapped to point A in Fig. 1.2. That figure reveals that it would have been technically possible to produce the outputs of the firm using as little as $0.56/1 = 56\%$ of its inputs. Thus, in the case of firm A, the input distance function takes the value $D_I^1(\iota, \iota, 1) = 1/0.56 = 1.786$.

1.2.6 *Other Sets and Functions*

If assumptions A1–A7 are true, then the input-output combinations that are possible using different technologies can also be represented by revenue and cost functions. A revenue function gives the maximum revenue that can be earned using given inputs. A cost function gives the minimum cost of producing given outputs. Other sets and functions that are discussed in this book include profit functions, production functions, input requirement functions, directional distance functions, hyperbolic distance functions, technology-and-environment-specific sets and functions, period-specific sets and functions, and state-contingent sets and functions.

1.3 Measures of Productivity Change

In this book, measures of productivity change are defined as measures of output quantity change divided by measures of input quantity change. Computing measures of output and input quantity change involves assigning numbers to baskets of outputs and inputs. Measurement theory says that so-called index numbers cannot be assigned in an arbitrary way. Rather, they must be assigned in such a way that the relationships between the numbers mirror the relationships between the baskets. To illustrate, consider the baskets of maple syrup and Vegemite and the associated sets of quantity index numbers presented in Table 1.3. Among other things, the index numbers in column L indicate that basket W contains twice as much syrup and Vegemite as basket A. The other index numbers in the table can be interpreted in a similar way. The index numbers in column L are the only numbers that are consistent with measurement

Table 1.3 Quantity index numbers

		L	F	CF	EKS
Basket A		1	1	1	1
Basket M		2.032	1.892	2.389	1.942
Basket R		2.032	1.893	2.854	1.943
Basket W		2	2	3.642	2.027

theory. Observe, for example, that basket M contains the same amount of syrup and Vegemite as basket R, and only in column L is the index number in row M the same as the index number in row R. Arguably the most important distinguishing feature of this book is that it assigns numbers to baskets of outputs and inputs in a way that is consistent with measurement theory. To clarify the approach, this section introduces firm and time subscripts into the notation. Thus, for example, $q_{it} = (q_{1it}, \ldots, q_{Nit})'$ and $x_{it} = (x_{1it}, \ldots, x_{Mit})'$ now denote the output and input vectors of firm i in period t.

1.3.1 Output Quantity Indices

An *index* is a rule or a formula that tells us how to use data to measure the change in one or more variables over time and/or space. An *index number* is the value obtained after data have been substituted into the formula. In this book, an output quantity index (or simply 'output index') that compares q_{it} with q_{ks} is defined as any variable of the form

$$QI(q_{ks}, q_{it}) \equiv Q(q_{it})/Q(q_{ks}) \tag{1.7}$$

where $Q(.)$ is a nonnegative, nondecreasing, linearly-homogeneous, scalar-valued aggregator function. All output indices of this type yield numbers that are consistent with measurement theory. They are also proper indices in the sense that, if outputs are positive, then they satisfy axioms Q1 to Q8 listed in O'Donnell (2016). Two of the most important axioms are a transitivity axiom and a proportionality axiom. The transitivity axiom says that a direct comparison of the outputs of two firms should yield the same index number as an indirect comparison through a third firm. If, for example, firm R produced the same amount of every output as firm M, and firm M produced λ times as much as firm A, then the index that compares the outputs of firm R with the outputs of firm A must take the value λ (indicating that firm R produced λ times as much as firm A). The proportionality axiom says that if firm W produced λ times as much as firm A, then the index that compares the outputs of firm W with the outputs of firm A must take the value λ. The class of proper output indices includes the Lowe index defined by O'Donnell (2012, Eq. 3). Output indices that do not satisfy the transitivity axiom and are therefore not proper include the well-known Fisher and Törnqvist indices. Output indices that do not satisfy the proportionality axiom and are therefore not proper include the chained Fisher (CF) index and an index proposed by Elteto and Koves (1964) and Szulc (1964) (hereafter, EKS).

To illustrate, consider the output quantities, output prices and output index numbers reported in Table 1.4. The output quantities reported in this table are the quantities reported earlier in Table 1.1. The index numbers in the different columns are Lowe (L), Fisher (F), CF and EKS index numbers that compare the output quantities in each row with the output quantities in row A. The Lowe index numbers were computed using the same aggregator function that was used to compute the aggregate

Table 1.4 Output quantities, output prices and output index numbers[a,b]

Row	q_1	q_2	p_1	p_2	L	F	CF	EKS
A	1	1	0.57	0.41	1	1	1	1
B	1	1	0.26	0.25	1	1	1	0.992*
C	2.37	2.37	0.57	0.41	2.37	2.37	2.37	2.37
D	2.11	2.11	0.58	0.53	2.11	2.11	2.11	2.096*
E	1.81	3.62	0.26	0.26	2.744	2.640*	2.695*	2.677*
F	1	1	0.59	0.76	1	1	0.972*	0.986*
G	1.777	3.503	0.63	0.65	2.668	2.575	2.626	2.608
H	0.96	0.94	0.34	0.31	0.950	0.951	0.950	0.944
I	5.82	0.001	0.46	0.58	2.817	2.952	2.800	2.672
J	6.685	0.001	0.61	1.43	3.236	2.789	3.217	2.508
K	1.381	4.732	0.57	0.41	3.110	2.783	3.716	2.883
L	0.566	4.818	0.49	0.65	2.760	2.648	3.251	2.737
M	1	3	0.51	0.46	2.032	1.892*	2.389*	1.942*
N	0.7	0.7	0.52	0.23	0.7	0.7	0.943*	0.711*
O	2	2	0.37	0.17	2	2	2.695*	2.029*
P	1	1	0.41	0.76	1	1	1.348*	0.982*
R	1	3	0.53	0.48	2.032	1.893*	2.854*	1.943*
S	1	1	0.53	0.37	1	1	1.514*	1.001*
T	1.925	3.722	0.91	0.53	2.852	2.631	3.973	2.706
U	1	1	0.31	1.03	1	1	1.359*	0.981*
V	1	5.166	0.47	0.08	3.150	2.099	3.530	2.296
W	2	2	0.57	0.27	2	2	3.642*	2.027*
X	1	1	0.31	0.51	1	1	1.821*	0.983*
Y	1	1	0.31	0.67	1	1	1.821*	0.981*
Z	1.81	3.62	0.42	0.69	2.744	2.745*	5.447*	2.759*

[a]L = Lowe; F = Fisher; CF = chained Fisher; EKS = Elteto-Koves-Szulc
[b]Numbers reported to less than three decimal places are exact; see the footnote to Table 1.2 on p. 8
*Incoherent (not because of rounding)

outputs in Table 1.2. Lowe index numbers are consistent with measurement theory. Observe, for example, that the output vector in row M is the same as the output vector in row R, and the Lowe index number in row M is the same as the Lowe index number in row R (the index numbers in these particular rows are, in fact, the index numbers reported above in Table 1.3). The Fisher, CF and EKS index numbers are *not* consistent with measurement theory.[2] Numbers that are clearly incoherent are marked with an asterisk (*). Observe, for example, that the outputs in row E are the

[2]In practice, CF (resp. EKS) indices are mainly used for time-series (resp. cross-section) comparisons. For this reason, the CF numbers in Table 1.4 were computed by treating the observations in the dataset as observations on one firm over twenty-five periods. The EKS numbers were computed by treating the observations in the dataset as observations on twenty-five firms in one period.

same as the outputs in row Z, but the CF index number in row E differs from the CF index number in row Z.

1.3.2 Input Quantity Indices

In this book, an input quantity index (or simply 'input index') that compares x_{it} with x_{ks} is defined as any variable of the form

$$XI(x_{ks}, x_{it}) \equiv X(x_{it})/X(x_{ks}) \tag{1.8}$$

where $X(.)$ is a nonnegative, nondecreasing, linearly-homogeneous, scalar-valued aggregator function. Again, all input indices of this type yield numbers that are consistent with measurement theory. They are also proper indices in the sense that, if inputs are positive, then they satisfy axioms X1 to X8 listed in O'Donnell (2016). The class of proper input indices includes the Lowe index defined by O'Donnell (2012, Eq. 4). Again, input indices that are not proper include the Fisher, CF and EKS indices.

To illustrate, consider the input quantities, input prices and input index numbers reported in Table 1.5. The input quantities reported in this table are the quantities reported earlier in Table 1.1. The index numbers in the different columns are Lowe (L), Fisher (F), CF and EKS index numbers that compare the input quantities in each row with the input quantities in row A. The Lowe index numbers were computed using the same aggregator function that was used to compute the aggregate inputs in Table 1.2. Again, these numbers are consistent with measurement theory. For example, the input vector in row D is the same as the input vector in row E, and the Lowe index number in row D is the same as the Lowe index number in row E. Again, the Fisher, CF and EKS index numbers are *not* consistent with measurement theory.[3] Again, numbers that are clearly incoherent are marked with an asterisk (*). Observe, for example, that the input vector in row Z is twice as big as the input vector in row E, but the EKS index number in row Z is not twice as big as the EKS index number in row E.

1.3.3 Productivity Indices

Productivity indices are measures of productivity change. Without loss of generality, this book focuses on measures of total factor productivity (TFP) change. An index that compares the TFP of firm i in period t with the TFP of firm k in period s is defined

[3] Again, the CF numbers were computed by treating the observations in the dataset as observations on one firm over twenty-five periods. The EKS index numbers were computed by treating the observations in the dataset as observations on twenty-five firms in one period.

Table 1.5 Input quantities, input prices and input index numbers[a,b]

Row	x_1	x_2	w_1	w_2	L	F	CF	EKS
A	1	1	0.28	1.91	1	1	1	1
B	0.56	0.56	0.22	0.58	0.56	0.56	0.56	0.525*
C	1	1	0.28	1.91	1	1	1	1
D	1.05	0.7	0.16	0.41	0.781	0.771*	0.771*	0.749*
E	1.05	0.7	0.07	1.02	0.781	0.734*	0.771*	0.797*
F	0.996	0.316	0.24	0.29	0.472	0.501	0.464	0.502
G	1.472	0.546	0.16	0.16	0.759	0.819	0.715	0.798
H	0.017	0.346	0.17	0.7	0.270	0.293	0.189	0.253
I	4.545	0.01	0.27	0.39	1.053	1.049	1.001	1.339
J	4.45	0.001	0.29	0.79	1.024	0.825	0.976	1.102
K	1	1	0.28	1.91	1	1	1.182*	1
L	1	1	0.21	0.56	1	1	1.182*	0.939*
M	1.354	1	0.16	0.74	1.081	1.054	1.276	1.056
N	0.33	0.16	0.24	2.3	0.199	0.179	0.223	0.196
O	1	1	0.24	0.15	1	1	1.032*	0.863*
P	0.657	0.479	0.26	0.61	0.520	0.517	0.578	0.495
R	1	1	0.16	0.22	1	1	1.064*	0.899*
S	1.933	0.283	0.19	0.62	0.663	0.575	0.861	0.668
T	1	1	0.17	0.26	1	1	1.088*	0.905*
U	1	0.31	0.27	0.91	0.469	0.432	0.568	0.464
V	1	1	0.29	0.78	1	1	1.178*	0.939*
W	0.919	0.919	0.39	0.81	0.919	0.919	1.083*	0.848*
X	1.464	0.215	0.21	0.31	0.502	0.519	0.787	0.572
Y	0.74	0.74	0.23	0.69	0.74	0.74	0.946*	0.700*
Z	2.1	1.4	0.31	0.22	1.561	1.642*	2.159*	1.479*

[a] L = Lowe; F = Fisher; CF = chained Fisher; EKS = Elteto-Koves-Szulc
[b] Numbers reported to less than three decimal places are exact; see the footnote to Table 1.2 on p. 8
*Incoherent (not because of rounding)

as any variable of the form $TFPI(x_{ks}, q_{ks}, x_{it}, q_{it}) \equiv QI(q_{ks}, q_{it})/XI(x_{ks}, x_{it})$ where $QI(.)$ is any proper output index and $XI(.)$ is any proper input index. Equivalently,

$$TFPI(x_{ks}, q_{ks}, x_{it}, q_{it}) \equiv TFP(x_{it}, q_{it})/TFP(x_{ks}, q_{ks}) \tag{1.9}$$

where $TFP(x_{it}, q_{it}) \equiv Q(q_{it})/X(x_{it})$ denotes the TFP of firm i in period t. All TFP indices (TFPIs) of this type are said to be proper. If outputs and inputs are positive, then they satisfy axioms T1 to T8 listed in O'Donnell (2017). The class of proper TFPIs includes the Lowe index defined by O'Donnell (2012, Eq. 5). TFPIs that are not proper include the Fisher, CF and EKS indices.

Table 1.6 Output quantities, input quantities and TFPI numbers[a,b]

Row	q_1	q_2	x_1	x_2	L	F	CF	EKS
A	1	1	1	1	1	1	1	1
B	1	1	0.56	0.56	1.786	1.786	1.786	1.889*
C	2.37	2.37	1	1	2.37	2.37	2.37	2.37
D	2.11	2.11	1.05	0.7	2.703	2.737	2.737	2.799
E	1.81	3.62	1.05	0.7	3.516	3.599*	3.495*	3.359*
F	1	1	0.996	0.316	2.117	1.994	2.096	1.963
G	1.777	3.503	1.472	0.546	3.515	3.145	3.670	3.269
H	0.96	0.94	0.017	0.346	3.513	3.250	5.028	3.728
I	5.82	0.001	4.545	0.01	2.675	2.815	2.798	1.996
J	6.685	0.001	4.45	0.001	3.159	3.378	3.296	2.276
K	1.381	4.732	1	1	3.110	2.783	3.144	2.883
L	0.566	4.818	1	1	2.760	2.648	2.750	2.916
M	1	3	1.354	1	1.879	1.795	1.872	1.840
N	0.7	0.7	0.33	0.16	3.516	3.913	4.233	3.629
O	2	2	1	1	2	2	2.611*	2.350*
P	1	1	0.657	0.479	1.923	1.935	2.332	1.985
R	1	3	1	1	2.032	1.893	2.682	2.162
S	1	1	1.933	0.283	1.509	1.738	1.757	1.498
T	1.925	3.722	1	1	2.852	2.631	3.652	2.991
U	1	1	1	0.31	2.134	2.317	2.391	2.117
V	1	5.166	1	1	3.150	2.099	2.996	2.445
W	2	2	0.919	0.919	2.176	2.176	3.364*	2.390*
X	1	1	1.464	0.215	1.991	1.926	2.313	1.719
Y	1	1	0.74	0.74	1.351	1.351	1.925*	1.401*
Z	1.81	3.62	2.1	1.4	1.758	1.672*	2.523*	1.866*

[a] L = Lowe; F = Fisher; CF = chained Fisher; EKS = Elteto-Koves-Szulc
[b] Numbers reported to less than three decimal places are exact; see the footnote to Table 1.2 on p. 8
*Incoherent (not because of rounding)

To illustrate, consider the output quantities, input quantities and TFPI numbers reported in Table 1.6. The output and input quantities reported in this table are the quantities reported earlier in Tables 1.1, 1.4 and 1.5. The TFPI numbers in the columns labelled L, F, CF and EKS were obtained by dividing the output index numbers in Table 1.4 by the corresponding input index numbers in Table 1.5. The index numbers in Table 1.6 compare the output-input combinations in each row with the output-input combinations in row A. The Lowe index numbers reported in column L are coherent. Observe, for example, that (a) the output vector in row W is twice as big as the output vector in row A, (b) the input vector in row W is only 0.919 times as big as the input vector in row A, and (c) the Lowe TFPI number is $2/0.919 = 2.176$. Again, the Fisher, CF and EKS index numbers are *not* coherent. Observe, for example, that (a) the output vector in row Z is the same as the output vector in row E, (b) the input vector in row Z is twice as big as the input vector in row E, but (c) the CF index number in row Z is not half as big as the CF index number in row E.

1.3.4 Other Indices

Other indices discussed in this book include output price indices, input price indices, terms-of-trade (TT) indices, implicit output indices, implicit input indices and implicit productivity indices. Implicit output (resp. input) indices are obtained by dividing revenue (resp. cost) indices by output price (resp. input price) indices. Implicit productivity indices are obtained by dividing profitability indices by TT indices. Except in restrictive special cases, implicit indices yield numbers that are not consistent with measurement theory.

1.4 Managerial Behaviour

To explain changes in outputs and inputs, and therefore changes in productivity, we need to know something about managerial behaviour. The existence of different sets and functions has few, if any, implications for behaviour. The existence of revenue functions, for example, does not mean that managers will choose outputs in order to maximise revenues, and the existence of cost functions does not mean they will choose inputs to minimise costs. Instead, different managers will tend to behave differently depending on what they value, and on what they can and cannot choose. Some of the simplest optimisation problems faced by firm managers involve maximising outputs, minimising inputs and/or maximising productivity.

1.4.1 Output Maximisation

The managers of some firms (e.g., the managers of government departments, benevolent societies, conservation groups and socially-responsible corporations) often value products and services differently to the market. There are also many products and services that are not exchanged in a market and therefore do not have a market price (e.g., city parks). If a firm manager places nonnegative values on outputs (not necessarily market values) and all other variables involved in the production process have been predetermined (i.e., have been determined in a previous period), then (s)he will generally aim to maximise a measure of total output. If there is more than one output, then the precise form of the output maximisation problem will depend on how easily the manager can choose the output mix. Suppose, for example, the manager of firm i can only choose output vectors that are scalar multiples of q_{it}. In this case, his/her period-t output-maximisation problem can be written as

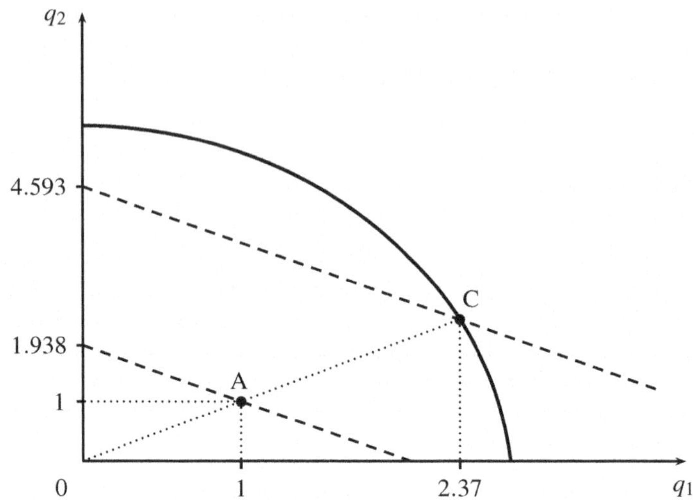

Fig. 1.5 Output maximisation. If the output mix of firm A had been predetermined, then the manager could have maximised total output by operating the firm at point C

$$\max_{q}\{Q(q) : q \propto q_{it},\ D_O^t(x_{it}, q, z_{it}) \leq 1\} \tag{1.10}$$

where $Q(.)$ is any nonnegative, nondecreasing, linearly-homogeneous, scalar-valued function satisfying $Q(q_{it}) > 0$. The output vector that solves this problem is $\bar{q}_{it} \equiv \bar{q}^t(x_{it}, q_{it}, z_{it}) = q_{it}/D_O^t(x_{it}, q_{it}, z_{it})$. The associated aggregate output is $Q(\bar{q}_{it}) = Q(q_{it})/D_O^t(x_{it}, q_{it}, z_{it})$.

For a numerical example, reconsider the toy data in Table 1.1. Also let $Q(q) = 0.484q_1 + 0.516q_2$. Figure 1.5 depicts the output maximisation problem that would have faced the manager of firm 1 in period 1 (i.e., firm A) had the firm's output mix been predetermined. In this figure, the frontier passing through point C is the frontier depicted earlier in Fig. 1.1. The outputs of firm 1 in period 1 map to point A. The aggregate output at this point is $Q(q_{11}) = 1$. The dashed line passing through point A is an iso-output line with a slope of -0.938 and a q_2 intercept of $Q(q_{11})/0.516 = 1.938$. The other dashed line is an iso-output line with the same slope but a higher intercept. Output maximisation involves choosing the iso-output line with the highest intercept that passes through a technically-feasible point. If the output mix of firm A had been predetermined, then the output-maximising iso-output line would have been the one passing through point C. The aggregate output at this point is $Q(\bar{q}_{11}) = 4.593 \times 0.516 = 2.37$.

1.4.2 Input Minimisation

If a firm manager places nonnegative values on inputs (again, not necessarily market values) and all other variables involved in the production process have been predetermined, then (s)he will generally aim to minimise a measure of total input. If there is more than one input, then the precise form of the input minimisation problem will depend on how easily the manager can choose the input mix. Suppose, for example, the manager of firm i can only use input vectors that are scalar multiples of x_{it}. In this case, his/her period-t input-minimisation problem can be written as

$$\min_{x}\{X(x) : x \propto x_{it},\ D_I^t(x, q_{it}, z_{it}) \geq 1\} \tag{1.11}$$

where $X(.)$ is any nonnegative, nondecreasing, linearly-homogeneous, scalar-valued aggregator function satisfying $X(x_{it}) > 0$. The input vector that solves this problem is $\bar{x}_{it} \equiv \bar{x}^t(x_{it}, q_{it}, z_{it}) = x_{it}/D_I^t(x_{it}, q_{it}, z_{it})$. The associated aggregate input is $X(\bar{x}_{it}) = X(x_{it})/D_I^t(x_{it}, q_{it}, z_{it})$.

For a numerical example, reconsider the toy data in Table 1.1. Also let $X(x) = 0.23x_1 + 0.77x_2$. Figure 1.6 depicts the input minimisation problem that would have faced the manager of firm 1 in period 1 (i.e., firm A) had the firm's input mix been predetermined. In this figure, the frontier passing through point B is the frontier depicted earlier in Fig. 1.2. The inputs of firm 1 in period 1 map to point A. The aggregate input at this point is $X(x_{11}) = 1$. The dashed line passing through point A is an iso-input line with a slope of -0.299 and an x_2 intercept of $X(x_{11})/0.77 = 1.299$. The other dashed line is an iso-input line with the same slope but a lower intercept.

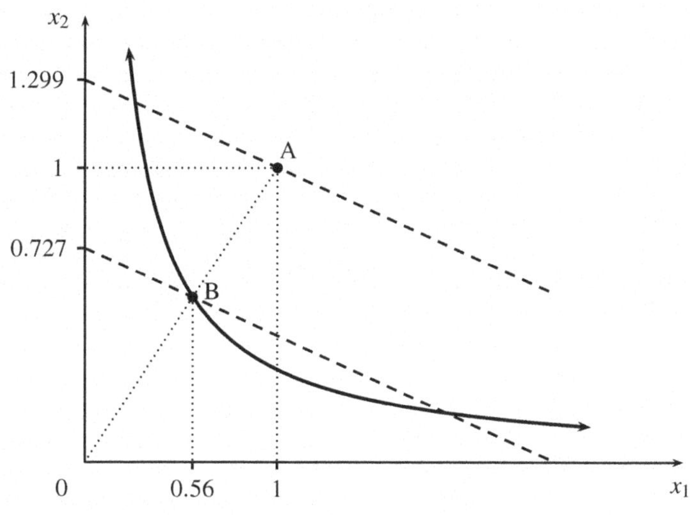

Fig. 1.6 Input minimisation. If the input mix of firm A had been predetermined, then the manager could have minimised total input use by operating the firm at point B

Input minimisation involves choosing the iso-input line with the lowest intercept that passes through a technically-feasible point. If the input mix of firm A had been predetermined, then the input-minimising iso-input line would have been the one passing through point B. The aggregate input at this point is $X(\bar{x}_{11}) = 0.727 \times 0.77 = 0.56$.

1.4.3 Productivity Maximisation

If a firm manager places nonnegative values on outputs and inputs (again, not necessarily market values) and all environmental variables have been predetermined, then (s)he may aim to maximise a measure of TFP. If there is more than one output and more than one input, then the precise form of the manager's TFP maximisation problem will depend on how easily (s)he can choose the output mix and the input mix. Suppose, for example, the manager of firm i can choose all outputs and inputs freely. In this case, his/her period-t TFP-maximisation problem can be written as

$$\max_{q,x}\{Q(q)/X(x) : D_O^t(x, q, z_{it}) \leq 1\} \tag{1.12}$$

where $Q(.)$ and $X(.)$ are nonnegative, nondecreasing, linearly-homogeneous, scalar-valued aggregator functions with parameters (or weights) that represent the values the manager places on outputs and inputs. There may be several pairs of output and input vectors that solve this problem. Let $q_{it}^* \equiv q^t(z_{it})$ and $x_{it}^* \equiv x^t(z_{it})$ denote one such pair. The associated maximum TFP is $TFP^t(z_{it}) = Q(q_{it}^*)/X(x_{it}^*)$.

For a numerical example, reconsider the toy data in Tables 1.1 and 1.2. Figure 1.7 depicts the TFP maximisation problem that would have faced the manager of firm 1 in period 1 (i.e., firm A). The frontier in this figure is the frontier depicted earlier in Fig. 1.3. The outputs and inputs of firm 1 in period 1 map to point A. The dashed line passing through point A is an iso-productivity ray with a slope of $TFP(x_{11}, q_{11}) =$ slope 0A $= 1/1 = 1$. The other dashed lines are iso-productivity rays with higher slopes. TFP maximisation involves choosing the iso-productivity ray that has the highest slope and passes through a technically-feasible point. If the manager of firm A had been able to choose all outputs and inputs freely, then the TFP-maximising iso-productivity ray would have been the one passing through points N and E. The TFP at any point on the line connecting these two points is $TFP^1(z_{11}) =$ slope 0N $=$ slope 0E $= 0.7/0.1991 = 2.744/0.7805 = 3.516$.

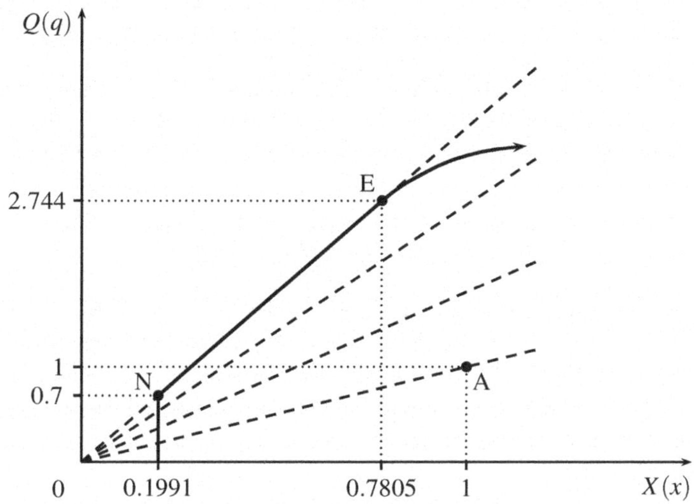

Fig. 1.7 Productivity maximisation. If the manager of firm A had been able to choose all outputs and inputs freely, then (s)he could have maximised TFP by operating the firm anywhere on the line connecting points N and E

1.4.4 Other Types of Behaviour

Other optimisation problems (and therefore other types of managerial behaviour) discussed in this book involve maximising revenue, minimising cost, maximising profit, maximising net output, and maximising return to the dollar.

1.5 Measures of Efficiency

Measures of efficiency can be viewed as *ex post* measures of how well firm managers have solved different optimisation problems. Except where explicitly stated otherwise, all measures of efficiency defined in this book take values in the closed unit interval. A firm manager is said to have been fully efficient by some measure if and only if that measure takes the value one.

1.5.1 Output-Oriented Measures

Output-oriented measures of efficiency are relevant measures of managerial performance in situations where managers have placed nonnegative values on outputs (not necessarily market values) and inputs have been predetermined. In these situations, the relevance of a particular measure depends on how easily the manager has been able to choose the output mix. If, for example, the output mix of the firm has been predetermined, then the most relevant measure is output-oriented technical efficiency (OTE). Several measures of OTE can be found in the literature. In this book, the OTE of manager i in period t is defined as $OTE^t(x_{it}, q_{it}, z_{it}) = D_O^t(x_{it}, q_{it}, z_{it})$. Equivalently,

$$OTE^t(x_{it}, q_{it}, z_{it}) = Q(q_{it})/Q(\bar{q}_{it}) \tag{1.13}$$

where $Q(q_{it})$ is the aggregate output of the firm and $Q(\bar{q}_{it}) = Q(q_{it})/D_O^t(x_{it}, q_{it}, z_{it})$ is the maximum aggregate output that is possible in period t when using x_{it} to produce a scalar multiple of q_{it} in an environment characterised by z_{it}. The right-hand side of (1.13) is, in fact, an output index. If environmental variables have been predetermined, then it can be viewed as a measure of how well the manager has solved problem (1.10).

For a numerical example, reconsider the output maximisation problem depicted earlier in Fig. 1.5. In that figure, the outputs of firm 1 in period 1 were represented by point A. The aggregate output at point A is $Q(q_{11}) = 1.938 \times 0.516 = 1$. The aggregate output at point C is $Q(\bar{q}_{11}) = 4.593 \times 0.516 = 2.37$. The OTE of manager 1 in period 1 is $OTE^1(x_{11}, q_{11}, z_{11}) = Q(q_{11})/Q(\bar{q}_{11}) = 0.422$ (i.e., the aggregate output at point A divided by the aggregate output at point C).

The fact that the OTE of a manager can be defined in terms of aggregate outputs means it can be depicted in input-output space. It can also be viewed as a TFPI. For example, points A and C in Fig. 1.5 map to points A and C in Fig. 1.8. The frontier depicted in this figure is the frontier depicted earlier in Fig. 1.4. The TFP at point A is $TFP(x_{11}, q_{11}) = Q(q_{11})/X(x_{11}) = \text{slope } 0A = 1$. The TFP at point

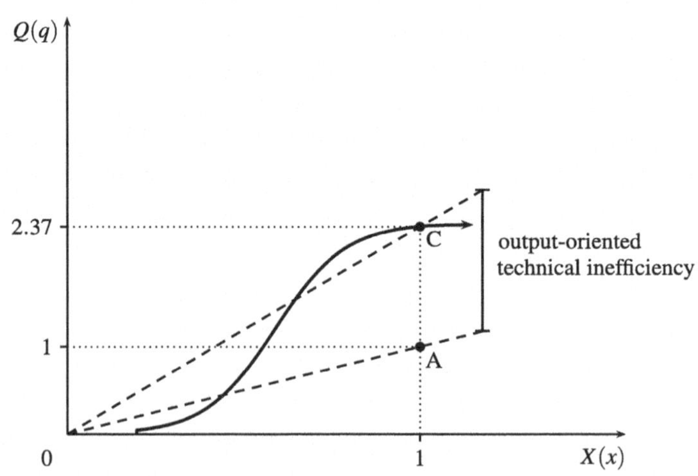

Fig. 1.8 Output-oriented technical inefficiency. The gap between the rays passing through points A and C is due to technical inefficiency

C is $TFP(x_{11}, \bar{q}_{11}) = Q(\bar{q}_{11})/X(x_{11}) =$ slope 0C $= 2.37$. The OTE of manager 1 in period 1 is $OTE^1(x_{11}, q_{11}, z_{11}) = TFP(x_{11}, q_{11})/TFP(x_{11}, \bar{q}_{11}) = 0.422$ (i.e., the TFP at point A divided by the TFP at point C).

1.5.2 Input-Oriented Measures

Input-oriented measures of efficiency are relevant measures of managerial performance in situations where managers have placed nonnegative values on inputs (again, not necessarily market values) and outputs have been predetermined. In these situations, the relevance of a particular measure depends on how easily the manager has been able to choose the input mix. If, for example, the input mix of the firm has been predetermined, then the most relevant measure is input-oriented technical efficiency (ITE). Again, several measures of ITE can be found in the literature. In this book, the ITE of manager i in period t is defined as $ITE^t(x_{it}, q_{it}, z_{it}) = 1/D_I^t(x_{it}, q_{it}, z_{it})$. Equivalently,

$$ITE^t(x_{it}, q_{it}, z_{it}) = X(\bar{x}_{it})/X(x_{it}) \tag{1.14}$$

where $X(x_{it})$ is the aggregate input of the firm and $X(\bar{x}_{it}) = X(x_{it})/D_I^t(x_{it}, q_{it}, z_{it})$ is the minimum aggregate input needed to produce q_{it} in period t when using a scalar multiple of x_{it} in an environment characterised by z_{it}. The right-hand side of (1.14) is an input index. If environmental variables have been predetermined, then it can be viewed as a measure of how well the manager has solved problem (1.11).

For a numerical example, reconsider the input minimisation problem depicted earlier in Fig. 1.6. In that figure, the inputs of firm 1 in period 1 were represented by point A. The aggregate input at point A is $X(x_{11}) = 1.299 \times 0.77 = 1$. The aggregate input at point B is $X(\bar{x}_{11}) = 0.727 \times 0.77 = 0.56$. The ITE of manager 1 in period 1 is $ITE^1(x_{11}, q_{11}, z_{11}) = X(\bar{x}_{11})/X(x_{11}) = 0.56/1 = 0.56$ (i.e., the aggregate input at point B divided by the aggregate input at point A).

The fact that the ITE of a manager can be defined in terms of aggregate inputs means it can also be depicted in input-output space. It can also be viewed as a TFPI. For example, points A and B in Fig. 1.6 map to points A and B in Fig. 1.9. The frontier passing through point B in Fig. 1.9 is the frontier depicted earlier in Figs. 1.4 and 1.8. The TFP at point A is $TFP(x_{11}, q_{11}) = Q(q_{11})/X(x_{11}) =$ slope 0A $= 1$. The TFP at point B is $TFP(\bar{x}_{11}, q_{11}) = Q(q_{11})/X(\bar{x}_{11}) =$ slope 0B$= 1.786$. The ITE of manager 1 in period 1 is $ITE^1(x_{11}, q_{11}, z_{11}) = TFP(x_{11}, q_{11})/TFP(\bar{x}_{11}, q_{11}) = 1/1.786 = 0.56$ (i.e., the TFP at point A divided by the TFP at point B).

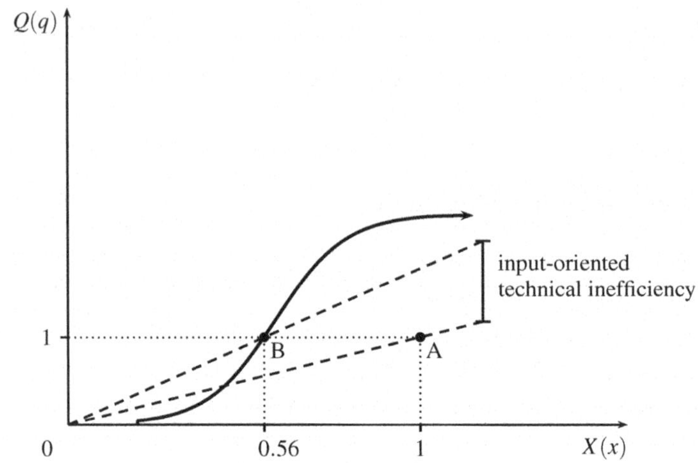

Fig. 1.9 Input-oriented technical inefficiency. The gap between the rays passing through points A and B is due to technical inefficiency

1.5.3 Productivity-Oriented Measures

Productivity-oriented measures of efficiency are relevant measures of managerial performance in situations where managers have placed nonnegative values on outputs and inputs (again, not necessarily market values) and chosen at least one output and at least one input freely. In these situations, the relevance of a particular measure depends on how easily the manager has been able to choose the output mix and the input mix. If, for example, all outputs and inputs have been chosen freely, then the most relevant measure is technical, scale and mix efficiency (TSME). The TSME of manager i in period t is

$$TSME^t(x_{it}, q_{it}, z_{it}) = TFP(x_{it}, q_{it})/TFP^t(z_{it}) \qquad (1.15)$$

where $TFP(x_{it}, q_{it}) = Q(q_{it})/X(x_{it})$ is the TFP of the firm and $TFP^t(z_{it})$ is the maximum TFP that is possible in period t in an environment characterised by z_{it}. The right-hand side of (1.15) is a TFPI. If environmental variables have been predetermined, then it can be viewed as a measure of how well the manager has solved problem (1.12).

For a numerical example, reconsider the TFP maximisation problem depicted earlier in Fig. 1.7. Relevant parts of that figure are now reproduced in Fig. 1.10. In these figures, the outputs and inputs of firm 1 in period 1 map to point A. The TFP at point A is $TFP(x_{11}, q_{11}) = \text{slope } 0A = 1/1 = 1$. The TFP at any point on the line connecting points N and E is $TFP^1(z_{11}) = \text{slope } 0E = 2.744/0.7805 = 3.516$. The TSME of manager 1 in period 1 is $TSME^1(x_{11}, q_{11}, z_{11}) = TFP(x_{11}, q_{11})/TFP^1(z_{11}) = 0.284$

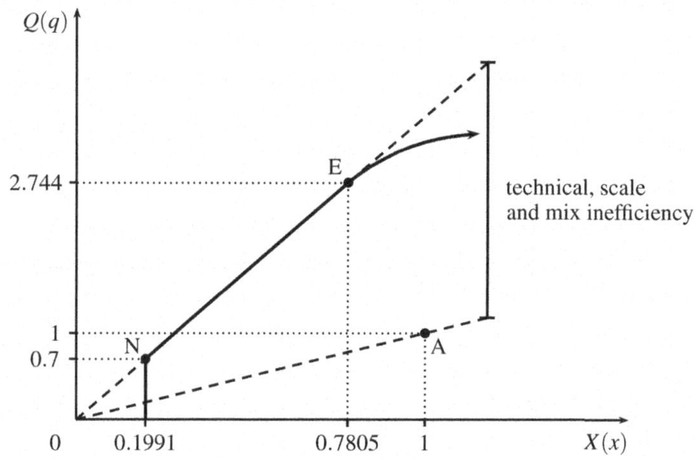

Fig. 1.10 Technical, scale and mix inefficiency. The gap between the rays passing through points A and E is due to technical, scale and mix inefficiency

(i.e., the TFP at point A divided by the TFP at any point on the line connecting points N and E).

The measure of TSME defined by (1.15) can be decomposed into a measure of technical efficiency and a measure of scale and mix efficiency. Both output- and input-oriented decompositions are available. The technical efficiency components are the measures of OTE and ITE defined by (1.13) and (1.14). The scale and mix efficiency components are productivity-oriented measures of economies of scale and substitution. Economies of scale and substitution are the benefits obtained by changing the scale of operations, the output mix, and the input mix. On the output side, the so-called output-oriented scale and mix efficiency (OSME) of manager i in period t is

$$OSME^t(x_{it}, q_{it}, z_{it}) = TFP(x_{it}, \bar{q}_{it})/TFP^t(z_{it}) \qquad (1.16)$$

where $TFP(x_{it}, \bar{q}_{it}) = Q(\bar{q}_{it})/X(x_{it})$ is the maximum TFP possible when using x_{it} to produce a scalar multiple of q_{it} in period t in an environment characterised by z_{it}. Equations (1.13), (1.15) and (1.16) imply that

$$OSME^t(x_{it}, q_{it}, z_{it}) = TSME^t(x_{it}, q_{it}, z_{it})/OTE^t(x_{it}, q_{it}, z_{it}). \qquad (1.17)$$

This equation says that OSME is the component of TSME that remains after accounting for OTE. On the input side, the so-called input-oriented scale and mix efficiency (ISME) of manager i in period t is

$$ISME^t(x_{it}, q_{it}, z_{it}) = TFP(\bar{x}_{it}, q_{it})/TFP^t(z_{it}) \qquad (1.18)$$

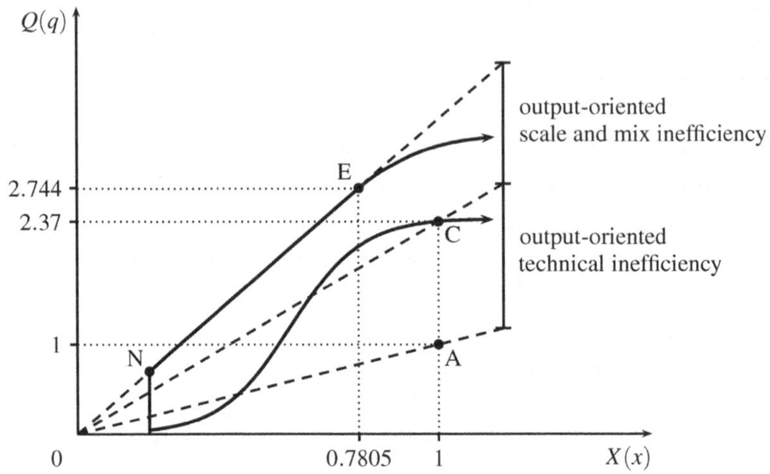

Fig. 1.11 Technical, scale and mix inefficiency. The gap between the rays passing through points A and C is due to technical inefficiency. The gap between the rays passing through points C and E is due to scale and mix inefficiency

where $TFP(\bar{x}_{it}, q_{it}) = Q(q_{it})/X(\bar{x}_{it})$ is the maximum TFP possible when using a scalar multiple of x_{it} to produce q_{it} in period t in an environment characterised by z_{it}. Equations (1.14), (1.15) and (1.18) imply that

$$ISME^t(x_{it}, q_{it}, z_{it}) = TSME^t(x_{it}, q_{it}, z_{it})/ITE^t(x_{it}, q_{it}, z_{it}). \tag{1.19}$$

This equation says that ISME is the component of TSME that remains after accounting for ITE.

For a numerical example, reconsider the measures of OTE, ITE and TSME depicted in Figs. 1.8, 1.9 and 1.10. Relevant parts of those figures are now reproduced in Figs. 1.11 and 1.12. In Fig. 1.11, the OSME of manager 1 in period 1 is $OSME^1(x_{11}, q_{11}, z_{11}) = TFP(x_{11}, \bar{q}_{11})/TFP^1(z_{11}) = 0.674$ (i.e., the TFP at point C divided by the TFP at any point on the line connecting points N and E). In Fig. 1.12, the ISME of manager 1 in period 1 is $ISME^1(x_{11}, q_{11}, z_{11}) = TFP(\bar{x}_{11}, q_{11})/TFP^1(z_{11}) = 0.508$ (i.e., the TFP at point B divided by the TFP at any point on the line connecting points N and E).

1.5.4 Other Measures

Other measures of efficiency discussed in this book include metatechnology ratios and measures of revenue, cost, profit, mix, allocative and scale efficiency. Metatechnology ratios can be viewed as measures of how well managers have chosen their production technologies (i.e., how well they have chosen their 'books of instructions').

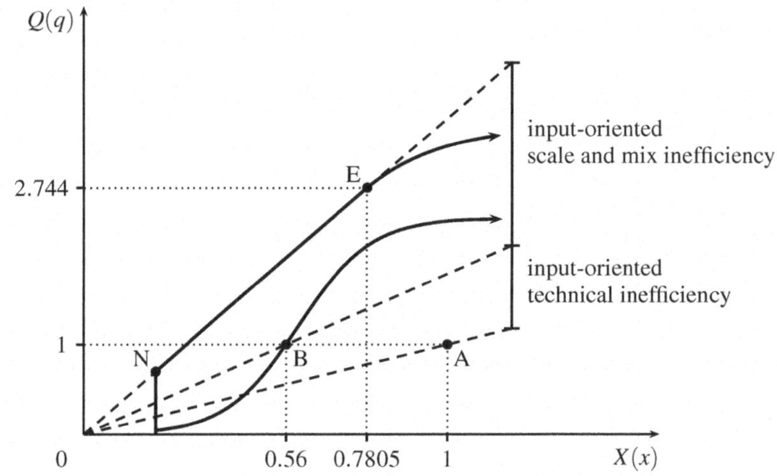

Fig. 1.12 Technical, scale and mix inefficiency. The gap between the rays passing through points A and B is due to technical inefficiency. The gap between the rays passing through points B and E is due to scale and mix inefficiency

Measures of revenue, cost and profit efficiency are measures of how well managers have maximised revenue, minimised cost and maximised profit. Measures of mix efficiency are measures of how well managers have captured economies of substitution (i.e., the benefits obtained by substituting some outputs for others, or by substituting some inputs for others). Measures of scale efficiency are measures of how well managers have captured economies of scale (i.e., the benefits obtained by changing the scale of operations).

1.6 Piecewise Frontier Analysis

Estimating and/or predicting levels of efficiency involves estimating production frontiers. A widely-used estimation approach involves enveloping scatterplots of data points as tightly as possible without violating any assumed properties of production technologies. Some of the most common assumptions lead to estimated frontiers that are comprised of multiple linear segments (or pieces). The associated frontiers are known as piecewise frontiers.[4]

[4]In mathematics, a piecewise function is a function defined on a sequence of intervals (or subdomains). Examples include the absolute value function and the Heaviside step function.

1.6.1 Basic Models

The most common piecewise frontier models (PFMs) are underpinned by the following assumptions:

PF1: production possibilities sets can be represented by distance, revenue, cost and/or profit functions;
PF2: all relevant quantities, prices and environmental variables are observed and measured without error;
PF3: production frontiers are locally (or piecewise) linear;
PF4: outputs, inputs and environmental variables are strongly disposable; and
PF5: production possibilities sets are convex.

If these assumptions are true, then most measures of efficiency can be estimated using linear programming (LP). The associated models and estimators are commonly known as data envelopment analysis (DEA) and estimators.

Output-Oriented Models

Output-oriented PFMs are mainly used to estimate the measure of OTE defined by (1.13). If there are I firms in the dataset and assumptions PF1 to PF5 are true, then the DEA estimation problem can be written as

$$\max_{\mu,\lambda_{11},\ldots,\lambda_{It}} \Big\{\mu : \mu q_{it} \leq \sum_{h=1}^{I}\sum_{r=1}^{t}\lambda_{hr}q_{hr},\ \sum_{h=1}^{I}\sum_{r=1}^{t}\lambda_{hr}z_{hr} \leq z_{it},$$
$$\sum_{h=1}^{I}\sum_{r=1}^{t}\lambda_{hr}x_{hr} \leq x_{it},\ \sum_{h=1}^{I}\sum_{r=1}^{t}\lambda_{hr} = 1,\ \lambda_{hr} \geq 0 \text{ for all } h \text{ and } r\Big\}. \tag{1.20}$$

This LP problem seeks to scale up the output vector while holding inputs and environmental variables fixed. The value of μ at the optimum is an estimate of the reciprocal of $OTE^t(x_{it}, q_{it}, z_{it})$.

For a numerical example, reconsider the toy data in Table 1.1. The estimation problem for manager 1 in period 1 is

$$\begin{aligned}
\max_{\mu,\lambda_{11},\ldots,\lambda_{51}} \quad & \mu \\
\text{s.t.} \quad & 1\mu - 1\lambda_{11} - 1\lambda_{21} - 2.37\lambda_{31} - 2.11\lambda_{41} - 1.81\lambda_{51} \leq 0 \\
& 1\mu - 1\lambda_{11} - 1\lambda_{21} - 2.37\lambda_{31} - 2.11\lambda_{41} - 3.62\lambda_{51} \leq 0 \\
& 1\lambda_{11} + 1\lambda_{21} + 1\lambda_{31} + 1\lambda_{41} + 1\lambda_{51} \leq 1 \\
& 1\lambda_{11} + 0.56\lambda_{21} + 1\lambda_{31} + 1.05\lambda_{41} + 1.05\lambda_{51} \leq 1 \\
& 1\lambda_{11} + 0.56\lambda_{21} + 1\lambda_{31} + 0.7\lambda_{41} + 0.7\lambda_{51} \leq 1 \\
& \lambda_{11} + \lambda_{21} + \lambda_{31} + \lambda_{41} + \lambda_{51} = 1 \\
\text{and} \quad & \lambda_{11}, \ldots, \lambda_{51} \geq 0.
\end{aligned}$$

The value of the μ at the optimum is 2.37. The associated estimate of OTE is $\hat{OTE}^1(x_{11}, q_{11}, z_{11}) = 1/2.37 = 0.422$. DEA estimates of OTE for other managers

Table 1.7 DEA estimates of OTE[a]

Row	Firm	Period	OTE
A	1	1	0.422
B	2	1	1
C	3	1	1
D	4	1	1
E	5	1	1
F	1	2	0.865
G	2	2	1
H	3	2	1
I	4	2	0.871
J	5	2	1
K	1	3	1
L	2	3	1
M	3	3	0.653
N	4	3	1
O	5	3	0.844
P	1	4	0.594
R	2	4	0.671
S	3	4	0.583
T	4	4	1
U	5	4	0.654
V	1	5	1
W	2	5	0.895
X	3	5	0.836
Y	4	5	0.516
Z	5	5	0.867

[a]Numbers reported to less than three decimal places are exact; see the footnote to Table 1.2 on p. 8

in other periods can be obtained in a similar way and are reported in Table 1.7. The solution for manager 1 in period 1 is depicted in Fig. 1.13. In this figure, the outputs of firm 1 in period 1 map to point A. The piecewise frontier passing through point C is an estimate of the true frontier depicted earlier in Fig. 1.5.

Input-Oriented Models

Input-oriented PFMs are mainly used to estimate the measure of ITE defined by (1.14). If there are I firms in the dataset and assumptions PF1 to PF5 are true, then the DEA estimation problem can be written as

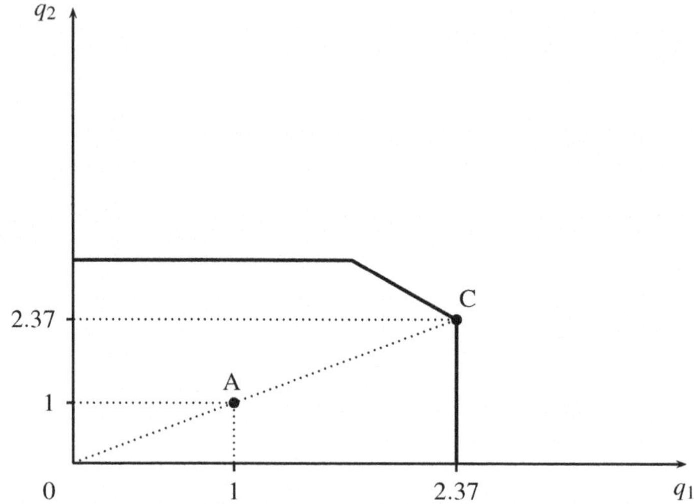

Fig. 1.13 An estimate of output-oriented technical efficiency. In the case of firm A, the DEA estimate of OTE is $\hat{OTE}^1(x_{11}, q_{11}, z_{11}) = 1/2.37 = 0.422$

$$\min_{\mu,\lambda_{11},\ldots,\lambda_{It}} \left\{\mu : \sum_{h=1}^{I}\sum_{r=1}^{t} \lambda_{hr} q_{hr} \geq q_{it}, \sum_{h=1}^{I}\sum_{r=1}^{t} \lambda_{hr} z_{hr} \leq z_{it}, \right.$$
$$\left. \mu x_{it} \geq \sum_{h=1}^{I}\sum_{r=1}^{t} \lambda_{hr} x_{hr}, \sum_{h=1}^{I}\sum_{r=1}^{t} \lambda_{hr} = 1, \ \lambda_{hr} \geq 0 \text{ for all } h \text{ and } r \right\}. \quad (1.21)$$

This LP problem seeks to scale down the input vector while holding outputs and environmental variables fixed. The value of μ at the optimum is an estimate of $ITE^t(x_{it}, q_{it}, z_{it})$.

For a numerical example, reconsider the toy data in Table 1.1. The estimation problem for firm 1 in period 1 is

$$\begin{array}{lllllll}
\min\limits_{\mu,\lambda_{11},\ldots,\lambda_{It}} & \mu & & & & & \\
\text{s.t.} & & 1\lambda_{11} + 1\lambda_{21} & + 2.37\lambda_{31} & + 2.11\lambda_{41} & + 1.81\lambda_{51} & \geq 1 \\
 & & 1\lambda_{11} + 1\lambda_{21} & + 2.37\lambda_{31} & + 2.11\lambda_{41} & + 3.62\lambda_{51} & \geq 1 \\
 & & 1\lambda_{11} + 1\lambda_{21} & + 1\lambda_{31} & + 1\lambda_{41} & + 1\lambda_{51} & \leq 1 \\
 & 1\mu & - 1\lambda_{11} - 0.56\lambda_{21} & - 1\lambda_{31} & - 1.05\lambda_{41} & - 1.05\lambda_{51} & \geq 0 \\
 & 1\mu & - 1\lambda_{11} - 0.56\lambda_{21} & - 1\lambda_{31} & - 0.7\lambda_{41} & - 0.7\lambda_{51} & \geq 0 \\
 & & \lambda_{11} + \lambda_{21} & + \lambda_{31} & + \lambda_{41} & + \lambda_{51} & = 1 \\
\text{and} & \lambda_{11}, \ldots, \lambda_{51} \geq 0. & & & & &
\end{array}$$

The value of μ at the optimum is $\hat{ITE}^1(x_{11}, q_{11}, z_{11}) = 0.56$. DEA estimates of ITE for other firms in other periods can be obtained in a similar way and are reported in

Table 1.8 DEA estimates of ITE[a]

Row	Firm	Period	ITE
A	1	1	0.56
B	2	1	1
C	3	1	1
D	4	1	1
E	5	1	1
F	1	2	0.954
G	2	2	1
H	3	2	1
I	4	2	0.955
J	5	2	1
K	1	3	1
L	2	3	1
M	3	3	0.604
N	4	3	1
O	5	3	0.777
P	1	4	0.551
R	2	4	0.657
S	3	4	0.669
T	4	4	1
U	5	4	0.689
V	1	5	1
W	2	5	0.846
X	3	5	0.881
Y	4	5	0.387
Z	5	5	0.5

[a]Numbers reported to less than three decimal places are exact; see the footnote to Table 1.2 on p. 8

Table 1.8. The solution for firm 1 in period 1 is depicted in Fig. 1.14. In this figure, the inputs of firm 1 in period 1 map to point A. The piecewise frontier passing through point B is an estimate of the true frontier depicted earlier in Fig. 1.6.

Productivity-Oriented Models

Productivity-oriented PFMs are mainly used to estimate the measure of TSME defined by (1.15). If estimates of OTE and ITE are available, then Eqs. (1.17) and (1.19) can subsequently be used to estimate the measures of OSME and ISME defined by (1.16) and (1.18).

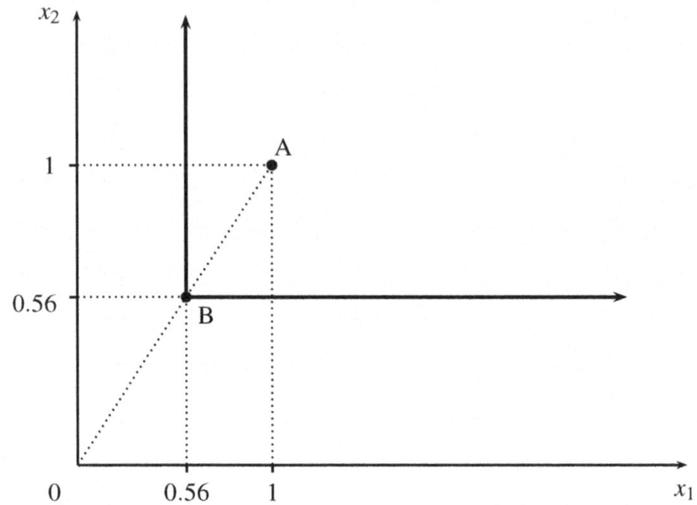

Fig. 1.14 An estimate of input-oriented technical efficiency. In the case of firm A, the DEA estimate of ITE is $\hat{ITE}^1(x_{11}, q_{11}, z_{11}) = 0.56/1 = 0.56$

Estimating the measure of TSME of defined by (1.15) involves estimating $TFP^t(z_{it})$. If there are I firms in the dataset and assumptions PF1 to PF5 are true, then the DEA estimation problem can be written as

$$\max_{q,x,\mu,\theta_{11},\ldots,\theta_{It}} \Big\{ Q(q) : q \leq \sum_{h=1}^{I}\sum_{r=1}^{t} \theta_{hr} q_{hr}, \ \sum_{h=1}^{I}\sum_{r=1}^{t} \theta_{hr} z_{hr} \leq \mu z_{it}, \ X(x) = 1, \\ \sum_{h=1}^{I}\sum_{r=1}^{t} \theta_{hr} x_{hr} \leq x, \ \sum_{h=1}^{I}\sum_{r=1}^{t} \theta_{hr} = \mu, \ \theta_{hr} \geq 0 \text{ for all } h \text{ and } r \Big\}. \tag{1.22}$$

If the aggregator functions are linear, then this problem is an LP problem. Whether or not the aggregator functions are linear, the value of the objective function at the optimum is an estimate of $TFP^t(z_{it})$. This can be substituted into (1.15) to obtain an estimate of $TSME^t(x_{it}, q_{it}, z_{it})$.

For a numerical example, reconsider the toy data in Table 1.1. Also suppose that $Q(q) = 0.484q_1 + 0.516q_2$ and $X(x) = 0.23x_1 + 0.77x_2$ (these functions were used earlier to compute the aggregate outputs and inputs in Table 1.2). The estimation problem for firm 1 in period 1 is

$$
\begin{array}{llllllll}
\max\limits_{q,x,\mu,\theta} & 0.484q_1 + 0.516q_2 \\
\text{s.t.} & q_1 - 1\theta_{11} - 1\theta_{21} & - 2.37\theta_{31} & - 2.11\theta_{41} & - 1.81\theta_{51} & & \leq 0 \\
& q_2 - 1\theta_{11} - 1\theta_{21} & - 2.37\theta_{31} & - 2.11\theta_{41} & - 3.62\theta_{51} & & \leq 0 \\
& 1\theta_{11} + 1\theta_{21} & + 1\theta_{31} & + 1\theta_{41} & + 1\theta_{51} & - 1\mu & \leq 0 \\
& & & & 0.23x_1 & + 0.77x_2 & = 1 \\
& 1\theta_{11} + 0.56\theta_{21} & + 1\theta_{31} & + 1.05\theta_{41} & + 1.05\theta_{51} & - x_1 & \leq 0 \\
& 1\theta_{11} + 0.56\theta_{21} & + 1\theta_{31} & + 0.7\theta_{41} & + 0.7\theta_{51} & - x_2 & \leq 0 \\
& \theta_{11} + \theta_{21} & + \theta_{31} & + \theta_{41} & + \theta_{51} & - \mu & = 0 \\
\text{and} & q_1, q_2, x_1, x_2, \theta_{11}, \ldots, \theta_{51} \geq 0.
\end{array}
$$

The value of the objective function at the optimum is $T\hat{F}P^1(z_{11}) = 3.516$. The TFP of firm 1 in period 1 is $TFP(x_{11}, q_{11}) = 1$. The associated DEA estimate of TSME is $T\hat{S}ME^1(x_{11}, q_{11}, z_{11}) = TFP(x_{11}, q_{11})/T\hat{F}P^1(z_{11}) = 0.284$. DEA estimates of TSME for other managers in other periods can be obtained in a similar way and are reported in Table 1.9. This table also reports estimates of OTE, OSME, ITE and ISME. The OTE and ITE estimates are the ones reported earlier in Tables 1.7 and 1.8. The OSME (resp. ISME) estimates were obtained by dividing the TSME estimates by the OTE (resp. ITE) estimates. The results for manager 1 in period 1 are depicted in Fig. 1.15. In this figure, the piecewise frontier passing through points B and E is an estimate of the true frontier passing through point E in Fig. 1.3. The piecewise frontier passing through points B and C is an estimate of the true frontier passing through points B and C in Fig. 1.4. The outputs and inputs of firm 1 in period 1 map to point A. The TFP-maximising point is point E. Points B and C are technically efficient points. The dashed lines passing through these points are iso-productivity rays with different slopes. The DEA estimates of TSME, OSME and ISME for manager 1 in period 1 are given by the ratios of these slopes.

Other Models

Other PFMs discussed in this book include revenue-, cost- and profit-oriented models. These models are mainly used to estimate measures of revenue, cost, profit, allocative, pure mix and pure scale efficiency.

1.6.2 Productivity Analysis

Productivity analysis involves both measuring and explaining changes in productivity. This section focuses on explaining changes in TFP. This involves decomposing proper TFPI numbers into measures of environmental change, technical change, and efficiency change. If production frontiers are piecewise linear, then the easiest way to proceed is to rewrite (1.15) as $TFP(x_{it}, q_{it}) = TFP^t(z_{it}) \times TSME^t(x_{it}, q_{it}, z_{it})$. A

Table 1.9 DEA estimates of TSME, OSME, OTE, ISME and ITE[a,b]

Row	Firm	Period	TSME	OTE	OSME	ITE	ISME
A	1	1	0.284	0.422	0.674	0.56	0.508
B	2	1	0.508	1	0.508	1	0.508
C	3	1	0.674	1	0.674	1	0.674
D	4	1	0.769	1	0.769	1	0.769
E	5	1	1	1	1	1	1
F	1	2	0.602	0.865	0.696	0.954	0.631
G	2	2	1	1	1	1	1
H	3	2	0.999	1	0.999	1	0.999
I	4	2	0.761	0.871	0.874	0.955	0.797
J	5	2	0.899	1	0.899	1	0.899
K	1	3	0.885	1	0.885	1	0.885
L	2	3	0.785	1	0.785	1	0.785
M	3	3	0.534	0.653	0.819	0.604	0.886
N	4	3	1	1	1	1	1
O	5	3	0.569	0.844	0.674	0.777	0.732
P	1	4	0.547	0.594	0.921	0.551	0.992
R	2	4	0.578	0.671	0.861	0.657	0.880
S	3	4	0.429	0.583	0.737	0.669	0.642
T	4	4	0.811	1	0.811	1	0.811
U	5	4	0.607	0.654	0.928	0.689	0.881
V	1	5	0.896	1	0.896	1	0.896
W	2	5	0.619	0.895	0.692	0.846	0.732
X	3	5	0.566	0.836	0.677	0.881	0.643
Y	4	5	0.384	0.516	0.745	0.387	0.994
Z	5	5	0.5	0.867	0.577	0.5	1

[a]TSME = OTE × OSME = ITE × ISME. Some estimates may be incoherent at the third decimal place due to rounding (e.g., the product of the OTE and OSME estimates in row Z is not exactly equal to 0.5 due to rounding)
[b]Numbers reported to less than three decimal places are exact; see the footnote to Table 1.2 on p. 8

similar equation holds for firm k in period s. Substituting these equations into (1.9) yields

$$TFPI(x_{ks}, q_{ks}, x_{it}, q_{it}) = TFP^t(z_{it})/TFP^s(z_{ks}) \times TSME^t(x_{it}, q_{it}, z_{it})/TSME^s(x_{ks}, q_{ks}, z_{ks}). \tag{1.23}$$

The first ratio on the right-hand side is an environment and technology index (ETI) (i.e., a combined measure of environmental and technical change). The second ratio is a technical, scale and mix efficiency index (TSMEI).

Output- and input-oriented decompositions of TFPI numbers are also available. For an output-oriented decomposition, the easiest way to proceed is to rewrite

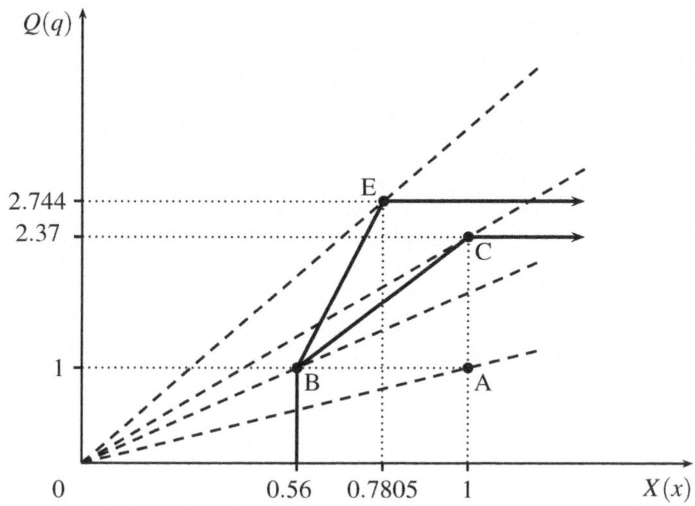

Fig. 1.15 Estimates of technical, scale and mix efficiency. The DEA estimates of TSME, OSME and ISME for manager 1 in period 1 are $T\hat{S}ME^1(x_{11}, q_{11}, z_{11})$ = (slope 0A)/(slope 0E) = 0.2844, $O\hat{S}ME^1(x_{11}, q_{11}, z_{11})$ = (slope 0C)/(slope 0E) = 0.674 and $I\hat{S}ME^1(x_{11}, q_{11}, z_{11})$ = (slope 0B)/(slope 0E) = 0.508

(1.17) as $TSME^t(x_{it}, q_{it}, z_{it}) = OTE^t(x_{it}, q_{it}, z_{it}) \times OSME^t(x_{it}, q_{it}, z_{it})$. A similar equation holds for firm k in period s. Substituting these equations into (1.23) yields

$$\begin{aligned} TFPI(x_{ks}, q_{ks}, x_{it}, q_{it}) &= TFP^t(z_{it})/TFP^s(z_{ks}) \\ &\quad \times OTE^t(x_{it}, q_{it}, z_{it})/OTE^s(x_{ks}, q_{ks}, z_{ks}) \\ &\quad \times OSME^t(x_{it}, q_{it}, z_{it})/OSME^s(x_{ks}, q_{ks}, z_{ks}). \end{aligned} \tag{1.24}$$

The first ratio on the right-hand side is the ETI in (1.23). The second ratio is an output-oriented technical efficiency index (OTEI). The last ratio is an output-oriented scale and mix efficiency index (OSMEI).

For an input-oriented decomposition, the easiest way to proceed is to rewrite (1.19) as $TSME^t(x_{it}, q_{it}, z_{it}) = ITE^t(x_{it}, q_{it}, z_{it}) \times ISME^t(x_{it}, q_{it}, z_{it})$. A similar equation holds for firm k in period s. Substituting these equations into (1.23) yields

$$\begin{aligned} TFPI(x_{ks}, q_{ks}, x_{it}, q_{it}) &= TFP^t(z_{it})/TFP^s(z_{ks}) \\ &\quad \times ITE^t(x_{it}, q_{it}, z_{it})/ITE^s(x_{ks}, q_{ks}, z_{ks}) \\ &\quad \times ISME^t(x_{it}, q_{it}, z_{it})/ISME^s(x_{ks}, q_{ks}, z_{ks}). \end{aligned} \tag{1.25}$$

The first ratio on the right-hand side is the ETI in (1.23) and (1.24). The second ratio is an input-oriented technical efficiency index (ITEI). The last ratio is an input-oriented scale and mix efficiency index (ISMEI).

For a numerical example, reconsider the toy data in Tables 1.1 and 1.2. Associated Lowe TFPI numbers were reported earlier in column L of Table 1.6. Associated DEA estimates of OTE, OSME, ITE and ISME were reported earlier in Table 1.9. Output- and input-oriented decompositions of the TFPI numbers are now reported in Table 1.10. The OTEI, OSMEI, ITEI and ISMEI numbers were obtained by dividing the estimates of OTE, OSME, ITE and ISME for each firm in each period by the corresponding estimates for firm 1 in period 1. The ETI numbers were obtained as residuals (i.e., ETI = TFPI/(OTEI×OSMEI) = TFPI/(ITEI×ISMEI)).

Table 1.10 Output- and input-oriented decompositions of Lowe TFPI numbers using DEA[a,b]

Firm	Period	TFPI	ETI	OTEI	OSMEI	ETI	ITEI	ISMEI
1	1	1	1	1	1	1	1	1
2	1	1.786	1	2.37	0.753	1	1.786	1
3	1	2.37	1	2.37	1	1	1.786	1.327
4	1	2.703	1	2.37	1.141	1	1.786	1.514
5	1	3.516	1	2.37	1.483	1	1.786	1.969
1	2	2.117	1	2.05	1.033	1	1.704	1.243
2	2	3.515	1	2.37	1.483	1	1.786	1.968
3	2	3.513	1	2.37	1.482	1	1.786	1.967
4	2	2.675	1	2.063	1.297	1	1.705	1.569
5	2	3.159	1	2.37	1.333	1	1.786	1.769
1	3	3.110	1.000	2.370	1.312	1.000	1.786	1.742
2	3	2.760	1.000	2.370	1.165	1.000	1.786	1.546
3	3	1.879	1.000	1.547	1.215	1.000	1.078	1.743
4	3	3.516	1.000	2.370	1.483	1.000	1.786	1.969
5	3	2	1.000	2.000	1.000	1.000	1.388	1.441
1	4	1.923	1.000	1.408	1.366	1.000	0.984	1.954
2	4	2.032	1.000	1.590	1.278	1.000	1.173	1.732
3	4	1.509	1.000	1.381	1.093	1.000	1.195	1.263
4	4	2.852	1.000	2.370	1.203	1.000	1.786	1.597
5	4	2.134	1.000	1.550	1.376	1.000	1.230	1.735
1	5	3.150	1.000	2.370	1.329	1.000	1.786	1.764
2	5	2.176	1.000	2.120	1.026	1.000	1.510	1.441
3	5	1.991	1.000	1.982	1.004	1.000	1.573	1.266
4	5	1.351	1.000	1.223	1.105	1.000	0.691	1.956
5	5	1.758	1.000	2.054	0.856	1.000	0.893	1.969

[a]TFPI = ETI × OTEI × OSMEI = ETI × ITEI × ISMEI. Some index numbers may be incoherent at the third decimal place due to rounding (e.g., the product of the ETI, OTEI and OSMEI numbers in row 2 is not exactly equal to the TFPI number due to rounding)

[b]Numbers reported to less than three decimal places are exact; see the footnote to Table 1.2 on p. 8

1.6.3 Other Models

Other PFMs discussed in this book include free disposal hull (FDH) and metafrontier models. FDH models are obtained by relaxing the assumption that production possibilities sets are convex. Metafrontier models can be used to decompose measures of technical efficiency into metatechnology ratios and associated measures of residual technical efficiency.

1.7 Deterministic Frontier Analysis

Production frontiers are often represented by distance, revenue, cost and/or profit functions. These functions can sometimes be written in the form of regression models in which the explanatory variables are deterministic (i.e., not random). The associated frontiers are known as deterministic frontiers.

1.7.1 Basic Models

Deterministic frontier models (DFMs) are underpinned by the following assumptions:

DF1 production possibilities sets can be represented by distance, revenue, cost and/or profit functions;

DF2 all relevant quantities, prices and environmental variables are observed and measured without error; and

DF3 the functional forms of relevant functions are known.

If these assumptions are true, then production frontiers can be estimated using single-equation regression models with error terms representing inefficiency.

Output-Oriented Models

Output-oriented DFMs are mainly used to estimate the measure of OTE defined by (1.13). This involves estimating the output distance function. Output distance functions can be written in the form of regression models with nonnegative errors representing output-oriented technical inefficiency. For example, consider the following output distance function:

$$D_O^t(x_{it}, q_{it}, z_{it}) = \left(A(t) \prod_{j=1}^{J} z_{jit}^{\delta_j} \prod_{m=1}^{M} x_{mit}^{\beta_m} \right)^{-1} \left(\sum_{n=1}^{N} \gamma_n q_{nit}^{\tau} \right)^{1/\tau} \tag{1.26}$$

where $A(t) > 0, A(t) \geq A(t-1), \beta = (\beta_1, \ldots, \beta_M)' \geq 0, \gamma = (\gamma_1, \ldots, \gamma_N)' \geq 0, \tau \geq 1$ and $\gamma'\iota = 1$. After some simple algebra, this function can be rewritten as

$$\ln q_{1it} = \alpha(t) + \sum_{j=1}^{J} \delta_j \ln z_{jit} + \sum_{m=1}^{M} \beta_m \ln x_{mit} - \frac{1}{\tau} \ln \left(\sum_{n=1}^{N} \gamma_n q_{nit}^{*\tau} \right) - u_{it} \quad (1.27)$$

where $\alpha(t) \equiv \ln A(t)$ is an output-oriented measure of technical change, $q_{nit}^{*} \equiv q_{nit}/q_{1it}$ denotes a normalised output, and $u_{it} \equiv -\ln OTE^t(x_{it}, q_{it}, z_{it}) \geq 0$ denotes an output-oriented technical inefficiency effect.

Input-Oriented Models

Input-oriented DFMs are mainly used to estimate the measure of ITE defined by (1.14). This involves estimating the input distance function. Input distance functions can be written in the form of regression models with nonnegative errors representing *input*-oriented technical inefficiency. For example, if the output distance function is given by (1.26), then the input distance function is

$$D_I^t(x_{it}, q_{it}, z_{it}) = \left(B(t) \prod_{j=1}^{J} z_{jit}^{\kappa_j} \prod_{m=1}^{M} x_{mit}^{\lambda_m} \right) \left(\sum_{n=1}^{N} \gamma_n q_{nit}^{\tau} \right)^{-1/(\tau\eta)} \quad (1.28)$$

where $\eta = \beta'\iota$, $B(t) = A(t)^{1/\eta}$, $\kappa_j = \delta_j/\eta$ and $\lambda_m = \beta_m/\eta$. After some simple algebra, this function can be rewritten as

$$-\ln x_{1it} = \xi(t) + \sum_{j=1}^{J} \kappa_j \ln z_{jit} + \sum_{m=2}^{M} \lambda_m \ln x_{mit}^{*} - \frac{1}{\tau\eta} \ln \left(\sum_{n=1}^{N} \gamma_n q_{nit}^{\tau} \right) - u_{it} \quad (1.29)$$

where $\xi(t) \equiv \ln B(t)$ is an input-oriented measure of technical change, $x_{mit}^{*} \equiv x_{mit}/x_{1it}$ denotes a normalised input, and, in a slight abuse of notation, $u_{it} \equiv -\ln ITE^t(x_{it}, q_{it}, z_{it}) \geq 0$ now denotes an input-oriented technical inefficiency effect.

Other Models

DFMs can also be used to estimate measures of revenue, cost and profit efficiency. This involves estimating revenue, cost and profit functions. These functions can also be written in the form of regression models with nonnegative errors representing inefficiency.

1.7.2 Least Squares Estimation

Least squares (LS) estimation of DFMs involves choosing the unknown parameters to minimise the sum of squared inefficiency effects. In the efficiency literature, it is common to assume that u_{it} is a random variable with the following properties:

LS1 $E(u_{it}) = \mu \geq 0$ for all i and t.
LS2 $var(u_{it}) \propto \sigma_u^2$ for all i and t.
LS3 $cov(u_{it}, u_{ks}) = 0$ if $i \neq k$ or $t \neq s$.
LS4 u_{it} is uncorrelated with the explanatory variables.

LS1 says the inefficiency effects have the same mean. LS2 says they are homoskedastic. LS3 says they are serially and spatially uncorrelated. LS4 is self-explanatory.

If a DFM contains an intercept and LS1 to LS4 are true, then LS estimators for the slope parameters are consistent. A consistent estimator for the intercept can be obtained by adjusting the LS estimator for the intercept upwards by an amount equal to the maximum of the LS residuals. In this book, the associated estimators for the intercept and slope parameters are collectively referred to as corrected least squares (CLS) estimators. In practice, it is common to impose restrictions on the parameters so that the estimated frontier is consistent with any assumed properties of production technologies. If the restrictions are true, then associated restricted least squares (RLS) estimators for the slope parameters are consistent. Again, a consistent estimator for the intercept can be obtained by adjusting the RLS estimator for the intercept upwards by an amount equal to the largest RLS residual. In this book, the associated estimators for the intercept and slope parameters are collectively referred to as corrected restricted least squares (CRLS) estimators.

For a numerical example, reconsider the toy data in Table 1.1. These data have been used to obtain CLS and CRLS estimates of the parameters in (1.27). The estimates are reported in Table 1.11. The CRLS estimates were obtained by restricting $\alpha(t) \geq \alpha(t-1)$, $\beta = (\beta_1, \ldots, \beta_M)' \geq 0$ and $\tau \geq 1$. The CRLS estimates have been used to predict levels of OTE and ITE. The predictions are reported in Table 1.12. The OTE

Table 1.11 LS parameter estimates

Parameter	CLS	CRLS
$\alpha(1) \equiv \ln A(1)$	0.954	1.159
$\alpha(2) \equiv \ln A(2)$	0.903	1.159
$\alpha(3) \equiv \ln A(3)$	0.702	1.159
$\alpha(4) \equiv \ln A(4)$	0.723	1.159
$\alpha(5) \equiv \ln A(5)$	0.782	1.159
δ_1	0.188	−0.056
β_1	0.093	0.280
β_2	0.259	0
γ_1	0.771	0.724
γ_2	0.229	0.276
τ	−0.083	1

Table 1.12 CRLS predictions of OTE and ITE[a]

Row	Firm	Period	OTE	ITE
A	1	1	0.314	0.016
B	2	1	0.369	0.029
C	3	1	0.744	0.348
D	4	1	0.653	0.219
E	5	1	0.715	0.302
F	1	2	0.327	0.018
G	2	2	0.660	0.226
H	3	2	0.938	0.795
I	4	2	0.900	0.686
J	5	2	1	1
K	1	3	0.724	0.315
L	2	3	0.546	0.115
M	3	3	0.447	0.057
N	4	3	0.300	0.014
O	5	3	0.652	0.218
P	1	4	0.353	0.024
R	2	4	0.487	0.077
S	3	4	0.271	0.009
T	4	4	0.790	0.430
U	5	4	0.314	0.016
V	1	5	0.675	0.245
W	2	5	0.668	0.237
X	3	5	0.293	0.013
Y	4	5	0.341	0.022
Z	5	5	0.589	0.151

[a]Numbers reported to less than three decimal places are exact; see the footnote to Table 1.2 on p. 8

predictions were obtained by evaluating (1.26). The ITE predictions were obtained by evaluating the reciprocal of (1.28). The predictions for manager 1 in period 1 are depicted in Figs. 1.16 and 1.17. In Fig. 1.16 (resp. 1.17), the outputs (resp. inputs) of firm 1 in period 1 map to point A. In Fig. 1.16, the frontier passing through point A* is an estimate of the true frontier depicted earlier in Fig. 1.5. In Fig. 1.17, the frontier passing through point B* is an estimate of the true frontier depicted earlier in Fig. 1.6.

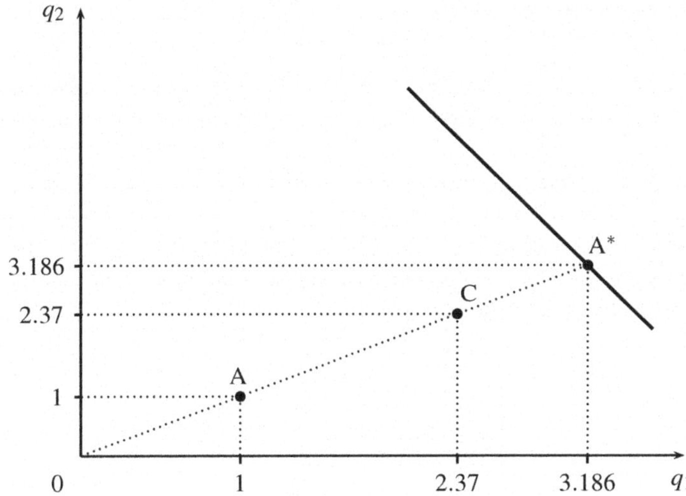

Fig. 1.16 A prediction of output-oriented technical efficiency. In the case of firm A, the CRLS prediction of OTE is $\hat{OTE}^1(x_{11}, q_{11}, z_{11}) = 1/3.186 = 0.314$

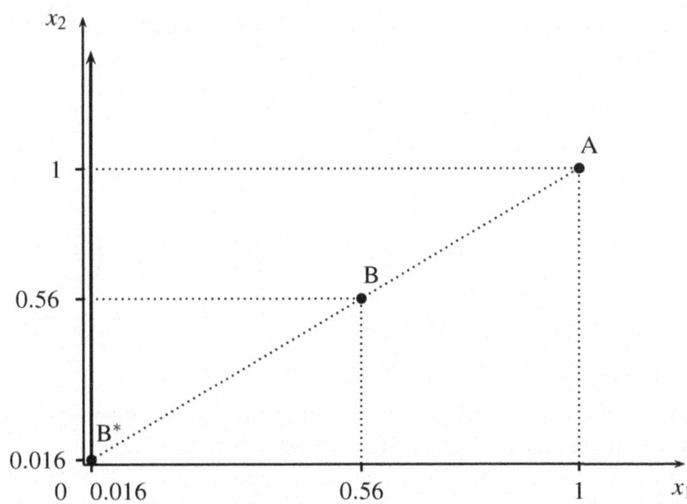

Fig. 1.17 A prediction of input-oriented technical efficiency. In the case of firm A, the CRLS prediction of ITE is $\hat{ITE}^1(x_{11}, q_{11}, z_{11}) = 0.016/1 = 0.016$

1.7.3 Productivity Analysis

For purposes of comparison with Sect. 1.6.2, this section focuses on decomposing proper TFPI numbers. Again, both output- and input-oriented decompositions are available.

For an output-oriented decomposition, a relatively easy way to proceed is to write $TFP(x_{it}, q_{it}) = TFP(x_{it}, q_{it}) \exp(-u_{it})/D_O^t(x_{it}, q_{it}, z_{it})$ where u_{it} denotes an output-oriented technical inefficiency effect. The precise form of this equation depends partly on the form of the output distance function. If the output distance function is given by (1.26), for example, then

$$TFP(x_{it}, q_{it}) = A(t)\left[\prod_{j=1}^{J} z_{jit}^{\delta_j}\right] \times \left[TFP(x_{it}, q_{it}) \prod_{m=1}^{M} x_{mit}^{\beta_m} \left(\sum_{n=1}^{N} \gamma_n q_{nit}^{\tau}\right)^{-1/\tau}\right] \exp(-u_{it}).$$

A similar equation holds for firm k in period s. Substituting these equations into (1.9) yields

$$TFPI(x_{ks}, q_{ks}, x_{it}, q_{it}) = \left[\frac{A(t)}{A(s)}\right]\left[\prod_{j=1}^{J}\left(\frac{z_{jit}}{z_{jks}}\right)^{\delta_j}\right] \times \left[TFPI(x_{ks}, q_{ks}, x_{it}, q_{it}) \prod_{m=1}^{M}\left(\frac{x_{mit}}{x_{mks}}\right)^{\beta_m}\left(\frac{\sum_n \gamma_n q_{nks}^{\tau}}{\sum_n \gamma_n q_{nit}^{\tau}}\right)^{1/\tau}\right] \times \left[\frac{\exp(-u_{it})}{\exp(-u_{ks})}\right]. \quad (1.30)$$

The first term on the right-hand side is an output-oriented technology index (OTI) (i.e., a measure of technical change). The second term is an output-oriented environment index (OEI) (i.e., a measure of environmental change). The third term is an output-oriented scale and mix efficiency index (OSMEI). The last term is an output-oriented technical efficiency index (OTEI). If there are no environmental variables involved in the production process, then the second term vanishes. The conditions under which other terms vanish is left as an exercise for the reader.

For an input-oriented decomposition, a relatively easy way to proceed is to write $TFP(x_{it}, q_{it}) = TFP(x_{it}, q_{it}) D_I^t(x_{it}, q_{it}, z_{it}) \exp(-u_{it})$ where u_{it} now denotes an *input*-oriented technical inefficiency effect. Again, the precise form of this equation depends partly on the form of the distance function. If the input distance function is given by (1.28), for example, then

$$TFP(x_{it}, q_{it}) = B(t)\left[\prod_{j=1}^{J} z_{jit}^{\kappa_j}\right] \times \left[TFP(x_{it}, q_{it}) \prod_{m=1}^{M} x_{mit}^{\lambda_m} \left(\sum_{n=1}^{N} \gamma_n q_{nit}^{\tau}\right)^{-1/(\tau\eta)}\right] \exp(-u_{it}).$$

A similar equation holds for firm k in period s. Substituting these equations into (1.9) yields

$$TFPI(x_{ks}, q_{ks}, x_{it}, q_{it}) = \left[\frac{B(t)}{B(s)}\right]\left[\prod_{j=1}^{J}\left(\frac{z_{jit}}{z_{jks}}\right)^{\kappa_j}\right] \times \left[TFPI(x_{ks}, q_{ks}, x_{it}, q_{it}) \prod_{m=1}^{M}\left(\frac{x_{mit}}{x_{mks}}\right)^{\lambda_m}\left(\frac{\sum_n \gamma_n q_{nks}^{\tau}}{\sum_n \gamma_n q_{nit}^{\tau}}\right)^{1/(\tau\eta)}\right] \times \left[\frac{\exp(-u_{it})}{\exp(-u_{ks})}\right]. \tag{1.31}$$

The first term on the right-hand side is an input-oriented technology index (ITI). The second term is an input-oriented environment index (IEI). The third term is an input-oriented scale and mix efficiency index (ISMEI). The last term is an input-oriented technical efficiency index (ITEI). Again, the conditions under which these terms vanish is left as an exercise for the reader.

For a numerical example, reconsider the toy data in Tables 1.1 and 1.2. Associated Lowe TFPI numbers were reported earlier in Table 1.6. Output- and input-oriented decompositions of these numbers are now reported in Table 1.13. The OTI, OEI, OSMEI, ITI, IEI and ISMEI numbers in each row were obtained by using the CRLS estimates reported in Table 1.11 to evaluate the relevant terms in (1.30) and (1.31). The OTEI and ITEI numbers were obtained as residuals (i.e., OTEI = TFPI/(OTI×OEI×OSMEI) and ITEI = TFPI/(ITI×IEI×ISMEI); these numbers could also have been obtained by taking ratios of the CRLS estimates of OTE and ITE reported earlier in Table 1.12).

1.7.4 Other Models

Other DFMs discussed in this book include various systems of equations. These systems can be used to explain variations in metafrontiers, output supplies and input demands.

Table 1.13 Output- and input-oriented decompositions of Lowe TFPI numbers using CRLS[a,b]

Firm	Period	TFPI	OTI	OEI	OTEI	OSMEI	ITI	IEI	ITEI	ISMEI
1	1	1	1	1	1	1	1	1	1	1
2	1	1.786	1	1	1.176	1.518	1	1	1.786	1
3	1	2.37	1	1	2.37	1	1	1	21.773	0.109
4	1	2.703	1	1	2.081	1.299	1	1	13.695	0.197
5	1	3.516	1	1	2.278	1.543	1	1	18.905	0.186
1	2	2.117	1	0.962	1.041	2.114	1	0.871	1.153	2.108
2	2	3.515	1	0.962	2.102	1.738	1	0.871	14.181	0.285
3	2	3.513	1	1	2.988	1.176	1	1	49.810	0.071
4	2	2.675	1	0.962	2.867	0.970	1	0.871	42.949	0.072
5	2	3.159	1	1	3.186	0.991	1	1	62.651	0.050
1	3	3.110	1	1	2.306	1.349	1	1	19.734	0.158
2	3	2.760	1	1	1.739	1.587	1	1	7.213	0.383
3	3	1.879	1	1	1.426	1.318	1	1	3.546	0.530
4	3	3.516	1	1	0.955	3.682	1	1	0.848	4.145
5	3	2	1	0.962	2.079	1	1	0.871	13.639	0.168
1	4	1.923	1	1	1.125	1.710	1	1	1.522	1.264
2	4	2.032	1	1	1.552	1.309	1	1	4.801	0.423
3	4	1.509	1	0.962	0.864	1.815	1	0.871	0.594	2.918
4	4	2.852	1	0.962	2.516	1.178	1	0.871	26.969	0.121
5	4	2.134	1	1	1	2.134	1	1	1	2.134
1	5	3.150	1	1	2.149	1.465	1	1	15.363	0.205
2	5	2.176	1	0.962	2.129	1.063	1	0.871	14.841	0.168
3	5	1.991	1	0.962	0.934	2.215	1	0.871	0.784	2.915
4	5	1.351	1	1	1.088	1.242	1	1	1.351	1
5	5	1.758	1	1	1.876	0.937	1	1	9.453	0.186

[a]TFPI = OTI × OEI × OTEI × OSMEI = ITI × IEI × ITEI × ISMEI. Some index numbers may be incoherent at the third decimal place due to rounding (e.g., the product of the OTI, OEI, OTEI and OSMEI numbers in row 2 is not exactly equal to the TFPI number due to rounding)
[b]Numbers reported to less than three decimal places are exact; see the footnote to Table 1.2 on p. 8

1.8 Stochastic Frontier Analysis

Distance, revenue, cost and profit functions can always be written in the form of regression models with unobserved error terms representing statistical noise and different types of inefficiency. In practice, the noise components are almost always assumed to be stochastic. The associated frontiers are known as stochastic frontiers.

1.8.1 Basic Models

Stochastic frontier models (SFMs) are underpinned by only one assumption, namely that production possibilities sets can be represented by distance, revenue, cost and/or profit functions.

Output-Oriented Models

Output-oriented SFMs are mainly used to estimate the measure of OTE defined by (1.13). This involves estimating the output distance function. Any output distance function can be written in the form of a regression model with an error representing statistical noise and another error representing output-oriented technical inefficiency. For example, any output distance function can be written as

$$\ln q_{1it} = \alpha + \lambda t + \sum_{j=1}^{J} \delta_j \ln z_{jit} + \sum_{m=1}^{M} \beta_m \ln x_{mit} - \sum_{n=1}^{N} \gamma_n \ln q^*_{nit} + v_{it} - u_{it} \tag{1.32}$$

where $q^*_{nit} \equiv q_{nit}/q_{1it}$ is a normalised output, $\gamma = (\gamma_1, \ldots, \gamma_N)'$ is a vector of parameters that sum to one, v_{it} is an error representing statistical noise, and $u_{it} \equiv -\ln D^t_O(x_{it}, q_{it}, z_{it})$ is a nonnegative output-oriented technical inefficiency effect. The exact nature of the noise component depends on the unknown output distance function. If the output distance function is given by (1.26), for example, then

$$v_{it} = [\alpha(t) - \alpha - \lambda t] + \left[\sum_{n=1}^{N} \gamma_n \ln q^*_{nit} - \frac{1}{\tau} \ln \left(\sum_{n=1}^{N} \gamma_n q^{*\tau}_{nit}\right)\right]. \tag{1.33}$$

These terms can be viewed as functional form errors.

Input-Oriented Models

Input-oriented SFMs are mainly used to estimate the measure of ITE defined by (1.14). This involves estimating the input distance function. Any input distance function can be written in the form of a regression model with an error representing statistical noise and another error representing *input*-oriented technical inefficiency. For example, any input distance function can be written as

$$-\ln x_{1it} = \xi(t) + \sum_{m=1}^{M} \lambda_m \ln x^*_{mit} - \sum_{n=1}^{N} \phi_n \ln q_{nit} + v_{it} - u_{it} \tag{1.34}$$

where $x^*_{mit} \equiv x_{mit}/x_{1it}$ is a normalised input, $\lambda = (\lambda_1, \ldots, \lambda_M)'$ is a vector of parameters that sum to one, v_{it} is an error representing statistical noise, and $u_{it} \equiv -\ln ITE^t(x_{it}, q_{it}, z_{it})$ is now a nonnegative input-oriented technical inefficiency effect. In this case, the exact nature of the noise component depends on the unknown input distance function. If the input distance function is given by (1.28), for example, then

$$v_{it} = \left[\sum_{j=1}^{J} \kappa_j \ln z_{jit}\right] + \left[\sum_{n=1}^{N} \phi_n \ln q_{nit} - \frac{1}{\tau\eta} \ln\left(\sum_{n=1}^{N} \gamma_n q_{nit}^{\tau}\right)\right]. \quad (1.35)$$

The first term is an omitted variable error. The second term can be viewed as a functional form error.

Other Models

Revenue-, cost- and profit-oriented SFMs are also available. These models are mainly used to estimate measures of revenue, cost and profit efficiency. This involves estimating revenue, cost and profit functions. These functions can also be written in the form of regression models with error terms representing statistical noise and different types of inefficiency.

1.8.2 Maximum Likelihood Estimation

Maximum likelihood (ML) estimation of SFMs involves choosing the unknown parameters to maximise the joint density (or 'likelihood') of the observed data. For simplicity, consider the output-oriented model defined by (1.32). This model can be written more compactly as

$$y_{it} = \alpha + \lambda t + \sum_{j=1}^{J} \delta_j \ln z_{jit} + \sum_{m=1}^{M} \beta_m \ln x_{mit} - \sum_{n=1}^{N} \gamma_n \ln q_{nit}^{*} + \epsilon_{it} \quad (1.36)$$

where $y_{it} \equiv \ln q_{1it}$ denotes the logarithm of the first output and $\epsilon_{it} \equiv v_{it} - u_{it}$ is a composite error representing statistical noise and output-oriented technical inefficiency. The likelihood of the observed data depends on the assumed probability distributions of v_{it} and u_{it}. It is common to assume that

ML3 v_{it} is an independent $N(0, \sigma_v^2)$ random variable, and
ML4 u_{it} is an independent $N^{+}(\mu, \sigma_u^2)$ random variable.

If these assumptions are true, then the ML estimators for the unknown parameters in the model are consistent, asymptotically efficient, and asymptotically normal. Following estimation, ML predictions of u_{it} can be obtained by using the ML parameter estimates to evaluate

$$E(u_{it}|\epsilon_{it}) = \mu_{it}^{*} + \sigma_{*}\left(\frac{\phi(\mu_{it}^{*}/\sigma_{*})}{\Phi(\mu_{it}^{*}/\sigma_{*})}\right) \quad (1.37)$$

where $\mu_{it}^{*} \equiv (\mu\sigma_v^2 - \epsilon_{it}\sigma_u^2)/(\sigma_v^2 + \sigma_u^2)$ and $\sigma_{*}^2 \equiv \sigma_v^2\sigma_u^2/(\sigma_v^2 + \sigma_u^2)$. Let $\tilde{u}_{it}$ denote the ML predictor for u_{it}. The associated predictor for OTE is $\exp(-\tilde{u}_{it})$.

Table 1.14 ML parameter estimates

Parameter	ML	RML
α	0.990	0.480
λ	−0.069	0
δ_1	0.258	0.110
β_1	0.148	0.092
β_2	0.279	0.289
γ_1	0.682	0.676
γ_2	0.318	0.324
σ_u^2	0.225	0.000
σ_v^2	0.000	0.083
μ	−0.139	−0.026

Table 1.15 ML predictions of OTE

Row	Firm	Period	ML	RML
A	1	1	0.398	0.995
B	2	1	0.510	0.995
C	3	1	0.944	0.995
D	4	1	0.921	0.995
E	5	1	0.985	0.995
F	1	2	0.492	0.995
G	2	2	0.880	0.995
H	3	2	1.000	0.995
I	4	2	0.381	0.995
J	5	2	0.956	0.995
K	1	3	0.933	0.995
L	2	3	0.511	0.995
M	3	3	0.620	0.995
N	4	3	0.628	0.995
O	5	3	0.765	0.995
P	1	4	0.640	0.995
R	2	4	0.694	0.995
S	3	4	0.528	0.995
T	4	4	0.972	0.995
U	5	4	0.679	0.995
V	1	5	0.884	0.995
W	2	5	0.910	0.995
X	3	5	0.637	0.995
Y	4	5	0.597	0.995
Z	5	5	0.965	0.995

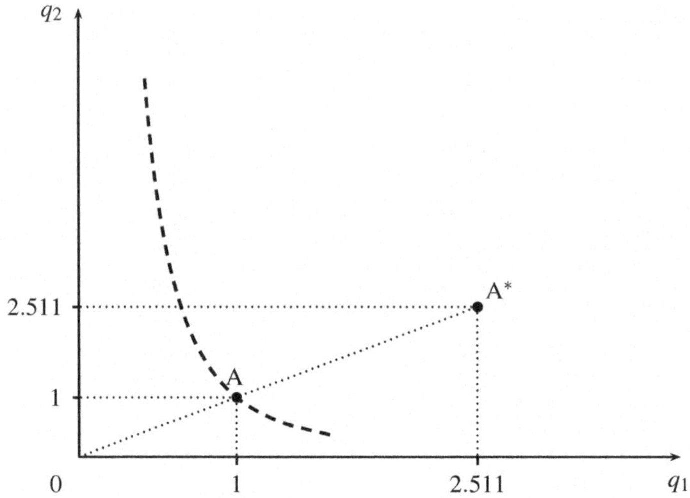

Fig. 1.18 A prediction of output-oriented technical efficiency. In the case of firm A, the ML prediction of OTE is $\hat{OTE}^1(x_{11}, q_{11}, z_{11}) = 1/2.511 = 0.398$

For a numerical example, reconsider the toy data in Table 1.1. These data have been used to obtain ML and restricted ML (RML) estimates of the unknown parameters in (1.32). The estimates are reported in Table 1.14. Both sets of estimates were obtained under assumptions ML3 and ML4. The RML estimates were obtained by restricting $\lambda \geq 0$. Both sets of estimates have been used to predict levels of OTE. The predictions are reported in Table 1.15. The ML prediction for manager 1 in period 1 is depicted in Fig. 1.18. In this figure, the outputs of firm 1 in period 1 map to point A. The associated predicted frontier output is represented by A*. The dashed line is an estimate of *a function that provides an approximation to* the true frontier depicted earlier in Fig. 1.5.

1.8.3 Productivity Analysis

For purposes of comparison with Sects. 1.6.2 and 1.7.3, this section again focuses on decomposing proper TFPI numbers. Again, both output- and input-oriented decompositions are available. In each case, the precise form of the decomposition depends partly on the SFM.

For an output-oriented example, consider the model defined by (1.32). After some simple algebra, the antilogarithm of this equation can be written as:

$$1 = \exp(\alpha + \lambda t) \left[\prod_{j=1}^{J} z_{jit}^{\delta_j} \right] \left[\prod_{m=1}^{M} x_{mit}^{\beta_m} \prod_{n=1}^{N} q_{nit}^{-\gamma_n} \right] \exp(-u_{it}) \exp(v_{it}). \quad (1.38)$$

Multiplying both sides of this equation by $TFP(x_{it}, q_{it})$ yields

$$TFP(x_{it}, q_{it}) = \exp(\alpha + \lambda t)\left[\prod_{j=1}^{J} z_{jit}^{\delta_j}\right]\left[TFP(x_{it}, q_{it})\prod_{m=1}^{M} x_{mit}^{\beta_m}\prod_{n=1}^{N} q_{nit}^{-\gamma_n}\right]$$
$$\times \exp(-u_{it})\exp(v_{it}) \quad (1.39)$$

A similar equation holds for firm k in period s. Substituting these equations into (1.9) yields

$$TFPI(x_{ks}, q_{ks}, x_{it}, q_{it}) = \left[\frac{\exp(\lambda t)}{\exp(\lambda s)}\right]\left[\prod_{j=1}^{J}\left(\frac{z_{jit}}{z_{jks}}\right)^{\delta_j}\right]$$
$$\times \left[TFPI(x_{ks}, q_{ks}, x_{it}, q_{it})\prod_{m=1}^{M}\left(\frac{x_{mit}}{x_{mks}}\right)^{\beta_m}\prod_{n=1}^{N}\left(\frac{q_{nks}}{q_{nit}}\right)^{\gamma_n}\right]$$
$$\times \left[\frac{\exp(-u_{it})}{\exp(-u_{ks})}\right]\left[\frac{\exp(v_{it})}{\exp(v_{ks})}\right] \quad (1.40)$$

In theory, the presence of statistical noise means we cannot interpret the first three terms in this equation in the same way we interpreted the first three terms in (1.30). However, in practice, the first term would normally be viewed as an output-oriented technology index (OTI), the second term would normally be viewed as an output-oriented environment index (OEI), and the third term would normally be viewed as an output-oriented scale and mix efficiency index (OSMEI). In both theory and practice, the fourth term is an output-oriented technical efficiency index (OTEI), and the last term is a statistical noise index (SNI). Again, the conditions under which these various terms vanish is left as an exercise for the reader.

For an input-oriented example, consider the model defined by (1.34). After some simple algebra, the antilogarithm of this equation can be written as:

$$1 = \exp[\xi(t)]\left[\prod_{m=1}^{M} x_{mit}^{\lambda_m}\prod_{n=1}^{N} q_{nit}^{-\phi_n}\right]\exp(-u_{it})\exp(v_{it}). \quad (1.41)$$

Multiplying both sides of this equation by $TFP(x_{it}, q_{it})$ yields

$$TFP(x_{it}, q_{it}) = \exp[\xi(t)]\left[TFP(x_{it}, q_{it})\prod_{m=1}^{M} x_{mit}^{\lambda_m}\prod_{n=1}^{N} q_{nit}^{-\phi_n}\right]$$
$$\times \exp(-u_{it})\exp(v_{it}) \quad (1.42)$$

A similar equation holds for firm k in period s. Substituting these equations into (1.9) yields

$$TFPI(x_{ks}, q_{ks}, x_{it}, q_{it}) = \left[\frac{\exp[\xi(t)]}{\exp[\xi(s)]}\right] \times \left[TFPI(x_{ks}, q_{ks}, x_{it}, q_{it}) \prod_{m=1}^{M} \left(\frac{x_{mit}}{x_{mks}}\right)^{\lambda_m} \prod_{n=1}^{N} \left(\frac{q_{nks}}{q_{nit}}\right)^{\phi_n}\right] \times \left[\frac{\exp(-u_{it})}{\exp(-u_{ks})}\right]\left[\frac{\exp(v_{it})}{\exp(v_{ks})}\right] \tag{1.43}$$

Again, the presence of statistical noise means we cannot interpret the first two terms in this equation in the same way we interpreted the first and third terms in (1.31). However, in practice, the first term would normally be viewed as an input-oriented

Table 1.16 An output-oriented decomposition of Lowe TFPI numbers using ML[a,b]

Firm	Period	TFPI	OTI	OEI	OTEI	OSMEI	SNI
1	1	1	1	1	1	1	1
2	1	1.786	1	1	1.281	1.394	1.000
3	1	2.37	1	1	2.37	1	1.000
4	1	2.703	1	1	2.314	1.168	1.000
5	1	3.516	1	1	2.474	1.421	1.000
1	2	2.117	0.933	1.196	1.236	1.534	1.000
2	2	3.515	0.933	1.196	2.209	1.426	1.000
3	2	3.513	0.933	1	2.511	1.499	1.000
4	2	2.675	0.933	1.196	0.958	2.503	1.000
5	2	3.159	0.933	1	2.400	1.410	1.000
1	3	3.110	0.871	1	2.344	1.523	1.000
2	3	2.760	0.871	1	1.283	2.469	1.000
3	3	1.879	0.871	1	1.556	1.386	1.000
4	3	3.516	0.871	1	1.578	2.557	1.000
5	3	2	0.871	1.196	1.920	1	1.000
1	4	1.923	0.813	1	1.607	1.472	1.000
2	4	2.032	0.813	1	1.743	1.433	1.000
3	4	1.509	0.813	1.196	1.327	1.170	1.000
4	4	2.852	0.813	1.196	2.441	1.202	1.000
5	4	2.134	0.813	1	1.705	1.539	1.000
1	5	3.150	0.759	1	2.220	1.869	1.000
2	5	2.176	0.759	1.196	2.285	1.050	1.000
3	5	1.991	0.759	1.196	1.599	1.372	1.000
4	5	1.351	0.759	1	1.498	1.188	1.000
5	5	1.758	0.759	1	2.424	0.955	1.000

[a]TFPI = OTI × OEI × OTEI × OSMEI × SNI. Some index numbers may be incoherent at the third decimal place due to rounding (e.g., the product of the OTI, OEI, OTEI, OSMEI and SNI numbers in row 6 is not exactly equal to the TFPI number due to rounding)

[b]Numbers reported to less than three decimal places are exact; see the footnote to Table 1.2 on p. 8

technology index (ITI), and the second term would normally be viewed as an input-oriented scale and mix efficiency index (ISMEI). In both theory and practice, the third term is an input-oriented technical efficiency index (ITEI), and the last term is a statistical noise index (SNI). Again, the conditions under which these terms vanish is left as an exercise for the reader.

For a numerical example, reconsider the toy data in Tables 1.1 and 1.2. The associated Lowe TFPI numbers were reported earlier in Table 1.6. An output-oriented decomposition of these numbers is now reported in Table 1.16. The OTI, OEI and OSMEI numbers in each row were obtained by using the ML estimates in Table 1.14 to evaluate the relevant terms in (1.40). The OTEI numbers were obtained by taking ratios of the ML predictions of OTE reported earlier in Table 1.15. The SNI numbers were obtained as residuals (i.e., SNI = TFPI/(OTI×OEI×OTEI×OSMEI)).

1.8.4 Other Models

Other SFMs discussed in this book include various systems of equations. These systems can be used to explain variations in metafrontiers, output supplies and input demands.

1.9 Practical Considerations

This section considers some of the steps involved in conducting a policy-oriented analysis of managerial performance. It also considers government policies that can be used to target the main drivers of performance. In this book, the term 'government' refers to a group of people with the authority to control any variables that are not controlled by firm managers.

1.9.1 The Main Steps

Policy-oriented performance analysis involves a number of steps that are best completed in a prescribed order or sequence. The main steps are the following (immediate predecessor steps are in parentheses):

1. Identify the manager(s).
2. Classify the variables that are physically involved in the production process (1).
3. Identify relevant measures of comparative performance (2).
4. Make assumptions about production technologies (2).
5. Assemble relevant data (3).
6. Select functions to represent production possibilities sets (4, 5).
7. Choose an estimation approach (4, 5).

8. Estimate the model and test the model assumptions (6, 7).
9. Check if the main results are robust to the assumptions and choices made in steps 4, 6 and 7 (8).

Researchers with little interest in policy often complete these steps in a different order. For example, academic researchers who are primarily interested in getting their work published often start at Step 7 (i.e., they choose the estimation approach first).

1.9.2 Government Policies

Changes in most measures of managerial performance can be attributed to four main factors: (a) technical progress, (b) environmental change, (c) technical efficiency change, and (c) scale, mix and/or allocative efficiency change. Different government policies affect, and can therefore be used to target, these different components. For example, governments can often increase rates of technical progress by conducting their own R&D, or by directly funding others to conduct R&D. They can often change production environments by, for example, regulating (or failing to regulate) the impact of production processes on the natural environment, and by providing and/or decommissioning different types of public infrastructure. They can often raise levels of technical efficiency by, for example, removing barriers to the adoption of particular technologies, and by providing education and training services to advise managers about the existence and proper use of new technologies. Finally, governments can often raise levels of scale and mix efficiency by changing the variables that drive managerial behaviour. For example, if firms are price-takers in output and input markets, and if managers seek to maximise profits, then governments can often raise levels of scale and mix efficiency by changing relative output and input prices (e.g., by changing minimum wages, interest rates, taxes and/or subsidies).

1.10 Summary and Further Reading

This book is concerned with measuring and explaining changes in managerial performance. The focus is on measures of performance that are useful for policy makers. Most, if not all, of these measures can be viewed as measures of efficiency and/or productivity. The measures of efficiency discussed in this book include measures of technical, scale, mix, revenue, cost, profit and allocative efficiency. Measures of efficiency that are *not* discussed include the measure of marginal cost efficiency discussed by Kutlu and Wang (2018), the measure of environmental efficiency defined by Coelli et al. (2007, Eq. 7), and the measure of irrigation water efficiency defined by Karagiannis et al. (2003, Eq. 2). Most of these other measures can, in fact, be viewed as special cases of the measures discussed in this book.

The measures of productivity discussed in this book include measures of total factor productivity (TFP), multifactor productivity (MFP) and partial factor productivity (PFP). In this book, TFP is defined as a measure of total output quantity divided by a measure of total input quantity. Measures of MFP and PFP can be viewed as measures of TFP in which one or more inputs have been assigned a weight of zero. The definition of TFP used in this book is consistent with concepts and definitions of TFP and/or TFP change that can be found in, for example, Barton and Cooper (1948, p. 123),[5] Jorgenson and Griliches (1967, pp. 249, 250), Christensen and Jorgenson (1970, p. 42), Nadiri (1970, pp. 1138, 1139), Chambers and Pope (1996, p. 1360), Prescott (1998, p. 526) and Good et al. (1999, Sect. 2.1). Elsewhere in the literature, measures of TFP and/or TFP change are often defined in terms of incomes, revenues and/or costs (e.g., Kendrick 1961, p. 10; Foster et al. 2008, p. 400; Lien et al. 2017, p. 253).

This book attributes changes in TFP to four main factors: technical change, environmental change, technical efficiency change, and scale and mix efficiency change. Elsewhere in the literature, it is common to attribute TFP change to (a) technical change only (e.g., Diewert and Morrison 1986, p. 659; Kumbhakar 2002, pp. 469, 471; Orea and Wall 2012, p. 103), (b) a combination of technical change and technical efficiency change (e.g., Nishimizu and Page 1982, pp. 920, 921; Färe et al. 1994, p. 71; Coelli et al. 2003, p. 323), or (c) a combination of technical change and economies of scale (e.g., Kumbhakar et al. 2000, p. 496; Hranaiova and Stefanou 2002, p. 79). In the macroeconomics literature, it is common to equate TFP change with the residuals from regression models (e.g., Olley and Pakes 1996, p. 1287). These alternative approaches are not generally consistent with the way TFP is defined in this book.

Finally, there are several other measures of managerial performance that are not explicitly discussed in this book. These include various measures of corporate social performance. Most of these measures can, in fact, be viewed as measures of TFP. The literature on these measures can be accessed from Siegel and Vitaliano (2007), Chen and Delmas (2011) and Gregory et al. (2016).

References

Barton G, Cooper M (1948) Relation of agricultural production to inputs. Rev Econ Statist 30(2):117–126

Chambers R, Pope R (1996) Aggregate productivity measures. Am J Agric Econ 78(5):1360–1365

Charnes A, Cooper W, Rhodes E (1981) Evaluating program and managerial efficiency: an application of data envelopment analysis to program follow through. Manage Sci 27(6):668–697

Chen CM, Delmas MA (2011) Measuring corporate social performance: an efficiency perspective. Prod Oper Manage 20(6):789–804

Christensen L, Jorgenson D (1970) U.S. real product and real factor input, 1929–1967. Rev Income Wealth 16(1):19–50

Coelli T, Rahman S, Thirtle C (2003) A stochastic frontier approach to total factor productivity measurement in Bangladesh crop agriculture, 1961–92. J Int Dev 15(3):321–333

Coelli T, Lauwers L, van Huylenbroeck G (2007) Environmental efficiency measurement and the materials balance condition. J Prod Anal 28(1–2):3–12

[5]Barton and Cooper (1948) use the term 'output per unit of input' instead of TFP.

Cooper W, Seiford L, Thanassoulis E, Zanakis S (2004) DEA and its uses in different countries. Eur J Oper Res 154(2):337–344
Diewert W, Morrison C (1986) Adjusting output and productivity indexes for changes in the terms of trade. Econ J 96(383):659–679
Elteto O, Koves P (1964) On a problem of index number computation relating to international comparison. Statisztikai Sz 42:507–518
Färe R, Grosskopf S (2010) Directional distance functions and slacks-based measures of efficiency. Eur J Oper Res 200(1):320–322
Färe R, Grosskopf S, Norris M, Zhang Z (1994) Productivity growth, technical progress, and efficiency change in industrialized countries. Am Econ Rev 84(1):66–83
Foster L, Haltiwanger J, Syverson C (2008) Reallocation, firm turnover, and efficiency: selection on productivity or profitability? Am Econ Rev 98(1):394–425
Good D, Nadiri M, Sickles R (1999) Index number and factor demand approaches to the estimation of poductivity, vol II. Microeconometrics, Basil Blackwell, Oxford
Gregory A, Whittaker J, Yan X (2016) Corporate social performance, competitive advantage, earnings persistence and firm value. J Bus Finan Acc 43(1&2):3–30
Hranaiova J, Stefanou S (2002) Scale, productivity growth and risk response under uncertainty. Economia Agrar y Recursos Naturales 2(2):73–91
Jorgenson D, Griliches Z (1967) The explanation of productivity change. Rev Econ Stud 34(3):249–283
Karagiannis G, Tzouvelekas T, Xepapadeas A (2003) Measuring irrigation water efficiency with a stochastic production frontier. Env Res Econ 26(1):57–72
Kendrick J (1961) Productivity trends in the United States. Princeton University Press
Kumbhakar S (2002) Risk preference and productivity measurement under output price uncertainty. Empirical Econ 27(3):461–472
Kumbhakar S, Nakamura S, Heshmati A (2000) Estimation of firm-specific technological bias, technical change and total factor productivity growth: a dual approach. Econometric Rev 19(4):162–173
Kutlu L, Wang R (2018) Estimation of cost efficiency without cost data. J Prod Anal 49(2–3):137–151
Lien G, Kumbhakar S, Hardaker J (2017) Accounting for risk in productivity analysis: an application to Norwegian dairy farming. J Prod Anal 47(3):247–257
Nadiri M (1970) Some approaches to the theory and measurement of total factor productivity: a survey. J Econ Lit 8(4):1137–1177
Nishimizu M, Page J (1982) Total factor productivity growth, technological progress and technical efficiency change: dimensions of productivity change in Yugoslavia, 1965–1978. Econ J 92(368):920–936
O'Donnell C (2012) Nonparametric estimates of the components of productivity and profitability change in U.S. agriculture. Am J Agric Econ 94(4):873–890
O'Donnell C (2016) Using information about technologies, markets and firm behaviour to decompose a proper productivity index. J Econ 190(2):328–340
O'Donnell C (2017) Estimating total factor productivity change when no price or value-share data are available. Centre for Efficiency and Productivity Analysis Working Papers WP01/2017, University of Queensland
Olley G, Pakes A (1996) The dynamics of productivity in the telecommunications equipment industry. Econometrica 64(6):1263–1297
Orea L, Wall A (2012) Productivity and producer welfare in the presence of production risk. J Agric Econ 63(1):102–118
Prescott E (1998) Lawrence R. Klein Lecture, (1997) Needed: a theory of total factor productivity. Int Econ Rev 39(3):525–551
Siegel D, Vitaliano D (2007) An empirical analysis of the strategic use of corporate social responsibility. J Econ Manage Strategy 16(3):773–792
Szulc B (1964) Indices for multi-regional comparisons. Prezeglad Statystyczny (Statistical Review) 3:239–254

Chapter 2
Production Technologies

To explain variations in managerial performance, we need to know something about what can and cannot be produced using different production technologies. In this book, a production technology (or simply 'technology') is defined as a technique, method or system for transforming inputs into outputs. For most practical purposes, it is convenient to think of a technology as a book of instructions, or recipe. In this book, the set of technologies that exist in a given period is referred to as a technology set. If we think of a technology as a book of instructions, then we can think of a technology set as a library. The input-output combinations that are possible using different technologies can be represented by output sets, input sets and production possibilities sets. Under certain conditions, they can also be represented by distance, revenue, cost and profit functions. This chapter defines, and discusses the properties of, these different sets and functions.

2.1 Output Sets

An output set is a set containing all outputs that can be produced using given inputs. A *period-and-environment-specific* output set is a set containing all outputs that can be produced using given inputs *in a given period in a given production environment.* For example, the set of outputs that can be produced using the input vector x in period t in a production environment characterised by z is

$$P^t(x, z) = \{q : x \text{ can produce } q \text{ in period } t \text{ in environment } z\}. \quad (2.1)$$

This set provides the foundation for much of the analysis in this book. If there are no environmental variables involved in the production process (i.e., if there is no environmental change), then all references to environment z can be deleted. If there is no technical change, then all references to period t can be deleted. If there is no

C. J. O'Donnell, *Productivity and Efficiency Analysis*,
https://doi.org/10.1007/978-981-13-2984-5_2

environmental change, then the set defined by (2.1) is equal to the output set defined by Balk (1998, Eq. 2.3). If there is no technical or environmental change, then it is equal to the output set defined by Shephard (1970, p. 179).

2.1.1 Assumptions

It is common to make assumptions about technologies by way of assumptions about what they can and cannot produce. For example, it is common to assume that, with a given set of technologies,

- A1 it is possible to produce zero output (i.e., inactivity is possible);
- A2 there is a limit to what can be produced using a finite amount of inputs (i.e., output sets are bounded);
- A3 a positive amount of at least one input is needed in order to produce a strictly positive amount of any output (i.e., inputs are weakly essential; there is 'no free lunch');
- A4 the set of outputs that can be produced using given inputs contains all the points on its boundary (i.e., output sets are closed);
- A5 the set of inputs that can produce given outputs contains all the points on its boundary (i.e., input sets are closed);
- A6 if particular inputs can be used to produce a given output vector, then they can also be used to produce a scalar contraction of that output vector (i.e., outputs are weakly disposable); and
- A7 if particular outputs can be produced using a given input vector, then they can also be produced using a scalar magnification of that input vector (i.e., inputs are weakly disposable).

Assumptions A1–A7 are maintained throughout this book. Other assumptions that are made from time to time include the following:

- A3s a positive amount of *every* input is needed to produce a nonzero amount of output (i.e., inputs are strictly essential);
- A4s the set of input-output combinations that are physically possible contains all the points on its boundary (i.e., production possibilities sets are closed);
- A6s if given inputs can be used to produce particular outputs, then they can also be used to produce fewer outputs (i.e., outputs are strongly disposable);
- A7s if given outputs can be produced using particular inputs, then they can also be produced using more inputs (i.e., inputs are strongly disposable);
- A8s if a given output-input combination is possible in a particular production environment, then it is also possible in a better production environment (i.e., environmental variables are strongly disposable)[1]; and

[1]Coelli et al. (2005, p. 192) refer to strongly disposable environmental variables as 'positive effect' environmental variables.

A9s (a) a suitable magnification of a positive input vector can produce any finite output vector, and (b) if some magnification of a non-zero input vector can produce a positive output vector, then it can, by another suitable magnification, produce any finite output vector (i.e., outputs are strongly attainable).

Assumptions A3s, A4s, A6s and A7s are stronger than assumptions A3, A4, A6 and A7 in the sense that the former imply the latter (i.e., A3s $\Rightarrow$ A3, A4s $\Rightarrow$ A4, ..., A7s $\Rightarrow$ A7). Assumptions concerning technologies can usually be written more precisely using output sets and mathematics. To illustrate, consider the period-and-environment-specific output set defined by (2.1). In this case, A1–A7 can be written as follows:

O1 $0 \in P^t(x, z)$ for all $(x, z) \in \mathbb{R}_+^{M+J}$ (inactivity);
O2 $P^t(x, z)$ is bounded for all $(x, z) \in \mathbb{R}_+^{M+J}$ (output sets are bounded);
O3 $q \geq 0 \Rightarrow q \notin P^t(0, z)$ (inputs weakly essential; no free lunch);
O4 $P^t(x, z)$ is closed for all $(x, z) \in \mathbb{R}_+^{M+J}$ (output sets closed);
O5 the set $\{x : q \in P^t(x, z)\}$ is closed for all $(q, z) \in \mathbb{R}_+^{N+J}$ (input sets closed);
O6 $q \in P^t(x, z)$ and $0 \leq \lambda \leq 1 \Rightarrow \lambda q \in P^t(x, z)$ (outputs weakly disposable); and
O7 $q \in P^t(x, z)$ and $\lambda \geq 1 \Rightarrow q \in P^t(\lambda x, z)$ (inputs weakly disposable).

If there is no technical or environmental change, then these assumptions are equivalent to the maintained axioms P.1–P.7 in Färe and Primont (1995, p. 27). In addition, A3s, A4s and A6s–A9s can be written as follows:

O3s $q \geq 0$ and $x_m = 0$ for any $m \Rightarrow q \notin P^t(x, z)$ (inputs strictly essential);
O4s the set $\{(x, q) : q \in P^t(x, z)\}$ is closed for all $z \in \mathbb{R}_+^J$ (prod. poss. sets closed);
O6s $q \in P^t(x, z)$ and $0 \leq \bar{q} \leq q \Rightarrow \bar{q} \in P^t(x, z)$ (outputs strongly disposable);
O7s $q \in P^t(x, z)$ and $\bar{x} \geq x \Rightarrow q \in P^t(\bar{x}, z)$ (inputs strongly disposable);
O8s $q \in P^t(x, z)$ and $\bar{z} \geq z \Rightarrow q \in P^t(x, \bar{z})$ (environ. variables strongly disp.); and
O9s if $x > 0$, or $x \geq 0$ and $\bar{q} \in P^t(\lambda x, z)$ for some $\bar{q} > 0$ and $\lambda > 0$, then, for any $q \in \mathbb{R}_+^N$, there exists a scalar $\phi > 0$ such that $q \in P^t(\phi x, z)$ (outputs strongly attainable).

If there is no technical or environmental change, then O6s and O7s are equivalent to P.2.s and P.6.s in Färe and Primont (1995, p. 27). Other assumptions that are made from time to time include the following:

O9 if $x \geq 0$, $q \geq 0$ and $q \in P^t(\lambda x, z)$ for some scalar $\lambda > 0$, then, for any scalar $\theta > 0$, there exists a scalar $\phi > 0$ such that $\theta q \in P^t(\phi x, z)$ (outputs weakly attainable),
O10 $q \in P^t(x, z) \Leftrightarrow \lambda^r q \in P^t(\lambda x, z)$ for all $\lambda > 0$ (homogeneity),
O11 $P^t(x, z) = G^t(x, z)P^t(\iota, z)$ (output homotheticity),
O13 $P^t(x, z) = E^t(x, z)P^1(x, \iota)$ (implicit Hicks output neutrality), and
O15 $P^t(x, z)$ is convex for all $(x, z) \in \mathbb{R}_+^{M+J}$ (output sets convex),

where ι is a vector of ones with a row dimension that can be inferred from the context (e.g., in O11 it is an $M \times 1$ input vector; in O13 it is a $J \times 1$ vector of environmental variables) and $G^t(.)$ and $E^t(.)$ are scalar-valued functions with properties that are consistent with the properties of $P^t(x, z)$ (e.g., if O10 is true, then $G^t(.)$ must be homogeneous of degree r in inputs). If there is no environmental change, then O11 and O13 are equivalent to definitions that can be found in Balk (1998, pp. 16, 18).[2] If there is no technical or environmental change, then O15 is equivalent to axiom P.9 in Färe and Primont (1995, p. 27).

Assumption O9 (weak attainability) says that if a non-zero input vector can be used to produce a non-zero output vector, then any scalar magnification of that output vector is attainable by a suitable scalar magnification of the input vector. Assumption O10 (homogeneity) says that if a firm is operating on the production frontier and its inputs are increased by one percent, then its outputs can be increased by r percent. In this book, the production frontier is said to exhibit decreasing returns to scale (DRS), nonincreasing returns to scale (NIRS), constant returns to scale (CRS), nondecreasing returns to scale (NDRS), increasing returns to scale (IRS) or variable returns to scale (VRS) as r is less than, no greater than, equal to, no less than, greater than, or not equal to one. Assumption O11 (output homotheticity) says that the outputs that can be produced using given inputs in a given period in a given environment are a scalar multiple of the outputs that can be produced using one unit of each input in the same period in the same environment. If there is only one output, then O11 is true. Assumption, O13 (implicit Hicks output neutrality) says that the outputs that can be produced using given inputs in a given period in a given environment are a scalar multiple of the outputs that can be produced using the same inputs in period one in an environment characterised by a vector of ones. Finally, assumption O15 (output sets convex) says that if an input vector can be used to produce two different output vectors, then it can also be used to produce a convex combination of those output vectors. Shephard (1970, p. 187) argues that O15 is valid for 'time divisible' technologies: the argument is that if $q \in P^t(x, z)$ and $\bar{q} \in P^t(x, z)$, then using x to produce the convex combination $(1 - \lambda)q + \lambda\bar{q}$ is equivalent to producing q a fraction $(1 - \lambda)$ of the time and producing $\bar{q}$ a fraction λ of the time. If market prices are not affected by the outputs of firms (i.e., if firms are 'price takers' in output markets) and both O6s and 015 are true (i.e., if outputs are strongly disposable and output sets are convex), then

O17 $P^t(x, z) = \{q : p'q \leq R^t(x, p, z) \text{ for all } p > 0\}$

where $R^t(x, p, z)$ is the revenue function defined by (2.16). This means that the output set is completely characterised by the revenue function. If there is no technical or environmental change, then this so-called duality result is equivalent to proposition (3.1.5) in Färe and Primont (1995, p. 49) .

[2]The reference vectors in O11 and O13 are arbitrary. Vectors of ones have been chosen here for notational convenience. The choice of reference period in O13 is also arbitrary. Again, period 1 has been chosen for notational convenience.

2.1.2 Example

Many of the examples presented in this book are built around the following period-and-environment-specific output set:

$$P^t(x,z) = \left\{ q : \left(\sum_{n=1}^{N} \gamma_n q_n^{\tau} \right)^{1/\tau} \leq A(t) \prod_{j=1}^{J} z_j^{\delta_j} \prod_{m=1}^{M} x_m^{\beta_m} \right\} \tag{2.2}$$

where $A(t) > 0$, $A(t) \geq A(t-1)$, $\beta = (\beta_1, \ldots, \beta_M)' \geq 0$, $\gamma = (\gamma_1, \ldots, \gamma_N)' \geq 0$, $\tau \geq 1$ and $\gamma'\iota = 1$. This set satisfies O3s, O4s, O6s, O7s, O10, O11 and O13.

2.2 Input Sets

An input set is a set containing all inputs that can produce given outputs. A *period-and-environment-specific* input set is a set containing all inputs that can produce given outputs *in a given period in a given production environment*. For example, the set of inputs that can produce the output vector q in period t in a production environment characterised by z is

$$L^t(q,z) = \{x : x \text{ can produce } q \text{ in period } t \text{ in environment } z\}. \tag{2.3}$$

If there is no technical change, then all references to period t can be deleted. If there are no environmental variables involved in the production process (i.e., if there is no environmental change), then all references to environment z can be deleted. If there is no environmental change, then the set defined by (2.3) is equal to the input set defined by Balk (1998, Eq. 2.2). If there is no technical or environmental change, then it is equal to the input set defined by Shephard (1970, p. 179).

2.2.1 Assumptions

Input sets and output sets are equivalent representations of the input-output combinations that are possible using different technologies. This means that assumptions concerning output sets imply, and are implied by, assumptions concerning input sets. Again, it is often convenient to write these assumptions using mathematics. To illustrate, consider the period-and-environment-specific input set defined by (2.3). Mathematically, $x \in L^t(q,z)$ if and only if $q \in P^t(x,z)$. This means that A1–A7 (equivalently, O1–O7) can be written as follows:

I1 $x \in L^t(0,z)$ for all $(x,z) \in \mathbb{R}_+^{M+J}$ (inactivity);
I2 the set $\{q : x \in L^t(q,z)\}$ is bounded for all $(x,z) \in \mathbb{R}_+^{M+J}$;

I3 $q \geq 0 \Rightarrow 0 \notin L^t(q, z)$ (inputs weakly essential; no free lunch);
I4 the set $\{q : x \in L^t(q, z)\}$ is closed for all $(x, z) \in \mathbb{R}_+^{M+J}$ (output sets closed);
I5 $L^t(q, z)$ is closed for all $(q, z) \in \mathbb{R}_+^{N+J}$ (input sets closed);
I6 $x \in L^t(q, z)$ and $0 \leq \lambda \leq 1 \Rightarrow x \in L^t(\lambda q, z)$ (outputs weakly disposable); and
I7 $x \in L^t(q, z)$ and $\lambda \geq 1 \Rightarrow \lambda x \in L^t(q, z)$ (inputs weakly disposable).

Furthermore, if O3s, O4s, O6s–O9s, O9 and O10 are true, then, and only then (respectively):

I3s $q \geq 0$ and $x_m = 0$ for any $m \Rightarrow x \notin L^t(q, z)$ (inputs strictly essential);
I4s the set $\{(x, q) : x \in L^t(q, z)\}$ is closed for all $z \in \mathbb{R}_+^J$ (prod. poss. sets closed);
I6s $x \in L^t(q, z)$ and $0 \leq \bar{q} \leq q \Rightarrow x \in L^t(\bar{q}, z)$ (outputs strongly disposable);
I7s $x \in L^t(q, z)$ and $\bar{x} \geq x \Rightarrow \bar{x} \in L^t(q, z)$ (inputs strongly disposable);
I8s $x \in L^t(q, z)$ and $\bar{z} \geq z \Rightarrow x \in L^t(q, \bar{z})$ (environ. variables strongly disp);
I9s If $x > 0$, or $x \geq 0$ and $\lambda x \in L^t(\bar{q}, z)$ for some $\bar{q} > 0$ and $\lambda > 0$, then, for any $q \in \mathbb{R}_+^N$, there exists a scalar $\phi > 0$ such that $\phi x \in L^t(q, z)$ (outputs strongly attainable);
I9 if $x \geq 0$, $q \geq 0$ and $\lambda x \in L^t(q, z)$ for some scalar $\lambda > 0$, then, for any scalar $\theta > 0$, there exists a scalar $\phi > 0$ such that $\phi x \in L^t(\theta q, z)$ (outputs weakly attainable); and
I10 $L^t(\lambda q, z) = \lambda^{1/r} L^t(q, z)$ for all $\lambda > 0$ (homogeneity).

Other assumptions that are made from time to time include the following

I12 $L^t(q, z) = K^t(q, z)L^t(\iota, z)$ (input homotheticity),
I14 $L^t(q, z) = J^t(q, z)L^1(q, \iota)$ (implicit Hicks input neutrality), and
I16 $L^t(q, z)$ is convex for all $(q, z) \in \mathbb{R}_+^{N+J}$ (input sets convex),

where $K^t(.)$ and $J^t(.)$ are scalar-valued functions with properties that are consistent with the properties of $L^t(q, z)$ (e.g., if I10 is true, then $K^t(.)$ must be homogeneous of degree $1/r$ in outputs). If there is no environmental change, then I12 and I14 are equivalent to definitions that can be found in Balk (1998, pp. 16, 17).[3] Assumption I12 (input homotheticity) says that the inputs that can produce a given output vector in a given period in a given environment are a scalar multiple of the inputs that can produce one unit of each output in the same period in the same environment. If there is only one input, then I12 is true. Assumption I14 (implicit Hicks input neutrality) says that the inputs that can produce a given output vector in a given period in a given environment are a scalar multiple of the inputs that can produce the same outputs in period one in an environment characterised by a vector of ones. Technical change is said to be Hicks-neutral (HN) if and only if it is both implicit Hicks output neutral (IHON) and implicit Hicks input neutral (IHIN). Finally, I16 (input sets convex) says that if an output vector can be produced using two different input vectors, then it can also be produced using a convex combination of those input vectors. Again, Shephard (1970, p. 15) argues that I16 is valid for time divisible technologies: in this case, the argument is that if $x \in L^t(q, z)$ and $\bar{x} \in L^t(q, z)$, then using the convex

[3]In I12 and I14, the reference vectors are again arbitrary. In I14, the choice of reference period is also arbitrary.

combination $(1-\lambda)x + \lambda\bar{x}$ to produce q is equivalent to using x a fraction $(1-\lambda)$ of the time and using $\bar{x}$ a fraction λ of the time. If market prices are not affected by the inputs demanded by the firm (i.e., if the firm is a 'price taker' in input markets) and both I7s and I16 are true (i.e., if inputs are strongly disposable and input sets are convex), then

I18 $L^t(q, z) = \{x : w'x \geq C^t(w, q, z) \text{ for all } w > 0\}$

where $C^t(w, q, z)$ is the cost function defined by (2.21). This means that the input set is completely characterised by the cost function. If there is no technical or environmental change, then this duality result is equivalent to proposition (3.1.2) in Färe and Primont (1995, p. 45).

2.2.2 Example

If the period-and-environment-specific output set is given by (2.2), then, and only then, the period-and-environment-specific input set is

$$L^t(q, z) = \left\{ x : \prod_{m=1}^{M} x_m^{\lambda_m} \geq \left(B(t) \prod_{j=1}^{J} z_j^{\kappa_j} \right)^{-1} \left(\sum_{n=1}^{N} \gamma_n q_n^{\tau} \right)^{1/(\tau\eta)} \right\} \quad (2.4)$$

where $\eta = \beta'\iota > 0$, $B(t) = A(t)^{1/\eta} > 0$, $B(t) \geq B(t-1)$, $\lambda = (\lambda_1, \ldots, \lambda_M)' = \beta/\eta \geq 0$, $\gamma = (\gamma_1, \ldots, \gamma_N)' \geq 0$, $\kappa_j = \delta_j/\eta$ for all j, $\tau \geq 1$ and $\gamma'\iota = \lambda'\iota = 1$. This set satisfies I3s, I4s, I6s, I7s, I10, I12 and I14.

2.3 Production Possibilities Sets

A production possibilities set is a set containing all input-output combinations that are physically possible. In this book, the focus is on two specific types of production possibilities set: *period-and-environment-specific* production possibilities sets and period-environment-*and-mix-specific* production possibilities sets.

A *period-and-environment-specific* production possibilities set is a set containing all input-output combinations that are physically possible *in a given period in a given production environment*. For example, the set of input-output combinations that are physically possible in period t in a production environment characterised by z is

$$T^t(z) = \{(x, q) : x \text{ can produce } q \text{ in period } t \text{ in environment } z\}. \quad (2.5)$$

This set can be found in O'Donnell (2016, p. 330). If there is no technical change, then all references to period t can be deleted. If there are no environmental variables involved in the production process (i.e., if there is no environmental change), then all references to environment z can be deleted. If there is no technical change, then the set defined by (2.5) is equal to the 'range of possible combinations of inputs × outputs' defined by Badin et al. (2012, Eq. 1.2). If there is no environmental change, then it is equal to the 'technology' defined by Balk (1998, Eq. 2.1). If there is no technical or environmental change, then it is equal to the 'graph' defined by Shephard (1970, p. 181).

A period-environment-*and-mix-specific* production possibilities set is a set containing all input-output combinations that are physically possible *when using a scalar multiple of a given input vector to produce a scalar multiple of a given output vector* in a given period in a given production environment. For example, the set of input-output combinations that are possible when using a scalar multiple of $\bar{x}$ to produce a scalar multiple of $\bar{q}$ in period t in an environment characterised by z is

$$T^t(\bar{x}, \bar{q}, z) = \{(x, q) : x \propto \bar{x},\ q \propto \bar{q},\ (x, q) \in T^t(z)\}. \tag{2.6}$$

This set can be found in O'Donnell (2016, p. 331). By construction, $T^t(\bar{x}, \bar{q}, z) \subseteq T^t(z)$.

2.3.1 Assumptions

Production possibilities sets, output sets and input sets are equivalent representations of the input-output combinations that are possible using different technologies. Again, this means that assumptions concerning output and input sets imply, and are implied by, assumptions concerning production possibilities sets. Again, it is often convenient to write these assumptions using mathematics. To illustrate, consider the period-and-environment specific production possibilities set defined by (2.5). Mathematically, $(x, q) \in T^t(z)$ if and only if $q \in P^t(x, z)$. This means that A1–A7 (equivalently, O1–O7) can be written as follows:

T1 $(x, 0) \in T^t(z)$ for all $(x, z) \in \mathbb{R}_+^{M+J}$ (inactivity);
T2 $\{q : (x, q) \in T^t(z)\}$ is bounded for all $(x, z) \in \mathbb{R}_+^{M+J}$ (output sets bounded);
T3 $q \geq 0 \Rightarrow (0, q) \notin T^t(z)$ (inputs weakly essential; no free lunch);
T4 the set $\{q : (x, q) \in T^t(z)\}$ is closed for all $(x, z) \in \mathbb{R}_+^{M+J}$ (output sets closed);
T5 the set $\{x : (x, q) \in T^t(z)\}$ is closed for all $(q, z) \in \mathbb{R}_+^{N+J}$ (input sets closed);
T6 $(x, q) \in T^t(z)$ and $0 \leq \lambda \leq 1 \Rightarrow (x, \lambda q) \in T^t(z)$ (outputs weakly disp.); and
T7 $(x, q) \in T^t(z)$ and $\lambda \geq 1 \Rightarrow (\lambda x, q) \in T^t(z)$ (inputs weakly disposable);

Furthermore, if O3s, O4s, O6s–O9s, O9, O10, O15 and I16 are true, then, and only then (respectively):

T3s $q \geq 0$ and $x_m = 0$ for any $m \Rightarrow (x, q) \notin T^t(z)$ (inputs strictly essential);
T4s $T^t(z)$ is closed for all $z \in \mathbb{R}_+^J$ (production possibilities sets closed);
T6s $(x, q) \in T^t(z)$ and $0 \leq \bar{q} \leq q \Rightarrow (x, \bar{q}) \in T^t(z)$ (outputs strongly disposable);
T7s $(x, q) \in T^t(z)$ and $\bar{x} \geq x \Rightarrow (\bar{x}, q) \in T^t(z)$ (inputs strongly disposable);

T8s $(x, q) \in T^t(z)$ and $\bar{z} \geq z \Rightarrow (x, q) \in T^t(\bar{z})$ (environ. variables strongly disp.);

T9s If $x > 0$, or $x \geq 0$ and $(\lambda x, \bar{q}) \in T^t(z)$ for some $\bar{q} > 0$ and $\lambda > 0$, then, for any $q \in \mathbb{R}_+^N$, there exists a scalar $\phi > 0$ such that $(\phi x, q) \in T^t(z)$ (outputs strongly attainable);

T9 If $x \geq 0, q \geq 0$ and $(\lambda x, q) \in T^t(z)$ for some scalar $\lambda > 0$, then, for any scalar $\theta > 0$, there exists a scalar $\phi > 0$ such that $(\phi x, \theta q) \in T^t(z)$ (outputs weakly attainable);

T10 $(x, q) \in T^t(z) \Leftrightarrow (\lambda x, \lambda^r q) \in T^t(z)$ for all $\lambda > 0$ (homogeneity);

T15 $\{q : (x, q) \in T^t(z)\}$ is convex for all $(x, z) \in \mathbb{R}_+^{M+J}$ (output sets convex); and

T16 $\{x : (x, q) \in T^t(z)\}$ is convex for all $(q, z) \in \mathbb{R}_+^{N+J}$ (input sets convex).

2.3.2 *Example*

If the period-and-environment-specific output set is given by (2.2), then, and only then, the period-and-environment-specific production possibilities set is

$$T^t(z) = \left\{ (x, q) : \left(\sum_{n=1}^{N} \gamma_n q_n^{\tau} \right)^{1/\tau} \leq A(t) \prod_{j=1}^{J} z_j^{\delta_j} \prod_{m=1}^{M} x_m^{\beta_m} \right\} \tag{2.7}$$

where $A(t) > 0$, $A(t) \geq A(t-1)$, $\beta = (\beta_1, \ldots, \beta_M)' \geq 0$, $\gamma = (\gamma_1, \ldots, \gamma_N)' \geq 0$, $\tau \geq 1$ and $\gamma' \iota = 1$. This set satisfies T3s, T4s, T6s and T7s.

2.4 Output Distance Functions

If output sets are bounded and outputs are weakly disposable, then the input-output combinations that are possible using different technologies can be represented by output distance functions. An output distance function gives the reciprocal of the largest factor by which it is possible to scale up a given output vector when using a given input vector. A *period-and-environment-specific* output distance function gives the reciprocal of the largest factor by which it is possible to scale up a given output vector when using a given input vector *in a given period in a given production environment*. For example, the reciprocal of the largest factor by which it is possible to scale up q when using x in period t in environment z is

$$D_O^t(x, q, z) = \inf\{\rho > 0 : q/\rho \in P^t(x, z)\}. \tag{2.8}$$

This particular output distance function can be found in O'Donnell (2016, p. 330). If there is no technical (resp. environmental) change, then all references to t (resp. z) can be deleted. If there is no environmental change, then it is equal to the '(direct) output distance function' defined by Balk (1998, Eq. 2.6). If there is no technical or environmental change, then it is equal to the (direct) output distance function defined by Färe and Primont (1995, Eq. 2.1.7). If output sets are closed and there is no technical or environmental change, then it is equal to the distance function defined by Shephard (1970, p. 207).

2.4.1 Properties

The properties of output distance functions can be derived from the properties of output sets. For example, consider the output distance function defined by (2.8). If $P^t(x, z)$ is bounded, then this function exists. If outputs are also weakly disposable, then $q \in P^t(x, z)$ if and only if $D^t_O(x, q, z) \leq 1$ (Färe and Primont 1995, p. 22). More generally, if O1–O7 are true, then the following are true[4]:

DO1 $0 \leq D^t_O(x, q, z)$ for all $(x, q, z) \in \mathbb{R}^{M+N+J}_+$ (nonnegative);
DO2 $D^t_O(x, \lambda q, z) = \lambda D^t_O(x, q, z)$ for all $\lambda > 0$ and $(x, q, z) \in \mathbb{R}^{M+N+J}_+$ (linearly homogeneous in q);
DO3 $0 \leq D^t_O(x, q, z) \leq 1$ for all $q \in P^t(x, z)$, $D^t_O(x, 0, z) = 0$ for all $(x, z) \in \mathbb{R}^{M+J}_+$, and $D^t_O(0, q, z) = +\infty$ for all $q \geq 0$;
DO4 $D^t_O(x, q, z)$ is continuous in q for all $(x, z) \in \mathbb{R}^{M+J}_+$; and
DO5 $D^t_O(x, q, z)$ is lower semi-continuous in x for all $(q, z) \in \mathbb{R}^{N+J}_+$.

If O6s, O7s, O9s, O15 and I16 are also true, then the following are true[5]:

DO6 $q \geq \bar{q} \geq 0 \Rightarrow D^t_O(x, q, z) \geq D^t_O(x, \bar{q}, z)$ for all $(x, z) \in \mathbb{R}^{M+J}_+$ (nondecreasing in q);
DO7 $\bar{x} \geq x \Rightarrow D^t_O(\bar{x}, q, z) \leq D^t_O(x, q, z)$ for all $(q, z) \in \mathbb{R}^{N+J}_+$ (nonincreasing in x);
DO8 $D^t_O(x, q, z)$ is convex in q for all $(x, z) \in \mathbb{R}^{M+J}_+$; and
DO9 $D^t_O(x, q, z)$ is quasiconvex in x for all $(q, z) \in \mathbb{R}^{N+J}_+$.

If O10, O11 and O13 are true, then, and only then, the following are true (respectively)[6]:

DO10 $D^t_O(\lambda x, q, z) = \lambda^{-r} D^t_O(x, q, z)$ for all $\lambda > 0$ (homogeneity);
DO11 $D^t_O(x, q, z) = D^t_O(\iota, q, z)/G^t(x, z)$ (output homotheticity); and
DO13 $D^t_O(x, q, z) = D^1_O(x, q, \iota)/E^t(x, z)$ (implicit Hicks output neutrality).

---

[4]If O1 and O2 are true, then DO1 and DO2 are true. The first part of DO3 is obvious. The last two parts of DO3 are equivalent to $D_o.1$ and $D_o.5$ in Färe and Primont (1995, pp. 17, 18). DO4 $\Leftrightarrow$ $\nabla.7$ in Shephard (1970, pp. 208, 211) which is satisfied under $D_o.4$ in Färe and Primont (1995). DO2 and O4 $\Rightarrow$ DO5. DO5 is equivalent to $D_o.4$ in Färe and Primont (1995).

[5]O6s $\Rightarrow$ DO6 and O7s $\Rightarrow$ DO7 (Shephard 1970, proof of $\nabla.5$ and $\nabla.8$ on pp. 210–211). If O1, O2, O4, O5, O6s, O7s, O9s, O15 and I16 are true, then $\overline{\text{A.1}}$–$\overline{\text{A.8}}$ in Shephard (1970) are true. Then DO8 and DO9 follow from Shephard (1970, pp. 207, 208, Prop. 61).

[6]Proofs of DO11 and DO13 are given in Appendix A.1 (Propositions 1 and 3).

Property DO10 says that the output distance function is homogeneous of degree $-r$ in inputs. If this is true, then $D_O^t(x, q, z) = D_I^t(x, q, z)^{-r}$ where $D_I^t(x, q, z)$ is the input distance function defined by (2.12) (e.g., O'Donnell 2016, Proposition 3). Properties DO11 and DO13 can be viewed as separability properties: if they are both true, then the output distance function can be written as $D_O^t(x, q, z) = Q(q)/F^t(x, z)$ where $Q(q) = D_O^1(\iota, q, \iota)$ can be viewed as an aggregate output and $F^t(x, z) = E^t(\iota, z)G^t(x, z)$ can be viewed as a production function.[7] For more details concerning production functions, see Sect. 2.9.1. If (a) output and input sets are homothetic, (b) technical change is HN, and (c) production frontiers exhibit CRS, then the output distance function can be written as $D_O^t(x, q, z) = Q(q)/[A^t(z)F(x)]$ where $Q(q) = D_O^1(\iota, q, \iota)$, $A^t(z) = E^t(\iota, z)$ and $F(x) = D_I^1(x, \iota, \iota)/D_I^1(\iota, \iota, \iota)$.[8] Finally, if firms are price takers in output markets and both O6s and 015 are true (i.e., if outputs are strongly disposable and output sets are convex), then

DO17 $D_O^t(x, q, z) = \sup_p\{p'q : R^t(x, p, z) \leq 1\}$

where $R^t(x, p, z)$ is the revenue function defined by (2.16). This means that the output distance function is completely characterised by the revenue function. If there is no technical or environmental change, then this result is equivalent to a duality result that can be found in Färe and Primont (1995, p. 50).

2.4.2 *Marginal Effects*

If output distance functions are continuously differentiable, then differential calculus can be used to define various marginal effects. For example, Table 2.1 presents several marginal effects that can be derived from a differentiable period-and-environment specific output distance function. The m-th *marginal product* (MP) can be interpreted as the radial expansion in the output vector that can be obtained from a marginal increase in input m, holding all other variables fixed. The n-th *normalised shadow output price* can be interpreted as the n-th shadow output price divided by the maximum revenue that a price-taking firm can earn using its inputs; shadow output prices can be interpreted as the prices that would induce price-taking revenue-maximising firms to operate at given points on the boundary of the output set; for more details, see, for example, Färe et al. (1993, p. 376) and Färe and Primont (1995, pp. 58, 59). The n-th *shadow revenue share* is the shadow revenue associated with the n-th output divided by total shadow revenue; shadow revenues are equal to shadow output prices multiplied by outputs. If the output set is homothetic (i.e., if DO11 is true), then shadow revenue shares do not depend on inputs. If technical change is IHON (i.e., if DO13 is true), then shadow revenue shares do not depend on environmental variables and do not change over time. The m-th *output elasticity* can be interpreted as the percent increase in all outputs that can be obtained from a one percent increase in

[7] A proof is given in Appendix A.1 (Proposition 5).

[8] A proof is given in Appendix A.1 (Proposition 17).

Table 2.1 Selected output-oriented marginal effects

Marginal product	$MP^t_m(x,q,z) = \frac{\partial(1/D^t_O(x,q,z))}{\partial x_m}$
Normalised shadow output price	$p^t_n(x,q,z) = \frac{\partial D^t_O(x,q,z)}{\partial q_n}$
Shadow revenue share	$r^t_n(x,q,z) = \frac{\partial \ln D^t_O(x,q,z)}{\partial \ln q_n}$
Output elasticity	$\eta^t_m(x,q,z) = -\frac{\partial \ln D^t_O(x,q,z)}{\partial \ln x_m}$
Elasticity of scale	$\eta^t(x,q,z) = \sum_{m=1}^M \eta^t_m(x,q,z)$
Marginal rate of transformation	$MRT^t_{kn}(x,q,z) = \frac{\partial D^t_O(x,q,z)/\partial q_n}{\partial D^t_O(x,q,z)/\partial q_k}$
Elasticity of transformation	$\sigma^t_{kn}(x,q,z) = \frac{d\ln(q_k/q_n)}{d\ln MRT^t_{kn}(x,q,z)}$

input m, holding all other variables fixed. If the output set is homothetic, then output elasticities do not depend on outputs. The *elasticity of scale* can be interpreted as the percent increase in all outputs that can be obtained from a one percent increase in *all* inputs, holding all other variables fixed. The production frontier is said to exhibit DRS, NIRS, CRS, NDRS or IRS as the elasticity of scale is less than, no greater than, equal to, no less than, or greater than one. If the output set is homothetic, then the elasticity of scale does not depend on outputs. The kn-th *marginal rate of transformation* (MRT) is the marginal rate at which output n can be substituted for output k on the boundary of the output set, holding all other variables fixed; it can also be viewed as the kn-th shadow output price ratio. If the output set is homothetic, then MRTs do not depend on inputs. If technical change is IHON, then MRTs do not depend on environmental variables and do not change over time. The kn-th *elasticity of transformation* can be interpreted as the percent change in the kn-th output quantity ratio associated with a one percent change in the kn-th shadow output price ratio.

2.4.3 Example

If the output set is given by (2.2), then the output distance function is

$$D^t_O(x,q,z) = \left(A(t)\prod_{j=1}^J z_j^{\delta_j}\prod_{m=1}^M x_m^{\beta_m}\right)^{-1}\left(\sum_{n=1}^N \gamma_n q_n^{\tau}\right)^{1/\tau} \tag{2.9}$$

where $A(t) > 0$, $A(t) \geq A(t-1)$, $\beta = (\beta_1, \ldots, \beta_M)' \geq 0$, $\gamma = (\gamma_1, \ldots, \gamma_N)' \geq 0$,$\tau \geq 1$ and $\gamma'\iota = 1$. This function satisfies DO6, DO7, DO10, DO11 and DO13 with $r = -\beta'\iota$. The m-th marginal product is $MP^t_m(x,q,z) = \beta_m D^t_O(x,q,z)/x_m \geq 0$. The n-th normalised shadow output price and the the n-th shadow revenue share are (respectively)

$$p_n^t(x, q, z) = \gamma_n q_n^{\tau-1} \left(\sum_{k=1}^{N} \gamma_k q_k^{\tau} \right)^{-1} D_O^t(x, q, z) \geq 0 \tag{2.10}$$

$$\text{and } r_n(q) = \gamma_n q_n^{\tau} \left(\sum_{k=1}^{N} \gamma_k q_k^{\tau} \right)^{-1} \geq 0. \tag{2.11}$$

The m-th output elasticity is $\beta_m \geq 0$. The elasticity of scale is $\eta = \beta'\iota > 0$. The kn-th marginal rate of transformation is $MRT_{kn}(q) = (\gamma_n/\gamma_k)(q_n/q_k)^{\tau-1}$. If $\tau > 1$, then the elasticity of transformation between any two outputs is $\sigma = 1/(1-\tau) < 0$.

2.5 Input Distance Functions

If inputs are weakly disposable, then the input-output combinations that are possible using different technologies can be represented by input distance functions. An input distance function gives the reciprocal of the smallest fraction of a given input vector that can produce a given output vector. A *period-and-environment-specific* input distance function gives the reciprocal of the smallest fraction of a given input vector that can produce a given output vector *in a given period in a given production environment*. For example, the reciprocal of the smallest fraction of x that can produce q in period t in environment z is

$$D_I^t(x, q, z) = \sup\{\theta > 0 : x/\theta \in L^t(q, z)\}. \tag{2.12}$$

This particular input distance function can be found in O'Donnell (2016, p. 330). If there is no technical (resp. environmental) change, then all references to t (resp. z) can be deleted. If there is no environmental change, then it is equal to the (direct) input distance function defined by Balk (1998, Eq. 2.4). If there is no technical or environmental change, then it is equal to the (direct) input distance function defined by Färe and Primont (1995, Eq. 2.1.19). If input sets are closed and there is no technical or environmental change, then it is equal to the distance function defined by Shephard (1970, p. 206).

2.5.1 *Properties*

The properties of input distance functions can be derived from the properties of input sets. For example, consider the input distance function defined by (2.12). If inputs are nonnegative, then this function exists. If inputs are also weakly disposable, then $x \in L^t(q, z)$ if and only if $D_I^t(x, q, z) \geq 1$ (Färe and Primont 1995, p. 22). More generally, if the input distance function exists, then the following are true (Färe and Primont 1995, pp. 22, 28):

DI1 $0 \leq D_I^t(x, q, z)$ for all $(x, q, z) \in \mathbb{R}_+^{M+N+J}$ (nonnegative);
DI2 $D_I^t(\lambda x, q, z) = \lambda D_I^t(x, q, z)$ for all $\lambda > 0$ and $(x, q, z) \in \mathbb{R}_+^{M+N+J}$ (linearly homogeneous in x); and
DI3 $D_I^t(x, q, z) \geq 1$ for all $x \in L^t(q, z)$.

If I6s, I7s, I9s, O15 and I16 are also true, then the following are true[9]:

DI4 $D_I^t(x, q, z)$ is upper semi-continuous in q for all $(x, z) \in \mathbb{R}_+^{M+J}$;
DI5 $D_I^t(x, q, z)$ is continuous in x for all $(q, z) \in \mathbb{R}_+^{N+J}$;
DI6 $\bar{q} \geq q \Rightarrow D_I^t(x, \bar{q}, z) \leq D_I^t(x, q, z)$ for all $(x, z) \in \mathbb{R}_+^{M+J}$ (nonincreasing in q);
DI7 $\bar{x} \geq x \Rightarrow D_I^t(\bar{x}, q, z) \geq D_I^t(x, q, z)$ for all $(q, z) \in \mathbb{R}_+^{N+J}$ (nondecreasing in x);
DI8 $D_I^t(x, q, z)$ is quasiconcave in q for all $(x, z) \in \mathbb{R}_+^{M+J}$; and
DI9 $D_I^t(x, q, z)$ is concave x for all $(q, z) \in \mathbb{R}_+^{N+J}$.

If I10, I12 and I14 are true, then, and only then, the following are true (respectively)[10]:

DI10 $D_I^t(x, \lambda q, z) = \lambda^{-1/r} D_I^t(x, q, z)$ for all $\lambda > 0$ (homogeneity);
DI12 $D_I^t(x, q, z) = D_I^t(x, \iota, z)/K^t(q, z)$ (input homotheticity); and
DI14 $D_I^t(x, q, z) = D_I^1(x, q, \iota)/J^t(q, z)$ (implicit Hicks input neutrality).

Property DI10 says that the input distance function is homogeneous of degree $-1/r$ in outputs. If this is true, then $D_I^t(x, q, z) = D_O^t(x, q, z)^{-1/r}$ (e.g., O'Donnell 2016, Proposition 3). Properties DI12 and DI14 can be viewed as separability properties: if they are both true, then the input distance function can be written as $D_I^t(x, q, z) = X(x)/H^t(q, z)$ where $X(x) = D_I^1(x, \iota, \iota)$ can be viewed as an aggregate input and $H^t(q, z) = J^t(\iota, z)K^t(q, z)$ can be viewed as an input requirement function.[11] For more details concerning input requirement functions, see Sect. 2.9.2. If (a) output and input sets are homothetic, (b) technical change is HN, and (c) production frontiers exhibit CRS, then the input distance function can be written as $D_I^t(x, q, z) = B^t(z)X(x)/H(q)$ where $B^t(z) = J^t(\iota, z)$, $X(x) = D_I^1(x, \iota, \iota)$ and $H(q) = D_O^1(\iota, q, \iota)/D_O^1(\iota, \iota, \iota)$.[12] Finally, if firms are price takers in input markets and both I7s and I16 are true (i.e., if inputs are strongly disposable and input sets are convex), then

DI18 $D_I^t(x, q, z) = \inf_w\{w'x : C^t(w, q, z) \geq 1\}$

where $C^t(w, q, z)$ is the cost function defined by (2.21). This means that the input distance function is completely characterised by the cost function. If there is no technical or environmental change, then this result is equivalent to a duality result that can be found in Färe and Primont (1995, p. 47).

---

[9] I6s $\Rightarrow$ DI6 and I7s $\Rightarrow$ DI7 (Shephard 1970, proof of D.4, D.5 and D.8 on pp. 68–70). If I1, I2, I4, I5, I6s, I7s, I9s, I15 and I16 are true, then $\overline{\text{A.1}}$–$\overline{\text{A.8}}$ in Shephard (1970) are true. Then DI4–DI9 follow from Shephard (1970, pp. 207, Proposition 60)

[10] Proofs of DI12 and DI14 are given in Appendix A.1 (Propositions 9 and 11).

[11] A proof is given in Appendix A.1 (Proposition 13).

[12] A proof is given in Appendix A.1 (Proposition 18).

2.5.2 *Marginal Effects*

If input distance functions are continuously differentiable, then differential calculus can be used to define various marginal effects. For example, Table 2.2 presents several marginal effects that can be derived from a differentiable period-and-environment specific input distance function. The n-th *marginal input* (MI) can be interpreted as the radial expansion in the input vector needed to produce a marginal increase in output n, holding all other variables fixed. The m-th *normalised shadow input price* can be interpreted as the m-th shadow input price divided by the minimum amount it will cost a price-taking firm to produce its outputs; shadow input prices can be interpreted as the prices that would induce price-taking cost-minimising firms to operate at given points on the boundary of the input set; for more details, see, for example, Färe and Primont (1995, p. 55). The m-th *shadow cost share* is the shadow cost associated with the m-th input divided by total shadow cost; shadow costs are equal to shadow input prices multiplied by inputs. If the input set is homothetic (i.e., if DI12 is true), then shadow cost shares do not depend on outputs. If technical change is IHIN (i.e., if DI14 is true), then shadow cost shares do not depend on environmental variables and do not change over time. The n-th *input elasticity* can be interpreted as the percent increase in all inputs needed to produce a one percent increase in output n, holding all other variables fixed. If the input set is homothetic, then input elasticities do not depend on inputs. The *elasticity of scale* can be interpreted as the percent increase in all inputs needed to produce a one percent increase in *all* outputs, holding all other variables fixed. The elasticity of scale defined in Table 2.2 is always equal to the elasticity of scale defined earlier in Table 2.1 (Färe et al. 1986, p. 180). If the input set is homothetic, then the elasticity of scale does not depend on inputs. The km-th *marginal rate of technical*[13] *substitution* (MRTS) is the marginal rate at which input m can be substituted for input k on the boundary of the input set, holding all other variables fixed; it can also be viewed as the km-th shadow input price ratio. If the input set is homothetic, then MRTSs do not depend on outputs. If technical change is IHIN, then MRTSs do not depend on environmental variables and do not change over time. The km-th *elasticity of substitution* can be interpreted as the percent change in the km-th input quantity ratio associated with a one percent change in the km-th shadow input price ratio.

2.5.3 *Example*

If the input set is given by (2.4), then the input distance function is

[13]The term 'technical' is used here to distinguish the MRTS from a similar concept in consumer demand theory. In consumer demand theory, the marginal rate of substitution (MRS) is the rate at which consumers can exchange one good for another while holding utility and all other variables fixed.

Table 2.2 Selected input-oriented marginal effects

Marginal input	$MI_n^t(x,q,z) = \frac{\partial(1/D_I^t(x,q,z))}{\partial q_n}$
Normalised shadow input price	$w_m^t(x,q,z) = \frac{\partial D_I^t(x,q,z)}{\partial x_m}$
Shadow cost share	$s_m^t(x,q,z) = \frac{\partial \ln D_I^t(x,q,z)}{\partial \ln x_m}$
Input elasticity	$\phi_n^t(x,q,z) = -\frac{\partial \ln D_I^t(x,q,z)}{\partial \ln q_n}$
Elasticity of scale	$\phi^t(x,q,z) = \left(\sum_{n=1}^N \phi_n^t(x,q,z)\right)^{-1}$
Marginal rate of technical substitution	$MRTS_{km}^t(x,q,z) = \frac{\partial D_I^t(x,q,z)/\partial x_m}{\partial D_I^t(x,q,z)/\partial x_k}$
Elasticity of substitution	$\delta_{km}^t(x,q,z) = \frac{d\ln(x_k/x_m)}{d\ln MRTS_{km}^t(x,q,z)}$

$$D_I^t(x,q,z) = \left(B(t)\prod_{j=1}^J z_j^{\kappa_j}\prod_{m=1}^M x_m^{\lambda_m}\right)\left(\sum_{n=1}^N \gamma_n q_n^\tau\right)^{-1/(\tau\eta)} \tag{2.13}$$

where $B(t) > 0$, $B(t) \geq B(t-1)$, $\lambda = (\lambda_1, \ldots, \lambda_M)' \geq 0$, $\gamma = (\gamma_1, \ldots, \gamma_N)' \geq 0$, $\tau \geq 1$, $\eta > 0$ and $\gamma'\iota = \lambda'\iota = 1$. This function satisfies DI6, DI7, DI10, DI12 and DI14 with $r = \eta$. The n-th input elasticity is

$$\phi_n(q) = \gamma_n q_n^\tau \left(\eta \sum_{k=1}^N \gamma_k q_k^\tau\right)^{-1} \geq 0. \tag{2.14}$$

The n-th marginal input is $MI_n^t(x,q,z) = \phi_n(q)/[q_n D_I^t(x,q,z)] \geq 0$. The m-th normalised shadow input price is $w_m^t(x,q,z) = \lambda_m D_I^t(x,q,z)/x_m \geq 0$. The m-th shadow cost share is $s_m = \lambda_m$. The elasticity of scale is $\phi = \eta > 0$. The km-th marginal rate of technical substitution is $MRTS_{km}(x) = (\lambda_m/\lambda_k)(x_k/x_m)$. The elasticity of substitution between any two inputs is $\delta = 1$.

2.6 Revenue Functions

A revenue function gives the maximum revenue that can be earned using given inputs. A *period-and-environment-specific* revenue function gives the maximum revenue that can be earned using given inputs *in a given period in a given production environment*. For example, the maximum revenue that can be earned using x in period t in environment z is

$$R^t(x,d,z) = \max_q\{p(q,d)'q : q \in P^t(x,z)\} \tag{2.15}$$

where d is a vector of nonnegative demand shifters that are not affected by the actions of the firm (e.g., population) and $p(q,d)$ is a vector of nonnegative inverse demand functions. If there is no technical (resp. environmental) change, then all references to t (resp. z) can be deleted. If market prices are not affected by the outputs supplied by the firm, then the firm is said to be a 'price taker' in output markets. For such a firm, the maximum revenue that can be earned using x in period t in environment z is

$$R^t(x, p, z) = \max_q\{p'q : q \in P^t(x, z)\} \tag{2.16}$$

where p is a vector of nonnegative prices that are not affected by the outputs of the firm. This function can be viewed as a special case of (2.15) corresponding to $\partial p(q, d)/\partial q = 0$. If there is no environmental change, then it is equal to the revenue function defined by Balk (1998, Eq. 4.1). If there is no technical or environmental change, then it is equal to the 'output maximal benefit function' defined by Shephard (1970, Eq. 98).

2.6.1 Properties

The properties of revenue functions can be derived from the properties of output sets. For example, consider the revenue function defined by (2.16). If $P^t(x, z)$ is closed and bounded, then this function exists (Shephard 1970, p. 207). If some outputs are regarded as undesirable (i.e., have a negative value), then it is possible to define a revenue function that has the same properties as (2.16) except it is defined over $p \in \mathbb{R}^N$ instead of $p \in \mathbb{R}^N_+$ (Shephard 1970, p. 229). If the revenue function defined by (2.16) exists, then the following are true:

R1 $R^t(0, p, z) = 0$ and $R^t(x, 0, z) = 0$ for all $(x, z) \in \mathbb{R}^{M+J}_+$ (no fixed income);
R2 $R^t(x, p, z) \geq 0$ for all $(x, p, z) \in \mathbb{R}^{M+N+J}_+$ (nonnegative);
R3 $R^t(x, \lambda p, z) = \lambda R^t(x, p, z)$ for all $\lambda > 0$ (linearly homogeneous in p);
R4 $\bar{p} \geq p \Rightarrow R^t(x, \bar{p}, z) \geq R^t(x, p, z)$ for all $(x, z) \in \mathbb{R}^{M+J}_+$ (nondecreasing in p);
R5 $R^t(x, p, z)$ is convex in p for all $(x, z) \in \mathbb{R}^{M+J}_+$; and
R6 $R^t(x, p, z)$ is continuous in p for all $(x, z) \in \mathbb{R}^{M+J}_+$.

If I7s, I16 and I5 are true, then the following are true (respectively) (Shephard 1970, pp. 230, 231):

R7 $\bar{x} \geq x \Rightarrow R^t(\bar{x}, p, z) \geq R^t(x, p, z)$ for all $(p, z) \in \mathbb{R}^{N+J}_+$ (nondecreasing in x);
R8 $R^t(x, p, z)$ is concave in x for all $(p, z) \in \mathbb{R}^{N+J}_+$; and
R9 $R^t(x, p, z)$ is upper semi-continuous in x for all $(p, z) \in \mathbb{R}^{N+J}_+$.

Finally, if O10, O11 and O13 are true, then the following are true (respectively)[14]:

R10 $R(\lambda x, p, z, t) = \lambda^r R^t(x, p, z)$ for all $\lambda > 0$ (homogeneity);
R11 $R^t(x, p, z) = G^t(x, z)R^t(\iota, p, z)$ (output homotheticity); and
R13 $R^t(x, p, z) = E^t(x, z)R^1(x, p, \iota)$ (implicit Hicks output neutrality).

[14]Proofs of R11 and R13 are given in Appendix A.1 (Propositions 2 and 4).

Table 2.3 Selected revenue-oriented marginal effects

Marginal revenue	$MR^t_m(x, p, z) = \frac{\partial R^t(x,p,z)}{\partial x_m}$
Revenue-maximising output supply	$\ddot{q}^t_n(x, p, z) = \frac{\partial R^t(x,p,z)}{\partial p_n}$
Revenue-maximising revenue share	$\ddot{r}^t_n(x, p, z) = \frac{\partial \ln R^t(x,p,z)}{\partial \ln p_n}$
Revenue elasticity	$\kappa^t_m(x, p, z) = \frac{\partial \ln R^t(x,p,z)}{\partial \ln x_m}$
Revenue elasticity of scale	$\kappa^t(x, p, z) = \sum_{m=1}^{M} \kappa^t_m(x, p, z)$

Property R10 says that the revenue function is homogeneous of degree r in inputs. Again, properties R11 and R13 can be viewed as separability properties: if they are both true, then the revenue function can be written as $R^t(x, p, z) = P(p)F^t(x, z)$ where $P(p) = R^1(\iota, p, \iota)$ can be viewed as an aggregate output price and $F^t(x, z) = E^t(\iota, z)G^t(x, z)$ can be viewed as a production function.[15]

2.6.2 *Marginal Effects*

If revenue functions are continuously differentiable, then differential calculus can be used to define various marginal effects. For example, Table 2.3 presents several marginal effects that can be derived from a differentiable period-and-environment specific revenue function. The m-th *marginal revenue* (MR) is the increase in maximum revenue that can be obtained from a marginal increase in input m, holding all other variables fixed. The n-th *revenue-maximising output supply* is the amount of output n that a price-taking firm must produce in order to maximise revenue. The n-th *revenue-maximising revenue share* is the associated revenue from output n as a proportion of maximum total revenue. If the output set is homothetic (i.e., if R11 is true), then revenue-maximising revenue shares do not depend on inputs. If technical change is IHON (i.e., if R13 is true), then revenue-maximising revenue shares do not depend on environmental variables and do not change over time. The m-th *revenue elasticity* is the percent increase in maximum revenue that can be obtained from a one percent increase in input m, holding all other variables fixed. If the output set is homothetic, then revenue elasticities do not depend on output prices. The *revenue elasticity of scale* is the percent increase in maximum revenue that can be obtained from a one percent increase in *all* inputs, holding all other variables fixed. If assumption O15 is true (i.e., if the output set is convex), then the revenue elasticity of scale is equal to the elasticity of scale defined earlier in Table 2.1 (Färe et al. 1986, p. 181). If the output set is homothetic, then the revenue elasticity of scale does not depend on output prices.

[15] A proof is given in Appendix A.1 (Proposition 6).

2.6.3 Example

If firms are a price takers in output markets and the output set is given by (2.2), then the revenue function depends on the value of τ. If $\tau > 1$, then

$$R^t(x, p, z) = \left(A(t) \prod_{j=1}^{J} z_j^{\delta_j} \prod_{m=1}^{M} x_m^{\beta_m} \right) \left(\sum_{n=1}^{N} \gamma_n^{\sigma} p_n^{1-\sigma} \right)^{1/(1-\sigma)} \quad (2.17)$$

where $A(t) > 0$, $A(t) \geq A(t-1)$, $\beta = (\beta_1, \ldots, \beta_M)' \geq 0$, $\gamma = (\gamma_1, \ldots, \gamma_N)' \geq 0$, $\gamma'\iota = 1$, and $\sigma = 1/(1-\tau) < 0$. This function satisfies R10, R11 and R13 with $r = \beta'\iota$. The m-th marginal revenue is $MR_m^t(x, p, z) = \beta_m R^t(x, p, z)/x_m \geq 0$. If the n-th output price is positive, then the n-th revenue-maximising output supply and revenue share are

$$\ddot{q}_n^t(x, p, z) = \left(A(t) \prod_{j=1}^{J} z_j^{\delta_j} \prod_{m=1}^{M} x_m^{\beta_m} \right) \left(\frac{\gamma_n}{p_n} \right)^{\sigma} \left(\sum_{k=1}^{N} \gamma_k^{\sigma} p_k^{1-\sigma} \right)^{\sigma/(1-\sigma)} \quad (2.18)$$

and $$\ddot{r}_n(p) = \gamma_n^{\sigma} p_n^{1-\sigma} \left(\sum_{k=1}^{N} \gamma_k^{\sigma} p_k^{1-\sigma} \right)^{-1}. \quad (2.19)$$

The m-th revenue elasticity is $\kappa_m = \beta_m \geq 0$. The revenue elasticity of scale is $\kappa = \beta'\iota > 0$.

2.7 Cost Functions

A cost function gives the minimum cost of producing given outputs. A *period-and-environment-specific* cost function gives the minimum cost of producing given outputs *in a given period in a given production environment*. For example, the minimum cost of producing q in period t in environment z is

$$C^t(s, q, z) = \min_x \{ w(x, s)'x : x \in L^t(q, z) \}. \quad (2.20)$$

where s is a vector of nonnegative supply shifters that are not affected by the actions of the firm (e.g., characteristics of production environments in upstream sectors) and $w(x, s)$ is a vector of nonnegative inverse supply functions. If there is no technical (resp. environmental) change, then all references to t (resp. z) can be deleted. If market prices are not affected by the inputs demanded by the firm, then the firm is said to be a 'price taker' in input markets. For such a firm, the minimum cost of producing q in period t in environment z is

$$C^t(w,q,z) = \min_x\{w'x : x \in L^t(q,z)\} \quad (2.21)$$

where w is a vector of nonnegative prices that are not affected by the inputs demanded by the firm. This function can be viewed as a special case of (2.20) corresponding to $\partial w(x,s)/\partial x = 0$. If there is no environmental change, then it is equal to the cost function defined by Balk (1998, Eq. 3.1). If there is no technical or environmental change, then it is equal to the cost function defined by Shephard (1970, Eq. 15).

2.7.1 Properties

The properties of cost functions can be derived from the properties of input sets. For example, consider the cost function defined by (2.21). If $L^t(q,z)$ is closed, then this function is well-defined for all positive input price vectors and all output vectors that are producible in environment $z \in \mathbb{R}^J_+$ (Färe and Primont 1995, p. 44). In this case, the following are true (Shephard 1970, pp. 84, 85, 228):

C1 $C^t(w,0,z) = 0$ and $C^t(0,q,z) = 0$ for all $(q,z) \in \mathbb{R}^{N+J}_+$ (no fixed cost);
C2 $C^t(w,q,z) \geq 0$ for all $(w,q,z) \in \mathbb{R}^{M+N+J}_+$ (nonnegative);
C3 $C^t(\lambda w,q,z) = \lambda C^t(w,q,z)$ for all $\lambda \geq 0$ (linearly homogeneous in w);
C4 $\bar{w} \geq w \Rightarrow C^t(\bar{w},q,z) \geq C^t(w,q,z)$ for all $(q,z) \in \mathbb{R}^{N+J}_+$ (nondecreasing in w);
C5 $C^t(w,q,z)$ is concave in w for all $(q,z) \in \mathbb{R}^{N+J}_+$; and
C6 $C^t(w,q,z)$ is continuous in w for all $(q,z) \in \mathbb{R}^{N+J}_+$.

If O6s, O15 and O4 are true, then the following are true (respectively) (Shephard 1970, pp. 190, 228):

C7 $\bar{q} \geq q \Rightarrow C^t(w,\bar{q},z) \geq C^t(w,q,z)$ for all $(w,z) \in \mathbb{R}^{M+J}_+$ (nondecreasing in q);
C8 $C^t(w,q,z)$ is convex in q for all $(w,z) \in \mathbb{R}^{M+J}_+$; and
C9 $C^t(w,q,z)$ is lower semi-continuous in q for all $w > 0$ and $z \in \mathbb{R}^J_+$.

Finally, if I10, I12 and I14 are true, then the following are true (respectively)[16]:

C10 $C^t(w,\lambda q,z) = \lambda^{1/r} C^t(w,q,z)$ for all $\lambda > 0$ (homogeneity);
C12 $C^t(w,q,z) = K^t(q,z)C^t(w,\iota,z)$ (input homotheticity); and
C14 $C^t(w,q,z) = J^t(q,z)C^1(w,q,\iota)$ (implicit Hicks input neutrality).

Property C10 says that the cost function is homogeneous of degree $1/r$ in outputs. Again, properties C12 and C14 can be viewed as separability properties: if they are both true, then the cost function can be written as $C^t(w,q,z) = W(w)H^t(q,z)$ where $W(w) = C^1(w,\iota,\iota)$ can be viewed as an aggregate input price and $H^t(q,z) = J^t(\iota,z)K^t(q,z)$ can be viewed as an input requirement function.[17]

[16]Proofs of C12 and C14 are given in Appendix A.1 (Propositions 10 and 12).
[17]A proof is given in Appendix A.1 (Proposition 14).

Table 2.4 Selected cost-oriented marginal effects

Marginal cost	$MC_n^t(w, q, z) = \frac{\partial C^t(w,q,z)}{\partial q_n}$
Cost-minimising input demand	$\ddot{x}_m^t(w, q, z) = \frac{\partial C^t(w,q,z)}{\partial w_m}$
Cost-minimising cost share	$\ddot{s}_m^t(w, q, z) = \frac{\partial \ln C^t(w,q,z)}{\partial \ln w_m}$
Cost elasticity	$\psi_n^t(w, q, z) = \frac{\partial \ln C^t(w,q,z)}{\partial \ln q_n}$
Cost elasticity of scale	$\psi^t(w, q, z) = \left(\sum_{n=1}^{N} \psi_n^t(w, q, z)\right)^{-1}$

2.7.2 Marginal Effects

If cost functions are continuously differentiable, then differential calculus can be used to define various marginal effects. For example, Table 2.4 presents several marginal effects that can be derived from a differentiable period-and-environment specific cost function. The m-th *marginal cost* (MC) is the increase in minimum cost when output n is increased by a marginal amount, holding all other variables fixed. The n-th *cost-minimising input demand* is the quantity of input m that a price-taking firm must use in order to minimise cost. The m-th *cost-minimising cost share* is the associated cost of input m as a proportion of minimum total cost. If the input set is homothetic (i.e., if C12 is true), then cost-minimising cost shares do not depend on outputs. If technical change is IHIN (i.e., if C14 is true), then cost-minimising cost shares do not depend on environmental variables and do not change over time. The n-th *cost elasticity* is the percent increase in minimum cost when output n is increased by one percent, holding all other variables fixed. If the input set is homothetic, then cost elasticities do not depend on input prices. The *cost elasticity of scale* is the percent increase in minimum cost when *all* outputs are increased by one percent, holding all other variables fixed. If assumption I16 is true (i.e., if the input set is convex), then the cost elasticity of scale is equal to the elasticity of scale defined earlier in Tables 2.1 and 2.2 (Färe et al. 1986, p. 180). If the input set is homothetic, then the cost elasticity of scale does not depend on input prices.

2.7.3 Example

If firms are price takers in input markets and the input distance function is given by (2.13), then

$$C^t(w, q, z) = \left(B(t)\prod_{j=1}^{J} z_j^{\kappa_j}\right)^{-1} \prod_{m=1}^{M} \left(\frac{w_m}{\lambda_m}\right)^{\lambda_m} \left(\sum_{n=1}^{N} \gamma_n q_n^{\tau}\right)^{1/(\tau\eta)} \tag{2.22}$$

where $B(t) > 0$, $B(t) \geq B(t-1)$, $\lambda = (\lambda_1, \ldots, \lambda_M)' \geq 0$, $\gamma = (\gamma_1, \ldots, \gamma_N)' \geq 0$, $\tau \geq 1, \eta > 0$ and $\gamma'\iota = \lambda'\iota = 1$. This function satisfies C10, C12 and C14 with $r = \eta$. The n-th cost elasticity is

$$\psi_n(q) = \gamma_n q_n^{\tau} \left(\eta \sum_{k=1}^{N} \gamma_k q_k^{\tau} \right)^{-1} \geq 0 \tag{2.23}$$

[this is equal to the n-th input elasticity given by (2.14)]. The n-th marginal cost is $MC_n^t(w, q, z) = \psi_n(q) C^t(w, q, z)/q_n \geq 0$. If the m-th input price is positive, then the m-th cost-minimising input demand is

$$\ddot{x}_m^t(w, q, z) = \left(B(t) \prod_{j=1}^{J} z_j^{\kappa_j} \right)^{-1} \left(\frac{\lambda_m}{w_m} \right) \prod_{k=1}^{M} \left(\frac{w_k}{\lambda_k} \right)^{\lambda_k} \left(\sum_{n=1}^{N} \gamma_n q_n^{\tau} \right)^{1/(\tau\eta)} . \tag{2.24}$$

The m-th cost-minimising cost share is $\lambda_m \geq 0$. The cost elasticity of scale is $\psi = \eta > 0$.

2.8 Profit Functions

A profit function gives the maximum profit that can be earned when inputs and outputs can be chosen freely. A *period-and-environment-specific* profit function gives the maximum profit that can be earned *in a given period in a given production environment* when inputs and outputs can be chosen freely. If outputs are weakly attainable and the set of technically-feasible input-output combinations that yield nonnegative profit is nonempty and compact,[18] then the maximum profit that can be earned in period t in environment z is

$$\Pi^t(s, d, z) = \max_{x,q} \{ p(q, d)'q - w(x, s)'x : (x, q) \in T^t(z) \} \tag{2.25}$$

where $p(q, d)$ and $w(x, s)$ are the vectors of inverse demand and supply functions introduced in Sects. 2.6 and 2.7. If there is no technical (resp. environmental) change, then all references to t (resp. z) can be deleted. If firms are price takers in output and input markets, then the maximum profit that can be earned in period t in environment z is

$$\Pi^t(w, p, z) = \max_{x,q} \{ p'q - w'x : (x, q) \in T^t(z) \} \tag{2.26}$$

[18] A set is compact if it is closed and bounded. If the set of technically-feasible output-input combinations that yield nonnegative profit is compact, then profit achieves a maximum on $T^t(z)$. This means the maximum operator can be used in (2.25) instead of the supremum operator.

where p and w are vectors of nonnegative output and input prices that are not affected by the outputs and inputs of the firm. This profit function can be viewed as a special case of (2.25) corresponding to $\partial p(q,d)/\partial q = 0$ and $\partial w(x,s)/\partial x = 0$. If there is no environmental change, then it is equal to the profit function defined by Balk (1998, Eq. 7.1).

2.8.1 Properties

The properties of profit functions can be derived from the properties of production possibilities sets. For example, consider the profit function defined by (2.26). If $T^t(z)$ is nonempty, closed and convex, then the following are true (Färe and Primont 1995, pp. 124, 125):

$\Pi 1$ $\Pi^t(w, p, z) \geq 0$ (nonnegative);
$\Pi 2$ $\Pi^t(\lambda w, \lambda p, z) = \lambda \Pi^t(w, p, z)$ for all $\lambda > 0$ (linearly homogeneous in prices);
$\Pi 3$ $\bar{w} \geq w \Rightarrow \Pi^t(\bar{w}, p, z) \leq \Pi^t(w, p, z)$ (nonincreasing in w);
$\Pi 4$ $\bar{p} \geq p \Rightarrow \Pi^t(w, \bar{p}, z) \geq \Pi^t(w, p, z)$ (nondecreasing in p); and
$\Pi 5$ $\Pi^t(w, p, z)$ is convex and continuous in $(w, p) > 0$.

2.8.2 Marginal Effects

If profit functions are continuously differentiable, then differential calculus can be used to define various marginal effects. For example, Table 2.5 presents two marginal effects that can be derived from a differentiable period-and-environment specific profit function. The n-th *profit-maximising output supply* is the amount of output n that a price-taking firm must produce in order to maximise profit. Similarly, the m-th *profit-maximising input demand* is the amount of input m that a price-taking firm must use in order to maximise profit. These two results together are known as Hotelling's lemma.

Table 2.5 Selected profit-oriented marginal effects

Profit-maximising output supply	$\mathring{q}^t_n(w, p, z) = \frac{\partial \Pi^t(w,p,z)}{\partial p_n}$
Profit-maximising input demand	$\mathring{x}^t_m(w, p, z) = -\frac{\partial \Pi^t(w,p,z)}{\partial w_m}$

2.8.3 Example

If firms are price takers in output and input markets and the production possibilities set is given by (2.7), then the profit function depends on $\eta = \beta'\iota$ and τ. If $\eta < 1$ and $\tau > 1$, then

$$\Pi^t(w, p, z) = (1-\eta)\left(A(t)\prod_{j=1}^{J} z_j^{\delta_j}\prod_{m=1}^{M}\left(\frac{\beta_m}{w_m}\right)^{\beta_m}\right)^{\frac{1}{1-\eta}}\left(\sum_{n=1}^{N}\gamma_n^{\sigma}p_n^{1-\sigma}\right)^{\frac{1}{(1-\sigma)(1-\eta)}} \tag{2.27}$$

where $A(t) > 0$, $A(t) \geq A(t-1)$, $\beta = (\beta_1, \ldots, \beta_M)' \geq 0$, $\gamma = (\gamma_1, \ldots, \gamma_N)' \geq 0$, $\gamma'\iota = 1$ and $\sigma = 1/(1-\tau) < 0$. If the n-th output price and the m-th input price are positive, then the n-th profit-maximising output and the m-th profit-maximising input are

$$\mathring{q}_n^t(w, p, z) = \left(A(t)\prod_{j=1}^{J} z_j^{\delta_j}\prod_{m=1}^{M}\left(\frac{\beta_m}{w_m}\right)^{\beta_m}\right)^{\frac{1}{1-\eta}}\left(\frac{\gamma_n}{p_n}\right)^{\sigma} \times\left(\sum_{k=1}^{N}\gamma_k^{\sigma}p_k^{1-\sigma}\right)^{\frac{1}{(1-\sigma)(1-\eta)}-1} \tag{2.28}$$

and

$$\mathring{x}_m^t(w, p, z) = \left(A(t)\prod_{j=1}^{J} z_j^{\delta_j}\prod_{k=1}^{M}\left(\frac{\beta_k}{w_k}\right)^{\beta_k}\right)^{\frac{1}{1-\eta}}\left(\frac{\beta_m}{w_m}\right) \times\left(\sum_{n=1}^{N}\gamma_n^{\sigma}p_n^{1-\sigma}\right)^{\frac{1}{(1-\sigma)(1-\eta)}}. \tag{2.29}$$

2.9 Other Sets and Functions

Other sets and functions that can be used to analyse efficiency and productivity include production functions, input requirement functions, directional distance functions, hyperbolic distance functions, technology-and-environment-specific sets and functions, period-specific sets and functions, and state-contingent sets and functions.

2.9.1 Production Functions

It is common[19] to assume that there is only one output. If there is only one output and assumptions A2, A4 and A6 are true, then the input-output combinations that are possible using different technologies can be represented by production functions. A production function gives the maximum output that a one-output firm can produce using a given input vector. A *period-and-environment-specific* production function gives the maximum output that a one-output firm can produce using a given input vector *in a given period in a given production environment*. For example, the maximum output that a one-output firm can produce when using x in period t in environment z is

$$F^t(x, z) = \max\{q : q \in P^t(x, z)\}. \tag{2.30}$$

An equivalent definition is $F^t(x, z) = 1/D^t_O(x, 1, z)$. If there is no technical (resp. environmental) change, then all references to t (resp. z) can be deleted. If there is no environmental change, then the production function defined by (2.30) is equal to the production function defined by Balk (1998, Eq. 2.8). If there is no technical or environmental change, then it is equal to the production function defined by Shephard (1970, p. 20). The properties of production functions are derived from the properties of output sets. For example, if O1–O7 are true, then the following are true:

F1 $F^t(x, z) < \infty$ for all $(x, z) \in \mathbb{R}^{M+J}_+$ (finite);
F2 $0 \leq F^t(x, z)$ for all $(x, z) \in \mathbb{R}^{M+J}_+$ (nonnegative); and
F3 $F^t(0, z) = 0$ for all $z \in \mathbb{R}^J_+$ (inputs weakly essential).

If O7s, O10, O11, O13 and I16 are also true, then (respectively)[20]:

F7s $\bar{x} \geq x \Rightarrow F^t(\bar{x}, z) \geq F^t(x, z)$ (nondecreasing in x);
F10 $F^t(\lambda x, z) = \lambda^r F^t(x, z)$ for all $\lambda > 0$ (homogeneity);
F11 $F^t(x, z) = G^t(x, z)F^t(\iota, z)$ (output homotheticity);
F13 $F^t(x, z) = E^t(x, z)F^1(x, \iota)$ (implicit Hicks output neutrality); and
F15 $F^t(x, z)$ is quasiconcave in x for all $z \in \mathbb{R}^J_+$.

If production functions are continuously differentiable, then differential calculus can be used to define various marginal effects. For example, Table 2.6 presents several marginal effects that can be derived from a differentiable period-and-environment-specific production function. The m-th *marginal product* (MP) gives the marginal increase in output that can be obtained from a marginal increase in input m, holding all other variables fixed. The m-th *output elasticity* gives the the percent increase in output that can be obtained from a one percent increase in input m, holding all other variables fixed. The *elasticity of scale* gives the percent increase in output that can be obtained from a one percent increase in *all* inputs, holding all other variables fixed.

[19] See, for example,Solow (1957, p. 312) and Hsieh and Klenow (2009, p. 1046).

[20] For proofs of F7s and F15, see Shephard (1970, p. 21). Proofs of F10, F11 and F13 are left as an exercise for the reader.

Table 2.6 Selected marginal effects

Marginal product	$MP^t_m(x, z) = \frac{\partial F^t(x,z)}{\partial x_m}$
Output elasticity	$\eta^t_m(x, z) = \frac{\partial \ln F^t(x,z)}{\partial \ln x_m}$
Elasticity of scale	$\eta^t(x, z) = \sum_{m=1}^{M} \eta^t_m(x, z)$

To make some of these concepts more concrete, suppose the output set is given by (2.2). If there is only one output, then

$$F^t(x, z) = A(t) \prod_{j=1}^{J} z_j^{\delta_j} \prod_{m=1}^{M} x_m^{\beta_m} \tag{2.31}$$

where $A(t) > 0$, $A(t) \geq A(t-1)$, and $\beta = (\beta_1, \ldots, \beta_M)' \geq 0$. The m-th marginal product is $MP^t_m(x, z) = \beta_m F^t(x, z)/x_m$. The m-th output elasticity is $\eta_m = \beta_m$. The elasticity of scale is $\eta = \beta'\iota$. The production frontier exhibits DRS, NIRS, CRS, NDRS or IRS as η is less than, no greater than, equal to, no less than, or greater than one. If $\eta = 1$ and there is no environmental change, then (2.31) reduces to a function that has the same structure, but not necessarily the same interpretation,[21] as the production function of Solow (1957, Eqs. 3, 4d). If $\eta = 1$ and there is no technical or environmental change, then it reduces to the production function of Hsieh and Klenow (2009, Eq. 1).

2.9.2 *Input Requirement Functions*

If there is only one input involved in the production process and assumptions A5 and A7 are true, then the input-output combinations that are possible using different technologies can be represented by input requirement functions. An input requirement function gives the minimum input that a one-input firm requires in order to produce a given output vector. A *period-and-environment-specific* input requirement function gives the minimum input that a one-input firm requires in order to produce a given output vector *in a given period in a given production environment*. For example, the minimum input that a one-input firm requires in order to produce q in period t in environment z is

$$H^t(q, z) = \min\{x : x \in L^t(q, z)\}. \tag{2.32}$$

[21] In this example, changes in $A(t)$ are attributed to the discovery of new technologies. In this book, such changes are referred to as technical change. Solow (1957) also attributes changes $A(t)$ to technical change. However, he "[uses] the phrase 'technical change' as a shorthand expression for *any kind of shift* in the production function. Thus, speedups, improvements in the education of the labor force, and all sorts of things will appear as 'technical change'" (Solow 1957, p. 312).

Table 2.7 Selected marginal effects

Marginal input	$MI_n^t(q, z) = \frac{\partial H^t(q,z)}{\partial q_n}$
Input elasticity	$\phi_n^t(q, z) = \frac{\partial \ln H^t(q,z)}{\partial \ln q_n}$
Elasticity of scale	$\phi^t(q, z) = \left(\sum_{n=1}^N \phi_n^t(q, z)\right)^{-1}$

An equivalent definition is $H^t(q, z) = 1/D_I^t(1, q, z)$. If there is no technical (resp. environmental) change, then all references to t (resp. z) can be deleted. If there is no technical or environmental change, then the input requirement function defined by (2.32) is equal to the 'inverse production function' defined by Shephard (1970, p. 197). The properties of input requirement functions are derived from the properties of input sets. For example, if I1–I7 are true, then the following are true:

H1 $H^t(q, z) < \infty$ for all $(q, z) \in \mathbb{R}_+^{N+J}$ (finite);
H2 $0 \leq H^t(q, z)$ for all $(q, z) \in \mathbb{R}_+^{N+J}$ (nonnegative); and
H3 $H^t(0, z) = 0$ for all $z \in \mathbb{R}_+^J$.

If I6s, I10, I12, I14 and O15 are also true, then (respectively)[22]:

H6s $\bar{q} \geq q \Rightarrow H^t(\bar{q}, z) \geq H^t(q, z)$ (nondecreasing in q);
H10 $H^t(\lambda q, z) = \lambda^{1/r} H^t(q, z)$ for all $\lambda > 0$ (homogeneity);
H12 $H^t(q, z) = K^t(q, z) H^t(\iota, z)$ (input homotheticity);
H14 $H^t(q, z) = J^t(q, z) H^1(q, \iota)$ (implicit Hicks input neutrality); and
H16 $H^t(q, z)$ is quasiconvex in q for all $z \in \mathbb{R}_+^J$.

If input requirement functions are continuously differentiable, then differential calculus can be used to define various marginal effects. For example, Table 2.7 presents several marginal effects that can be derived from a differentiable period-and-environment-specific input requirement function. The n-th *marginal input* (MI) gives the marginal increase in input needed to produce a marginal increase in output n, holding all other variables fixed. The n-th *input elasticity* gives the percent increase in input needed to produce a one percent increase in output n, holding all other variables fixed. The *elasticity of scale* gives the percent increase in input needed to produce a one percent increase in *all* outputs, holding all other variables fixed.

To make some of these concepts more concrete, suppose the input set is given by (2.4). If there is only one input, then

$$H^t(q, z) = \left(B(t) \prod_{j=1}^{J} z_j^{\kappa_j}\right)^{-1} \left(\sum_{n=1}^{N} \gamma_n q_n^{\tau}\right)^{1/(\tau\eta)} \tag{2.33}$$

[22]For proofs of H6s and H16, see Shephard (1970, p. 198). Proofs of H10, H12 and H14 are left as an exercise for the reader.

where $B(t) > 0$, $B(t) \geq B(t-1)$, $\gamma = (\gamma_1, \ldots, \gamma_N)' \geq 0$, $\tau \geq 1$, $\eta > 0$ and $\gamma'\iota = 1$. The n-th input elasticity is

$$\phi_n(q) = \gamma_n q_n^\tau \left(\eta \sum_{k=1}^{N} \gamma_k q_k^\tau \right)^{-1} \geq 0. \tag{2.34}$$

The n-th marginal input is $MI_n^t(q, z) = \phi_n(q) H^t(q, z)/q_n$. The elasticity of scale is $\phi = \eta$. The production frontier exhibits DRS, NIRS, CRS, NDRS or IRS as η is less than, no greater than, equal to, no less than, or greater than one.

2.9.3 Directional Distance Functions

If assumptions A2, A6 and A7 are true, then the input-output combinations that are possible using different technologies can be represented by directional distance functions. A directional distance function measures the distance in a given direction from a given point to the boundary of a production possibilities set. A *period-and-environment-specific* directional distance function measures the distance in a given direction from a given point to the boundary of a *period-and-environment-specific* production possibilities set. For example, the directional distance function that measures the distance in the direction $(-g_x, g_q)$ from the point (x, q) to the boundary of $T^t(z)$ is

$$D_D^t(x, q, z, g_x, g_q) = \sup\{\beta : (x - \beta g_x, q + \beta g_q) \in T^t(z)\}. \tag{2.35}$$

If there is no technical (resp. environmental) change, then all references to t (resp. z) can be deleted. If $g_x = 0$ and $g_q = q$, then $D_D^t(x, q, z, g_x, g_q) = D_O^t(x, q, z)^{-1} - 1$. If $g_x = x$ and $g_q = 0$, then $D_D^t(x, q, z, g_x, g_q) = 1 - D_I^t(x, q, z)^{-1}$. If there is no environmental change, then the directional distance function defined by (2.35) is equal to the distance function defined by Balk (1998, Eq. 7.22). If there is no technical or environmental change, then it is equal to the distance function defined by Färe and Grosskopf (2000, Eq. 3) . The properties of directional distance functions are derived from the properties of production possibilities sets. For example, $D_D^t(x, q, z, g_x, g_q) \geq 0$ if and only if $(x, q) \in T^t(z)$. More generally, if T1, T3, T4s, T6s and T7s are true, then (Chambers et al. 1998, Lemma 2.2) :

DD1 $D_D^t(x - \alpha g_x, q + \alpha g_q, z, g_x, g_q) = D_D^t(x, q, z, g_x, g_q) - \alpha$ (translation);
DD2 $D_D^t(x, q, z, g_x, g_q)$ is upper semicontinuous in x and q (jointly) for all $z \in \mathbb{R}_+^J$;
DD3 $D_D^t(x, q, z, \lambda g_x, \lambda g_q) = (1/\lambda) D_D^t(x, q, z, g_x, g_q)$ for all $\lambda > 0$;
DD4 $\bar{q} \geq q \Rightarrow D_D^t(x, \bar{q}, z, g_x, g_q) \leq D_D^t(x, q, z, g_x, g_q)$ (nonincreasing in q); and
DD5 $\bar{x} \geq x \Rightarrow D_D^t(\bar{x}, q, z, g_x, g_q) \geq D_D^t(x, q, z, g_x, g_q)$ (nondecreasing in x).

For more details concerning directional distance functions and their properties, see Chambers et al. (1996), Chambers et al. (1998) and Färe and Grosskopf (2000).

2.9.4 Hyperbolic Distance Functions

If assumptions A2, A6 and A7 are true, then the input-output combinations that are possible using different technologies can also be represented by hyperbolic distance functions. A hyperbolic distance function measures the distance along a rectangular hyperbola from a given point to the boundary of a production possibilities set. A *period-and-environment-specific* hyperbolic distance function measures the distance along a rectangular hyperbola from a given point to the boundary of a *period-and-environment-specific* production possibilities set. For example, the hyperbolic distance function that measures the distance along a rectangular hyperbola from the point (x, q) to the boundary of $T^t(z)$ is

$$D_H^t(x, q, z) = \inf\{\rho > 0 : (\rho x, q/\rho) \in T^t(z)\}. \tag{2.36}$$

If there is no technical (resp. environmental) change, then all references to t (resp. z) can be deleted. If there is no technical or environmental change, then the hyperbolic distance function defined by (2.36) is equal to the distance function defined by Cuesta and Zofio (2005, Eq. 2). The properties of hyperbolic distance functions are derived from the properties of production possibilities sets. For example, if T1–T7 are true, then[23]

DH1 $0 \leq D_H^t(x, q, z) < +\infty$ for all $(x, q) \in D^t(z)$;
DH2 $D_H^t(0, 0, z) = 0$ for all $z \in \mathbb{R}_+^J$;
DH3 $D_H^t(\lambda x, q/\lambda, z) = \lambda^{-1} D_H^t(x, q, z)$ for all $\lambda > 0$, $(x, q) \in D^t(z)$ and $z \in \mathbb{R}_+^J$ (almost homogeneous);
DH4 $D_H^t(\lambda x, q, z) \leq D_H^t(x, q, z)$ for all $\lambda \geq 1$ (nonincreasing in inputs); and
DH5 $D_H^t(x, \lambda q, z) \leq D_H^t(x, q, z)$ for all $0 < \lambda \leq 1$ (nondecreasing in outputs)

where $D^t(z) = \{(x, q) :$ there exists a $\rho > 0$ such that $(\rho x, q/\rho) \in T^t(z)\}$ is the effective domain of the function. For more details concerning hyperbolic distance functions and their properties, see, for example, Färe et al. (1985, pp. 110–112) and Färe et al. (2002) .

2.9.5 Technology-and-Environment-Specific Sets and Functions

Technology-and-environment-specific sets are subsets of the period-and-environment-specific sets defined in Sects. 2.1, 2.2 and 2.3. A *technology*-and-environment-specific output set, for example, is a set containing all outputs that can be produced

[23] T1–T7 $\Rightarrow$ GR.1–GR.5 in Färe et al. (1985, p. 111). DH2–DH5 are equivalent to $F_g.1$, $F_g.3$, $F_g.4$ and $F_g.5$ in Färe et al. (1985, pp. 111, 112) (respectively). A function $F(x, y)$ is said to be almost homogeneous of degree a, b, and c, respectively, if and only if $F(\lambda^a x, \lambda^b y) = \lambda^c F(x, y)$ for any $\lambda > 0$ (Lau 1972, p. 282).

using given inputs *and a given technology* in a given production environment. For example, the set of outputs that can be produced using the input vector x and technology g in an environment characterised by z is

$$p^g(x, z) = \{q : x \text{ and technology } g \text{ can produce } q \text{ in environment } z\}. \tag{2.37}$$

The associated *period*-and-environment-specific output set is $P^t(x, z) = \cup_{g \in G_t} p^g(x, z)$ where G_t is the period-t technology set. Thus, by construction, $p^g(x, z) \subseteq P^t(x, z)$ for all $g \in G_t$. Many of the examples presented in this book are underpinned by the following technology-and-environment-specific output set:

$$p^g(x, z) = \left\{ q : \left(\sum_{n=1}^{N} \gamma_n q_n^{\tau} \right)^{1/\tau} \leq a(g) \prod_{j=1}^{J} z_j^{\delta_j} \prod_{m=1}^{M} x_m^{\beta_m} \right\} \tag{2.38}$$

where $a(g) > 0$, $\beta = (\beta_1, \ldots, \beta_M)' \geq 0$, $\gamma = (\gamma_1, \ldots, \gamma_N)' \geq 0$, $\tau \geq 1$ and $\gamma' \iota = 1$. The associated period-and-environment-specific output set is given by (2.2), where $A(t) = \max_{g \in G_t} a(g)$.

Under weak conditions, technology-and-environment-specific sets can be represented by technology-and-environment-specific analogues of the functions discussed in Sects. 2.4, 2.5, 2.6, 2.7 and 2.8. For example, if output sets are bounded and outputs are weakly disposable, then the input-output combinations that are possible using different technologies can be represented by technology-and-environment-specific output distance functions. A *technology*-and-environment-specific output distance function gives the reciprocal of the largest factor by which it is possible to scale up a given output vector when using a given input vector *and a given technology* in a given production environment. For example, the reciprocal of the largest factor by which it is possible to scale up q when using x and technology g in environment z is

$$d_O^g(x, q, z) = \inf\{\rho > 0 : q/\rho \in p^g(x, z)\}. \tag{2.39}$$

This distance function can be found in O'Donnell et al. (2017, Eq. 1). The associated *period*-and-environment-specific output distance function is $D_O^t(x, q, z) = \min_{g \in G_t} d_O^g(x, q, z)$. Thus, by construction, $d_O^g(x, q, z) \geq D_O^t(x, q, z)$ for all $g \in G_t$. The properties of technology-and-environment-specific output distance functions are generally similar to those of period-and-environment-specific output distance functions. For example, if outputs are strongly disposable, then the output distance function defined by (2.39) is nonnegative, nondecreasing and linearly homogeneous in outputs. If the technology-and-environment-specific production possibilities set is given by (2.38), for example, then the technology-and-environment-specific output distance function is

$$d_O^g(x, q, z) = \left(a(g) \prod_{j=1}^{J} z_j^{\delta_j} \prod_{m=1}^{M} x_m^{\beta_m} \right)^{-1} \left(\sum_{n=1}^{N} \gamma_n q_n^{\tau} \right)^{1/\tau}. \tag{2.40}$$

The associated period-and-environment-specific output distance function is given by (2.9), where $A(t) = \max_{g \in G_t} a(g)$.

2.9.6 *Period-Specific Sets and Functions*

Period-specific sets are *supersets* of the period-and-environment-specific sets defined in Sects. 2.1, 2.2 and 2.3. A *period*-specific production possibilities set, for example, is a set containing all input-output combinations that are physically possible *in a given period.* For example, the set of input-output combinations that are physically possible in period t is

$$T^t = \{(x, q) : x \text{ can produce } q \text{ in period } t\}. \tag{2.41}$$

An equivalent definition is $T^t = \cup_{z \in Z} T^t(z)$ where Z denotes the set of all possible vectors of environmental variables. Thus, by construction, $T^t \supseteq T^t(z)$ for all $z \in Z$. If there is no technical change, then all references to period t can be deleted. In this case, the set defined by (2.41) is equal to the 'metatechnology set' defined by O'Donnell et al. (2008, Eq. 1) and the 'marginal (unconditional) attainable set' defined by Badin et al. (2012, Eq. 1.4).

Period-specific sets can generally be represented by period-specific analogues of the functions discussed in Sects. 2.4, 2.5, 2.6, 2.7 and 2.8. For example, if output sets are bounded and outputs are weakly disposable, then the input-output combinations that are possible in different periods can be represented by period-specific output distance functions. A *period*-specific output distance function gives the reciprocal of the largest factor by which it is possible to scale up a given output vector when using a given input vector *in a given period*. For example, the reciprocal of the largest factor by which it is possible to scale up q when using x in period t is

$$D_O^t(x, q) = \inf\{\rho > 0 : (x, q/\rho) \in T^t\}. \tag{2.42}$$

This distance function can be found in Balk (1998, p. 13). An equivalent definition is $D_O^t(x, q) = \min_{z \in Z} D_O^t(x, q, z)$. Thus, by construction, $D_O^t(x, q) \leq D_O^t(x, q, z)$ for all $z \in Z$. Again, if there is no technical change, then all references to period t can be deleted. In this case, the output distance function defined by (2.42) is equal to the output distance function defined by Färe and Primont (1995, Eq. 2.1.11) and the 'output metadistance function' defined by O'Donnell et al. (2008, Eq. 3). Again, the properties of period-specific functions are generally similar to those of period-and-environment-specific functions. For example, if outputs are strongly disposable, then the output distance function defined by (2.42) is nonnegative, nondecreasing and linearly homogeneous in outputs.

2.9.7 State-Contingent Sets and Functions

Characteristics of production environments are often chosen by Nature. If *all* characteristics of production environments are chosen by Nature, then production environments are often referred to as 'states of Nature'. In such cases, environment-specific sets and functions are sometimes referred to as *state-contingent* sets and functions. For example, period-and-environment-specific production possibilities sets are sometimes referred to as period-and-state-contingent production possibilities sets. In mathematical terms, the set of input-output combinations that are physically possible in period t in state of Nature s is

$$T^t(s) = \{(x, q) : x \text{ can produce } q \text{ in period } t \text{ in state } s\}. \quad (2.43)$$

If there are S possible states of Nature, then the period-specific production possibilities set (2.41) can be defined as $T^t = \cup_{s \in \Omega} T^t(s)$ where $\Omega = \{1, \ldots, S\}$. As another example, period-and-environment-specific output distance functions are sometimes referred to as period-and-state-contingent output distance functions. In mathematical terms, the reciprocal of the largest factor by which it is possible to scale up q when using x in state s is

$$D_O^t(x, q, s) = \inf\{\rho > 0 : (x, q/\rho) \in T^t(s)\}. \quad (2.44)$$

The period-specific output distance function (2.42) can be defined as $D_O^t(x, q) = \min_{s \in \Omega} D_O^t(x, q, s)$. The properties of state-contingent sets and functions are identical to those of environment-specific sets and functions.

2.10 Summary and Further Reading

In this book, a production technology (or simply 'technology') is defined as a technique, method or system for transforming inputs into outputs. Examples include the Bessemer and Hlsarna processes for making steel, and phonics methods for teaching children to read. For most practical purposes, it is convenient to follow O'Donnell (2016, p. 328) and Caselli and Coleman (2006, p. 509) and think of a technology as book of instructions, or blueprint. Some authors use the term 'technology' quite differently. For example, Griliches (1987, p. 8084) thinks of a technology 'as consisting of both the average set of recipes for doing things ...and the currently known *best* way of doing things". Balk (1998, p. 12) uses the term 'technology' to describe a set of feasible input-output combinations.

In this book, the set of technologies that exist in any given period is called a 'technology set'. If we think of a technology as a book of instructions, or blueprint, then we can follow O'Donnell (2016, p. 328) and Caselli and Coleman (2006, p. 509) and think of a technology set as a library.[24] Again, some authors use the term 'technology set' quite differently. For example, Färe and Primont (1995, p. 8) and Coelli et al. (2005, p. 42) use the term 'technology set' to describe a set of feasible input-output combinations.

The input-output combinations that are possible using different technologies can be represented by output sets. An output set is a set containing all outputs that can be produced using given inputs. Many researchers work with output sets that are not specific to particular time periods or production environments; see, for example, Shephard (1970, p. 179), Färe and Primont (1995, Eq. 2.1.8), Kumbhakar and Lovell (2000, p. 22), Coelli et al. (2005, Eq. 3.2) and Fried et al. (2008, Eq. 1.8). In this book, the focus is on *period-and-environment-specific* output sets. A period-and-environment-specific output set is a set containing all outputs that can be produced using given inputs *in a given period in a given production environment.*

The input-output combinations that are possible using different technologies can also be represented by input sets. An input set is a set containing all inputs that can produce given outputs. Again, many researchers work with input sets that are not specific to particular time periods or production environments; see, for example, Shephard (1970, p. 179), Färe and Primont (1995, Eq. 2.1.16), Kumbhakar and Lovell (2000, p. 21), Coelli et al. (2005, Eq. 3.3) and Fried et al. (2008, Eq. 1.2). In this book, the focus is on *period-and-environment-specific* input sets. A period-and-environment-specific input set is a set containing all inputs that can produce given outputs *in a given period in a given production environment.*

The input-output combinations that are possible using different technologies can also be represented by production possibilities sets. A production possibilities set is a set containing all input-output combinations that are physically possible. Again, many researchers work with production possibilities sets that are not specific to particular time periods or production environments; see, for example, Shephard (1970, p. 181), Kumbhakar and Lovell (2000, p. 18), Färe and Primont (1995, p. 8), Coelli et al. (2005, Eq. 3.1), and Fried et al. (2008, Eq. 1.1).[25] In this book, the focus is on two specific production possibilities sets: *period-and-environment-specific* production possibilities sets and period-environment-*and-mix-specific* production possibilities sets. A period-and-environment-specific production possibilities set is a set containing all input-output combinations that are physically possible *in a given period in a given production environment*; examples of such sets can be found in O'Donnell (2016, p. 330) and O'Donnell et al. (2017, p. 119). A period-environment-and-mix-specific production possibilities set is a set containing all input-output combinations that are physically possible *when using a scalar multiple of a given input vector*

[24]O'Donnell (2016) refers to a technology set as a 'metatechnology'. This terminology is common in the metafrontier literature. See, for example, Casu et al. (2013).

[25]Shephard (1970) and Kumbhakar and Lovell (2000) refer to production possibilities sets as graphs; Färe and Primont (1995) and Coelli et al. (2005) refer to them as technology sets.

to produce a scalar multiple of a given output vector in a given period in a given production environment; an example of such a set can be found in O'Donnell (2016, p. 331).

It is common to make assumptions about technologies by way of assumptions about what they can and cannot produce. For example, it is common to assume that, with a given set of technologies, (A1) inactivity is possible, (A2) output sets are bounded, (A3) inputs are weakly essential (i.e., there is 'no free lunch'), (A4) output sets are closed, (A5) input sets are closed, (A6) outputs are weakly disposable, and (A7) inputs are weakly disposable. These seven assumptions are the 'maintained set of axioms' in Färe and Primont (1995, pp. 26, 27). They are also maintained throughout this book. In the production economics literature, the following additional assumptions are also made from time to time: (A6s) outputs are strongly disposable, (A7s) inputs are strongly disposable, (A8s) environmental variables are strongly disposable, (A15) output sets are convex, and (A16) input sets are convex.

If output sets are bounded and outputs are weakly disposable, then the input-output combinations that are possible using different technologies can be represented by output distance functions. An output distance function gives the reciprocal of the largest factor by which it is possible to scale up a given output vector when using a given input vector. Again, many researchers work with output distance functions that are not specific to particular time periods or production environments; see, for example, Shephard (1970, p. 207),Färe and Primont (1995, Eqs. 2.1.6, 2.1.11), Kumbhakar and Lovell (2000, Eq. 1.11), Coelli et al. (2005, Eq. 3.5) and Fried et al. (2008, Eq. 1.11). In this book, the focus is on *period-and-environment-specific* output distance functions. A period-and-environment-specific output distance function gives the reciprocal of the largest factor by which it is possible to scale up a given output vector when using a given input vector *in a given period in a given production environment*; examples of such functions can be found in O'Donnell (2016, p. 330) and O'Donnell et al. (2017, Eq. 3). Output distance functions are nonnegative and linearly homogeneous in outputs. If outputs are strongly disposable, then they are also nondecreasing in outputs. If they are continuously differentiable, then differential calculus can be used to derive various marginal effects (e.g., marginal products and normalised shadow output prices).

If inputs are weakly disposable, then the input-output combinations that are possible using different technologies can be represented by input distance functions. An input distance function gives the reciprocal of the smallest fraction of inputs that a firm needs to produce its outputs. Again, many researchers work with input distance functions that are not specific to particular time periods or production environments; see, for example, Shephard (1953, p. 5; 1970, p. 206), Färe and Primont (1995, Eq. 2.1.19), Kumbhakar and Lovell (2000, Eq. 1.5), Coelli et al. (2005, Eq. 3.6) and Fried et al. (2008, Eq. 1.5). In this book, the focus is on *period-and-environment-specific* input distance functions. A period-and-environment-specific input distance function gives the reciprocal of the smallest fraction of inputs that a firm needs to produce its outputs *in a given period in a given production environment*; examples of such functions can be found in O'Donnell (2016, p. 330) and O'Donnell et al. (2017, Eq. 4). Input distance functions are nonnegative and linearly homogeneous in inputs. If inputs are strongly disposable, then they are also nondecreasing in inputs. If they are continuously differentiable, then differential calculus can be used to derive various marginal effects (e.g., normalised shadow input prices and the elasticity of scale).

If output sets are bounded and outputs are weakly disposable, then the input-output combinations that are possible using different technologies can be represented by revenue functions. A revenue function gives the maximum revenue that can be earned using given inputs. Again, many researchers work with revenue functions that are not specific to particular time periods or production environments; see, for example, Färe and Primont (1995, Eq. 3.1.4) and Fried et al. (2008, Eq. 1.24). In this book, the focus is on *period-and-environment-specific* revenue functions. A period-and-environment-specific revenue function gives the maximum revenue that can be earned using given inputs *in a given period in a given production environment*. If firms are price takers in output markets, then revenue functions are nonnegative, nondecreasing and linearly homogeneous in output prices. If they are continuously differentiable, then differential calculus can be used to derive various marginal effects (e.g., marginal revenues and revenue-maximising revenue shares).

If inputs are weakly disposable, then the input-output combinations that are possible using different technologies can be represented by cost functions. A cost function gives the minimum cost of producing given outputs. Again, many researchers work with with cost functions that are not specific to particular time periods or production environments; see, for example, Färe and Primont (1995, Eq. 3.1.1) and Fried et al. (2008, Eq. 1.20). In this book, the focus is on *period-and-environment-specific* cost functions. A period-and-environment-specific cost function gives the minimum cost of producing given outputs *in a given period in a given production environment*. If firms are price takers in input markets, then cost functions are nonnegative, nondecreasing and linearly homogeneous in input prices. If they are continuously differentiable, then differential calculus can be used to derive various marginal effects (e.g., marginal costs and cost-minimising cost shares).

If outputs are weakly attainable and the set of technically-feasible input-output combinations that yield nonnegative profit is compact, then profit functions exist. A profit function gives the maximum profit that can be earned when inputs and outputs can be chosen freely. Again, many researchers work with profit functions that are not specific to particular time periods or production environments; see, for example, Färe and Primont (1995, Eq. 6.1.3) and Fried et al. (2008, Eq. 1.28). In this book, the focus is on *period-and-environment-specific* profit functions. A period-and-environment-specific profit function gives the maximum profit that can be earned *in a given period in a given production environment* when inputs and outputs can be chosen freely. If firms are price takers in output and input markets, then profit functions are nonnegative and nonincreasing (resp. nondecreasing) in input prices (resp. output prices). If they are continuously differentiable, then differential calculus can be used to derive profit-maximising output supplies and input demands.

Other sets and functions discussed in this book include production functions, input requirement functions, directional distance functions, hyperbolic distance functions, technology-and-environment-specific sets and functions, period-specific sets and functions, and state-contingent sets and functions. A production function gives the maximum output that a one-output firm can produce using a given input vector; examples of production functions that are not specific to particular time periods or production environments can be found in Shephard (1970, p. 20) and Färe and Primont (1995, p. 8). An input requirement function gives the minimum input that a one-input firm needs in order to produce a given output vector; an example of an input requirement function that is not specific to a particular time period or production environment is the 'inverse production function' defined by Shephard (1970, p. 197). A directional distance function measures the distance in a given direction from a given point to the boundary of a production possibilities set; an example of a directional distance function that is not specific to a particular time period or production environment can be found in Färe and Grosskopf (2000, Eq. 3). The basic idea behind directional distance functions can be traced back at least as far as the shortage function of Luenberger (1992, p. 242, Definition 4.1). A hyperbolic distance function measures the distance along a rectangular hyperbola from a given point to the boundary of a production possibilities set; an example of a hyperbolic distance function that is not specific to a particular time period or production environment can be found in Cuesta and Zofio (2005, Eq. 2). Technology-and-environment-specific sets are subsets of period-and-environment-specific sets. A *technology*-and-environment-specific production possibilities set, for example, is a set containing all input-output combinations that are physically possible *using a given technology* in a given production environment; an example of such a set can be found in O'Donnell et al. (2017, p. 118). Under weak conditions, technology-and-environment-specific sets can be represented by technology-and-environment-specific functions. For example, if output sets are bounded and outputs are weakly disposable, then the input-output combinations that are possible using different technologies can be represented by technology-and-environment-specific output distance functions. A *technology*-and-environment-specific output distance function gives the reciprocal of the largest factor by which it is possible to scale up a given output vector when using a given input vector *and a given technology* in a given production environment; an example of such a function can be found in O'Donnell et al. (2017, Eq. 1). Period-specific sets are *supersets* of period-and-environment-specific sets. A *period*-specific production possibilities set, for example, is a set containing all input-output combinations that are physically possible *in a given period*; an example of such a set can be found in Balk (1998, Eq. 2.1). Under weak conditions, period-specific sets can be represented by period-specific functions. For example, if output sets are bounded and outputs are weakly disposable, then the input-output combinations that are possible in different periods can be represented by period-specific output distance functions. A *period*-specific output distance function gives the reciprocal of the largest factor by which it is possible to scale up a given output vector when using a given input vector *in a given period*; an example of such a function can be found in Balk (1998, Eq. 2.6). Finally, if *all* characteristics of production environments are chosen by Nature, then production environments are often referred to as 'states of Nature'. In such cases, environment-specific sets and functions are sometimes referred to as *state-contingent* sets and functions. For example, period-and-environment-specific production possibilities sets are sometimes referred to as period-and-state-contingent production possibilities sets. More details (and much of the jargon) surrounding state-contingent sets and functions can be accessed from Chambers and Quiggin (2000) and Rasmussen (2003).

Finally, other functions that are *not* discussed in this book include indirect output distance functions, indirect input distance functions, cost indirect revenue functions, revenue indirect cost functions, and nonstandard profit functions. An indirect output distance function gives the reciprocal of the largest factor by which it is possible to scale up a given output vector for a given cost. An indirect input distance function gives the reciprocal of the smallest fraction of a given input vector that can earn a given revenue. A cost indirect revenue function gives the maximum revenue that can be earned for a given cost. A revenue indirect cost function gives the minimum cost of earning a given revenue. Finally, a nonstandard profit function gives the maximum profit that a firm can earn when output quantities and input prices are predetermined but output prices and input quantities can be chosen freely. For more details on indirect functions, see Färe and Primont (1994). For more details on nonstandard profit functions, see Humphrey and Pulley (1997, p. 81) and Kumbhakar (2006).[26]

References

Badin L, Daraio C, Simar L (2012) How to measure the impact of environmental factors in a nonparametric production model. Eur J Oper Res 223(3):818–833

Balk B (1998) Industrial price, quantity, and productivity indices: the micro-economic theory and an application. Kluwer Academic Publishers, Boston

Caselli F, Coleman W (2006) The world technology frontier. Am Econ Rev 93(3):499–522

Casu B, Ferrari A, Zhao T (2013) Regulatory reform and productivity change in Indian banking. Rev Econ Stat 95(3):1066–1077

Chambers R, Quiggin J (2000) Uncertainty, production, choice and agency: the state-contingent approach. Cambridge University Press, Cambridge

Chambers R, Chung Y, Färe R (1996) Benefit and distance functions. J Econ Theory 70:407–419

Chambers R, Chung Y, Färe R (1998) Profit, directional distance functions, and Nerlovian efficiency. J Optim Theory Appl 98(2):351–364

Coelli T, Rao D, O'Donnell C, Battese G (2005) An introduction to efficiency and productivity analysis, 2nd edn. Springer, New York

Cuesta R, Zofio J (2005) Hyperbolic efficiency and parametric distance functions: with application to Spanish savings banks. J Prod Anal 24(1):31–48

Färe R, Grosskopf S (2000) Theory and application of directional distance functions. J Prod Anal 13(2000):93–103

Färe R, Primont D (1994) The unification of Ronald W. Shephard's duality theory. J Econ 60(2):199–207

Färe R, Primont D (1995) Multi-output production and duality: theory and applications. Kluwer Academic Publishers, Boston

Färe R, Grosskopf S, Lovell C (1985) The measurement of efficiency of production. Kluwer Academic Publishers, Boston

Färe R, Grosskopf S, Lovell C (1986) Scale economies and duality. J Econ 46(2):175–182

[26]Humphrey and Pulley (1997) refer to their nonstandard profit function as an 'alternative indirect profit function'.

Färe R, Grosskopf S, Lovell C, Yaisawarng S (1993) Derivation of shadow prices for undesirable outputs: a distance function approach. Rev Econ Stat 75(2):374–380

Färe R, Grosskopf S, Zaim O (2002) Hyperbolic efficiency and return to the dollar. Eur J Oper Res 136(3):671–679

Fried H, Lovell CAK, Schmidt S (2008) Efficiency and productivity. In: Fried H, Lovell CAK, Schmidt S (eds) The measurement of productive efficiency and productivity growth. Oxford University Press, New York, pp 3–91

Griliches Z (1987) Productivity: measurement problems. In: Eatwell J, Milgate M, Newman P (eds) The new Palgrave: a dictionary of economics, 1st edn. Palgrave Macmillan, New York

Hsieh CT, Klenow P (2009) Misallocation and manufacturing TFP in China and India. Q J Econ 124(4):1403–1448

Humphrey DB, Pulley LB (1997) Banks' responses to deregulation: profits, technology, and efficiency. J Money Credit Bank 29(1):73–93

Kumbhakar S (2006) Specification and estimation of nonstandard profit functions. Empir Econ 31(1):243–260

Kumbhakar S, Lovell C (2000) Stochastic frontier analysis. Cambridge University Press, Cambridge

Lau L (1972) Profit functions of technologies with multiple inputs and outputs. Rev Econ Stat 54(3):281–289

Luenberger D (1992) New optimality principles for economic efficiency and equilibrium. J Optim Theory Appl 75(2):221–264

O'Donnell C (2016) Using information about technologies, markets and firm behaviour to decompose a proper productivity index. J Econ 190(2):328–340

O'Donnell C, Rao D, Battese G (2008) Metafrontier frameworks for the study of firm-level efficiencies and technology ratios. Empir Econ 34(2):231–255

O'Donnell C, Fallah-Fini S, Triantis K (2017) Measuring and analysing productivity change in a metafrontier framework. J Prod Anal 47(2):117–128

Rasmussen S (2003) Criteria for optimal production under uncertainty. The state-contingent approach. Aust J Agric Resour Econ 47(4):447–476

Shephard R (1953) Cost and production functions. Princeton University Press, Princeton

Shephard R (1970) The theory of cost and production functions. Princeton University Press, Princeton

Solow R (1957) Technical change and the aggregate production function. Rev Econ Stat 39(3):312–320

Chapter 3
Measures of Productivity Change

In this book, measures of productivity change are defined as measures of output quantity change divided by measures of input quantity change. Computing measures of output and input quantity change involves assigning numbers to baskets of outputs and inputs. Measurement theory[1] says that so-called index numbers must be assigned in such a way that the relationships between the numbers mirror the relationships between the baskets. For example, if we are computing a measure of output quantity change, and if basket A contains exactly twice as much of every output as basket B, then the index number assigned to basket A should be exactly twice as big as the number assigned to basket B. This chapter explains how to compute output and input quantity index numbers (and therefore productivity index numbers) that are consistent with measurement theory.

3.1 Output Quantity Indices

An *index* is a rule or formula that explains how to use data to measure the change in one or more variables across time and/or space. An *index number* is the value obtained after data have been substituted into the formula.[2] In this book, an output quantity index (or simply 'output index') that compares the outputs of firm i in period

---

[1]Measurement theory is the study of how numbers are assigned to objects. Classical measurement theory holds that only quantitative attributes of objects are measurable. The representational theory of measurement holds that qualitative attributes of objects are also measureable. For more details, see Sarle (1997), Hosch (2011, pp. 227–229) and Tal (2016, Sect. 3).

[2]Similar distinctions can be found in other areas of science. In econometrics, for example, an *estimator* is a rule or formula that explains how to use data to estimate the value of a population parameter, while an *estimate* is the value obtained after data have been substituted into the formula. See, for example, Hill et al. (2011, p. 53).

C. J. O'Donnell, *Productivity and Efficiency Analysis*,
https://doi.org/10.1007/978-981-13-2984-5_3

t with the outputs of firm k in period s is defined as any variable of the form[3]

$$QI(q_{ks}, q_{it}) \equiv Q(q_{it})/Q(q_{ks}) \tag{3.1}$$

where $Q(.)$ is a nonnegative, nondecreasing, linearly-homogeneous, scalar-valued aggregator function. If outputs are positive,[4] then all output indices of this type satisfy the following axioms[5]:

QI1 $q_{rl} \geq q_{it} \Rightarrow QI(q_{ks}, q_{rl}) \geq QI(q_{ks}, q_{it})$ (weak monotonicity),
QI2 $QI(q_{ks}, \lambda q_{it}) = \lambda QI(q_{ks}, q_{it})$ for $\lambda > 0$ (homogeneity type I),
QI3 $QI(\lambda q_{ks}, \lambda q_{it}) = QI(q_{ks}, q_{it})$ for $\lambda > 0$ (homogeneity type II),
QI4 $QI(q_{ks}, \lambda q_{ks}) = \lambda$ for $\lambda > 0$ (proportionality),
QI5 $QI(q_{ks}, q_{it}) = 1/QI(q_{it}, q_{ks})$ (time-space reversal) and
QI6 $QI(q_{ks}, q_{rl})QI(q_{rl}, q_{it}) = QI(q_{ks}, q_{it})$ (transitivity).

The interpretation of these axioms is straightforward. In a cross-section context, for example, axiom QI1 (weak monotonicity) says that if firm C produced more than firm B, then the index that compares the outputs of firm C with the outputs of firm A cannot take a value less than the index that compares the outputs of firm B with the outputs of firm A. Axiom QI2 (homogeneity type I) says that if firm C produced λ times as much as firm B, then the index number that compares the outputs of firm C with the outputs of firm A must be λ times the index number that compares the outputs of firm B with the outputs of firm A. Axiom QI3 (homogeneity type II) says that if firm D produced λ times as much as firm B, and firm C produced λ times as much as firm A, then the index that compares the outputs of firm D with the outputs of firm C must take the same value as the index that compares the outputs of firm B with the outputs of firm A. Axiom QI4 (proportionality) says that if firm B produced λ times as much as firm A, then the index that compares the outputs of firm B with the outputs of firm A must take the value λ. Axiom QI5 (time-space reversal) says that the index number that compares the outputs of firm B with the outputs of firm A must be the reciprocal of the index number that compares the outputs of firm A with the outputs of firm B. Thus, for example, if we find that firm B produced twice as much as firm A, then we must also find that firm A produced half as much as firm B. Axiom QI6 (transitivity) says that if we compare the outputs of firms C and A indirectly through firm B, then we must get the same index number as when we compare the outputs of firms C and A directly. Thus, for example, if we find that

---

[3]This definition can be traced back at least as far as O'Donnell (2012a). Elsewhere in the literature, output and input indices are rarely defined in terms of aggregate quantities. When they are, the aggregator functions are often observation-varying (e.g., they depend on observation-varying prices or value shares) and/or their monotonicity and homogeneity properties are not all specified. See, for example, Diewert (1976).

[4]If some outputs are zero, then some output indices may be mathematically undefined and may therefore not satisfy some axioms.

[5]These statements, and similar statements elsewhere in this chapter, are axioms in the sense that they are substantive assertions about elements of the domain of index number theory.

firm C produced twice as much as firm B, and that firm B produced twice as much as firm A, then we must also find that firm C produced four times as much as firm A.

In O'Donnell (2016), an output index is said to be proper if and only if QI1 to QI6 are satisfied.[6] The geometric average of any set of proper output indices is also a proper output index. Depending on the aggregator functions, proper output indices may have other properties. For example, if aggregator functions are strictly increasing in outputs, then the associated output indices are *strongly* monotonic. Strong monotonicity means that if firm C produced more than firm B, then the index number that compares the outputs of firm C with the outputs of firm A will be *greater than* the index number that compares the outputs of firm B with the outputs of firm A.

Any nonnegative, nondecreasing, linearly-homogeneous, scalar-valued aggregator function can be used for purposes of constructing a proper output index. Linear (resp. double-log) functions can be used to construct additive (resp. multiplicative) indices. If outputs are strongly disposable, then output distance functions can be used to construct primal indices. If cost functions are homogeneous in outputs, then they can be used to construct dual indices. Locally-linear functions (i.e., linear functions with parameters that are permitted to vary from one observation to the next) can be used to construct benefit-of-the-doubt (BOD) indices. In practice, the choice of function is generally a matter of taste.[7]

3.1.1 Additive Indices

Additive output indices are constructed using aggregator functions of the form $Q(q_{it}) \propto a'q_{it}$ where a is any nonnegative vector of weights. The associated index that compares the outputs of firm i in period t with the outputs of firm k in period s is[8]

[6]In O'Donnell (2016), an output index is said to be proper if and only if *eight* axioms are satisfied. If QI4 and QI6 are satisfied, then, and only then, the extra two axioms of O'Donnell (2016), an identity axiom and a circularity axiom, are also satisfied. The use of the term 'proper' in an index number context can be traced back to O'Donnell (2012b, p. 6).

[7]If output distance functions and/or cost functions are unknown, then the choice set will obviously be limited. Samuelson and Swamy (1974) write that "we cannot hope for one ideal formula for the index number: if it works for the tastes of Jack Spratt, it won't work for his wife's tastes; if say, a Cobb-Douglas function can be found that works for him with one set of parameters and for her with another set, their daughter will in general require a non-Cobb-Douglas formula! Just as there is an uncountable infinity of different indifference contours—there is no counting tastes—there is an uncountable infinity of different index-number formulas, which dooms Fisher's search for *the* ideal one. It does not exist even in Plato's heaven." (p. 568).

[8]The use of the term 'additive' to describe an index of this type can be traced back at least as far as Aczel and Eichhorn (1974). The index is additive in the sense that $QI^A(q_{ks}, q_{it} + q_{rl}) = QI^A(q_{ks}, q_{it}) + QI^A(q_{ks}, q_{rl})$ and $1/QI^A(q_{ks} + q_{rl}, q_{it}) = 1/QI^A(q_{ks}, q_{it}) + 1/QI^A(q_{rl}, q_{it})$ (Aczel and Eichhorn 1974, p. 525).

$$QI^{A}(q_{ks}, q_{it}) \equiv (a'q_{it})/(a'q_{ks}). \tag{3.2}$$

Any nonnegative observation-invariant measures of relative value can be used as weights. In practice, the choice of weights is a matter of taste. One possibility is to use average market prices as weights. In this case, the index defined by (3.2) takes the form of the Lowe index defined by O'Donnell (2012c, p. 877); this index should be used by analysts who regard output prices as appropriate measures of relative value (e.g., analysts who might otherwise use a Fisher, chained Fisher or EKS index). Alternatively, let Q denote a matrix of mean-corrected[9] outputs with N columns and as many rows as there are observations in the dataset. If the eigenvector associated with the largest eigenvalue of $Q'Q$ is nonnegative, then it can be used as vector of weights. In this case, the index defined by (3.2) takes the form of the 'output factor' defined by Daraio and Simar (2007, Eq. 6.2, p. 149).

3.1.2 Multiplicative Indices

Multiplicative output indices are constructed using aggregator functions of the form $Q(q_{it}) \propto \prod_{n=1}^{N} q_{nit}^{a_n}$ where $a_1, \ldots, a_N$ are any nonnegative weights that sum to one. The associated index that compares the outputs of firm i in period t with the outputs of firm k in period s is[10]

$$QI^{M}(q_{ks}, q_{it}) \equiv \prod_{n=1}^{N} \left(\frac{q_{nit}}{q_{nks}} \right)^{a_n}. \tag{3.3}$$

Any nonnegative observation-invariant measures of relative value can be used as weights, provided they sum to one. Again, the choice of weights is a matter of taste. One possibility is to use average revenue shares as weights. In this case, the index defined by (3.3) takes the form of the geometric Young (GY) index defined by O'Donnell (2012b, Eq. 5); this index should be used by analysts who regard revenue shares as appropriate measures of relative value (e.g., analysts who might otherwise use a Törnqvist, chained Törnqvist or CCD index). Another possibility is to estimate the weights in a linear regression framework. For example, Eq. (3.3) can be rewritten as

$$\ln(q_{1it}/q_{1ks}) = \sum_{n=2}^{N} a_n[\ln(q_{1it}/q_{1ks}) - \ln(q_{nit}/q_{nks})] + e_{it} \tag{3.4}$$

---

[9]Here, the term 'mean-corrected' means all variables have been re-scaled to have unit means.

[10]The use of the term 'multiplicative' to describe an index of this type can be traced back at least as far as Coelli et al. (2005, p. 131). The index is multiplicative in the sense that $QI^{M}(q_{ks} \odot q_{gh}, q_{it} \odot q_{rl}) = QI^{M}(q_{ks}, q_{it})QI^{M}(q_{gh}, q_{rl})$.

where $e_{it} = \ln QI^M(q_{ks}, q_{it})$ is an unobserved log-index that in most other contexts would be interpreted as statistical noise. The unknown parameters/weights in this regression model can be estimated using, for example, least squares methods. The associated output index numbers are the antilogarithms of the residuals. This index should be used by analysts who want to minimise the amount of variation in the index numbers. It can also be used by analysts who have no information about output prices, revenue shares or production technologies.

It is worth noting that multiplicative output indices fail a determinateness test. The determinateness test says that the index should not go to zero or infinity as any output goes to zero. If there is only one output, then all well-known output indices fail the determinateness test. Partly for this reason, many authors view the determinateness test as an undesirable one; see, for example, Samuelson and Swamy (1974, p. 572) (these authors discuss the determinateness test in the context of price indices).

3.1.3 Primal Indices

Primal[11] output indices are constructed using output distance functions as aggregator functions. For a primal output index to be a proper index, the output distance function must be nondecreasing in outputs, implying that outputs must be strongly disposable. In this case, a suitable aggregator function is $Q(q_{it}) \propto D_O^{\bar{t}}(\bar{x}, q_{it}, \bar{z})$ where $\bar{t}$ is a fixed time period and $\bar{x}$ and $\bar{z}$ are fixed vectors of inputs and environmental variables (again, the choices of $\bar{t}$, $\bar{x}$ and $\bar{z}$ are a matter of taste). The associated primal index that compares the outputs of firm i in period t with the outputs of firm k in period s is

$$QI^P(q_{ks}, q_{it}) \equiv D_O^{\bar{t}}(\bar{x}, q_{it}, \bar{z}) / D_O^{\bar{t}}(\bar{x}, q_{ks}, \bar{z}). \tag{3.5}$$

This index can be traced back to O'Donnell (2016, Eq. 2). It should be used by analysts who regard marginal rates of transformation as appropriate measures of relative value (e.g., analysts who might otherwise use a generalised Malmquist index). If there is no technical or environmental change, then it reduces to the output index defined by Färe and Primont (1995, p. 38). If output sets are homothetic, then it does not depend on $\bar{x}$. If technical change is IHON, then it does not depend on $\bar{t}$ or $\bar{z}$. Ultimately, the exact form of the index depends on the output distance function. If the output distance function is given by (2.9), for example, then

$$QI^P(q_{ks}, q_{it}) = \left(\frac{\sum_n \gamma_n q_{nit}^{\tau}}{\sum_n \gamma_n q_{nks}^{\tau}} \right)^{1/\tau}. \tag{3.6}$$

[11] Balk (1998, p. 100) also uses the term 'primal' in reference to an index that is constructed using an output distance function.

Observe that this index does not depend on the choices of $\bar{t}$, $\bar{x}$ or $\bar{z}$. This is because the output distance function given by (2.9) represents a homothetic output set with a boundary that exhibits IHON technical change.

3.1.4 Dual Indices

Dual[12] output indices are constructed using cost functions as aggregator functions. For a dual output index to be a proper index, the cost function must be homogeneous in outputs. If the cost function is homogeneous of degree $1/r$ in outputs, for example, then a suitable output aggregator function is $Q(q_{it}) \propto C^{\bar{t}}(\bar{w}, q_{it}, \bar{z})^r$ where $\bar{t}$ is a fixed time period and $\bar{w}$ and $\bar{z}$ are fixed vectors of input prices and environmental variables (again, the choices of $\bar{t}$, $\bar{w}$ and $\bar{z}$ are a matter of taste). The associated dual index that compares the outputs of firm i in period t with the outputs of firm k in period s is

$$QI^D(q_{ks}, q_{it}) \equiv C^{\bar{t}}(\bar{w}, q_{it}, \bar{z})^r / C^{\bar{t}}(\bar{w}, q_{ks}, \bar{z})^r. \tag{3.7}$$

This index should be used by analysts who regard marginal costs as appropriate measures of relative value. If there is no technical change, then it reduces to the output index defined by O'Donnell (2012b, Eq. 3). If input sets are homothetic, then it does not depend on $\bar{w}$. Ultimately, the exact form of the index depends on the cost function. If the cost function is given by (2.22), for example, then

$$QI^D(q_{ks}, q_{it}) = \left(\frac{\sum_n \gamma_n q_{nit}^{\tau}}{\sum_n \gamma_n q_{nks}^{\tau}} \right)^{1/\tau}. \tag{3.8}$$

Observe that this index is the same as the index defined by (3.6). This is because the output distance function given by (2.9) and the cost function given by (2.22) are equivalent representations of a homothetic output set with a boundary that exhibits IHON technical change.

3.1.5 Benefit-of-the-Doubt Indices

Benefit-of-the-doubt (BOD)[13] output indices are constructed using aggregator functions of the form $Q(q_{it}) = a_{it}' q_{it}$ where a_{it} is an unknown vector of nonnegative weights. If $Q(.)$ is continuously differentiable, then, by Euler's homogeneous function theorem, $a_{it} = \partial Q(q_{it})/\partial q_{it}$. Computing BOD output indices involves choosing the weight vector to maximise $Q(q_{it})$. The only constraint is that if the chosen weight

[12] In production economics, the term 'dual' is usually used to describe cost, revenue and profit functions (e.g., Beavis and Dobbs 1990, p. 99).

[13] Cherchye et al. (2007) attribute the term 'benefit-of-the-doubt' to Melyn and Moesen (1991).

vector is used to aggregate any output vector in the dataset, then the resulting aggregate output can be no greater than one.[14] Thus, the optimisation problem is

$$\max_{a_{it}} \left\{ a_{it}' q_{it} : a_{it} \geq 0, a_{it}' q_{hr} \leq 1 \text{ for all } h \text{ and } r \right\}. \tag{3.9}$$

This optimisation problem can be found in O'Donnell and Nguyen (2013, Eq. 22). Let $Q^B(q_{it})$ denote the maximised value of the objective function. The associated BOD index that compares the outputs of firm i in period t with the outputs of firm k in period s is

$$QI^B(q_{ks}, q_{it}) \equiv Q^B(q_{it})/Q^B(q_{ks}). \tag{3.10}$$

A strongly monotonic version of this index can be obtained by adding the constraint $a_{it} > 0$ to problem (3.9). Whether the weights in problem (3.9) are positive or merely nonnegative, the fact that they vary with i and t means the index defined by (3.10) has high 'characteristicity'. Characteristicity refers to "the degree to which weights are specific to the comparison at hand" (Caves et al. 1982b, p. 74).[15] The BOD output index should be used by analysts who believe measures of relative value should vary from one output comparison to the next. It can also be used by analysts who have no information about output prices, revenue shares or production technologies.

3.1.6 *Other Indices*

Other types of output indices include binary, chained and multilateral indices. These are not proper output indices in the sense that they do not generally satisfy all of axioms QI1–QI6. Binary output indices are designed for comparing two output vectors only. Chained output indices are mainly used for comparing the outputs of a single firm over several time periods. Multilateral output indices are mainly used for comparing the outputs of several firms in a single time period.

3.1.6.1 Binary Indices

Binary output indices do not generally satisfy axiom QI6 (transitivity). The class of binary output indices includes Fisher, Törnqvist and generalised Malmquist (GM) indices. The Fisher index that compares the outputs of firm i in period t with the

[14]The choice of one as the maximum aggregate output is arbitrary.

[15]The BOD output index is a proper index, implying it satisfies a circularity axiom (among others). Characteristicity and circularity are generally in conflict with each other. Drechsler (1973, p.17) claims, incorrectly, that they are *always* in conflict with each other. This erroneous claim can be traced back to Fisher (1922, p. 275).

outputs of firm k in period s is[16]

$$QI^F(q_{ks}, q_{it}, \ldots) \equiv \left(\frac{p'_{it}q_{it}}{p'_{it}q_{ks}} \frac{p'_{ks}q_{it}}{p'_{ks}q_{ks}} \right)^{1/2}. \tag{3.11}$$

If observed output prices are firm- and time-invariant, then Fisher output index numbers are equal to Lowe output index numbers. The Törnqvist index that compares the outputs of firm i in period t with the outputs of firm k in period s is

$$QI^T(q_{ks}, q_{it}, \ldots) \equiv \prod_{n=1}^{N} \left(\frac{q_{nit}}{q_{nks}} \right)^{(r_{nit}+r_{nks})/2} \tag{3.12}$$

where $r_{nit} \equiv p_{nit}q_{nit}/R_{it}$ is the n-th observed revenue share. If observed revenue shares are firm- and time-invariant, then Törnqvist output index numbers are equal to GY output index numbers. Finally, there are several Malmquist indices defined in the literature. In this book, the GM index that compares the outputs of firm i in period t with the outputs of firm k in period s is defined as

$$QI^{GM}(q_{ks}, q_{it}, \ldots) \equiv \left(\frac{D^t_O(x_{it}, q_{it}, z_{it})}{D^t_O(x_{it}, q_{ks}, z_{it})} \frac{D^s_O(x_{ks}, q_{it}, z_{ks})}{D^s_O(x_{ks}, q_{ks}, z_{ks})} \right)^{1/2}. \tag{3.13}$$

If output sets are homothetic and technical change is IHON, then this particular Malmquist index is equivalent to the primal index defined by (3.5). If the output distance function is given by (2.9), then it is equivalent to the primal index defined by (3.6). If there is only one firm involved in the comparison and there is no environmental change, then the two ratios in (3.13) are equivalent to the Malmquist output indices defined by Diewert (1992, Eqs. 118, 119) (hence the use of the term 'generalised'). If (a) there is no environmental change, (b) firms are price takers in output markets, (c) firm managers maximise revenue, (d) output prices and quantities are strictly positive, (e) the period-s and period-t output distance functions are nondecreasing in outputs, and (f) the period-s and period-t output distance functions are translog functions with identical second-order coefficients, then the GM index defined by (3.13) is equivalent to the Törnqvist index defined by (3.12) (Caves et al. 1982a, Thm. 2.). For this reason, Törnqvist output indices are said to be exact for translog output distance functions. Unfortunately, properties (e) and (f) cannot both be true.[17] This means that Törnqvist output indices are merely 'superlative'. Superlative output indices are

[16]The right-hand side of this equation is a function of q_{ks}, q_{it}, p_{ks} and p_{it}. However, only q_{ks} and q_{it} have been listed on the left-hand side. In this book, dots and ellipses are used in functions to indicate that one or more variables have been omitted.

[17]If the output distance function is nondecreasing in outputs, then the partial derivatives of the distance function with respect to the outputs must be nonnegative for all feasible input-output combinations. If the output distance function is a translog function, then it is possible to find feasible input-output combinations such that at least one partial derivative is negative. Ergo, the output distance function cannot be a translog function.

exact for functions that can generally only provide second-order *approximations* to output distance functions.

3.1.6.2 Chained Indices

Chained output indices do not generally satisfy axiom QI4 (proportionality). The class of chained output indices includes chained Fisher (CF), chained Törnqvist (CT) and chained generalised Malmquist (CGM) indices. The CF index that compares the outputs of firm i in period t with the outputs of firm i in period 1 is

$$QI^{CF}(q_{i1}, q_{it}, \ldots) \equiv \prod_{s=1}^{t-1} QI^{F}(q_{is}, q_{i,s+1}, \ldots) \tag{3.14}$$

where $QI^{F}(q_{is}, q_{i,s+1}, \ldots)$ is a binary Fisher index. If observed output prices are firm- and time-invariant, then CF output index numbers are equal to Lowe output index numbers. The CT index that compares the outputs of firm i in period t with the outputs of firm i in period 1 is

$$QI^{CT}(q_{i1}, q_{it}, \ldots) \equiv \prod_{s=1}^{t-1} QI^{T}(q_{is}, q_{i,s+1}, \ldots) \tag{3.15}$$

where $QI^{T}(q_{is}, q_{i,s+1}, \ldots)$ is a binary Törnqvist index. If observed revenue shares are firm- and time-invariant, then CT output index numbers are equal to GY output index numbers. Finally, the CGM index that compares the outputs of firm i in period t with the outputs of firm i in period 1 is

$$QI^{CGM}(q_{i1}, q_{it}, \ldots) \equiv \prod_{s=1}^{t-1} QI^{GM}(q_{is}, q_{i,s+1}, \ldots) \tag{3.16}$$

where $QI^{GM}(q_{is}, q_{i,s+1}, \ldots)$ is a binary GM index. If output sets are homothetic and technical change is IHON, then CGM output index numbers are equal to primal output index numbers computed using (3.5).

3.1.6.3 Multilateral Indices

Multilateral output indices do not generally satisfy axiom QI4 (proportionality). They are also particularly sensitive to the addition or removal of observations from the dataset. This means, for example, that the index number that compares the outputs of firm A with the outputs of firm B will generally change when firm Z is added to the dataset (even if the outputs of firm Z are the same as the outputs of a firm that is already represented in the dataset).

The class of multilateral output indices includes an index proposed by Elteto and Koves (1964) and Szulc (1964) (hereafter, EKS), an index proposed by Caves et al. (1982b) (hereafter CCD), and a multilateral generalised Malmquist (MGM) index. The EKS index that compares the outputs of firm i in period t with the outputs of firm k in period t is

$$QI^{EKS}(q_{kt}, q_{it}, \ldots) \equiv \left(\prod_{r=1}^{I_t} QI^F(q_{kt}, q_{rt}, \ldots) QI^F(q_{rt}, q_{it}, \ldots) \right)^{1/I_t} \tag{3.17}$$

where I_t is the number of firms in the dataset in period t and $QI^F(q_{kt}, q_{rt}, \ldots)$ is a binary Fisher index. If observed output prices are firm- and time-invariant, then EKS output index numbers are equal to Lowe output index numbers. The CCD index that compares the outputs of firm i in period t with the outputs of firm k in period t is

$$QI^{CCD}(q_{kt}, q_{it}, \ldots) \equiv \left(\prod_{r=1}^{I_t} QI^T(q_{kt}, q_{rt}, \ldots) QI^T(q_{rt}, q_{it}, \ldots) \right)^{1/I_t} \tag{3.18}$$

where $QI^T(q_{kt}, q_{rt}, \ldots)$ is a binary Törnqvist index. If observed revenue shares are firm- and time-invariant, then CCD output index numbers are equal to GY output index numbers. Finally, the MGM index that compares the outputs of firm i in period t with the outputs of firm k in period t is

$$QI^{MGM}(q_{kt}, q_{it}, \ldots) \equiv \left(\prod_{r=1}^{I_t} QI^{GM}(q_{kt}, q_{rt}, \ldots) QI^{GM}(q_{rt}, q_{it}, \ldots) \right)^{1/I_t} \tag{3.19}$$

where $QI^{GM}(q_{kt}, q_{rt}, \ldots)$ is a binary GM index. If output sets are homothetic and technical change is IHON, then MGM output index numbers are equal to primal output index numbers computed using (3.5).

3.1.7 Toy Example

Reconsider the output quantity and price data reported earlier in Table 1.4. Sets of associated output index numbers are reported in Table 3.1. In this table, the index numbers in any given row compare the outputs in that row with the outputs in row A. For example, in any given column, the index number in row O indicates that the output vector $(2, 2)'$ is twice as big as the output vector $(1, 1)'$. The numbers in column AEW are additive index numbers obtained by assigning the outputs equal weight. The numbers in column L (resp. GY) are Lowe (resp. geometric Young) index numbers. The numbers in column OLS are multiplicative index numbers obtained

Table 3.1 Proper output index numbers[a,b]

Row	q_1	q_2	AEW	L	GY	OLS	P	D	BOD	Ave.
A	1	1	1	1	1	1	1	1	1	1
B	1	1	1	1	1	1	1	1	1	1
C	2.37	2.37	2.37	2.37	2.37	2.37	2.37	2.37	2.37	2.37
D	2.11	2.11	2.11	2.11	2.11	2.11	2.11	2.11	2.11	2.11
E	1.81	3.62	2.715	2.744	2.603	2.062	3.617	3.617	2.758	2.827
F	1	1	1	1	1	1	1	1	1	1
G	1.777	3.503	2.64	2.668	2.537	2.019	3.500	3.500	2.681	2.748
H	0.96	0.94	0.95	0.950	0.949	0.956	0.940	0.940	0.950	0.948
I	5.82	0.001	2.911	2.817	0.062	1.140	0.011	0.011	2.771	0.298
J	6.685	0.001	3.343	3.236	0.066	1.276	0.013	0.013	3.183	0.336
K	1.381	4.732	3.057	3.110	2.634	1.741	4.726	4.726	3.137	3.147
L	0.566	4.818	2.692	2.760	1.740	0.847	4.810	4.810	2.968	2.576
M	1	3	2	2.032	1.779	1.229	2.996	2.996	2.048	2.071
N	0.7	0.7	0.7	0.7	0.7	0.7	0.7	0.7	0.7	0.7
O	2	2	2	2	2	2	2	2	2	2
P	1	1	1	1	1	1	1	1	1	1
R	1	3	2	2.032	1.779	1.229	2.996	2.996	2.048	2.071
S	1	1	1	1	1	1	1	1	1	1
T	1.925	3.722	2.824	2.852	2.720	2.179	3.719	3.719	2.867	2.939
U	1	1	1	1	1	1	1	1	1	1
V	1	5.166	3.083	3.150	2.366	1.362	5.159	5.159	3.183	3.083
W	2	2	2	2	2	2	2	2	2	2
X	1	1	1	1	1	1	1	1	1	1
Y	1	1	1	1	1	1	1	1	1	1
Z	1.81	3.62	2.715	2.744	2.603	2.062	3.617	3.617	2.758	2.827

[a]AEW = additive with equal weights; L = Lowe; GY = geometric Young; OLS = multiplicative with OLS weights; P = primal with CNLS parameter estimates; D = dual with CNLS parameter estimates; BOD = benefit-of-the-doubt

[b]Numbers reported to less than three decimal places are exact; see the footnote to Table 1.2 on p. 8

by using the method of ordinary least squares (OLS) to estimate the weights in (3.4). The numbers in columns P and D are primal and dual index numbers obtained by replacing the unknown parameters in (3.6) and (3.8) with corrected nonlinear least squares (CNLS) estimates of the parameters in (7.2).[18] The numbers in column BOD are benefit-of-the-doubt index numbers. The numbers in the last column are unweighted geometric averages of the index numbers in the other seven columns. All of the index numbers in Table 3.1 are proper in the sense that they have been obtained using indices that satisfy axioms QI1 to QI6. They are also consistent with measurement theory. Measurement theory says that the relationships between the

[18]The CNLS estimates of τ, γ_1 and γ_2 are 1, 0.0018 and 0.9982 respectively.

index numbers must mirror the relationships between the output vectors. Observe, for example, that the output vector in row M is the same as the output vector in row R, and, in any given column, the index number in row M is the same as the index number in row R.

Output indices that do not generally satisfy one or more of axioms QI1 to QI6 include Fisher, Törnqvist, CF, CT, EKS and CCD indices. Index numbers obtained using these indices are reported in Table 3.2. For illustrative purposes, the CF and CT index numbers were computed by treating the observations in the dataset as observations on a single firm over twenty-five periods. The EKS and CCD index numbers were computed by treating the observations in the dataset as observations on

Table 3.2 Other output index numbers[a,b]

Row	q_1	q_2	F	T	CF	CT	EKS	CCD
A	1	1	1	1	1	1	1	1
B	1	1	1	1	1	1	0.992*	1.011*
C	2.37	2.37	2.37	2.37	2.37	2.37	2.37	2.37
D	2.11	2.11	2.11	2.11	2.11	2.11	2.096*	2.129*
E	1.81	3.62	2.640*	2.636*	2.695*	2.691*	2.677*	2.840*
F	1	1	1	1	0.972*	0.971*	0.986*	1.022*
G	1.777	3.503	2.575	2.571	2.626	2.622	2.608	2.769
H	0.96	0.94	0.951	0.951	0.950	0.950	0.944	0.958
I	5.82	0.001	2.952	0.948	2.800	0.748	2.672	0.562
J	6.685	0.001	2.789	1.058	3.217	0.860	2.508	0.622
K	1.381	4.732	2.783	2.769	3.716	6.323*	2.883	3.090
L	0.566	4.818	2.648	2.369	3.251	5.440*	2.737	2.862
M	1	3	1.892*	1.879*	2.389*	4.068*	1.942*	2.088*
N	0.7	0.7	0.7	0.7	0.943*	1.611*	0.711*	0.688*
O	2	2	2	2	2.695*	4.604*	2.029*	1.969*
P	1	1	1	1	1.348*	2.302*	0.982*	1.036*
R	1	3	1.893*	1.880*	2.854*	4.914*	1.943*	2.089*
S	1	1	1	1	1.514*	2.624*	1.001*	0.999*
T	1.925	3.722	2.631	2.631	3.973	6.888	2.706	2.771
U	1	1	1	1	1.359*	2.332*	0.981*	1.054*
V	1	5.166	2.099	2.070	3.530	6.437*	2.296	2.276
W	2	2	2	2	3.642*	6.734*	2.027*	1.971*
X	1	1	1	1	1.821*	3.367*	0.983*	1.031*
Y	1	1	1	1	1.821*	3.367*	0.981*	1.041*
Z	1.81	3.62	2.745*	2.729*	5.447*	10.075*	2.759*	2.985*

[a]F = Fisher; T = Törnqvist; CF = chained Fisher; CT = chained Törnqvist; EKS = Elteto-Koves-Szulc; CCD = Caves-Christensen-Diewert

[b]Numbers reported to less than three decimal places are exact; see the footnote to Table 1.2 on p. 8

*Incoherent (not because of rounding)

twenty-five firms in a single period. The index numbers in Table 3.2 are inconsistent with measurement theory. Numbers that are clearly incoherent are marked with an asterisk (*). Observe, for example, that the output vector in row E is the same as the output vector in row Z, but the index numbers in row E differ from the index numbers in row Z. As another example, the outputs in row L are both less than five times greater than the outputs in row A, but the CT index number in row L is 5.44. In this book, these types of errors are viewed as measurement errors.

3.2 Input Quantity Indices

In this book, an input quantity index (or simply 'input index') that compares the inputs of firm i in period t with the inputs of firm k in period s is defined as any variable of the form[19]

$$XI(x_{ks}, x_{it}) \equiv X(x_{it})/X(x_{ks}) \tag{3.20}$$

where $X(.)$ is a nonnegative, nondecreasing, linearly-homogeneous, scalar-valued aggregator function. If inputs are positive,[20] then all input indices of this type satisfy the following axioms:

XI1 $x_{rl} \geq x_{it} \Rightarrow XI(x_{ks}, x_{rl}) \geq XI(x_{ks}, x_{it})$ (weak monotonicity);
XI2 $XI(x_{ks}, \lambda x_{it}) = \lambda XI(x_{ks}, x_{it})$ for $\lambda > 0$ (homogeneity type I);
XI3 $XI(\lambda x_{ks}, \lambda x_{it}) = XI(x_{ks}, x_{it})$ for $\lambda > 0$ (homogeneity type II);
XI4 $XI(x_{ks}, \lambda x_{ks}) = \lambda$ for $\lambda > 0$ (proportionality);
XI5 $XI(x_{ks}, x_{it}) = 1/XI(x_{it}, x_{ks})$ (time-space reversal); and
XI6 $XI(x_{ks}, x_{rl})XI(x_{rl}, x_{it}) = XI(x_{ks}, x_{it})$ (transitivity).

The interpretation of these axioms is analogous to the interpretation of axioms QI1 to QI6 in Sect. 3.1. In a time-series context, for example, axiom XI6 (transitivity) says that if we compare the inputs used in periods 1 and 3 indirectly through period 2, then we must get the same index number as when we compare the inputs used in periods 1 and 3 directly. Thus, if a firm used twice as much of every input in period 3 as it did in period 2, and it used three times as much of every input in period 2 as it did in period 1, then all direct and indirect comparisons should say that it used six times as much of every input in period 3 as it did in period 1.

In O'Donnell (2016), an input index is said to be proper if and only if XI1 to XI6 are satisfied.[21] The geometric average of any set of proper input indices is also a proper input index. Again, depending on the aggregator functions, proper input indices may have other properties. For example, if aggregator functions are strictly

[19]This definition can be traced back at least as far as O'Donnell (2012a). See footnote 3 on p. 94.

[20]If some inputs are zero, then some input indices may be mathematically undefined and may therefore not satisfy some axioms.

[21]In O'Donnell (2016), an input index is said to be proper if and only if *eight* axioms are satisfied. If XI1 to XI6 are satisfied, then, and only then, all eight of the O'Donnell (2016) axioms are satisfied.

increasing in inputs, then the associated input indices are *strongly* monotonic. Strong monotonicity means that if more inputs were used in period 3 than in period 2, then the index number that compares the inputs in period 3 with the inputs in period 1 will be *greater than* the index number that compares the inputs in period 2 with the inputs in period 1.

Any nonnegative, nondecreasing, linearly-homogeneous, scalar-valued aggregator function can be used for purposes of constructing a proper input index. Again, the choice of function is generally a matter of taste. Again, linear (resp. double-log) functions can be used to construct additive (resp. multiplicative) indices. If inputs are strongly disposable, then input distance functions can be used to construct primal indices. If revenue functions are homogeneous in inputs, then they can be used to construct dual indices. Finally, locally-linear functions can be used to construct BOD indices.

3.2.1 Additive Indices

Additive input indices are constructed using aggregator functions of the form $X(x_{it}) \propto b'x_{it}$ where b is any nonnegative vector of weights. The associated index that compares the inputs of firm i in period t with the inputs of firm k in period s is

$$XI^A(x_{ks}, x_{it}) \equiv (b'x_{it})/(b'x_{ks}). \tag{3.21}$$

Any nonnegative observation-invariant measures of relative value can be used as weights. Again, the choice of weights is a matter of taste. One possibility is to use average market prices as weights. In this case, the index defined by (3.21) takes the form of the Lowe index defined by O'Donnell (2012c, p. 877); this index should be used by analysts who regard input prices as appropriate measures of relative value (e.g., analysts who might otherwise use a Fisher, chained Fisher or EKS index). Alternatively, let X denote a matrix of mean-corrected inputs with M columns and as many rows as there are observations in the dataset. If the eigenvector associated with the largest eigenvalue of $X'X$ is nonnegative, then it can be used as vector of weights. In this case, the index defined by (3.21) takes the form of the 'input factor' defined by Daraio and Simar (2007, Eq. 6.1, p. 148).

3.2.2 Multiplicative Indices

Multiplicative input indices are constructed using aggregator functions of the form $X(x_{it}) \propto \prod_{m=1}^{M} x_{mit}^{b_m}$ where $b_1, \ldots, b_M$ are any nonnegative weights that sum to one. The associated index that compares the inputs of firm i in period t with the inputs of firm k in period s is

$$XI^M(x_{ks}, x_{it}) \equiv \prod_{m=1}^{M} \left(\frac{x_{mit}}{x_{mks}} \right)^{b_m}. \tag{3.22}$$

Any nonnegative observation-invariant measures of relative value can be used as weights, provided they sum to one. Again, the choice of weights is a matter of taste. One possibility is to use average cost shares as weights. In this case, the index defined by (3.22) takes the form of the GY index defined by O'Donnell (2016, p. 333); this index should be used by analysts who regard cost shares as appropriate measures of relative value (e.g., analysts who might otherwise use a Törnqvist, chained Törnqvist or CCD index). Another possibility is to estimate the weights in a linear regression framework. For example, Eq. (3.22) can be rewritten as

$$\ln(x_{1it}/x_{1ks}) = \sum_{m=2}^{M} b_m[\ln(x_{1it}/x_{1ks}) - \ln(x_{mit}/x_{mks})] + e_{it} \tag{3.23}$$

where $e_{it} = \ln XI^M(x_{ks}, x_{it})$ is an unobserved log-index that in most other contexts would be interpreted as statistical noise. The unknown parameters/weights in this regression model can be estimated using, for example, least squares methods. The associated input index numbers are the antilogarithms of the residuals. This index should be used by analysts who want to minimise the amount of variation in the index numbers. It can also be used by analysts who have no information about input prices, cost shares or production technologies. Finally, it is worth noting that multiplicative input indices fail an input-oriented version of the determinateness test discussed at the end of Sect. 3.1.2.

3.2.3 Primal Indices

Primal[22] input indices are constructed using input distance functions as aggregator functions. For a primal input index to be a proper index, the input distance function must be nondecreasing in inputs, implying that inputs must be strongly disposable. In this case, a suitable aggregator function is $X(x_{it}) \propto D_I^{\bar{t}}(x_{it}, \bar{q}, \bar{z})$ where $\bar{t}$ is a fixed time period and $\bar{q}$ and $\bar{z}$ are fixed vectors of outputs and environmental variables (again, the choices of $\bar{t}$, $\bar{q}$ and $\bar{z}$ are a matter of taste). The associated primal index that compares the inputs of firm i in period t with the inputs of firm k in period s is

$$XI^P(x_{ks}, x_{it}) \equiv D_I^{\bar{t}}(x_{it}, \bar{q}, \bar{z})/D_I^{\bar{t}}(x_{ks}, \bar{q}, \bar{z}). \tag{3.24}$$

This index can be traced back to O'Donnell (2016, Eq. 3). It should be used by analysts who regard marginal rates of technical substitution as appropriate measures

[22]Balk (1998, p. 59) also uses the term 'primal' in reference to an index that is constructed using an input distance function.

of relative value (e.g., analysts who might otherwise use a generalised Malmquist index). If there is no technical or environmental change, then it reduces to the input index defined by Färe and Primont (1995, p. 36). If input sets are homothetic, then it does not depend on $\bar{q}$. If technical change is IHIN, then it does not depend on $\bar{t}$ or $\bar{z}$. Ultimately, the exact form of the index depends on the input distance function. If the input distance function is given by (2.13), for example, then

$$XI^P(x_{ks}, x_{it}) = \prod_{m=1}^{M} \left(\frac{x_{mit}}{x_{mks}} \right)^{\lambda_m}. \tag{3.25}$$

This index can be viewed as a multiplicative index with weights given by shadow cost shares. Observe that it does not depend on the choices of $\bar{t}$, $\bar{q}$ or $\bar{z}$. This is because the input distance function given by (2.13) represents a homothetic input set with a boundary that exhibits IHIN technical change.

3.2.4 Dual Indices

Dual input indices are constructed using revenue functions as aggregator functions. For a dual input index to be a proper index, the revenue function must be homogeneous in inputs. If the revenue function is homogeneous of degree r in inputs, for example, then a suitable input aggregator function is $X(x_{it}) \propto R^{\bar{t}}(x_{it}, \bar{p}, \bar{z})^{1/r}$ where $\bar{t}$ is a fixed time period and $\bar{p}$ and $\bar{z}$ are fixed vectors of output prices and environmental variables (again, the choices of $\bar{t}$, $\bar{p}$ and $\bar{z}$ are a matter of taste). The associated dual index that compares the inputs of firm i in period t with the inputs of firm k in period s is

$$XI^D(x_{ks}, x_{it}) \equiv R^{\bar{t}}(x_{it}, \bar{p}, \bar{z})^{1/r} / R^{\bar{t}}(x_{ks}, \bar{p}, \bar{z})^{1/r}. \tag{3.26}$$

This index should be used by analysts who regard marginal revenues as appropriate measures of relative value. If output sets are homothetic, then it does not depend on $\bar{p}$. Ultimately, the exact form of the index depends on the revenue function. If the revenue function is given by (2.17), for example, then

$$XI^D(x_{ks}, x_{it}) = \prod_{m=1}^{M} \left(\frac{x_{mit}}{x_{mks}} \right)^{\lambda_m} \tag{3.27}$$

where $\lambda_m = \beta_m/\eta$ is a shadow cost share and $\eta = \sum_m \beta_m$ is the elasticity of scale. Observe that this index is the same as the index defined by (3.25). This is because the input distance function given by (2.13) and the revenue function given by (2.17) are equivalent representations of a homothetic input set with a boundary that exhibits IHIN technical change.

3.2.5 Benefit-of-the-Doubt Indices

BOD input indices are constructed using aggregator functions of the form $X(x_{it}) = b_{it}'x_{it}$ where b_{it} is an unknown vector of nonnegative weights. If $X(.)$ is continuously differentiable, then $b_{it} = \partial X(x_{it})/\partial x_{it}$. Computing BOD input indices involves choosing the weight vector to minimise $X(x_{it})$. The only constraint is that if the chosen weight vector is used to aggregate any input vector in the dataset, then the resulting aggregate input can be no less than one.[23] Thus, the optimisation problem is

$$\min_{b_{it}} \left\{ b_{it}'x_{it} : b_{it} \geq 0, b_{it}'x_{hr} \geq 1 \text{ for all } h \text{ and } r \right\}. \tag{3.28}$$

This optimisation problem can be found in O'Donnell and Nguyen (2013, Eq. 23). Let $X^B(x_{it})$ denote the minimised value of the objective function. The associated BOD index that compares the inputs of firm i in period t with the inputs of firm k in period s is

$$X^B(x_{ks}, x_{it}) \equiv X^B(x_{it})/X^B(x_{ks}). \tag{3.29}$$

Like the BOD output index, this is a proper index with high characteristicity. A strongly monotonic version can be obtained by adding the constraint $b_{it} > 0$ to problem (3.28). The BOD input index should be used by analysts who believe measures of relative value should vary from one input comparison to the next. It can also be used by analysts who have no information about input prices, cost shares or production technologies.

3.2.6 Other Indices

Other types of input indices include binary, chained and multilateral indices. These are not proper input indices in the sense that they do not generally satisfy all of axioms XI1 to XI6. Binary input indices are designed for comparing two input vectors only. Chained input indices are mainly used for comparing the inputs of a single firm over several time periods. Multilateral input indices are mainly used for comparing the inputs of several firms in a single time period.

3.2.6.1 Binary Indices

Binary input indices do not generally satisfy axiom XI6 (transitivity). The class of binary input indices includes Fisher, Törnqvist and GM indices. The Fisher index

---

[23]The choice of one as the minimum aggregate input is arbitrary.

that compares the inputs of firm i in period t with the inputs of firm k in period s is

$$XI^F(x_{ks}, x_{it}, \ldots) \equiv \left(\frac{w'_{it}x_{it}}{w'_{it}x_{ks}} \frac{w'_{ks}x_{it}}{w'_{ks}x_{ks}} \right)^{1/2}. \tag{3.30}$$

If observed input prices are firm- and time-invariant, then Fisher input index numbers are equal to Lowe input index numbers. The Törnqvist index that compares the inputs of firm i in period t with the inputs of firm k in period s is

$$XI^T(x_{ks}, x_{it}, \ldots) \equiv \prod_{m=1}^{M} \left(\frac{x_{mit}}{x_{mks}} \right)^{(s_{mit}+s_{mks})/2} \tag{3.31}$$

where $s_{mit} \equiv w_{mit}x_{mit}/C_{it}$ is the m-th observed cost share. If observed cost shares are firm- and time-invariant, then Törnqvist input index numbers are equal to GY input index numbers. Finally, the GM index that compares the inputs of firm i in period t with the inputs of firm k in period s is

$$XI^{GM}(x_{ks}, x_{it}, \ldots) \equiv \left(\frac{D_I^t(x_{it}, q_{it}, z_{it})}{D_I^t(x_{ks}, q_{it}, z_{it})} \frac{D_I^s(x_{it}, q_{ks}, z_{ks})}{D_I^s(x_{ks}, q_{ks}, z_{ks})} \right)^{1/2}. \tag{3.32}$$

If input sets are homothetic and technical change is IHIN, then this index is equivalent to the primal index defined by (3.24). If the input distance function is given by (2.13), then it is equivalent to the primal index defined by (3.25). If there is only one firm involved in the comparison and there is no environmental change, then the two ratios in (3.32) are equivalent to the Malmquist input indices defined by Diewert (1992, Eqs. 97, 98) (hence the use of the term 'generalised'). If (a) there is no environmental change, (b) firms are price takers in input markets, (c) firm managers minimise cost, (d) input prices and quantities are strictly positive, (e) the period-t and period-s input distance functions are nondecreasing in inputs, and (f) the period-t and period-s input distance functions are translog functions with identical second-order coefficients, then the GM index defined by (3.32) is equivalent to the Törnqvist index defined by (3.31) (Caves et al. 1982a, Thm. 1). For this reason, Törnqvist input indices are said to be exact for translog input distance functions. Unfortunately, properties (e) and (f) cannot both be true.[24] This means that Törnqvist input indices are merely superlative. Superlative input indices are exact for functions that can generally only provide second-order *approximations* to input distance functions.

[24] If the input distance function is nondecreasing in inputs, then the partial derivative of the distance function with respect to the inputs must be nonnegative for all feasible input-output combinations. If the input distance function is a translog function, then it is possible to find feasible input-output combinations such that at least one partial derivative is negative. Ergo, the input distance function cannot be a translog function.

3.2.6.2 Chained Indices

Chained input indices do not generally satisfy axiom XI4 (proportionality). The class of chained input indices includes CF, CT and CGM indices. The CF index that compares the inputs of firm i in period t with the inputs of firm i in period 1 is

$$XI^{CF}(x_{i1}, x_{it}, \ldots) \equiv \prod_{s=1}^{t-1} XI^{F}(x_{is}, x_{i,s+1}, \ldots) \tag{3.33}$$

where $XI^{F}(x_{is}, x_{i,s+1}, \ldots)$ is a binary Fisher index. If observed input prices are firm- and time-invariant, then CF input index numbers are equal to Lowe input index numbers. The CT index that compares the inputs of firm i in period t with the inputs of firm i in period 1 is

$$XI^{CT}(x_{i1}, x_{it}, \ldots) \equiv \prod_{s=1}^{t-1} XI^{T}(x_{is}, x_{i,s+1}, \ldots) \tag{3.34}$$

where $XI^{T}(x_{is}, x_{i,s+1}, \ldots)$ is a binary Törnqvist index. If observed cost shares are firm- and time-invariant, then CT input index numbers are equal to GY input index numbers. Finally, the CGM index that compares the inputs of firm i in period t with the inputs of firm i in period 1 is

$$XI^{CGM}(x_{i1}, x_{it}, \ldots) \equiv \prod_{s=1}^{t-1} XI^{GM}(x_{is}, x_{i,s+1}, \ldots) \tag{3.35}$$

where $XI^{GM}(x_{is}, x_{i,s+1}, \ldots)$ is a binary GM index. If input sets are homothetic and technical change is IHIN, then CGM input index numbers are equal to primal input index numbers computed using (3.24).

3.2.6.3 Multilateral Indices

Multilateral input indices do not generally satisfy axiom XI4 (proportionality). They are also particularly sensitive to the addition or removal of observations from the dataset. The class of multilateral input indices includes the EKS, CCD and MGM indices. The EKS index that compares the inputs of firm i in period t with the inputs of firm k in period t is

$$XI^{EKS}(x_{kt}, x_{it}, \ldots) \equiv \left(\prod_{r=1}^{I_t} XI^{F}(x_{kt}, x_{rt}, \ldots) XI^{F}(x_{rt}, x_{it}, \ldots) \right)^{1/I_t} \tag{3.36}$$

where I_t is the number of firms in period t and $XI^F(x_{kt}, x_{rt}, \ldots)$ is a binary Fisher index. If observed input prices are firm- and time-invariant, then EKS input index numbers are equal to Lowe input index numbers. The CCD index that compares the inputs of firm i in period t with the inputs of firm k in period t is

$$XI^{CCD}(x_{kt}, x_{it}, \ldots) \equiv \left(\prod_{r=1}^{I_t} XI^T(x_{kt}, x_{rt}, \ldots) XI^T(x_{rt}, x_{it}, \ldots) \right)^{1/I_t} \quad (3.37)$$

where $XI^T(x_{kt}, x_{rt}, \ldots)$ is a binary Törnqvist index. If observed cost shares are firm- and time-invariant, then CCD input index numbers are equal to GY input index numbers. Finally, the MGM index that compares the inputs of firm i in period t with the inputs of firm k in period t is

$$XI^{MGM}(x_{kt}, x_{it}, \ldots) \equiv \left(\prod_{r=1}^{I_t} XI^{GM}(x_{kt}, x_{rt}, \ldots) XI^{GM}(x_{rt}, x_{it}, \ldots) \right)^{1/I_t} \quad (3.38)$$

where $XI^{GM}(x_{kt}, x_{rt}, \ldots)$ is a binary GM index. If input sets are homothetic and technical change is IHIN, then MGM input index numbers are equal to primal input index numbers computed using (3.24).

3.2.7 Toy Example

Reconsider the input quantity and price data reported earlier in Table 1.5. Sets of associated input index numbers are reported in Table 3.3. In this table, the index numbers in any given row compare the inputs in that row with the inputs in row A. For example, in any given column, the index number in row Y indicates that the input vector $(0.74, 0.74)'$ is only 0.74 times as big as the input vector $(1, 1)'$. The numbers in column AEW are additive index numbers obtained by assigning the inputs equal weight. The numbers in column L (resp. GY) are Lowe (resp. geometric Young) index numbers. The numbers in column OLS are multiplicative index numbers obtained by using OLS to estimate the weights in (3.23). The numbers in columns P and D are primal and dual index numbers obtained by replacing the unknown parameters in (3.25) and (3.27) with CNLS estimates of the relevant parameters in (7.2).[25] The numbers in column BOD are benefit-of-the-doubt index numbers. The numbers in the last column are unweighted geometric averages of the index numbers in the other seven columns. All of the index numbers in Table 3.3 are proper in the sense that they have been obtained using indices that satisfy axioms XI1 to XI6. They are also consistent with measurement theory. Observe, for example, that the input vector in

[25]The CNLS estimates of λ_1 and λ_2 are 0.2367 and 0.7633 respectively.

Table 3.3 Proper input index numbers[a,b]

Row	x_1	x_2	AEW	L	GY	OLS	P	D	BOD	Ave.
A	1	1	1	1	1	1	1	1	1	1
B	0.56	0.56	0.56	0.56	0.56	0.56	0.56	0.56	0.56	0.56
C	1	1	1	1	1	1	1	1	1	1
D	1.05	0.7	0.875	0.781	0.831	0.938	0.770	0.770	0.830	0.826
E	1.05	0.7	0.875	0.781	0.831	0.938	0.770	0.770	0.830	0.826
F	0.996	0.316	0.656	0.472	0.513	0.724	0.415	0.415	0.458	0.511
G	1.472	0.546	1.009	0.759	0.830	1.117	0.690	0.690	0.779	0.827
H	0.017	0.346	0.182	0.27	0.097	0.039	0.170	0.170	0.223	0.143
I	4.545	0.01	2.278	1.053	0.133	0.829	0.043	0.043	0.240	0.274
J	4.45	0.001	2.226	1.024	0.035	0.431	0.007	0.007	0.223	0.122
K	1	1	1	1	1	1	1	1	1	1
L	1	1	1	1	1	1	1	1	1	1
M	1.354	1	1.177	1.081	1.137	1.245	1.074	1.074	1.132	1.130
N	0.33	0.16	0.245	0.199	0.217	0.270	0.190	0.190	0.223	0.218
O	1	1	1	1	1	1	1	1	1	1
P	0.657	0.479	0.568	0.52	0.547	0.602	0.516	0.516	0.545	0.544
R	1	1	1	1	1	1	1	1	1	1
S	1.933	0.283	1.108	0.663	0.638	1.133	0.446	0.446	0.462	0.650
T	1	1	1	1	1	1	1	1	1	1
U	1	0.31	0.655	0.469	0.509	0.722	0.409	0.409	0.451	0.506
V	1	1	1	1	1	1	1	1	1	1
W	0.919	0.919	0.919	0.919	0.919	0.919	0.919	0.919	0.919	0.919
X	1.464	0.215	0.840	0.502	0.484	0.859	0.339	0.339	0.351	0.493
Y	0.74	0.74	0.74	0.74	0.74	0.74	0.74	0.74	0.74	0.74
Z	2.1	1.4	1.750	1.561	1.662	1.876	1.541	1.541	1.661	1.652

[a]AEW = additive with equal weights; L = Lowe; GY = geometric Young; OLS = multiplicative with OLS weights; P = primal with CNLS parameter estimates; D = dual with CNLS parameter estimates; BOD = benefit-of-the-doubt

[b]Numbers reported to less than three decimal places are exact; see the footnote to Table 1.2 on p. 8. Some numbers may be incoherent at the third decimal place due to rounding (e.g., the number in row Z of column L is not exactly twice as big as the number in row E of column L due to rounding)

row D is the same as the input vector in row E, and, in any given column, the index number in row D is the same as the index number in row E.

Input indices that do not generally satisfy one or more of axioms XI1 to XI6 include Fisher, Törnqvist, CF, CT, EKS and CCD indices. Index numbers obtained using these indices are reported in Table 3.4. Again, for illustrative purposes, the CF and CT index numbers were computed by treating the observations in the dataset as observations on a single firm over twenty-five periods. The EKS and CCD index numbers were computed by treating the observations in the dataset as observations on twenty-five firms in a single period. The index numbers in Table 3.4 are inconsistent

Table 3.4 Other input index numbers[a,b]

Row	x_1	x_2	F	T	CF	CT	EKS	CCD
A	1	1	1	1	1	1	1	1
B	0.56	0.56	0.56	0.56	0.56	0.56	0.525*	0.526*
C	1	1	1	1	1	1	1	1
D	1.05	0.7	0.771*	0.774*	0.771*	0.774*	0.749*	0.742*
E	1.05	0.7	0.734*	0.732*	0.771*	0.774*	0.797*	0.789*
F	0.996	0.316	0.501	0.515	0.464	0.473	0.502	0.474
G	1.472	0.546	0.819	0.835	0.715	0.730	0.798	0.749
H	0.017	0.346	0.293	0.280	0.189	0.105	0.253	0.189
I	4.545	0.01	1.049	0.312	1.001	0.303	1.339	0.532
J	4.45	0.001	0.825	0.114	0.976	0.296	1.102	0.272
K	1	1	1	1	1.182*	2.596*	1	1
L	1	1	1	1	1.182*	2.596*	0.939*	0.940*
M	1.354	1	1.054	1.055	1.276	2.800*	1.056	1.058
N	0.33	0.16	0.179	0.179	0.223	0.488*	0.196	0.195
O	1	1	1	1	1.032*	2.288*	0.863*	0.813*
P	0.657	0.479	0.517	0.518	0.578	1.280*	0.495	0.490
R	1	1	1	1	1.064*	2.359*	0.899*	0.883*
S	1.933	0.283	0.575	0.613	0.861	1.917	0.668	0.645
T	1	1	1	1	1.088*	2.418*	0.905*	0.893*
U	1	0.31	0.432	0.445	0.568	1.258	0.464	0.454
V	1	1	1	1	1.178*	2.601*	0.939*	0.941*
W	0.919	0.919	0.919	0.919	1.083*	2.390*	0.848*	0.845*
X	1.464	0.215	0.519	0.535	0.787	1.680*	0.572	0.528
Y	0.74	0.74	0.74	0.74	0.946*	2.068*	0.700*	0.703*
Z	2.1	1.4	1.642*	1.649*	2.159*	4.724*	1.479*	1.385*

[a]F = Fisher; T = Törnqvist; CF = chained Fisher; CT = chained Törnqvist; EKS = Elteto-Koves-Szulc; CCD = Caves-Christensen-Diewert

[b]Numbers reported to less than three decimal places are exact; see the footnote to Table 1.2 on p. 8

*Incoherent (not because of rounding)

with measurement theory. Again, numbers that are clearly incoherent are marked with an asterisk (*). Observe, for example, that the input vector in row Z is twice as big as the input vector in row E, but the index numbers in row Z are not twice as big as the index numbers in row E. As another example, the inputs in row M are not even twice as big as the inputs in row A, but the CT index number in row M is 2.8. Again, in this book, these types of errors are viewed as measurement errors.

3.3 Productivity Indices

Productivity indices are measures of productivity change. This section focuses on TFP indices (TFPIs). Multifactor productivity (MFP) indices and partial factor productivity (PFP) indices can be treated as special cases of TFP indices in which one or more inputs are given a weight of zero.

In this book, an index that compares the TFP of firm i in period t with the TFP of firm k in period s is defined as any variable of the form

$$TFPI(x_{ks}, q_{ks}, x_{it}, q_{it}) \equiv QI(q_{ks}, q_{it})/XI(x_{ks}, x_{it}) \tag{3.39}$$

where $QI(.)$ is any proper output index and $XI(.)$ is any proper input index. This definition can be traced back at least as far as O'Donnell (2013, p. 10). An equivalent definition is

$$TFPI(x_{ks}, q_{ks}, x_{it}, q_{it}) \equiv TFP(x_{it}, q_{it})/TFP(x_{ks}, q_{ks}) \tag{3.40}$$

where $TFP(x_{it}, q_{it}) \equiv Q(q_{it})/X(x_{it})$ denotes the TFP of firm i in period t. If outputs and inputs are positive,[26] then all TFPIs of this type satisfy the following axioms:

TI1 $q_{rl} \geq q_{it}$ and $x_{rl} \leq x_{it} \Rightarrow TFPI(x_{ks}, q_{ks}, x_{rl}, q_{rl}) \geq TFPI(x_{ks}, q_{ks}, x_{it}, q_{it})$ (weak monotonicity);

TI2 $TFPI(x_{ks}, q_{ks}, \delta x_{it}\, \lambda q_{it}) = (\lambda/\delta) TFPI(x_{ks}, q_{ks}, x_{it}, q_{it})$ for $\lambda > 0$ and $\delta > 0$ (homogeneity type I);

TI3 $TFPI(\delta x_{ks}, \lambda q_{ks}, \delta x_{it}, \lambda q_{it}) = TFPI(x_{ks}, q_{ks}, x_{it}, q_{it})$ for $\lambda > 0$ and $\delta > 0$ (homogeneity type II);

TI4 $TFPI(x_{ks}, q_{ks}, \delta x_{ks}, \lambda q_{ks}) = \lambda/\delta$ for $\lambda > 0$ and $\delta > 0$ (proportionality);

TI5 $TFPI(x_{ks}, q_{ks}, x_{it}, q_{it}) = 1/TFPI(x_{it}, q_{it}, x_{ks}, q_{ks})$ (time-space reversal); and

TI6 $TFPI(x_{ks}, q_{ks}, x_{it}, q_{it}) = TFPI(x_{ks}, q_{ks}, x_{rl}, q_{rl}) TFPI(x_{rl}, q_{rl}, x_{it}, q_{it})$ (transitivity).

Again, the interpretation of these axioms is straightforward. In a cross-section context, for example, axiom TI6 (transitivity) says that if we compare the TFP of firms C and A indirectly through firm B, then we must get the same index number as when we compare the TFP of firms C and A directly. Thus, if we find that firm C is twice as productive as firm B, and firm B is twice as productive as firm A, then we must also find that firm C is four times as productive as firm A.

In O'Donnell (2016), a TFPI is said to be proper if and only if it can be written as a proper output index divided by a proper input index. Any proper output and input indices can be used for this purpose. Again, the choice of indices is generally a matter of taste. In practice, it is common, but not necessary, to divide output indices of a given type by input indices of the same type.

[26] If some outputs or inputs are zero, then some TFPIs may be either zero or mathematically undefined and may therefore not satisfy some axioms.

3.3.1 Additive Indices

Additive TFPIs are constructed by dividing additive output indices by additive input indices. For example, the additive index that compares the TFP of firm i in period t with the TFP of firm k in period s is

$$TFPI^{A}(x_{ks}, q_{ks}, x_{it}, q_{it}) \equiv \frac{a'q_{it}}{a'q_{ks}} \frac{b'x_{ks}}{b'x_{it}} \tag{3.41}$$

where a is any nonnegative vector of output weights and b is any nonnegative vector of input weights. If some inputs are given a weight of zero, then this index can be viewed as an MFP index. If all inputs except one are given a weight of zero, then it can be viewed as a PFP index. If all inputs except labour (resp. capital) are given a weight of zero, then it can be viewed as a labour (resp. capital) productivity index. If average market prices are used as weights, then it takes the form of the Lowe TFPI defined by O'Donnell (2012c, p. 877); this index should be used by analysts who regard market prices as appropriate measures of relative value (e.g., analysts who might otherwise use a Fisher, chained Fisher or EKS index).

3.3.2 Multiplicative Indices

Multiplicative TFPIs are constructed by dividing multiplicative output indices by multiplicative input indices. For example, the multiplicative index that compares the TFP of firm i in period t with the TFP of firm k in period s is

$$TFPI^{M}(x_{ks}, q_{ks}, x_{it}, q_{it}) \equiv \prod_{n=1}^{N} \left(\frac{q_{nit}}{q_{nks}}\right)^{a_n} \prod_{m=1}^{M} \left(\frac{x_{mks}}{x_{mit}}\right)^{b_m} \tag{3.42}$$

where $a_1, \ldots, a_N$ are nonnegative output weights that sum to one and $b_1, \ldots, b_M$ are nonnegative input weights that sum to one. Again, if some inputs are given a weight of zero, then this index can be viewed as an MFP index. If all inputs except one are given a weight of zero, then it can be viewed as a PFP index. If all inputs except labour (resp. capital) are given a weight of zero, then it can be viewed as a labour (resp. capital) productivity index. If all outputs are given equal weight and all inputs are given equal weight, then it takes the form of the GDF-based index defined by Portela and Thanassoulis (2006, Eq. 4) (these authors define their index in a time-series context). If average revenue shares are used as output weights and average cost shares are used as input weights, then it takes the form of the GY index defined by O'Donnell (2016, Eq. 5); this index should be used by analysts who regard revenue and cost shares as appropriate measures of relative value (e.g., analysts who might otherwise use a Törnqvist, chained Törnqvist or CCD index). Another possibility is to estimate the weights in a linear regression framework. For example, Eq. (3.42) can be rewritten as

$$\begin{aligned}\ln(q_{1it}/q_{1ks}) - \ln(x_{1it}/x_{1ks}) = &\sum_{n=2}^{N} a_n[\ln(q_{1it}/q_{1ks}) - \ln(q_{nit}/q_{nks})] \\ &- \sum_{m=2}^{M} b_m[\ln(x_{1it}/x_{1ks}) - \ln(x_{mit}/x_{mks})] + e_{it}\end{aligned} \tag{3.43}$$

where $e_{it} = \ln TFPI^M(x_{ks}, q_{ks}, x_{it}, q_{it})$ is an unobserved log-TFPI that in most other contexts would be interpreted as statistical noise. The unknown parameters/weights in this model can be estimated using, for example, least squares methods. The associated TFPI numbers are the antilogarithms of the residuals. This index should be used by analysts who want to minimise the amount of variation in the index numbers. It can also be used by analysts who have no information about output prices, input prices, revenue shares, cost shares or production technologies.

3.3.3 *Primal Indices*

Primal TFPIs are constructed by dividing primal output indices by primal input indices. For example, the primal index that compares the TFP of firm i in period t with the TFP of firm k in period s is

$$TFPI^P(x_{ks}, q_{ks}, x_{it}, q_{it}) \equiv \frac{D_O^{\bar{t}}(\bar{x}, q_{it}, \bar{z})}{D_O^{\bar{t}}(\bar{x}, q_{ks}, \bar{z})} \frac{D_I^{\bar{t}}(x_{ks}, \bar{q}, \bar{z})}{D_I^{\bar{t}}(x_{it}, \bar{q}, \bar{z})} \tag{3.44}$$

where $\bar{t}$ is a fixed time period and $\bar{x}$, $\bar{q}$ and $\bar{z}$ are fixed vectors of inputs, outputs and environmental variables. This index can traced back to O'Donnell (2016, Eq. 4). It should be used by analysts who regard marginal rates of transformation and marginal rates of technical substitution as appropriate measures of relative value (e.g., analysts who might otherwise use a generalised Malmquist or Hicks-Moorsteen index). For it to be a proper index, the output distance function must be nondecreasing in outputs and the input distance function must be nondecreasing in inputs, implying that outputs and inputs must be strongly disposable. If there is no environmental change, then it reduces to the Färe-Primont (FP) index defined by O'Donnell (2014, Eq. 11). If output (resp. input) sets are homothetic, then it does not depend on $\bar{x}$ (resp. $\bar{q}$). If technical change is HN, then it does not depend on $\bar{t}$ or $\bar{z}$. Ultimately, the exact form of the index depends on the output and input distance functions. If the output distance function is given by (2.9), for example, then, and only then, the input distance function is given by (2.13). In this case,

$$TFPI^P(x_{ks}, q_{ks}, x_{it}, q_{it}) = \left(\frac{\sum_n \gamma_n q_{nit}^\tau}{\sum_n \gamma_n q_{nks}^\tau}\right)^{1/\tau} \prod_{m=1}^{M} \left(\frac{x_{mks}}{x_{mit}}\right)^{\lambda_m}. \tag{3.45}$$

Observe that this index does not depend on the choices of $\bar{t}$, $\bar{x}$, $\bar{q}$ or $\bar{z}$. This is because the output and input distance functions given by (2.9) and (2.13) represent homothetic output and input sets with boundaries that exhibit HN technical change. If $\tau = 1$, then (3.45) takes the form of an additive output index divided by a multiplicative input index. If some shadow cost shares are equal to zero, then it can be viewed as an MFP index. If all shadow cost shares except one are equal to zero, then it can be viewed as a PFP index. If all shadow cost shares except the shadow cost share for labour (resp. capital) are equal to zero, then it can be viewed as a labour (resp. capital) productivity index.

3.3.4 Dual Indices

Dual TFPIs are constructed by dividing dual output indices by dual input indices. For a dual TFPI to be a proper index, the cost function must be homogeneous in outputs and the revenue function must be homogeneous in inputs. If, for example, the cost function is homogeneous of degree $1/r$ in outputs and the revenue function is homogeneous of degree r in inputs, then the dual index that compares the TFP of firm i in period t with the TFP of firm k in period s is

$$TFPI^D(x_{ks}, q_{ks}, x_{it}, q_{it}) \equiv \left(\frac{C^{\bar{t}}(\bar{w}, q_{it}, \bar{z})}{C^{\bar{t}}(\bar{w}, q_{ks}, \bar{z})}\right)^r \left(\frac{R^{\bar{t}}(x_{ks}, \bar{p}, \bar{z})}{R^{\bar{t}}(x_{it}, \bar{p}, \bar{z})}\right)^{1/r} \tag{3.46}$$

where $\bar{t}$ is a fixed time period and $\bar{w}$, $\bar{p}$ and $\bar{z}$ are fixed vectors of input prices, output prices and environmental variables. This index should be used by analysts who regard marginal revenues and marginal costs as appropriate measures of relative value. If output (resp. input) sets are homothetic, then it does not depend on $\bar{p}$ (resp. $\bar{w}$). Ultimately, the exact form of the index depends on the revenue and cost functions. If the revenue function is given by (2.17), for example, then, and only then, the cost function is given by (2.22). In this case,

$$TFPI^D(x_{ks}, q_{ks}, x_{it}, q_{it}) = \left(\frac{\sum_n \gamma_n q_{nit}^\tau}{\sum_n \gamma_n q_{nks}^\tau}\right)^{1/\tau} \prod_{m=1}^{M} \left(\frac{x_{mks}}{x_{mit}}\right)^{\lambda_m}. \tag{3.47}$$

Observe that this index is the same as the index defined by (3.45). This is because the distance, revenue and cost functions given by (2.9), (2.13), (2.17) and (2.22) are equivalent representations of homothetic output and input sets with boundaries that exhibits HN technical change.

3.3.5 Benefit-of-the-Doubt Indices

BOD TFPIs are constructed by dividing BOD output indices by BOD input indices. For example, the BOD index that compares the TFP of firm i in period t with the TFP of firm k in period s is

$$TFPI^B(x_{ks}, q_{ks}, x_{it}, q_{it}) \equiv \frac{Q^B(q_{it})}{Q^B(q_{ks})} \frac{X^B(x_{ks})}{X^B(x_{it})} \tag{3.48}$$

where $Q^B(q_{it})$ denotes the maximised value of the objective function in problem (3.9) and $X^B(x_{it})$ denotes the minimised value of the objective function in problem (3.28). This is a proper TFPI with high characteristicity. It should be used by analysts who believe measures of relative value should vary from one TFP comparison to the next. It can also be used by analysts who have no information about output prices, input prices, revenue shares, cost shares or production technologies.

3.3.6 Other Indices

Other types of productivity indices include binary, chained and multilateral TFPIs. These are not proper TFPIs in the sense that they cannot generally be written as proper output indices divided by proper input indices. Binary TFPIs are designed for comparing two observations only. Chained TFPIs are mainly used for comparing the TFP of a single firm over several time periods. Multilateral TFPIs are mainly used for comparing the TFP of several firms in a single time period.

3.3.6.1 Binary Indices

Binary TFPIs do not generally satisfy axiom TI6 (transitivity). The class of binary TFPIs includes Fisher, Törnqvist and GM indices. Fisher TFPIs are constructed by dividing Fisher output indices by Fisher input indices. For example, the Fisher index that compares the TFP of firm i in period t with the TFP of firm k in period s is

$$TFPI^F(x_{ks}, q_{ks}, x_{it}, q_{it}, \ldots) = \left(\frac{p'_{it}q_{it}}{p'_{it}q_{ks}} \frac{p'_{ks}q_{it}}{p'_{ks}q_{ks}} \frac{w'_{it}x_{ks}}{w'_{it}x_{it}} \frac{w'_{ks}x_{ks}}{w'_{ks}x_{it}} \right)^{1/2}. \tag{3.49}$$

If observed output and input prices are firm- and time-invariant, then Fisher TFPI numbers are equal to Lowe TFPI numbers. Törnqvist TFPIs are constructed by dividing Törnqvist output indices by Törnqvist input indices. For example, the Törnqvist index that compares the TFP of firm i in period t with the TFP of firm k in period s is

$$TFPI^{T}(x_{ks}, q_{ks}, x_{it}, q_{it}, \ldots) \equiv \prod_{n=1}^{N} \left(\frac{q_{nit}}{q_{nks}} \right)^{(r_{nit}+r_{nks})/2} \prod_{m=1}^{M} \left(\frac{x_{mks}}{x_{mit}} \right)^{(s_{mit}+s_{mks})/2}. \tag{3.50}$$

If observed revenue and cost shares are firm- and time-invariant, then Törnqvist TFPI numbers are equal to GY TFPI numbers. Finally, GM TFPIs are constructed by dividing GM output indices by GM input indices. For example, the GM index that compares the TFP of firm i in period t with the TFP of firm k in period s is

$$\begin{aligned} TFPI^{GM}(x_{ks}, q_{ks}, x_{it}, q_{it}, \ldots) \equiv & \left(\frac{D_O^t(x_{it}, q_{it}, z_{it})}{D_O^t(x_{it}, q_{ks}, z_{it})} \frac{D_O^s(x_{ks}, q_{it}, z_{ks})}{D_O^s(x_{ks}, q_{ks}, z_{ks})} \right. \\ & \left. \times \frac{D_I^t(x_{ks}, q_{it}, z_{it})}{D_I^t(x_{it}, q_{it}, z_{it})} \frac{D_I^s(x_{ks}, q_{ks}, z_{ks})}{D_I^s(x_{it}, q_{ks}, z_{ks})} \right)^{1/2}. \end{aligned} \tag{3.51}$$

If output and input sets are homothetic and technical change is HN, then this index is equivalent to the primal index defined by (3.44). If the output and input distance functions are given by (2.9) and (2.13), then it is equivalent to the primal index defined by (3.45). If there is no environmental change, then it takes the form of the Malmquist TFPI of Bjurek (1996, Eq. 9)[27] (hence the use of the term 'generalised'). The main idea behind the Bjurek index can be traced back to Diewert (1992, p. 240). However, Diewert attributes the concept to Hicks (1961) and Moorsteen (1961). For this reason, the Bjurek index is commonly referred to as a Hicks-Moorsteen (HM) index (e.g., Briec and Kerstens 2011; Kerstens and Van de Woestyne 2014; Mizobuchi 2017)

At least three other binary. Malmquist indices can be found in the literature. Except in restrictive special cases, these indices cannot be written as output indices divided by input indices, implying they cannot generally be viewed as productivity indices. First, the output-oriented Malmquist (OM) index that compares the 'productivity' of firm i in period t with the 'productivity' of firm k in period s is

$$TFPI^{OM}(x_{ks}, x_{it}, q_{ks}, q_{it}, s, t) \equiv \left(\frac{D_O^s(x_{it}, q_{it})}{D_O^s(x_{ks}, q_{ks})} \frac{D_O^t(x_{it}, q_{it})}{D_O^t(x_{ks}, q_{ks})} \right)^{1/2} \tag{3.52}$$

[27] Bjurek (1996) defines his index in a time-series context. In such a context, all notation pertaining to firms can be suppressed.

where $D_O^t(x_{it}, q_{it})$ is a period-specific output distance function. The basic idea behind this index can be traced back at least as far as Caves et al. (1982a, p. 1404) (these authors define their index in a cross-section context).[28] Except in restrictive special cases, it yields systematically biased estimates of productivity change: for more details and an empirical demonstration, see Grifell-Tatjé and Lovell (1995).

Second, the input-oriented Malmquist (IM) index that compares the 'productivity' of firm i in period t with the 'productivity' of firm k in period s is

$$TFPI^{IM}(x_{ks}, x_{it}, q_{ks}, q_{it}, s, t) \equiv \left(\frac{D_I^s(x_{ks}, q_{ks})\ D_I^t(x_{ks}, q_{ks})}{D_I^s(x_{it}, q_{it})\ D_I^t(x_{it}, q_{it})} \right)^{1/2} \tag{3.53}$$

where $D_I^t(x_{it}, q_{it})$ is a period-specific input distance function. The idea behind this index can be traced back to as far as Caves et al. (1982a, p. 1408) (again, these authors define their index in a cross-section context). The IM index has the same pathological properties as the OM index. If the period-t and period-s production frontiers exhibit CRS, then the IM and OM indices are equivalent. If the output set is homothetic and the period-t and period-s production frontiers exhibit CRS, then the IM and OM indices are equivalent to the HM index (Mizobuchi 2017).

Finally, the reciprocal of the IM TFPI has the same form as the 'input-based Malmquist productivity index' defined by Färe et al. (1992, Eq. 9) (these authors define their index in a time-series context). The Färe et al. (1992) index has some counterintuitive properties: if, for example, inputs are strongly disposable, then increases in inputs and decreases in outputs will generally be associated with *increases* in the value of their index, indicating that productivity has increased.

3.3.6.2 Chained Indices

Chained TFPIs do not generally satisfy axiom TI4 (proportionality). The class of chained TFPIs includes CF, CT and chained CGM indices. The CF index that compares the TFP of firm i in period t with the TFP of firm i in period 1 is

[28]The output distance functions that underpin the Caves et al. (1982a) index are firm-specific functions. A firm-specific output distance function is presumably a representation of a firm-specific output set. A firm-specific output set is presumably a set containing all outputs that can be produced by a given firm using given inputs. Thus, Caves et al. (1982a) presumably have in mind that it was technically possible for a given firm to transform a given input vector into a given output vector, but, because it operates in a different production environment, it was not technically possible for another firm to do the same. In contrast, Färe et al. (1994, Eq. 6). define an 'output-based Malmquist productivity change index' in a time-series context. The output distance functions that define their index are period-specific functions. Thus, Färe et al. (1994) presumably have in mind that it was technically possible to transform a given input vector into a given output vector in a given period, but, because the requisite technologies may not have been developed, it may not have been technically possible to do the same thing in an earlier period.

$$TFPI^{CF}(x_{i1}, q_{i1}, x_{it}, q_{it}, \ldots) \equiv \prod_{s=1}^{t-1} TFPI^{F}(x_{is}, q_{is}, x_{i,s+1}, q_{i,s+1}, \ldots) \quad (3.54)$$

where $TFPI^{F}(x_{is}, q_{is}, x_{i,s+1}, q_{i,s+1}, \ldots)$ is a binary Fisher index. If observed output and input prices are firm- and time-invariant, then CF TFPI numbers are equal to Lowe TFPI numbers. The CT index that compares the TFP of firm i in period t with the TFP of firm i in period 1 is

$$TFPI^{CT}(x_{i1}, q_{i1}, x_{it}, q_{it}, \ldots) \equiv \prod_{s=1}^{t-1} TFPI^{T}(x_{is}, q_{is}, x_{i,s+1}, q_{i,s+1}, \ldots) \quad (3.55)$$

where $TFPI^{T}(x_{is}, q_{is}, x_{i,s+1}, q_{i,s+1}, \ldots)$ is a binary Törnqvist index. If observed revenue and cost shares are firm- and time-invariant, then CT TFPI numbers are equal to GY TFPI numbers. Finally, the CGM index that compares the TFP of firm i in period t with the TFP of firm i in period 1 is

$$TFPI^{CGM}(x_{i1}, q_{i1}, x_{it}, q_{it}, \ldots) \equiv \prod_{s=1}^{t-1} TFPI^{GM}(x_{is}, q_{is}, x_{i,s+1}, q_{i,s+1}, \ldots) \quad (3.56)$$

where $TFPI^{GM}(x_{is}, q_{is}, x_{i,s+1}, q_{i,s+1}, \ldots)$ is a binary GM index. If output and input sets are homothetic and technical change is HN, then CGM TFPI numbers are equal to primal index numbers computed using (3.44).

3.3.6.3 Multilateral Indices

Multilateral TFPIs do not generally satisfy axiom TI4 (proportionality). They are also particularly sensitive to the addition or removal of observations from the dataset. The class of multilateral TFPIs includes EKS, CCD and MGM TFPIs. The EKS index that compares the TFP of firm i in period t with the TFP of firm k in period t is

$$TFPI^{EKS}(x_{kt}, q_{kt}, x_{it}, q_{it}, \ldots) \equiv \left(\prod_{r=1}^{I_t} TFPI^{F}(x_{kt}, q_{kt}, x_{rt}, q_{rt}, \ldots) \times TFPI^{F}(x_{rt}, q_{rt}, x_{it}, q_{it}, \ldots) \right)^{1/I_t} \quad (3.57)$$

where I_t is the number of firms in period t and $TFPI^{F}(x_{kt}, q_{kt}, x_{rt}, q_{rt}, \ldots)$ is a binary Fisher index. If observed output and input prices are firm- and time-invariant, then EKS TFPI numbers are equal to Lowe TFPI numbers. The CCD index that compares the TFP of firm i in period t with the TFP of firm k in period t is

$$TFPI^{CCD}(x_{kt}, q_{kt}, x_{it}, q_{it}, \ldots) \equiv \left(\prod_{r=1}^{I_t} TFPI^{T}(x_{kt}, q_{kt}, x_{rt}, q_{rt}, \ldots) \times TFPI^{T}(x_{rt}, q_{rt}, x_{it}, q_{it}, \ldots) \right)^{1/I_t} \tag{3.58}$$

where $TFPI^{T}(x_{kt}, q_{kt}, x_{rt}, q_{rt}, \ldots)$ is a binary Törnqvist index. If observed revenue and cost shares are firm- and time-invariant, then CCD TFPI numbers are equal to GY TFPI numbers. Finally, the MGM index that compares the TFP of firm i in period t with the TFP of firm k in period t is

$$TFPI^{MGM}(x_{kt}, q_{kt}, x_{it}, q_{it}, \ldots) \equiv \left(\prod_{r=1}^{I_t} TFPI^{GM}(x_{kt}, q_{kt}, x_{rt}, q_{rt}, \ldots) \times TFPI^{GM}(x_{rt}, q_{rt}, x_{it}, q_{it}, \ldots) \right)^{1/I_t} \tag{3.59}$$

where $TFPI^{GM}(x_{kt}, q_{kt}, x_{rt}, q_{rt}, \ldots)$ is a binary GM index. If output and input sets are homothetic and technical change is HN, then MGM TFPI numbers are equal to primal index numbers computed using (3.44).

3.3.7 Toy Example

Reconsider the output and input quantity and price data reported earlier in Tables 1.4 and 1.5. Sets of associated TFPI numbers are reported in Table 3.5. These numbers were obtained by dividing the output index numbers in Table 3.1 by the corresponding input index numbers in Table 3.3. In Table 3.5, the index numbers in any given row compare the inputs and outputs in that row with the inputs and outputs in row A. All of these index numbers are proper in the sense that they have been obtained by dividing proper output index numbers by proper input index numbers. They all satisfy TI1 to TI6. Observe, for example, that (a) the output vector in row W is twice as big as the output vector in row A, (b) the input vector in row W is only 0.919 times as big as the input vector in row A, and (c), in any given column, the index number in row W is equal to $2/0.919 = 2.176$.

TFPIs that do not generally satisfy one or more of axioms TI1 to TI6 include Fisher, Törnqvist, CF, CT, EKS and CCD indices. Index numbers obtained using these indices are reported in Table 3.6. These numbers were obtained by dividing the output index numbers in Table 3.2 by the corresponding input index numbers in

Table 3.5 Proper TFPI numbers[a,b]

Row	q_1	q_2	x_1	x_2	AEW	L	GY	OLS	P	D	BOD	Ave.
A	1	1	1	1	1	1	1	1	1	1	1	1
B	1	1	0.56	0.56	1.786	1.786	1.786	1.786	1.786	1.786	1.786	1.786
C	2.37	2.37	1	1	2.37	2.37	2.37	2.37	2.37	2.37	2.37	2.37
D	2.11	2.11	1.05	0.7	2.411	2.703	2.539	2.249	2.738	2.738	2.541	2.554
E	1.81	3.62	1.05	0.7	3.103	3.516	3.133	2.198	4.694	4.694	3.321	3.422
F	1	1	0.996	0.316	1.524	2.117	1.948	1.381	2.412	2.412	2.182	1.958
G	1.777	3.503	1.472	0.546	2.616	3.515	3.054	1.807	5.069	5.069	3.440	3.324
H	0.96	0.94	0.017	0.346	5.234	3.513	9.811	24.340	5.543	5.543	4.251	6.647
I	5.82	0.001	4.545	0.01	1.278	2.675	0.464	1.375	0.268	0.268	11.558	1.089
J	6.685	0.001	4.45	0.001	1.502	3.159	1.890	2.962	1.773	1.773	14.249	2.750
K	1.381	4.732	1	1	3.057	3.110	2.634	1.741	4.726	4.726	3.137	3.147
L	0.566	4.818	1	1	2.692	2.760	1.740	0.847	4.810	4.810	2.968	2.576
M	1	3	1.354	1	1.699	1.879	1.565	0.988	2.789	2.789	1.809	1.833
N	0.7	0.7	0.33	0.16	2.857	3.516	3.221	2.594	3.686	3.686	3.134	3.218
O	2	2	1	1	2	2	2	2	2	2	2	2
P	1	1	0.657	0.479	1.761	1.923	1.827	1.662	1.937	1.937	1.834	1.838
R	1	3	1	1	2	2.032	1.779	1.229	2.996	2.996	2.048	2.071
S	1	1	1.933	0.283	0.903	1.509	1.568	0.883	2.243	2.243	2.163	1.540
T	1.925	3.722	1	1	2.824	2.852	2.720	2.179	3.719	3.719	2.867	2.939
U	1	1	1	0.31	1.527	2.134	1.966	1.385	2.445	2.445	2.218	1.976
V	1	5.166	1	1	3.083	3.150	2.366	1.362	5.159	5.159	3.183	3.083
W	2	2	0.919	0.919	2.176	2.176	2.176	2.176	2.176	2.176	2.176	2.176
X	1	1	1.464	0.215	1.191	1.991	2.067	1.164	2.954	2.954	2.848	2.030
Y	1	1	0.74	0.74	1.351	1.351	1.351	1.351	1.351	1.351	1.351	1.351
Z	1.81	3.62	2.1	1.4	1.551	1.758	1.567	1.099	2.347	2.347	1.661	1.711

[a]AEW = additive with equal weights; L = Lowe; GY = geometric Young; OLS = multiplicative with OLS weights; P = primal with CNLS parameter estimates; D = dual with CNLS parameter estimates; BOD = benefit-of-the-doubt

[b]Numbers reported to less than three decimal places are exact; see the footnote to Table 1.2 on p. 8. Some numbers may be incoherent at the third decimal place due to rounding (e.g., the number in row Z of column AEW is not exactly half as big as the number in row E of column AEW due to rounding)

Table 3.4. Again, numbers that are clearly incoherent are marked with an asterisk (*). Observe, for example, that the output vector in row Z is the same as the output vector in row E, and the input vector in row Z is twice as big as the input vector in row E, but the TFPI numbers in row Z are not half as big as the index numbers in row E. Again, in this book, these types of errors are viewed as measurement errors.

Table 3.6 Other TFPI numbers[a,b]

Row	q_1	q_2	x_1	x_2	F	T	CF	CT	EKS	CCD
A	1	1	1	1	1	1	1	1	1	1
B	1	1	0.56	0.56	1.786	1.786	1.786	1.786	1.889*	1.922*
C	2.37	2.37	1	1	2.37	2.37	2.37	2.37	2.37	2.37
D	2.11	2.11	1.05	0.7	2.737	2.725	2.737	2.725	2.799	2.870
E	1.81	3.62	1.05	0.7	3.599*	3.601*	3.495*	3.476*	3.359*	3.600*
F	1	1	0.996	0.316	1.994	1.942	2.096	2.052	1.963	2.157
G	1.777	3.503	1.472	0.546	3.145	3.078	3.670	3.592	3.269	3.697
H	0.96	0.94	0.017	0.346	3.250	3.392	5.028	9.059	3.728	5.072
I	5.82	0.001	4.545	0.01	2.815	3.037	2.798	2.469	1.996	1.056
J	6.685	0.001	4.45	0.001	3.378	9.289	3.296	2.909	2.276	2.292
K	1.381	4.732	1	1	2.783	2.769	3.144	2.436	2.883	3.090
L	0.566	4.818	1	1	2.648	2.369	2.750	2.096	2.916	3.044
M	1	3	1.354	1	1.795	1.781	1.872	1.453	1.840	1.973
N	0.7	0.7	0.33	0.16	3.913	3.918	4.233	3.304	3.629	3.535
O	2	2	1	1	2	2	2.611*	2.012*	2.350*	2.421*
P	1	1	0.657	0.479	1.935	1.930	2.332	1.798	1.985	2.113
R	1	3	1	1	1.893	1.880	2.682	2.083	2.162	2.366
S	1	1	1.933	0.283	1.738	1.631	1.757	1.369	1.498	1.549
T	1.925	3.722	1	1	2.631	2.631	3.652	2.848	2.991	3.104
U	1	1	1	0.31	2.317	2.248	2.391	1.853	2.117	2.324
V	1	5.166	1	1	2.099	2.070	2.996	2.475	2.445	2.418
W	2	2	0.919	0.919	2.176	2.176	3.364*	2.817*	2.390*	2.332*
X	1	1	1.464	0.215	1.926	1.871	2.313	2.004	1.719	1.951
Y	1	1	0.74	0.74	1.351	1.351	1.925*	1.628*	1.401*	1.482*
Z	1.81	3.62	2.1	1.4	1.672*	1.655*	2.523*	2.133*	1.866*	2.154*

[a]F = Fisher; T = Törnqvist; CF = chained Fisher; CT = chained Törnqvist; EKS = Elteto-Koves-Szulc; CCD = Caves-Christensen-Diewert

[b]Numbers reported to less than three decimal places are exact; see the footnote to Table 1.2 on p. 8

*Incoherent (not because of rounding)

3.4 Other Indices

Other types of indices include output price, input price, terms-of-trade, implicit output, implicit input and implicit productivity indices.

3.4.1 Output Price Indices

In this book, an index that compares the output prices received by firm i in period t with the output prices received by firm k in period s is defined as any variable of the form

$$PI(p_{ks}, p_{it}) \equiv P(p_{it})/P(p_{ks}) \tag{3.60}$$

where $P(.)$ is a nonnegative, nondecreasing, linearly-homogeneous, scalar-valued aggregator function. If output prices are positive, then all indices of this type satisfy the following axioms:

PI1 $p_{rl} \geq p_{it} \Rightarrow PI(p_{ks}, p_{rl}) \geq PI(p_{ks}, p_{it})$ (weak monotonicity),
PI2 $PI(p_{ks}, \lambda p_{it}) = \lambda PI(p_{ks}, p_{it})$ for $\lambda > 0$ (homogeneity type I),
PI3 $PI(\lambda p_{ks}, \lambda p_{it}) = PI(p_{ks}, p_{it})$ for $\lambda > 0$ (homogeneity type II),
PI4 $PI(p_{ks}, \lambda p_{ks}) = \lambda$ for $\lambda > 0$ (proportionality),
PI5 $PI(p_{ks}, p_{it}) = 1/PI(p_{it}, p_{ks})$ (time-space reversal) and
PI6 $PI(p_{ks}, p_{rl})PI(p_{rl}, p_{it}) = PI(p_{ks}, p_{it})$ (transitivity).

The interpretation of these axioms is analogous to the interpretation of QI1 to QI6. In a cross-section context, for example, the proportionality axiom says that if the output prices received by firm A are exactly λ times the output prices received by firm B, then the index that compares the two sets of prices must take the value λ. In this book, an output price index is said to be proper if and only if PI1 to PI6 are satisfied.[29] Again, any nonnegative, nondecreasing, linearly-homogeneous, scalar-valued aggregator function can be used for purposes of constructing a proper output price index. Again, the choice of function is generally a matter of taste. Linear functions can be used to construct additive indices; an example is the Lowe price index defined by Balk and Diewert (2003, Eq. 5).[30] Double-log functions can be used to construct multiplicative indices; an example is the GY output price index defined by IMF (2004, p. 10). Locally-linear functions can be used to construct BOD indices. Finally, if firms are price takers in output markets, then revenue functions can be used to construct dual indices. In this last case, a suitable aggregator function is $P(p_{it}) \propto R^{\bar{t}}(\bar{x}, p_{it}, \bar{z})$ where $\bar{t}$ is a fixed time period and $\bar{x}$ and $\bar{z}$ are fixed vectors of inputs and environmental variables (as usual, the choices of $\bar{t}$, $\bar{x}$ and $\bar{z}$ are a matter of taste). The associated dual index that compares the output prices received by firm i in period t with the output prices received by firm k in period s is

$$PI^D(p_{ks}, p_{it}) \equiv R^{\bar{t}}(\bar{x}, p_{it}, \bar{z})/R^{\bar{t}}(\bar{x}, p_{ks}, \bar{z}). \tag{3.61}$$

---

[29] In O'Donnell (2012b), an output price index is said to be proper if and only if *nine* axioms are satisfied. If PI1 to PI6 are satisfied, then, and only then, eight of the O'Donnell (2012b) axioms are satisfied. If the aggregator function is differentiable, then the ninth axiom is also satisfied.

[30] Balk and Diewert (2003) define their price index in a consumer context. According to Hill (2008, p. 2), many consumer price indices produced by statistical agencies turn out to be Lowe indices.

If there is no technical change, then this index is equivalent to the output price index defined by O'Donnell (2012b, Eq. 7). If there is no technical or environmental change, then it is equivalent to the output price index defined by Färe and Primont (1995, Eq. 3.5.6). If output sets are homothetic, then it does not depend on $\bar{x}$. If technical change is IHON, then it does not depend on $\bar{t}$ or $\bar{z}$. Ultimately, the exact form of the index depends on the revenue function. If the revenue function is given by (2.17), for example, then

$$PI^D(p_{ks}, p_{it}) = \left(\frac{\sum_n \gamma_n^\sigma p_{nit}^{1-\sigma}}{\sum_n \gamma_n^\sigma p_{nks}^{1-\sigma}} \right)^{1/(1-\sigma)} . \tag{3.62}$$

Most other output price indices are not proper in the sense that they do not satisfy one or more of axioms PI1 to PI6. These include various binary, chained and multilateral indices. Binary output price indices are designed for comparing two output price vectors only; they do not generally satisfy PI6 (transitivity). The class of binary output price indices includes Fisher and Törnqvist indices. Chained output price indices are mainly used for comparing the prices received by a single firm over several time periods; they do not generally satisfy PI4 (proportionality). The class of chained output price indices includes CF and CT indices. Finally, multilateral output price indices are mainly used for comparing the prices received by several firms in a single time period; again, they do not generally satisfy PI4 (proportionality). The class of multilateral output price indices includes EKS and CCD indices.

To illustrate, reconsider the output quantities and prices reported in Table 1.4. Sets of associated output price index numbers are reported in Table 3.7. In this table, the index numbers in any given row compare the output prices in that row with the output prices in row A. The numbers in the L, GY and BOD columns are Lowe, geometric Young and benefit-of-the-doubt index numbers; these are all proper index numbers in the sense that they have been obtained using indices that satisfy axioms PI1 to PI6. On the other hand, the numbers in the T, CT and CCD columns are Törnqvist, chained Törnqvist and Caves-Christensen-Diewert index numbers that have been obtained using indices that do not generally satisfy one or more of those axioms. Again, for illustrative purposes, the CT index numbers were computed by treating the observations in the dataset as observations on a single firm over twenty-five periods, while the CCD index numbers were computed by treating the observations in the dataset as observations on twenty-five firms in a single period. Again, numbers that are clearly incoherent are marked with an asterisk (*). Observe, for example, that the output prices in row K are the same as the output prices in row A, but the CT and CCD index numbers in row K are less than one (indicating that prices fell). As another example, the output prices in row T are both higher than the output prices in row A, but the CT index number in row T is less than one. Again, in this book, these types of errors are viewed as measurement errors.

Table 3.7 Output price index numbers[a,b]

Row	p_1	p_2	L	GY	BOD	T	CT	CCD
A	0.57	0.41	1	1	1	1	1	1
B	0.26	0.25	0.529	0.531	0.486	0.520	0.520	0.523
C	0.57	0.41	1	1	1	1	1	1
D	0.58	0.53	1.147	1.154	1.071	1.133	1.133	1.138
E	0.26	0.26	0.54	0.542	0.491	0.545	0.535	0.536
F	0.59	0.76	1.421	1.405	1.193	1.378	1.418	1.392
G	0.63	0.65	1.332	1.335	1.198	1.345	1.320	1.323
H	0.34	0.31	0.672	0.675	0.627	0.663	0.664*	0.666
I	0.46	0.58	1.094	1.083	0.925	0.908	0.970	0.992
J	0.61	1.43	2.211	1.988	1.538	1.370	1.286	1.548
K	0.57	0.41	1	1	1	1	0.789*	0.960*
L	0.49	0.65	1.202	1.185	1	1.294	1.117	1.246
M	0.51	0.46	1.002	1.007	0.939	1.019	0.846	0.987
N	0.52	0.23	0.747	0.707	0.879	0.765	0.596*	0.757
O	0.37	0.17	0.538	0.513	0.625	0.551	0.429	0.546
P	0.41	0.76	1.255	1.182	0.939	1.192	0.932	1.214
R	0.53	0.48	1.043	1.049	0.976	1.061	0.735	1.028
S	0.53	0.37	0.917	0.915	0.925	0.918	0.633*	0.918
T	0.91	0.53	1.453	1.429	1.538	1.444	0.999*	1.406
U	0.31	1.03	1.473	1.213	1.108	1.349	1.053	1.392
V	0.47	0.08	0.528	0.387	0.794	0.435	0.254	0.401
W	0.57	0.27	0.839	0.803	0.963	0.857	0.462*	0.850
X	0.31	0.51	0.874	0.839	0.679	0.836	0.452	0.849
Y	0.31	0.67	1.058	0.968	0.755	0.997	0.540	1.018
Z	0.42	0.69	1.183	1.136	0.920	1.202	0.600	1.196

[a]L = Lowe; GY = geometric Young; BOD = benefit-of-the-doubt; T = Törnqvist; CT = chained Törnqvist; CCD = Caves-Christensen-Diewert
[b]Numbers reported to less than three decimal places are exact; see the footnote to Table 1.2 on p. 8
*Incoherent (not because of rounding)

3.4.2 Input Price Indices

In this book, an index that compares the input prices paid by firm i in period t with the input prices paid by firm k in period s is defined as any variable of the form

$$WI(w_{ks}, w_{it}) \equiv W(w_{it})/W(w_{ks}) \tag{3.63}$$

where $W(.)$ is a nonnegative, nondecreasing, linearly-homogeneous, scalar-valued aggregator function. If input prices are positive, then all indices of this type satisfy the following axioms:

WI1 $w_{rl} \geq w_{it} \Rightarrow WI(w_{ks}, w_{rl}) \geq WI(w_{ks}, w_{it})$ (weak monotonicity),
WI2 $WI(w_{ks}, \lambda w_{it}) = \lambda WI(w_{ks}, w_{it})$ for $\lambda > 0$ (homogeneity type I),
WI3 $WI(\lambda w_{ks}, \lambda w_{it}) = WI(w_{ks}, w_{it})$ for $\lambda > 0$ (homogeneity type II),
WI4 $WI(w_{ks}, \lambda w_{ks}) = \lambda$ for $\lambda > 0$ (proportionality),
WI5 $WI(w_{ks}, w_{it}) = 1/WI(w_{it}, w_{ks})$ (time-space reversal) and
WI6 $WI(w_{ks}, w_{rl})WI(w_{rl}, w_{it}) = WI(w_{ks}, w_{it})$ (transitivity).

The interpretation of these axioms is analogous to the interpretation of PI1 to PI6. In this book, an input price index is said to be proper if and only if WI1 to WI6 are satisfied. Again, any nonnegative, nondecreasing, linearly-homogeneous, scalar-valued aggregator function can be used for purposes of constructing a proper input price index. Again, the choice of function is generally a matter of taste. Linear functions can be used to construct additive indices. Double-log functions can be used to construct multiplicative indices. Locally-linear functions can be used to construct BOD indices. Finally, if firms are price takers in input markets, then cost functions can be used to construct dual indices. In this last case, a suitable aggregator function is $W(w_{it}) \propto C^{\bar{t}}(w_{it}, \bar{q}, \bar{z})$ where $\bar{t}$ is a fixed time period and $\bar{q}$ and $\bar{z}$ are fixed vectors of outputs and environmental variables (again, the choices of $\bar{t}$, $\bar{q}$ and $\bar{z}$ are a matter of taste). The associated dual index that compares the input prices paid by firm i in period t with the input prices paid by firm k in period s is

$$WI^D(w_{ks}, w_{it}) \equiv C^{\bar{t}}(w_{it}, \bar{q}, \bar{z})/C^{\bar{t}}(w_{ks}, \bar{q}, \bar{z}). \tag{3.64}$$

If there is no technical or environmental change, then this index is equivalent to the input price index defined by Färe and Primont (1995, Eq. 3.5.1). If input sets are homothetic, then it does not depend on $\bar{q}$. If technical change is IHIN, then it does not depend on $\bar{t}$ or $\bar{z}$. Ultimately, the exact form of the index depends on the cost function. If the cost function is given by (2.22), for example, then

$$WI^D(w_{ks}, w_{it}) = \prod_{m=1}^{M} \left(\frac{w_{mit}}{w_{mks}} \right)^{\lambda_m}. \tag{3.65}$$

This index can be viewed as a multiplicative index with weights given by shadow cost shares.

Most other input price indices are not proper in the sense that they do not satisfy one or more of axioms WI1 to WI6. These include various binary, chained and multilateral indices. Binary input price indices are designed for comparing two input price vectors only; they do not generally satisfy WI6 (transitivity). The class of binary input price indices includes Fisher and Törnqvist indices. Chained input price indices are mainly used for comparing the prices paid by a single firm over several time periods; they do not generally satisfy WI4 (proportionality). The class of chained input price indices includes CF and CT indices. Finally, multilateral input price indices are mainly used for comparing the prices paid by several firms in a single time period; again, they do not generally satisfy WI4 (proportionality). The class of multilateral input price indices includes EKS and CCD indices.

To illustrate, reconsider the input quantities and prices reported in Table 1.5. Sets of associated input price index numbers are reported in Table 3.8. In this table, the index numbers in any given row compare the input prices in that row with the input prices in row A. The numbers in the L, GY and BOD columns are Lowe, geometric Young and benefit-of-the-doubt index numbers; these are all proper index numbers in the sense that they have been obtained using indices that satisfy axioms WI1 to WI6. On the other hand, the numbers in the T, CT and CCD columns are Törnqvist, chained Törnqvist and Caves-Christensen-Diewert index numbers that have been obtained using indices that do not generally satisfy one or more of those axioms. Again, for illustrative purposes, the CT index numbers were computed by treating

Table 3.8 Input price index numbers[a,b]

Row	w_1	w_2	L	GY	BOD	T	CT	CCD
A	0.28	1.91	1	1	1	1	1	1
B	0.22	0.58	0.411	0.454	0.590	0.368	0.368*	0.395
C	0.28	1.91	1	1	1	1	1	1
D	0.16	0.41	0.294	0.325	0.427	0.274	0.274	0.282
E	0.07	1.02	0.471	0.387	0.443	0.491	0.456	0.446
F	0.24	0.29	0.309	0.316	0.615	0.317	0.358	0.309
G	0.16	0.16	0.192	0.189	0.410	0.191	0.227*	0.191
H	0.17	0.7	0.420	0.454	0.510	0.380	0.587	0.432
I	0.27	0.39	0.374	0.394	0.692	0.489	0.554*	0.408
J	0.29	0.79	0.552	0.610	0.783	0.694	0.596*	0.527
K	0.28	1.91	1	1	1	1	0.859*	1
L	0.21	0.56	0.395	0.436	0.565	0.354	0.304	0.38
M	0.16	0.74	0.428	0.457	0.497	0.415	0.350	0.420
N	0.24	2.3	1.127	1.043	1	1.143	0.939	1.063
O	0.24	0.15	0.252	0.216	0.615	0.191	0.181	0.216
P	0.26	0.61	0.455	0.502	0.682	0.416	0.383	0.435
R	0.16	0.22	0.217	0.227	0.410	0.179	0.171*	0.197
S	0.19	0.62	0.403	0.443	0.535	0.437	0.299	0.376
T	0.17	0.26	0.241	0.256	0.436	0.201	0.188*	0.221
U	0.27	0.91	0.585	0.642	0.766	0.592	0.465*	0.554
V	0.29	0.78	0.548	0.605	0.781	0.492	0.434*	0.527
W	0.39	0.81	0.640	0.701	1	0.555	0.487*	0.603
X	0.21	0.31	0.293	0.310	0.538	0.336	0.227	0.304
Y	0.23	0.69	0.464	0.511	0.635	0.422	0.345*	0.450
Z	0.31	0.22	0.336	0.300	0.795	0.287	0.215*	0.309

[a]L = Lowe; GY = geometric Young; BOD = benefit-of-the-doubt; T = Törnqvist; CT = chained Törnqvist; CCD = Caves-Christensen-Diewert

[b]Numbers reported to less than three decimal places are exact; see the footnote to Table 1.2 on p. 8

*Incoherent (not because of rounding)

the observations in the dataset as observations on a single firm over twenty-five periods, while the CCD index numbers were computed by treating the observations in the dataset as observations on twenty-five firms in a single period. Again, numbers that are clearly incoherent are marked with an asterisk (*). Observe, for example, that the input prices in row K are the same as the input prices in row A, but the CT index number in row K is less than one (indicating that prices fell).

3.4.3 Terms-of-Trade Indices

The terms of trade (TT) is a measure of prices received divided by a measure of prices paid. In this book, a proper index that compares the TT of firm i in period t with the TT of firm k in period s is defined as any variable of the form

$$TTI(w_{ks}, p_{ks}, w_{it}, p_{it}) \equiv PI(p_{ks}, p_{it})/WI(w_{ks}, w_{it}) \tag{3.66}$$

where $PI(.)$ is any proper output price index and $WI(.)$ is any proper input price index. If all output and input prices are positive, then all terms-of-trade indices (TTIs) of this type satisfy the following axioms:

TT1 $p_{rl} \geq p_{it}$ and $w_{rl} \leq w_{it} \Rightarrow TTI(w_{ks}, p_{ks}, w_{rl}, p_{rl}) \geq TTI(w_{ks}, p_{ks}, w_{it}, p_{it})$ (weak monotonicity);

TT2 $TTI(w_{ks}, p_{ks}, \delta w_{it}\, \lambda p_{it}) = (\lambda/\delta) TTI(w_{ks}, p_{ks}, w_{it}, p_{it})$ for $\lambda > 0$ and $\delta > 0$ (homogeneity type I);

TT3 $TTI(\delta w_{ks}, \lambda p_{ks}, \delta w_{it}, \lambda p_{it}) = TTI(w_{ks}, p_{ks}, w_{it}, p_{it})$ for $\lambda > 0$ and $\delta > 0$ (homogeneity type II);

TT4 $TTI(w_{ks}, p_{ks}, \delta w_{ks}, \lambda p_{ks}) = \lambda/\delta$ for $\lambda > 0$ and $\delta > 0$ (proportionality);

TT5 $TTI(w_{ks}, p_{ks}, w_{it}, p_{it}) = 1/TTI(w_{it}, p_{it}, w_{ks}, p_{ks})$ (time-space reversal); and

TT6 $TTI(w_{ks}, p_{ks}, w_{it}, p_{it}) = TTI(w_{ks}, p_{ks}, w_{rl}, p_{rl}) TTI(w_{rl}, p_{rl}, w_{it}, p_{it})$ (transitivity).

Again, the interpretation of these axioms is straightforward. In a time-series context, for example, axiom TT4 (proportionality) says that if all output and input prices in period 5 were exactly double what they had been in period 1, then the index that compares the TT in the two periods must take the value one (indicating that there was no change in the TT). Any proper price indices can be used for purposes of constructing a proper TTI. Again, the choice of indices is generally a matter of taste. Additive (resp. multiplicative) TTIs are constructed by dividing additive (resp. multiplicative) output price indices by additive (resp. multiplicative) input price indices. Dual (resp. BOD) TTIs are constructed by dividing dual (resp. BOD) output price indices by dual (resp. BOD) input price indices.

Most other TTIs are not proper in the sense that they do not satisfy one or more of axioms TT1 to TT6. These include various binary, chained and multilateral indices. Binary TTIs do not generally satisfy TT6 (transitivity); the class of binary TTIs includes Fisher and Törnqvist indices. Chained TTIs do not generally satisfy TT4 (proportionality); the class of chained TTIs includes CF and CT indices. Finally, multilateral input price indices do not generally satisfy TT4 (proportionality); the class of multilateral TTIs includes EKS and CCD indices.

To illustrate, reconsider the output and input quantities and prices reported in Tables 1.4 and 1.5. Sets of associated TTI numbers are reported in Table 3.9. These numbers were obtained by dividing the output price index numbers in Table 3.7 by the corresponding input price index numbers in Table 3.8. In Table 3.9, the index numbers in any given row compare the prices received and paid in that row with the prices received and paid in row A. The L, GY and BOD index numbers are proper in the sense that they have been obtained by dividing proper output price index numbers by proper input price index numbers; they all satisfy axioms TT1 to TT6. On the other hand, the T, CT and CCD numbers have been obtained using indices that do not generally satisfy one or more of those axioms. Again, numbers that are clearly incoherent are marked with an asterisk (*). Observe, for example, that the prices received and paid in row K are the same as the prices received and paid in row A, but the CT and CCD index numbers in row K are less than one.

3.4.4 Implicit Output Indices

Implicit output indices are constructed by dividing revenue indices by output price indices. For example, the implicit dual (ID) index that compares the outputs of firm i in period t with the outputs of firm k in period s is

$$QI^{ID}(q_{ks}, q_{it}, p_{ks}, p_{it}) \equiv RI(p_{ks}, q_{ks}, p_{it}, q_{it})/PI^{D}(p_{ks}, p_{it}) \qquad (3.67)$$

where $RI(p_{ks}, q_{ks}, p_{it}, q_{it}) = R_{it}/R_{ks}$ is a revenue index and $PI^{D}(p_{ks}, p_{it})$ is the dual output price index defined by (3.61). Other implicit output indices are obtained in a similar way. Implicit output indices are not proper indices in the sense that they do not generally satisfy QI1 to QI6. Much depends on the characteristics of production technologies and managerial behaviour. For example, if (a) firms are price takers in output markets, (b) output sets are homothetic, (c) technical change is IHON, and (d) the OAE of firm k in period s is equal to the OAE of firm i in period t, then the ID output index defined by (3.67) is equal to the primal output index defined by (3.5) (implying it satisfies QI1 to QI6).[31]

To illustrate, reconsider the output quantities and prices reported earlier in Table 1.4. Sets of associated implicit output index numbers are reported in Table 3.10. The index numbers in this table were obtained by dividing revenue index numbers by the output price index numbers in Table 3.7. In Table 3.10, the index numbers in each row compare the outputs in that row with the outputs in row A. Again, numbers that are clearly incoherent are marked with an asterisk (*). Observe, for example, that

[31] A proof is given in Appendix A.1 (Proposition 19).

Table 3.9 Terms-of-trade index numbers[a,b]

Row	p_1	p_2	w_1	w_2	L	GY	BOD	T	CT	CCD
A	0.57	0.41	0.28	1.91	1	1	1	1	1	1
B	0.26	0.25	0.22	0.58	1.286	1.17	0.823	1.415	1.415	1.325
C	0.57	0.41	0.28	1.91	1	1	1	1	1	1
D	0.58	0.53	0.16	0.41	3.9	3.552	2.509	4.137	4.137	4.029
E	0.26	0.26	0.07	1.02	1.147	1.399	1.106	1.111	1.173	1.201
F	0.59	0.76	0.24	0.29	4.6	4.451	1.939	4.345	3.961	4.501
G	0.63	0.65	0.16	0.16	6.92	7.078	2.92	7.051	5.827	6.934
H	0.34	0.31	0.17	0.7	1.599	1.489	1.231	1.746	1.132	1.542
I	0.46	0.58	0.27	0.39	2.928	2.752	1.335	1.857	1.749	2.428
J	0.61	1.43	0.29	0.79	4.004	3.261	1.963	1.975	2.157	2.935
K	0.57	0.41	0.28	1.91	1	1	1	1	0.919*	0.960*
L	0.49	0.65	0.21	0.56	3.043	2.717	1.771	3.657	3.675	3.281
M	0.51	0.46	0.16	0.74	2.339	2.206	1.889	2.455	2.416	2.352
N	0.52	0.23	0.24	2.3	0.662	0.678	0.879	0.669	0.635	0.713
O	0.37	0.17	0.24	0.15	2.136	2.378	1.016	2.885	2.375	2.527
P	0.41	0.76	0.26	0.61	2.756	2.356	1.377	2.864	2.431	2.789
R	0.53	0.48	0.16	0.22	4.812	4.628	2.38	5.938	4.304	5.213
S	0.53	0.37	0.19	0.62	2.272	2.065	1.728	2.103	2.115	2.440
T	0.91	0.53	0.17	0.26	6.027	5.579	3.528	7.176	5.298	6.355
U	0.31	1.03	0.27	0.91	2.517	1.89	1.445	2.278	2.265	2.511
V	0.47	0.08	0.29	0.78	0.962	0.64	1.017	0.886	0.586	0.760
W	0.57	0.27	0.39	0.81	1.311	1.146	0.963	1.543	0.948	1.409
X	0.31	0.51	0.21	0.31	2.981	2.707	1.261	2.491	1.993	2.797
Y	0.31	0.67	0.23	0.69	2.282	1.894	1.189	2.363	1.565	2.265
Z	0.42	0.69	0.31	0.22	3.519	3.789	1.157	4.189	2.791	3.867

[a]L = Lowe; GY = geometric Young; BOD = benefit-of-the-doubt; T = Törnqvist; CT = chained Törnqvist; CCD = Caves-Christensen-Diewert
[b]Numbers reported to less than three decimal places are exact; see the footnote to Table 1.2 on p. 8
*Incoherent (not because of rounding)

the output vector in row E is the same as the output vector in row Z, but the index numbers in row E differ from the index numbers in row Z.

3.4.5 *Implicit Input Indices*

Implicit input indices are constructed by dividing cost indices by input price indices. For example, the implicit dual (ID) index that compares the inputs of firm i in period t with the inputs of firm k in period s is

Table 3.10 Implicit output index numbers[a,b]

Row	q_1	q_2	IL	IGY	IBOD	IT	ICT	ICCD
A	1	1	1	1	1	1	1	1
B	1	1	0.984*	0.980*	1.071*	1	1	0.995*
C	2.37	2.37	2.37	2.37	2.37	2.37	2.37	2.37
D	2.11	2.11	2.083*	2.072*	2.232*	2.11	2.11	2.101*
E	1.81	3.62	2.667*	2.657*	2.937*	2.641*	2.695*	2.688*
F	1	1	0.969*	0.980*	1.154*	1	0.972*	0.989*
G	1.777	3.503	2.602	2.595	2.893	2.577	2.626	2.619
H	0.96	0.94	0.938	0.933	1.005	0.951	0.950	0.946
I	5.82	0.001	2.498	2.523	2.955	3.011	2.818	2.755
J	6.685	0.001	1.883	2.093	2.707	3.037	3.237	2.690
K	1.381	4.732	2.783	2.783	2.783	2.783	3.526	2.900
L	0.566	4.818	2.894	2.936	3.479	2.688	3.114	2.792
M	1	3	1.925*	1.914*	2.055*	1.893*	2.280*	1.954*
N	0.7	0.7	0.718*	0.758*	0.610*	0.7	0.899*	0.707*
O	2	2	2.047*	2.148*	1.763*	2.001*	2.567*	2.019*
P	1	1	0.952*	1.010*	1.272*	1.001*	1.281*	0.984*
R	1	3	1.926*	1.916*	2.059*	1.894*	2.736*	1.955*
S	1	1	1.002*	1.003*	0.993*	1	1.450*	1.001*
T	1.925	3.722	2.615	2.659	2.471	2.631	3.806*	2.703
U	1	1	0.929*	1.127*	1.235*	1.014*	1.298*	0.982*
V	1	5.166	1.708	2.327	1.135	2.070	3.543	2.250
W	2	2	2.044*	2.134*	1.780*	2.001*	3.710*	2.018*
X	1	1	0.957*	0.997*	1.232*	1	1.851*	0.985*
Y	1	1	0.945*	1.033*	1.325*	1.003*	1.851*	0.982*
Z	1.81	3.62	2.810*	2.926*	3.614*	2.766*	5.542*	2.781*

[a]IL = implicit Lowe; IGY = implicit geometric Young; IBOD = implicit benefit-of-the-doubt; IT = implicit Törnqvist; ICT = implicit chained Törnqvist; ICCD = implicit Caves-Christensen-Diewert
[b]Numbers reported to less than three decimal places are exact; see the footnote to Table 1.2 on p. 8
*Incoherent (not because of rounding)

$$XI^{ID}(x_{ks}, x_{it}, w_{ks}, w_{it}) \equiv CI(w_{ks}, x_{ks}, w_{it}, x_{it})/WI^{D}(w_{ks}, w_{it}) \tag{3.68}$$

where $CI(w_{ks}, x_{ks}, w_{it}, x_{it}) = C_{it}/C_{ks}$ is a cost index and $WI^D(w_{ks}, w_{it})$ is the dual input price index defined by (3.64). Other implicit input indices are obtained in a similar way. Implicit input indices are not proper indices in the sense that they do not generally satisfy XI1 to XI6. Again, much depends on the characteristics of production technologies and managerial behaviour. For example, if (a) firms are price takers in input markets, (b) input sets are homothetic, (c) technical change is IHIN, and (d) the IAE of firm k in period s is equal to the IAE of firm i in period t, then the ID input index defined by (3.68) is equal to the primal input index defined by (3.24) (implying it satisfies XI1 to XI6).[32]

To illustrate, reconsider the input quantities and prices reported earlier in Table 1.5. Sets of associated implicit input index numbers are reported in Table 3.11. The index numbers in this table were obtained by dividing cost index numbers by the input price index numbers in Table 3.8. In Table 3.11, the index numbers in each row compare the inputs in that row with the inputs in row A. Again, numbers that are clearly incoherent are marked with an asterisk (*). Observe, for example, that the input vector in row T is the same as the input vector in row A, but the index numbers in row T differ from one.

3.4.6 Implicit Productivity Indices

Implicit productivity indices are constructed by dividing implicit output indices by implicit input indices (equivalently, by dividing profitability indices by terms-of-trade indices). For example, the implicit dual (ID) index that compares the TFP of firm i in period t with the TFP of firm k in period s is

$$TFPI^{ID}(x_{ks}, q_{ks}, x_{it}, q_{it}, \ldots) \equiv QI^{ID}(q_{ks}, q_{it}, \ldots)/XI^{ID}(x_{ks}, x_{it}, \ldots) \quad (3.69)$$

where $QI^{ID}(q_{ks}, q_{it}, \ldots)$ is the ID output index defined by (3.67) and $XI^{ID}(x_{ks}, x_{it}, \ldots)$ is the ID input index defined by (3.68). Other implicit TFPIs are obtained in a similar way. These are not proper indices in the sense that they cannot generally be written as proper output indices divided by proper input indices; this implies they do not generally satisfy TI1 to TI6. Again, much depends on the characteristics of production technologies and managerial behaviour. For example, (a) if firms are price takers in output and input marketsindexprice taker!in input markets, (b) output and input sets are homothetic, (c) technical change is HN, and (d) the OAE and IAE of firm k in period s are equal to the OAE and IAE of firm i in period t, then the ID TFPI defined by (3.69) is equal to the primal TFPI defined by (3.44) (implying it satisfies TI1 to TI6).[33]

To illustrate, reconsider the output and input quantities and prices reported in Tables 1.4 and 1.5. Sets of associated implicit TFPI numbers are reported in Table 3.12. These numbers were obtained by dividing the implicit output index numbers in Table 3.10 by the corresponding implicit input index numbers in Table 3.11. In Table 3.12, the index numbers in any given row compare the inputs and outputs in that row with the inputs and outputs in row A. Again, numbers that are clearly incoherent are marked with an asterisk (*). Observe, for example, that the output

[32] A proof is given in Appendix A.1 (Proposition 20).

[33] A proof is given in Appendix A.1 (Proposition 21).

Table 3.11 Implicit input index numbers[a,b]

Row	x_1	x_2	IL	IGY	IBOD	IT	ICT	ICCD
A	1	1	1	1	1	1	1	1
B	0.56	0.56	0.498*	0.451*	0.347*	0.556*	0.556*	0.518*
C	1	1	1	1	1	1	1	1
D	1.05	0.7	0.706*	0.640*	0.487*	0.759*	0.759*	0.736*
E	1.05	0.7	0.764*	0.928*	0.811*	0.732*	0.789*	0.806*
F	0.996	0.316	0.489	0.478	0.245*	0.476	0.422	0.488
G	1.472	0.546	0.766	0.781	0.359	0.773	0.651	0.773
H	0.017	0.346	0.266	0.247	0.220	0.295	0.191	0.259
I	4.545	0.01	1.505	1.428	0.812	1.150	1.014	1.376
J	4.45	0.001	1.068	0.967	0.753	0.850	0.989	1.118
K	1	1	1	1	1	1	1.164*	1
L	1	1	0.890*	0.806*	0.623*	0.994*	1.157*	0.926*
M	1.354	1	1.020	0.957	0.879	1.052	1.248	1.041
N	0.33	0.16	0.181	0.196	0.204	0.179	0.217	0.192
O	1	1	0.707*	0.825*	0.289*	0.933*	0.985*	0.825*
P	0.657	0.479	0.465*	0.422*	0.310*	0.508	0.552	0.486
R	1	1	0.800*	0.765*	0.423*	0.971*	1.016*	0.880*
S	1.933	0.283	0.614	0.559	0.463	0.567	0.828	0.659
T	1	1	0.814*	0.767*	0.450*	0.975*	1.042*	0.887*
U	1	0.31	0.431	0.393	0.329	0.426	0.542	0.455
V	1	1	0.891*	0.807*	0.625*	0.994*	1.125*	0.927*
W	0.919	0.919	0.787*	0.718*	0.504*	0.907*	1.034*	0.835*
X	1.464	0.215	0.582	0.551	0.317	0.509	0.753	0.563
Y	0.74	0.74	0.670*	0.608*	0.490*	0.737*	0.901*	0.691*
Z	2.1	1.4	1.302*	1.460*	0.551*	1.526*	2.037*	1.416*

[a]IL = implicit Lowe; IGY = implicit geometric Young; IBOD = implicit benefit-of-the-doubt; IT = implicit Törnqvist; ICT = implicit chained Törnqvist; ICCD = implicit Caves-Christensen-Diewert
[b]Numbers reported to less than three decimal places are exact; see the footnote to Table 1.2 on p. 8
*Incoherent (not because of rounding)

vector in row Z is the same as the output vector in row E, and the input vector in row Z is twice as big as the input vector in row E, but the index numbers in row Z are not half as big as the index numbers in row E.

3.5 Summary and Further Reading

Measuring changes in productivity involves assigning numbers to baskets of outputs and inputs. Measurement theory says that so-called index numbers should be assigned in such a way that the relationships between the numbers mirror the relationships

Table 3.12 Implicit TFPI numbers[a,b]

Row	q_1	q_2	x_1	x_2	IL	IGY	IBOD	IT	ICT	ICCD
A	1	1	1	1	1	1	1	1	1	1
B	1	1	0.56	0.56	1.978*	2.174*	3.091*	1.798*	1.798*	1.920*
C	2.37	2.37	1	1	2.37	2.37	2.37	2.37	2.37	2.37
D	2.11	2.11	1.05	0.7	2.949	3.238	4.585	2.781	2.781	2.855
E	1.81	3.62	1.05	0.7	3.492*	2.863*	3.622*	3.607*	3.415*	3.336*
F	1	1	0.996	0.316	1.983	2.050	4.704	2.099	2.303	2.027
G	1.777	3.503	1.472	0.546	3.397	3.321	8.049	3.334	4.034	3.390
H	0.96	0.94	0.017	0.346	3.523	3.784	4.575	3.226	4.978	3.652
I	5.82	0.001	4.545	0.01	1.660	1.766	3.640	2.618	2.779	2.002
J	6.685	0.001	4.45	0.001	1.763	2.165	3.597	3.574	3.272	2.405
K	1.381	4.732	1	1	2.783	2.783	2.783	2.783	3.029	2.900
L	0.566	4.818	1	1	3.251	3.642	5.588	2.705	2.692	3.015
M	1	3	1.354	1	1.888	2.001	2.337	1.798	1.827	1.877
N	0.7	0.7	0.33	0.16	3.960	3.870	2.986	3.922	4.134	3.681
O	2	2	1	1	2.897*	2.602*	6.091*	2.145*	2.606*	2.449*
P	1	1	0.657	0.479	2.049	2.397	4.100	1.972	2.322	2.024
R	1	3	1	1	2.408	2.503	4.868	1.951	2.692	2.222
S	1	1	1.933	0.283	1.631	1.795	2.145	1.762	1.752	1.518
T	1.925	3.722	1	1	3.211	3.469	5.487	2.697	3.653	3.046
U	1	1	1	0.31	2.155	2.869	3.753	2.381	2.395	2.160
V	1	5.166	1	1	1.917	2.883	1.815	2.083	3.150	2.428
W	2	2	0.919	0.919	2.597*	2.972*	3.534*	2.206*	3.590*	2.416*
X	1	1	1.464	0.215	1.643	1.809	3.883	1.966	2.457	1.751
Y	1	1	0.74	0.74	1.410*	1.698*	2.706*	1.361*	2.055*	1.421*
Z	1.81	3.62	2.1	1.4	2.157*	2.004*	6.561*	1.812*	2.720*	1.963*

[a]IL = implicit Lowe; IGY = implicit geometric Young; IBOD = implicit benefit-of-the-doubt; IT = implicit Törnqvist; ICT = implicit chained Törnqvist; ICCD = implicit Caves-Christensen-Diewert
[b]Numbers reported to less than three decimal places are exact; see the footnote to Table 1.2 on p. 8
*Incoherent (not because of rounding)

between the baskets. In practice, assigning numbers to baskets of outputs and inputs involves weighting the outputs and inputs in each basket. One way of ensuring that the numbers are consistent with measurement theory is to use weights that do not vary from one basket to the next. Some authors claim this fixed-weight approach is absurd; for a recent discussion, see Diewert and Fox (2017, p. 279). The scientific basis for these claims is unclear.[34]

In this book, an index that compares the outputs of firm i in period t with the outputs of firm k in period s is defined as any variable of the form $QI(q_{ks}, q_{it}) \equiv$

[34]Some observers put these claims down to hubris. See, for example, Samuelson and Swamy (1974, p. 575).

$Q(q_{it})/Q(q_{ks})$ where $Q(.)$ is a nonnegative, nondecreasing, linearly-homogeneous, scalar-valued aggregator function. Similarly, on the input side, an index that compares the inputs of firm i in period t with the inputs of firm k in period s is defined as any variable of the form $XI(x_{ks}, x_{it}) \equiv X(x_{it})/X(x_{ks})$ where $X(.)$ is also a nonnegative, nondecreasing, linearly-homogeneous, scalar-valued function. Output and input indices of this type yield numbers that are consistent with measurement theory. They are also proper in the sense that, if outputs and inputs are positive, then they satisfy a set of axioms listed in O'Donnell (2016). Two of the most important axioms are a transitivity axiom and a proportionality axiom. The O'Donnell (2016) axioms are weaker than most of the axioms (often called tests) discussed in the mainstream index number literature (e.g., Diewert 1992; Balk 2008, pp. 58–61). These other axioms/tests are relatively strong because they say something about price change as well as quantity change. Not all of these other axioms/tests can be satisfied simultaneously; details can be accessed from Diewert (1992) and Balk (2008, Ch. 3).

Any nonnegative, nondecreasing, linearly-homogeneous, scalar-valued aggregator function can be used for purposes of constructing a proper quantity index. The choice of function is generally a matter of taste. Linear functions can be used to construct additive indices; examples include the Lowe output and input indices defined by O'Donnell (2012c, p. 877) and the output and input 'factors' defined by Daraio and Simar (2007, Eqs. 6.1, 6.2). Double-log functions can be used to construct multiplicative indices; examples include the geometric young (GY) output and input indices defined by O'Donnell (2012b, 2016). Other functions that have been used to construct quantity indices include constant elasticity of substitution (CES) and fixed-proportions functions; the use of these functions in an index number context can be traced back at least as far as Samuelson and Swamy (1974, p. 574). If outputs (resp. inputs) are strongly disposable, then output (resp. input) distance functions can be used to construct primal output (resp. input) indices; examples include the output and input indices of Färe and Primont (1995, pp. 36, 38) and O'Donnell (2016, Eqs. 2, 3). If cost (resp. revenue) functions are homogeneous in outputs (resp. inputs), then they can be used to construct dual output (resp. input) indices; an example is the output index defined by O'Donnell (2012b, Eq. 3). Finally, locally-linear functions can be used to construct benefit-of-the-doubt (BOD) indices; examples include the output and input indices described by O'Donnell and Nguyen (2013), the 'human development' indices of Mahlberg and Obersteiner (2001) and Despotis (2005), and the 'technology achievement' index of Cherchye et al. (2008). The additive, multiplicative, primal and dual indices discussed in this book are all fixed-weight indices, whereas the BOD indices are variable-weight indices. They are all proper indices, and they all yield numbers that are consistent with measurement theory.

Quantity indices that are not proper include various binary, chained and multilateral indices. Binary quantity indices are designed for comparing two quantity vectors only. They do not generally satisfy the transitivity axiom. The binary output and input indices discussed in this chapter include Fisher, Törnqvist and generalised Malmquist (GM) indices. Chained quantity indices are mainly used for comparing the outputs or inputs of a single firm over several time periods. They do not generally satisfy the proportionality axiom. The chained quantity indices discussed in this chapter include chained Fisher (CF), chained Törnqvist (CT) and chained GM (CGM) indices. Finally, multilateral quantity indices are mainly used for comparing the outputs or inputs of several firms in a single time period. Again, they do not generally satisfy the proportionality axiom. The multilateral quantity indices discussed in this chapter include Elteto-Koves-Szulc (EKS), Caves-Christensen-Diewert (CCD) and multilateral GM (MGM) indices.

Measuring changes in outputs and inputs is a precursor to measuring changes in TFP. In this book, a proper TFP index (TFPI) is defined as any proper output index divided by any proper input index. Again, the choice of indices is generally a matter of taste. Additive TFPIs are constructed by dividing additive output indices by additive input indices; an example is the Lowe TFPI defined by O'Donnell (2012c, p. 877). Multiplicative TFPIs are constructed by dividing multiplicative output indices by multiplicative input indices; examples include the GDF-based index defined by Portela and Thanassoulis (2006, Eq. 4) and the GY index defined by O'Donnell (2016, Eq. 5). Primal TFPIs are constructed by dividing primal output indices by primal input indices; examples include the Färe-Primont index defined by O'Donnell (2014, Eq. 11) and the 'general' index defined by O'Donnell (2016, Eq. 4). Dual TFPIs are constructed by dividing dual output indices by dual input indices. BOD TFPIs are constructed by dividing BOD output indices by BOD input indices. For empirical applications of proper TFPIs, see, for example, O'Donnell (2012c), Tozer and Villano (2013), Islam et al. (2014), Laurenceson and O'Donnell (2014), Khan et al. (2015), Pan and Walden (2015), Fissel et al. (2015), Mugera et al. (2016), Carrington et al. (2016), Anik et al. (2017), Baráth and Fertö (2017) and Briec et al. (2018).[35]

There are many productivity indices that cannot be written as proper output indices divided by proper input indices. These include various binary, chained and multilateral TFP indices. Again, binary TFP indices are designed for making binary comparisons. Again, they are not generally transitive. The binary TFP indices discussed in this chapter include Fisher, Törnqvist, GM, Hicks-Moorsteen (HM), output-oriented Malmquist (OM), and input-oriented Malmquist (IM) indices. Other binary TFP indices include the 'indirect Malmquist (input based)' productivity index of Färe and Grosskopf (1990, Eq. 3.3) and the 'cost Malmquist' productivity index of Maniadakis and Thanassoulis (2004, Eq. 15). Even though these indices are binary indices, they are often used, inappropriately, to make multiperiod and/or multilateral comparisons: for applications of Fisher TFPIs in a multiperiod and/or multilateral setting, see Ray and Mukherjee (1996), Kuosmanen and Sipiläinen (2009), Sheng et al. (2011) and Khan et al. (2017); for an application of the Törnqvist TFPI, see Elnasri and Fox (2017); for applications of the HM TFPI, see O'Donnell (2010b), Arora and Arora (2013), Arjomandi et al. (2014), Arjomandi et al. (2015), See and Li (2015) and Deaza et al. (2016); for applications of the OM TFPI, see Färe et al. (1994),

[35]Many of these authors use either the DPIN software of O'Donnell (2010a) or the R package of Dakpo et al. (2016) to compute 'Färe-Primont' TFPI numbers. In this book, these index numbers are viewed as additive index numbers obtained using estimated representative normalised shadow prices as weights.

Coelli and Rao (2005) and Worthington and Lee (2008); for applications of the IM TFPI, see Suhariyanto and Thirtle (2001) and Rahman (2007).

Chained productivity indices are mainly used for comparing the TFP of a single firm over several time periods. Again, they do not generally satisfy a proportionality axiom. The chained TFPIs discussed in this chapter include CF, CT and CGM indices. For an empirical application of the CF TFPI, see Economic Inisights (2014). For an empirical application of the CT TFPI, see See and Coelli (2013, Table 4).

Multilateral productivity indices are mainly used for comparing the TFP of several firms in a single time period. Again, they do not generally satisfy a proportionality axiom. The multilateral TFPIs discussed in this chapter include EKS, CCD and MGM indices. For an empirical application of the CCD TFPI, see Bao (2014).

Other types of indices discussed in this chapter include output price, input price, terms-of-trade, implicit output, implicit input and implicit productivity indices. Implicit output (resp. input) indices are obtained by dividing revenue (resp. cost) indices by output price (resp. input price) indices. Implicit productivity indices are obtained by dividing profitability indices by terms-of-trade indices. Implicit indices are not generally consistent with measurement theory. For empirical applications of implicit output indices, see Fox et al. (2003), Ball et al. (2004) and Lawrence et al. (2006).

Measures of change that are not discussed in this book include various indicators. The composite quantity indicator of Blancas et al. (2013, Eq. 5) can be viewed as a multiplicative BOD index; it yields numbers that are not consistent with measurement theory. The Luenberger productivity indicator of Chambers et al. (1996) is based on differences rather than ratios; it cannot be written as a proper output quantity index divided by a proper input quantity index.

References

Aczel J, Eichhorn W (1974) A note on additive indices. J Econ Theory 8(4):525–529

Anik AR, Rahman S, Sarker J (2017) Agricultural productivity growth and the role of capital in South Asia (1980–2013). Sustainability 9(3):470

Arjomandi A, Valadkhani A, O'Brien M (2014) Analysing banks' intermediation and operational performance using the Hicks-Moorsteen TFP index: the case of Iran. Res Int Bus Finance 30:111–125

Arjomandi A, Salleh MI, Mohammadzadeh A (2015) Measuring productivity change in higher education: an application of Hicks-Moorsteen total factor productivity index to Malaysian public universities. J Asia Pac Econ 20(4):630–643

Arora H, Arora P (2013) Measuring and decomposing productivity change using Hicks-Moorsteen index numbers: evidence from Indian banks. Int J Prod Qual Manag 11(1):74–95

Balk B (1998) Industrial price, quantity, and productivity indices: the micro-economic theory and an application. Kluwer Academic Publishers, Boston

Balk B (2008) Price and quantity index numbers: models for measuring aggregate change and difference. Cambridge University Press, New York

Balk B, Diewert W (2003) The Lowe consumer price index and its substitution bias. Department of Economics Discussion Paper 04-07, University of British Colombia

Ball V, Hallahan C, Nehring R (2004) Convergence of productivity: an analysis of the catch-up hypothesis within a panel of states. Am J Agric Econ 86(5):1315–1321

Bao H (2014) Provincial total factor productivity in Vietnamese agriculture and its determinants. J Econ Dev 16(2):5–20

Baráth L, Fertö I (2017) Productivity and convergence in European agriculture. J Agric Econ 68(1):228–248

Beavis B, Dobbs I (1990) Optimization and stability theory for economic analysis. Cambridge University Press, Cambridge

Bjurek H (1996) The Malmquist total factor productivity index. Scand J Econ 98(2):303–313

Blancas F, Contreras I, Ramirez-Hurtado J (2013) Constructing a composite indicator with multiplicative aggregation under the objective of ranking alternatives. J Oper Res Soc 64(5):668–678

Briec W, Kerstens K (2011) The Hicks-Moorsteen productivity index satisfies the determinateness axiom. Manch Sch 79(4):765–775

Briec W, Kerstens K, Prior D, Van de Woestyne I (2018) Testing general and special Färe-Primont indices: a proposal for public and private sector synthetic indices of European regional expenditures and tourism. Eur J Oper Res (forthcoming)

Carrington R, O'Donnell C, Rao D (2016) Australian university productivity growth and public funding revisited. Stud High Educ pp 1–22. https://doi.org/10.1080/03075,079.2016.1259,306

Caves D, Christensen L, Diewert W (1982a) The economic theory of index numbers and the measurement of input, output, and productivity. Econometrica 50(6):1393–1414

Caves D, Christensen L, Diewert W (1982b) Multilateral comparisons of output, input, and productivity using superlative index numbers. Econ J 92(365):73–86

Chambers R, Färe R, Grosskopf S (1996) Productivity growth in APEC countries. Pac Econ Rev 1(3):181–190

Cherchye L, Moesen W, Rogge N, van Puyenbroeck T (2007) An introduction to 'benefit of the doubt' composite indicators. Soc Indic Res 82(1):111–145

Cherchye L, Moesen W, Rogge N, van Puyenbroeck T, Saisana M, Saltelli A, Liska R, Tarantola S (2008) Creating composite indicators with DEA and robustness analysis: the case of the Technology Achievement Index. J Oper Res Soc 59(2):239–251

Coelli T, Rao D (2005) Total factor productivity growth in agriculture: a Malmquist index analysis of 93 countries, 1980–2000. Agric Econ 32(s1):115–134

Coelli T, Rao D, O'Donnell C, Battese G (2005) An introduction to efficiency and productivity analysis, 2nd edn. Springer, New York

Dakpo K, Desjeax Y, Latruffe L (2016) Productivity: indices of productivity using Data Envelopment Analysis (DEA). R Package Version 0.1.0, https://cran.r-project.org/web/packages/productivity/productivity.pdf

Daraio C, Simar L (2007) Advanced robust and nonparametric methods in efficiency analysis: methodology and applications. Springer, Berlin

Deaza J, Gilles E, Vivas A (2016) Productivity measurements for South Korea and three countries of the Pacific Alliance: Colombia, Chile and Mexico, 2008–2012. Appl Econ Int Dev 16(2):75–92

Despotis D (2005) A reassessment of the Human Development Index via data envelopment analysis. J Oper Res Soc 56(8):969–980

Diewert W (1976) Exact and superlative index numbers. J Econ 4(2):115–145

Diewert W (1992) Fisher ideal output, input, and productivity indexes revisited. J Prod Anal 3(3):211–248

Diewert W, Fox K (2017) Decomposing productivity indexes into explanatory factors. Eur J Oper Res 256(1):275–291

Drechsler L (1973) Weighting of index numbers in multilateral international comparisons. Rev Income Wealth 19(1):17–34

Economic Inisights (2014) Economic benchmarking assessment of operating expenditure for NSW and Tasmanian electricity TNSPs. Report prepared by Denis Lawrence, Tim Coelli and John Kain for the Australian Energy Regulator

Elnasri A, Fox K (2017) The contribution of research and innovation to productivity. J Prod Anal 47(3):291–308

Elteto O, Koves P (1964) On a problem of index number computation relating to international comparison. Statisztikai Szemle 42:507–518
Färe R, Grosskopf S (1990) The Fisher ideal index and the indirect Malmquist productivity index: a comparison. New Zealand Econ Pap 24(1):66–72
Färe R, Primont D (1995) Multi-output production and duality: theory and applications. Kluwer Academic Publishers, Boston
Färe R, Grosskopf S, Lindgren B, Roos P (1992) Productivity changes in Swedish pharmacies 1980–1989: a non-parametric Malmquist approach. J Prod Anal 3:85–101
Färe R, Grosskopf S, Norris M, Zhang Z (1994) Productivity growth, technical progress, and efficiency change in industrialized countries. Am Econ Rev 84(1):66–83
Fisher I (1922) The making of index numbers. Houghton Mifflin, Boston
Fissel B, Felthoven R, Kaperski S, O'Donnell C (2015) Decomposing productivity and efficiency changes in the Alaska head and gut factory trawl fleet. Mar Policy. https://doi.org/10.1016/j.marpol.2015.06.018i
Fox K, Grafton Q, Kirkley J, Squires D (2003) Property rights in a fishery: regulatory change and firm performance. J Environ Econ Manage 46(1):156–177
Grifell-Tatjé E, Lovell C (1995) A note on the Malmquist productivity index. Econ Lett 47:169–175
Hicks J (1961) Measurement of capital in relation to the measurement of other economic aggregates. Macmillan, London
Hill P (2008) Lowe indices. In: Paper presented at the 2008 World Congress on national accounts and economic performance measures for nations, Washington, DC
Hill R, Griffiths W, Lim G (2011) Principles of econometrics, 4th edn. Wiley, Hoboken
Hosch W (ed) (2011) The britannica guide to numbers and measurement, 1st edn. Britannica Educational Publishing, Chicago
IMF (2004) Producer price index manual: theory and practice. published for the ILO, IMF, OECD, UNECE and World Bank by the International Monetary Fund, Washington, DC
Islam N, Xayavong V, Kingwell R (2014) Broadacre farm productivity and profitability in South-Western Australia. Aust J Agric Resour Econ 58(2):147–170
Kerstens K, Van de Woestyne I (2014) Comparing the Malmquist and Hicks-Moorsteen productivity indices: Exploring the impact of unbalanced versus balanced panel data. Eur J Oper Res 233:749–758
Khan F, Salim R, Bloch H (2015) Nonparametric estimates of productivity and efficiency change in Australian broadacre agriculture. Aust J Agric Resour Econ 59(3):393–411
Khan F, Salim R, Bloch H, Islam N (2017) The public R&D and productivity growth in Australia's broadacre agriculture: Is there a link? Aust J Agric Resour Econ 61(2):285–303
Kuosmanen T, Sipiläinen T (2009) Exact decomposition of the Fisher ideal total factor productivity index. J Prod Anal 31(3):137–150
Laurenceson J, O'Donnell CJ (2014) New estimates and a decomposition of provincial productivity change in China. China Econ Rev 30:86–97
Lawrence D, Diewert W, Fox K (2006) The contributions of productivity, price changes and firm size to profitability. J Prod Anal 26(1):1–13
Mahlberg B, Obersteiner M (2001) Remeasuring the HDI by data envelopment analysis. Interim Report IR-01-069, International Institute for Applied Systems Analysis (IIASA), Laxenburg, Austria
Maniadakis N, Thanassoulis E (2004) A cost Malmquist productivity index. Eur J Oper Res 154(2):396–409
Melyn W, Moesen W (1991) Towards a synthetic indicator of macroeconomic performance: unequal weighting when limited information is available. Public Economics Research Paper 17, CES, KU Leuven
Mizobuchi H (2017) Productivity indexes under Hicks neutral technical change. J Prod Anal 48:63–68
Moorsteen R (1961) On measuring productive potential and relative efficiency. Q J Econ 75(3):151–167

Mugera A, Langemeier M, Ojede A (2016) Contributions of productivity and relative price change to farm-level profitability change. Am J Agric Econ 98(4):1210–1229
O'Donnell C (2010a) DPIN version 1.0: A program for decomposing productivity index numbers. Centre for Efficiency and Productivity Analysis Working Papers WP01/2010, University of Queensland
O'Donnell C (2010b) Measuring and decomposing agricultural productivity and profitability change. Aust J Agric Resour Econ 54(4):527–560
O'Donnell C (2012a) An aggregate quantity framework for measuring and decomposing productivity change. J Prod Anal 38(3):255–272
O'Donnell C (2012b) Alternative indexes for multiple comparisons of quantities and prices. Centre for Efficiency and Productivity Analysis Working Papers WP05/2012 (Version 21 May 2013), University of Queensland
O'Donnell C (2012c) Nonparametric estimates of the components of productivity and profitability change in U.S. agriculture. Am J Agric Econ 94(4):873–890
O'Donnell C (2013) Econometric estimates of productivity and efficiency change in the Australian northern prawn fishery. In: Mamula A, Walden J (eds) Proceedings of the National Marine Fisheries Service Workshop, U.S. Department of Commerce National Oceanic and Atmospheric Administration
O'Donnell C (2014) Econometric estimation of distance functions and associated measures of productivity and efficiency change. J Prod Anal 41(2):187–200
O'Donnell C (2016) Using information about technologies, markets and firm behaviour to decompose a proper productivity index. J Econ 190(2):328–340
O'Donnell C, Nguyen K (2013) An econometric approach to estimating support prices and measures of productivity change in public hospitals. J Prod Anal 40(3):323–335
Pan M, Walden J (2015) Measuring productivity in a shared stock fishery: a case study of the Hawaii longline fishery. Mar Policy 62:302–308
Rahman S (2007) Regional productivity and convergence in Bangladesh agriculture. J Dev Areas 41(1):221–236
Ray S, Mukherjee K (1996) Decomposition of the Fisher ideal index of productivity: a non-parametric dual analysis of US airlines data. Econ J 106(439):1659–1678
Samuelson P, Swamy S (1974) Invariant economic index numbers and canonical duality: survey and synthesis. Am Econ Rev 64(4):566–593
Sarle W (1997) Measurement theory: frequently asked questions. ftp://ftp.sas.com/pub/neural/measurement.html
See K, Coelli T (2013) Estimating and decomposing productivity growth of the electricity generation industry in Malaysia: a stochastic frontier analysis. Energy Policy 62(207–214)
See K, Li F (2015) Total factor productivity analysis of the UK airport industry: a Hicks-Moorsteen index method. J Air Transp Manag 43(March):1–10
Sheng Y, Mullen J, Zhao S (2011) A turning point in agricultural productivity: consideration of the causes. Research Report 11.4, Australian Bureau of Agricultural and Resource Economics and Sciences
Silva Portela M, Thanassoulis E (2006) Malmquist indexes using a geometric distance function (GDF). Application to a sample of Portuguese bank branches. J Prod Anal 25(1):25–41
Suhariyanto K, Thirtle C (2001) Asian agricultural productivity and convergence. J Agric Econ 52(3):96–110
Szulc B (1964) Indices for multi-regional comparisons. Prezeglad Statystyczny (Stat Rev) 3:239–254
Tal E (2016) Measurement in science. In: Zalta EN (ed) The Stanford encyclopedia of philosophy, winter, 2016th edn. Stanford University, Metaphysics Research Lab
Tozer P, Villano R (2013) Decomposing productivity and efficiency among Western Australian grain producers. J Agric Resour Econ 38(3):312–326
Worthington A, Lee B (2008) Efficiency, technology and productivity change in Australian universities, 1998–2003. Econ Educ Rev 27(3):285–298

Chapter 4
Managerial Behaviour

To explain changes in outputs and inputs, and therefore changes in productivity, we need to know something about managerial behaviour. The existence of different sets and functions has few, if any, implications for behaviour. The existence of revenue functions, for example, does not mean that managers will choose outputs in order to maximise revenues, and the existence of cost functions does not mean they will choose inputs to minimise costs. Instead, different managers will tend to behave differently depending on what they value, and on what they can and cannot choose. For example, if managers value goods and services at market prices, then, if possible, they will tend to choose outputs and inputs to maximise profits. On the other hand, if managers value products and services differently to the market, then they may instead choose outputs and inputs to maximise measures of productivity. This chapter discusses some of the simplest optimisation problems faced by firm managers.

4.1 Output Maximisation

If a firm manager places nonnegative values on outputs (not necessarily market values) and all other variables involved in the production process have been predetermined (i.e., determined in a previous period), then (s)he will generally aim to maximise a measure of total output. If there is more than one output, then the precise form of the manager's output maximisation problem will depend on how easily (s)he can choose the output mix.

4.1.1 Output Mix Predetermined

If the manager of firm i can only choose output vectors that are scalar multiples of q_{it}, then his/her period-t output-maximisation problem can be written as

C. J. O'Donnell, *Productivity and Efficiency Analysis*,
https://doi.org/10.1007/978-981-13-2984-5_4

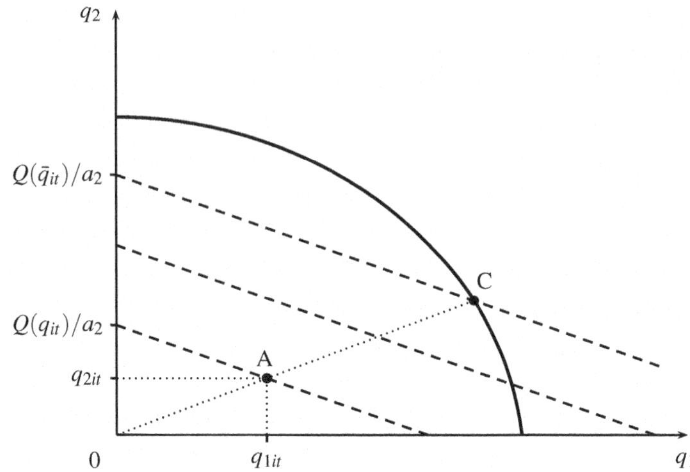

Fig. 4.1 Output maximisation when the output mix has been predetermined. If the output mix of firm i had been predetermined, then the manager could have maximised total output by operating at point C

$$\max_q \{Q(q) : q \propto q_{it},\ D_O^t(x_{it}, q, z_{it}) \le 1\} \tag{4.1}$$

where $Q(.)$ is any nonnegative, nondecreasing, linearly-homogeneous, scalar-valued aggregator function satisfying $Q(q_{it}) > 0$. The output vector that solves this problem is $\bar{q}_{it} \equiv \bar{q}^t(x_{it}, q_{it}, z_{it}) = q_{it}/D_O^t(x_{it}, q_{it}, z_{it})$. This vector is unique and does not depend on the particular form of the aggregator function. The associated aggregate output is $Q(\bar{q}_{it}) = Q(q_{it})/D_O^t(x_{it}, q_{it}, z_{it})$. The associated value of the output distance function is $D_O^t(x_{it}, \bar{q}_{it}, z_{it}) = 1$. This implies that the output-maximising point lies on the boundary of $P^t(x_{it}, z_{it})$ (i.e., on the production frontier).

To illustrate, suppose there are only two outputs. Also suppose that $Q(q) = a_1q_1 + a_2q_2$ where a_1 and a_2 are both positive. Figure 4.1 depicts the output maximisation problem that would have faced the manager of firm i in period t had the firm's output mix been predetermined. In this figure, the curve passing through point C represents the boundary of $P^t(x_{it}, z_{it})$. The outputs of firm i in period t map to point A. The aggregate output at this point is $Q(q_{it})$. The dashed line passing through point A is an iso-output line[1] with a slope of $-a_1/a_2$ and a vertical intercept of $Q(q_{it})/a_2$. The other dashed lines are iso-output lines with the same slope but higher intercepts. Output maximisation involves choosing the iso-output line with the highest intercept that passes through a technically-feasible point. If the output mix of firm i had been predetermined, then the manager could have maximised total output by operating at point C. The aggregate output at this point is $Q(\bar{q}_{it})$. For a numerical example, see Sect. 1.4.1.

[1] If $Q(q_{it}) = a_1q_{1it} + a_2q_{2it}$, then $q_{2it} = Q(q_{it})/a_2 - (a_1/a_2)q_{1it}$. This is the equation of a line with a slope of $-a_1/a_2$ and an intercept of $Q(q_{it})/a_2$. The term *iso*-output derives from the fact that all points on this line yield the *same* aggregate output, namely $Q(q_{it})$.

4.1.2 Outputs Chosen Freely

If outputs are strongly disposable, then it is technically possible for firm managers to choose them freely. If the manager of firm i can choose outputs freely, then his/her period-t output-maximisation problem can be written as

$$\max_{q}\{Q(q) : D_O^t(x_{it}, q, z_{it}) \leq 1\} \tag{4.2}$$

where $Q(.)$ is a nonnegative, nondecreasing, linearly-homogeneous, scalar-valued aggregator function with parameters (or weights) that represent the values the manager places on outputs. If there is more than one output, then there may be several output vectors that solve this problem. Let $\hat{q}_{it} \equiv \hat{q}^t(x_{it}, z_{it})$ denote one such vector. The associated maximum aggregate output is $Q(\hat{q}_{it})$. If both the aggregator function and the output distance function are differentiable, then this solution can be characterised in terms of the marginal effects discussed in Sect. 2.4.2. For example, let $\hat{q}_{nit}$ denote the n-th element of $\hat{q}_{it}$. If there exists an n such that $\partial Q(\hat{q}_{it})/\partial \hat{q}_{nit} > 0$ and $p_n^t(x_{it}, \hat{q}_{it}, z_{it}) > 0$, then $D_O^t(x_{it}, \hat{q}_{it}, z_{it}) = 1$. This implies that the output-maximising point lies on the production frontier. As another example, if both $\hat{q}_{nit}$ and $\hat{q}_{kit}$ are positive, then $MRT_{kn}^t(x_{it}, \hat{q}_{it}, z_{it}) = [\partial Q(\hat{q}_{it})/\partial \hat{q}_{nit}]/'[\partial Q(\hat{q}_{it})/\partial \hat{q}_{kit}]$. This implies that total output will be maximised at a point where an iso-output line (or curve, if the aggregator function is nonlinear) is tangent to the production frontier.

To illustrate, reconsider the output-maximisation problem depicted in Fig. 4.1. Relevant parts of that figure are now reproduced in Fig. 4.2. In these figures, the dashed lines are iso-output lines with a slope of $-a_1/a_2$. Output maximisation involves choosing the iso-output line with the highest intercept that passes through

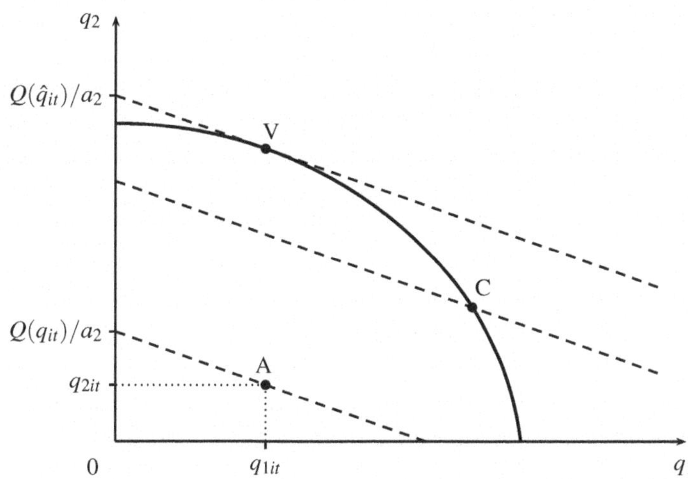

Fig. 4.2 Output maximisation when outputs can be chosen freely. If the manager of firm i had been able to choose outputs freely, then (s)he could have maximised total output by operating at point V

a technically-feasible point. If the manager of firm i had been able to choose outputs freely, then (s)he could have maximised total output by operating at point V. The aggregate output at this point is $Q(\hat{q}_{it})$.

4.1.3 Example

The output vector that solves (4.1) depends on the output distance function. If the output distance function is given by (2.9), then

$$\bar{q}^t(x_{it}, q_{it}, z_{it}) = q_{it}\left(A(t)\prod_{j=1}^{J} z_{jit}^{\delta_j}\prod_{m=1}^{M} x_{mit}^{\beta_m}\right)\left(\sum_{n=1}^{N}\gamma_n q_{nit}^{\tau}\right)^{-1/\tau}. \tag{4.3}$$

The output vector that solves (4.2) depends on both the output distance function and the aggregator function. Suppose that $Q(q) = a'q$ where $a = (a_1, \ldots, a_N)' > 0$. If the output distance function is given by (2.9) and $\tau > 1$, then the n-th element of $\hat{q}^t(x_{it}, z_{it})$ is

$$\hat{q}_n^t(x_{it}, z_{it}) = \left(A(t)\prod_{j=1}^{J} z_{jit}^{\delta_j}\prod_{m=1}^{M} x_{mit}^{\beta_m}\right)\left(\frac{\gamma_n}{a_n}\right)^{\sigma}\left(\sum_{k=1}^{N}\gamma_k^{\sigma} a_k^{1-\sigma}\right)^{\sigma/(1-\sigma)} \tag{4.4}$$

where $\sigma = 1/(1-\tau) < 0$.

4.2 Input Minimisation

If a firm manager places nonnegative values on inputs (again, not necessarily market values) and all other variables involved in the production process have been predetermined, then (s)he will generally aim to minimise a measure of total input. If there is more than one input, then the exact form of the manager's input minimisation problem will depend on how easily (s)he can choose the input mix.

4.2.1 Input Mix Predetermined

If the manager of firm i can only use input vectors that are scalar multiples of x_{it}, then his/her period-t input-minimisation problem can be written as

$$\min_{x}\{X(x) : x \propto x_{it},\ D_I^t(x, q_{it}, z_{it}) \geq 1\} \tag{4.5}$$

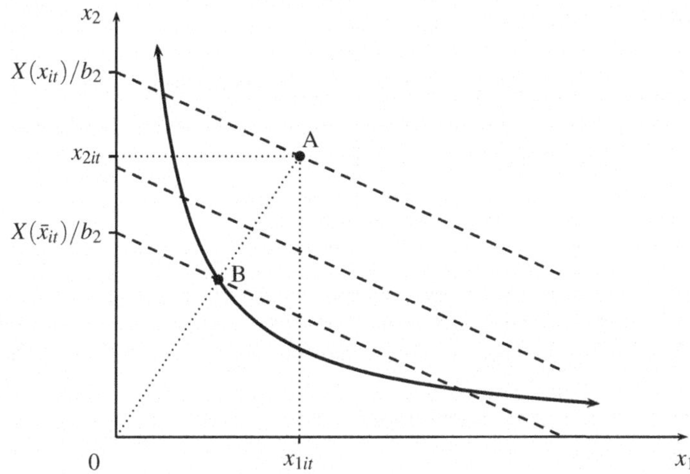

Fig. 4.3 Input minimisation when the input mix is predetermined. If the input mix of firm i had been predetermined, then the manager could have minimised total input by operating at point B

where $X(.)$ is any nonnegative, nondecreasing, linearly-homogeneous, scalar-valued aggregator function satisfying $X(x_{it}) > 0$. The input vector that solves this problem is $\bar{x}_{it} \equiv \bar{x}^t(x_{it}, q_{it}, z_{it}) = x_{it}/D_I^t(x_{it}, q_{it}, z_{it})$. This vector is unique and does not depend on the particular form of the aggregator function. The associated aggregate input is $X(\bar{x}_{it}) = X(x_{it})/D_I^t(x_{it}, q_{it}, z_{it})$. The associated value of the input distance function is $D_I^t(\bar{x}_{it}, q_{it}, z_{it}) = 1$. This implies that the input-minimising point lies on the boundary of $L^t(q_{it}, z_{it})$ (i.e., on the production frontier).

To illustrate, suppose there are only two inputs. Also suppose that $X(x) = b_1x_1 + b_2x_2$ where b_1 and b_2 are both positive. Figure 4.3 depicts the input minimisation problem that would have faced the manager of firm i in period t had the firm's input mix been predetermined. In this figure, the curve passing through point B represents the boundary of $L^t(q_{it}, z_{it})$. The inputs of firm i in period t map to point A. The aggregate input at this point is $X(x_{it})$. The dashed line passing through point A is an iso-input line[2] with a slope of $-b_1/b_2$ and an vertical intercept of $X(x_{it})/b_2$. The other dashed lines are iso-input lines with the same slope but lower intercepts. Input minimisation involves choosing the iso-input line with the lowest intercept that passes through a technically-feasible point. If the input mix of firm i had been predetermined, then the manager could have minimised total input by operating at point B. The aggregate input at this point is $X(\bar{x}_{it})$. For a numerical example, see Sect. 1.4.2.

---

[2]If $X(x_{it}) = b_1x_{1it} + b_2x_{2it}$, then $x_{2it} = X(x_{it})/b_2 - (b_1/b_2)x_{1it}$. This is the equation of a line with a slope of $-b_1/b_2$ and an intercept of $X(x_{it})/b_2$. The term *iso*-input derives from the fact that all points on this line yield the *same* aggregate input, namely $X(x_{it})$.

4.2.2 Inputs Chosen Freely

If inputs are strongly disposable, then it is technically possible for firm managers to choose them freely. If the manager of firm i can choose inputs freely, then his/her period-t input-minimisation problem can be written as

$$\min_x \{X(x) : D_I^t(x, q_{it}, z_{it}) \geq 1\} \tag{4.6}$$

where $X(.)$ is a nonnegative, nondecreasing, linearly-homogeneous, scalar-valued aggregator function with parameters (or weights) that represent the values the manager places on inputs. If there is more than one input, then there may be several input vectors that solve this problem. Let $\hat{x}_{it} \equiv \hat{x}^t(q_{it}, z_{it})$ denote one such vector. The associated minimum aggregate input is $X(\hat{x}_{it})$. If both the aggregator function and the input distance function are differentiable, then this solution can be characterised in terms of the marginal effects discussed in Sect. 2.5.2. For example, let $\hat{x}_{mit}$ denote the m-th element of $\hat{x}_{it}$. If there exists an m such that $\partial X(\hat{x}_{it})/\partial \hat{x}_{mit} > 0$ and $w_m^t(\hat{x}_{it}, q_{it}, z_{it}) > 0$, then $D_I^t(\hat{x}_{it}, q_{it}, z_{it}) = 1$. This implies that the input-minimising point lies on the production frontier. As another example, if both $\hat{x}_{mit}$ and $\hat{x}_{kit}$ are positive, then $MRTS_{km}^t(\hat{x}_{it}, q_{it}, z_{it}) = [\partial X(\hat{x}_{it})/\partial \hat{x}_{mit}]/[\partial X(\hat{x}_{it})/\partial \hat{x}_{kit}]$. This implies that total input will be minimised at a point where an iso-input line (or curve, if the aggregator function is nonlinear) is tangent to the production frontier.

To illustrate, reconsider the input-minimisation problem depicted in Fig. 4.3. Relevant parts of that figure are now reproduced in Fig. 4.4. In these figures, the dashed lines are iso-input lines with a slope of $-b_1/b_2$. Input minimisation involves choosing the iso-input line with the lowest intercept that passes through a

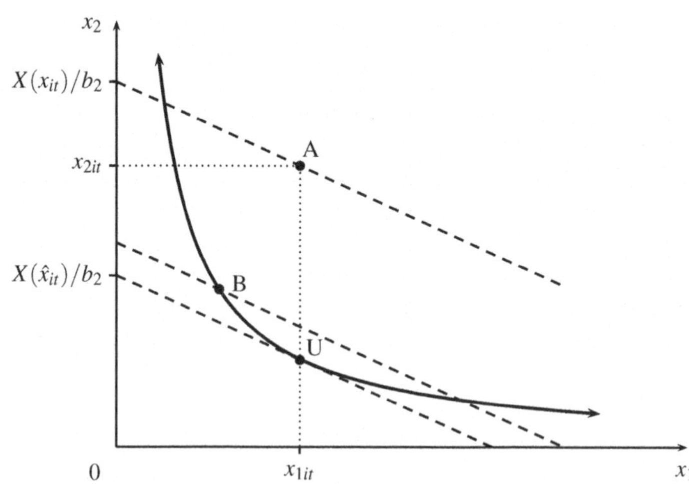

Fig. 4.4 Input minimisation when inputs can be chosen freely. If the manager of firm i had been able to choose inputs freely, then (s)he could have minimised total input by operating at point U

technically-feasible point. If the manager of firm i had been able to choose inputs freely, then (s)he could have minimised total input by operating at point U. The aggregate input at this point is $X(\hat{x}_{it})$.

4.2.3 Example

The input vector that solves (4.5) depends on the input distance function. If the input distance function is given by (2.13), then

$$\bar{x}^t(x_{it}, q_{it}, z_{it}) = x_{it}\left(B(t)\prod_{j=1}^{J} z_{jit}^{\kappa_j}\prod_{m=1}^{M} x_{mit}^{\lambda_m}\right)^{-1}\left(\sum_{n=1}^{N}\gamma_n q_{nit}^{\tau}\right)^{1/(\tau\eta)}. \quad (4.7)$$

The input vector that solves (4.6) depends on both the input distance function and the aggregator function. Suppose that $X(x) = b'x$ where $b = (b_1, \ldots, b_M)' > 0$. If the input distance function is given by (2.13), then the m-th element of $\hat{x}^t(q_{it}, z_{it})$ is

$$\hat{x}_m^t(q_{it}, z_{it}) = \left(B(t)\prod_{j=1}^{J} z_{jit}^{\kappa_j}\right)^{-1}\left(\frac{\lambda_m}{b_m}\right)\left(\prod_{k=1}^{M}\lambda_k^{-\lambda_k}b_k^{\lambda_k}\right)\left(\sum_{n=1}^{N}\gamma_n q_{nit}^{\tau}\right)^{1/(\tau\eta)}. \quad (4.8)$$

4.3 Revenue Maximisation

If a firm manager values outputs at market prices and all other variables involved in the production process have been predetermined, then (s)he will generally aim to maximise revenue. The exact form of the manager's revenue maximisation problem will depend on whether market prices are affected by the outputs of the firm. If market prices *are* affected by the outputs of the firm, then the firm is said to be a price setter in output markets. If market prices are *not* affected by the outputs of the firm, then the firm is said to be a price taker in output markets.

4.3.1 Price Setters in Output Markets

If firm i is a price setter in output markets, then the manager's period-t revenue-maximisation problem can be written as

$$\max_q\{p(q, d_{it})'q : D_O^t(x_{it}, q, z_{it}) \leq 1\} \quad (4.9)$$

where d_{it} is a vector of nonnegative exogenous[3] demand shifters and $p(q, d_{it})$ is a vector of nonnegative inverse demand functions. If there is more than one output, then there may be several output vectors that solve this problem. Let $\ddot{q}_{it} \equiv \ddot{q}^t(x_{it}, d_{it}, z_{it})$ denote one such vector. The associated maximum revenue is $R^t(x_{it}, d_{it}, z_{it}) = p(\ddot{q}_{it}, d_{it})'\ddot{q}_{it}$. If consumer demand is sufficiently weak, then it is possible that $D^t_O(x_{it}, \ddot{q}_{it}, z_{it}) < 1$. This implies that the revenue-maximising point may lie inside the production frontier (O'Donnell 2016, p. 331). Conceptually, if consumer demand is sufficiently weak, then it may be possible to maximise revenue by selling a small quantity at a high price rather than selling a large quantity at a low price.

For a numerical example, reconsider the toy data in Table 1.1. Suppose the two inverse demand functions are the following:

$$p_1(q, d_{it}) = 0.8 + 0.1d_{1it} + 0.24d_{2it} - 0.57q_1 \quad (4.10)$$

$$\text{and} \quad p_2(q, d_{it}) = 0.1 + 0.72d_{2it} - 0.41q_2. \quad (4.11)$$

Figure 4.5 depicts the revenue maximisation problem that would have faced the manager of any firm that used one unit of each input in period 1 in environment 1. In this figure, the curve passing through point C is the frontier depicted earlier in Fig. 1.1; it represents the boundary of $P^1(\iota, 1)$. If the vector of demand shifters had been $d_{i1} = (4.1, 4.1)'$, then any manager could have maximised revenue by choosing $\ddot{q}_{i1} = (1.925, 3.722)'$. This vector maps to point T in Fig. 4.5. The associated vector of output prices would have been $p(\ddot{q}_{i1}, 4.1\iota) = (1.097, 1.526)'$. The associated maximum revenue would have been $R^1(\iota, 4.1\iota, 1) = 7.791$. The dashed line passing through point T is a pseudo-iso-revenue line[4] with a slope of $-p_1(\ddot{q}_{i1}, 4.1\iota)/p_2(\ddot{q}_{i1}, 4.1\iota) = -0.719$ and a vertical intercept of $R^1(\iota, 4.1\iota, 1)/p_2(\ddot{q}_{i1}, 4.1\iota) = 5.105$. On the other hand, if the vector of demand shifters had been $d_{i1} = (1, 1)'$ ($\Rightarrow$ consumer demand had been relatively weak), then the manager of any firm using one unit of each input could have maximised revenue by choosing $\ddot{q}_{i1} = (1, 1)'$. This vector maps to point A in Fig. 4.5. In this case, the vector of output prices would have been $p(\ddot{q}_{i1}, \iota) = (0.57, 0.41)'$. The associated maximum revenue would have been $R^1(\iota, \iota, 1) = 0.98$. The dashed line passing through point A is a pseudo-iso-revenue line with a slope of $-p_1(\ddot{q}_{i1}, \iota)/p_2(\ddot{q}_{i1}, \iota) = -1.39$ and a vertical intercept of $R^1(\iota, \iota, 1)/p_2(\ddot{q}_{i1}, \iota) = 2.39$.

[3]Here, the term 'exogenous' means that demand shifters (e.g., population, tastes) are not affected by the actions of the firm (or, more precisely, the firm manager).

[4]If $R^t(x_{it}, d_{it}, z_{it}) = p_1(\ddot{q}_{it}, d_{it})\ddot{q}_{1it} + p_2(\ddot{q}_{it}, d_{it})\ddot{q}_{2it}$, then $\ddot{q}_{2it} = R^t(x_{it}, d_{it}, z_{it})/p_2(\ddot{q}_{it}, d_{it}) - [p_1(\ddot{q}_{it}, d_{it})/p_2(\ddot{q}_{it}, d_{it})]\ddot{q}_{1it}$. This is the equation of a line with a slope of $-p_1(\ddot{q}_{it}, d_{it})/p_2(\ddot{q}_{it}, d_{it})$ and a vertical intercept of $R^t(x_{it}, d_{it}, z_{it})/p_2(\ddot{q}_{it}, d_{it})$. The term *iso*-revenue derives from the fact that if $p(\ddot{q}_{it}, d_{it})$ did not vary with $\ddot{q}_{it}$, then all output combinations on this line would yield the *same* revenue. The term *pseudo* is used here because $p(\ddot{q}_{it}, d_{it})$ *does* vary with $\ddot{q}_{it}$.

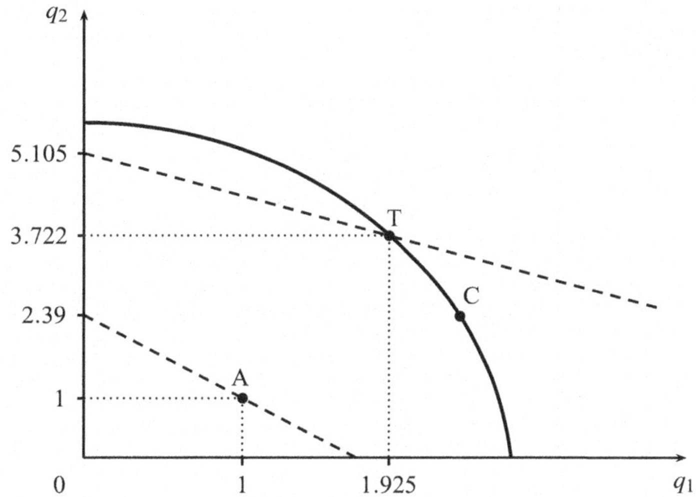

Fig. 4.5 Revenue maximisation for a price-setting firm. If consumer demand had been relatively strong (resp. weak), then the manager of any firm using one unit of each input could have maximised revenue by operating at point T (resp. A)

4.3.2 Price Takers in Output Markets

If firm i is a price taker in output markets, then the manager's period-t revenue-maximisation problem can be written as

$$\max_{q}\{p_{it}'q : D_O^t(x_{it}, q, z_{it}) \leq 1\} \tag{4.12}$$

where p_{it} is a vector of nonnegative prices that are not affected by the outputs of the firm. This problem can be viewed as a special case of (4.9) corresponding to $\partial p(q, d_{it})/\partial q = 0$. Again, if there is more than one output, then there may be several output vectors that solve this problem. In a slight abuse of notation, let $\ddot{q}_{it} \equiv \ddot{q}^t(x_{it}, p_{it}, z_{it})$ denote one such vector. The associated maximum revenue is $R^t(x_{it}, p_{it}, z_{it}) = p_{it}'\ddot{q}_{it}$. If the output distance function is differentiable, then this solution can be characterised in terms of the marginal effects discussed in Sect. 2.4.2. For example, let p_{nit} (resp. $\ddot{q}_{nit}$) denote the n-th element of p_{it} (resp. $\ddot{q}_{it}$). If there exists an n such that $p_{nit}\ddot{q}_{nit} > 0$ and $p_n^t(x_{it}, \ddot{q}_{it}, z_{it}) > 0$, then $D_O^t(x_{it}, \ddot{q}_{it}, z_{it}) = 1$. This implies that the revenue-maximising point lies on the boundary of $P^t(x_{it}, z_{it})$. As another example, if both $\ddot{q}_{nit}$ and $\ddot{q}_{kit}$ are positive, then $MRT_{kn}^t(x_{it}, \ddot{q}_{it}, z_{it}) = p_{nit}/p_{kit}$. This implies that revenue will be maximised at a point where an iso-revenue line is tangent to the frontier. For more details, see, for example, Färe and Primont (1995, Sect. 3.3) and O'Donnell (2016, Propositions 11, 13).

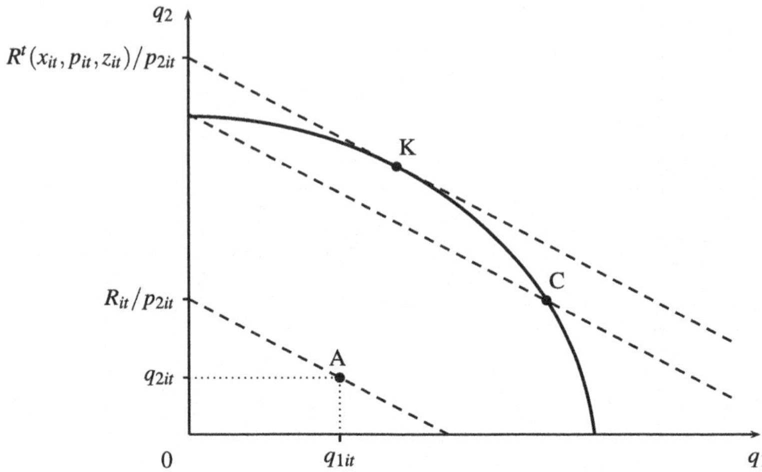

Fig. 4.6 Revenue maximisation for a price-taking firm. If firm i had been a price taker in output markets, then the manager could have maximised revenue by operating at point K

To illustrate, suppose there are only two outputs. Figure 4.6 depicts the revenue maximisation problem that would have faced the manager of firm i in period t. In this figure, the curve passing through point C is the frontier depicted earlier in Figs. 4.1 and 4.2; it represents the boundary of $P^t(x_{it}, z_{it})$. The outputs of firm i in period t map to point A. The revenue at this point is $R_{it} = p'_{it}q_{it}$. The dashed line passing through point A is an iso-revenue line[5] with a slope of $-p_{1it}/p_{2it}$ and a vertical intercept of R_{it}/p_{2it}. The other dashed lines are iso-revenue lines with the same slope but higher intercepts. For the manager of a price-taking firm, revenue maximisation involves choosing the iso-revenue line with the highest intercept that passes through a technically-feasible point. If firm i had been a price taker in output markets and its inputs had been predetermined, then the manager could have maximised revenue by operating at point K. The revenue at this point is $R^t(x_{it}, p_{it}, z_{it})$. Observe that the revenue-maximising point in Fig. 4.6 is not the same as the output-maximising point in either Fig. 4.1 or Fig. 4.2. This illustrates that maximising revenue is not generally the same as maximising total output.

4.3.3 Example

Suppose that firm i is a price taker in output markets. If the output distance function is given by (2.9), then the output vector that solves (4.12) depends on output prices

[5]If $R_{it} = p_{1it}q_{1it} + p_{2it}q_{2it}$, then $q_{2it} = R_{it}/p_{2it} - (p_{1it}/p_{2it})q_{1it}$. This is the equation of a line with a slope of $-p_{1it}/p_{2it}$ and an intercept of R_{it}/p_{2it}. The term *iso*-revenue derives from the fact that all points on this line yield the *same* revenue, namely R_{it}.

and the value of τ. If the n-th output price is positive and $\tau > 1$, then the n-th element of $\ddot{q}^t(x_{it}, p_{it}, z_{it})$ is

$$\ddot{q}^t_n(x_{it}, p_{it}, z_{it}) = \left(A(t)\prod_{j=1}^{J} z_{jit}^{\delta_j}\prod_{m=1}^{M} x_{mit}^{\beta_m}\right)\left(\frac{\gamma_n}{p_{nit}}\right)^{\sigma}\left(\sum_{k=1}^{N}\gamma_k^{\sigma}p_{kit}^{1-\sigma}\right)^{\sigma/(1-\sigma)} \tag{4.13}$$

where $\sigma = 1/(1-\tau) < 0$.

4.4 Cost Minimisation

If a firm manager values inputs at market prices and all other variables involved in the production process have been predetermined, then (s)he will generally aim to minimise cost. The exact form of the manager's cost-minimisation problem will depend on whether market prices are affected by the inputs demanded by the firm. If market prices *are* affected by the inputs demanded by the firm, then the firm is said to be a price setter in input markets. If market prices are *not* affected by the inputs of the firm, then the firm is said to be a price taker in input markets.

4.4.1 Price Setters in Input Markets

If firm i is a price setter in input markets, then the manager's period-t cost-minimisation problem can be written as

$$\min_x \{w(x, s_{it})'x : D^t_I(x, q_{it}, z_{it}) \geq 1\} \tag{4.14}$$

where s_{it} is a vector of nonnegative exogenous[6] supply shifters and $w(x, s_{it})$ is a vector of nonnegative inverse supply functions. If there is more than one input, then there may be several input vectors that solve this problem. Let $\ddot{x}_{it} \equiv \ddot{x}^t(s_{it}, q_{it}, z_{it})$ denote one such vector. The associated minimum cost is $C^t(s_{it}, q_{it}, z_{it}) = w(\ddot{x}_{it}, s_{it})'\ddot{x}_{it}$. If the inverse supply function and the input distance function are differentiable, then this solution can be characterised in terms of marginal effects. For example, let $w_m(\ddot{x}_{it}, s_{it})$ (resp. $\ddot{x}_{mit}$) denote the m-th element of $w(\ddot{x}_{it}, s_{it})$ (resp. $\ddot{x}_{it}$). If there exists an m such that $w_m(\ddot{x}_{it}, s_{it})\ddot{x}_{mit} > 0$ and $\partial w_m(\ddot{x}_{it}, s_{it})/\partial \ddot{x}_{mit} > 0$, then $D^t_I(\ddot{x}_{it}, q_{it}, z_{it}) = 1$. This implies that the cost-minimising point lies on the boundary of $L^t(q_{it}, z_{it})$.

[6]Here, the term 'exogenous' means that supply shifters (e.g., characteristics of production environments in upstream sectors) are not affected by the actions of the firm (or, more precisely, firm managers).

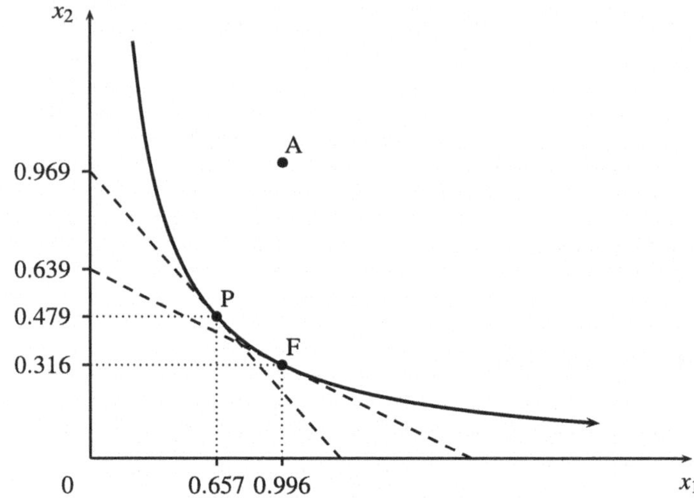

Fig. 4.7 Cost minimisation for a price-setting firm. If input supplies had been relatively scarce (resp. abundant), then the manager of any firm producing one unit of each output could have minimised cost by operating at point F (resp. P)

For a numerical example, reconsider the toy data in Table 1.1. Suppose the two inverse supply functions are the following:

$$w_1(x, s_{it}) = \exp(0.27 \ln x_1 - 1.6 - 0.1 s_{2it}) \quad (4.15)$$

and

$$w_2(x, s_{it}) = \exp(0.3 \ln x_2 - 0.01 - 1.2 s_{1it} - 0.09 s_{2it}). \quad (4.16)$$

Figure 4.7 depicts the cost minimisation problem that would have faced the manager of any firm that produced one unit of each output in period 1 in environment 1. In this figure, the curve passing through points P and F is the frontier depicted earlier in Fig. 1.2; it represents the boundary of $L^1(\iota, 1)$. If the vector of supply shifters had been $s_{i1} = (1, 1)'$, then the manager of any firm producing one unit of each output could have minimised cost by using $\ddot{x}_{i1} = (0.657, 0.479)'$. This vector maps to point P in Fig. 4.7. The associated vector of input prices would have been $w(\ddot{x}_{i1}, \iota) = (0.163, 0.218)'$. The associated minimum cost would have been $C^1(\iota, \iota, 1) = 0.212$. The dashed line passing through point P is a pseudo-iso-cost line[7] with a slope of $-w_1(\ddot{x}_{i1}, \iota)/w_2(\ddot{x}_{i1}, \iota) = -0.746$ and a vertical intercept of $C^1(\iota, \iota, 1)/w_2(\ddot{x}_{i1}, \iota) = 0.969$. As another example, if the vector of supply shifters had been $s_{i1} = (0.1, 0.1)'$ ($\Rightarrow$ input supplies had been relatively scarce), then the manager of any firm producing one unit of each output could have minimised cost by

[7] If $C^t(s_{it}, q_{it}, z_{it}) = w_1(\ddot{x}_{it}, s_{it})\ddot{x}_{1it} + w_2(\ddot{x}_{it}, s_{it})\ddot{x}_{2it}$, then $\ddot{x}_{2it} = C^t(s_{it}, q_{it}, z_{it})/w_2(\ddot{x}_{it}, s_{it}) - [w_1(\ddot{x}_{it}, s_{it})/w_2(\ddot{x}_{it}, s_{it})]\ddot{x}_{1it}$. This is the equation of a line with a slope of $-w_1(\ddot{x}_{it}, s_{it})/w_2(\ddot{x}_{it}, s_{it})$ and a vertical intercept of $C^t(s_{it}, q_{it}, z_{it})/w_2(\ddot{x}_{it}, s_{it})$. The term *iso*-cost derives from the fact that if $w(\ddot{x}_{it}, s_{it})$ did not vary with $\ddot{x}_{it}$, then all input combinations on this line would yield the *same* cost. The term *pseudo* is used here because $w(\ddot{x}_{it}, s_{it})$ *does* vary with $\ddot{x}_{it}$.

using $\ddot{x}_{i1} = (0.996, 0.316)'$. This vector maps to point F in Fig. 4.7. In this case, the vector of input prices would have been $w(\ddot{x}_{i1}, 0.1\iota) = (0.2, 0.616)'$. The associated minimum cost would have been $C^1(0.1\iota, \iota, 1) = 0.393$. The associated pseudo-iso-cost line has a slope of $-w_1(\ddot{x}_{i1}, 0.1\iota)/w_2(\ddot{x}_{i1}, 0.1\iota) = -0.324$ and a vertical intercept of $C^1(0.1\iota, \iota, 1)/w_2(\ddot{x}_{i1}, 0.1\iota) = 0.639$.

4.4.2 Price Takers in Input Markets

If firm i is a price taker in input markets, then the manager's period-t cost-minimisation problem can be written as

$$\min_{x}\{w_{it}'x : D_I^t(x, q_{it}, z_{it}) \geq 1\} \tag{4.17}$$

where w_{it} is a vector of nonnegative prices that are not affected by the input demands of the firm. This problem can be viewed as a special case of (4.14) corresponding to $\partial w(x, s_{it})/\partial x = 0$. Again, if there is more than one input, then there may be several input vectors that solve this problem. In another slight abuse of notation, let $\ddot{x}_{it} \equiv \ddot{x}^t(w_{it}, q_{it}, z_{it})$ denote one such vector. The associated minimum cost is $C^t(w_{it}, q_{it}, z_{it}) = w_{it}'\ddot{x}_{it}$. If the input distance function is differentiable, then this solution can be characterised in terms of the marginal effects discussed in Sect. 2.5.2. For example, let w_{mit} (resp. $\ddot{x}_{mit}$) denote the m-th element of w_{it} (resp. $\ddot{x}_{it}$). If there exists an m such that $w_{mit}\ddot{x}_{mit} > 0$ and $w_m^t(\ddot{x}_{it}, q_{it}, z_{it}) > 0$, then $D_I^t(\ddot{x}_{it}, q_{it}, z_{it}) = 1$. This implies that the cost-minimising point lies on the production frontier. As another example, if both $\ddot{x}_{mit}$ and $\ddot{x}_{kit}$ are positive, then $MRTS_{km}^t(\ddot{x}_{it}, q_{it}, z_{it}) = w_{mit}/w_{kit}$. This implies that cost will be minimised at a point where an isocost line is tangent to the frontier. For more details, see, for example, Färe and Primont (1995, Sect. 3.3) and O'Donnell (2016, Proposition 16).

To illustrate, suppose there are only two inputs. Figure 4.8 depicts the cost minimisation problem that would have faced the manager of firm i in period t. In this figure, the curve passing through point X is the frontier depicted earlier in Figs. 4.3 and 4.4; it represents the boundary of $L^t(q_{it}, z_{it})$. The inputs of firm i in period t map to point A. The cost at this point is $C_{it} = w_{it}'x_{it}$. The dashed line passing through point A is an iso-cost line[8] with a slope of $-w_{1it}/w_{2it}$ and an vertical intercept of C_{it}/w_{2it}. The other dashed lines are iso-cost lines with the same slope but lower intercepts. For the manager of a price-taking firm, cost minimisation involves choosing the iso-cost line with the lowest intercept that passes through a technically-feasible point. If firm i had been a price taker in input markets and its outputs had been predetermined, then the manager could have minimised cost by operating at point X. The cost at this

[8]If $C_{it} = w_{1it}x_{1it} + w_{2it}x_{2it}$, then $x_{2it} = C_{it}/w_{2it} - (w_{1it}/w_{2it})x_{1it}$. This is the equation of a line with a slope of $-w_{1it}/w_{2it}$ and an intercept of C_{it}/w_{2it}. The term *iso*-cost derives from the fact that all points on this line yield the *same* cost, namely C_{it}.

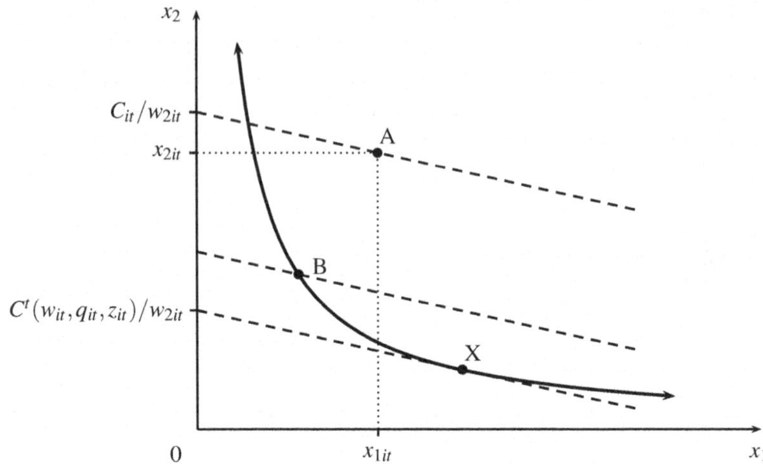

Fig. 4.8 Cost minimisation for a price-taking firm. If firm i had been a price taker in input markets, then the manager could have minimised cost by operating at point X

point is $C^t(w_{it}, q_{it}, z_{it})$. Observe that the cost-minimising point in Fig. 4.8 is not the same as the input-minimising point in either Fig. 4.3 or Fig. 4.4. This illustrates that minimising cost is not generally the same as minimising total input.

4.4.3 Example

Suppose that firm i is a price taker in input markets. If the input distance function is given by (2.13), then the input vector that solves (4.17) depends on input prices. If the m-th input price is positive, then the m-th element of $\ddot{x}^t(w_{it}, q_{it}, z_{it})$ is

$$\ddot{x}^t_m(w_{it}, q_{it}, z_{it}) = \left(B(t)\prod_{j=1}^{J} z_{jit}^{\kappa_j}\right)^{-1} \left(\frac{\lambda_m}{w_{mit}}\right) \prod_{k=1}^{M} \left(\frac{w_{kit}}{\lambda_k}\right)^{\lambda_k} \left(\sum_{n=1}^{N} \gamma_n q_{nit}^{\tau}\right)^{1/(\tau\eta)}. \tag{4.18}$$

4.5 Profit Maximisation

If a firm manager values outputs and inputs at market prices and all environmental variables have been predetermined, then (s)he will generally aim to maximise profit. The exact form of the manager's profit maximisation problem will depend on whether the firm is a price setter or price taker in output and/or input markets.

4.5.1 Price Setters in Output and Input Markets

If firm i is a price setter in output and input markets, then the manager's period-t profit-maximisation problem can be written as

$$\max_{q,x}\{p(q, d_{it})'q - w(x, s_{it})'x : D_O^t(x, q, z_{it}) \leq 1\} \tag{4.19}$$

where d_{it} and s_{it} are vectors of nonnegative exogenous[9] demand and supply shifters, $p(q, d_{it})$ is a vector of nonnegative inverse demand functions, and $w(x, s_{it})$ is a vector of nonnegative inverse supply functions. There may be several pairs of output and input vectors that solve this problem. Let $\mathring{q}_{it} \equiv \mathring{q}^t(s_{it}, d_{it}, z_{it})$ and $\mathring{x}_{it} \equiv \mathring{x}^t(s_{it}, d_{it}, z_{it})$ denote one such pair. The associated maximum profit is $\Pi^t(s_{it}, d_{it}, z_{it}) = p(\mathring{q}_{it}, d_{it})'\mathring{q}_{it} - w(\mathring{x}_{it}, s_{it})'\mathring{x}_{it}$. Equivalently, $\Pi^t(s_{it}, d_{it}, z_{it}) = P(\mathring{q}_{it}, d_{it})Q(\mathring{q}_{it}) - W(\mathring{x}_{it}, s_{it})X(\mathring{x}_{it})$ where $Q(\mathring{q}_{it})$ is a scalar-valued aggregate output, $X(\mathring{x}_{it})$ is a scalar-valued aggregate input, $P(\mathring{q}_{it}, d_{it}) = p(\mathring{q}_{it}, d_{it})'\mathring{q}_{it}/Q(\mathring{q}_{it})$ is a scalar-valued aggregate output price, and $W(\mathring{x}_{it}, s_{it}) = w(\mathring{x}_{it}, s_{it})'\mathring{x}_{it}/X(\mathring{x}_{it})$ is a scalar-valued aggregate input price. Except in restrictive special cases (e.g., when inverse supply functions are nonincreasing in inputs), associated values of the output and input distance functions are $D_O^t(\mathring{x}_{it}, \mathring{q}_{it}, z_{it}) = D_I^t(\mathring{x}_{it}, \mathring{q}_{it}, z_{it}) = 1$. This implies that the profit-maximising point lies on the boundary of $T^t(z_{it})$.

For a numerical example, reconsider the toy data in Table 1.1. Suppose the inverse demand and supply functions are given by (4.10), (4.11), (4.15) and (4.16). Also suppose that $Q(q) = 0.484q_1 + 0.516q_2$ and $X(x) = 0.23x_1 + 0.77x_2$. Figure 4.9 depicts the profit maximisation problem that would have faced the manager of any firm that operated in period 1 in environment 1. In this figure, the curve passing through points H and G is the frontier depicted earlier in Fig. 1.3; it represents the boundary of $T^1(1)$. If the vectors of demand and supply shifters had been $d_{i1} = s_{i1} = (1, 1)'$, then the manager of any firm that operated in period 1 in environment 1 could have maximised profit by using $\mathring{x}_{i1} = (0.017, 0.346)'$ to produce $\mathring{q}_{i1} = (0.960, 0.940)'$. The associated vectors of output and input prices would have been $p(\mathring{q}_{i1}, \iota) = (0.593, 0.435)'$ and $w(\mathring{x}_{i1}, \iota) = (0.061, 0.198)'$. The associated aggregate quantities and prices would have been $Q(\mathring{q}_{i1}) = 0.950$, $X(\mathring{x}_{i1}) = 0.270$, $P(\mathring{q}_{i1}, \iota) = 1.030$ and $W(\mathring{x}_{i1}, \iota) = 0.257$. Maximised profit would have been $\Pi^1(\iota, \iota, 1) = 0.908$. This solution maps to point H in Fig. 4.9. The dashed line passing through this point is a pseudo-iso-profit line[10] with a slope of $W(\mathring{x}_{i1}, \iota)/P(\mathring{q}_{i1}, \iota) = 0.250$ and a vertical intercept of $\Pi^1(\iota, \iota, 1)/P(\mathring{q}_{i1}, \iota) = 0.882$. As another example,

---

[9]Here, the term 'exogenous' means that demand and supply shifters are not affected by the actions of the firm (or, more precisely, the firm manager).

[10]If $\Pi^t(s_{it}, d_{it}, z_{it}) = P(\mathring{q}_{it}, d_{it})Q(\mathring{q}_{it}) - W(\mathring{x}_{it}, s_{it})X(\mathring{x}_{it})$, then $Q(\mathring{q}_{it}) = \Pi^t(s_{it}, d_{it}, z_{it})/P(\mathring{q}_{it}, d_{it}) + [W(\mathring{x}_{it}, s_{it})/P(\mathring{q}_{it}, d_{it})]X(\mathring{x}_{it})$. This is the equation of a line with a slope of $W(\mathring{x}_{it}, s_{it})/P(\mathring{q}_{it}, d_{it})$ and a vertical intercept of $\Pi^t(s_{it}, d_{it}, z_{it})/P(\mathring{q}_{it}, d_{it})$. The term *iso*-profit derives from the fact that if $W(\mathring{x}_{it}, s_{it})$ and $P(\mathring{q}_{it}, d_{it})$ did not depend on $\mathring{x}_{it}$ and $\mathring{q}_{it}$, then all points on this line would yield the *same* profit. The term *pseudo* is used here because $W(\mathring{x}_{it}, s_{it})$ and $P(\mathring{q}_{it}, d_{it})$ *do* depend on $\mathring{x}_{it}$ and $\mathring{q}_{it}$.

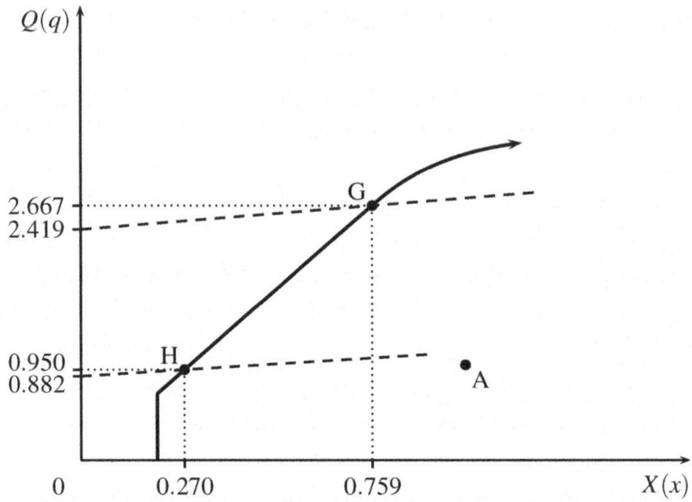

Fig. 4.9 Profit maximisation for a price-setting firm. If consumer demand had been relatively strong (resp. weak) and input supplies had been relatively scarce (resp. abundant), then the manager of a price-setting firm could have maximised profit by operating at point G (resp. H)

if the vectors of demand and supply shifters had been $d_{i1} = (4.1, 4.1)'$ ($\Rightarrow$ consumer demand had been relatively strong) and $s_{i1} = (0.1, 0.1)'$ ($\Rightarrow$ input supplies had been relatively scarce), then the manager of any firm that operated in period 1 in environment 1 could have maximised profit by using $\mathring{x}_{i1} = (1.472, 0.546)'$ to produce $\mathring{q}_{i1} = (1.777, 3.503)'$. The associated vectors of output and input prices would have been $p(\mathring{q}_{i1}, 4.1\iota) = (1.181, 1.616)'$ and $w(\mathring{x}_{i1}, 0.1\iota) = (0.222, 0.726)'$. The associated aggregate quantities and prices would have been $Q(\mathring{q}_{i1}) = 2.667$, $X(\mathring{x}_{i1}) = 0.759$, $P(\mathring{q}_{i1}, 4.1\iota) = 2.909$ and $W(\mathring{x}_{i1}, 0.1\iota) = 0.952$. Maximised profit would have been $\Pi^1(0.1\iota, 4.1\iota, 1) = 7.036$. This solution maps to point G in Fig. 4.9. The pseudo-iso-profit line passing through this point has a slope of $W(\mathring{x}_{i1}, 0.1\iota)/P(\mathring{q}_{i1}, 4.1\iota) = 0.327$ and a vertical intercept of $\Pi^1(0.1\iota, 4.1\iota, 1)/P(\mathring{q}_{i1}, 4.1\iota) = 2.419$.

4.5.2 Price Takers in Output and Input Markets

If firm i is a price taker in output and input markets, then the manager's period-t profit-maximisation problem can be written as

$$\max_{q,x}\{p'_{it}q - w'_{it}x : D^t_O(x, q, z_{it}) \leq 1\} \tag{4.20}$$

where p_{it} and w_{it} are vectors of nonnegative prices that are not affected by the outputs supplied or inputs demanded by the firm. This problem can be viewed as a special case of (4.19) corresponding to $\partial p(q, d_{it})/\partial q = 0$ and $\partial w(x, s_{it})/\partial x = 0$. Again, there may be several pairs of output and input vectors that solve this problem. In another slight abuse of notation, let $\mathring{q}_{it} \equiv \mathring{q}^t(w_{it}, p_{it}, z_{it})$ and $\mathring{x}_{it} \equiv \mathring{x}^t(w_{it}, p_{it}, z_{it})$ denote one such pair. The associated maximum profit is $\Pi^t(w_{it}, p_{it}, z_{it}) = p'_{it}\mathring{q}_{it} - w'_{it}\mathring{x}_{it}$. Equivalently, $\Pi^t(w_{it}, p_{it}, z_{it}) = P(\mathring{q}_{it}, p_{it})Q(\mathring{q}_{it}) - W(\mathring{x}_{it}, w_{it})X(\mathring{x}_{it})$ where $Q(\mathring{q}_{it})$ is a scalar-valued aggregate output, $X(\mathring{x}_{it})$ is a scalar-valued aggregate input, $P(\mathring{q}_{it}, p_{it}) = p'_{it}\mathring{q}_{it}/Q(\mathring{q}_{it})$ is a scalar-valued aggregate output price, and $W(\mathring{x}_{it}, w_{it}) = w'_{it}\mathring{x}_{it}/X(\mathring{x}_{it})$ is a scalar-valued aggregate input price. Thus, except in restrictive special cases (e.g., there is only one output and only one input), and despite the fact that the firm is a price taker in output and input markets, aggregate output and input prices depend on the outputs supplied and inputs demanded by the firm. If the output distance function is differentiable, then the solution to (4.20) can be characterised in terms of the marginal effects discussed in Sect. 2.4.2. For example, let w_{mit} (resp. $\mathring{x}_{mit}$) denote the m-th element of w_{it} (resp. $\mathring{x}_{it}$). If there exists an m such that $w_{mit}\mathring{x}_{mit} > 0$ and $MP^t_m(\mathring{x}_{it}, \mathring{q}_{it}, z_{it}) > 0$, then $D^t_O(\mathring{x}_{it}, \mathring{q}_{it}, z_{it}) = 1$. This implies that the profit-maximising point lies on the production frontier.

For a numerical example, reconsider the toy data in Tables 1.1, 1.4 and 1.5. Also suppose that $Q(q) = 0.484q_1 + 0.516q_2$ and $X(x) = 0.23x_1 + 0.77x_2$. Figure 4.10 depicts the profit maximisation problem that would have faced the manager of firm 3 in period 1. In this figure, the curve passing through point J is the frontier depicted in Figs. 1.3 and 4.9; it represents the boundary of $T^1(1)$. The outputs and inputs of firm 3 map to point C. The aggregate output and input quantities at this point are $Q(q_{31}) = 2.37$ and $X(x_{31}) = 1$. The associated aggregate prices are $P(q_{31}, p_{31}) = 0.98$ and $W(x_{31}, w_{31}) = 2.19$. The profit of the firm was $\Pi_{31} = 0.133$. The dashed line passing through point C is a pseudo-isoprofit line[11] with a slope of $W(x_{31}, w_{31})/P(q_{31}, p_{31}) = 2.235$ and a vertical intercept of $\Pi_{31}/P(q_{31}, p_{31}) = 0.135$. It turns out that the manager of firm 3 could have maximised profit by using $\mathring{x}_{31} = (4.450, 0.001)'$ to produce $\mathring{q}_{31} = (6.685, 0.001)'$. These outputs and inputs map to point J. The aggregate quantities at this point are $Q(\mathring{q}_{31}) = 3.236$ and $X(\mathring{x}_{31}) = 1.024$. The associated aggregate prices are $P(\mathring{q}_{31}, p_{31}) = 1.178$ and $W(\mathring{x}_{31}, w_{31}) = 1.218$. The associated profit is $\Pi^1(w_{31}, p_{31}, 1) = 2.564$. The dashed line passing through point J is a pseudo-isoprofit line with a slope of $W(\mathring{x}_{31}, w_{31})/P(\mathring{q}_{31}, p_{31}) = 1.034$ and a vertical intercept of $\Pi^1(w_{31}, p_{31}, 1)/P(\mathring{q}_{31}, p_{31}) = 2.177$.

[11] If $\Pi_{31} = P(q_{31}, p_{31})Q(q_{31}) - W(x_{31}, w_{31})X(x_{31})$, then $Q(q_{31}) = \Pi_{31}/P(q_{31}, p_{31}) + [W(x_{31}, w_{31})/P(q_{31}, p_{31})]X(x_{31})$. This is the equation of a line with a slope of $W(x_{31}, w_{31})/P(q_{31}, p_{31})$ and a vertical intercept of $\Pi_{31}/P(q_{31}, p_{31})$. The term *iso*-profit derives from the fact that if $P(q_{31}, p_{31})$ and $W(x_{31}, w_{31})$ did not vary with q_{31} and x_{31}, then all points on this line would yield the *same* profit. The term *pseudo* is used here because, except in restrictive special cases (e.g., there is only one input and only one output), $P(q_{31}, p_{31})$ and $W(x_{31}, w_{31})$ *do* vary with q_{31} and x_{31}.

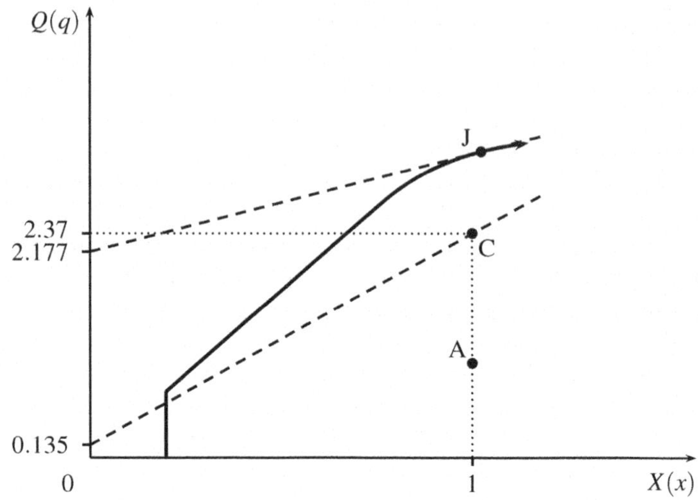

Fig. 4.10 Profit maximisation for a price-taking firm. If firm 3 had been a price taker in output and input markets, then the manager could have maximised profit by operating at point J

4.5.3 Example

Suppose that firm i is a price taker in output and input markets and the output distance function is given by (2.9). The outputs and inputs that solve (4.20) depend on $\eta = \beta'\iota$ and τ. If $\eta < 1$ and $\tau > 1$, for example, then the n-th element of $\mathring{q}^t(w_{it}, p_{it}, z_{it})$ and the m-th element of $\mathring{x}^t(w_{it}, p_{it}, z_{it})$ are

$$\mathring{q}^t_n(w_{it}, p_{it}, z_{it}) = \left(A(t) \prod_{j=1}^{J} z_{jit}^{\delta_j} \prod_{m=1}^{M} \left(\frac{\beta_m}{w_{mit}} \right)^{\beta_m} \right)^{\frac{1}{1-\eta}} \left(\frac{\gamma_n}{p_{nit}} \right)^{\sigma} \times \left(\sum_{k=1}^{N} \gamma_k^{\sigma} p_{kit}^{1-\sigma} \right)^{\frac{1}{(1-\sigma)(1-\eta)} - 1} \tag{4.21}$$

$$\text{and } \mathring{x}^t_m(w_{it}, p_{it}, z_{it}) = \left(A(t) \prod_{j=1}^{J} z_{jit}^{\delta_j} \prod_{k=1}^{M} \left(\frac{\beta_k}{w_{kit}} \right)^{\beta_k} \right)^{\frac{1}{1-\eta}} \left(\frac{\beta_m}{w_{mit}} \right) \times \left(\sum_{n=1}^{N} \gamma_n^{\sigma} p_{nit}^{1-\sigma} \right)^{\frac{1}{(1-\sigma)(1-\eta)}} \tag{4.22}$$

where $\sigma = 1/(1 - \tau) < 0$.

4.6 Productivity Maximisation

If a firm manager places nonnegative values on outputs and inputs (again, not necessarily market values) and all environmental variables have been predetermined, then (s)he may aim to maximise a measure of TFP. If there is more than one output and more than one input, then the precise form of the manager's TFP maximisation problem will depend on how easily (s)he can choose the output mix and the input mix.

4.6.1 Output and Input Mixes Predetermined

If the manager of firm i can only use a scalar multiple of x_{it} to produce a scalar multiple of q_{it}, then his/her period-t TFP-maximisation problem can be written as

$$\max_{q,x}\{Q(q)/X(x) : x \propto x_{it},\ q \propto q_{it},\ D_O^t(x, q, z_{it}) \leq 1\} \tag{4.23}$$

where $Q(.)$ and $X(.)$ are nonnegative, nondecreasing, linearly-homogeneous, scalar-valued aggregator functions that satisfy $TFP(x_{it}, q_{it}) = Q(q_{it})/X(x_{it}) > 0$. There may be several pairs of output and input vectors that solve this problem. Let $\breve{q}_{it} \equiv \breve{q}^t(x_{it}, q_{it}, z_{it})$ and $\breve{x}_{it} \equiv \breve{x}^t(x_{it}, q_{it}, z_{it})$ denote one such pair. The associated maximum TFP is $TFP^t(x_{it}, q_{it}, z_{it}) = Q(\breve{q}_{it})/X(\breve{x}_{it})$. The associated values of the output and input distance functions are $D_O^t(\breve{x}_{it}, \breve{q}_{it}, z_{it}) = D_I^t(\breve{x}_{it}, \breve{q}_{it}, z_{it}) = 1$. This implies that the TFP-maximising point lies on the boundary of $T^t(x_{it}, q_{it}, z_{it})$.

To illustrate, let $Q(q) = a'q$ and $X(x) = b'x$ where a and b are positive vectors satisfying $a'\iota = b'\iota = 1$. Figure 4.11 depicts the TFP maximisation problem that would have faced the manager of firm i in period t. In this figure, the curve passing through point D represents the boundary of $T^t(x_{it}, q_{it}, z_{it})$. The outputs and inputs of firm i in period t map to point A. The aggregate output and input at this point are $Q(q_{it})$ and $X(x_{it})$. The dashed line passing through point A is an iso-productivity ray[12] with a slope of $TFP(x_{it}, q_{it}) = Q(q_{it})/X(x_{it})$. The other dashed lines are iso-productivity rays with higher slopes. TFP maximisation involves choosing the iso-productivity ray with the highest slope that passes through a technically-feasible point. If the manager of firm i had only been able to use a scalar multiple of x_{it} to produce a scalar multiple of q_{it}, then (s)he could have maximised TFP by operating at point D. The TFP at this point is $TFP^t(x_{it}, q_{it}, z_{it}) = Q(\breve{q}_{it})/X(\breve{x}_{it})$.

[12]The equation of the dashed line through point A is $Q(q_{it}) = TFP(x_{it}, q_{it})X(x_{it})$. This is the equation of a line with a slope of $TFP(x_{it}, q_{it})$ and an intercept of zero. The term *iso*-productivity ray derives from the fact that all points on this ray map to the *same* level of TFP, namely $TFP(x_{it}, q_{it}) = Q(q_{it})/X(x_{it})$.

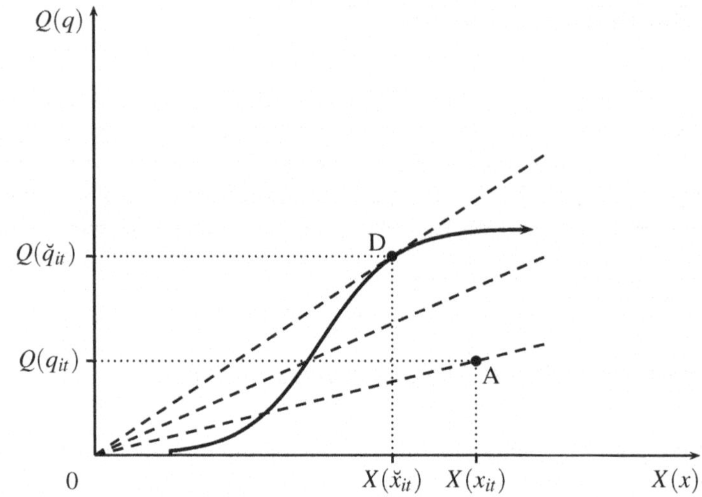

Fig. 4.11 TFP maximisation when the output mix and input mix have been predetermined. If the manager of firm i had only been able to use a scalar multiple of x_{it} to produce a scalar multiple of q_{it}, then (s)he could have maximised TFP by operating at point D

4.6.2 Outputs and Inputs Chosen Freely

If outputs and inputs are strongly disposable, then it is technically possible for firm managers to choose them freely. If the manager of firm i can choose outputs and inputs freely, then his/her period-t TFP-maximisation problem can be written as

$$\max_{q,x}\{Q(q)/X(x) : D_O^t(x, q, z_{it}) \leq 1\} \tag{4.24}$$

where $Q(.)$ and $X(.)$ are nonnegative, nondecreasing, linearly-homogeneous, scalar-valued aggregator functions with parameters (or weights) that represent the values the manager places on outputs and inputs. Again, there may be several pairs of output and input vectors that solve this problem. Let $q_{it}^* \equiv q^t(z_{it})$ and $x_{it}^* \equiv x^t(z_{it})$ denote one such pair. The associated maximum TFP is $TFP^t(z_{it}) = Q(q_{it}^*)/X(x_{it}^*)$. Except in restrictive special cases (e.g., outputs are of no value to the manager), the associated values of the output and input distance functions are $D_O^t(x_{it}^*, q_{it}^*, z_{it}) = D_I^t(x_{it}^*, q_{it}^*, z_{it}) = 1$. Again, this implies that the TFP-maximising point lies on the boundary of $T^t(z_{it})$.

To illustrate, reconsider the TFP maximisation problem depicted in Fig. 4.11. The curve passing through point D in that figure is now reproduced in Fig. 4.12; it represents the boundary of $T^t(x_{it}, q_{it}, z_{it})$. In Fig. 4.12, the curve passing through point E represents the boundary of $T^t(z_{it})$. If the firm manager had only been able to use a scalar multiple of x_{it} to produce a scalar multiple of q_{it}, then (s)he could have maximised TFP by operating at point D. The TFP at this point is

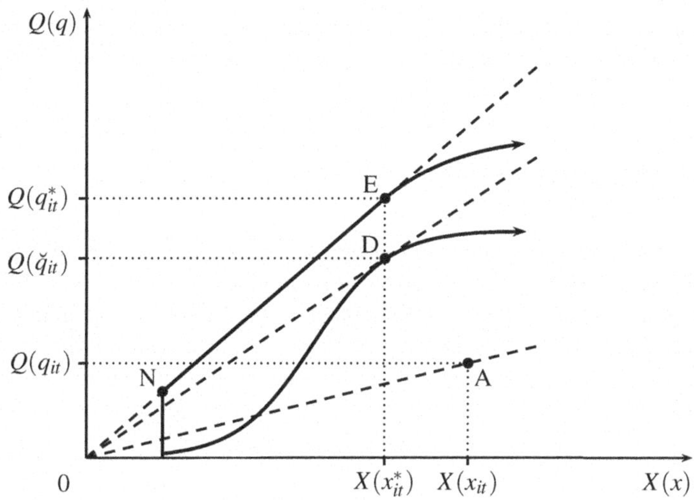

Fig. 4.12 TFP maximisation when outputs and inputs can be chosen freely. If the manager of firm i had been able to choose outputs and inputs freely, then (s)he could have maximised TFP by operating anywhere on the line connecting points N and E

$TFP(\check{x}_{it}, \check{q}_{it}) = Q(\check{q}_{it})/X(\check{x}_{it})$.[13] However, if the manager had been able to choose outputs and inputs freely, then (s)he could have maximised TFP by operating at any point on the line connecting points N and E. The TFP at any point on this line is $TFP^t(z_{it}) = Q(q^*_{it})/X(x^*_{it})$. For a numerical example, see Sect. 1.4.3.

4.6.3 Example

If the output distance function is given by (2.9), then the solutions to (4.23) and (4.24) depend on the elasticity of scale. If η is greater (resp. less) than one, then, whether or not output and input mixes are predetermined, TFP becomes infinitely large as the firm becomes infinitely large (resp. infinitesimally small). If $\eta = 1$, then there are an infinite number of output-input combinations that maximise TFP.

4.7 Other Types of Behaviour

Other optimisation problems faced by managers (and therefore other types of managerial behaviour) involve choosing technologies, maximising net output, and maximising return to the dollar. Many managers make decisions in the face of uncertainty.

---

[13]To avoid clutter, the axis label for $X(\check{x}_{it})$ has been omitted from Fig. 4.12. In this particular example, $X(\check{x}_{it}) = X(x^*_{it})$.

Some managers exhibit bounded rationality in the sense that they have limited capacity to make rational (i.e., optimal) decisions within the time that is available.

4.7.1 Choosing Technologies

If more than one technology exists in period t, then the optimisation problems discussed in Sects. 4.1–4.6 can be solved as either maximax or minimin problems. The output maximisation problem (4.1), for example, can be solved as a maximax problem. This involves (1) finding the maximum aggregate output possible using each technology, then (2) finding the maximum of these maxima. In the first step, the problem of finding the maximum aggregate output possible using technology g can be written as

$$\max_{q}\{Q(q) : q \propto q_{it},\ d_O^g(x_{it}, q_{it}, z_{it}) \leq 1\} \tag{4.25}$$

where $d_O^g(.)$ is the technology-and-environment-specific output distance function defined by (2.39). The output vector that solves this problem is $\bar{q}_{it}^g \equiv q_{it}/d_O^g(x_{it}, q_{it}, z_{it})$. The associated aggregate output is $Q(\bar{q}_{it}^g) = Q(q_{it})/d_O^g(x_{it}, q_{it}, z_{it})$. The associated value of the output distance function is $d_O^g(x_{it}, \bar{q}_{it}^g, z_{it}) = 1$. This implies that the output-maximising point lies on the boundary of the technology-and-environment-specific output set defined by $p^g(x_{it}, z_{it}) = \{q : (x_{it}, q) \in t^g(z_{it})\}$. In the second step, the manager's optimisation problem can be written as

$$\max_{g \in G_t}\{Q(\bar{q}_{it}^g)\} \tag{4.26}$$

where G_t is the period-t technology set. The output vector that solves this problem is $\bar{q}_{it} = q_{it}/D_O^t(x_{it}, q_{it}, z_{it})$ where $D_O^t(x_{it}, q_{it}, z_{it}) = \min_{g \in G_t} d_O^g(x_{it}, q_{it}, z_{it})$. The associated value of the output distance function is $D_O^t(x_{it}, \bar{q}_{it}, z_{it}) = 1$. This implies that the output-maximising point lies on the boundary of $P^t(x_{it}, z_{it}) = \cup_{g \in G_t} p^g(x_{it}, z_{it})$.

To illustrate, reconsider the output maximisation problem depicted earlier in Fig. 4.1, and suppose that technologies 1 and 2 were the only technologies that existed in period t. The output maximisation problem faced by the manager is now depicted in Fig. 4.13. In this figure, the curves passing through points Z and C represent the boundaries of $p^1(x_{it}, z_{it})$ and $p^2(x_{it}, z_{it})$ respectively. The outputs of firm i in period t map to point A. The aggregate output at this point is $Q(q_{it})$. The dashed line passing through point A is an iso-output line with a slope of $-a_1/a_2$ and a vertical intercept of $Q(q_{it})/a_2$. The other dashed lines are iso-output lines with the same slope but higher intercepts. Output maximisation involves choosing the iso-output line with the highest intercept that passes through a technically-feasible point. If the output mix of firm i had been predetermined and the manager had only been able to choose technology 1, then (s)he could have maximised total output by operating at point Z. The aggregate output at this point is $Q(\bar{q}_{it}^1)$. If the output mix of the firm had

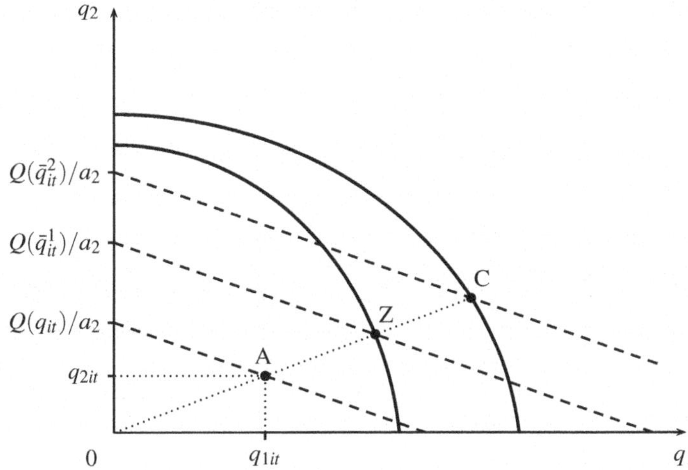

Fig. 4.13 Output maximisation when the output mix is predetermined. If the output mix of firm i had been predetermined and the manager had been able to use either technology, then (s)he could have maximised output by operating at point C

been predetermined and the manager had been able to choose either technology, then (s)he could have maximised total output by choosing technology 2 and operating at point C. The aggregate output at this point is $Q(\bar{q}_{it}) = \max\{Q(\bar{q}_{it}^1), Q(\bar{q}_{it}^2)\} = Q(\bar{q}_{it}^2)$. This is the solution depicted earlier in Fig. 4.1.

4.7.2 Maximising Net Output

If a firm manager places nonnegative values on outputs and inputs (not necessarily market values) and all environmental variables have been predetermined, then (s)he may aim to maximise a measure of net output (NO). If there is more than one output and more than one input, then the precise form of the manager's NO maximisation problem will depend on how easily (s)he can choose the output mix and input mix. If, for example, the manager of firm i can choose outputs and inputs freely, then his/her period-t NO-maximisation problem can be written as

$$\max_{q,x}\{Q(q) - X(x) : D_O^t(x, q, z_{it}) \leq 1\} \tag{4.27}$$

where $Q(.)$ and $X(.)$ are nonnegative, nondecreasing, linearly-homogeneous, scalar-valued aggregator functions with parameters (or weights) that represent the values the firm manager places on outputs and inputs. There may be several pairs of output and input vectors that solve this problem. All such pairs lie on the boundary of

$T^t(z_{it})$. If $Q(q) = p'_{it}q$ and $X(x) = w'_{it}x$, then problem (4.27) is is equivalent to the profit-maximisation problem (4.20).

4.7.3 Maximising Return to the Dollar

If a firm manager values outputs and inputs at market prices and all other variables involved in the production process have been predetermined, then (s)he may aim to maximise revenue divided by cost (or 'return to the dollar'). The exact form of the manager's return to the dollar (RTD) maximisation problem will depend on whether the firm is a price setter or price taker in output and/or input markets. If, for example, firm i is a price-taker in output and input markets, then the manager's period-t RTD maximisation problem can be written as

$$\max_{q,x}\{(p'_{it}q)/(w'_{it}x) : D^t_O(x, q, z_{it}) \leq 1\} \tag{4.28}$$

where p_{it} and w_{it} are vectors of output and input prices that are not affected by the actions the firm. Again, there may be several pairs of output and input vectors that solve this problem. Again, all such pairs lie on the boundary of $T^t(z_{it})$. Problem (4.28) can be viewed as a special case of problem (4.24) corresponding to $Q(q) = p'_{it}q$ and $X(x) = w'_{it}x$.

4.7.4 Behaviour in the Face of Environmental Uncertainty

Managers often make production decisions in the face of uncertainty about characteristics of their production environments. If so-called environmental variables are discrete variables chosen by Nature, then managerial behaviour is best analysed in a state-contingent framework. In the state-contingent literature, it is common to break each production period into two sub-periods: in the first sub-period, the firm manager makes production decisions in the face of uncertainty about characteristics of his/her production environment; in the second sub-period, Nature resolves any uncertainty by choosing a value from the set $\Omega = \{1, \ldots, S\}$. For a simple example, suppose that *all* environmental variables are unknown at the time production decisions are made. Also suppose there is only one output and that all inputs involved in the production process have been predetermined. Let q_s denote the output produced when Nature chooses state $s \in \Omega$. If the manager of firm i seeks to maximise expected output, then the optimisation problem (s)he faces at the beginning of period t can be written as

$$\max_{q_1,\ldots,q_S}\left\{\sum_{s\in\Omega}\pi_{sit}q_s : q_s \leq F^t(x_{it}, s) \text{ for all } s \in \Omega\right\} \tag{4.29}$$

where $F^t(x, s) = 1/D_O^t(x, 1, s)$ is a period-and-state-contingent production function and π_{sit} is the subjective probability that manager i attaches to state s in period t. There may be several state-contingent output vectors that solve this problem. In a slight abuse of notation, let $\hat{q}_{it} \equiv \hat{q}^t(x_{it}, \pi_{1it}, \ldots, \pi_{Sit})$ denote one such vector. The associated expected output is $E(\hat{q}_{it}) = \sum_{s\in\Omega} \pi_{sit}\hat{q}_{sit}$ where $\hat{q}_{sit}$ denotes the s-th element of $\hat{q}_{it}$. Note that if the manager wanted to avoid all environmental risk, then (s)he could choose a solution vector in which all state-contingent outputs were equal.

To illustrate, consider a rice farmer who must decide when to drain his/her fields in the face of uncertainty about whether pre-harvest evaporation will be either high ($s = 1$) or low ($s = 2$). If a field is drained now and evaporation is high, then the plants will suffer moisture stress before they reach maturity and yield will be reduced to the point where the field is not worth harvesting. If a field is drained next month and evaporation is low, then, by the time the field is dry enough for mechanical harvesting, the mature grain will have degraded to the point where, again, the field is not worth harvesting. If a field is drained now (resp. next month) and evaporation is low (resp. high), then the plants will reach maturity without moisture stress and the field will dry out sufficiently for a timely harvest. If a farmer believes evaporation is likely to be low (i.e., if he/she attaches relatively high probability to state 2), then he/she will drain most of his/her fields now; in this case, output will be relatively high (resp. low) if evaporation turns out to be low (resp. high). Suppose that farmer i believes evaporation is likely to be low in period t (i.e., $\pi_{2it} > \pi_{1it}$). Figure 4.14 depicts the expected-output maximisation problem that would have faced this farmer in this period. In Fig. 4.14, the curve passing through point C represents the boundary of the output set defined by $P^t(x_{it}) = \{(q_1, q_2) : q_s \leq F^t(x_{it}, s) \text{ for } s = 1, 2\}$. The ray from the origin through point A is known as the 'bisector'; all points on this ray are riskless insofar as the same output will be produced in each state of Nature. The (riskless) state-contingent outputs of farmer i map to point A. The dashed line passing through point A is an iso-expected-output line[14] with a slope of $-\pi_{1it}/\pi_{2it}$ and a vertical intercept of $E(q_{it})/\pi_{2it}$. The other dashed lines are iso-expected-output lines with the same slope but higher intercepts. Expected-output maximisation involves choosing the iso-expected-output line with the highest intercept that passes through a technically-feasible point. Given his/her subjective probabilities, farmer i could have maximised expected output by operating at point V. The expected output at this point is $E(\hat{q}_{it})$. If farmer i had wanted to avoid all environmental risk, then (s)he could have maximised (expected) output by operating at point C. The (expected) output at this point is $E(\bar{q}_{it})$. The gap between the iso-expected-output lines passing through points C and V represents the risk premium.

[14]If $E(q_{it}) = \pi_{1it}q_{1it} + \pi_{2it}q_{2it}$, then $q_{2it} = E(q_{it})/\pi_{2it} - (\pi_{1it}/\pi_{2it})q_{1it}$. This is the equation of a line with a slope of $-\pi_{1it}/\pi_{2it}$ and an intercept of $E(q_{it})/\pi_{2it}$. The term *iso*-expected-output derives from the fact that all points on this line yield the *same* expected output, namely $E(q_{it})$.

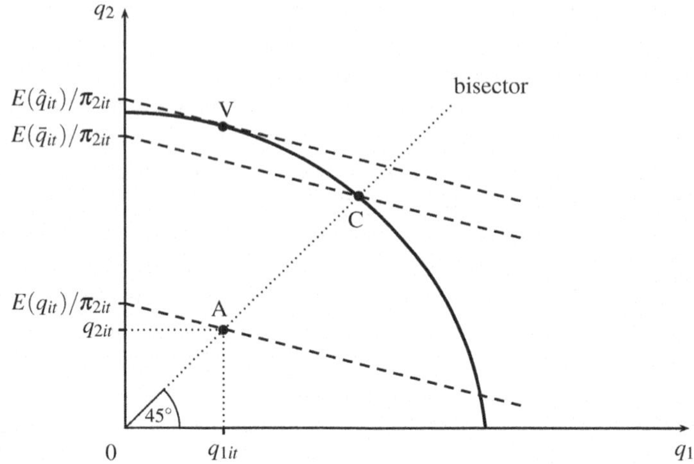

Fig. 4.14 Expected output maximisation in the face of environmental uncertainty. If a manager attaches a relatively high probability to state 2, then (s)he will maximise expected output by operating above the bisector

4.7.5 Behaviour in the Face of Other Types of Uncertainty

It is common to assume that firm managers make output and/or input decisions in the face of many other types of uncertainty. For example, Olley and Pakes (1996) assume that managers make input decisions in the face of uncertainty about productivity.[15] In their widely-cited analysis of the U.S. telecommunications industry, they assume, *inter alia*, that (a) there is only one output, (b) all inputs can be classified as either labour or capital goods, (c) the maximum output that can be produced using given inputs (i.e., the production function) depends on the age of the firm (implying it is firm- and time-varying), (d) the prices of labour and capital goods are firm-invariant, (e) irrespective of the amount of labour that is used, a fixed proportion of the capital stock is consumed in each period, (f) at the beginning of each period, the manager chooses the volume of labour to be used in that period and the volume of capital goods that will be added to the capital stock, (g) *at the beginning of each period, the manager knows how productive he/she will be in that period, but does not know how productive he/she will be in subsequent periods*, and (h) the manager makes his/her labour and capital investment decisions to maximise the expected discounted value of future net returns. If at any time the salvage (or sell-off) value of the firm is greater than the expected returns from staying in business, then the firm will exit the industry. Solving the manager's optimisation problem yields (a) an exit rule and (b) time-varying demand functions for labour and capital goods.

[15] It is not entirely clear what Olley and Pakes (1996) mean by the term 'productivity'. They appear to use the terms 'productivity' and 'efficiency' interchangeably.

4.7.6 *Bounded Rationality*

Firm managers have limited capacity to make rational (i.e., optimal) decisions within the time that is available. So-called 'bounded rationality' may be due to (a) lack of knowledge about the set of choice alternatives that are available (e.g., the set of technologies that exist), (b) lack of knowledge about characteristics of the production environment (e.g., because some characteristics have not been observed), (c) lack of knowledge about the payoffs associated with different choices (e.g., because distance, revenue, cost and/or profit functions are unknown) and/or (d) lack of skill in calculating the payoffs associated with different choices (e.g., because of lack of training and/or experience). In these situations, firm managers often make decisions using heuristics. A heuristic is a practical method for finding a solution that is satisfactory but not necessarily optimal. In layman's terms, a heuristic is a 'rule of thumb'. Managers who use heuristics act as 'satisficers'. Satisficing means choosing a course of action that is 'good enough'. Heuristics can save time, effort and resources. However, they can also lead to systematic errors. In this book, these types of errors are referred to as 'inefficiency'. In the behavioural economics literature, they are sometimes[16] referred to as 'cognitive biases'.

4.8 Summary and Further Reading

To explain changes in productivity, we need to explain how output and input quantities are determined. There are many economic models that can be used for this purpose. Different models are distinguished by different assumptions about what firm managers value, and what they can and cannot choose.

If a firm manager places nonnegative values on outputs (not necessarily market values) and all inputs and environmental variables have been predetermined (i.e., determined in a previous period), then (s)he will generally choose outputs to maximise a measure of total output. If there is more than one output, then the precise form of the manager's output maximisation problem will depend on how easily (s)he can choose the output mix. Irrespective of how easily the output mix can be chosen, the output-maximising point will always lie on the boundary of the output set.

If a firm manager places nonnegative values on inputs and all outputs and environmental variables have been predetermined, then (s)he will generally choose inputs to minimise a measure of total input. If there is more than one input, then the precise form of the manager's input minimisation problem will depend on how easily (s)he can choose the input mix. Irrespective of how easily the input mix can be chosen, the input-minimising point will always lie on the boundary of the input set.

If a firm manager values outputs at market prices and all inputs and environmental variables have been predetermined, then (s)he will generally choose outputs to maximise total revenue. For any given manager, the exact form of the revenue

[16] See, for example, Tversky and Kahneman (1974, p. 1130).

maximisation problem will depend on whether the firm is a price setter or price taker in output markets. If the firm is a price setter in output markets and consumer demand is sufficiently weak, then it may be possible to maximise revenue by selling a small quantity at a high price rather than selling a large quantity at a low price; in this case, the revenue-maximising point may lie inside the boundary of the output set. If the firm is a price taker in output markets, then the revenue-maximising point will always lie on the boundary.

If a firm manager values inputs at market prices and all outputs and environmental variables have been predetermined, then (s)he will generally choose inputs to minimise total cost. For any given manager, the exact form of cost minimisation problem will depend on whether the firm is a price setter or price taker in input markets. In either case, the cost-minimising point will generally lie on the boundary of the input set.

If a firm manager values outputs and inputs at market prices and all environmental variables have been predetermined, then (s)he will tend to choose outputs and inputs to maximise either profit or return-to-the-dollar. For any given manager, the exact form of his/her optimisation problem will depend on whether the firm is a price setter or price taker in output and input markets. In any case, the profit-maximising and return-to-the-dollar-maximising output-input combinations will generally lie on the boundary of the production possibilities set.

If a firm manager places nonnegative values on outputs and inputs (again, not necessarily market values) and all environmental variables have been predetermined, then (s)he will tend to choose outputs and inputs to maximise a measure of either TFP or net output. If there is more than one output and more than one input, then the precise form of the manager's optimisation problem will depend on how easily (s)he can choose the output mix and input mix. Irrespective of how easily the output and input mixes can be chosen, the TFP-maximising and net-output-maximising output-input combinations will always lie on the boundary of the production possibilities set.

If more than one technology exists in a given period, then each of the optimisation problems discussed above can be solved as either a maximax problem or a minimin problem. For example, an output maximisation problem can be solved by (1) finding the maximum aggregate output possible using each technology, then (2) finding the maximum of these maxima. As another example, a cost minimisation problem can be solved by (1) finding the minimum cost of production using each technology, then (2) finding the minimum of these minima.

Some optimisation problems involve price, demand and/or environmental uncertainty. Decision-making in the face of uncertainty is often analysed within a state-contingent framework. For more details concerning state-contingent models of behaviour, see Chambers and Quiggin (2000), Quiggin and Chambers (2006), Serra et al. (2010), O'Donnell et al. (2010) and Rasmussen (2011). Some managers have limited capacity to solve complex optimisation problems. For more details concerning so-called bounded rationality, see the seminal work of Simon (1955). Boundedly-rational managers often make decisions using heuristics (i.e., 'rules of thumb').

References

Chambers R, Quiggin J (2000) Uncertainty, production, choice and agency: the state-contingent approach. Cambridge University Press, Cambridge, UK

Färe R, Primont D (1995) Multi-output production and duality: theory and applications. Kluwer Academic Publishers, Boston

O'Donnell C (2016) Using information about technologies, markets and firm behaviour to decompose a proper productivity index. J Econometrics 190(2):328–340

O'Donnell C, Chambers R, Quiggin J (2010) Efficiency analysis in the presence of uncertainty. J Prod Anal 33(1):1–17

Olley G, Pakes A (1996) The dynamics of productivity in the telecommunications equipment industry. Econometrica 64(6):1263–1297

Quiggin J, Chambers R (2006) The state-contingent approach to production under uncertainty. Aust J Agric Resour Econ 50(2):153–169

Rasmussen S (2011) Optimisation of production under uncertainty: the state-contingent approach. Springer, Heidelberg

Serra T, Stefanou S, Oude Lansink A (2010) A dynamic dual model under state-contingent production uncertainty. Eur Rev Agric Econ 37(3):293–312

Simon H (1955) A behavioral model of rational choice. Q J Econ 69(1):99–118

Tversky A, Kahneman D (1974) Judgment under uncertainty: heuristics and biases. Science 185(4157):1124–1131

Chapter 5
Measures of Efficiency

Measures of efficiency can be viewed as *ex post* measures of how well firm managers have solved different optimisation problems. For example, measures of output-oriented technical efficiency can be viewed as measures of how well managers have maximised outputs when inputs and output mixes have been predetermined. Similarly, measures of profit efficiency can be viewed as measures of how well managers have maximised profits when inputs and outputs have been chosen freely. This chapter discusses various output-, input-, revenue-, cost-, profit- and productivity-oriented measures of efficiency. Except where explicitly stated otherwise, all measures of efficiency defined in this chapter take values in the closed unit interval. A firm manager is said to have been fully efficient by some measure if and only if that measure takes the value one.

5.1 Output-Oriented Measures

Output-oriented measures of efficiency are relevant measures of managerial performance in situations where managers have placed nonnegative values on outputs (not necessarily market values) and inputs have been predetermined (i.e., chosen in a previous period). In these situations, the relevance of a particular measure depends on how easily the manager has been able to choose the output mix. If the output mix of the firm has been predetermined, then the most relevant measure is output-oriented technical efficiency (OTE). If the manager has been able to choose outputs freely, then the most relevant measure is output-oriented technical and mix efficiency (OTME). Measures of OTME can be decomposed into separate measures of technical and mix efficiency.

C. J. O'Donnell, *Productivity and Efficiency Analysis*,
https://doi.org/10.1007/978-981-13-2984-5_5

5.1.1 Output-Oriented Technical Efficiency

Several measures of OTE can be found in the literature. In this book, the OTE of manager i in period t is defined as $OTE^t(x_{it}, q_{it}, z_{it}) = D_O^t(x_{it}, q_{it}, z_{it})$. Equivalently,

$$OTE^t(x_{it}, q_{it}, z_{it}) = Q(q_{it})/Q(\bar{q}_{it}) \tag{5.1}$$

where $Q(q_{it})$ is the aggregate output of the firm and $Q(\bar{q}_{it}) = Q(q_{it})/D_O^t(x_{it}, q_{it}, z_{it})$ is the maximum aggregate output that is possible in period t when using x_{it} to produce a scalar multiple of q_{it} in an environment characterised by z_{it}. This particular measure of OTE can be found in O'Donnell (2016, p. 332). If environmental variables have been predetermined, then it can be viewed as a measure of how well the manager has solved problem (4.1). If there is no environmental change, then it is equivalent to the measure of 'output technical efficiency' defined by Balk (1998, Eq. 2.16). If there is no technical or environmental change, then it is equivalent to the *reciprocal* of the measure of 'technical output efficiency' defined by Färe and Primont (1995, Eq. 3.4.14).

To illustrate, reconsider the output maximisation problem depicted earlier in Fig. 4.1. For convenience, relevant parts of that figure are now reproduced in Fig. 5.1. In these figures, the frontier passing through point C represents the boundary of $P^t(x_{it}, z_{it})$. The outputs of firm i in period t map to point A. The dashed lines passing through points A and C are iso-output lines with the same slope but different intercepts. The OTE of manager i in period t is given by the ratio of these intercepts. Equivalently, $OTE^t(x_{it}, q_{it}, z_{it}) = ||0A||/||0C||$ (i.e., the length of the line segment 0A divided by the length of the line segment 0C).

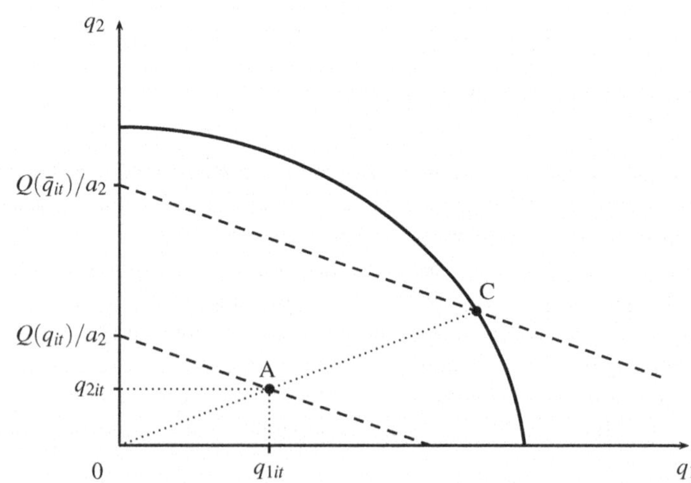

Fig. 5.1 Output-oriented technical inefficiency. The gap between the dashed lines passing through A and C is due to technical inefficiency

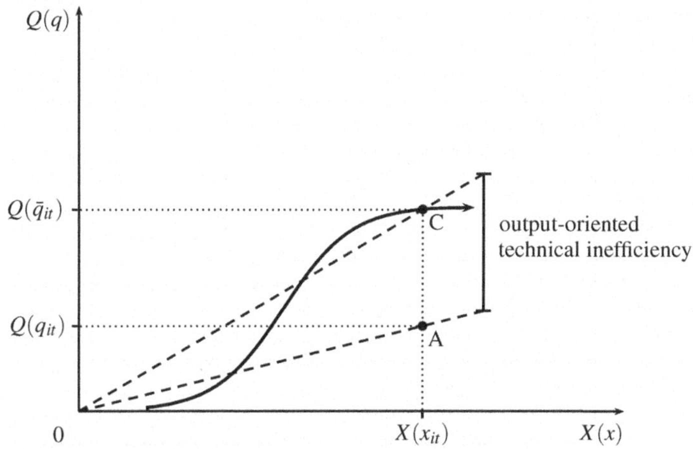

Fig. 5.2 Output-oriented technical inefficiency. The gap between the rays passing through A and C is due to technical inefficiency

The fact that the OTE of a manager can be defined in terms of aggregate outputs means it can also be depicted in output-input space. It can also be viewed as a TFP index. For example, points A and C in Fig. 5.1 map to points A and C in Fig. 5.2. In Fig. 5.2, the frontier passing through point C represents the boundary of $T^t(x_{it}, q_{it}, z_{it})$. The TFP at point A is $TFP(x_{it}, q_{it}) = Q(q_{it})/X(x_{it}) =$ slope 0A. The TFP at point C is $TFP(x_{it}, \bar{q}_{it}) = Q(\bar{q}_{it})/X(x_{it}) =$ slope 0C. The OTE of manager i in period t is $OTE^t(x_{it}, q_{it}, z_{it}) = TFP(x_{it}, q_{it})/TFP(x_{it}, \bar{q}_{it}) =$ (slope 0A)/(slope 0C) (i.e., an index that compares the TFP at point A with the TFP at point C). For a numerical example, see Sect. 1.5.1.

5.1.2 *Output-Oriented Technical and Mix Efficiency*

The OTME of manager i in period t is defined as

$$OTME^t(x_{it}, q_{it}, z_{it}) = Q(q_{it})/Q(\hat{q}_{it}) \tag{5.2}$$

where $Q(q_{it})$ is the aggregate output of the firm and $Q(\hat{q}_{it})$ is the maximum aggregate output that is possible in period t when using x_{it} in an environment characterised by z_{it}. This measure of efficiency appears to be new. If environmental variables have been predetermined, then it can be viewed as a measure of how well the manager has solved problem (4.2).

To illustrate, reconsider the output maximisation problem depicted earlier in Fig. 5.14. Relevant parts of that figure are now reproduced in Fig. 5.3. In this figure,

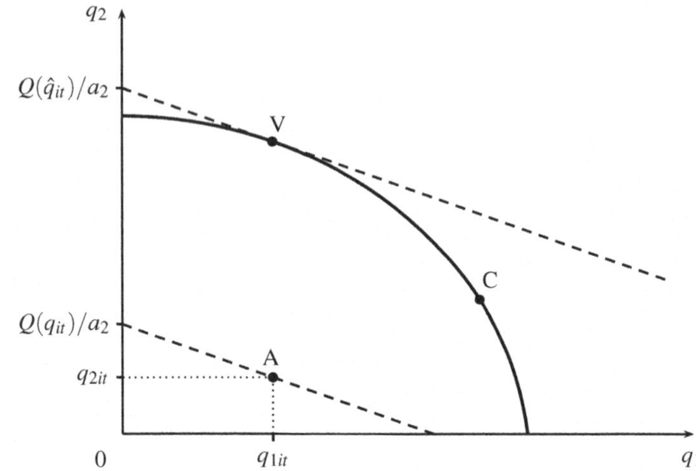

Fig. 5.3 Output-oriented technical and mix inefficiency. The gap between the dashed lines passing through A and V is due to technical and mix inefficiency

the frontier passing through point C is the frontier depicted earlier in Fig. 5.1; it represents the boundary of $P^t(x_{it}, z_{it})$. The outputs of firm i in period t map to point A. The dashed lines passing through points A and V are iso-output lines with the same slope but different intercepts. The OTME of manager i in period t is given by the ratio of these intercepts.

Again, the fact that the OTME of a manager can be defined in terms of aggregate outputs means it can be depicted in output-input space. Again, this means it can be viewed as a TFP index. For example, points A and V in Fig. 5.3 map to points A and V in Fig. 5.4. In this figure, the frontier passing through point E (and just above point V) represents the boundary of $T^t(z_{it})$. The TFP at point A is $TFP(x_{it}, q_{it}) = Q(q_{it})/X(x_{it}) =$ slope 0A. The TFP at point V is $TFP(x_{it}, \hat{q}_{it}) = Q(\hat{q}_{it})/X(x_{it}) =$ slope 0V. The OTME of manager i in period t is $OTME^t(x_{it}, q_{it}, z_{it}) = TFP(x_{it}, q_{it})/TFP(x_{it}, \hat{q}_{it}) =$ (slope 0A)/(slope 0V) (i.e., an index that compares the TFP at point A with the TFP at point V).

5.1.3 *Output-Oriented Mix Efficiency*

The measure of OTME defined by (5.2) can be decomposed into separate measures of technical and mix efficiency. The technical efficiency component is the measure of OTE defined by (5.1). The mix efficiency component is an output-oriented measure of how well the manager has captured economies of output substitution. Economies of output substitution are the benefits obtained by substituting some outputs for

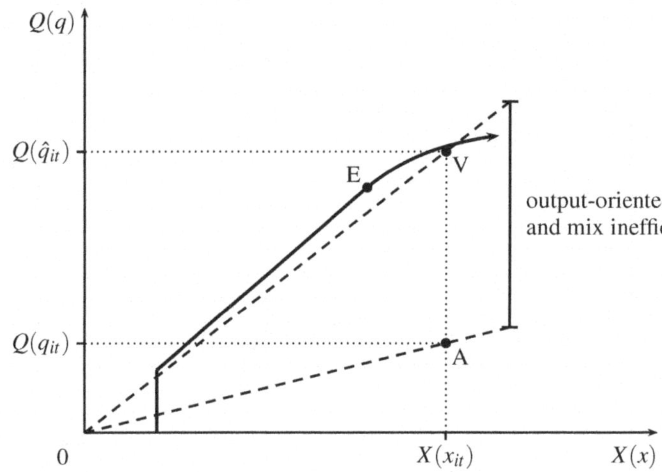

Fig. 5.4 Output-oriented technical and mix inefficiency. The gap between the rays passing through A and V is due to technical and mix inefficiency

others (e.g., producing less of output 1 in order to produce more of output 2). In this book, the so-called output-oriented mix efficiency (OME) of manager i in period t is defined as

$$OME^t(x_{it}, q_{it}, z_{it}) = Q(\bar{q}_{it})/Q(\hat{q}_{it}) \tag{5.3}$$

where $Q(\bar{q}_{it}) = Q(q_{it})/D^t_O(x_{it}, q_{it}, z_{it})$ is the maximum aggregate output that is possible in period t when using x_{it} to produce a scalar multiple of q_{it} in an environment characterised by z_{it}. Equations (5.1), (5.2) and (5.3) imply that

$$OME^t(x_{it}, q_{it}, z_{it}) = OTME^t(x_{it}, q_{it}, z_{it})/OTE^t(x_{it}, q_{it}, z_{it}). \tag{5.4}$$

This equation says that OME is the component of OTME that remains after accounting for OTE. If there is no environmental change, then the measure of OME defined by (5.3) is equivalent to the measure of OME defined by O'Donnell (2010, Eq. 3.4). If there is only one output, then it takes the value one.

To illustrate, reconsider the measures of OTE and OTME depicted in Figs. 5.1 and 5.3. For convenience, those figures are now combined into Fig. 5.5. In this figure, the outputs of firm i in period t map to point A. The dashed lines passing through points A, C and V are iso-output lines with the same slope but different intercepts. The OTME, OTE and OME of manager i in period t are given by the ratios of these intercepts.

Again, the fact that the OME of a manager can be defined in terms of aggregate outputs means it can be depicted in output-input space. Again, this means it can be viewed as a TFP index. For example, points A, C and V in Fig. 5.5 map to points A, C and V in Fig. 5.6. In this figure, the frontier passing through point C is the frontier

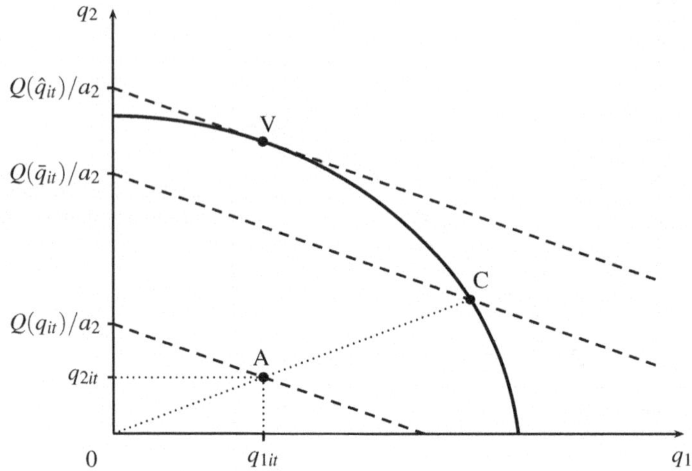

Fig. 5.5 Output-oriented technical and mix inefficiency. The gap between the dashed lines passing through A and C is due to technical inefficiency. The gap between the dashed lines passing through C and V is due to mix inefficiency

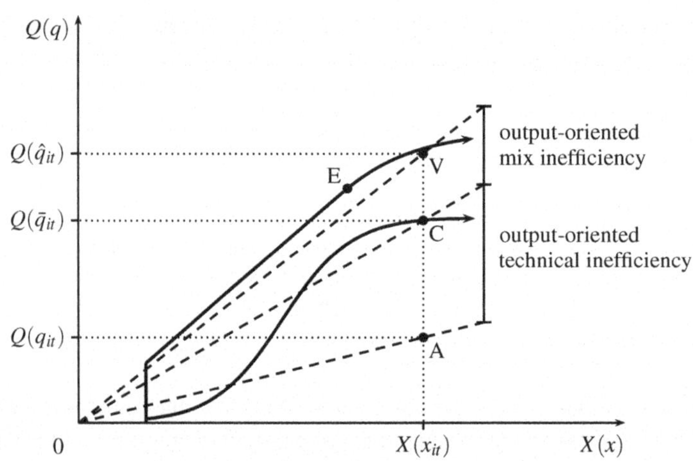

Fig. 5.6 Output-oriented technical and mix inefficiency. The gap between the rays passing through A and C is due to technical inefficiency. The gap between the rays passing through C and V is due to mix inefficiency

depicted earlier in Fig. 5.2; it represents the boundary of $T^t(x_{it}, q_{it}, z_{it})$. The frontier passing through point E is the frontier depicted in Fig. 5.4; it represents the boundary of $T^t(z_{it})$. The TFP at point C is $TFP(x_{it}, \bar{q}_{it}) = Q(\bar{q}_{it})/X(x_{it})$ = slope 0C. The TFP at point V is $TFP(x_{it}, \hat{q}_{it}) = Q(\hat{q}_{it})/X(x_{it})$ = slope 0V. The OME of manager i in period t is $OME^t(x_{it}, q_{it}, z_{it}) = TFP(x_{it}, \bar{q}_{it})/TFP(x_{it}, \hat{q}_{it})$ = (slope 0C)/(slope 0V) (i.e., an index that compares the TFP at point C with the TFP at point V).

5.1.4 Example

If the output distance function is given by (2.9), then the OTE of manager i in period t is

$$OTE^t(x_{it}, q_{it}, z_{it}) = \left(A(t)\prod_{j=1}^{J} z_{jit}^{\delta_j}\prod_{m=1}^{M} x_{mit}^{\beta_m}\right)^{-1}\left(\sum_{n=1}^{N}\gamma_n q_{nit}^{\tau}\right)^{1/\tau}. \tag{5.5}$$

The OTME and OME of the manager depend on both the aggregator function and the value of τ. Suppose $Q(q) = a'q$ where $a = (a_1, \ldots, a_N)' > 0$. If $\tau > 1$, then

$$OTME^t(x_{it}, q_{it}, z_{it}) = a'q_{it}\left(A(t)\prod_{j=1}^{J} z_{jit}^{\delta_j}\prod_{m=1}^{M} x_{mit}^{\beta_m}\right)^{-1}\left(\sum_{n=1}^{N}\gamma_n^{\sigma} a_n^{1-\sigma}\right)^{1/(\sigma-1)}$$

and $$OME^t(x_{it}, q_{it}, z_{it}) = a'q_{it}\left(\sum_{n=1}^{N}\gamma_n q_{nit}^{\tau}\right)^{-1/\tau}\left(\sum_{n=1}^{N}\gamma_n^{\sigma} a_n^{1-\sigma}\right)^{1/(\sigma-1)} \tag{5.6}$$

where $\sigma = 1/(1-\tau) < 0$. As $\tau \to 1$,[1]

$$OTE^t(x_{it}, q_{it}, z_{it}) \to \left(A(t)\prod_{j=1}^{J} z_{jit}^{\delta_j}\prod_{m=1}^{M} x_{mit}^{\beta_m}\right)^{-1}\left(\sum_{n=1}^{N}\gamma_n q_{nit}\right),$$

$$OTME^t(x_{it}, q_{it}, z_{it}) \to a'q_{it}\left(A(t)\prod_{j=1}^{J} z_{jit}^{\delta_j}\prod_{m=1}^{M} x_{mit}^{\beta_m}\max\left\{\frac{a_1}{\gamma_1}, \ldots, \frac{a_N}{\gamma_N}\right\}\right)^{-1}$$

and $$OME^t(x_{it}, q_{it}, z_{it}) \to \left(\frac{a'q_{it}}{\gamma'q_{it}}\right)\left(\max\left\{\frac{a_1}{\gamma_1}, \ldots, \frac{a_N}{\gamma_N}\right\}\right)^{-1}. \tag{5.7}$$

5.2 Input-Oriented Measures

Input-oriented measures of efficiency are relevant measures of managerial performance in situations where managers have placed nonnegative values on inputs (not necessarily market values) and outputs have been predetermined. In these situations, the relevance of a particular measure depends on how easily the manager has been able to choose the input mix. If the input mix of the firm has been predetermined, then the most relevant measure is input-oriented technical efficiency (ITE). If the manager

---

[1] As $\tau \to 1$, $\sigma \to -\infty$. By a limiting argument originally due to Hardy et al. (1934, pp. 13, 15), $\lim_{\sigma\to-\infty}\left(\sum_n \gamma_n^{\sigma} a_n^{1-\sigma}\right)^{1/(1-\sigma)} = \max\{a_1/\gamma_1, \ldots, a_N/\gamma_N\}$.

has been able to choose inputs freely, then the most relevant measure is input-oriented technical and mix efficiency (ITME). Measures of ITME can be decomposed into separate measures of technical and mix efficiency.

5.2.1 Input-Oriented Technical Efficiency

Again, several measures of ITE can be found in the literature. The basic idea behind these measures can be traced back to the 'coefficient of resource utilization' defined by Debreu (1951, p. 285). In this book, the ITE of manager i in period t is defined as $ITE^t(x_{it}, q_{it}, z_{it}) = 1/D_I^t(x_{it}, q_{it}, z_{it})$. Equivalently,

$$ITE^t(x_{it}, q_{it}, z_{it}) = X(\bar{x}_{it})/X(x_{it}) \tag{5.8}$$

where $X(x_{it})$ is the aggregate input of the firm and $X(\bar{x}_{it}) = X(x_{it})/D_I^t(x_{it}, q_{it}, z_{it})$ is the minimum aggregate input needed to produce q_{it} in period t when using a scalar multiple of x_{it} in an environment characterised by z_{it}. This particular measure of ITE can be found in O'Donnell (2016, p. 331). If environmental variables have been predetermined, then it can be viewed as a measure of how well the manager has solved problem (4.5). If there is no environmental change, then it is equivalent to the measure of 'input technical efficiency' defined by Balk (1998, Eq. 2.15). If there is no technical or environmental change, then it is equivalent to the measure of 'technical efficiency' defined by Färe and Primont (1995, Eq. 3.4.7).

To illustrate, reconsider the input minimisation problem depicted earlier in Fig. 4.3. Relevant parts of that figure are now reproduced in Fig. 5.7. In these figures, the frontier passing through point B represents the boundary of $L^t(q_{it}, z_{it})$. The inputs of firm i in period t map to point A. The dashed lines passing through points A and B are iso-input lines with the same slope but different intercepts. The ITE of manager i in period t is given by the ratio of these intercepts. Equivalently, $ITE^t(x_{it}, q_{it}, z_{it}) = ||0B||/||0A||$ (i.e., the length of the line segment 0B divided by the length of the line segment 0A).

The fact that the ITE of a manager can be defined in terms of aggregate inputs means it can also be depicted in output-input space. It can also be viewed as a TFP index. For example, points A and B in Fig. 5.7 map to points A and B in Fig. 5.8. In Fig. 5.8, the frontier passing through point B is the frontier depicted earlier in Fig. 5.2; it represents the boundary of $T^t(x_{it}, q_{it}, z_{it})$. The TFP at point A is $TFP(x_{it}, q_{it}) = Q(q_{it})/X(x_{it}) =$ slope 0A. The TFP at point B is $TFP(\bar{x}_{it}, q_{it}) = Q(q_{it})/X(\bar{x}_{it}) =$ slope 0B. The ITE of manager i in period t is $ITE^t(x_{it}, q_{it}, z_{it}) = TFP(x_{it}, q_{it})/TFP(\bar{x}_{it}, q_{it}) =$ (slope 0A)/(slope 0B) (i.e., an index that compares the TFP at point A with the TFP at point B). For a numerical example, see Sect. 1.5.2.

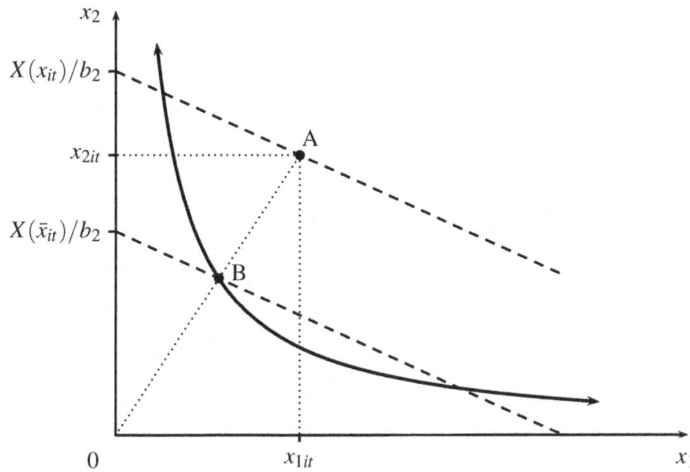

Fig. 5.7 Input-oriented technical inefficiency. The gap between the dashed lines passing through A and B is due to technical inefficiency

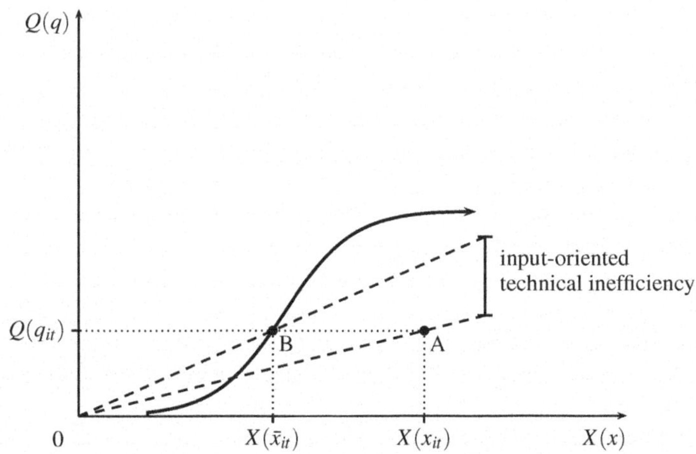

Fig. 5.8 Input-oriented technical inefficiency. The gap between the rays through A and B is due to technical inefficiency

5.2.2 *Input-Oriented Technical and Mix Efficiency*

The ITME of manager i in period t is defined as

$$ITME^t(x_{it}, q_{it}, z_{it}) = X(\hat{x}_{it})/X(x_{it}) \tag{5.9}$$

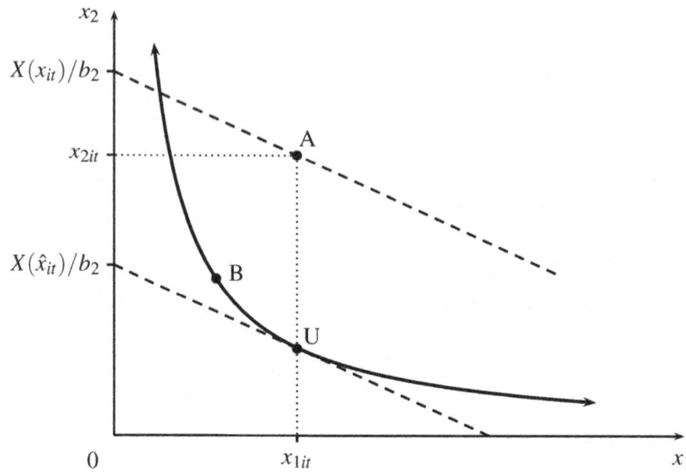

Fig. 5.9 Input-oriented technical and mix inefficiency. The gap between the dashed lines passing through A and U is due to technical and mix inefficiency

where $X(x_{it})$ is the aggregate input of the firm and $X(\hat{x}_{it})$ is the minimum aggregate input needed to produce q_{it} in period t in an environment characterised by z_{it}. Again, this measure of efficiency appears to be new. If environmental variables have been predetermined, then it can be viewed as a measure of how well the manager has solved problem (4.6).

To illustrate, reconsider the input minimisation problem depicted earlier in Fig. 4.4. Relevant parts of that figure are now reproduced in Fig. 5.9. In this figure, the frontier passing through point B is the frontier depicted earlier in Fig. 5.7; it represents the boundary of $L^t(q_{it}, z_{it})$. The inputs of firm i in period t map to point A. The dashed lines passing through points A and U are iso-input lines with the same slope but different intercepts. The ITME of manager i in period t is given by the ratio of these intercepts.

Again, the fact that the ITME of a manager can be defined in terms of aggregate inputs means it can be depicted in output-input space. Again, this means it can be viewed as a TFP index. For example, points A and U in Fig. 5.9 map to points A and U in Fig. 5.10. In this figure, the frontier passing through point E is the frontier depicted earlier in Fig. 5.4; it represents the boundary of $T^t(z_{it})$. The TFP at point A is $TFP(x_{it}, q_{it}) = Q(q_{it})/X(x_{it}) =$ slope 0A. The TFP at point U is $TFP(\hat{x}_{it}, q_{it}) = Q(q_{it})/X(\hat{x}_{it}) =$ slope 0U. The ITME of manager i in period t is $ITME^t(x_{it}, q_{it}, z_{it}) = TFP(x_{it}, q_{it})/TFP(\hat{x}_{it}, q_{it}) =$ (slope 0A)/(slope 0U) (i.e., an index that compares the TFP at point A with the TFP at point U).

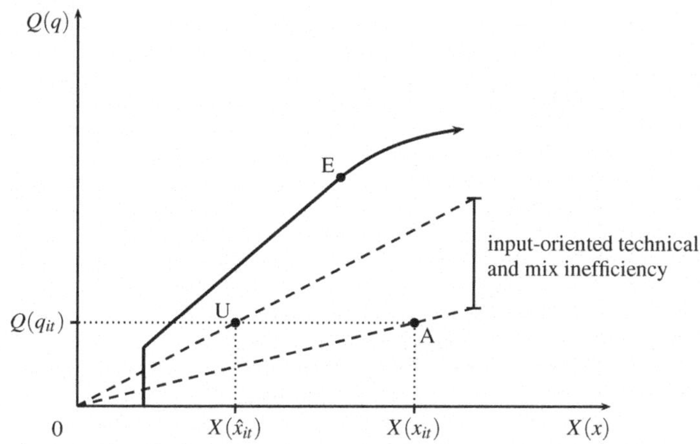

Fig. 5.10 Input-oriented technical and mix inefficiency. The gap between the rays passing through A and U is due to technical and mix inefficiency

5.2.3 *Input-Oriented Mix Efficiency*

The measure of ITME defined by (5.9) can be decomposed into separate measures of technical and mix efficiency. The technical efficiency component is the measure of ITE defined by (5.8). The mix efficiency component is an input-oriented measure of how well the manager has captured economies of input substitution. Economies of input substitution are the benefits obtained by substituting some inputs for others (e.g., substituting capital for labour). In this book, the so-called input-oriented mix efficiency (IME) of manager i in period t is defined as

$$IME^t(x_{it}, q_{it}, z_{it}) = X(\hat{x}_{it})/X(\bar{x}_{it}) \tag{5.10}$$

where $X(\bar{x}_{it}) = X(x_{it})/D_I^t(x_{it}, q_{it}, z_{it})$ is the minimum aggregate input needed to produce q_{it} in period t when using a scalar multiple of x_{it} in an environment characterised by z_{it}. Equations (5.8), (5.9) and (5.10) imply that

$$IME^t(x_{it}, q_{it}, z_{it}) = ITME^t(x_{it}, q_{it}, z_{it})/ITE^t(x_{it}, q_{it}, z_{it}). \tag{5.11}$$

This equation says that IME is the component of ITME that remains after accounting for ITE. If there is no environmental change, then the measure of IME defined by (5.10) is equivalent to the measure of IME defined by O'Donnell (2010, Eq. 4.6). If there is only one input, then it takes the value one.

To illustrate, reconsider the measures of ITE and ITME depicted in Figs. 5.7 and 5.9. For convenience, those figures are now combined into Fig. 5.11. In this figure, the inputs of firm i in period t map to point A. The dashed lines passing through points A, B and U are iso-input lines with the same slope but different intercepts.

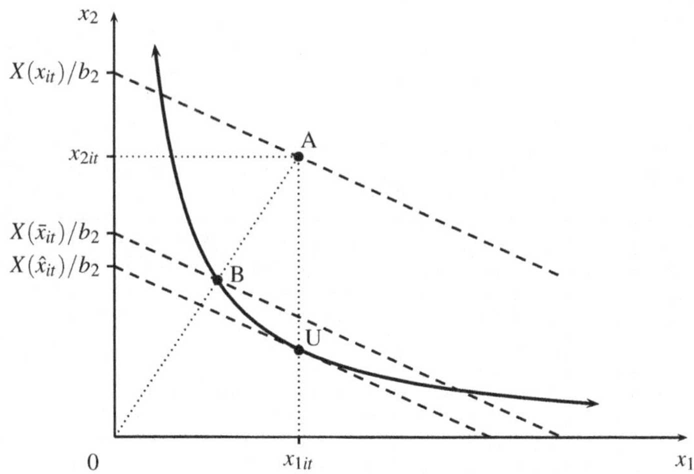

Fig. 5.11 Input-oriented technical and mix inefficiency. The gap between the dashed lines passing through A and B is due to technical inefficiency. The gap between the dashed lines passing through U and B is due to mix inefficiency

The ITME, ITE and IME of manager i in period t are given by the ratios of these intercepts.

Again, the fact that the IME of a manager can be defined in terms of aggregate inputs means it can be depicted in output-input space. Again, this means it can be viewed as a TFP index. For example, points A, B and U in Fig. 5.11 map to points A, B and U in Fig. 5.12. In this figure, the frontier passing through point B is the frontier depicted earlier in Fig. 5.8; it represents the boundary of $T^t(x_{it}, q_{it}, z_{it})$. The frontier passing through point E is the frontier depicted in Fig. 5.10; it represents the boundary of $T^t(z_{it})$. The TFP at point B is $TFP(\bar{x}_{it}, q_{it}) = Q(q_{it})/X(\bar{x}_{it}) =$ slope 0B. The TFP at point U is $TFP(\hat{x}_{it}, q_{it}) = Q(q_{it})/X(\hat{x}_{it}) =$ slope 0U. The IME of manager i in period t is $IME^t(x_{it}, q_{it}, z_{it}) = TFP(\bar{x}_{it}, q_{it})/TFP(\hat{x}_{it}, q_{it}) =$ (slope 0B)/(slope 0U) (i.e., an index that compares the TFP at point B with the TFP at point U).

5.2.4 Example

If the input distance function is given by (2.13), then the ITE of manager i in period t is

$$ITE^t(x_{it}, q_{it}, z_{it}) = \left(B(t) \prod_{j=1}^{J} z_{jit}^{\kappa_j} \prod_{m=1}^{M} x_{mit}^{\lambda_m} \right)^{-1} \left(\sum_{n=1}^{N} \gamma_n q_{nit}^{\tau} \right)^{1/(\tau\eta)}. \quad (5.12)$$

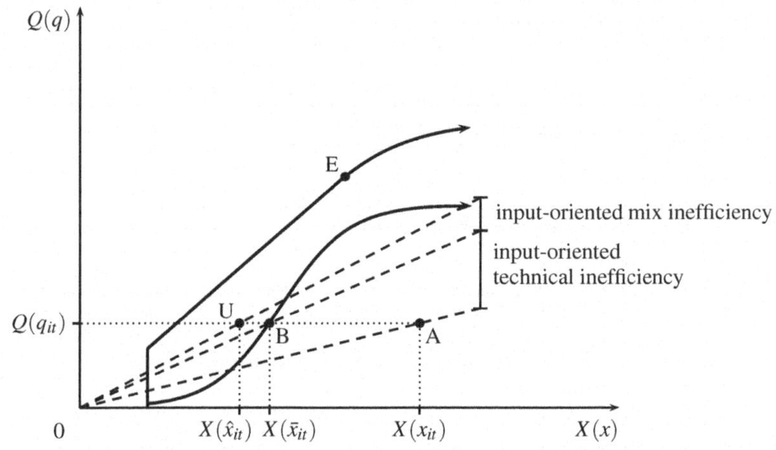

Fig. 5.12 Input-oriented technical and mix inefficiency. The gap between the rays passing through A and B is due to technical inefficiency. The gap between the rays passing through U and B is due to mix inefficiency

The ITME and IME of the manager depend on the aggregator function. If $X(x) = b'x$ where $b = (b_1, \ldots, b_M)' > 0$, then

$$ITME^t(x_{it}, q_{it}, z_{it}) = \left(\left(b'x_{it}\, B(t) \prod_{j=1}^{J} z_{jit}^{\kappa_j} \right)^{-1} \prod_{m=1}^{M} \left(\frac{b_m}{\lambda_m} \right)^{\lambda_m} \left(\sum_{n=1}^{N} \gamma_n q_{nit}^{\tau} \right) \right)^{1/(\tau\eta)}$$

and $$IME^t(x_{it}, q_{it}, z_{it}) = \left(b'x_{it} \right)^{-1} \prod_{m=1}^{M} \left(\frac{b_m x_{mit}}{\lambda_m} \right)^{\lambda_m}. \qquad (5.13)$$

5.3 Revenue-Oriented Measures

Revenue-oriented measures of efficiency are relevant measures of managerial performance in situations where managers have valued outputs at market prices and inputs have been predetermined. The most widely-used revenue-oriented measure of efficiency is revenue efficiency (RE). If a firm is a price taker in output markets, then the RE of its manager can be decomposed into separate measures of technical and allocative efficiency.

5.3.1 Revenue Efficiency

For any given manager, the exact definition of RE depends on whether the firm is a price setter or price taker in output markets.

5.3.1.1 Price Setters in Output Markets

If firm i is a price setter in output markets, then the RE of manager i in period t is

$$RE^t(x_{it}, d_{it}, q_{it}, z_{it}) = R_{it}/R^t(x_{it}, d_{it}, z_{it}) \quad (5.14)$$

where $R_{it} = p(q_{it}, d_{it})'q_{it}$ is the revenue of the firm and $R^t(x_{it}, d_{it}, z_{it})$ is the maximum revenue that can be earned using x_{it} in period t when the production environment and the demand market are characterised by z_{it} and d_{it} respectively. This particular measure of RE appears to be new. If environmental variables have been predetermined, then it can be viewed as a measure of how well the manager has solved problem (4.9).

For a numerical example, reconsider the revenue maximisation problem depicted earlier in Fig. 4.5. Relevant parts of that figure are now reproduced in Fig. 5.13. In these figures, the frontier passing through point C represents the boundary of $P^1(\iota, 1)$. If the vector of demand shifters had been $d_{i1} = (4.1, 4.1)'$, then the revenue-maximising point would have been point T. The associated maximum revenue would

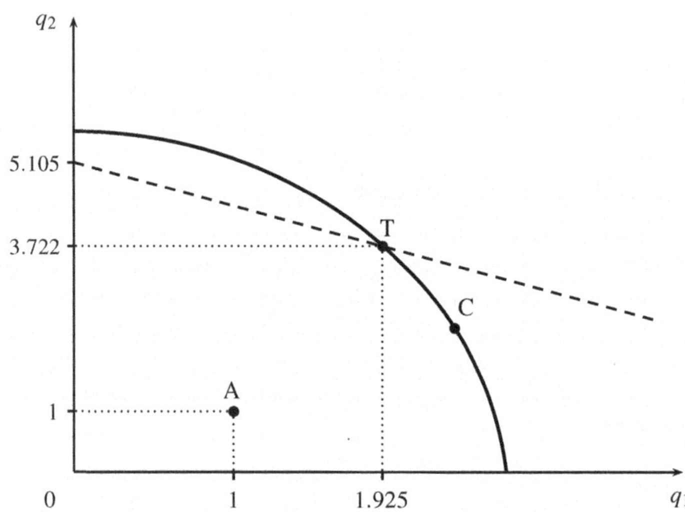

Fig. 5.13 The revenue efficiency of the manager of a price-setting firm. If consumer demand had been relatively strong, then the RE of the manager of firm A would have been $RE^1(\iota, 4.1\iota, \iota, 1) = 0.548$

have been $R^1(\iota, 4.1\iota, 1) = 7.791$. On the other hand, the revenue at point A would have been $R_{11} = 4.266$. Thus, the RE of the manager of firm A would have been $RE^1(\iota, 4.1\iota, \iota, 1) = R_{11}/R^1(\iota, 4.1\iota, 1) = 4.266/7.791 = 0.548$.

5.3.1.2 Price Takers in Output Markets

If firm i is a price taker in output markets, then the RE of manager i in period t is[2]

$$RE^t(x_{it}, p_{it}, q_{it}, z_{it}) = R_{it}/R^t(x_{it}, p_{it}, z_{it}) \tag{5.15}$$

where $R_{it} = p'_{it}q_{it}$ is the revenue of the firm and $R^t(x_{it}, p_{it}, z_{it})$ is the maximum revenue that can be earned using x_{it} in period t in a production environment characterised by z_{it} when output prices are given by p_{it}. Again, this particular measure of RE appears to be new. If environmental variables have been predetermined, then it can be viewed as a measure of how well the manager has solved problem (4.12). If there is no environmental change, then it is equivalent to the measure of RE defined by Balk (1998, Eq. 4.4). If there is no technical or environmental change, then it is equivalent to the *reciprocal* of the measure of 'overall output efficiency' defined by Färe et al. (1985, Eq. 4.4.5).

To illustrate, reconsider the revenue maximisation problem depicted earlier in Fig. 4.6. Relevant parts of that figure are now reproduced in Fig. 5.14. In these figures, the frontier passing through point C is the frontier depicted earlier in Fig. 5.3; it represents the boundary of $P^t(x_{it}, z_{it})$. The outputs of firm i in period t map to point A. The dashed lines passing through points A and K are iso-revenue lines with the same slope but different intercepts. The RE of manager i in period t is given by the ratio of these intercepts. It is worth noting that the ratio of the intercepts in Fig. 5.14 is not the same as the ratio of the intercepts in Fig. 5.3. This illustrates that RE does not generally equal OTME.

5.3.2 *Output-Oriented Allocative Efficiency*

The measure of RE defined by (5.15) can be decomposed into separate measures of technical and allocative efficiency. The technical efficiency component is the measure of OTE defined by (5.1). If firm i is a price taker in output markets, then this component can be written as

$$OTE^t(x_{it}, q_{it}, z_{it}) = R_{it}/R^t(x_{it}, p_{it}, q_{it}, z_{it}) \tag{5.16}$$

[2]Equation (5.15) can be viewed as a special case of (5.14) corresponding to $\partial p(q_{it}, d_{it})/\partial q_{it} = 0$.

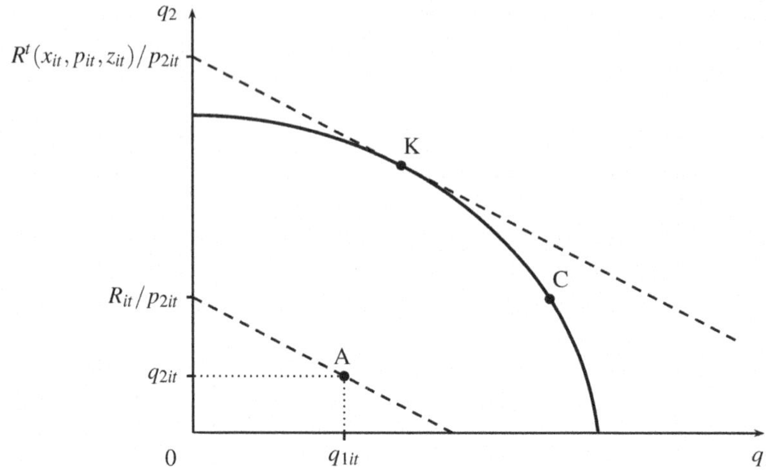

Fig. 5.14 The revenue inefficiency of the manager of a price-taking firm. The gap between the dashed lines passing through A and K is due to revenue inefficiency

where $R^t(x_{it}, p_{it}, q_{it}, z_{it}) = R_{it}/D^t_O(x_{it}, q_{it}, z_{it})$ is the maximum revenue that can be earned using x_{it} in period t in a production environment characterised by z_{it} when output prices are given by p_{it} and outputs are a scalar multiple of q_{it}. The allocative efficiency component is a revenue-oriented measure of how well the manager has captured economies of output substitution. If firm i is a price taker in output markets, then the so-called output-oriented allocative efficiency (OAE) of manager i in period t is

$$OAE^t(x_{it}, p_{it}, q_{it}, z_{it}) = R^t(x_{it}, p_{it}, q_{it}, z_{it})/R^t(x_{it}, p_{it}, z_{it}). \tag{5.17}$$

An implication of Eqs. (5.15), (5.16) and (5.17) is that

$$OAE^t(x_{it}, p_{it}, q_{it}, z_{it}) = RE^t(x_{it}, p_{it}, q_{it}, z_{it})/OTE^t(x_{it}, q_{it}, z_{it}). \tag{5.18}$$

This equation says that OAE is the component of RE that remains after accounting for OTE. If there is no environmental change, then the measure of OAE defined by (5.17) is equivalent to the measure of 'output allocative efficiency' defined by Balk (1998, Eq. 4.6). If there is no technical or environmental change, then it is equivalent to the *reciprocal* of the measure of 'allocative output efficiency' defined by Färe et al. (1985, Eq. 4.6.1). If there is only one output, then it takes the value one.

To illustrate, reconsider the measure of RE depicted in Fig. 5.14. Relevant parts of that figure are now reproduced in Fig. 5.15. In this figure, the outputs of firm i in period t map to point A. The dashed lines passing through points A, C and K are iso-revenue lines with the same slope but different intercepts. The RE, OTE and OAE of manager i in period t are given by the ratios of these intercepts.

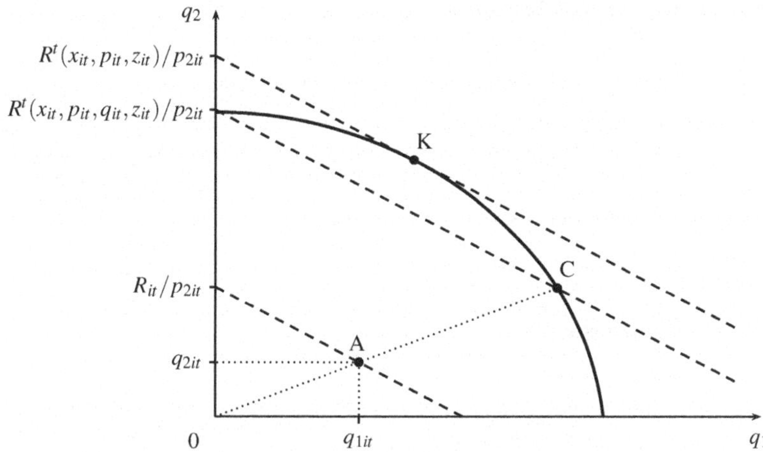

Fig. 5.15 The revenue inefficiency of the manager of a price-taking firm. The gap between the dashed lines passing through A and C is due to technical inefficiency. The gap between the dashed lines passing through C and K is due to allocative inefficiency

5.3.3 Example

If the output distance function is given by (2.9), then the OTE of manager i in period t is given by (5.5). The RE and OAE of the manager depend on the market power of the firm and the value of τ. If, for example, the firm is a price taker in output markets and $\tau > 1$, then

$$RE^t(x_{it}, p_{it}, q_{it}, z_{it}) = p_{it}'q_{it}\left(A(t)\prod_{j=1}^{J} z_{jit}^{\delta_j}\prod_{m=1}^{M} x_{mit}^{\beta_m}\right)^{-1}\left(\sum_{n=1}^{N}\gamma_n^{\sigma}p_{nit}^{1-\sigma}\right)^{1/(\sigma-1)}$$

and $$OAE^t(x_{it}, p_{it}, q_{it}, z_{it}) = p_{it}'q_{it}\left(\sum_{n=1}^{N}\gamma_n q_{nit}^{\tau}\right)^{-1/\tau}\left(\sum_{n=1}^{N}\gamma_n^{\sigma}p_{nit}^{1-\sigma}\right)^{1/(\sigma-1)}$$

where $\sigma = 1/(1-\tau) < 0$. As $\tau \to 1$,

$$RE^t(x_{it}, p_{it}, q_{it}, z_{it}) \to p_{it}'q_{it}\left(A(t)\prod_{j=1}^{J} z_{jit}^{\delta_j}\prod_{m=1}^{M} x_{mit}^{\beta_m}\max\left\{\frac{p_{1it}}{\gamma_1},\ldots,\frac{p_{Nit}}{\gamma_N}\right\}\right)^{-1}$$

and $$OAE^t(x_{it}, p_{it}, q_{it}, z_{it}) \to \left(\frac{p_{it}'q_{it}}{\gamma' q_{it}}\right)\left(\max\left\{\frac{p_{1it}}{\gamma_1},\ldots,\frac{p_{Nit}}{\gamma_N}\right\}\right)^{-1}.$$

5.4 Cost-Oriented Measures

Cost-oriented measures of efficiency are relevant measures of managerial performance in situations where managers have valued inputs at market prices and outputs have been predetermined. The most widely-used cost-oriented measure of efficiency is cost efficiency (CE). The CE of any manager can be decomposed into separate measures of technical and allocative efficiency.

5.4.1 Cost Efficiency

For any given manager, the exact definition of CE depends on whether the firm is a price setter or price taker in input markets.

5.4.1.1 Price Setters in Input Markets

If firm i is a price setter in input markets, then the CE of manager i period t is

$$CE^t(s_{it}, x_{it}, q_{it}, z_{it}) = C^t(s_{it}, q_{it}, z_{it})/C_{it} \tag{5.19}$$

where $C_{it} = w(x_{it}, s_{it})'x_{it}$ is the cost of the firm's inputs and $C^t(s_{it}, q_{it}, z_{it})$ is the minimum cost of producing q_{it} in period t when the production environment and the supply sector are characterised by z_{it} and s_{it} respectively. This particular measure of CE appears to be new. If environmental variables have been predetermined, then it can be viewed as a measure of how well the manager has solved problem (4.14).

For a numerical example, reconsider the cost minimisation problem depicted earlier in Fig. 4.7. Relevant parts of that figure are now reproduced in Fig. 5.16. In these figures, the frontier passing through point P represents the boundary of $L^1(\iota, 1)$. If the vector of supply shifters had been $s_{i1} = (1, 1)'$, then the cost-minimising point would have been point P. The associated minimum cost would have been $C^1(\iota, \iota, 1) = 0.212$. On the other hand, the cost of the inputs at point A would have been $C_{11} = 0.4552$. Thus, the CE of the manager of firm A would have been $CE^1(\iota, \iota, \iota, 1) = C_{11}/C^1(\iota, \iota, 1) = 0.212/0.4552 = 0.466$.

5.4.1.2 Price Takers in Input Markets

If firm i is a price taker in input markets, then the CE of manager i in period t is[3]

$$CE^t(w_{it}, x_{it}, q_{it}, z_{it}) = C^t(w_{it}, q_{it}, z_{it})/C_{it} \tag{5.20}$$

[3]Equation (5.20) can be viewed as a special case of (5.19) corresponding to $\partial w(x_{it}, s_{it})/\partial x_{it} = 0$.

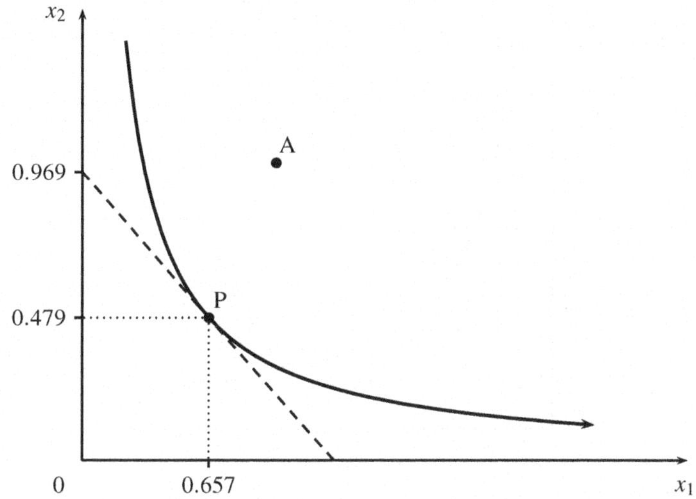

Fig. 5.16 The cost efficiency of the manager of a price-setting firm. If input-supplies had been relatively abundant, then the CE of the manager of firm A would have been $CE^1(\iota, \iota, \iota, 1) = 0.466$

where $C_{it} = w_{it}' x_{it}$ is the cost of the firm's inputs and $C^t(w_{it}, q_{it}, z_{it})$ is the minimum cost of producing q_{it} in period t in a production environment characterised by z_{it} when input prices are given by w_{it}. Again, this particular measure of CE appears to be new. If environmental variables have been predetermined, then it can be viewed as a measure of how well the manager has solved problem (4.17). If there is no environmental change, then it is equivalent to the measure of CE defined by Balk (1998, Eq. 3.10). If there is no technical or environmental change, then it is equivalent to the measure of 'overall input efficiency' defined by Färe et al. (1985, Eq. 3.4.4).

To illustrate, reconsider the cost minimisation problem depicted earlier in Fig. 4.8. Relevant parts of that figure are now reproduced in Fig. 5.17. In these figures, the frontier passing through point X is the frontier depicted earlier in Fig. 5.9; it represents the boundary of $L^t(q_{it}, z_{it})$. The inputs of firm i in period t map to point A. The dashed lines passing through points A and X are iso-cost lines with the same slope but different intercepts. The CE of manager i in period t is given by the ratio of these intercepts. It is worth noting that the ratio of the intercepts in Fig. 5.17 is not the same as the ratio of the intercepts in Fig. 5.9. This illustrates that CE does not generally equal ITME.

5.4.2 Input-Oriented Allocative Efficiency

The measure of CE defined by (5.20) can be decomposed into separate measures of technical and allocative efficiency. The technical efficiency component is the measure

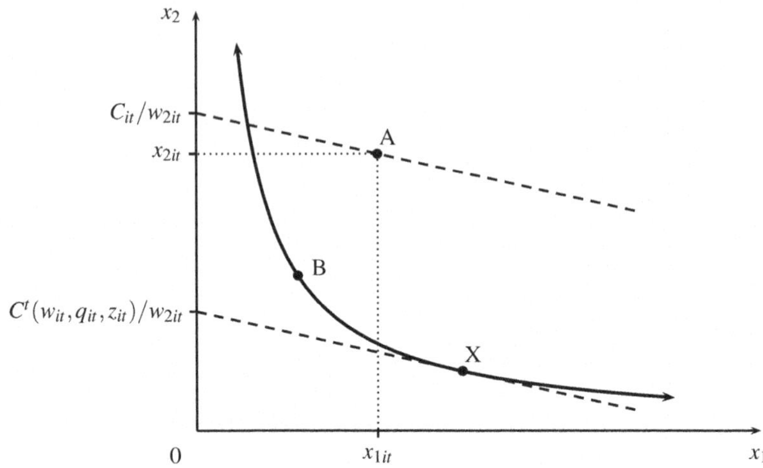

Fig. 5.17 The cost inefficiency of the manager of a price-taking firm. The gap between the dashed lines passing through A and X is due to cost inefficiency

of ITE defined by (5.8). If firm i is a price taker in input markets, then this component can be written as

$$ITE^t(x_{it}, q_{it}, z_{it}) = C^t(w_{it}, x_{it}, q_{it}, z_{it})/C_{it} \tag{5.21}$$

where $C^t(w_{it}, x_{it}, q_{it}, z_{it}) = C_{it}/D_I^t(x_{it}, q_{it}, z_{it})$ is the minimum cost of producing q_{it} in period t in a production environment characterised by z_{it} when input prices are given by w_{it} and inputs are a scalar multiple of x_{it}. The allocative efficiency component is a cost-oriented measure of how well the manager has captured economies of input substitution. If firm i is a price taker in input markets, then the so-called input-oriented allocative efficiency (IAE) of manager i in period t is

$$IAE^t(w_{it}, x_{it}, q_{it}, z_{it}) = C^t(w_{it}, q_{it}, z_{it})/C^t(w_{it}, x_{it}, q_{it}, z_{it}). \tag{5.22}$$

An implication of Eqs. (5.20), (5.21) and (5.22) is that

$$IAE^t(w_{it}, x_{it}, q_{it}, z_{it}) = CE^t(w_{it}, x_{it}, q_{it}, z_{it})/ITE^t(x_{it}, q_{it}, z_{it}). \tag{5.23}$$

This equation says that IAE is the component of CE that remains after accounting for ITE. If there is no environmental change, then the measure of IAE defined by (5.22) is equivalent to the measure of 'input allocative efficiency' defined by Balk (1998, Eq. 3.13). If there is no technical or environmental change, then it is equivalent to the measure of 'allocative input efficiency' defined by Färe et al. (1985, Eq. 3.6.1). If there is only one input, then it takes the value one.

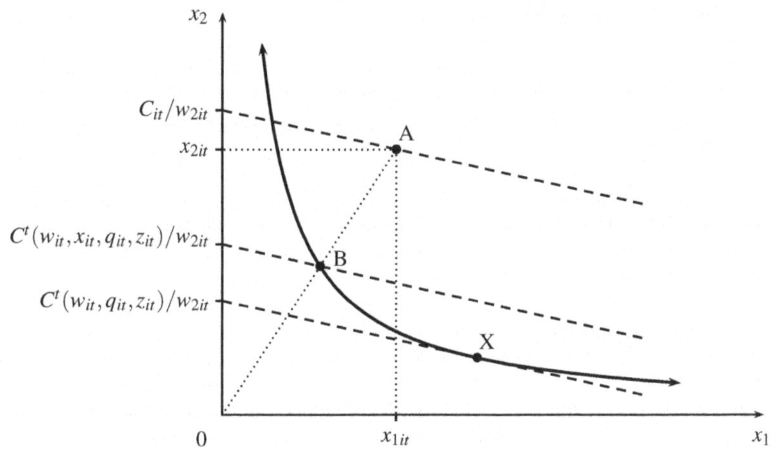

Fig. 5.18 The cost inefficiency of the manager of a price-taking firm. The gap between the dashed lines passing through A and B is due to technical inefficiency. The gap between the dashed lines passing through B and X is due to allocative inefficiency

To illustrate, reconsider the measure of CE depicted in Fig. 5.17. Relevant parts of that figure are now reproduced in Fig. 5.18. In this figure, the inputs of firm i in period t map to point A. The dashed lines passing through points A, B and X are iso-cost lines with the same slope but different intercepts. The CE, ITE and IAE of manager i in period t are given by the ratios of these intercepts.

5.4.3 Example

If the input distance function is given by (2.13), then the ITE of manager i in period t is given by (5.12). The CE and IAE of the manager depend on the market power of the firm. If, for example, firm i is a price taker in input markets, then

$$CE^t(w_{it}, x_{it}, q_{it}, z_{it}) = \left(w_{it}'x_{it} \; B(t) \prod_{j=1}^{J} z_{jit}^{\kappa_j} \right)^{-1} \prod_{m=1}^{M} \left(\frac{w_{mit}}{\lambda_m} \right)^{\lambda_m} \times \left(\sum_{n=1}^{N} \gamma_n q_{nit}^{\tau} \right)^{1/(\tau\eta)} \tag{5.24}$$

and
$$IAE^t(w_{it}, x_{it}, q_{it}, z_{it}) = \prod_{m=1}^{M} \left(\frac{s_{mit}}{\lambda_m} \right)^{\lambda_m} \tag{5.25}$$

where $s_{mit} = w_{mit}x_{mit}/w_{it}'x_{it}$ is the m-th observed cost share.

5.5 Profit-Oriented Measures

Profit-oriented measures of efficiency are relevant measures of managerial performance in situations where managers have valued outputs and inputs at market prices and then chosen them freely. The most widely-used profit-oriented measure of efficiency is profit efficiency (PE). Measures of PE can be decomposed into output- and input-oriented measures of technical, scale and allocative efficiency.

5.5.1 *Profit Efficiency*

For any given manager, the exact definition of PE depends on whether the firm is a price setter or price taker in output and input markets.

5.5.1.1 Price Setters in Output and Input Markets

If firm i is a price setter in output and input markets, then the PE of manager i in period t is

$$PE^t(s_{it}, x_{it}, d_{it}, q_{it}, z_{it}) = \Pi_{it} I(\Pi_{it} \geq 0)/\Pi^t(s_{it}, d_{it}, z_{it}) \tag{5.26}$$

where $\Pi_{it} = p(q_{it}, d_{it})'q_{it} - w(x_{it}, s_{it})'x_{it}$ is the profit of the firm, $I(.)$ is an indicator function that takes the value 1 if the argument is true (and 0 otherwise), and $\Pi^t(s_{it}, d_{it}, z_{it})$ is the maximum profit that can be earned in period t in a production environment characterised by z_{it} when supply and demand markets are characterised by s_{it} and d_{it} respectively. This particular measure of PE appears to be new. If environmental variables have been predetermined, then it can be viewed as a measure of how well the manager has solved problem (4.19).

For a numerical example, reconsider the profit maximisation problem depicted earlier in Fig. 4.9. Relevant parts of that figure are now reproduced in Fig. 5.19. The frontier in both figures represents the boundary of $T^1(1)$. If the vectors of demand and supply shifters had been $d_{i1} = (4.1, 4.1)'$ and $s_{i1} = (0.1, 0.1)'$, then the profit maximising point would have been point G. The associated maximum profit would have been $\Pi^1(0.1\iota, 4.1\iota, 1) = 7.036$. On the other hand, the profit at point A would have been $\Pi_{11} = 3.196$. Thus, the PE of the manager of firm A would have been $PE^1(0.1\iota, \iota, 4.1\iota, \iota, 1) = \Pi_{11} I(\Pi_{11} \geq 0)/\Pi^1(0.1\iota, 4.1\iota, 1) = 3.196/7.036 = 0.454$.

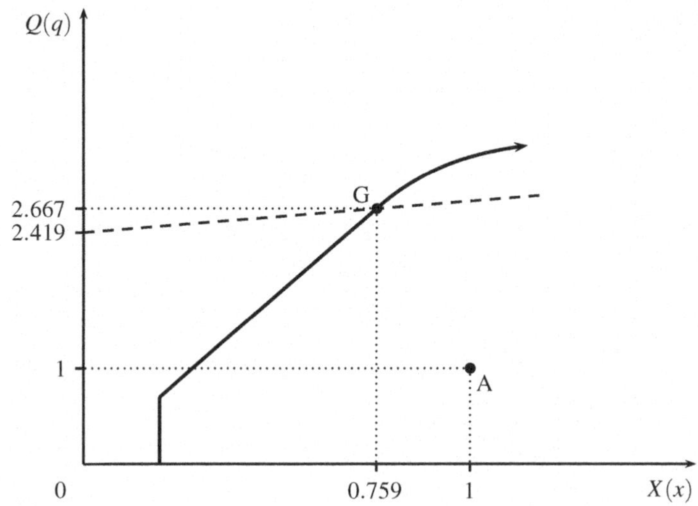

Fig. 5.19 The profit efficiency of the manager of a price-setting firm. If consumer demand had been relatively strong and input supplies had been relatively scarce, then the PE of the manager of firm A would have been $PE^1(0.1\iota, \iota, 4.1\iota, \iota, 1) = 0.454$

5.5.1.2 Price Takers in Output and Input Markets

If firm i is a price taker in output and input markets, then the PE of manager i in period t is[4]

$$PE^t(w_{it}, x_{it}, p_{it}, q_{it}, z_{it}) = \Pi_{it} I(\Pi_{it} \geq 0)/\Pi^t(w_{it}, p_{it}, z_{it}) \tag{5.27}$$

where $\Pi_{it} = p'_{it}q_{it} - w'_{it}x_{it}$ is the profit of the firm and $\Pi^t(w_{it}, p_{it}, z_{it})$ is the maximum profit that can be earned in period t in a production environment characterised by z_{it} when the output and input price vectors are p_{it} and w_{it} respectively. Again, this particular measure of PE appears to be new. If environmental variables have been predetermined, then it can be viewed as a measure of how well the manager has solved problem (4.20). If the firm makes a profit and there is no technical or environmental change, then it is equivalent to the reciprocal of the measure of 'aggregate efficiency' defined by Banker and Maindiratta (1988, p. 1320). Alternative measures of PE that can be found in the literature include the measure of 'Nerlovian profit efficiency' defined by Färe and Grosskopf (1997, Eq. 6) and the 'profit-based efficiency measure' of Chambers et al. (1998, Eq. 23). These alternative measures do not necessarily take values in the closed unit interval.

---

[4]Equation (5.27) can be viewed as a special case of (5.26) corresponding to $\partial p(q_{it}, d_{it})/\partial q_{it} = 0$ and $\partial w(x_{it}, s_{it})/\partial x_{it} = 0$.

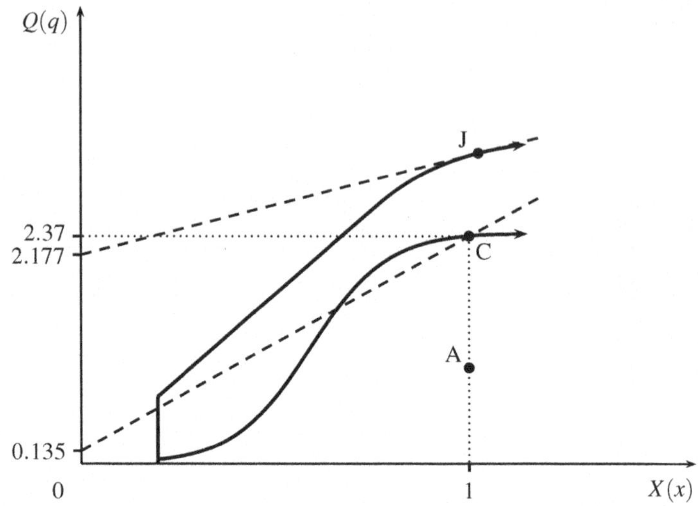

Fig. 5.20 The profit efficiency of the manager of a price-taking firm. If firm C had been a price taker in output and input markets, then the PE of its manager would have been $PE^1(w_{31}, x_{31}, p_{31}, q_{31}, 1) = 0.052$

For a numerical example, reconsider the profit maximisation problem depicted earlier in Fig. 4.10. Relevant parts of that figure are now reproduced in Fig. 5.20. In this figure, the frontier passing through point J is the frontier depicted in Fig. 5.19; it represents the boundary of $T^1(1)$. The frontier passing through point C represents the boundary of $T^1(x_{31}, q_{31}, 1)$. If firm C had been a price taker in output and input markets, then profit-maximising point would have been point J. The associated maximum profit would have been $\Pi^1(w_{31}, p_{31}, 1) = 2.564$. On the other hand, the profit at point C would have been $\Pi_{13} = 0.133$. Thus, the PE of the manager of firm C would have been $PE^1(w_{31}, x_{31}, p_{31}, q_{31}, 1) = \Pi_{31} I(\Pi_{31} \geq 0)/\Pi^1(w_{31}, p_{31}, 1) = 0.133/2.564 = 0.052$.

5.5.2 Output-Oriented Scale and Allocative Efficiency

The measure of PE defined by (5.27) can be decomposed into an output-oriented measure of technical efficiency and an output-oriented measure of scale and allocative efficiency. The technical efficiency component is the measure of OTE defined by (5.1). The scale and allocative efficiency component is a profit-oriented measure of how well the manager has captured economies of scale and substitution. Economies of scale and substitution are the benefits obtained by changing the scale of operations, the output mix, and the input mix. If firm i is a price taker in output and input markets, then the so-called output-oriented scale and allocative efficiency (OSAE) of manager i in period t is

$$OSAE^t(w_{it}, x_{it}, p_{it}, q_{it}, z_{it}) = \frac{(R^t(x_{it}, p_{it}, q_{it}, z_{it}) - C_{it})I(R^t(x_{it}, p_{it}, q_{it}, z_{it}) \geq C_{it})}{\Pi^t(w_{it}, p_{it}, z_{it})} \tag{5.28}$$

where $R^t(x_{it}, p_{it}, q_{it}, z_{it}) = R_{it}/D^t_O(x_{it}, q_{it}, z_{it})$ is the maximum revenue that can be earned using x_{it} in period t in a production environment characterised by z_{it} when output prices are given by p_{it} and outputs are a scalar multiple of q_{it}. Equations (5.16), (5.27) and (5.28) imply that if OTE equals one, then PE equals OSAE. Thus, OSAE can be viewed as the component of PE that remains after accounting for OTE.

For a numerical example, reconsider the measure of PE depicted in Fig. 5.20. In this figure, the OTE of the manager of firm C is one. Thus, if the firm had been a price taker in output and input markets, then the OSAE of the manager would have been $OSAE^1(w_{31}, x_{31}, p_{31}, q_{31}, 1) = 0.052$.

5.5.3 Input-Oriented Scale and Allocative Efficiency

The measure of PE defined by (5.27) can also be decomposed into an *input-oriented* measure of technical efficiency and an *input-oriented* measure of scale and allocative efficiency. The technical efficiency component is the measure of ITE defined by (5.8). Again, the scale and allocative efficiency component is a profit-oriented measure of how well the manager has captured economies of scale and substitution. If firm i is a price taker in output and input markets, then its so-called input-oriented scale and allocative efficiency (ISAE) in period t is

$$ISAE^t(w_{it}, x_{it}, p_{it}, q_{it}, z_{it}) = \frac{(R_{it} - C^t(w_{it}, x_{it}, q_{it}, z_{it}))I(R_{it} \geq C^t(w_{it}, x_{it}, q_{it}, z_{it}))}{\Pi^t(w_{it}, p_{it}, z_{it})} \tag{5.29}$$

where $C^t(w_{it}, x_{it}, q_{it}, z_{it}) = C_{it}/D^t_I(x_{it}, q_{it}, z_{it})$ is the minimum cost of producing q_{it} in period t in a production environment characterised by z_{it} when input prices are given by w_{it} and inputs are a scalar multiple of x_{it}. Equations (5.21), (5.27) and (5.29) imply that if ITE equals one, then PE equals ISAE. Thus, ISAE can be viewed as the component of PE that remains after accounting for ITE.

For a numerical example, reconsider the measure of PE depicted in Fig. 5.20. In this figure, the ITE of the manager of firm C is one. Thus, if the firm had been a price taker in output and input markets, then the ISAE of the manager would have been $ISAE^1(w_{31}, x_{31}, p_{31}, q_{31}, 1) = 0.052$.

5.5.4 Example

If the output distance function is given by (2.9), then the OTE of manager i in period t is given by (5.5). The PE, OSAE and ISAE of the manager depend on both the market power and the profit of the firm. For example, if the firm is a price taker in output and input markets and it makes a profit, then

$$PE^t(w_{it}, x_{it}, p_{it}, q_{it}, z_{it}) = \left(A(t) \prod_{j=1}^{J} z_{jit}^{\delta_j} \prod_{m=1}^{M} \left(\frac{\beta_m}{w_{mit}} \right)^{\beta_m} \right)^{\frac{1}{\eta-1}} \times \left(\frac{p'_{it} q_{it} - w'_{it} x_{it}}{1-\eta} \right) \left(\sum_{n=1}^{N} \gamma_n^{\sigma} p_{nit}^{1-\sigma} \right)^{\frac{1}{(1-\sigma)(\eta-1)}}. \quad (5.30)$$

Associated expressions for the measures of OSAE and ISAE are messy; the derivations are left as an exercise for the reader.

5.6 Productivity-Oriented Measures

Productivity-oriented measures of efficiency are relevant measures of managerial performance in situations where managers have placed nonnegative values on outputs and inputs (again, not necessarily market values) and chosen at least one output and at least one input freely. In these situations, the relevance of a particular measure depends on how easily the manager has been able to choose the output mix and the input mix. If both the output mix and input mix have been predetermined, then the most relevant measure is technical and scale efficiency (TSE). If the manager has been able to choose all outputs and inputs freely, then the most relevant measure is technical, scale and mix efficiency (TSME). Measures of TSE and TSME can be decomposed into various measures of technical, scale and mix efficiency.

5.6.1 Technical and Scale Efficiency

In this book, the TSE of manager i in period t is defined as

$$TSE^t(x_{it}, q_{it}, z_{it}) = TFP(x_{it}, q_{it})/TFP^t(x_{it}, q_{it}, z_{it}) \quad (5.31)$$

where $TFP(x_{it}, q_{it}) = Q(q_{it})/X(x_{it})$ is the TFP of the firm and $TFP^t(x_{it}, q_{it}, z_{it})$ is the maximum TFP that is possible in period t in an environment characterised by z_{it} when using a scalar multiple of x_{it} to produce a scalar multiple of q_{it}. This particular measure

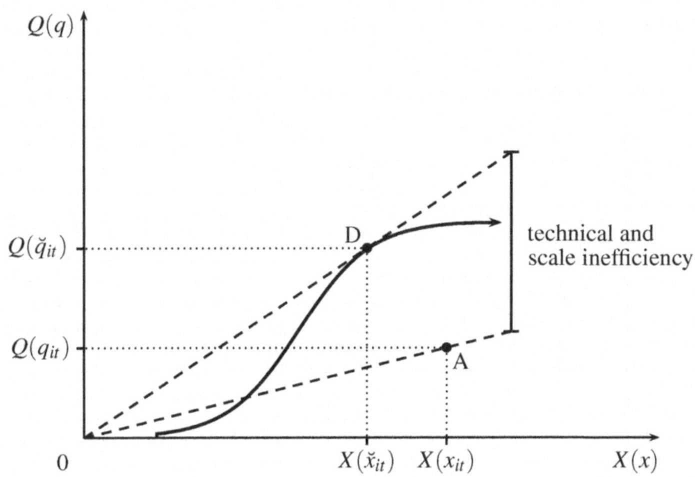

Fig. 5.21 Technical and scale inefficiency. The gap between the rays through A and D is due to technical and scale inefficiency

of TSE appears to be new. If environmental variables have been predetermined, then it can be viewed as a measure of how well the manager has solved problem (4.23). If there is no technical or environmental change, then it is equivalent to the measure of TSE defined by Banker et al. (1984, p. 1089).

To illustrate, reconsider the TFP maximisation problem depicted earlier in Fig. 4.11. Relevant parts of that figure are now reproduced in Fig. 5.21. In these figures, the frontier passing through point D is the frontier depicted earlier in Fig. 5.2; it represents the boundary of $T^t(x_{it}, q_{it}, z_{it})$. The outputs and inputs of firm i in period t map to point A. The TFP at point A is $TFP(x_{it}, q_{it}) =$ slope 0A. If the manager had only been able to use a scalar multiple of x_{it} to produce a scalar multiple of q_{it}, then (s)he could have maximised TFP by operating at point D. The TFP at point D is $TFP^t(x_{it}, q_{it}, z_{it}) =$ slope 0D. Thus, the TSE of the manager is $TSE^t(x_{it}, q_{it}, z_{it}) = TFP(x_{it}, q_{it})/TFP^t(x_{it}, q_{it}, z_{it}) =$ (slope 0A)/(slope 0D) (i.e., an index that compares the TFP at point A with the TFP at point D).

5.6.2 Technical, Scale and Mix Efficiency

In this book, the TSME of manager i in period t is defined as

$$TSME^t(x_{it}, q_{it}, z_{it}) = TFP(x_{it}, q_{it})/TFP^t(z_{it}) \tag{5.32}$$

where $TFP(x_{it}, q_{it}) = Q(q_{it})/X(x_{it})$ is the TFP of the firm and $TFP^t(z_{it})$ is the maximum TFP that is possible in period t in an environment characterised by z_{it}. This

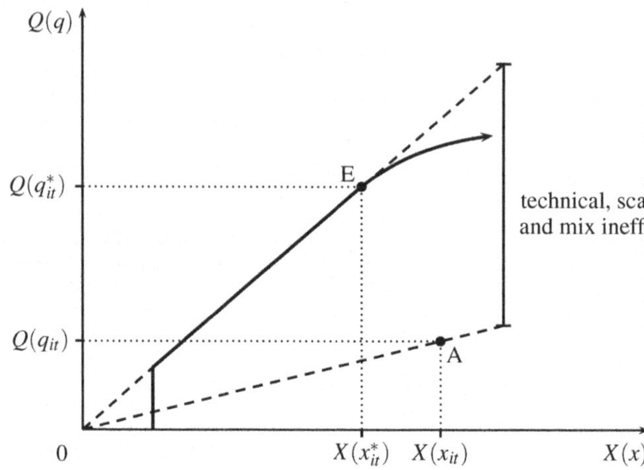

Fig. 5.22 Technical, scale and mix inefficiency. The gap between the rays through A and E is due to technical, scale and mix inefficiency

measure of efficiency is equivalent to the measure of 'firm efficiency' defined by O'Donnell (2016, p. 331). If environmental variables have been predetermined, then it can be viewed as a measure of how well the manager has solved problem (4.25). If there is no environmental change, then it is equivalent to the measure of 'TFP efficiency' defined by O'Donnell (2010, Eq. 3.1).

To illustrate, reconsider the TFP maximisation problem depicted earlier in Fig. 4.12. Relevant parts of that figure are now reproduced in Fig. 5.22. In these figures, the frontier passing through point E is the frontier depicted earlier in Fig. 5.4; it represents the boundary of $T^t(z_{it})$. The outputs and inputs of firm i in period t map to point A. The TFP at point A is $TFP(x_{it}, q_{it}) =$ slope 0A. If the manager of firm i had been able to choose outputs and inputs freely, then (s)he could have maximised TFP by operating at point E. The TFP at point E is $TFP^t(z_{it}) =$ slope 0E. Thus, the TSME of the manager is $TSME^t(x_{it}, q_{it}, z_{it}) = TFP(x_{it}, q_{it})/TFP^t(z_{it}) =$ (slope 0A)/(slope 0E) (i.e., an index that compares the TFP at point A with the TFP at point E).

5.6.3 *Residual Mix Efficiency*

The measure of TSME defined by (5.32) can be decomposed into a measure of technical and scale efficiency and a residual measure of mix efficiency. The technical and scale efficiency component is the measure of TSE defined by (5.31). The associated measure of residual mix efficiency (RME) is

$$RME^t(x_{it}, q_{it}, z_{it}) = TFP^t(x_{it}, q_{it}, z_{it})/TFP^t(z_{it}) \tag{5.33}$$

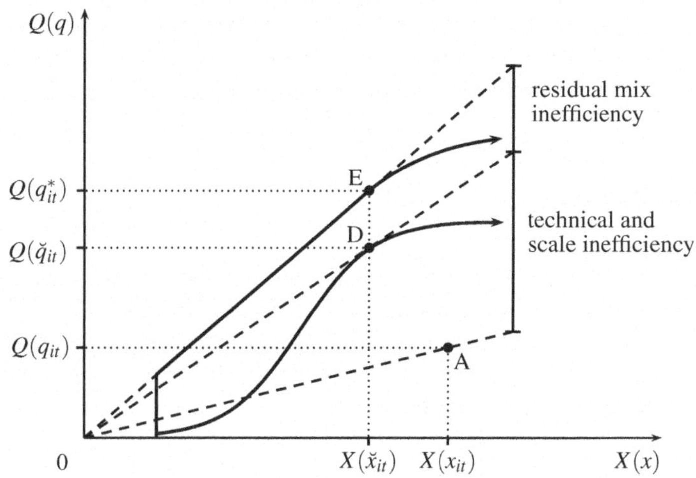

Fig. 5.23 Technical, scale and mix inefficiency. The gap between the rays through A and D is due to technical and scale inefficiency. The gap between the rays through D and E is due to residual mix inefficiency

where $TFP^t(x_{it}, q_{it}, z_{it})$ and $TFP^t(z_{it})$ are the measures of maximum TFP that appear in Eqs. (5.31) and (5.32). This particular measure of RME appears to be new. Equations (5.31), (5.32) and (5.33) imply that

$$RME^t(x_{it}, q_{it}, z_{it}) = TSME^t(x_{it}, q_{it}, z_{it})/TSE^t(x_{it}, q_{it}, z_{it}). \tag{5.34}$$

This equation says that RME is the component of TSME that remains after accounting for TSE (hence the use of the term 'residual'). If there is no environmental change, then the measure of RME defined by (5.33) is equivalent to the measure of RME defined by O'Donnell (2010, Eq. 3.6).

To illustrate, reconsider the measures of TSE and TSME depicted in Figs. 5.21 and 5.22. Relevant parts of those figures are now reproduced in Fig. 5.23. Recall from Figs. 5.21 and 5.22 that the TSE and TSME of the manager of firm A are $TSE^t(x_{it}, q_{it}, z_{it}) =$ (slope 0A)/(slope 0D) and $TSME^t(x_{it}, q_{it}, z_{it}) =$ (slope 0A)/(slope 0E). Consequently, the RME of the manager is $RME^t(x_{it}, q_{it}, z_{it}) = TSME^t(x_{it}, q_{it}, z_{it})/TSE^t(x_{it}, q_{it}, z_{it}) =$ (slope 0D)/(slope 0E) (i.e., an index that compares the TFP at point D with the TFP at point E).

5.6.4 Example

If the output distance function is given by (2.9), then measures of TSME and TSE depend on the elasticity of scale. If $\eta = 1$, then the TSME and TSE of manager i in period t are given by the equations for OTME and OTE presented in Sect. 5.1.4 (or the equations for ITME and ITE presented in Sect. 5.2.4). If $\eta \neq 1$, then the TSME and TSE of manager i in period t are both infinitesimally small.

5.7 Other Measures

Measures of TSE and TSME can be decomposed into various measures of output- and input-oriented technical, scale and mix efficiency. If more than one technology exists in a given period, then most measures of efficiency can be decomposed into metatechnology ratios and residual measures of efficiency. Several nonradial measures of efficiency are also available.

5.7.1 Output-Oriented Scale Efficiency

The measure of TSE defined by (5.31) can be decomposed into separate output-oriented measures of technical and scale efficiency. The technical efficiency component is the measure of OTE defined by (5.1). The scale efficiency component is a measure of how well the manager has captured economies of scale. Economies of scale are the benefits obtained by changing the scale of operations. In this book, the so-called output-oriented scale efficiency (OSE) of manager i in period t is defined as $OSE^t(x_{it}, q_{it}, z_{it}) = \inf_{\lambda} D_O^t(\lambda x_{it}, \lambda q_{it}, z_{it})/D_O^t(x_{it}, q_{it}, z_{it})$. An equivalent definition is

$$OSE^t(x_{it}, q_{it}, z_{it}) = TFP(x_{it}, \bar{q}_{it})/TFP^t(x_{it}, q_{it}, z_{it}) \quad (5.35)$$

where $TFP(x_{it}, \bar{q}_{it}) = Q(\bar{q}_{it})/X(x_{it})$ is the maximum TFP possible when using x_{it} to produce a scalar multiple of q_{it} in period t in a production environment characterised by z_{it}. Equations (5.1), (5.31) and (5.35) imply that

$$OSE^t(x_{it}, q_{it}, z_{it}) = TSE^t(x_{it}, q_{it}, z_{it})/OTE^t(x_{it}, q_{it}, z_{it}). \quad (5.36)$$

This equation says that OSE is the component of TSE that remains after accounting for OTE. If there is no environmental change, then the measure of OSE defined by (5.35) is equivalent to the output-oriented measure of scale efficiency defined by Balk (1998, Eq. 2.42). If the production frontier exhibits CRS, then it takes the value one.

To illustrate, reconsider the measures of OTE and TSE depicted in Figs. 5.2 and 5.21. Relevant parts of those figures are now reproduced in Fig. 5.24. Recall from Figs. 5.2 and 5.21 that the OTE and TSE of the manager of firm A are $OTE^t(x_{it}, q_{it}, z_{it}) =$ (slope 0A)/(slope 0C) and $TSE^t(x_{it}, q_{it}, z_{it}) =$ (slope 0A)/(slope

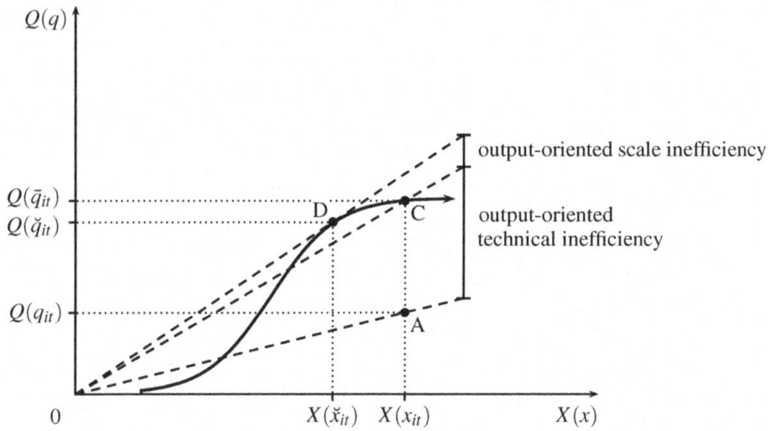

Fig. 5.24 Output-oriented technical and scale inefficiency. The gap between the rays through A and C is due to technical inefficiency. The gap between the rays through C and D is due to scale inefficiency

0D). Consequently, the OSE of the manager is $OSE^t(x_{it}, q_{it}, z_{it}) = TSE^t(x_{it}, q_{it}, z_{it})/OTE^t(x_{it}, q_{it}, z_{it})$ = (slope 0C)/(slope 0D) (i.e., an index that compares the TFP at point C with the TFP at point D).

5.7.2 Output-Oriented Scale and Mix Efficiency

The measure of TSME defined by (5.32) can be decomposed into an output-oriented measure of technical efficiency and an output-oriented measure of scale and mix efficiency. The technical efficiency component is the measure of OTE defined by (5.1). The scale and mix efficiency component is a productivity-oriented measure of how well the manager has captured economies of scale and substitution. In this book, the so-called output-oriented scale and mix efficiency (OSME) of manager i in period t is defined as

$$OSME^t(x_{it}, q_{it}, z_{it}) = TFP(x_{it}, \bar{q}_{it})/TFP^t(z_{it}) \tag{5.37}$$

where $TFP(x_{it}, \bar{q}_{it}) = Q(\bar{q}_{it})/X(x_{it})$ is the maximum TFP possible when using x_{it} to produce a scalar multiple of q_{it} in period t in a production environment characterised by z_{it}. Equations (5.1), (5.32) and (5.37) imply that

$$OSME^t(x_{it}, q_{it}, z_{it}) = TSME^t(x_{it}, q_{it}, z_{it})/OTE^t(x_{it}, q_{it}, z_{it}). \tag{5.38}$$

This equation says that OSME is the component of TSME that remains after accounting for OTE. If there is no environmental change, then the measure of OSME defined

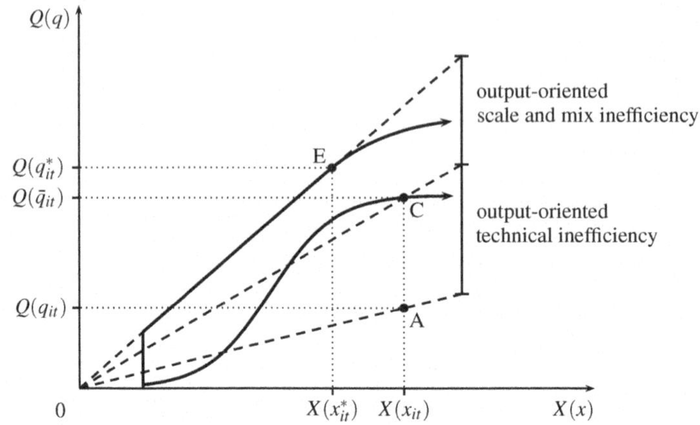

Fig. 5.25 Technical, scale and mix inefficiency. The gap between the rays through A and C is due to technical inefficiency. The gap between the rays through C and E is due to scale and mix inefficiency

by (5.37) is equivalent to the measure of OSME defined by O'Donnell (2012 , p. 881). If the production frontier exhibits CRS, then it is equal to the measure of OME defined by (5.3).

To illustrate, reconsider the measures of OTE and TSME depicted in Figs. 5.2 and 5.22. Relevant parts of those figures are now reproduced in Fig. 5.25. Recall from Figs. 5.2 and 5.22 that the OTE and TSME of the manager of firm A are $OTE^t(x_{it}, q_{it}, z_{it})$ = (slope 0A)/(slope 0C) and $TSME^t(x_{it}, q_{it}, z_{it})$ = (slope 0A)/(slope 0E). Consequently, the OSME of the manager is $OSME^t(x_{it}, q_{it}, z_{it}) = TSME^t(x_{it}, q_{it}, z_{it})/OTE^t(x_{it}, q_{it}, z_{it})$ = (slope 0C)/(slope 0E) (i.e., an index that compares the TFP at point C with the TFP at point E).

5.7.3 Residual Output-Oriented Scale Efficiency

The measure of OSME defined by (5.37) can be decomposed into separate measures of mix and scale efficiency. The mix efficiency component is the measure of OME defined by (5.3). The associated measure of residual output-oriented scale efficiency (ROSE) is

$$ROSE^t(x_{it}, q_{it}, z_{it}) = TFP(x_{it}, \hat{q}_{it})/TFP^t(z_{it}) \tag{5.39}$$

where $TFP(x_{it}, \hat{q}_{it})$ is the maximum TFP that is possible in period t when using x_{it} in an environment characterised by z_{it}. Equations (5.3), (5.37) and (5.39) imply that

$$ROSE^t(x_{it}, q_{it}, z_{it}) = OSME^t(x_{it}, q_{it}, z_{it})/OME^t(x_{it}, q_{it}, z_{it}). \tag{5.40}$$

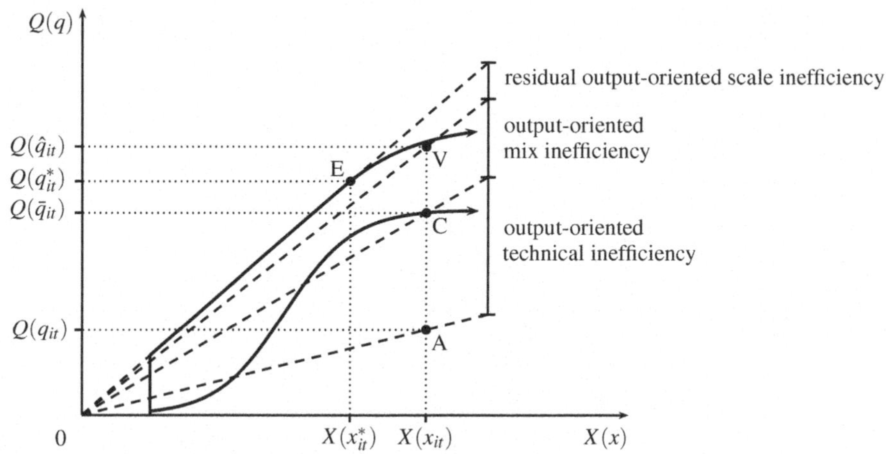

Fig. 5.26 Technical, scale and mix inefficiency. The gap between the rays through A and C is due to technical inefficiency. The gap between the rays through C and V is due to mix inefficiency. The gap between the rays through V and E is due to residual scale inefficiency

This equation says that ROSE is the component of OSME that remains after accounting for OME (hence the use of the term 'residual'). If there is no environmental change, then the measure of ROSE defined by (5.39) is equivalent to the measure of ROSE defined by O'Donnell (2010, Eq. 3.5).

To illustrate, reconsider the measures of OME and OSME depicted in Figs. 5.6 and 5.25. Relevant parts of those figures are now reproduced in Fig. 5.26. Recall from Figs. 5.6 and 5.25 that the OME and OSME of the manager of firm A are $OME^t(x_{it}, q_{it}, z_{it})$ = (slope 0C)/(slope 0V) and $OSME^t(x_{it}, q_{it}, z_{it})$ = (slope 0C)/(slope 0E). Consequently, the ROSE of the manager is $ROSE^t(x_{it}, q_{it}, z_{it}) = OSME^t(x_{it}, q_{it}, z_{it})/OME^t(x_{it}, q_{it}, z_{it})$ = (slope 0V)/(slope 0E) (i.e., an index that compares the TFP at point V with the TFP at point E).

5.7.4 *Input-Oriented Scale Efficiency*

The measure of TSE defined by (5.31) can also be decomposed into separate *input-oriented* measures of technical and scale efficiency. The technical efficiency component is the measure of ITE defined by (5.8). Again, the scale efficiency component is a measure of how well the manager has captured economies of scale. In this book, the input-oriented scale efficiency (ISE) of manager i in period t is defined as $ISE^t(x_{it}, q_{it}, z_{it}) = D_I^t(x_{it}, q_{it}, z_{it})/\sup_{\lambda} D_I^t(\lambda x_{it}, \lambda q_{it}, z_{it})$. An equivalent definition is

$$ISE^t(x_{it}, q_{it}, z_{it}) = TFP(\bar{x}_{it}, q_{it})/TFP^t(x_{it}, q_{it}, z_{it}) \quad (5.41)$$

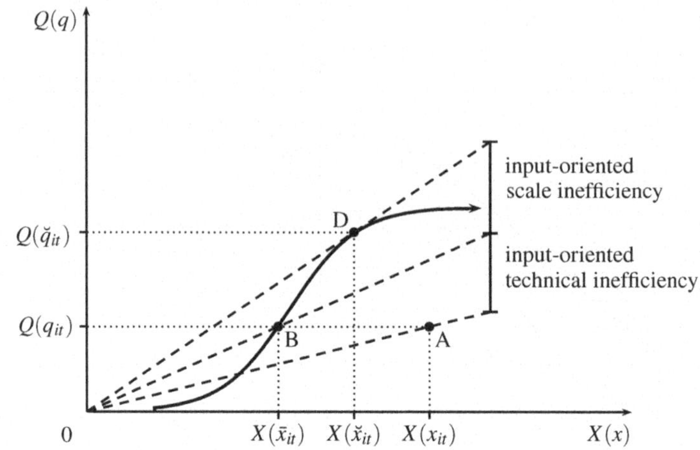

Fig. 5.27 Input-oriented technical and scale inefficiency. The gap between the rays through A and B is due to technical inefficiency. The gap between the rays through B and D is due to scale inefficiency

where $TFP(\bar{x}_{it}, q_{it}) = Q(q_{it})/X(\bar{x}_{it})$ is the maximum TFP possible when using a scalar multiple of x_{it} to produce q_{it} in period t in a production environment characterised by z_{it}. Equations (5.8), (5.31) and (5.41) imply that

$$ISE^t(x_{it}, q_{it}, z_{it}) = TSE^t(x_{it}, q_{it}, z_{it})/ITE^t(x_{it}, q_{it}, z_{it}). \tag{5.42}$$

This equation says that ISE is the component of TSE that remains after accounting for ITE. If there is no environmental change, then the measure of ISE defined by (5.41) is equivalent to the input-oriented measure of scale efficiency defined by Balk (1998, Eq. 2.33). If there is no technical or environmental change, then it is equivalent to the measure of (input) scale efficiency defined by Banker et al. (1984, p.1089). Again, if the production frontier exhibits CRS, then it takes the value one.

To illustrate, reconsider the measures of ITE and TSE depicted earlier in Figs. 5.8 and 5.21. Relevant parts of those figures are now reproduced in Fig. 5.27. Recall from Figs. 5.8 and 5.21 that the ITE and TSE of the manager of firm A are $ITE^t(x_{it}, q_{it}, z_{it}) =$ (slope 0A)/(slope 0B) and $TSE^t(x_{it}, q_{it}, z_{it}) = TFP(x_{it}, q_{it})/TFP^t(x_{it}, q_{it}, z_{it}) =$(slope 0A)/(slope 0D). Consequently, the ISE of the manager is $ISE^t(x_{it}, q_{it}, z_{it}) = TSE^t(x_{it}, q_{it}, z_{it})/ITE^t(x_{it}, q_{it}, z_{it}) =$ (slope 0B)/(slope 0D) (i.e., an index that compares the TFP at point B with the TFP at point D).

5.7.5 Input-Oriented Scale and Mix Efficiency

The measure of TSME defined by (5.32) can also be decomposed into an *input-oriented* measure of technical efficiency and an *input-oriented* measure of scale and mix efficiency. The technical efficiency component is the measure of ITE defined by (5.8). Again, the scale and mix efficiency component is a productivity-oriented measure of how well the manager has captured economies of scale and substitution. In this book, the so-called input-oriented scale and mix efficiency (ISME) of manager i in period t is defined as

$$ISME^t(x_{it}, q_{it}, z_{it}) = TFP(\bar{x}_{it}, q_{it})/TFP^t(z_{it}) \quad (5.43)$$

where $TFP(\bar{x}_{it}, q_{it}) = Q(q_{it})/X(\bar{x}_{it})$ is the maximum TFP possible when using a scalar multiple of x_{it} to produce q_{it} in period t in a production environment characterised by z_{it}. Equations (5.8), (5.32) and (5.43) imply that

$$ISME^t(x_{it}, q_{it}, z_{it}) = TSME^t(x_{it}, q_{it}, z_{it})/ITE^t(x_{it}, q_{it}, z_{it}). \quad (5.44)$$

This equation says that ISME is the component of TSME that remains after accounting for ITE. If there is no technical change, then the measure of ISME defined by (5.43) is equivalent to the measure of ISME defined by O'Donnell and Nguyen (2013, p. 325). If the production frontier exhibits CRS, then it is equal to the measure of IME defined by (5.10).

To illustrate, reconsider the measures of ITE and TSME depicted in Figs. 5.8 and 5.22. Relevant parts of those figures are now reproduced in Fig. 5.28. Recall from Figs. 5.8 and 5.28 that the ITE and TSME of the manager of firm A are $ITE^t(x_{it}, q_{it}, z_{it})$ = (slope 0A)/(slope 0B) and $TSME^t(x_{it}, q_{it}, z_{it})$ = (slope 0A)/(slope 0E). Consequently, the ISME of the manager is $ISME^t(x_{it}, q_{it}, z_{it}) = TSME^t(x_{it}, q_{it}, z_{it})/ITE^t(x_{it}, q_{it}, z_{it})$ = (slope 0B)/(slope 0E) (i.e., an index that compares the TFP at point B with the TFP at point E).

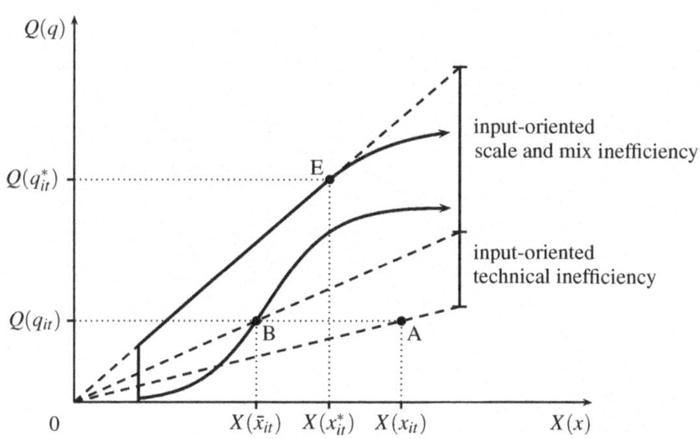

Fig. 5.28 Technical, scale and mix inefficiency. The gap between the rays through A and B is due to technical inefficiency. The gap between the rays through B and E is due to scale and mix inefficiency

5.7.6 Residual Input-Oriented Scale Efficiency

The measure of ISME defined by (5.43) can be decomposed into separate measures of mix and scale efficiency. The mix efficiency component is the measure of IME defined by (5.10).The associated measure of residual input-oriented scale efficiency (RISE) is

$$RISE^t(x_{it}, q_{it}, z_{it}) = TFP(\hat{x}_{it}, q_{it})/TFP^t(z_{it}) \tag{5.45}$$

where $TFP(\hat{x}_{it}, q_{it})$ is the maximum TFP that is possible in period t when producing q_{it} in an environment characterised by z_{it}. Equations (5.10), (5.43) and (5.45) imply that

$$RISE^t(x_{it}, q_{it}, z_{it}) = ISME^t(x_{it}, q_{it}, z_{it})/IME^t(x_{it}, q_{it}, z_{it}). \tag{5.46}$$

This equation says that RISE is the component of ISME that remains after accounting for IME (hence the use of the term 'residual'). If there is no environmental change, then the measure of RISE defined by (5.45) is equivalent to the measure of RISE defined by O'Donnell (2010, Eq. 4.7).

To illustrate, reconsider the measures of IME and ISME depicted in Figs. 5.12 and 5.28. Relevant parts of those figures are now reproduced in Fig. 5.29. Recall from Figs. 5.12 and 5.28 that the IME and ISME of the manager of firm A are $IME^t(x_{it}, q_{it}, z_{it})$ = (slope 0B)/(slope 0U) and $ISME^t(x_{it}, q_{it}, z_{it})$ = (slope 0B)/(slope 0E). Consequently, the RISE of the manager is $RISE^t(x_{it}, q_{it}, z_{it}) = ISME^t(x_{it}, q_{it}, z_{it})/IME^t(x_{it}, q_{it}, z_{it})$ = (slope 0U)/(slope 0E) (i.e., an index that compares the TFP at point U with the TFP at point E).

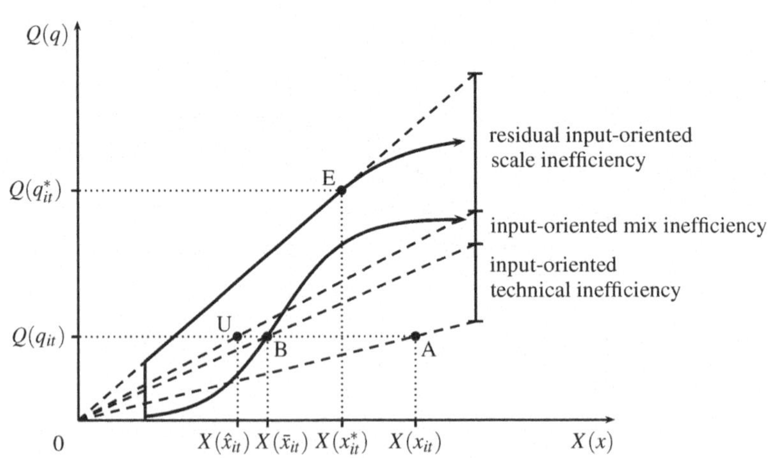

Fig. 5.29 Technical, scale and mix inefficiency. The gap between the rays through A and B is due to technical inefficiency. The gap between the rays through B and U is due to mix inefficiency. The gap between the rays through U and E is due to residual scale inefficiency

5.7.7 Metatechnology Ratios

If more than one technology exists in period t, then most measures of efficiency can be written as metatechnology ratios multiplied by residual measures of efficiency. For example, the measure of OTE defined by (5.1) can be written as the product of an output-oriented metatchnology ratio (OMR) and a measure of residual output-oriented technical efficiency (ROTE). The OMR can be viewed as an output-oriented measure of how well the manager has *chosen* the production technology (i.e., how well (s)he has chosen the 'book of instructions'). ROTE can be viewed as an output-oriented measure of how well the manager has *used* his/her chosen technology (i.e., how well (s)he has 'followed the instructions'). For a precise definition, let g_{it} denote the technology chosen by manager i in period t. The OMR and ROTE of the manager in this period are

$$OMR^{g_{it}t}(x_{it}, q_{it}, z_{it}) = Q(\bar{q}_{it}^{g_{it}})/Q(\bar{q}_{it}) \tag{5.47}$$

$$\text{and} \quad ROTE^{g_{it}}(x_{it}, q_{it}, z_{it}) = Q(q_{it})/Q(\bar{q}_{it}^{g_{it}}) \tag{5.48}$$

where $Q(q_{it})$ is the aggregate output of the firm, $Q(\bar{q}_{it}^{g_{it}}) = Q(q_{it})/d_O^{g_{it}}(x_{it}, q_{it}, z_{it})$ is the maximum aggregate output that is possible when using x_{it} *and technology* g_{it} to produce a scalar multiple of q_{it} in an environment characterised by z_{it}, and $Q(\bar{q}_{it}) = Q(q_{it})/D_O^t(x_{it}, q_{it}, z_{it})$ is the maximum aggregate output that is possible when using x_{it} *and any technology that existed in period t* to produce a scalar multiple of q_{it} in an environment characterised by z_{it}. Equivalent definitions are $OMR^{g_{it}t}(x_{it}, q_{it}, z_{it}) = D_O^t(x_{it}, q_{it}, z_{it})/d_O^{g_{it}}(x_{it}, q_{it}, z_{it})$ and $ROTE^{g_{it}}(x_{it}, q_{it}, z_{it}) = d_O^{g_{it}}(x_{it}, q_{it}, z_{it})$. These definitions can be found in O'Donnell et al. (2017, Eqs. 10, 11). Equations (5.1), (5.47) and (5.48) imply that

$$ROTE^{g_{it}}(x_{it}, q_{it}, z_{it}) = OTE^t(x_{it}, q_{it}, z_{it})/OMR^{g_{it}t}(x_{it}, q_{it}, z_{it}). \tag{5.49}$$

This equation says that ROTE is the component of OTE that remains after accounting for the OMR (hence the use of the term 'residual'). If environmental variables have been predetermined, then the OMR (resp. measure of ROTE) defined by (5.47) (resp. 5.48) can be viewed as a measure of how well the manager has solved problem (4.26) (resp. 4.25). If there is no environmental change, then the OMR defined by (5.47) has the same structure, but not necessarily the same interpretation,[5] as the metatechnology ratio defined by O'Donnell et al. (2008, Eq. 9). If there is only one technology in period t, then it takes the value one.

To illustrate, reconsider the output maximisation problem depicted earlier in Fig. 4.13. For convenience, that figure is now reproduced in Fig. 5.30. In these figures, the curves passing through points Z and C represent the boundaries of $p^1(x_{it}, z_{it})$ and $p^2(x_{it}, z_{it})$. The outputs of firm i in period t map to point A. The dashed lines

[5]The 'group-k' distance function in O'Donnell et al. (2008) is not necessarily a technology-specific distance function. It could, for example, be a period-and-environment-specific distance function.

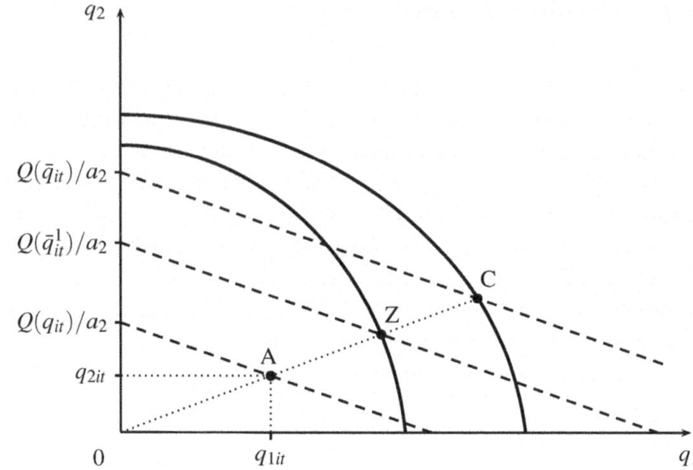

Fig. 5.30 Output-oriented technical efficiency. The gap between the dashed lines passing through points Z and C is due to the choice of technology. The gap between the dashed lines passing through points A and Z is due to residual technical inefficiency (i.e., how the chosen technology is used)

passing through points A, Z and C are iso-output lines with the same slope but different intercepts. The OTE, OMR and ROTE of manager i in period t are given by the ratios of these intercepts. For example, if the firm manager had used technology 1, then $OTE^t(x_{it}, q_{it}, z_{it}) = Q(q_{it})/Q(\bar{q}_{it})$, $OMR^{1t}(x_{it}, q_{it}, z_{it}) = Q(\bar{q}^1_{it})/Q(\bar{q}_{it})$ and $ROTE^1(x_{it}, q_{it}, z_{it}) = Q(q_{it})/Q(\bar{q}^1_{it})$. Equivalently, if the firm manager had used technology 1, then $OTE^t(x_{it}, q_{it}, z_{it}) = ||0A||/||0C||$ (i.e., the length of the line segment 0A divided by the length of the line segment 0C), $OMR^{1t}(x_{it}, q_{it}, z_{it}) = ||0Z||/||0C||$ (i.e., the length of 0Z divided by the length of 0C) and $ROTE^1(x_{it}, q_{it}, z_{it}) = ||0A||/||0Z||$ (i.e., the length of 0A divided by the length of 0Z).

Again, the fact that OMRs and measures of ROTE can be defined in terms of aggregate outputs means they can be depicted in output-input space. Again, this means they can be viewed as TFP indices. For example, points A, C and Z in Fig. 5.30 map to points A, C and Z in Fig. 5.31. In this figure, the frontier passing through point C is the frontier depicted earlier in Fig. 5.2; it represents the boundary of $T^t(x_{it}, q_{it}, z_{it})$. The frontier passing through point Z represents the boundary of $t^1(x_{it}, q_{it}, z_{it}) = \{(x, q) : x \propto x_{it},\ q \propto q_{it},\ q \in p^1(x, z_{it})\}$. The TFP at point A is $TFP(x_{it}, q_{it}) = Q(q_{it})/X(x_{it}) =$ slope 0A. The TFP at point Z is $TFP(x_{it}, \bar{q}^1_{it}) = Q(\bar{q}^1_{it})/X(x_{it}) =$ slope 0Z. The TFP at point C is $TFP(x_{it}, \bar{q}_{it}) = Q(\bar{q}_{it})/X(x_{it}) =$ slope 0C. If the firm manager had used technology 1, then the OTE, OMR and ROTE of the manager would have been

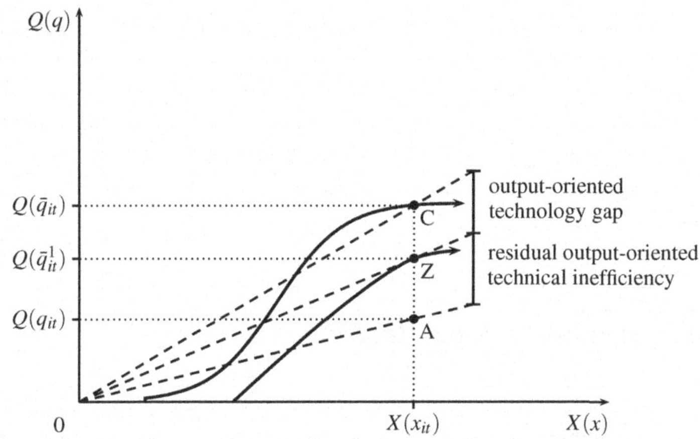

Fig. 5.31 Output-oriented technical efficiency. The gap between the rays passing through points Z and C is due to the choice of technology. The gap between the rays passing through points A and Z is due to residual output-oriented technical inefficiency (i.e., how the chosen technology is used)

$$OTE^{t}(x_{it}, q_{it}, z_{it}) = TFP(x_{it}, q_{it})/TFP(x_{it}, \bar{q}_{it}) = (\text{slope 0A})/(\text{slope 0C}),$$
$$OMR^{1t}(x_{it}, q_{it}, z_{it}) = TFP(x_{it}, \bar{q}_{it}^{1})/TFP(x_{it}, \bar{q}_{it}) = (\text{slope 0Z})/(\text{slope 0C})$$
and
$$ROTE^{1}(x_{it}, q_{it}, z_{it}) = TFP(x_{it}, q_{it})/TFP(x_{it}, \bar{q}_{it}^{1}) = (\text{slope 0A})/(\text{slope 0Z}).$$

5.7.8 Nonradial Measures

Each measure of efficiency defined in this chapter can be viewed as a measure of the difference between two vectors. For example, the measure of OTE defined by (5.1) can be viewed as a measure of the difference between the output vectors q_{it} and $\bar{q}_{it}$, while the measure of TSME defined by (5.32) can be viewed as a measure of the difference between the netput vectors $(-x_{it}, q_{it})$ and $(-x_{it}^{*}, q_{it}^{*})$. In the efficiency literature, a measure of efficiency is said be *radial* if the vectors involved in the comparison are scalar multiples (i.e., radial expansions or contractions) of each other. All other measures of efficiency are said to be *nonradial*. The class of radial efficiency measures includes the OMR defined by (5.47) and the measures of OTE, ITE and ROTE defined by (5.1), (5.8) and (5.48). All other measures of efficiency defined in this chapter are nonradial measures. All of these (radial and nonradial) measures have two important properties: (a) they are invariant to changes in units of measurement, and (b) they take values in the closed unit interval. Other nonradial measures of efficiency include the asymmetric 'input efficiency function' of Färe (1975, p. 21), the 'Russell measure of input efficiency' defined by Färe and Lovell (1978, p. 158), the 'Russell-extended Farrell efficiency index' defined by Zieschang (1984, p. 390), the 'modified asymmetric Färe efficiency measure' defined by Dervaux et al. (1998, p. 301), the GDF-based measures of technical and profit efficiency defined by Portela and Thanassoulis (2007, Eqs. 3, 5), and the DDF-based 'metafrontier performance indexes' of Zhang et al. (2013, Eqs. 6, 8, 12). Many of these measures are critically discussed in the surveys of Russell and Schworm (2009, 2011). Not all of them are invariant to changes in units of measurement, and not all of them lie in the closed unit interval.

5.8 Summary and Further Reading

Measures of efficiency can be viewed as *ex post* measures of how well firm managers have solved different optimisation problems. Except where explicitly stated otherwise, all measures of efficiency defined in this book take values in the closed unit interval. A firm manager is said to have been fully efficient by some measure if and only if that measure takes the value one.

Output-oriented measures of efficiency can be viewed as measures of how well firm managers have maximised outputs when inputs and environmental variables have been predetermined (i.e., determined in a previous period). In these situations, the relevance of a particular measure depends on how easily the manager has been able to choose the output mix. If the output mix of the firm has been predetermined, then the most relevant measure is output-oriented technical efficiency (OTE). The basic concept behind OTE can be traced back at least as far as Farrell (1957, p. 259). If the manager has been able to choose outputs freely, then the most relevant measure is output-oriented technical and mix efficiency (OTME). This concept appears to be new. The OTME of any manager can be decomposed in to separate measures of OTE and output-oriented mix efficiency (OME). The concept of OME can be traced back at least as far as O'Donnell (2010, Eq. 3.4). The OME of a manager can be viewed as an output-oriented measure of how well (s)he has captured economies of output substitution. Economies of output substitution are the benefits obtained by substituting some outputs for others (e.g., producing less of output 1 in order to produce more of output 2). Economies of output substitution differ from economies of scope; in the economics, literature, the term 'economies of scope' usually refers to the benefits obtained by producing several goods together rather than producing each one separately (e.g., Panzar and Willig 1981).

Input-oriented measures of efficiency can be viewed as measures of how well firm managers have minimised inputs when outputs and environmental variables have been predetermined. In these situations, the relevance of a particular measure now depends on how easily the manager has been able to choose the input mix. If the input mix of the firm has been predetermined, then the most relevant measure is input-oriented technical efficiency (ITE). The concept of ITE can be traced back to the 'coefficient of resource utilization' defined by Debreu (1951, p. 285). If the manager has been able to choose inputs freely, then the most relevant measure is input-oriented technical and mix efficiency (ITME). This concept also appears to be new. The ITME of any manager can be decomposed in to separate measures of ITE and input-oriented mix efficiency (IME). The IME of a manager is an input-oriented measure of how well (s)he has captured economies of input substitution. Economies of input substitution are the benefits obtained by substituting some inputs for others (e.g., substituting capital for labour). The concept of IME can be traced back at least as far as O'Donnell (2010, Eq. 4.6).

Revenue-oriented measures of efficiency can be viewed as measures of how well firm managers have maximised revenues when inputs and environmental variables have been predetermined and outputs have been chosen freely. The most common revenue-oriented measure of efficiency is revenue efficiency (RE). For any given firm, the exact definition of RE depends on whether the firm is a price setter or price taker in output markets. If the firm is a price setter (resp. price taker) in output markets, then the RE of the manager depends, *inter alia*, on 'demand shifters' (resp. output prices). If the firm is a price taker in output markets, then the RE of the manager can be decomposed into separate measures of OTE and output-oriented allocative efficiency (OAE). The OAE of the manager is a revenue-oriented measure of how well (s)he has captured economies of output substitution. The concept of OAE can be traced back at least as far as Färe et al. (1985, Sect. 4.6).

Cost-oriented measures of efficiency can be viewed as measures of how well firm managers have minimised costs when outputs and environmental variables have been predetermined and inputs have been chosen freely. The most common cost-oriented measure of efficiency is cost efficiency (CE). For any given firm, the exact definition of CE depends on whether the firm is a price setter or price taker in input markets. If the firm is a price setter (resp. price taker) in input markets, then the CE of the manager depends, *inter alia*, on 'supply shifters' (resp. input prices). The concept of CE can be traced back to the measure of 'overall efficiency' defined by Farrell (1957, p. 255). The CE of any manager can be decomposed into separate measures of ITE and input-oriented allocative efficiency (IAE). The IAE of the manager is a cost-oriented measure of how well (s)he has captured economies of input substitution. The concept of IAE can be traced back to the measure of 'price efficiency' defined by Farrell (1957, p. 255).

Profit-oriented measures of efficiency can be viewed as measures of how well firm managers have maximised profits when environmental variables have been predetermined and outputs and inputs have been chosen freely. The most widely-used profit-oriented measure of efficiency is profit efficiency (PE). For any given firm, the exact definition of PE depends on whether the firm is a price setter or price taker in output and input markets. If the firm is a price setter (resp. price taker) in output and input markets, then the PE of the manager depends, *inter alia*, on demand and supply shifters (resp. output and input prices). Measures of PE can be decomposed into separate measures of technical, scale and allocative efficiency. Both output- and input-oriented decompositions are available. The technical efficiency components are measures of OTE and ITE. The associated scale and allocative efficiency components are measures of output-oriented scale and allocative efficiency (OSAE) and input-oriented scale and allocative efficiency (ISAE). The OSAE and ISAE of a manager are profit-oriented measures of how well (s)he has captured economies of scale and substitution. Economies of scale and substitution are the benefits obtained by changing the scale of operations, the output mix, and the input mix. The concepts of OSAE and ISAE appear to be new.

Productivity-oriented measures of efficiency can be viewed as measures of how well firm managers have maximised productivity when environmental variables have been predetermined. In these situations, the relevance of a particular measure depends on how easily the manager has been able to choose the output mix and the input mix. If both the output mix and the input mix have been predetermined, then the most relevant measure is technical and scale efficiency (TSE). The concept of TSE can be traced back at least as far as Banker et al. (1984, p. 1089). Measures of TSE can be decomposed into separate output- and input-oriented measures of technical and scale efficiency. The technical efficiency components are measures of OTE and ITE. The associated scale efficiency components are measures of output-oriented scale efficiency (OSE) and input-oriented scale efficiency (ISE). The OSE (resp. ISE) of a manager is an output-oriented (resp. input-oriented) measure of how well (s)he has captured economies of scale. Economies of scale are the benefits obtained by changing the scale of operations. If the manager has been able to choose outputs and inputs freely, then the most relevant productivity-oriented measure of efficiency is technical, scale and mix efficiency (TSME). This concept can be traced back at least as far as the measure of 'TFP efficiency' defined by O'Donnell (2010). The TSME of any manager can be decomposed into a measure of TSE and a measure of residual mix efficiency (RME). The concept of RME can be traced back to O'Donnell (2010). Measures of TSME can also be decomposed into separate output- and input-oriented measures of technical, scale and mix efficiency. The technical efficiency components are measures of OTE and ITE. The associated scale and mix efficiency components are measures of output-oriented scale and mix efficiency (OSME) and input-oriented scale and mix efficiency (ISME). The OSME and ISME of a manager are productivity-oriented measures of how well (s)he has captured economies of scale and substitution. The concepts of OSME and ISME can be traced back at least as far as O'Donnell (2012). Measures of OSME and ISME can be further decomposed into separate measures of mix and scale efficiency. The mix efficiency components are measures of OME and IME. The associated scale efficiency components are measures of residual output-oriented scale efficiency (ROSE) and residual input-oriented scale efficiency (RISE). The concepts of ROSE and RISE can be traced back to O'Donnell (2010).

If more than one technology exists in a given period, then each measure of efficiency discussed above can be decomposed into the product of a metatchnology ratio and a measure of residual efficiency. On the output side, for example, the OTE of any firm can be decomposed into an output-oriented metatechnology ratio (OMR) and a measure of residual output-oriented technical efficiency (ROTE). The OMR can be viewed as an output-oriented measure of how well the firm manager has chosen the production technology (i.e., how well (s)he has chosen the 'book of instructions'). The ROTE of the manager can be viewed as an output-oriented measure of how well (s)he has used his/her chosen technology (i.e., how well (s)he has 'followed the instructions'). The concept of an OMR can be traced back at least as far as the 'technology gap ratio' of Battese and Rao (2002); the concept of ROTE can be traced back to their measure of technical efficiency with respect to the 'group frontier'. On the input side, the ITE of any firm can be decomposed into an input-oriented metatechnology ratio (IMR) and a measure of residual input-oriented technical efficiency (RITE). The IMR can be viewed as an input-oriented measure of how well the firm manager has chosen the production technology; the RITE of the manager can be viewed as an input-oriented measure of how well (s)he has used his/her chosen technology. The concept of an IMR can be traced back at least as far as the measure of 'inter-envelope efficiency' defined by Charnes et al. (1981).

Other interesting measures of efficiency include various non-radial measures. Many of these measures are defined in terms of directional or hyperbolic distance functions. Examples include the 'metafrontier performance indexes' of Zhang et al. (2013, Eqs. 6, 8, 12). These measures of efficiency do not necessarily lie in the closed unit interval.

References

Balk B (1998) Industrial price, quantity, and productivity indices: the micro-economic theory and an application. Kluwer Academic Publishers, Boston

Banker R, Maindiratta A (1988) Nonparametric analysis of technical and allocative efficiencies in production. Econometrica 56(6):1315–1332

Banker R, Charnes A, Cooper W (1984) Some models for estimating technical and scale inefficiencies in data envelopment analysis. Manage Sci 30(9):1078–1092

Battese G, Rao DSP (2002) Technology gap, efficiency, and a stochastic metafrontier function. Int J Bus Econ 1(2):87–93

Chambers R, Chung Y, Färe R (1998) Profit, directional distance functions, and Nerlovian efficiency. J Optim Theory Appl 98(2):351–364

Charnes A, Cooper W, Rhodes E (1981) Evaluating program and managerial efficiency: an application of data envelopment analysis to program follow through. Manage Sci 27(6):668–697

Debreu G (1951) The coefficient of resource utilization. Econometrica 19(3):273–292

Dervaux B, Kerstens K, Vanden Eeckaut P (1998) Radial and nonradial static efficiency decompositions: a focus on congestion measurement. Transp Res Part B: Methodol 32(5):299–312

Färe R (1975) Efficiency and the production function Zeitschrift für Nationalökonomie. J Econ 35(3–4):317–324

Färe R, Grosskopf S (1997) Profit efficiency, farrell decompositions and the mahler inequality. Econ Lett 57(3):283–287

Färe R, Lovell C (1978) Measuring the technical efficiency of production. J Econ Theory 19(August):150–162

Färe R, Primont D (1995) Multi-output production and duality: theory and applications. Kluwer Academic Publishers, Boston

Färe R, Grosskopf S, Lovell C (1985) The measurement of efficiency of production. Kluwer Academic Publishers, Boston

Farrell M (1957) The measurement of productive efficiency. J R Stat Soc, Series A (General) 120(3):253–290

Hardy G, Littlewood J, Polya G (1934) Inequalities. Cambridge University Press, Cambridge

O'Donnell C (2010) Measuring and decomposing agricultural productivity and profitability change. Aust J Agric Resour Econ 54(4):527–560

O'Donnell C (2012) Nonparametric estimates of the components of productivity and profitability change in U.S. agriculture. Am J Agric Econ 94(4):873–890
O'Donnell C (2016) Using information about technologies, markets and firm behaviour to decompose a proper productivity index. J Econometrics 190(2):328–340
O'Donnell C, Nguyen K (2013) An econometric approach to estimating support prices and measures of productivity change in public hospitals. J Prod Anal 40(3):323–335
O'Donnell C, Rao D, Battese G (2008) Metafrontier frameworks for the study of firm-level efficiencies and technology ratios. Empirical Econ 34(2):231–255
O'Donnell C, Fallah-Fini S, Triantis K (2017) Measuring and analysing productivity change in a metafrontier framework. J Prod Anal 47(2):117–128
Panzar J, Willig R (1981) Economies of scope. Am Econ Rev 72(1):268–272
Portela M, Thanassoulis E (2007) Developing a decomposable measure of profit efficiency using DEA. J Oper Res Soc 58(4):481–490
Russell R, Schworm W (2009) Axiomatic foundations of efficiency measurement on data-generated technologies. J Prod Anal 31(2):77–86
Russell R, Schworm W (2011) Properties of inefficiency indexes on <input, output> space. J Prod Anal 36(2):143–156
Zhang N, Zhou P, Choi Y (2013) Energy efficiency, CO_2 emission performance and technology gaps in fossil fuel electricity generation in Korea: a meta-frontier non-radial directional distance function analysis. Energy Policy 56(May):653–662
Zieschang K (1984) An extended farrell technical efficiency measure. J Econ Theory 33(2):387–396

Chapter 6
Piecewise Frontier Analysis

Estimating/predicting levels of efficiency involves estimating production frontiers. A widely-used estimation approach involves enveloping scatterplots of data points as tightly as possible without violating any assumptions that have been made about production technologies. Some of the most common assumptions lead to estimated frontiers that are comprised of multiple linear segments (or pieces). The associated frontiers are known as piecewise frontiers. This chapter explains how to estimate the unknown parameters of so-called piecewise frontier models (PFMs). It then explains how the estimated parameters can be used to analyse efficiency and productivity change. The focus is on what are commonly known as data envelopment analysis (DEA) estimators. These estimators date back at least as far as Farrell (1957).

6.1 Basic Models

The most common PFMs are underpinned by the following assumptions:

PF1 production possibilities sets can be represented by distance, revenue, cost and/or profit functions;
PF2 all relevant quantities, prices and environmental variables are observed and measured without error;
PF3 production frontiers are locally (or piecewise) linear;
PF4 inputs, outputs and environmental variables are strongly disposable; and
PF5 production possibilities sets are convex.

If these assumptions are true, then production frontiers and most measures of efficiency can be estimated using linear programming (LP). The associated models and estimators are commonly known as DEA models and estimators.

C. J. O'Donnell, *Productivity and Efficiency Analysis*,
https://doi.org/10.1007/978-981-13-2984-5_6

6.1.1 Output-Oriented Models

Output-oriented PFMs are mainly used to estimate the measure of OTE defined by (5.1). They can also be used to estimate the measure of OTME defined by (5.2). Subsequently, Eq. (5.4) can be used to estimate the measure of OME defined by (5.3).

Estimating the measure of OTE defined by (5.1) involves estimating the period-and-environment-specific output distance function. If assumptions PF1 to PF3 are true, then this function takes the form

$$D_O^{it}(x_{it}, q_{it}, z_{it}) = \gamma_{it}' q_{it} / (\alpha_{it} + \delta_{it}' z_{it} + \beta_{it}' x_{it}) \tag{6.1}$$

where α_{it} is an unknown scalar and $\gamma_{it} = (\gamma_{1it}, \ldots, \gamma_{Nit})'$, $\delta_{it} = (\delta_{1it}, \ldots, \delta_{Jit})'$ and $\beta_{it} = (\beta_{1it}, \ldots, \beta_{Mit})'$ are unknown vectors. The superscripts i and t appear on the left-hand side of this equation to indicate that the unknown parameters are permitted to vary from one data point to the next (i.e., locally). The term 'locally-linear frontier' derives from the fact that if $D_O^{it}(x_{it}, q_{it}, z_{it}) = 1$ (i.e., if the firm operates on the frontier), then the relationship between the inputs, outputs and environmental variables is $\gamma_{it}' q_{it} = \alpha_{it} + \delta_{it}' z_{it} + \beta_{it}' x_{it}$ (i.e., a linear function with parameters that are permitted to vary locally). Estimation involves choosing the unknown parameters to maximise $D_O^{it}(x_{it}, q_{it}, z_{it})$ subject to the requirement that assumptions PF4 and PF5 are satisfied. Assumption PF4 will be satisfied if and only if $\gamma_{it} \geq 0$, $\delta_{it} \geq 0$ and $\beta_{it} \geq 0$. If there are I firms in the dataset, then assumption PF5 will be satisfied if and only if $\gamma_{it}' q_{hr} \leq \alpha_{it} + \delta_{it}' z_{hr} + \beta_{it}' x_{hr}$ for all $h \leq I$ and $r \leq t$. With these constraints, the estimation problem becomes the following:

$$\max_{\alpha_{it}, \delta_{it}, \beta_{it}, \gamma_{it}} \Big\{ \gamma_{it}' q_{it} / (\alpha_{it} + \delta_{it}' z_{it} + \beta_{it}' x_{it}) : \gamma_{it} \geq 0,\ \delta_{it} \geq 0,\ \beta_{it} \geq 0,$$
$$\alpha_{it} + \delta_{it}' z_{hr} + \beta_{it}' x_{hr} - \gamma_{it}' q_{hr} \geq 0 \text{ for all } h \leq I \text{ and } r \leq t \Big\}. \tag{6.2}$$

This problem can be found in O'Donnell et al. (2017, Eq. 17). If the data are cross-section data, then all references to time periods can be deleted. If there are no environmental variables involved in the production process (i.e., if there is no environmental change), then the environmental variables and their coefficients can be deleted. If the data are cross-section data and there is no environmental change, then problem (6.2) reduces to the fractional programming problem of Banker et al. (1984, Eq. 22).

Solving (6.2) is complicated by the fact that the parameters are unidentified. A unique set of parameters can be identified by setting $\gamma_{it}' q_{it} = 1$. With this so-called normalising constraint, problem (6.2) can be rewritten as

$$\min_{\alpha_{it}, \delta_{it}, \beta_{it}, \gamma_{it}} \Big\{ \alpha_{it} + \delta_{it}' z_{it} + \beta_{it}' x_{it} : \gamma_{it} \geq 0,\ \delta_{it} \geq 0,\ \beta_{it} \geq 0,\ \gamma_{it}' q_{it} = 1,$$
$$\alpha_{it} + \delta_{it}' z_{hr} + \beta_{it}' x_{hr} - \gamma_{it}' q_{hr} \geq 0 \text{ for all } h \leq I \text{ and } r \leq t \Big\}. \tag{6.3}$$

This LP problem can be found in O'Donnell et al. (2017, Eq. 18). The value of the objective function at the optimum is an estimate of the reciprocal of $OTE^t(x_{it}, q_{it}, z_{it})$. Most efficiency researchers would refer to problem (6.3) as the 'multiplier' form of the DEA estimation problem. If there is no environmental change, then it reduces to problem (6.6) in O'Donnell (2010b, p. 543).

Every LP problem has a dual form with the property that if the so-called primal problem and its dual both have feasible solutions, then the optimised values of the two objective functions are equal. The dual form of problem (6.3) is

$$\max_{\mu,\lambda_{11},\ldots,\lambda_{It}} \left\{ \mu : \mu q_{it} \leq \sum_{h=1}^{I} \sum_{r=1}^{t} \lambda_{hr} q_{hr}, \sum_{h=1}^{I} \sum_{r=1}^{t} \lambda_{hr} z_{hr} \leq z_{it}, \sum_{h=1}^{I} \sum_{r=1}^{t} \lambda_{hr} x_{hr} \leq x_{it}, \sum_{h=1}^{I} \sum_{r=1}^{t} \lambda_{hr} = 1, \lambda_{hr} \geq 0 \text{ for all } h \text{ and } r \right\}. \quad (6.4)$$

This problem can be found in O'Donnell et al. (2017, Eq. 19). It seeks to scale up the output vector while holding inputs and environmental variables fixed. The value of μ at the optimum is an estimate of the reciprocal of $OTE^t(x_{it}, q_{it}, z_{it})$. Again, if the data are cross-section data, then all references to time periods can be deleted. If there is no environmental change, then the constraint involving the environmental variables can be deleted. Most efficiency researchers would refer to problem (6.4) as the 'envelopment' form of the DEA estimation problem. If there is no environmental change, then it reduces to problem (6.9) in O'Donnell (2010b, p. 544). If the data are cross-section data and there is no environmental change, then it reduces to a problem that can be found in Färe et al. (1994, p. 103).

Estimating the measure of OTME defined by (5.2) involves estimating $Q(q_{it})/Q(\hat{q}_{it})$. If there are I firms in the dataset and assumptions PF1 to PF5 are true, then the estimation problem is

$$\max_{q,\lambda_{11},\ldots,\lambda_{It}} \left\{ Q(q)/Q(q_{it}) : q \leq \sum_{h=1}^{I} \sum_{r=1}^{t} \lambda_{hr} q_{hr}, \sum_{h=1}^{I} \sum_{r=1}^{t} \lambda_{hr} z_{hr} \leq z_{it}, \sum_{h=1}^{I} \sum_{r=1}^{t} \lambda_{hr} x_{hr} \leq x_{it}, \sum_{h=1}^{I} \sum_{r=1}^{t} \lambda_{hr} = 1, \lambda_{hr} \geq 0 \text{ for all } h \text{ and } r \right\}. \quad (6.5)$$

If the aggregator function is linear (resp. nonlinear), then this is a linear (resp. nonlinear) programming problem. Whether or not the aggregator function is linear, the value of the objective function at the optimum is an estimate of the reciprocal of $OTME^t(x_{it}, q_{it}, z_{it})$. If there is no environmental change and $Q(.)$ is a linear function that gives all outputs equal weight, then problem (6.5) reduces to problem (A.15) in O'Donnell (2010b, p. 560).

For a numerical example, reconsider the toy data reported earlier in Table 1.1. Associated DEA estimates of OTME, OTE and OME are reported in Table 6.1. The

Table 6.1 DEA estimates of OTME, OTE and OME[a,b]

Row	Firm	Period	OTME	OTE	OME
A	1	1	0.390	0.422	0.924
B	2	1	1	1	1
C	3	1	0.924	1	0.924
D	4	1	0.769	1	0.769
E	5	1	1	1	1
F	1	2	0.626	0.865	0.724
G	2	2	1	1	1
H	3	2	1	1	1
I	4	2	0.871	0.871	1
J	5	2	1	1	1
K	1	3	1	1	1
L	2	3	0.887	1	0.887
M	3	3	0.651	0.653	0.997
N	4	3	1	1	1
O	5	3	0.643	0.844	0.762
P	1	4	0.547	0.594	0.921
R	2	4	0.653	0.671	0.974
S	3	4	0.448	0.583	0.769
T	4	4	0.917	1	0.917
U	5	4	0.622	0.654	0.950
V	1	5	1	1	1
W	2	5	0.683	0.895	0.764
X	3	5	0.592	0.836	0.708
Y	4	5	0.411	0.516	0.797
Z	5	5	0.864	0.867	0.997
Geometric mean			0.749	0.828	0.905

[a]OTME = OTE × OME. Some estimates may be incoherent at the third decimal place due to rounding (e.g., in any given row, the product of the OTE and OME estimates may not be exactly equal to the OTME estimate due to rounding)

[b]Numbers reported to less than three decimal places are exact; see the footnote to Table 1.2 on p. 8

OTE and OTME estimates were obtained by solving problems (6.4) and (6.5) for each firm in each period. The OME estimates were obtained by dividing the OTME estimates by the OTE estimates (i.e., the OME estimates were obtained as residuals). If there is more than one output, as there is in this example, then measures of OTME and OME depend on the aggregator function. The aggregator function used in this example was $Q(q) = 0.484q_1 + 0.516q_2$. This function was used earlier to compute the aggregate outputs in Table 1.2. It is also the aggregator function that was used to compute the Lowe output index numbers in Table 3.1.

6.1.2 Input-Oriented Models

Input-oriented PFMs are mainly used to estimate the measure of ITE defined by (5.8). They can also be used to estimate the measure of ITME defined by (5.9). Subsequently, Eq. (5.11) can be used to estimate the measure of IME defined by (5.10).

Estimating the measure of ITE defined by (5.8) involves estimating the period-and-environment-specific input distance function. If assumptions PF1 to PF3 are true, then this function takes the form

$$D_I^{it}(x_{it}, q_{it}, z_{it}) = (\theta_{it}' x_{it})/(\xi_{it}' q_{it} - \kappa_{it}' z_{it} - \phi_{it}) \tag{6.6}$$

where ϕ_{it} is an unknown scalar and $\xi_{it} = (\xi_{1it}, \ldots, \xi_{Nit})'$, $\kappa_{it} = (\kappa_{1it}, \ldots, \kappa_{Jit})'$ and $\theta_{it} = (\theta_{1it}, \ldots, \theta_{Mit})'$ are unknown vectors. Again, the superscripts i and t appear on the left-hand side of this equation to indicate that the unknown parameters are permitted to vary locally. Estimation involves choosing the unknown parameters to minimise $D_I^{it}(x_{it}, q_{it}, z_{it})$ subject to the requirement that assumptions PF4 and PF5 are satisfied. Assumption PF4 will be satisfied if and only if $\xi_{it} \geq 0$, $\kappa_{it} \geq 0$ and $\theta_{it} \geq 0$. If there are I firms in the dataset, then assumption PF5 will be satisfied if and only if $\theta_{it}' x_{hr} \geq \xi_{it}' q_{hr} - \kappa_{it}' z_{hr} - \phi_{hr}$ for all $h \leq I$ and $r \leq t$. With these constraints, the estimation problem becomes the following:

$$\min_{\xi_{it}, \kappa_{it}, \phi_{it}, \theta_{it}} \Big\{ \theta_{it}' x_{it}/(\xi_{it}' q_{it} - \kappa_{it}' z_{it} - \phi_{it}) : \xi_{it} \geq 0,\ \kappa_{it} \geq 0,\ \theta_{it} \geq 0, \\ \xi_{it}' q_{hr} - \kappa_{it}' z_{hr} - \phi_{it} - \theta_{it}' x_{hr} \leq 0 \text{ for all } h \leq I \text{ and } r \leq t \Big\}. \tag{6.7}$$

This is a fractional programming problem with an infinite number of solutions. A unique solution can be obtained by setting $\theta_{it}' x_{it} = 1$. With this normalising constraint, the problem can be rewritten as

$$\max_{\xi_{it}, \kappa_{it}, \phi_{it}, \theta_{it}} \Big\{ \xi_{it}' q_{it} - \kappa_{it}' z_{it} - \phi_{it} : \xi_{it} \geq 0,\ \kappa_{it} \geq 0,\ \theta_{it} \geq 0,\ \theta_{it}' x_{it} = 1, \\ \xi_{it}' q_{hr} - \kappa_{it}' z_{hr} - \phi_{it} - \theta_{it}' x_{hr} \leq 0 \text{ for all } h \leq I \text{ and } r \leq t \Big\}. \tag{6.8}$$

This LP problem can be found in O'Donnell et al. (2017, Eq. A8). The value of the objective function at the optimum is an estimate of $ITE^t(x_{it}, q_{it}, z_{it})$. Again, if the data are cross-section data, then all references to time periods can be deleted. If there is no environmental change, then the environmental variables and their coefficients can be deleted. Again, most efficiency researchers would refer to problem (6.8) as the multiplier form of the DEA estimation problem. If there is no environmental change, then it reduces to problem (6.5) in O'Donnell (2010b, p. 543). If the data are cross-section data and there is no environmental change, then it reduces to problem (20) in Banker et al. (1984).

The dual form of problem (6.8) is

$$\min_{\mu,\lambda_{11},\ldots,\lambda_{It}} \left\{ \mu : \sum_{h=1}^{I}\sum_{r=1}^{t} \lambda_{hr} q_{hr} \geq q_{it},\ \sum_{h=1}^{I}\sum_{r=1}^{t} \lambda_{hr} z_{hr} \leq z_{it}, \right.$$
$$\left. \mu x_{it} \geq \sum_{h=1}^{I}\sum_{r=1}^{t} \lambda_{hr} x_{hr},\ \sum_{h=1}^{I}\sum_{r=1}^{t} \lambda_{hr} = 1,\ \lambda_{hr} \geq 0 \text{ for all } h \text{ and } r \right\}. \quad (6.9)$$

This problem can be found in O'Donnell et al. (2017, Eq. A9). It seeks to scale down the input vector while holding outputs and environmental variables fixed. The value of μ at the optimum is an estimate of $ITE^t(x_{it}, q_{it}, z_{it})$. Again, if the data are cross-section data, then all references to time periods can be deleted. If there is no environmental change, then the constraint involving the environmental variables can be deleted. Again, most efficiency researchers would refer to problem (6.9) as the envelopment form of the DEA estimation problem. If the data are cross-section data, then it reduces to problem (7.6) in Coelli et al. (2005, p. 192). If there is no environmental change, then it reduces to problem (6.7) in O'Donnell (2010b, p. 543). If the data are cross-section data and there is no environmental change, then it reduces to problem (19) in Banker et al. (1984).

Estimating the measure of ITME defined by (5.9) involves estimating $X(\hat{x}_{it})/X(x_{it})$. If there are I firms in the dataset and assumptions PF1 to PF5 are true, then the estimation problem is

$$\min_{x,\lambda_{11},\ldots,\lambda_{It}} \left\{ X(x)/X(x_{it}) : \sum_{h=1}^{I}\sum_{r=1}^{t} \lambda_{hr} q_{hr} \geq q_{it},\ \sum_{h=1}^{I}\sum_{r=1}^{t} \lambda_{hr} z_{hr} \leq z_{it}, \right.$$
$$\left. x \geq \sum_{h=1}^{I}\sum_{r=1}^{t} \lambda_{hr} x_{hr},\ \sum_{h=1}^{I}\sum_{r=1}^{t} \lambda_{hr} = 1,\ \lambda_{hr} \geq 0 \text{ for all } h \text{ and } r \right\}. \quad (6.10)$$

If the aggregator function is linear (resp. nonlinear), then this is a linear (resp. nonlinear) programming problem. Whether or not the aggregator function is linear, the value of the objective function at the optimum is an estimate of $ITME^t(x_{it}, q_{it}, z_{it})$. If there is no environmental change and $X(.)$ is a linear function that gives all inputs equal weight, then problem (6.10) reduces to problem (6.15) in O'Donnell (2010b, p. 547).

For a numerical example, reconsider the toy data reported earlier in Table 1.1. Associated DEA estimates of ITME, ITE and IME are reported in Table 6.2. The ITE and ITME estimates were obtained by solving problems (6.9) and (6.10) for each firm in each period. The IME estimates were obtained by dividing the ITME estimates by the ITE estimates (i.e., the IME estimates were obtained as residuals). If there is more than one input, as there is in this example, then measures of ITME and IME depend on the aggregator function. The aggregator function used in this example was $X(x) = 0.23x_1 + 0.77x_2$. This function was used earlier to compute the aggregate inputs in Table 1.2. It is also the aggregator function that was used to compute the Lowe input index numbers in Table 3.3.

Table 6.2 DEA estimates of ITME, ITE and IME[a,b]

Row	Firm	Period	ITME	ITE	IME
A	1	1	0.56	0.56	1
B	2	1	1	1	1
C	3	1	1	1	1
D	4	1	1	1	1
E	5	1	1	1	1
F	1	2	0.603	0.954	0.632
G	2	2	1	1	1
H	3	2	1	1	1
I	4	2	0.864	0.955	0.905
J	5	2	1	1	1
K	1	3	1	1	1
L	2	3	1	1	1
M	3	3	0.602	0.604	0.997
N	4	3	1	1	1
O	5	3	0.581	0.777	0.748
P	1	4	0.548	0.551	0.994
R	2	4	0.651	0.657	0.990
S	3	4	0.430	0.669	0.643
T	4	4	0.843	1	0.843
U	5	4	0.608	0.689	0.883
V	1	5	1	1	1
W	2	5	0.632	0.846	0.748
X	3	5	0.567	0.881	0.644
Y	4	5	0.385	0.387	0.996
Z	5	5	0.5	0.5	1
Geometric mean			0.741	0.814	0.911

[a]ITME = ITE × IME. Some estimates may be incoherent at the third decimal place due to rounding (e.g., in any given row, the product of the ITE and IME estimates may not be exactly equal to the ITME estimate due to rounding)

[b]Numbers reported to less than three decimal places are exact; see the footnote to Table 1.2 on p. 8

6.1.3 Revenue-Oriented Models

Revenue-oriented PFMs are mainly used to estimate the measure of RE defined by (5.15). If estimates of OTE are available, then Eq. (5.18) can subsequently be used to estimate the measure of OAE defined by (5.17).

Estimating the measure of RE defined by (5.15) involves estimating $R^t(x_{it}, p_{it}, z_{it})$. If there are I firms in the dataset and assumptions PF1 to PF5 are true, then the estimation problem is

$$\max_{q,\lambda_{11},\ldots,\lambda_{It}} \left\{ p'_{it}q : q \leq \sum_{h=1}^{I}\sum_{r=1}^{t} \lambda_{hr}q_{hr}, \sum_{h=1}^{I}\sum_{r=1}^{t} \lambda_{hr}z_{hr} \leq z_{it}, \right.$$
$$\left. \sum_{h=1}^{I}\sum_{r=1}^{t} \lambda_{hr}x_{hr} \leq x_{it}, \sum_{h=1}^{I}\sum_{r=1}^{t} \lambda_{hr} = 1, \lambda_{hr} \geq 0 \text{ for all } h \text{ and } r \right\}. \quad (6.11)$$

The value of the objective function at the optimum is an estimate of $R^t(x_{it}, p_{it}, z_{it})$. This can be substituted into (5.15) to obtain an estimate of $RE^t(x_{it}, p_{it}, q_{it}, z_{it})$. Observe that the constraints in problem (6.11) are the same as the constraints in problem (6.5); the only difference between the two problems is the objective function. Again, if the data are cross-section data, then all references to time periods can be deleted. If there is no environmental change, then the constraint involving the environmental variables can be deleted. If the data are cross-section data and there is no environmental change, then problem (6.11) reduces to problem (7.2) in Coelli et al. (2005).

For a numerical example, reconsider the toy data reported earlier in Table 1.1. Associated DEA estimates of RE, OTE and OAE are reported in Table 6.3. The OTE estimates are those reported earlier in Table 6.1. The RE estimates were obtained by first solving problem (6.11) for each firm in each period. This step yielded estimates of $R^t(x_{it}, p_{it}, z_{it})$. The RE estimates were then obtained by dividing observed revenues by these estimates of $R^t(x_{it}, p_{it}, z_{it})$. Finally, the OAE estimates were obtained by dividing the RE estimates by the OTE estimates (i.e., the OAE estimates were obtained as residuals).

6.1.4 Cost-Oriented Models

Cost-oriented PFMs are mainly used to estimate the measure of CE defined by (5.20). If estimates of ITE are available, then Eq. (5.23) can subsequently be used to estimate the measure of IAE defined by (5.22).

Estimating the measure of CE defined by (5.20) involves estimating $C^t(w_{it}, q_{it}, z_{it})$. If there are I firms in the dataset and assumptions PF1 to PF5 are true, then the estimation problem is

$$\min_{x,\lambda_{11},\ldots,\lambda_{It}} \left\{ w'_{it}x : \sum_{h=1}^{I}\sum_{r=1}^{t} \lambda_{hr}q_{hr} \geq q_{it}, \sum_{h=1}^{I}\sum_{r=1}^{t} \lambda_{hr}z_{hr} \leq z_{it}, \right.$$
$$\left. x \geq \sum_{h=1}^{I}\sum_{r=1}^{t} \lambda_{hr}x_{hr}, \sum_{h=1}^{I}\sum_{r=1}^{t} \lambda_{hr} = 1, \lambda_{hr} \geq 0 \text{ for all } h \text{ and } r \right\}.$$
$$(6.12)$$

Table 6.3 DEA estimates of RE, OTE and OAE[a,b]

Row	Firm	Period	RE	OTE	OAE
A	1	1	0.415	0.422	0.984
B	2	1	1	1	1
C	3	1	0.984	1	0.984
D	4	1	0.789	1	0.789
E	5	1	1	1	1
F	1	2	0.643	0.865	0.744
G	2	2	1	1	1
H	3	2	1	1	1
I	4	2	0.871	0.871	1
J	5	2	1	1	1
K	1	3	1	1	1
L	2	3	0.908	1	0.908
M	3	3	0.644	0.653	0.987
N	4	3	1	1	1
O	5	3	0.821	0.844	0.973
P	1	4	0.511	0.594	0.861
R	2	4	0.656	0.671	0.978
S	3	4	0.413	0.583	0.709
T	4	4	0.989	1	0.989
U	5	4	0.638	0.654	0.976
V	1	5	0.678	1	0.678
W	2	5	0.848	0.895	0.947
X	3	5	0.633	0.836	0.757
Y	4	5	0.353	0.516	0.684
Z	5	5	0.818	0.867	0.943
Geometric mean			0.752	0.828	0.908

[a]RE = OTE × OAE. Some estimates may be incoherent at the third decimal place due to rounding (e.g., in any given row, the product of the OTE and OAE estimates may not be exactly equal to the RE estimate due to rounding)

[b]Numbers reported to less than three decimal places are exact; see the footnote to Table 1.2 on p. 8

The value of the objective function at the optimum is an estimate of $C^t(w_{it}, q_{it}, z_{it})$. This can be substituted into (5.20) to obtain an estimate of $CE^t(w_{it}, x_{it}, q_{it}, z_{it})$. Observe that the constraints in problem (6.12) are the same as the constraints in problem (6.10); the only difference between the two problems is the objective function. Again, if the data are cross-section data, then all references to time periods can be deleted. If there is no environmental change, then the constraint involving the environmental variables can be deleted. If the data are cross-section data and there is no environmental change, then problem (6.12) reduces to problem (7.1) in Coelli et al. (2005).

Table 6.4 DEA estimates of CE, ITE and IAE[a,b]

Row	Firm	Period	CE	ITE	IAE
A	1	1	0.56	0.56	1
B	2	1	1	1	1
C	3	1	1	1	1
D	4	1	1	1	1
E	5	1	1	1	1
F	1	2	0.351	0.954	0.368
G	2	2	0.839	1	0.839
H	3	2	1	1	1
I	4	2	0.846	0.955	0.886
J	5	2	1	1	1
K	1	3	1	1	1
L	2	3	1	1	1
M	3	3	0.603	0.604	0.999
N	4	3	1	1	1
O	5	3	0.776	0.777	0.999
P	1	4	0.497	0.551	0.902
R	2	4	0.634	0.657	0.965
S	3	4	0.423	0.669	0.633
T	4	4	0.917	1	0.917
U	5	4	0.610	0.689	0.886
V	1	5	1	1	1
W	2	5	0.687	0.846	0.812
X	3	5	0.325	0.881	0.368
Y	4	5	0.377	0.387	0.975
Z	5	5	0.5	0.5	1
Geometric mean			0.712	0.814	0.875

[a]CE = ITE × IAE. Some estimates may be incoherent at the third decimal place due to rounding (e.g., in any given row, the product of the ITE and IAE estimates may not be exactly equal to the CE estimate due to rounding)

[b]Numbers reported to less than three decimal places are exact; see the footnote to Table 1.2 on p. 8

For a numerical example, reconsider the toy data reported earlier in Table 1.1. Associated DEA estimates of CE, ITE and IAE are reported in Table 6.4. The ITE estimates are those reported earlier in Table 6.2. The CE estimates were obtained by first solving problem (6.12) for each firm in each period. This step yielded estimates of $C^t(w_{it}, q_{it}, z_{it})$. The CE estimates were then obtained by dividing these estimates by observed costs. Finally, the IAE estimates were obtained by dividing the CE estimates by the ITE estimates (i.e., the IAE estimates were obtained as residuals).

6.1.5 Profit-Oriented Models

Profit-oriented PFMs are mainly used to estimate the measure of PE defined by (5.27). If estimates of OTE and ITE are available, then Eqs. (5.28) and (5.29) can subsequently be used to obtain estimates of OSAE and ISAE.

Estimating the measure of PE defined by (5.27) involves estimating $\Pi^t(w_{it}, p_{it}, z_{it})$. If there are I firms in the dataset and assumptions PF1 to PF5 are true, then the estimation problem is

$$\max_{q,x,\lambda_{11},\ldots,\lambda_{It}} \left\{ p_{it}'q - w_{it}'x : q \leq \sum_{h=1}^{I}\sum_{r=1}^{t}\lambda_{hr}q_{hr}, \sum_{h=1}^{I}\sum_{r=1}^{t}\lambda_{hr}z_{hr} \leq z_{it}, \right.$$
$$\left. \sum_{h=1}^{I}\sum_{r=1}^{t}\lambda_{hr}x_{hr} \leq x, \sum_{h=1}^{I}\sum_{r=1}^{t}\lambda_{hr} = 1, \ \lambda_{hr} \geq 0 \text{ for all } h \text{ and } r \right\}. \quad (6.13)$$

The value of the objective function at the optimum is an estimate of $\Pi^t(w_{it}, p_{it}, z_{it})$. This can be substituted into (5.27) to obtain an estimate of $PE^t(w_{it}, x_{it}, p_{it}, q_{it}, z_{it})$. Again, if the data are cross-section data, then all references to time periods can be deleted. In this case, problem (6.13) has the same structure, but not the same interpretation,[1] as problem (2) in Färe et al. (1990). If there is no environmental change, then the constraint involving the environmental variables can be deleted. If the data are cross-section data and there is no environmental change, then problem (6.13) reduces to problem (7.3) in Coelli et al. (2005).

For a numerical example, reconsider the toy data reported earlier in Table 1.1. Associated DEA estimates of PE, OTE, OSAE, ITE and ISAE are reported in Table 6.5. The PE estimates were obtained by first solving problem (6.13) for each firm in each period. This step yielded estimates of $\Pi^t(w_{it}, p_{it}, z_{it})$. The PE estimates were then obtained using (5.27). The OTE and ITE estimates are those reported earlier in Tables 6.1 and 6.2. These technical efficiency estimates were used to obtain estimates of $R^t(x_{it}, p_{it}, q_{it}, z_{it}) = R_{it}/D_O^t(x_{it}, q_{it}, z_{it})$ and $C^t(w_{it}, x_{it}, q_{it}, z_{it}) = C_{it}/D_I^t(x_{it}, q_{it}, z_{it})$. The OSAE and ISAE estimates were then obtained using (5.28) and (5.29).

6.1.6 Productivity-Oriented Models

Productivity-oriented PFMs are mainly used to estimate the measure of TSME defined by (5.32). They can also be used to estimate the measure of TSE defined by

[1] Färe et al. (1990) consider the case where a subset of inputs are pre-determined (or 'fixed'). The fixed-input constraint in their so-called short-run profit maximisation problem plays the same role as, but has a different interpretation to, the environmental variable constraint in problem (6.13).

Table 6.5 DEA estimates of PE, OTE, OSAE, ITE and ISAE[a]

Row	Firm	Period	PE	OTE	OSAE	ITE	ISAE
A	1	1	0	0.422	0.150	0.56	0
B	2	1	0.084	1	0.084	1	0.084
C	3	1	0.150	1	0.150	1	0.150
D	4	1	0.751	1	0.751	1	0.751
E	5	1	1	1	1	1	1
F	1	2	0.303	0.865	0.366	0.954	0.308
G	2	2	0.878	1	0.878	1	0.878
H	3	2	0.246	1	0.246	1	0.246
I	4	2	0.609	0.871	0.776	0.955	0.632
J	5	2	0.514	1	0.514	1	0.514
K	1	3	0.210	1	0.210	1	0.210
L	2	3	0.885	1	0.885	1	0.885
M	3	3	0.346	0.653	0.719	0.604	0.487
N	4	3	0.032	1	0.032	1	0.032
O	5	3	0.491	0.844	0.633	0.777	0.553
P	1	4	0.215	0.594	0.458	0.551	0.278
R	2	4	0.562	0.671	0.903	0.657	0.608
S	3	4	0.132	0.583	0.371	0.669	0.199
T	4	4	0.618	1	0.618	1	0.618
U	5	4	0.191	0.654	0.363	0.689	0.233
V	1	5	0	1	0	1	0
W	2	5	0.278	0.895	0.374	0.846	0.360
X	3	5	0.184	0.836	0.250	0.881	0.202
Y	4	5	0.105	0.516	0.428	0.387	0.251
Z	5	5	0.666	0.867	0.811	0.5	0.804
Arithmetic mean			0.378	0.851	0.479	0.841	0.411

[a]Numbers reported to less than three decimal places are exact; see the footnote to Table 1.2 on p. 8

(5.31). Subsequently, Eq. (5.34) can be used to estimate the measure of RME defined by (5.33). If estimates of OTE, OME, ITE and IME are available, then Eqs. (5.36), (5.38), (5.40), (5.42), (5.44) and (5.46) can also be used to estimate the measures of OSE , OSME , ROSE, ISE , ISME and RISE defined by (5.35), (5.37), (5.39), (5.41), (5.43) and (5.45).

Estimating the measure of TSME defined by (5.32) involves estimating $TFP^t(z_{it})$. If there are I firms in the dataset and assumptions PF1 to PF5 are true, then the estimation problem is

$$\max_{q,x,\lambda_{11},\ldots,\lambda_{It}} \left\{ Q(q)/X(x) : q \le \sum_{h=1}^{I}\sum_{r=1}^{t} \lambda_{hr} q_{hr}, \; \sum_{h=1}^{I}\sum_{r=1}^{t} \lambda_{hr} z_{hr} \le z_{it}, \right.$$
$$\left. \sum_{h=1}^{I}\sum_{r=1}^{t} \lambda_{hr} x_{hr} \le x, \; \sum_{h=1}^{I}\sum_{r=1}^{t} \lambda_{hr} = 1, \; \lambda_{hr} \ge 0 \text{ for all } h \text{ and } r \right\}. \quad (6.14)$$

Observe that the constraints in this problem are the same as the constraints in problem (6.13); the only difference between the two problems is the objective function. The optimised value of the objective function in problem (6.14) is an estimate of $TFP^t(z_{it})$. This can be substituted into (5.32) to obtain an estimate of $TSME^t(x_{it}, q_{it}, z_{it})$. Let q_{it}^* and x_{it}^* denote values of q and x that solve (4.24). The values of q and x that solve (6.14) are estimates of q_{it}^* and x_{it}^*.

Problem (6.14) is a fractional programming problem. The Charnes and Cooper (1962) transformation for fractional programs can be used to rewrite it as

$$\max_{q,x,\mu,\theta_{11},\ldots,\theta_{It}} \left\{ Q(q) : q \le \sum_{h=1}^{I}\sum_{r=1}^{t} \theta_{hr} q_{hr}, \; \sum_{h=1}^{I}\sum_{r=1}^{t} \theta_{hr} z_{hr} \le \mu z_{it}, \; X(x) = 1, \right.$$
$$\left. \sum_{h=1}^{I}\sum_{r=1}^{t} \theta_{hr} x_{hr} \le x, \; \sum_{h=1}^{I}\sum_{r=1}^{t} \theta_{hr} = \mu, \; \theta_{hr} \ge 0 \text{ for all } h \text{ and } r \right\}. \quad (6.15)$$

The value of the objective function at the optimum is still an estimate of $TFP^t(z_{it})$. However, whereas the values of q and x that solve (6.14) are estimates of q_{it}^* and x_{it}^*, the values of q and x that solve (6.15) are estimates of $q_{it}^*/X(x_{it}^*)$ and $x_{it}^*/X(x_{it}^*)$. The value of μ at the optimum is an estimate of $1/X(x_{it}^*)$. If there is no environmental change, then all constraints involving μ can be deleted. If the aggregator functions are linear (resp. nonlinear), then problem (6.15) is a linear (resp. nonlinear) programming problem. If there is no environmental change and the aggregator functions are linear with coefficients equal to one, then it reduces to problem (6.16) in O'Donnell (2010b, p. 548).

Estimating the measure of TSE defined by Eq. (5.31) involves estimating $TFP^t(x_{it}, q_{it}, z_{it})$. If there are I firms in the dataset and assumptions PF1 to PF5 are true, then the estimation problem is[2]

$$\max_{\rho,\mu,\theta_{11},\ldots,\theta_{It}} \left\{ \rho Q(q_{it}) : \rho q_{it} \le \sum_{h=1}^{I}\sum_{r=1}^{t} \theta_{hr} q_{hr}, \; \sum_{h=1}^{I}\sum_{r=1}^{t} \theta_{hr} z_{hr} \le \mu z_{it}, \right.$$
$$\left. \sum_{h=1}^{I}\sum_{r=1}^{t} \theta_{hr} x_{hr} \le x_{it}/X(x_{it}), \; \sum_{h=1}^{I}\sum_{r=1}^{t} \theta_{hr} = \mu, \; \theta_{hr} \ge 0 \text{ for all } h \text{ and } r \right\}. \quad (6.16)$$

[2]This estimation problem is obtained by replacing q and x in problem (6.15) with ρq_{it} and δx_{it}, then using the linear homogeneity properties of the aggregator functions to simplify. For example, the constraint $X(\delta x_{it}) = 1$ implies that $\delta = 1/X(x_{it})$, which in turn implies that $\delta x_{it} = x_{it}/X(x_{it})$.

Whether or not the output and input aggregator functions are linear, this is an LP problem. The value of the objective function at the optimum is an estimate of $TFP^t(x_{it}, q_{it}, z_{it})$. This can be substituted into (5.31) to obtain an estimate of $TSE^t(x_{it}, q_{it}, z_{it})$.

For a numerical example, reconsider the toy data reported earlier in Table 1.1. Associated DEA estimates of TSME, TSE and RME are reported in Table 6.6. Estimates of TSME, OTE, OSME, OME, OSE, ROSE and RME are reported in Table 6.7. Estimates of TSME, ITE, ISME, IME, ISE, RISE and RME are reported in Table 6.8. The TSME and TSE estimates were obtained by first solving problems

Table 6.6 DEA estimates of TSME, TSE and RME[a,b]

Row	Firm	Period	TSME	TSE	RME
A	1	1	0.284	0.422	0.674
B	2	1	0.508	0.753	0.674
C	3	1	0.674	1	0.674
D	4	1	0.769	1	0.769
E	5	1	1	1	1
F	1	2	0.602	0.615	0.978
G	2	2	1	1	1
H	3	2	0.999	1	0.999
I	4	2	0.761	0.849	0.896
J	5	2	0.899	1	0.899
K	1	3	0.885	1	0.885
L	2	3	0.785	1	0.785
M	3	3	0.534	0.592	0.903
N	4	3	1	1	1
O	5	3	0.569	0.569	1
P	1	4	0.547	0.547	1
R	2	4	0.578	0.642	0.901
S	3	4	0.429	0.551	0.779
T	4	4	0.811	0.838	0.968
U	5	4	0.607	0.624	0.973
V	1	5	0.896	1	0.896
W	2	5	0.619	0.619	1
X	3	5	0.566	0.725	0.781
Y	4	5	0.384	0.384	1
Z	5	5	0.500	0.5	1.000
Geometric mean			0.656	0.737	0.890

[a]TSME = TSE × RME. Some estimates may be incoherent at the third decimal place due to rounding (e.g., in any given row, the product of the TSE and RME estimates may not be exactly equal to the TSME estimate due to rounding)

[b]Numbers reported to less than three decimal places are exact; see the footnote to Table 1.2 on p. 8

Table 6.7 DEA estimates of TSME, OTE, OSME, OME, ROSE, OSE and RME[a,b]

Row	Firm	Period	TSME	OTE	OSME	OTE	OME	ROSE	OTE	OSE	RME
A	1	1	0.284	0.422	0.674	0.422	0.924	0.730	0.422	1	0.674
B	2	1	0.508	1	0.508	1	1	0.508	1	0.753	0.674
C	3	1	0.674	1	0.674	1	0.924	0.730	1	1	0.674
D	4	1	0.769	1	0.769	1	0.769	1	1	1	0.769
E	5	1	1	1	1	1	1	1	1	1	1
F	1	2	0.602	0.865	0.696	0.865	0.724	0.962	0.865	0.711	0.978
G	2	2	1	1	1	1	1	1	1	1	1
H	3	2	0.999	1	0.999	1	1	0.999	1	1	0.999
I	4	2	0.761	0.871	0.874	0.871	1	0.874	0.871	0.976	0.896
J	5	2	0.899	1	0.899	1	1	0.899	1	1	0.899
K	1	3	0.885	1	0.885	1	1	0.885	1	1	0.885
L	2	3	0.785	1	0.785	1	0.887	0.885	1	1	0.785
M	3	3	0.534	0.653	0.819	0.653	0.997	0.821	0.653	0.907	0.903
N	4	3	1	1	1	1	1	1	1	1	1
O	5	3	0.569	0.844	0.674	0.844	0.762	0.885	0.844	0.674	1
P	1	4	0.547	0.594	0.921	0.594	0.921	1	0.594	0.921	1
R	2	4	0.578	0.671	0.861	0.671	0.974	0.885	0.671	0.956	0.901
S	3	4	0.429	0.583	0.737	0.583	0.769	0.958	0.583	0.946	0.779
T	4	4	0.811	1	0.811	1	0.917	0.885	1	0.838	0.968
U	5	4	0.607	0.654	0.928	0.654	0.95	0.976	0.654	0.954	0.973
V	1	5	0.896	1	0.896	1	1	0.896	1	1	0.896
W	2	5	0.619	0.895	0.692	0.895	0.764	0.906	0.895	0.692	1
X	3	5	0.566	0.836	0.677	0.836	0.708	0.956	0.836	0.867	0.781
Y	4	5	0.384	0.516	0.745	0.516	0.797	0.935	0.516	0.745	1
Z	5	5	0.500	0.867	0.577	0.867	0.997	0.579	0.867	0.577	1.000
Geometric mean			0.656	0.828	0.792	0.828	0.905	0.875	0.828	0.890	0.890

[a]TSME = OTE × OSME = OTE × OME × ROSE = OTE × OSE × RME. Some estimates may be incoherent at the third decimal place due to rounding (e.g., in any given row, the product of the OTE, OSE and RME estimates may not be exactly equal to the TSME estimate due to rounding)
[b]Numbers reported to less than three decimal places are exact; see the footnote to Table 1.2 on p. 8

(6.15) and (6.16) for each firm in each period. This step yielded estimates of $TFP^t(z_{it})$ and $TFP^t(x_{it}, q_{it}, z_{it})$. The aggregator functions used in this step were $Q(q) = 0.484q_1 + 0.516q_2$ and $X(x) = 0.23x_1 + 0.77x_2$. These functions were used earlier to compute the aggregate outputs and inputs in Table 1.2. The next step was to use the aggregate outputs and inputs in Table 1.2 to compute measures of TFP. The TSME and TSE estimates were then obtained by dividing these measures of TFP by the corresponding estimates of $TFP^t(z_{it})$ and $TFP^t(x_{it}, q_{it}, z_{it})$. The RME estimates were obtained by dividing the TSME estimates by the TSE estimates (i.e., the RME estimates were obtained as residuals). The OTE, ITE, OME and IME estimates are

Table 6.8 DEA estimates of TSME, ITE, ISME, IME, RISE, ISE and RME[a,b]

Row	Firm	Period	TSME	ITE	ISME	ITE	IME	RISE	ITE	ISE	RME
A	1	1	0.284	0.56	0.508	0.56	1	0.508	0.56	0.753	0.674
B	2	1	0.508	1	0.508	1	1	0.508	1	0.753	0.674
C	3	1	0.674	1	0.674	1	1	0.674	1	1	0.674
D	4	1	0.769	1	0.769	1	1	0.769	1	1	0.769
E	5	1	1	1	1	1	1	1	1	1	1
F	1	2	0.602	0.954	0.631	0.954	0.632	0.998	0.954	0.645	0.978
G	2	2	1	1	1	1	1	1	1	1	1
H	3	2	0.999	1	0.999	1	1	0.999	1	1	0.999
I	4	2	0.761	0.955	0.797	0.955	0.905	0.880	0.955	0.889	0.896
J	5	2	0.899	1	0.899	1	1	0.899	1	1	0.899
K	1	3	0.885	1	0.885	1	1	0.885	1	1	0.885
L	2	3	0.785	1	0.785	1	1	0.785	1	1	0.785
M	3	3	0.534	0.604	0.886	0.604	0.997	0.888	0.604	0.981	0.903
N	4	3	1	1	1	1	1	1	1	1	1
O	5	3	0.569	0.777	0.732	0.777	0.748	0.979	0.777	0.732	1
P	1	4	0.547	0.551	0.992	0.551	0.994	0.998	0.551	0.993	1
R	2	4	0.578	0.657	0.880	0.657	0.990	0.888	0.657	0.977	0.901
S	3	4	0.429	0.669	0.642	0.669	0.643	0.998	0.669	0.824	0.779
T	4	4	0.811	1	0.811	1	0.843	0.962	1	0.838	0.968
U	5	4	0.607	0.689	0.881	0.689	0.883	0.998	0.689	0.906	0.973
V	1	5	0.896	1	0.896	1	1	0.896	1	1	0.896
W	2	5	0.619	0.846	0.732	0.846	0.748	0.979	0.846	0.732	1
X	3	5	0.566	0.881	0.643	0.881	0.644	0.998	0.881	0.823	0.781
Y	4	5	0.384	0.387	0.994	0.387	0.996	0.998	0.387	0.994	1
Z	5	5	0.500	0.5	1.000	0.5	1	1.000	0.5	1	1.000
Geometric mean			0.656	0.814	0.806	0.814	0.911	0.885	0.814	0.906	0.890

[a]TSME = ITE × ISME = ITE × IME × RISE = ITE × ISE × RME. Some estimates may be incoherent at the third decimal place due to rounding (e.g., in any given row, the product of the ITE, ISE and RME estimates may not be exactly equal to the TSME estimate due to rounding)
[b]Numbers reported to less than three decimal places are exact; see the footnote to Table 1.2 on p. 8

those reported earlier in Tables 6.1 and 6.2. The OSME and ISME (resp. OSE and ISE) estimates were obtained by dividing the TSME (resp. TSE) estimates by the OTE and ITE estimates. The ROSE and RISE estimates were obtained by dividing the OSME and ISME estimates by the OME and IME estimates (i.e., they were obtained as residuals).

6.2 Models with Stronger Assumptions

In addition to assumptions PF1 to PF5, it is common to assume there is no technical change. It is also common to assume that production frontiers exhibit NIRS, CRS or NDRS. Imposing these types of assumptions requires modifications to the basic DEA models described in Sect. 6.1. To avoid unnecessary repetition, this section focuses on the modifications that must be made to basic output- and input-oriented models; the modifications that must be made to other types of models are left as an exercise for the reader.

6.2.1 *No Technical Change*

If there is no technical change, then production frontiers are time-invariant. In this case, each (environment-specific) frontier should be estimated using data from all time periods. This is equivalent to treating all the observations in the dataset as observations from a single time period. For example, if the dataset covers T time periods, then the multiplier and envelopment forms of the output-oriented DEA models become (respectively)

$$\min_{\alpha_{it},\delta_{it},\beta_{it},\gamma_{it}} \Big\{\alpha_{it} + \delta_{it}'z_{it} + \beta_{it}'x_{it} : \gamma_{it} \geq 0,\ \delta_{it} \geq 0,\ \beta_{it} \geq 0,\ \gamma_{it}'q_{it} = 1,$$
$$\alpha_{it} + \delta_{it}'z_{hr} + \beta_{it}'x_{hr} - \gamma_{it}'q_{hr} \geq 0 \text{ for all } h \leq I \text{ and } r \leq T\Big\} \quad (6.17)$$

and

$$\max_{\mu,\lambda_{11},\ldots,\lambda_{IT}} \Big\{\mu : \mu q_{it} \leq \sum_{h=1}^{I}\sum_{r=1}^{T}\lambda_{hr}q_{hr},\ \sum_{h=1}^{I}\sum_{r=1}^{T}\lambda_{hr}z_{hr} \leq z_{it},$$
$$\sum_{h=1}^{I}\sum_{r=1}^{T}\lambda_{hr}x_{hr} \leq x_{it},\ \sum_{h=1}^{I}\sum_{r=1}^{T}\lambda_{hr} = 1,\ \lambda_{hr} \geq 0 \text{ for all } h \text{ and } r\Big\}. \quad (6.18)$$

On the input side, if there is no technical change and the dataset covers T time periods, then the multiplier and envelopment forms of the input-oriented DEA models become (respectively)

$$\max_{\xi_{it},\kappa_{it},\phi_{it},\theta_{it}} \Big\{\xi_{it}'q_{it} - \kappa_{it}'z_{it} - \phi_{it} : \xi_{it} \geq 0,\ \kappa_{it} \geq 0,\ \theta_{it} \geq 0,\ \theta_{it}'x_{it} = 1,$$
$$\xi_{it}'q_{hr} - \kappa_{it}'z_{hr} - \phi_{it} - \theta_{it}'x_{hr} \leq 0 \text{ for all } h \leq I \text{ and } r \leq T\Big\} \qquad (6.19)$$

and

$$\min_{\mu,\lambda_{11},\ldots,\lambda_{IT}} \Big\{\mu : \sum_{h=1}^{I}\sum_{r=1}^{T}\lambda_{hr}q_{hr} \geq q_{it},\ \sum_{h=1}^{I}\sum_{r=1}^{T}\lambda_{hr}z_{hr} \leq z_{it},$$
$$\mu x_{it} \geq \sum_{h=1}^{I}\sum_{r=1}^{T}\lambda_{hr}x_{hr},\ \sum_{h=1}^{I}\sum_{r=1}^{T}\lambda_{hr} = 1,\ \lambda_{hr} \geq 0 \text{ for all } h \text{ and } r\Big\}. \qquad (6.20)$$

6.2.2 Nonincreasing Returns to Scale

If production frontiers exhibit NIRS, then the unknown parameters in (6.1) must satisfy $\alpha_{it} + \delta_{it}'z_{it} \geq 0$. With this constraint, the multiplier form of the output-oriented DEA model becomes

$$\min_{\alpha_{it},\delta_{it},\beta_{it},\gamma_{it}} \Big\{\alpha_{it} + \delta_{it}'z_{it} + \beta_{it}'x_{it} : \gamma_{it} \geq 0,\ \delta_{it} \geq 0,\ \beta_{it} \geq 0,\ \gamma_{it}'q_{it} = 1,\ \alpha_{it} + \delta_{it}'z_{it} \geq 0,$$
$$\alpha_{it} + \delta_{it}'z_{hr} + \beta_{it}'x_{hr} - \gamma_{it}'q_{hr} \geq 0 \text{ for all } h \leq I \text{ and } r \leq t\Big\}. \qquad (6.21)$$

Again, if the data are cross-section data, then all references to time periods can be deleted. If there is no environmental change, then the environmental variables and their coefficients can be deleted. If the data are cross-section data and there is no environmental change, then problem (6.21) reduces to problem DO_1 in Seiford and Thrall (1990, p. 15). The dual (or envelopment) form of the problem is

$$\max_{\mu,\rho,\lambda_{11},\ldots,\lambda_{It}} \Big\{\mu : \mu q_{it} \leq \sum_{h=1}^{I}\sum_{r=1}^{t}\lambda_{hr}q_{hr},\ \sum_{h=1}^{I}\sum_{r=1}^{t}\lambda_{hr}z_{hr} \leq \rho z_{it},\ \sum_{h=1}^{I}\sum_{r=1}^{t}\lambda_{hr} = \rho,$$
$$\sum_{h=1}^{I}\sum_{r=1}^{t}\lambda_{hr}x_{hr} \leq x_{it},\ \rho \leq 1,\ \lambda_{hr} \geq 0 \text{ for all } h \text{ and } r\Big\}. \qquad (6.22)$$

If there is no environmental change, then the constraint involving the environmental variables can be deleted. If the data are cross-section data and there is no environmental change, then problem (6.22) reduces to problem PO_1 in Seiford and Thrall (1990, p. 15).

On the input side, the NIRS assumption implies that the unknown parameters in (6.6) must satisfy $\phi_{it} + \kappa'_{it} z_{it} \geq 0$. With this constraint, the multiplier form of the input-oriented DEA model becomes

$$\max_{\xi_{it},\kappa_{it},\phi_{it},\theta_{it}} \Big\{ \xi'_{it} q_{it} - \kappa'_{it} z_{it} - \phi_{it} : \xi_{it} \geq 0,\ \kappa_{it} \geq 0,\ \theta_{it} \geq 0,\ \theta'_{it} x_{it} = 1,\ \phi_{it} + \kappa'_{it} z_{it} \geq 0,$$
$$\xi'_{it} q_{hr} - \kappa'_{it} z_{hr} - \phi_{it} - \theta'_{it} x_{hr} \leq 0 \text{ for all } h \leq I \text{ and } r \leq t \Big\}. \tag{6.23}$$

Again, if there is no environmental change, then the environmental variables and their coefficients can be deleted. If the data are cross-section data and there is no environmental change, then problem (6.23) reduces to problem DI_1 in Seiford and Thrall (1990, p. 15). The dual (or envelopment) form of the problem is

$$\min_{\mu,\rho,\lambda_{11},\ldots,\lambda_{It}} \Big\{ \mu : q_{it} \leq \sum_{h=1}^{I} \sum_{r=1}^{t} \lambda_{hr} q_{hr},\ \sum_{h=1}^{I} \sum_{r=1}^{t} \lambda_{hr} z_{hr} \leq \rho z_{it},\ \sum_{h=1}^{I} \sum_{r=1}^{t} \lambda_{hr} = \rho,$$
$$\sum_{h=1}^{I} \sum_{r=1}^{t} \lambda_{hr} x_{hr} \leq \mu x_{it},\ \rho \leq 1,\ \lambda_{hr} \geq 0 \text{ for all } h \text{ and } r \Big\}. \tag{6.24}$$

Again, if there is no environmental change, then the constraint involving the environmental variables can be deleted. If the data are cross-section data and there is no environmental change, then problem (6.24) reduces to problem PI_1 in Seiford and Thrall (1990, p. 15).

6.2.3 *Constant Returns to Scale*

If production frontiers exhibit CRS, then the unknown parameters in (6.1) must satisfy $\alpha_{it} + \delta'_{it} z_{it} = 0$. With this constraint, the multiplier form of the output-oriented DEA model becomes

$$\min_{\alpha_{it},\delta_{it},\beta_{it},\gamma_{it}} \Big\{ \beta'_{it} x_{it} : \gamma_{it} \geq 0,\ \delta_{it} \geq 0,\ \beta_{it} \geq 0,\ \gamma'_{it} q_{it} = 1,\ \alpha_{it} + \delta'_{it} z_{it} = 0,$$
$$\alpha_{it} + \delta'_{it} z_{hr} + \beta'_{it} x_{hr} - \gamma'_{it} q_{hr} \geq 0 \text{ for all } h \leq I \text{ and } r \leq t \Big\}. \tag{6.25}$$

Again, if there is no environmental change, then the environmental variables and their coefficients can be deleted. If the data are cross-section data and there is no environmental change, then problem (6.25) reduces to problem (4) in Charnes et al. (1978). The dual (or envelopment) form of the problem is

$$\max_{\mu,\rho,\lambda_{11},\ldots,\lambda_{It}} \left\{ \mu : \mu q_{it} \le \sum_{h=1}^{I} \sum_{r=1}^{t} \lambda_{hr} q_{hr}, \ \sum_{h=1}^{I} \sum_{r=1}^{t} \lambda_{hr} z_{hr} \le \rho z_{it}, \right.$$
$$\left. \sum_{h=1}^{I} \sum_{r=1}^{t} \lambda_{hr} x_{hr} \le x_{it}, \ \sum_{h=1}^{I} \sum_{r=1}^{t} \lambda_{hr} \le \rho, \ \lambda_{hr} \ge 0 \text{ for all } h \text{ and } r \right\}. \tag{6.26}$$

If there is no environmental change, then the constraints involving ρ can be deleted. If the data are cross-section data and there is no environmental change, then problem (6.26) reduces to problem (3) in Charnes et al. (1978).

On the input side, the CRS assumption implies that the unknown parameters in (6.6) must satisfy $\phi_{it} + \kappa_{it}' z_{it} = 0$. With this constraint, the multiplier form of the input-oriented DEA model becomes

$$\max_{\xi_{it},\kappa_{it},\phi_{it},\theta_{it}} \left\{ \xi_{it}' q_{it} : \xi_{it} \ge 0, \ \kappa_{it} \ge 0, \ \theta_{it} \ge 0, \ \theta_{it}' x_{it} = 1, \ \phi_{it} + \kappa_{it}' z_{it} = 0, \right.$$
$$\left. \xi_{it}' q_{hr} - \kappa_{it}' z_{hr} - \phi_{it} - \theta_{it}' x_{hr} \le 0 \text{ for all } h \le I \text{ and } r \le t \right\}. \tag{6.27}$$

Again, if there is no environmental change, then the environmental variables and their coefficients can be deleted. If the data are cross-section data and there is no environmental change, then problem (6.27) reduces to problem (10) in Banker et al. (1984). The dual (or envelopment) form of the problem is

$$\min_{\mu,\rho,\lambda_{11},\ldots,\lambda_{It}} \left\{ \mu : \sum_{h=1}^{I} \sum_{r=1}^{t} \lambda_{hr} q_{hr} \ge q_{it}, \ \sum_{h=1}^{I} \sum_{r=1}^{t} \lambda_{hr} z_{hr} \le \rho z_{it}, \right.$$
$$\left. \mu x_{it} \ge \sum_{h=1}^{I} \sum_{r=1}^{t} \lambda_{hr} x_{hr}, \ \sum_{h=1}^{I} \sum_{r=1}^{t} \lambda_{hr} \le \rho, \ \lambda_{hr} \ge 0 \text{ for all } h \text{ and } r \right\}. \tag{6.28}$$

Again, if there is no environmental change, then the constraints involving ρ can be deleted. If the data are cross-section data and there is no environmental change, then problem (6.28) reduces to problem (9) in Banker et al. (1984).

Finally, it is common to make the CRS assumption, not because production frontiers exhibit CRS, but because estimates of technical efficiency that have been obtained under a CRS assumption can be used to obtain estimates of scale efficiency. To be more specific, estimates of scale efficiency can be obtained by dividing estimates of technical efficiency obtained under a CRS assumption by corresponding estimates of technical efficiency obtained under a variable returns to scale (VRS) assumption. For example, the measure of OSE defined by (5.35) can be estimated by dividing the value of μ that solves (6.4) by the value of μ that solves (6.26). On the input side, the measure of ISE defined by (5.41) can be estimated by dividing the value of μ that solves (6.28) by the value of μ that solves (6.9).

6.2.4 Nondecreasing Returns to Scale

If production frontiers exhibit NDRS, then the unknown parameters in (6.1) must satisfy $\alpha_{it} + \delta_{it}' z_{it} \leq 0$. With this constraint, the multiplier form of the output-oriented DEA model becomes

$$\min_{\alpha_{it},\delta_{it},\beta_{it},\gamma_{it}} \Big\{\alpha_{it} + \delta_{it}' z_{it} + \beta_{it}' x_{it} : \gamma_{it} \geq 0,\ \delta_{it} \geq 0,\ \beta_{it} \geq 0,\ \gamma_{it}' q_{it} = 1,\ \alpha_{it} + \delta_{it}' z_{it} \leq 0,$$
$$\alpha_{it} + \delta_{it}' z_{hr} + \beta_{it}' x_{hr} - \gamma_{it}' q_{hr} \geq 0 \text{ for all } h \leq I \text{ and } r \leq t\Big\}. \quad (6.29)$$

Again, if there is no environmental change, then the environmental variables and their coefficients can be deleted. If the data are cross-section data and there is no environmental change, then problem (6.29) reduces to problem DO_2 in Seiford and Thrall (1990, p. 15). The dual (or envelopment) form of the problem is

$$\max_{\mu,\rho,\lambda_{11},\ldots,\lambda_{It}} \Big\{\mu : \mu q_{it} \leq \sum_{h=1}^{I}\sum_{r=1}^{t} \lambda_{hr} q_{hr},\ \sum_{h=1}^{I}\sum_{r=1}^{t} \lambda_{hr} z_{hr} \leq \rho z_{it},\ \sum_{h=1}^{I}\sum_{r=1}^{t} \lambda_{hr} = \rho,$$
$$\sum_{h=1}^{I}\sum_{r=1}^{t} \lambda_{hr} x_{hr} \leq x_{it},\ \rho \geq 1,\ \lambda_{hr} \geq 0 \text{ for all } h \text{ and } r\Big\}. \quad (6.30)$$

If there is no environmental change, then the constraint involving the environmental variables can be deleted. If the data are cross-section data and there is no environmental change, then problem (6.30) reduces to problem PO_2 in Seiford and Thrall (1990, p. 15).

On the input side, the NDRS assumption implies that the unknown parameters in (6.6) must satisfy $\phi_{it} + \kappa_{it}' z_{it} \leq 0$. With this constraint, the multiplier form of the input-oriented DEA model becomes

$$\max_{\xi_{it},\kappa_{it},\phi_{it},\theta_{it}} \Big\{\xi_{it}' q_{it} - \kappa_{it}' z_{it} - \phi_{it} : \xi_{it} \geq 0,\ \kappa_{it} \geq 0,\ \theta_{it} \geq 0,\ \theta_{it}' x_{it} = 1,\ \phi_{it} + \kappa_{it}' z_{it} \leq 0,$$
$$\xi_{it}' q_{hr} - \kappa_{it}' z_{hr} - \phi_{it} - \theta_{it}' x_{hr} \leq 0 \text{ for all } h \leq I \text{ and } r \leq t\Big\}. \quad (6.31)$$

Again, if there is no environmental change, then the environmental variables and their coefficients can be deleted. If the data are cross-section data and there is no environmental change, then problem (6.31) reduces to problem DI_2 in Seiford and Thrall (1990, p. 15). The dual (or envelopment) form of the problem is

$$\min_{\mu,\rho,\lambda_{11},\ldots,\lambda_{It}} \left\{\mu : q_{it} \leq \sum_{h=1}^{I}\sum_{r=1}^{t}\lambda_{hr}q_{hr},\ \sum_{h=1}^{I}\sum_{r=1}^{t}\lambda_{hr}z_{hr} \leq \rho z_{it},\ \sum_{h=1}^{I}\sum_{r=1}^{t}\lambda_{hr} = \rho,\right.$$

$$\left.\sum_{h=1}^{I}\sum_{r=1}^{t}\lambda_{hr}x_{hr} \leq \mu x_{it},\ \rho \geq 1,\ \lambda_{hr} \geq 0 \text{ for all } h \text{ and } r\right\}. \quad (6.32)$$

Again, if there is no environmental change, then the constraint involving the environmental variables can be deleted. If the data are cross-section data and there is no environmental change, then problem (6.32) reduces to problem PI_2 in Seiford and Thrall (1990, p. 15).

6.2.5 Toy Example

Reconsider the output and input quantity data reported earlier in Table 1.1. Some associated DEA estimates of OTE and ITE are reported in Table 6.9. In this table, the estimates reported in the columns labelled NTC were obtained under the assumption there is no technical change (i.e., by treating the observations in the dataset as observations on twenty-five firms in a single time period). The estimates reported in the columns labelled VRS, NIRS, NDRS and CRS were obtained under the assumption that the production frontier exhibits VRS, NIRS, NDRS and CRS (respectively). The estimates reported in the VRS columns are the estimates reported earlier in Tables 6.1 and 6.2. Dividing the CRS estimates of OTE (resp. ITE) by the VRS estimates yields the OSE (resp. ISE) estimates reported earlier in Table 6.7 (resp. 6.8). By construction, the VRS estimates are no less than the NIRS and NDRS estimates, the NIRS and NDRS estimates are no less than the CRS estimates, and the two sets of CRS estimates are identical. The relationships between these different estimates can sometimes be used to estimate whether firms are operating in regions of increasing or decreasing returns to scale. In the one-input-one-output case, for example, if a VRS estimate of OTE (resp. ITE) is larger than the corresponding NDRS (resp. NIRS) estimate, then the associated firm is estimated to be operating in a region of DRS (resp. IRS).

6.3 Models with Weaker Assumptions

It is common to relax assumptions PF4 and PF5. Relaxing these assumptions also requires modifications to the basic DEA models described in Sect. 6.1. Again, to avoid unnecessary repetition, this section focuses on the modifications that must be made to basic output- and input-oriented models; the modifications that must be made to other types of models are left as an exercise for the reader.

Table 6.9 DEA estimates of OTE and ITE under relatively strong assumptions[a]

			OTE					ITE				
Row	Firm	Period	NTC	VRS	NIRS	NDRS	CRS	NTC	VRS	NIRS	NDRS	CRS
A	1	1	0.422	0.422	0.422	0.422	0.422	0.286	0.56	0.422	0.56	0.422
B	2	1	0.610	1	0.753	1	0.753	0.511	1	0.753	1	0.753
C	3	1	1	1	1	1	1	1	1	1	1	1
D	4	1	0.949	1	1	1	1	0.926	1	1	1	1
E	5	1	1	1	1	1	1	1	1	1	1	1
F	1	2	0.614	0.865	0.615	0.865	0.615	0.629	0.954	0.615	0.954	0.615
G	2	2	1	1	1	1	1	1	1	1	1	1
H	3	2	1	1	1	1	1	1	1	1	1	1
I	4	2	0.871	0.871	0.871	0.849	0.849	0.932	0.955	0.849	0.955	0.849
J	5	2	1	1	1	1	1	1	1	1	1	1
K	1	3	1	1	1	1	1	1	1	1	1	1
L	2	3	0.933	1	1	1	1	0.938	1	1	1	1
M	3	3	0.643	0.653	0.653	0.592	0.592	0.589	0.604	0.592	0.604	0.592
N	4	3	1	1	1	1	1	1	1	1	1	1
O	5	3	0.844	0.844	0.844	0.569	0.569	0.777	0.777	0.777	0.569	0.569
P	1	4	0.594	0.594	0.594	0.547	0.547	0.551	0.551	0.551	0.547	0.547
R	2	4	0.671	0.671	0.671	0.642	0.642	0.624	0.657	0.642	0.657	0.642
S	3	4	0.583	0.583	0.551	0.583	0.551	0.669	0.669	0.551	0.669	0.551
T	4	4	1	1	1	0.838	0.838	1	1	1	0.838	0.838
U	5	4	0.654	0.654	0.624	0.654	0.624	0.689	0.689	0.624	0.689	0.624
V	1	5	1	1	1	1	1	1	1	1	1	1
W	2	5	0.895	0.895	0.895	0.619	0.619	0.846	0.846	0.846	0.619	0.619
X	3	5	0.836	0.836	0.725	0.836	0.725	0.881	0.881	0.725	0.881	0.725
Y	4	5	0.516	0.516	0.516	0.384	0.384	0.387	0.387	0.387	0.384	0.384
Z	5	5	0.867	0.867	0.867	0.5	0.5	0.5	0.5	0.5	0.5	0.5
Geometric mean			0.796	0.828	0.800	0.763	0.737	0.751	0.814	0.762	0.788	0.737

[a]Numbers reported to less than three decimal places are exact; see the footnote to Table 1.2 on p. 8

6.3.1 *Inputs Not Strongly Disposable*

If inputs are not strongly disposable, then the coefficients of the input variables in (6.1) and (6.6) are unsigned. In this case, the multiplier form of the output-oriented DEA model becomes

$$\min_{\alpha_{it},\delta_{it},\beta_{it},\gamma_{it}} \Big\{\alpha_{it} + \delta_{it}'z_{it} + \beta_{it}'x_{it} : \gamma_{it} \geq 0,\ \delta_{it} \geq 0,\ \gamma_{it}'q_{it} = 1,$$

$$\alpha_{it} + \delta_{it}'z_{hr} + \beta_{it}'x_{hr} - \gamma_{it}'q_{hr} \geq 0 \text{ for all } h \leq I \text{ and } r \leq t\Big\}. \tag{6.33}$$

The dual (or envelopment) form of this problem is

$$\max_{\mu,\lambda_{11},\ldots,\lambda_{It}} \left\{\mu : \mu q_{it} \leq \sum_{h=1}^{I}\sum_{r=1}^{t}\lambda_{hr}q_{hr}, \sum_{h=1}^{I}\sum_{r=1}^{t}\lambda_{hr}z_{hr} \leq z_{it}, \right.$$
$$\left. \sum_{h=1}^{I}\sum_{r=1}^{t}\lambda_{hr}x_{hr} = x_{it}, \sum_{h=1}^{I}\sum_{r=1}^{t}\lambda_{hr} = 1, \lambda_{hr} \geq 0 \text{ for all } h \text{ and } r\right\}. \tag{6.34}$$

On the input side, the multiplier form of the input-oriented DEA model becomes

$$\max_{\xi_{it},\kappa_{it},\phi_{it},\theta_{it}} \left\{\xi_{it}'q_{it} - \kappa_{it}'z_{it} - \phi_{it} : \xi_{it} \geq 0, \kappa_{it} \geq 0, \theta_{it}'x_{it} = 1, \right.$$
$$\left. \xi_{it}'q_{hr} - \kappa_{it}'z_{hr} - \phi_{it} - \theta_{it}'x_{hr} \leq 0 \text{ for all } h \leq I \text{ and } r \leq t\right\}. \tag{6.35}$$

The dual (or envelopment) form of this problem is

$$\min_{\mu,\lambda_{11},\ldots,\lambda_{It}} \left\{\mu : \sum_{h=1}^{I}\sum_{r=1}^{t}\lambda_{hr}q_{hr} \geq q_{it}, \sum_{h=1}^{I}\sum_{r=1}^{t}\lambda_{hr}z_{hr} \leq z_{it}, \right.$$
$$\left. \mu x_{it} = \sum_{h=1}^{I}\sum_{r=1}^{t}\lambda_{hr}x_{hr}, \sum_{h=1}^{I}\sum_{r=1}^{t}\lambda_{hr} = 1, \lambda_{hr} \geq 0 \text{ for all } h \text{ and } r\right\}. \tag{6.36}$$

Again, if the data are cross-section data, then all references to time periods can be deleted. If there is no environmental change, then the constraint involving the environmental variables can be deleted. If the data are cross-section data and there is no environmental change, then problem (6.36) reduces to problem (3) in Cooper et al. (2000, p. 5).

6.3.2 Outputs Not Strongly Disposable

If outputs are not strongly disposable, then the coefficients of the output variables in (6.1) and (6.6) are unsigned. In this case, the multiplier form of the output-oriented DEA model becomes

$$\min_{\alpha_{it},\delta_{it},\beta_{it},\gamma_{it}} \left\{\alpha_{it} + \delta_{it}'z_{it} + \beta_{it}'x_{it} : \delta_{it} \geq 0, \beta_{it} \geq 0, \gamma_{it}'q_{it} = 1, \right.$$
$$\left. \alpha_{it} + \delta_{it}'z_{hr} + \beta_{it}'x_{hr} - \gamma_{it}'q_{hr} \geq 0 \text{ for all } h \leq I \text{ and } r \leq t\right\}. \tag{6.37}$$

The dual (or envelopment) form of this problem is

$$\max_{\mu,\lambda_{11},\ldots,\lambda_{It}} \left\{ \mu : \mu q_{it} = \sum_{h=1}^{I}\sum_{r=1}^{t} \lambda_{hr} q_{hr}, \ \sum_{h=1}^{I}\sum_{r=1}^{t} \lambda_{hr} z_{hr} \le z_{it}, \right.$$
$$\left. \sum_{h=1}^{I}\sum_{r=1}^{t} \lambda_{hr} x_{hr} \le x_{it}, \ \sum_{h=1}^{I}\sum_{r=1}^{t} \lambda_{hr} = 1, \ \lambda_{hr} \ge 0 \text{ for all } h \text{ and } r \right\}. \tag{6.38}$$

Again, if the data are cross-section data, then all references to time periods can be deleted. If there is no environmental change, then the constraint involving the environmental variables can be deleted. If the data are cross-section data and there is no environmental change, then problem (6.38) reduces to problem (9.4) in Zhu (2009, p. 188).

On the input side, if outputs are not strongly disposable, then the multiplier form of the input-oriented DEA model becomes

$$\max_{\xi_{it},\kappa_{it},\phi_{it},\theta_{it}} \left\{ \xi_{it}' q_{it} - \kappa_{it}' z_{it} - \phi_{it} : \kappa_{it} \ge 0, \ \theta_{it} \ge 0, \ \theta_{it}' x_{it} = 1, \right.$$
$$\left. \xi_{it}' q_{hr} - \kappa_{it}' z_{hr} - \phi_{it} - \theta_{it}' x_{hr} \le 0 \text{ for all } h \le I \text{ and } r \le t \right\}. \tag{6.39}$$

The dual (or envelopment) form of this problem is

$$\min_{\mu,\lambda_{11},\ldots,\lambda_{It}} \left\{ \mu : \sum_{h=1}^{I}\sum_{r=1}^{t} \lambda_{hr} q_{hr} = q_{it}, \ \sum_{h=1}^{I}\sum_{r=1}^{t} \lambda_{hr} z_{hr} \le z_{it}, \right.$$
$$\left. \mu x_{it} \ge \sum_{h=1}^{I}\sum_{r=1}^{t} \lambda_{hr} x_{hr}, \ \sum_{h=1}^{I}\sum_{r=1}^{t} \lambda_{hr} = 1, \ \lambda_{hr} \ge 0 \text{ for all } h \text{ and } r \right\}. \tag{6.40}$$

6.3.3 Environmental Variables Not Strongly Disposable

If environmental variables are not strongly disposable, then the coefficients of the environmental variables in (6.1) and (6.6) are unsigned. In this case, the multiplier form of the output-oriented DEA model becomes

$$\min_{\alpha_{it},\delta_{it},\beta_{it},\gamma_{it}} \left\{ \alpha_{it} + \delta_{it}' z_{it} + \beta_{it}' x_{it} : \gamma_{it} \ge 0, \ \beta_{it} \ge 0, \ \gamma_{it}' q_{it} = 1, \right.$$
$$\left. \alpha_{it} + \delta_{it}' z_{hr} + \beta_{it}' x_{hr} - \gamma_{it}' q_{hr} \ge 0 \text{ for all } h \le I \text{ and } r \le t \right\}. \tag{6.41}$$

The dual (or envelopment) form of this problem is

$$\max_{\mu,\lambda_{11},\ldots,\lambda_{It}} \left\{\mu : \mu q_{it} \leq \sum_{h=1}^{I}\sum_{r=1}^{t} \lambda_{hr} q_{hr}, \sum_{h=1}^{I}\sum_{r=1}^{t} \lambda_{hr} z_{hr} = z_{it}, \right.$$
$$\left. \sum_{h=1}^{I}\sum_{r=1}^{t} \lambda_{hr} x_{hr} \leq x_{it}, \sum_{h=1}^{I}\sum_{r=1}^{t} \lambda_{hr} = 1, \lambda_{hr} \geq 0 \text{ for all } h \text{ and } r \right\}. \tag{6.42}$$

On the input side, the multiplier form of the input-oriented DEA model becomes

$$\max_{\xi_{it},\kappa_{it},\phi_{it},\theta_{it}} \left\{\xi_{it}' q_{it} - \kappa_{it}' z_{it} - \phi_{it} : \xi_{it} \geq 0, \theta_{it} \geq 0, \theta_{it}' x_{it} = 1, \right.$$
$$\left. \xi_{it}' q_{hr} - \kappa_{it}' z_{hr} - \phi_{it} - \theta_{it}' x_{hr} \leq 0 \text{ for all } h \leq I \text{ and } r \leq t \right\}. \tag{6.43}$$

The dual (or envelopment) form of this problem is

$$\min_{\mu,\lambda_{11},\ldots,\lambda_{It}} \left\{\mu : \sum_{h=1}^{I}\sum_{r=1}^{t} \lambda_{hr} q_{hr} \geq q_{it}, \sum_{h=1}^{I}\sum_{r=1}^{t} \lambda_{hr} z_{hr} = z_{it}, \right.$$
$$\left. \mu x_{it} \geq \sum_{h=1}^{I}\sum_{r=1}^{t} \lambda_{hr} x_{hr}, \sum_{h=1}^{I}\sum_{r=1}^{t} \lambda_{hr} = 1, \lambda_{hr} \geq 0 \text{ for all } h \text{ and } r \right\}. \tag{6.44}$$

Again, if the data are cross-section data, then all references to time periods can be deleted. In this case, problem (6.44) reduces to problem (7.8) in Coelli et al. (2005, p. 193).

6.3.4 Production Possibilities Sets Not Convex

If production possibilities sets are not convex, then there is no LP duality theory to link the multiplier and envelopment forms of PFMs. In the efficiency literature, researchers have focused on the envelopment forms. If production possibilities sets are not convex, then the envelopment form of the output-oriented DEA model becomes

$$\max_{\mu,\rho,\lambda_{11},\ldots,\lambda_{It}} \left\{\mu : \mu q_{it} \leq \sum_{h=1}^{I}\sum_{r=1}^{t} \lambda_{hr} q_{hr}, \sum_{h=1}^{I}\sum_{r=1}^{t} \lambda_{hr} z_{hr} \leq z_{it}, \right.$$
$$\left. \sum_{h=1}^{I}\sum_{r=1}^{t} \lambda_{hr} x_{hr} \leq x_{it}, \sum_{h=1}^{I}\sum_{r=1}^{t} \lambda_{hr} = 1, \lambda_{hr} \in \{0, 1\} \text{ for all } h \text{ and } r \right\}. \tag{6.45}$$

If there is no environmental change, then the constraint involving the environmental variables can be deleted. In this case, problem (6.45) reduces to problem 1.2 in Tulkens and Vanden Eeckaut (1995, p. 481). In the efficiency literature, these types of models are known as free disposal hull (FDH) models. This terminology derives from the fact that, aside from PF1 to PF3, the only assumption that is being made is that inputs, outputs and environmental variables are strongly (or freely) disposable.

On the input side, if production possibilities sets are not convex, then the envelopment form of the input-oriented DEA model becomes

$$\min_{\mu,\lambda_{11},\ldots,\lambda_{It}} \left\{\mu : \sum_{h=1}^{I}\sum_{r=1}^{t} \lambda_{hr} q_{hr} \geq q_{it}, \sum_{h=1}^{I}\sum_{r=1}^{t} \lambda_{hr} z_{hr} \leq z_{it}, \right.$$
$$\left. \mu x_{it} \geq \sum_{h=1}^{I}\sum_{r=1}^{t} \lambda_{hr} x_{hr}, \sum_{h=1}^{I}\sum_{r=1}^{t} \lambda_{hr} = 1, \ \lambda_{hr} \in \{0, 1\} \text{ for all } h \text{ and } r \right\}. \tag{6.46}$$

Again, if there is no environmental change, then the constraint involving the environmental variables can be deleted. In this case, problem (6.46) reduces to problem 1.1 in Tulkens and Vanden Eeckaut (1995, p. 481). If the data are cross-section data and there is only one input, then the Tulkens and Vanden Eeckaut (1995) problem is equivalent to problem (12) in Deprins et al. (1984, p. 296).

6.3.5 *Toy Example*

Reconsider the output and input quantity data reported earlier in Table 1.1. Some associated estimates of OTE and ITE are reported in Table 6.10. In this table, the estimates reported in the columns labelled PF4 have been obtained under the assumption that inputs, outputs and environmental variables are strongly disposable; these are the estimates reported earlier in Tables 6.1 and 6.2. The estimates reported in the columns labelled XNSD, QNSD and ZNSD have been obtained under the assumption that inputs, outputs and environmental variables are *not* strongly disposable (respectively). The estimates reported in the FDH columns have been obtained under the assumption that production possibilities sets are not convex. By construction, the estimates obtained under assumption PF4 are no greater than the XNSD, QNSD, ZNSD and FDH estimates.

6.4 Inference

If the assumptions underpinning PFMs are true, then, under weak regularity conditions concerning the probability density functions (PDFs) of the (in)efficiency effects (e.g., that they are monotonic), piecewise frontier estimators for (in)efficiency are

Table 6.10 DEA estimates of OTE and ITE under relatively weak assumptions[a]

			OTE					ITE				
Row	Firm	Period	PF4	XNSD	QNSD	ZNSD	FDH	PF4	XNSD	QNSD	ZNSD	FDH
A	1	1	0.422	0.422	0.422	0.422	0.422	0.56	0.56	0.56	0.56	0.56
B	2	1	1	1	1	1	1	1	1	1	1	1
C	3	1	1	1	1	1	1	1	1	1	1	1
D	4	1	1	1	1	1	1	1	1	1	1	1
E	5	1	1	1	1	1	1	1	1	1	1	1
F	1	2	0.865	0.865	1	1	1	0.954	0.954	1	1	1
G	2	2	1	1	1	1	1	1	1	1	1	1
H	3	2	1	1	1	1	1	1	1	1	1	1
I	4	2	0.871	1	0.871	1	1	0.955	0.955	1	1	0.979
J	5	2	1	1	1	1	1	1	1	1	1	1
K	1	3	1	1	1	1	1	1	1	1	1	1
L	2	3	1	1	1	1	1	1	1	1	1	1
M	3	3	0.653	1	0.653	0.653	0.724	0.604	0.604	0.612	0.604	0.775
N	4	3	1	1	1	1	1	1	1	1	1	1
O	5	3	0.844	0.844	0.844	1	0.844	0.777	0.777	0.777	1	1
P	1	4	0.594	0.594	0.594	0.594	1	0.551	0.551	0.551	0.551	1
R	2	4	0.671	0.671	0.671	0.671	0.724	0.657	0.657	0.657	0.657	1
S	3	4	0.583	0.583	0.612	0.833	1	0.669	0.669	0.705	0.947	1
T	4	4	1	1	1	1	1	1	1	1	1	1
U	5	4	0.654	0.654	0.656	0.654	1	0.689	0.689	0.692	0.689	1
V	1	5	1	1	1	1	1	1	1	1	1	1
W	2	5	0.895	0.895	0.895	1	1	0.846	0.846	0.846	1	1
X	3	5	0.836	0.836	0.894	1	1	0.881	0.881	0.928	1	1
Y	4	5	0.516	0.516	0.516	0.516	1	0.387	0.387	0.387	0.387	0.757
Z	5	5	0.867	1	0.867	0.867	1	0.5	0.5	0.5	0.5	0.5
Geometric mean			0.828	0.852	0.837	0.865	0.935	0.814	0.814	0.821	0.846	0.930

[a]Numbers reported to less than three decimal places are exact; see the footnote to Table 1.2 on p. 8

consistent.[3] This provides a basis for conducting basic asymptotic inference (i.e., constructing confidence intervals and testing hypotheses in large samples). For notational simplicity, let E_{it} denote a measure of the efficiency of manager i in period t. An associated measure of inefficiency is $u_{it} \equiv -\ln E_{it} \geq 0$. In practice, the methods used to conduct inference depend on whether the PDFs of E_{it} and u_{it} are known.

[3]In this context, 'consistent' means that the sampling distributions of the estimators collapse to the true levels of (in)efficiency as the numbers of firms used to estimate production frontiers become infinitely large.

6.4.1 PDFs Known

If the PDFs of E_{it} and u_{it} are known, then standard statistical methods can be used to conduct asymptotic inference. This section considers methods for (a) constructing confidence intervals for measures of efficiency, (b) testing for differences in average efficiency, and (c) testing assumptions about production technologies.

6.4.1.1 Confidence Intervals for Measures of Efficiency

Suppose we are interested in constructing a $100(1-\alpha)\%$ confidence interval for $E_{it} = \exp(-u_{it})$. The choice of confidence interval formula depends on the PDF of u_{it}. For example, if u_{it} is an independent exponential random variable with scale parameter $\sigma_t > 0$, then a $100(1-\alpha)\%$ confidence interval for E_{it} is[4]

$$(\alpha/2)^{\hat{\sigma}_t} \leq E_{it} \leq (1-\alpha/2)^{\hat{\sigma}_t} \tag{6.47}$$

where $\hat{\sigma}_t$ denotes a consistent estimator for σ_t. If there are I_t firms in the dataset in period t, then a consistent estimator for σ_t is $\hat{\sigma}_t = \sum_{i=1}^{I_t} \hat{u}_{it}/I_t$ where $\hat{u}_{it}$ denotes a consistent estimator for u_{it}. The validity of this procedure depends on I_t being large.

For a numerical example, reconsider the toy data reported in Table 1.1. Suppose we are interested in constructing 95% confidence intervals for measures of OTE. For purposes of illustration, and bearing in mind that the numbers of firms used to estimate production frontiers need to be large, let us treat the observations in the dataset as observations on twenty-five firms in a single time period; this implies that all references to time periods can be deleted. Let us also assume that u_i is an independent exponential random variable with scale parameter $\sigma > 0$. DEA estimates of E_i and u_i are reported in Table 6.11 (the efficiency estimates are the OTE estimates reported earlier in the NTC column of Table 6.9). The estimate of the scale parameter is $\hat{\sigma} = 0.228$. The associated 95% confidence interval is $0.432 \leq E_i \leq 0.994$.

6.4.1.2 Testing for Differences in Average Efficiency

Suppose that all the observations in the dataset can be classified into two or more groups (e.g., by type of environment). Let S_{gt} (resp. I_{gt}) denote the set (resp. number) of firms in group g in period t. Suppose that $E(u_{it}) = \mu_g$ if $i \in S_{gt}$. Also suppose we are interested in testing $H_0 : \mu_1 \leq \mu_2$ against $H_1 : \mu_1 > \mu_2$. The choice of test statistic depends on the PDF of u_{it}. For example, if u_{it} is an independent exponential random variable, then the test statistic is

---

[4]This formula is based on the result that if u_{it} is an independent exponential random variable with scale parameter $\sigma_t > 0$, then $P[-\sigma_t \ln(1-\alpha/2) \leq u_{it} \leq -\sigma_t \ln(\alpha/2)] = 1 - \alpha \Rightarrow P[(\alpha/2)^{\sigma_t} \leq \exp(-u_{it}) \leq (1-\alpha/2)^{\sigma_t}] = 1 - \alpha$.

Table 6.11 Estimates of efficiency and inefficiency[a]

Firm	E_i	u_i
A	0.422	0.863
B	0.610	0.495
C	1	0
D	0.949	0.052
E	1	0
F	0.614	0.488
G	1	0
H	1	0
I	0.871	0.139
J	1	0
K	1	0
L	0.933	0.070
M	0.643	0.441
N	1	0
O	0.844	0.170
P	0.594	0.521
R	0.671	0.399
S	0.583	0.540
T	1	0
U	0.654	0.424
V	1	0
W	0.895	0.111
X	0.836	0.179
Y	0.516	0.662
Z	0.867	0.143

[a]Numbers reported to less than three decimal places are exact; see the footnote to Table 1.2 on p. 8

$$F = \frac{\sum_t \sum_{i \in S_{1t}} \hat{u}_{it} / \sum_t I_{1t}}{\sum_t \sum_{i \in S_{2t}} \hat{u}_{it} / \sum_t I_{2t}}. \tag{6.48}$$

If the null hypothesis is true, then this statistic has an F distribution with $2\sum_t I_{1t}$ numerator and $2\sum_t I_{2t}$ denominator degrees of freedom. Thus, we should reject the null hypothesis at the α level of significance if $F > F_{(1-\alpha, 2\sum_t I_{1t}, 2\sum_t I_{2t})}$. As another example, if u_{it} is an independent half-normal random variable, then the test statistic is

$$F = \frac{\sum_t \sum_{i \in S_{1t}} \hat{u}_{it}^2 / \sum_t I_{1t}}{\sum_t \sum_{i \in S_{2t}} \hat{u}_{it}^2 / \sum_t I_{2t}}. \tag{6.49}$$

If the null hypothesis is true, then this statistic has an F distribution with $\sum_t I_{1t}$ numerator and $\sum_t I_{2t}$ denominator degrees of freedom. Thus, we should reject the null hypothesis at the α level of significance if $F > F_{(1-\alpha,\sum_t I_{1t},\sum_t I_{2t})}$. If the data are cross-section data, then these tests are equivalent to tests proposed by Banker (1993). The validity of both tests depends on $\sum_g \sum_t I_{gt}$ being large. However, neither $\sum_t I_{1t}$ nor $\sum_t I_{2t}$ need to be large (Banker 1993, p. 1272). Moreover, the assumption made about the PDF of u_{it} (i.e., exponential or half-normal) need only be true for $i \in S_{1t} \cup S_{2t}$ (Banker 1993, fn. 8).

For a numerical example, reconsider the toy data reported in Table 1.1. Suppose we are interested in testing the null hypothesis that the average output-oriented technical inefficiency of firms operating in environment 1 is no greater than the average output-oriented technical inefficiency of firms operating in environment 2. Again, for purposes of illustration, let us treat the observations in the dataset as observations on twenty-five firms in a single time period; this implies that all references to time periods can be deleted. In this case, $S_1 = \{$A, B, C, D, E, H, J, K, L, M, N, P, R, U, V, Y, Z$\}$, $S_2 = \{$F, G, I, O, S, T, W, X$\}$, $I_1 = 17$ and $I_2 = 8$. DEA estimates of E_i and u_i were reported earlier in Table 6.11. If u_i is an independent exponential random variable, then the test statistic takes the value $F = (4.069/17)/(1.627/8) = 1.177$. The critical value at the $\alpha = 0.05$ level of significance is $F_{(0.95,34,16)} = 2.174$. The value of the test statistic is less than this critical value, so we should not reject the null hypothesis (at the 5% level of significance).

6.4.1.3 Testing Assumptions About Production Technologies

Suppose we are interested in testing a null hypothesis concerning the technologies that exist in period t (e.g., the null hypothesis that the period-t production frontier exhibits CRS, or the null hypothesis that the period-t production possibilities set is convex). Again, the choice of test statistic depends on the PDF of u_{it}. For example, if there are I_t firms in the dataset in period t and u_{it} is an independent exponential random variable, then the test statistic is

$$F = \frac{\sum_{i=1}^{I_t} \hat{u}_{it}^r}{\sum_{i=1}^{I_t} \hat{u}_{it}^u} \tag{6.50}$$

where $\hat{u}_{it}^r$ and $\hat{u}_{it}^u$ denote restricted and unrestricted estimators for u_{it} (i.e., the estimators used under the null and alternative hypotheses). If the null hypothesis is true, then this statistic has a half-F distribution with $2I_t$ numerator and $2I_t$ denominator degrees of freedom. Thus, we should reject the null hypothesis at the α level of significance if $F > F_{(1-\alpha/2,2I_t,2I_t)}$.[5] As another example, if u_{it} is an independent half-normal random variable, then the test statistic is

---

[5]Consider an F distribution with the numerator degrees of freedom equal to the denominator degrees of freedom. A half-F distribution is such a distribution truncated from below at 1. The critical value that leaves an area of α in the right-hand tail of a half-F distribution is the value that leaves an area of $\alpha/2$ in the right-hand tail of the corresponding untruncated F distribution.

$$F = \frac{\sum_{i=1}^{I_t} (\hat{u}_{it}^r)^2}{\sum_{i=1}^{I_t} (\hat{u}_{it}^u)^2}. \tag{6.51}$$

If the null hypothesis is true, then this statistic has a half-F distribution with I_t numerator and I_t denominator degrees of freedom. Thus, we should reject the null hypothesis at the α level of significance if $F > F_{(1-\alpha/2, I_t, I_t)}$. The validity of these tests depends on I_t being large. Both tests are also underpinned by the assumption that the inefficiency effects are *independent* random variables. This suggests that independent random samples should be used to estimate the inefficiency effects under the null and alternative hypotheses. In practice, random sampling without replacement can be used to divide the sample into two groups of equal size. One sub-sample can then be used to estimate u_{it} under the null hypothesis. The other sub-sample can be used to estimate u_{it} under the alternative hypothesis.

For a numerical example, reconsider the toy data reported in Table 1.1. Again, for purposes of illustration, let us treat the observations in the dataset as observations on twenty-five firms in a single time period; this implies that all references to time periods can be deleted. Suppose we are interested in testing the null hypothesis that the production frontier exhibits CRS. For this particular numerical example, random sampling without replacement was used to select two groups of size 12 from the 25 observations. The first group comprised firms B, E, F, H, I, L, M, O, R, S, V and Y. The second group comprised firms A, C, D, G, J, K, N, P, U, W, X and Z. Data from the first (resp. second) group were used to estimate levels of output-oriented technical inefficiency under a VRS (resp. CRS) assumption. If u_i is an independent exponential random variable, then the test statistic takes the value $F = 2.726/1.663 = 1.639$. The critical value at the $\alpha = 0.05$ level of significance is $F_{(0.975, 24, 24)} = 2.269$. The value of the test statistic is less than this critical value, so we should not reject the null hypothesis (at the 5% level of significance).

6.4.2 PDFs Unknown

If the PDFs of E_{it} and u_{it} are unknown, then bootstrapping methods can be used to conduct asymptotic inference. This section considers bootstrapping methods for (a) constructing confidence intervals for measures of efficiency, (b) testing for differences in average efficiency, and (c) bias correction.

6.4.2.1 Confidence Intervals for Measures of Efficiency

Suppose we are interested in constructing a $100(1-\alpha)\%$ confidence interval for E_{it}. In this context, bootstrapping involves using the data to somehow generate B artificial samples of observations. Each so-called bootstrap sample is then used to compute an estimate of E_{it}. If B is sufficiently large, then the distribution of these computed estimates can be used as an estimate of the distribution of E_{it}. Thus, constructing a bootstrap confidence interval for E_{it} involves the following steps:

1. Specify a data generating process (DGP) and set $b = 1$.
2. Use the DGP to generate a bootstrap sample of observations that includes data on firm i in period t.
3. Use the bootstrap sample to compute an estimate of E_{it}, denoted $\hat{E}_{it}^{b}$.
4. If $b < B$, then set $b = b + 1$ and return to step 2. Otherwise, stop.

After completing these steps, the $100(1-\alpha)\%$ confidence interval limits are given by the $\alpha/2$-th percentile and the $(1-\alpha/2)$-th percentile of the set $\{\hat{E}_{it}^{1}, \ldots, \hat{E}_{it}^{B}\}$. These confidence interval limits may be sensitive to the DGP.

For a numerical example, reconsider the toy data reported in Table 1.1. Suppose we are interested in constructing 95% confidence intervals for measures of OTE. Again, for purposes of illustration, let us treat the observations in the dataset as observations on twenty-five firms in a single time period. For this particular numerical example, the `dea.boot` function in Bogetoft and Otto (2015) was used to generate $B = 2000$ bootstrap samples and associated 95% confidence interval limits. These limits are reported in Table 6.12.

6.4.2.2 Testing for Differences in Average Efficiency

Suppose that all the observations in the dataset can be classified into two or more groups, and that we are interested in testing the null hypothesis from Sect. 6.4.1.2. If the probability distribution of u_{it} is unknown, then the probability distributions of the test statistics (6.48) and (6.49) are also unknown. However, they can be estimated using bootstrapping. In this context, bootstrapping still involves using the data to somehow generate B bootstrap samples. However, each bootstrap sample is now used to compute a value of a test statistic. If B is sufficiently large, then the distribution of these computed values can be used as an estimate of the probability distribution of the test statistic. Thus, a bootstrap test of the type of null hypothesis discussed in Sect. 6.4.1.2 involves the following steps:

1. Specify a DGP and set $b = 1$.
2. Use the DGP to generate a bootstrap sample of observations.
3. Use the bootstrap sample to compute the value of the test statistic, denoted F^{b}.
4. If $b < B$, then set $b = b + 1$ and return to step 2. Otherwise, stop.

After completing these steps, we should reject the null hypothesis at the α level of significance if the value of the test statistic computed from the original sample is greater than the $(1-\alpha)$-th percentile of the set $\{F^{1}, \ldots, F^{B}\}$. Again, test outcomes may be sensitive to the DGP.

For a numerical example, reconsider the toy data reported in Table 1.1. Suppose we are interested in testing the null hypothesis that the average output-oriented technical inefficiency of firms operating in environment 1 is no greater than the average output-oriented technical inefficiency of firms operating in environment 2. Again,

Table 6.12 CI limits

Firm	2.5%	97.5%
A	0.340	0.420
B	0.506	0.605
C	0.807	0.996
D	0.797	0.942
E	0.801	0.992
F	0.505	0.609
G	0.767	0.992
H	0.636	0.990
I	0.621	0.867
J	0.644	0.991
K	0.801	0.991
L	0.727	0.928
M	0.533	0.639
N	0.644	0.989
O	0.715	0.841
P	0.487	0.590
R	0.549	0.665
S	0.467	0.579
T	0.847	0.990
U	0.524	0.648
V	0.778	0.990
W	0.766	0.890
X	0.675	0.831
Y	0.433	0.512
Z	0.727	0.860

for purposes of illustration, let us treat the observations in the dataset as observations on twenty-five firms in a single time period. Recall from the example in Sect. 6.4.1.2 that the test statistic (6.48) took the value $F = 1.177$. To find the critical value at the $\alpha = 0.05$ level of significance, the `dea.boot` function in Bogetoft and Otto (2015) was used to generate $B = 2000$ bootstrap samples and associated values of the test statistic. The 95-th percentile of these values (i.e., the critical value) was 2.973. The value of the F statistic is less than this critical value, so we should not reject the null hypothesis (at the 5% level of significance).

6.4.2.3 Bias Correction

Let $\hat{E}_{it}$ denote a piecewise frontier estimator for E_{it}. If E_{it} is a measure of technical efficiency, then $\hat{E}_{it}$ is upwardly biased. Correcting for this bias involves the following bootstrap steps:

1. Specify a DGP and set $b = 1$.
2. Use the DGP to generate a bootstrap sample of observations that includes data on firm i in period t.
3. Use the bootstrap sample to compute an estimate of E_{it}, denoted $\hat{E}_{it}^b$.
4. If $b < B$, then set $b = b + 1$ and return to step 2. Otherwise, stop.

Note that these are the same steps that were followed in Sect. 6.4.2.1. After completing these steps, an estimator for the bias is

$$\hat{b}_{it} = \bar{E}_{it}^B - \hat{E}_{it} \tag{6.52}$$

where $\bar{E}_{it}^B = \sum_b \hat{E}_{it}^b / B$. A bias-corrected estimator for E_{it} is

$$\tilde{E}_{it} = \hat{E}_{it} - \hat{b}_{it} = \hat{E}_{it} - (\bar{E}_{it}^B - \hat{E}_{it}) = 2\hat{E}_{it} - \bar{E}_{it}^B. \tag{6.53}$$

For more details, see Simar and Wilson (1998, p. 51). In practice, it is possible that $\bar{E}_{it}^B > 2\hat{E}_{it}$, implying that $\tilde{E}_{it} < 0$. Such a result indicates that either the frontier model is misspecified or the bootstrap procedure has failed.

For a numerical example, reconsider the toy data reported in Table 1.1. Suppose we want to compute bias-corrected estimates of OTE. Again, for purposes of illustration, let us treat the observations in the dataset as observations on twenty-five firms in a single time period. For this particular numerical example, the `dea.boot` function in Bogetoft and Otto (2015) was used to generate $B = 2000$ bootstrap samples and associated estimates of bias. The estimates of bias are reported in Table 6.13. This table also reports associated estimates of efficiency. The efficiency estimates in column E are the (uncorrected) estimates reported earlier in Table 6.11. The estimates reported in column BCE are bias-corrected estimates. Only the bias-corrected estimates lie within the confidence interval limits reported earlier in Table 6.12.

6.5 Productivity Analysis

Productivity analysis involves both measuring and explaining changes in productivity. This section focuses on measuring and explaining changes in TFP. Methods for measuring and explaining changes in MFP and PFP can be handled as special cases in which one or more inputs are assigned a value (or weight) of zero.

Table 6.13 Estimates of efficiency[a]

Firm	E	bias	BCE
A	0.422	0.038	0.383
B	0.610	0.050	0.560
C	1	0.091	0.909
D	0.949	0.080	0.870
E	1	0.120	0.880
F	0.614	0.057	0.557
G	1	0.137	0.863
H	1	0.182	0.818
I	0.871	0.102	0.769
J	1	0.180	0.820
K	1	0.096	0.904
L	0.933	0.090	0.843
M	0.643	0.050	0.594
N	1	0.178	0.822
O	0.844	0.056	0.788
P	0.594	0.058	0.536
R	0.671	0.058	0.613
S	0.583	0.057	0.526
T	1	0.085	0.915
U	0.654	0.067	0.587
V	1	0.110	0.890
W	0.895	0.055	0.840
X	0.836	0.080	0.756
Y	0.516	0.039	0.477
Z	0.867	0.067	0.800

[a]Numbers reported to less than three decimal places are exact; see the footnote to Table 1.2 on p. 8

6.5.1 Measuring Changes in TFP

Measuring changes in TFP involves computing proper TFP index (TFPI) numbers. Except in restrictive special cases, PFMs cannot be used to compute primal or dual TFPI numbers.[6] However, they can be used to compute additive and multiplicative TFPI numbers. Additive TFPI numbers can be computed by using average estimated normalised shadow prices as weights in Eq. (3.41).[7] If the output and input distance

---

[6]Primal and dual indices are only proper indices if the parameters of distance, revenue and cost functions do not vary across observations. Except in restrictive special cases (e.g., there is only one input and one output, there is no environmental change, and production frontiers exhibit CRS), PFMs are underpinned by functions with parameters that *do* vary across observations.

[7]Additive TFPI numbers can also be computed using estimated representative normalised shadow prices as weights. The DPIN software of O'Donnell (2010a) computes so-called 'Färe-Primont'

functions take the form of (6.1) and (6.6), then the n-th normalised shadow output price and the m-th normalised shadow input price are

$$p_n^{it}(x_{it}, q_{it}, z_{it}) = \gamma_{nit}/(\alpha_{it} + \delta_{it}' z_{it} + \beta_{it}' x_{it}) \tag{6.54}$$

$$\text{and} \quad w_m^{it}(x_{it}, q_{it}, z_{it}) = \theta_{mit}/(\xi_{it}' q_{it} - \kappa_{it}' z_{it} - \phi_{it}). \tag{6.55}$$

Multiplicative TFPI numbers can be computed by using average estimated shadow value shares as weights in Eq. (3.42).[8] If the output and input distance functions take the form of (6.1) and (6.6), then the n-th shadow revenue share and the m-th shadow cost share are

$$r_n^{it}(x_{it}, q_{it}, z_{it}) = \gamma_{nit} q_{nit}/\gamma_{it}' q_{it} \tag{6.56}$$

$$\text{and} \quad s_m^{it}(x_{it}, q_{it}, z_{it}) = \theta_{mit} x_{mit}/\theta_{it}' x_{it}. \tag{6.57}$$

Estimates of the unknown parameters in Eqs. (6.54)–(6.57) (and therefore estimates of normalised shadow prices and shadow value shares) can be obtained by solving the multiplier forms of the output- and input-oriented models described in Sects. 6.1.1 and 6.1.2.

To illustrate, reconsider the output and input quantity data reported earlier in Table 1.1. Associated DEA estimates of normalised shadow prices and shadow value shares are reported in Table 6.14. The arithmetic averages reported in the last row of this table were used to compute the additive and multiplicative TFPI numbers reported in Table 6.15. These index numbers are proper in the sense that they have been obtained by dividing proper output index numbers by proper input index numbers. They are also consistent with measurement theory. Observe, for example, that (a) the output vector in row O is twice as big as the output vector in row A, (b) the input vector in row O is the same as the input vector in row A, and (c) the index numbers in row O are twice as big as the numbers in row A.

6.5.2 Explaining Changes in TFP

Explaining changes in TFP generally involves decomposing proper TFPI numbers into measures of environmental change, technical change, and efficiency change. This section focuses on productivity-, output- and input-oriented decompositions.

TFPI numbers in this way. If average estimated normalised shadow prices are proportional to average observed prices, then the associated additive index numbers are equal to Lowe index numbers.

[8]If average estimated shadow value shares are equal to average observed value shares, then the associated multiplicative index numbers are equal to geometric Young index numbers.

Table 6.14 DEA estimates of normalised shadow prices and shadow value shares[a,b]

Row	Firm	Period	$p_1^{it}(.)$	$p_2^{it}(.)$	$w_1^{it}(.)$	$w_2^{it}(.)$	$r_1^{it}(.)$	$r_2^{it}(.)$	$s_1^{it}(.)$	$s_2^{it}(.)$
A	1	1	0.422	0	1.786	0	1	0	1	0
B	2	1	1	0	1.786	0	1	0	1	0
C	3	1	0.422	0	1	0	1	0	1	0
D	4	1	0.474	0	0.611	0.513	1	0	0.641	0.359
E	5	1	0	0.276	0.952	0	0	1	1	0
F	1	2	0	0.865	0.155	2.829	0	1	0.147	0.853
G	2	2	0	0.285	0	1.832	0	1	0	1
H	3	2	0.808	0.238	0.158	2.882	0.776	0.224	0.003	0.997
I	4	2	0.15	0.201	0.224	2.879	1	0	0.973	0.027
J	5	2	0.15	0	0.224	2.879	1	0	0.997	0.003
K	1	3	0.15	0.168	0	1	0.207	0.793	0	1
L	2	3	0	0.208	0	1	0	1	0	1
M	3	3	0.15	0.168	0.288	1.267	0.229	0.771	0.235	0.765
N	4	3	0	1.429	0.086	6.072	0	1	0.029	0.971
O	5	3	0.422	0	0.776	0.511	1	0	0.603	0.397
P	1	4	0.459	0.135	0.789	2.705	0.772	0.228	0.286	0.714
R	2	4	0.297	0.125	0.409	1.113	0.443	0.557	0.269	0.731
S	3	4	0	0.583	0.069	4.813	0	1	0.089	0.911
T	4	4	0.317	0.104	0.684	0.316	0.611	0.389	0.684	0.316
U	5	4	0	0.654	0.032	4.581	0	1	0.022	0.978
V	1	5	0	0.194	0	1	0	1	0	1
W	2	5	0.345	0.102	0.776	0.511	0.772	0.228	0.603	0.397
X	3	5	0	0.836	0.069	4.813	0	1	0.088	0.912
Y	4	5	0.398	0.117	0.789	2.705	0.772	0.228	0.226	0.774
Z	5	5	0.15	0.165	0	1.429	0.312	0.688	0	1
Arithmetic mean			0.245	0.274	0.466	1.906	0.476	0.524	0.396	0.604

[a] $p_n^{it}(.)$ = n-th estimated normalised shadow output price; $w_m^{it}(.)$ = m-th estimated normalised shadow input price; $r_n^{it}(.)$ = n-th estimated shadow revenue share; $s_m^{it}(.)$ = m-th estimated shadow cost share
[b] Numbers reported to less than three decimal places are exact; see the footnote to Table 1.2 on p. 8

6.5.2.1 Productivity-Oriented Decompositions

Productivity-oriented decompositions of TFPI numbers tend to be most relevant in situations where managers have placed nonnegative values on outputs and inputs, and where they have chosen at least one output and one input freely (i.e., situations where productivity-oriented measures of efficiency are most relevant). In these situations, arguably the easiest way to proceed is to rewrite (5.32) as $TFP(x_{it}, q_{it}) = TFP^t(z_{it}) \times$

Table 6.15 Additive and multiplicative TFPI numbers[a,b]

Row	Firm	Period	q_1	q_2	x_1	x_2	A	M
A	1	1	1	1	1	1	1	1
B	2	1	1	1	0.56	0.56	1.786	1.786
C	3	1	2.37	2.37	1	1	2.37	2.37
D	4	1	2.11	2.11	1.05	0.7	2.744	2.567
E	5	1	1.81	3.62	1.05	0.7	3.599	3.167
F	1	2	1	1	0.996	0.316	2.224	2.009
G	2	2	1.777	3.503	1.472	0.546	3.694	3.137
H	3	2	0.96	0.94	0.017	0.346	3.375	9.042
I	4	2	5.82	0.001	4.545	0.01	3.044	0.549
J	5	2	6.685	0.001	4.45	0.001	3.600	2.378
K	1	3	1.381	4.732	1	1	3.152	2.634
L	2	3	0.566	4.818	1	1	2.813	1.739
M	3	3	1	3	1.354	1	1.923	1.578
N	4	3	0.7	0.7	0.33	0.16	3.619	3.285
O	5	3	2	2	1	1	2	2
P	1	4	1	1	0.657	0.479	1.946	1.842
R	2	4	1	3	1	1	2.057	1.779
S	3	4	1	1	1.933	0.283	1.646	1.652
T	4	4	1.925	3.722	1	1	2.875	2.72
U	5	4	1	1	1	0.31	2.244	2.029
V	1	5	1	5.166	1	1	3.202	2.365
W	2	5	2	2	0.919	0.919	2.176	2.176
X	3	5	1	1	1.464	0.215	2.171	2.177
Y	4	5	1	1	0.74	0.74	1.351	1.351
Z	5	5	1.81	3.62	2.1	1.4	1.799	1.584

[a] A = additive index with averages of DEA estimates of normalised shadow prices used as weights; M = multiplicative index with averages of DEA estimates of shadow value shares used as weights. Some index numbers may be incoherent at the third decimal place due to rounding (e.g., the number in row Z of column A is not exactly half as big as the number in row E of column A due to rounding)
[b] Numbers reported to less than three decimal places are exact; see the footnote to Table 1.2 on p. 8

$TSME^t(x_{it}, q_{it}, z_{it})$. A similar equation holds for firm k in period s. Substituting these equations into (3.40) yields

$$TFPI(x_{ks}, q_{ks}, x_{it}, q_{it}) = TFP^t(z_{it})/TFP^s(z_{ks}) \times TSME^t(x_{it}, q_{it}, z_{it})/TSME^s(x_{ks}, q_{ks}, z_{ks}). \quad (6.58)$$

This equation appears in O'Donnell et al. (2017, Eq. 12). The first ratio on the right-hand side is an environment and technology index (ETI) (i.e., a combined measure of environmental and technical change). The second ratio is a technical, scale and mix efficiency index (TSMEI). For a finer decomposition, Eq. (5.34) can be rewritten as $TSME^t(x_{it}, q_{it}, z_{it}) = TSE^t(x_{it}, q_{it}, z_{it}) \times RME^t(x_{it}, q_{it}, z_{it})$. A similar equation holds for firm k in period s. Substituting these equations into (6.58) yields

$$\begin{aligned} TFPI(x_{ks}, q_{ks}, x_{it}, q_{it}) &= TFP^t(z_{it})/TFP^s(z_{ks}) \\ &\times TSE^t(x_{it}, q_{it}, z_{it})/TSE^s(x_{ks}, q_{ks}, z_{ks}) \\ &\times RME^t(x_{it}, q_{it}, z_{it})/RME^s(x_{ks}, q_{ks}, z_{ks}). \end{aligned} \tag{6.59}$$

The first ratio on the right-hand side is the ETI in (6.58). The second ratio is a technical and scale efficiency index (TSEI). The last ratio is a residual mix efficiency index (RMEI). In practice, estimates of the TSMEI and TSEI can be obtained by solving (6.15) and (6.16). Estimates of the other components can be obtained as residuals.

For a numerical example, reconsider the Lowe TFPI numbers reported earlier in column L of Table 3.5. Two productivity-oriented decompositions of these index numbers are reported in Table 6.16. The TSMEI, TSEI and RMEI numbers in this table were obtained by dividing the TSME, TSE and RME estimates in each row of Table 6.6 by the corresponding estimates for firm 1 in period 1. The ETI numbers were then obtained as residuals (i.e., ETI = TFPI/TSMEI).

6.5.2.2 Output-Oriented Decompositions

Output-oriented decompositions of TFPI numbers tend to be most relevant in situations where managers have placed nonnegative values on outputs, and where inputs have been predetermined (i.e., situations where output-oriented measures of efficiency are most relevant). In these situations, arguably the easiest way to proceed is to rewrite (5.38) as $TSME^t(x_{it}, q_{it}, z_{it}) = OTE^t(x_{it}, q_{it}, z_{it}) \times OSME^t(x_{it}, q_{it}, z_{it})$. A similar equation holds for firm k in period s. Substituting these equations into (6.58) yields

$$\begin{aligned} TFPI(x_{ks}, q_{ks}, x_{it}, q_{it}) &= TFP^t(z_{it})/TFP^s(z_{ks}) \\ &\times OTE^t(x_{it}, q_{it}, z_{it})/OTE^s(x_{ks}, q_{ks}, z_{ks}) \\ &\times OSME^t(x_{it}, q_{it}, z_{it})/OSME^s(x_{ks}, q_{ks}, z_{ks}). \end{aligned} \tag{6.60}$$

If there is no environmental change, then this equation is equivalent to equation (11) in O'Donnell (2012, p. 881). The first ratio on the right-hand side is the ETI in (6.58). The second ratio is an output-oriented technical efficiency index (OTEI). The last ratio is an output-oriented scale and mix efficiency index (OSMEI). For a finer decomposition, Eq. (5.40) can be rewritten as $OSME^t(x_{it}, q_{it}, z_{it}) = OME^t(x_{it}, q_{it}, z_{it}) \times ROSE^t(x_{it}, q_{it}, z_{it})$. A similar equation holds for firm k in period s. Substituting these equations into (6.60) yields

Table 6.16 Productivity-oriented decompositions of Lowe TFPI numbers[a,b]

Row	Firm	Period	TFPI	ETI	TSMEI	ETI	TSEI	RMEI
A	1	1	1	1	1	1	1	1
B	2	1	1.786	1	1.786	1	1.786	1
C	3	1	2.37	1	2.37	1	2.37	1
D	4	1	2.703	1	2.703	1	2.37	1.141
E	5	1	3.516	1	3.516	1	2.37	1.483
F	1	2	2.117	1	2.117	1	1.459	1.451
G	2	2	3.515	1	3.515	1	2.37	1.483
H	3	2	3.513	1	3.513	1	2.37	1.482
I	4	2	2.675	1	2.675	1	2.013	1.329
J	5	2	3.159	1	3.159	1	2.37	1.333
K	1	3	3.110	1.000	3.110	1.000	2.37	1.312
L	2	3	2.760	1.000	2.760	1.000	2.37	1.165
M	3	3	1.879	1.000	1.879	1.000	1.403	1.339
N	4	3	3.516	1.000	3.516	1.000	2.37	1.483
O	5	3	2	1.000	2.000	1.000	1.349	1.483
P	1	4	1.923	1.000	1.923	1.000	1.297	1.483
R	2	4	2.032	1.000	2.032	1.000	1.521	1.336
S	3	4	1.509	1.000	1.509	1.000	1.306	1.156
T	4	4	2.852	1.000	2.852	1.000	1.987	1.435
U	5	4	2.134	1.000	2.133	1.000	1.479	1.443
V	1	5	3.150	1.000	3.149	1.000	2.37	1.329
W	2	5	2.176	1.000	2.176	1.000	1.467	1.483
X	3	5	1.991	1.000	1.991	1.000	1.719	1.158
Y	4	5	1.351	1.000	1.351	1.000	0.911	1.483
Z	5	5	1.758	1.000	1.758	1.000	1.185	1.483
Geometric mean			2.306	1.000	2.305	1.000	1.747	1.320

[a]TFPI = ETI × TSMEI = ETI × TSEI × RMEI. Some index numbers may be incoherent at the third decimal place due to rounding (e.g., in any given row, the product of the ETI and TSMEI numbers may not be exactly equal to the TFPI number due to rounding)
[b]Numbers reported to less than three decimal places are exact; see the footnote to Table 1.2 on p. 8

$$
\begin{aligned}
TFPI(x_{ks}, q_{ks}, x_{it}, q_{it}) = {} & TFP^t(z_{it})/TFP^s(z_{ks}) \\
& \times OTE^t(x_{it}, q_{it}, z_{it})/OTE^s(x_{ks}, q_{ks}, z_{ks}) \\
& \times OME^t(x_{it}, q_{it}, z_{it})/OME^s(x_{ks}, q_{ks}, z_{ks}) \\
& \times ROSE^t(x_{it}, q_{it}, z_{it})/ROSE^s(x_{ks}, q_{ks}, z_{ks}).
\end{aligned} \tag{6.61}
$$

If there is no environmental change, then this equation is equivalent to the first part of equation (4.2) in O'Donnell (2010b, p. 537). The first two ratios on the right-hand side are the ETI and OTEI in (6.60). The third ratio is an output-oriented mix efficiency index (OMEI). The last ratio is a residual output-oriented scale efficiency index (ROSEI). For an alternative decomposition, equation (5.36) can be rewritten as $TSE^t(x_{it}, q_{it}, z_{it}) = OTE^t(x_{it}, q_{it}, z_{it}) \times OSE^t(x_{it}, q_{it}, z_{it})$. A similar equation holds for firm k in period s. Substituting these equations into (6.59) yields

$$\begin{aligned} TFPI(x_{ks}, q_{ks}, x_{it}, q_{it}) = {} & TFP^t(z_{it})/TFP^s(z_{ks}) \\ & \times OTE^t(x_{it}, q_{it}, z_{it})/OTE^s(x_{ks}, q_{ks}, z_{ks}) \\ & \times OSE^t(x_{it}, q_{it}, z_{it})/OSE^s(x_{ks}, q_{ks}, z_{ks}) \\ & \times RME^t(x_{it}, q_{it}, z_{it})/RME^s(x_{ks}, q_{ks}, z_{ks}). \end{aligned} \tag{6.62}$$

If there is no environmental change, then this equation is equivalent to the second part of equation (4.2) in O'Donnell (2010b, p. 537). The first two ratios on the right-hand side are the ETI and OTEI in (6.60) and (6.61). The third ratio is an output-oriented scale efficiency index (OSEI). The last ratio is the RMEI in (6.59).

For a numerical example, reconsider the Lowe TFPI numbers reported earlier in column L of Table 3.5. Three output-oriented decompositions of these index numbers are reported in Table 6.17. The OTEI, OSMEI, OMEI, ROSEI, OSEI and RMEI numbers in this table were obtained by dividing the OTE, OSME, OME, ROSE, OSE and RME estimates in each row of Table 6.7 by the corresponding estimates for firm 1 in period 1. The ETI numbers are the index numbers reported in Table 6.16.

6.5.2.3 Input-Oriented Decompositions

Input-oriented decompositions of TFPI numbers tend to be most relevant in situations where managers have placed nonnegative values on inputs, and where outputs have been predetermined (i.e., situations where input-oriented measures of efficiency are most relevant). In these situations, an easy way to proceed is to rewrite (5.44) as $TSME^t(x_{it}, q_{it}, z_{it}) = ITE^t(x_{it}, q_{it}, z_{it}) \times ISME^t(x_{it}, q_{it}, z_{it})$. A similar equation holds for firm k in period s. Substituting these equations into (6.58) yields

$$\begin{aligned} TFPI(x_{ks}, q_{ks}, x_{it}, q_{it}) = {} & TFP^t(z_{it})/TFP^s(z_{ks}) \\ & \times ITE^t(x_{it}, q_{it}, z_{it})/ITE^s(x_{ks}, q_{ks}, z_{ks}) \\ & \times ISME^t(x_{it}, q_{it}, z_{it})/ISME^s(x_{ks}, q_{ks}, z_{ks}). \end{aligned} \tag{6.63}$$

If there is no technical change, then this equation is equivalent to equation (12) in O'Donnell and Nguyen (2013, p. 326). The first ratio on the right-hand side is the ETI in (6.58). The second ratio is an input-oriented technical efficiency index (ITEI). The last ratio is an input-oriented scale and mix efficiency index (ISMEI). For a finer decomposition, equation (5.46) can be rewritten as $ISME^t(x_{it}, q_{it}, z_{it}) = IME^t(x_{it}, q_{it}, z_{it}) \times RISE^t(x_{it}, q_{it}, z_{it})$. A similar equation holds for firm k in period s. Substituting these equations into (6.63) yields

Table 6.17 Output-oriented decompositions of Lowe TFPI numbers[a,b]

Row	Firm	Period	TFPI	ETI	OTEI	OSMEI	ETI	OTEI	OMEI	ROSEI	ETI	OTEI	OSEI	RMEI
A	1	1	1	1	1	1	1	1	1	1	1	1	1	1
B	2	1	1.786	1	2.37	0.753	1	2.37	1.083	0.696	1	2.37	0.753	1
C	3	1	2.37	1	2.37	1	1	2.37	1	1	1	2.37	1	1
D	4	1	2.703	1	2.37	1.141	1	2.37	0.833	1.37	1	2.37	1	1.141
E	5	1	3.516	1	2.37	1.483	1	2.37	1.083	1.37	1	2.37	1	1.483
F	1	2	2.117	1	2.05	1.033	1	2.05	0.784	1.318	1	2.05	0.711	1.451
G	2	2	3.515	1	2.37	1.483	1	2.37	1.083	1.37	1	2.37	1	1.483
H	3	2	3.513	1	2.37	1.482	1	2.37	1.083	1.369	1	2.37	1	1.482
I	4	2	2.675	1	2.063	1.297	1	2.063	1.083	1.198	1	2.063	0.976	1.329
J	5	2	3.159	1	2.37	1.333	1	2.37	1.083	1.231	1	2.37	1	1.333
K	1	3	3.11	1.000	2.370	1.312	1.000	2.370	1.083	1.212	1.000	2.370	1	1.312
L	2	3	2.76	1.000	2.370	1.165	1.000	2.370	0.961	1.212	1.000	2.370	1	1.165
M	3	3	1.879	1.000	1.547	1.215	1.000	1.547	1.079	1.125	1.000	1.547	0.907	1.339
N	4	3	3.516	1.000	2.370	1.483	1.000	2.370	1.083	1.370	1.000	2.370	1	1.483
O	5	3	2	1.000	2.000	1.000	1.000	2.000	0.825	1.212	1.000	2.000	0.674	1.483
P	1	4	1.923	1.000	1.408	1.366	1.000	1.408	0.997	1.370	1.000	1.408	0.921	1.483
R	2	4	2.032	1.000	1.590	1.278	1.000	1.590	1.054	1.212	1.000	1.590	0.956	1.336
S	3	4	1.509	1.000	1.381	1.093	1.000	1.381	0.833	1.312	1.000	1.381	0.946	1.156
T	4	4	2.852	1.000	2.370	1.203	1.000	2.370	0.993	1.212	1.000	2.370	0.838	1.435
U	5	4	2.134	1.000	1.550	1.376	1.000	1.550	1.029	1.337	1.000	1.550	0.954	1.443
V	1	5	3.15	1.000	2.370	1.329	1.000	2.370	1.083	1.227	1.000	2.370	1	1.329

(continued)

Table 6.17 (continued)

Row	Firm	Period	TFPI	ETI	OTEI	OSMEI	ETI	OTEI	OMEI	ROSEI	ETI	OTEI	OSEI	RMEI
W	2	5	2.176	1.000	2.120	1.026	1.000	2.120	0.827	1.241	1.000	2.120	0.692	1.483
X	3	5	1.991	1.000	1.982	1.004	1.000	1.982	0.767	1.310	1.000	1.982	0.867	1.158
Y	4	5	1.351	1.000	1.223	1.105	1.000	1.223	0.863	1.281	1.000	1.223	0.745	1.483
Z	5	5	1.758	1.000	2.054	0.856	1.000	2.054	1.079	0.793	1.000	2.054	0.577	1.483
Geometric mean			2.306	1.000	1.962	1.175	1.000	1.962	0.980	1.199	1.000	1.962	0.890	1.320

[a]TFPI = ETI × OTEI × OSMEI = ETI × OTEI × OMEI × ROSEI = ETI × OTEI × OSEI × RMEI. Some index numbers may be incoherent at the third decimal place due to rounding (e.g., in any given row, the product of the ETI, OTEI and OSMEI numbers may not be exactly equal to the TFPI number due to rounding)

[b]Numbers reported to less than three decimal places are exact; see the footnote to Table 1.2 on p. 8

$$\begin{aligned}TFPI(x_{ks}, q_{ks}, x_{it}, q_{it}) &= TFP^t(z_{it})/TFP^s(z_{ks}) \\ &\times ITE^t(x_{it}, q_{it}, z_{it})/ITE^s(x_{ks}, q_{ks}, z_{ks}) \\ &\times IME^t(x_{it}, q_{it}, z_{it})/IME^s(x_{ks}, q_{ks}, z_{ks}) \\ &\times RISE^t(x_{it}, q_{it}, z_{it})/RISE^s(x_{ks}, q_{ks}, z_{ks}). \end{aligned} \tag{6.64}$$

The first two ratios on the right-hand side are the ETI and ITEI in (6.63). The third ratio is an input-oriented mix efficiency index (IMEI). The last ratio is a residual input-oriented scale efficiency index (RISEI). For an alternative decomposition, equation (5.42) can be rewritten as $TSE^t(x_{it}, q_{it}, z_{it}) = ITE^t(x_{it}, q_{it}, z_{it}) \times ISE^t(x_{it}, q_{it}, z_{it})$. A similar equation holds for firm k in period s. Substituting these equations into (6.59) yields

$$\begin{aligned}TFPI(x_{ks}, q_{ks}, x_{it}, q_{it}) &= TFP^t(z_{it})/TFP^s(z_{ks}) \\ &\times ITE^t(x_{it}, q_{it}, z_{it})/ITE^s(x_{ks}, q_{ks}, z_{ks}) \\ &\times ISE^t(x_{it}, q_{it}, z_{it})/ISE^s(x_{ks}, q_{ks}, z_{ks}) \\ &\times RME^t(x_{it}, q_{it}, z_{it})/RME^s(x_{ks}, q_{ks}, z_{ks}). \end{aligned} \tag{6.65}$$

The first two ratios on the right-hand side are the ETI and ITEI in (6.63) and (6.64). The third ratio is an input-oriented scale efficiency index (ISEI). The last ratio is the RMEI in (6.59).

For a numerical example, reconsider the Lowe TFPI numbers reported earlier in column L of Table 3.5. Three input-oriented decompositions of these index numbers are reported in Table 6.17. The ITEI, ISMEI, IMEI, RISEI, ISEI and RMEI numbers in this table were obtained by dividing the ITE, ISME, IME, RISE, ISE and RME estimates in each row of Table 6.8 by the corresponding estimates for firm 1 in period 1. The ETI numbers are the index numbers reported in Table 6.16.

6.5.2.4 Other Decompositions

There are many TFPI numbers that are not proper in the sense that they cannot generally be written as proper output index numbers divided by proper input index numbers. If decision makers view measures of productivity change as measures of output quantity change divided by measures of input quantity change, then it is not clear why they would want to decompose TFPI numbers of this type. Putting this issue to one side, one way of decomposing TFPI numbers that are *not* proper is to explicitly allow for statistical noise.

In this book, statistical noise is viewed as a combination of four errors: functional form errors (e.g., when translog revenue and cost functions are used to compute dual indices), measurement errors (e.g., when aggregator functions are not linearly homogeneous), omitted variable errors (e.g., when labour productivity indices are used as measures of TFP change), and included variable errors (e.g., when personal attributes of the manager are treated as environmental variables). One way of decomposing

TFPI numbers that are not proper is to first write them as the product of proper TFPI numbers and statistical noise index (SNI) numbers. Subsequently, the proper TFPI numbers can be decomposed into measures of technical change, environmental change and various measures of efficiency change.

For a numerical example, reconsider the EKS TFPI numbers reported earlier in Table 3.6. Two decompositions of these numbers are reported in Table 6.19. EKS TFPI numbers are closely related to Lowe TFPI numbers (if observed output and input prices are firm- and time-invariant, then they are equal). Output- and input-oriented decompositions of the Lowe TFPI numbers were presented earlier in Tables 6.17 and 6.18. The ETI, OTEI, OSMEI, ITEI and ISMEI numbers in those tables are now reported in Table 6.19. The numbers in the SNI columns in Table 6.19 were obtained by dividing the EKS TFPI numbers by the Lowe TFPI numbers. In this context, the SNI can be viewed as an output price index divided by an input price index; if output and input prices had been firm- and time-invariant, then all the SNI numbers would have been equal one.

6.6 Other Models

Other PFMs include models that can be used to explain variations in metafrontiers and inefficiency.

6.6.1 Metafrontier Models

Metafrontier models are used in situations where firm managers can be classified into two or more groups, and where managers in different groups choose input-output combinations from potentially different production possibilities sets. To illustrate, this section considers situations where firm managers can be classified into two or more groups according to the technologies they use. To avoid repetition, attention is restricted to the estimation of output-oriented metafrontier models; the estimation of input-, revenue-, cost-, profit- and productivity-oriented metafrontier models is analogous to the estimation of output-oriented models.

If we observe the technologies used by firm managers, then output-oriented metafrontier models can be used to estimate the output-oriented metatechnology ratio (OMR) defined by (5.47), the measure of output-oriented technical efficiency (OTE) defined by (5.1), and the measure of residual output-oriented technical efficiency (ROTE) defined by (5.48). If assumptions PF1 to PF5 are true, then this can be done in three steps. The first step is to estimate the measure of OTE defined by (5.1). The second step is to estimate the measure of ROTE defined by (5.48). The final step is to use equation (5.49) to estimate the OMR defined by (5.47).

The output-oriented LP problems presented in Sect. 6.1.1 are only suitable for estimating OTE when the technologies used by managers are *not* observed. In such

Table 6.18 Input-oriented decompositions of Lowe TFPI numbers[a,b]

Row	Firm	Period	TFPI	ETI	ITEI	ISMEI	ETI	ITEI	IMEI	RISEI	ETI	ITEI	ISEI	RMEI
A	1	1	1	1	1	1	1	1	1	1	1	1	1	1
B	2	1	1.786	1	1.786	1	1	1.786	1	1	1	1.786	1	1
C	3	1	2.37	1	1.786	1.327	1	1.786	1	1.327	1	1.786	1.327	1
D	4	1	2.703	1	1.786	1.514	1	1.786	1	1.514	1	1.786	1.327	1.141
E	5	1	3.516	1	1.786	1.969	1	1.786	1	1.969	1	1.786	1.327	1.483
F	1	2	2.117	1	1.704	1.243	1	1.704	0.632	1.965	1	1.704	0.856	1.451
G	2	2	3.515	1	1.786	1.968	1	1.786	1	1.969	1	1.786	1.327	1.483
H	3	2	3.513	1	1.786	1.967	1	1.786	1	1.967	1	1.786	1.327	1.482
I	4	2	2.675	1	1.705	1.569	1	1.705	0.905	1.733	1	1.705	1.181	1.329
J	5	2	3.159	1	1.786	1.769	1	1.786	1	1.769	1	1.786	1.327	1.333
K	1	3	3.11	1.000	1.786	1.742	1.000	1.786	1.000	1.742	1.000	1.786	1.327	1.312
L	2	3	2.76	1.000	1.786	1.546	1.000	1.786	1.000	1.546	1.000	1.786	1.327	1.165
M	3	3	1.879	1.000	1.078	1.743	1.000	1.078	0.997	1.749	1.000	1.078	1.302	1.339
N	4	3	3.516	1.000	1.786	1.969	1.000	1.786	1.000	1.969	1.000	1.786	1.327	1.483
O	5	3	2	1.000	1.388	1.441	1.000	1.388	0.748	1.927	1.000	1.388	0.972	1.483
P	1	4	1.923	1.000	0.984	1.954	1.000	0.984	0.994	1.965	1.000	0.984	1.317	1.483
R	2	4	2.032	1.000	1.173	1.732	1.000	1.173	0.990	1.749	1.000	1.173	1.296	1.336
S	3	4	1.509	1.000	1.195	1.263	1.000	1.195	0.643	1.965	1.000	1.195	1.093	1.156
T	4	4	2.852	1.000	1.786	1.597	1.000	1.786	0.843	1.894	1.000	1.786	1.113	1.435
U	5	4	2.134	1.000	1.230	1.735	1.000	1.230	0.883	1.965	1.000	1.230	1.202	1.443

(continued)

Table 6.18 (continued)

Row	Firm	Period	TFPI	ETI	ITEI	ISMEI	ETI	ITEI	IMEI	RISEI	ETI	ITEI	ISEI	RMEI
V	1	5	3.15	1.000	1.786	1.764	1.000	1.786	1.000	1.764	1.000	1.786	1.327	1.329
W	2	5	2.176	1.000	1.510	1.441	1.000	1.510	0.748	1.927	1.000	1.510	0.972	1.483
X	3	5	1.991	1.000	1.573	1.266	1.000	1.573	0.644	1.965	1.000	1.573	1.093	1.158
Y	4	5	1.351	1.000	0.691	1.956	1.000	0.691	0.996	1.965	1.000	0.691	1.319	1.483
Z	5	5	1.758	1.000	0.893	1.969	1.000	0.893	1.000	1.969	1.000	0.893	1.327	1.483
Geometric mean			2.306	1.000	1.453	1.587	1.000	1.453	0.911	1.743	1.000	1.453	1.203	1.320

[a]TFPI = ETI × ITEI × ISMEI = ETI × ITEI × IMEI × RISEI = ETI × ITEI × ISEI × RMEI. Some index numbers may be incoherent at the third decimal place due to rounding (e.g., in any given row, the product of the ETI, ITEI and ISMEI numbers may not be exactly equal to the TFPI number due to rounding)

[b]Numbers reported to less than three decimal places are exact; see the footnote to Table 1.2 on p. 8

Table 6.19 Output- and input-oriented decompositions of EKS TFPI numbers[a,b]

Row	Firm	Period	TFPI	ETI	OTEI	OSMEI	SNI	ETI	ITEI	ISMEI	SNI
A	1	1	1	1	1	1	1	1	1	1	1
B	2	1	1.889*	1	2.37	0.753	1.058	1	1.786	1	1.058
C	3	1	2.37	1	2.37	1	1	1	1.786	1.327	1
D	4	1	2.799	1	2.37	1.141	1.035	1	1.786	1.514	1.035
E	5	1	3.359*	1	2.37	1.483	0.955	1	1.786	1.969	0.955
F	1	2	1.963	1	2.050	1.033	0.927	1	1.704	1.243	0.927
G	2	2	3.269	1	2.37	1.483	0.93	1	1.786	1.968	0.930
H	3	2	3.728	1	2.37	1.482	1.061	1	1.786	1.967	1.061
I	4	2	1.996	1	2.063	1.297	0.746	1	1.705	1.569	0.746
J	5	2	2.276	1	2.37	1.333	0.720	1	1.786	1.769	0.720
K	1	3	2.883	1.000	2.370	1.312	0.927	1.000	1.786	1.742	0.927
L	2	3	2.916	1.000	2.370	1.165	1.057	1.000	1.786	1.546	1.057
M	3	3	1.840	1.000	1.547	1.215	0.979	1.000	1.078	1.743	0.979
N	4	3	3.629	1.000	2.370	1.483	1.032	1.000	1.786	1.969	1.032
O	5	3	2.350*	1.000	2.000	1.000	1.175	1.000	1.388	1.441	1.175
P	1	4	1.985	1.000	1.408	1.366	1.032	1.000	0.984	1.954	1.032
R	2	4	2.162	1.000	1.590	1.278	1.064	1.000	1.173	1.732	1.064
S	3	4	1.498	1.000	1.381	1.093	0.993	1.000	1.195	1.263	0.993

(continued)

Table 6.19 (continued)

Row	Firm	Period	TFPI	ETI	OTEI	OSMEI	SNI	ETI	ITEI	ISMEI	SNI
T	4	4	2.991	1.000	2.370	1.203	1.049	1.000	1.786	1.597	1.049
U	5	4	2.117	1.000	1.550	1.376	0.992	1.000	1.230	1.735	0.992
V	1	5	2.445	1.000	2.370	1.329	0.776	1.000	1.786	1.764	0.776
W	2	5	2.390*	1.000	2.120	1.026	1.098	1.000	1.510	1.441	1.098
X	3	5	1.719	1.000	1.982	1.004	0.863	1.000	1.573	1.266	0.863
Y	4	5	1.401	1.000	1.223	1.105	1.037	1.000	0.691	1.956	1.037
Z	5	5	1.866*	1.000	2.054	0.856	1.062	1.000	0.893	1.969	1.062
Geometric mean			2.251	1.000	1.962	1.175	0.976	1.000	1.453	1.587	0.976

[a]TFPI = ETI × OTEI × OSMEI × SNI = ETI × ITEI × ISMEI × SNI. Some index numbers may be incoherent at the third decimal place due to rounding (e.g., in any given row, the product of the ETI, ITEI, ISMEI and SNI numbers may not be exactly equal to the TFPI number due to rounding)
[b]Numbers reported to less than three decimal places are exact; see the footnote to Table 1.2 on p. 8
*Incoherent (not because of rounding)

cases, the OTE of manager i in period t should be estimated using observations on all managers in all periods up to and including period t. However, if the technologies used by managers *are* observed, then the OTE of manager i in period t should be estimated using observations on all managers who used a technology *that existed* in period t. If, for example, there are I firms in the dataset, then the envelopment form of the basic DEA estimation problem is

$$\max_{\mu,\lambda_{11},\ldots,\lambda_{IT}} \Big\{\mu : \mu q_{it} \leq \sum_{h=1}^{I}\sum_{r=1}^{T} \lambda_{hr} d_{hrt} q_{hr},\ \sum_{h=1}^{I}\sum_{r=1}^{T} \lambda_{hr} d_{hrt} z_{hr} \leq z_{it},$$
$$\sum_{h=1}^{I}\sum_{r=1}^{T} \lambda_{hr} d_{hrt} x_{hr} \leq x_{it},\ \sum_{h=1}^{I}\sum_{r=1}^{T} \lambda_{hr} d_{hrt} = 1,$$
$$\lambda_{hr} \geq 0 \text{ for all } h \text{ and } r\Big\} \tag{6.66}$$

where $d_{hrt} = I(g_{hr} \in G_t)$ is a dummy variable that takes the value 1 if, in period r, the manager of firm h used a technology that existed in period t (and 0 otherwise). This dummy variable effectively deletes from the dataset any observations on any firms in any periods when the manager did not use a technology that existed in period t. Problem (6.66) can be found in O'Donnell et al. (2017, Eq. 20). The value of μ at the optimum is an estimate of the reciprocal of $OTE^t(x_{it}, q_{it}, z_{it})$. If assumptions PF1 to PF5 are true, then the value of μ that solves problem (6.66) is a more reliable estimate of the reciprocal of $OTE^t(x_{it}, q_{it}, z_{it})$ than the value of μ that solves problem (6.4).

Estimating the measure of ROTE defined by (5.48) involves estimating the g_{it}-th technology-and-environment-specific output distance function. If assumptions PF1 to PF3 are true, then this function takes the form $d_O^{g_{it}}(x_{it}, q_{it}, z_{it}) = (\gamma'_{it} q_{it})/(\alpha_{it} + \delta'_{it} z_{it} + \beta'_{it} x_{it})$ where γ_{it}, α_{it}, δ_{it} and β_{it} are unknown parameters to be estimated. If PF4 and PF5 are also true, then the envelopment form of the estimation problem is

$$\max_{\mu,\lambda_{11},\ldots,\lambda_{IT}} \Big\{\mu : \mu q_{it} \leq \sum_{h=1}^{I}\sum_{r=1}^{T} \lambda_{hr} d_{hrit} q_{hr},\ \sum_{h=1}^{I}\sum_{r=1}^{T} \lambda_{hr} d_{hrit} z_{hr} \leq z_{it},$$
$$\sum_{h=1}^{I}\sum_{r=1}^{T} \lambda_{hr} d_{hrit} x_{hr} \leq x_{it},\ \sum_{h=1}^{I}\sum_{r=1}^{T} \lambda_{hr} d_{hrit} = 1,$$
$$\lambda_{hr} \geq 0 \text{ for all } h \text{ and } r\Big\} \tag{6.67}$$

where $d_{hrit} = I(g_{hr} = g_{it})$ is a dummy variable that takes the value 1 if the manager of firm h used technology g_{it} in period r (and 0 otherwise). This dummy variable effectively deletes from the dataset any observations on any firms in any periods when the manager did not use the technology that manager i used in period t. The value of the objective function at the optimum is an estimate of the reciprocal of $ROTE^{g_{it}}(x_{it}, q_{it}, z_{it})$. This problem can be found in O'Donnell et al. (2017, Eq. 21).

If there is no environmental change, then it is equivalent to problem (17) in Battese et al. (2004, p. 238).

For a numerical example, reconsider the toy data reported in Table 1.1. For purposes of this example, suppose that (a) technologies 1 and 2 existed in each period, (b) no other technologies existed in any period, (c) the managers of firms 1, 2 and 3 always used technology 1, and (d) the managers of firms 4 and 5 always used technology 2. Associated estimates of OTE, ROTE and the OMRs are reported in Table 6.20. The OTE estimates are the estimates reported earlier in the NTC column of Table 6.9. The ROTE estimates were obtained by solving problem (6.67) for each firm/manager in each period. The OMRs were obtained by dividing the OTE estimates by the ROTE estimates (i.e., the OMRs were obtained as residuals). Among other things, the estimates in this table indicate that the manager of firm 1 chose the right technology in period 1 but did not use it properly (i.e., he/she 'chose the right book' but 'did not follow the instructions').

6.6.2 *Inefficiency Models*

Measures of efficiency can be viewed as measures of how well firm managers have solved different optimisation problems. It is common to assume that the underlying causes of optimisation errors are known. For example, theories of bounded rationality tell us that managers make optimisation errors due to lack of knowledge, training and/or experience (see Sect. 4.7.6). Let a_{it} be a vector of predetermined personal attributes (e.g., education, training and/or experience) that affect the optimisation errors that manager i makes in period t. The relationship between these attributes and the estimated inefficiency of the manager can be written as

$$\hat{u}_{it} = g^t(a_{it}) + v_{it} \tag{6.68}$$

where $\hat{u}_{it} \geq 0$ is an estimator for inefficiency, $g^t(.)$ is an approximating function chosen by the researcher, and v_{it} denotes a measure of statistical noise. The unknown parameters of the approximating function can be estimated within a truncated regression framework. In the productivity literature, this modelling approach is often referred to as a two-stage DEA (TSDEA) approach (in the first stage, DEA is used to estimate u_{it}; in the second stage, the relationship between $\hat{u}_{it}$ and a_{it} is estimated within a truncated regression framework). More details on TSDEA estimation can be accessed from Ray (1988), Hoff (2007), Simar and Wilson (2007, 2011b), McDonald (2009), Zelenyuk (2009) and Johnson and Kuosmanen (2011, 2012). It is worth noting that many of these authors implicitly define measures of efficiency in a way that is fundamentally different to the way they are defined in this book. For example, many authors omit characteristics of the production environment from the first stage of the TSDEA estimation procedure. Thus, they implicitly define technical (in)efficiency as a measure of the distance from an observed point to a point on a *period-specific* frontier. In this book, technical (in)efficiency is instead defined

Table 6.20 DEA estimates of OTE, ROTE and OMRs[a,b]

Row	Firm	Period	OTE	OMR	ROTE
A	1	1	0.422	1	0.422
B	2	1	0.610	0.864	0.706
C	3	1	1	1	1
D	4	1	0.949	0.949	1
E	5	1	1	1	1
F	1	2	0.614	0.690	0.889
G	2	2	1	1	1
H	3	2	1	1	1
I	4	2	0.871	1	0.871
J	5	2	1	1	1
K	1	3	1	1	1
L	2	3	0.933	1	0.933
M	3	3	0.643	0.959	0.671
N	4	3	1	1	1
O	5	3	0.844	0.849	0.994
P	1	4	0.594	0.738	0.805
R	2	4	0.671	1	0.671
S	3	4	0.583	0.676	0.862
T	4	4	1	1	1
U	5	4	0.654	1	0.654
V	1	5	1	1	1
W	2	5	0.895	0.988	0.905
X	3	5	0.836	0.836	1
Y	4	5	0.516	0.775	0.665
Z	5	5	0.867	0.867	1
Geometric mean			0.796	0.921	0.865

[a]OTE = OMR × ROTE. Some estimates may be incoherent at the third decimal place due to rounding (e.g., in any given row, the product of the OMR and ROTE estimates may not be exactly equal to the OTE estimate due to rounding)
[b]Numbers reported to less than three decimal places are exact; see the footnote to Table 1.2 on p. 8

as a measure of the distance from an observed point to a point on a *period-and-environment-specific* frontier. The practical implications are profound: if (a) there are any environmental variables involved in the production process, and (b) technical (in)efficiency is defined as a measure of the distance from an observed point to a point on a period-specific frontier, then managers will be held responsible for variables that are outside their control (e.g., good crop farmers will be labelled as technically inefficient when relatively low yields are due to low rainfall).

6.7 Summary and Further Reading

The most common piecewise frontier models (PFMs) are underpinned by five assumptions: assumption PF1 says that production possibilities sets can be represented by distance, revenue, cost and/or profit functions; assumption PF2 says that all relevant quantities, prices and environmental variables are observed and measured without error; assumption PF3 says that production frontiers are piecewise linear; assumption PF4 says that outputs, inputs and environmental variables are strongly disposable; and assumption PF5 says that production possibilities sets are convex. If these assumptions are true, then production frontiers and most measures of efficiency can be estimated using linear programming (LP). The associated models are commonly known as data envelopment analysis (DEA) models. The idea behind DEA can be traced back at least as far as Farrell (1957) and Farrell and Fieldhouse (1962). According to Färe et al. (1994, p. 12), the formulation of DEA estimation problems as LP problems is due to Boles (1966), Bressler (1966), Seitz (1966) and Sitorus (1966). For more details on the origins of DEA, see Forsund and Sarafoglou (2002). This chapter has focused on relatively simple PFMs that can be used to estimate the measures of efficiency defined in Chap. 5.

Output-oriented PFMs are mainly used to estimate measures of output-oriented technical efficiency (OTE), output-oriented technical and mix efficiency (OTME), and output-oriented mix efficiency (OME). If assumptions PF1 to PF5 are true, then estimates of OTE can be obtained by solving problem (19) in O'Donnell et al. (2017). If the data are cross-section data and there are no environmental variables involved in the production process (i.e., if there is no environmental change), then that particular problem reduces to a problem that can be found in Färe et al. (1994, p. 103). PFMs for estimating OTME can be traced back to O'Donnell (2010b, p. 560). Piecewise frontier estimates of OME can be obtained by dividing estimates of OTME by estimates of OTE (i.e., OME estimates can be obtained as residuals). For empirical applications of output-oriented PFMs to macroeconomic data (i.e., to data that have been aggregated to the industry or total economy level), see, for example, Burley (1980), Färe et al. (2001), Kumar and Russell (2002), Milner and Weyman-Jones (2003), Färe et al. (2004a), Demchuk and Zelenyuk (2009) and Shiu and Zelenyuk (2012); for an application to crop farms, see Tozer and Villano (2013); for an application to banks, see Curi et al. (2013); for an application to electric utilities, see Färe et al. (1989); for an application to nursing homes, see Chattopadhyay and Heffley (1994).

Input-oriented PFMs are mainly used to estimate measures of input-oriented technical efficiency (ITE), input-oriented technical and mix efficiency (ITME), and input-oriented mix efficiency (IME). If assumptions PF1 to PF5 are true, then estimates of ITE can be obtained by solving problem (A9) in O'Donnell et al. (2017). If the data are cross-section data and there is no environmental change, then that particular problem reduces to problem (19) in Banker et al. (1984). PFMs for estimating ITME can be traced back to O'Donnell (2010b, Eq. 6.15). Piecewise frontier estimates of

IME can be obtained by dividing estimates of ITME by estimates of ITE (i.e., IME estimates can be obtained as residuals).

Revenue-oriented PFMs are mainly used to estimate measures of revenue efficiency (RE) and output-oriented allocative efficiency (OAE). Estimating RE involves estimating the maximum revenue that can be obtained using given inputs in given periods in given production environments. Estimates of RE can then be obtained by dividing observed revenues by estimates of maximum revenue. PFMs for estimating maximum revenue can traced back at least as far as Färe et al. (1985, Eq. 4.7.7). If firms are price takers in output markets and estimates of OTE are available, then estimates of OAE can be obtained by dividing estimates of RE by estimates of OTE.

Cost-oriented PFMs are mainly used to estimate measures of cost efficiency (CE) and input-oriented allocative efficiency (IAE). Estimating CE involves estimating the minimum cost of producing given outputs in given periods in given production environments. Estimates of CE can then be obtained by dividing estimates of minimum cost by observed costs. PFMs for estimating minimum cost can traced back at least as far as Färe et al. (1985, Eq. 3.7.5). If estimates of ITE are available, then estimates of IAE can be obtained by dividing estimates of CE by estimates of ITE.

Profit-oriented PFMs are mainly used to estimate measures of profit efficiency (PE). This involves estimating the maximum profit that can be obtained in given periods in given production environments. Estimates of PE can then be obtained by dividing observed profits by estimates of maximum profit. PFMs for estimating maximum profit can traced back at least as far as Färe et al. (1990). If firms are price takers in output and input markets, then estimates of PE and OTE can be used to obtain estimates of output-oriented scale and allocative efficiency (OSAE). On the input side, if firms are price takers in output and input markets, then estimates of PE and ITE can be used to obtain estimates of input-oriented scale and allocative efficiency (ISAE). For an empirical application of profit-oriented PFMs to airlines, see Coelli et al. (2002); for an application to crop farms, see Färe et al. (1990); for applications to banks, see Färe et al. (2004b), Portela and Thanassoulis (2005) and Koutsomanoli-Filippaki et al. (2012); for applications to pulp and paper mills, see Brännlund et al. (1995) and Brännlund et al. (1998).

Productivity-oriented PFMs are mainly used to estimate measures of technical, scale and mix efficiency (TSME). They can also be used to estimate measures of technical and scale efficiency (TSE). Estimating measures of TSME involves estimating the maximum TFP possible in given periods in given production environments. Estimates of TSME can then be obtained by dividing observed levels of TFP by estimates of maximum TFP. Estimating measures of TSE involves estimating the maximum TFP possible when using scalar multiples of given input vectors to produce scalar multiples of given output vectors in given periods in given production environments. Again, estimates of TSE can then be obtained by dividing observed levels of TFP by estimates of maximum TFP. PFMs for estimating maximum TFP can traced back at least as far as O'Donnell (2010b). Piecewise frontier estimates of residual mix efficiency (RME) can be obtained by dividing estimates of TSME by estimates of TSE (i.e., RME estimates can be obtained as residuals). If estimates of OTE are available, then estimates of output-oriented scale efficiency (OSE) can be obtained by dividing estimates of TSE by estimates of OTE (i.e., OSE estimates can be obtained as residuals). If estimates of ITE are available, then estimates of input-oriented scale efficiency (ISE) can be obtained by dividing estimates of TSE by estimates of ITE (i.e., ISE estimates can also be obtained as residuals).

It is possible to relax assumptions PF2 to PF5. Models that relax PF2 include the semiparametric stochastic frontier models of Fan et al. (1996), Huang and Fu (1999), Kumbhakar et al. (2007) and Kuosmanen and Kortelainen (2012). Models that relax PF3 include the piecewise double-log frontier model of Banker et al. (1981). Models that relax PF4 include the models of 'input congestion' discussed by Färe et al. (1983), Färe and Grosskopf (1998, 2000, 2001), Cooper et al. (2000, 2001), Zhu (2009, Ch. 9) and Briec et al. (2016, 2018). Models that relax PF5 are known as free disposal hull (FDH) models; these models can be traced back to Deprins et al. (1984).

In practice, it is more common to estimate PFMs under *stronger* assumptions than PF1 to PF5. For example, the popular output-oriented DEA model of Charnes et al. (1978, Eq. 3) is based on the additional assumption that production frontiers exhibit CRS. The input-oriented DEA model of Banker et al. (1984, Eq. 9) is also based on the assumption that production frontiers exhibit CRS. Seiford and Thrall (1990, p. 15) present DEA models that are based on the assumption that production frontiers exhibit either NDRS or NIRS; Kerstens and Vanden Eeckaut (1999) present FDH models that are based on these alternative returns to scale assumptions. Finally, if assumption PF4 is true, then the slope coefficients in output distance functions must be nonnegative. It is possible to strengthen PF4 by requiring these coefficients to lie within certain bounds. Models with so-called weight restrictions can be accessed from Allen et al. (1997), Podinovski (2004a, b, 2007) and Podinovski and Bouzdine-Chameeva (2013).

If the assumptions underpinning PFMs are true, then, under weak regularity conditions concerning the probability density functions (PDFs) of the (in)efficiency effects, piecewise frontier estimators for (in)efficiency are consistent. Results of this type can be found in Banker (1993), Korostelev et al. (1995), Kneip et al. (1998, 2015), Gijbels et al. (1999), Park et al. (2000) and Simar and Wilson (2013, Sect. 2.5). These results provide a basis for conducting asymptotic inference. If the PDFs of measures of inefficiency are known, then we can use standard statistical methods for this purpose. If the PDFs of measures of inefficiency are *not* known, then we can use bootstrapping methods. In this chapter, the focus has been on methods for (a) constructing confidence intervals for measures of efficiency, (b) testing for differences in average efficiency, and (c) testing assumptions about production technologies. Several other asymptotic hypothesis testing procedures can be found in the literature. For example, if the PDFs of measures of inefficiency are not known, then it is possible to test for differences in PDFs across groups using nonparametric tests proposed by Li (1996, 1999) and bootstrapping tests proposed by Li (1999) and Simar and Zelenyuk (2006). For historical background on using PFMs for inference, see Grosskopf (1996). For more details on asymptotic test procedures, see Banker (1996). For more details on bootstrap procedures, see Kneip et al. (2008, 2011, 2015) and Simar and Wilson (1998, 2000, 2013, 2011a, 2015).

PFMs can be used to both measure and explain changes in TFP. *Measuring* changes in TFP involves computing proper TFP index (TFPI) numbers. PFMs cannot generally be used to compute primal or dual index numbers. However, they can be used to compute additive and multiplicative index numbers. *Explaining* changes in TFP generally involves decomposing proper TFPI numbers into measures of environmental change, technical change, and efficiency change. Several decompositions are available. *Productivity-oriented* decompositions involve decomposing TFPI numbers into measures of environmental change, technical change and *productivity-oriented* measures of efficiency change (i.e., changes in TSME, TSE and RME). *Output-oriented* decompositions involve decomposing TFPI numbers into measures of environmental change, technical change and *output-oriented* measures of efficiency change (i.e., changes in OTE, OTME, OSME, OME, OSE and ROSE). *Input-oriented* decompositions involve decomposing TFPI numbers into measures of environmental change, technical change and *input-oriented* measures of efficiency change (i.e., changes in ITE, ITME, ISME, IME, ISE and RISE). In principle, PFMs can be used to decompose any proper TFPI numbers into these different measures. However, to avoid the need to solve nonlinear programming problems, they are mainly used to decompose additive TFPI numbers: for an empirical application involving macroeconomic data, see Laurenceson and O'Donnell (2014); for applications in agriculture, see O'Donnell (2012), Rahman and Salim (2013), Tozer and Villano (2013), Islam et al. (2014), Khan et al. (2015), Temoso et al. (2015), Baležentis (2015), Mugera et al. (2016), Anik et al. (2017) and Baráth and Fertö (2017); for applications to banks, see Mohammad (2015) and Nguyen and Simioni (2015); for an application to universities, see Carrington et al. (2016); for an application to ports, see Kumtong et al. (2017).

There are many TFPI numbers that are not proper in the sense that they cannot generally be written as proper output index numbers divided by proper input index numbers. Examples include Fisher, Törnqvist, Hicks-Moorsteen, Malmquist, EKS and CCD TFPI numbers. If decision makers view measures of productivity change as measures of output quantity change divided by measures of input quantity change, then it is not clear why they would be interested in TFPI numbers of this type. Putting this issue to one side, one way of decomposing such numbers is to first write them as the product of proper TFPI numbers and statistical noise index (SNI) numbers. Subsequently, PFMs can be used to decompose the proper TFPI numbers into measures of technical change, environmental change and various measures of efficiency change. For alternative decomposition methodologies that involve PFMs but do not explicitly involve SNI numbers, see, for example, Färe et al. (1994), Suhariyanto and Thirtle (2001), Kuosmanen and Sipiläinen (2009), Pastor et al. (2011) and Afsharian and Ahn (2015).

Other models that are widely used in the piecewise frontier literature include metafrontier models and inefficiency-effects models. Metafrontier models are used in situations where firm managers can be classified into two or more groups, and where managers in different groups choose input-output combinations from potentially different production possibilities sets. Estimation of basic piecewise metafrontier models can be traced back to Charnes et al. (1981). For a discussion of assumption

PF5 (convexity) in a metafrontier context, see Kerstens et al. (2015) and Afsharian and Podinovski (2018). For empirical applications of piecewise metafrontier models in agriculture, see O'Donnell et al. (2008) and Beltran-Esteve et al. (2014); for applications to banks, see Casu et al. (2013), Johnes et al. (2014) and Huang et al. (2015); for an application to schools, see Charnes et al. (1981); for an application to electricity generators, see Zhang et al. (2013); for an application to highway maintenance contractors, see O'Donnell et al. (2017). Finally, inefficiency-effects models are regression models that can be used to explain variations in estimates of inefficiency. In the productivity literature, inefficiency-effects models are generally estimated within a two-stage DEA (TSDEA) framework (in the first stage, piecewise frontier estimators are used to estimate inefficiency; in the second stage, the relationship between inefficiency and its determinants is estimated within a truncated regression framework). For an empirical application of TSDEA methodology to universities, see Carrington et al. (2005).

References

Afsharian M, Ahn H (2015) The overall Malmquist index: a new approach for measuring productivity changes over time. Ann Oper Re 226(1):1–27

Afsharian M, Podinovski V (2018) A linear programming approach to efficiency evaluation in nonconvex metatechnologies. Eur J Oper Res 268(1):268–280

Allen R, Athanassopoulos A, Dyson R, Thanassoulis E (1997) Weight restrictions and value judgements in data envelopment analysis: evolution, development and future directions. Ann Oper Res 73:13–34

Anik AR, Rahman S, Sarker J (2017) Agricultural productivity growth and the role of capital in South Asia (1980–2013). Sustainability 9(3):470

Baležentis T (2015) The sources of the total factor productivity growth in Lithuanian family farms: A Färe-Primont index approach. Prague Econ Papers 24(2):225–241

Banker R (1993) Maximum likelihood, consistency and data envelopment analysis: a statistical foundation. Manag Sci 39(10):1265–1273

Banker R (1996) Hypothesis tests using data envelopment analysis. J Prod Anal 7(2–3):139–159

Banker R, Charnes A, Cooper W (1984) Some models for estimating technical and scale inefficiencies in data envelopment analysis. Manag Sci 30(9):1078–1092

Banker RD, Charnes A, Cooper WW, Schinnar AP (1981) A bi-extremal principle for frontier estimation and efficiency evaluations. Manag Sci 27(12):1370–1382

Baráth L, Fertö I (2017) Productivity and convergence in European agriculture. J Agri Econ 68(1):228–248

Battese G, Rao D, O'Donnell C (2004) A metafrontier production function for estimation of technical efficiencies and technology gaps for firms operating under different technologies. J Prod Anal 21(1):91–103

Beltran-Esteve M, Gomez-Limon J, Picazo-Tadeo A, Reig-Martinez E (2014) A metafrontier directional distance function approach to assessing eco-efficiency. J Prod Anal 41:69–83

Bogetoft P, Otto L (2015) Benchmarking: benchmark and frontier analysis using DEA and SFA. R package version 2015-7-8

Boles J (1966) Efficiency squared-efficient computation of efficiency indexes. In: Thirty Ninth annual meeting of the Western farm economics association, pp 137–142

Brännlund R, Färe R, Grosskopf S (1995) Environmental regulation and profitability: an application to Swedish pulp and paper mills. Environ Resour Econ 6:23–36

Brännlund R, Chung Y, Färe R, Grosskopf S (1998) Emissions trading and profitability: the Swedish pulp and paper industry. Environ Resour Econ 12:345–356

Bressler R (1966) The measurement of productive efficiency. In: Thirty Ninth annual meeting of the Western farm economics association, pp 129–136

Briec W, Kerstens K, Van de Woestyne I (2016) Congestion in production correspondences. J Econ 119(1):65–90

Briec W, Kerstens K, Van de Woestyne I (2018) Hypercongestion in production correspondences: an empirical exploration. Appl Econ 50(27):2938–2956

Burley H (1980) Productive efficiency in U.S. manufacturing: a linear programming approach. Rev Econ Stat 62(4):619–622

Carrington R, Coelli T, Rao D (2005) The performance of Australian universities: conceptual issues and preliminary results. Econ Papers 24(2):145–163

Carrington R, O'Donnell C, Rao D (2016) Australian university productivity growth and public funding revisited. Stud High Educ 1–22: https://doi.org/10.1080/03075,079.2016.1259,306

Casu B, Ferrari A, Zhao T (2013) Regulatory reform and productivity change in Indian banking. Rev Econ Stat 95(3):1066–1077

Charnes A, Cooper W (1962) Programming with linear fractional functionals. Naval Res Logistics Q 9(3–4):181–186

Charnes A, Cooper W, Rhodes E (1978) Measuring the efficiency of decision-making unit. Eur J Oper Res 2(6):429–444 (see also "Corrections" op.cit. 3(4):339)

Charnes A, Cooper W, Rhodes E (1981) Evaluating program and managerial efficiency: an application of data envelopment analysis to Program follow through. Manag Sci 27(6):668–697

Chattopadhyay S, Heffley D (1994) Are for-profit nursing homes more efficient? Data envelopment analysis with a case-mix constraint. East Econ J 20(2):171–186

Coelli T, Grifell-Tatje E, Perelman S (2002) Capacity utilisation and profitability: a decomposition of short-run profit efficiency. Int J Prod Econ 79(3):261–278

Coelli T, Rao D, O'Donnell C, Battese G (2005) An introduction to efficiency and productivity analysis, 2nd edn. Springer, New York

Cooper W, Seiford L, Zhu J (2000) A unified additive model approach for evaluating inefficiency and congestion with associated measures in DEA. Socio-Econ Plann Sci 34(1):1–25

Cooper W, Seiford L, Zhu J (2001) Slacks and congestion: response to a comment by R. Fare and S. Grosskopf. Socio-Econ Plann Sci 35(3):205–215

Curi C, Guarda P, Lozano-Vivas A, Zelenyuk V (2013) Is foreign-bank efficiency in financial centers driven by home or host country characteristics? J Prod Anal 40:367–385

Demchuk P, Zelenyuk V (2009) Testing differences in efficiency of regions within a country: the case of Ukraine. J Prod Anal 32(2):81–102

Deprins D, Simar L, Tulkens H (1984) Measuring labor efficiency in post offices. In: Marchand M, Pestieau P, Tulkens H (eds) The performance of public enterprises: concepts and measurements. North Holland Publishing Company, Amsterdam

Fan Y, Li Q, Weersink A (1996) Semiparametric estimation of stochastic production frontier models. J Bus Econ Stat 14(4):460–468

Färe R, Grosskopf S (1998) Congestion: a note. Socio-Econ Plann Sci 32(1):21–23

Färe R, Grosskopf S (2000) Slacks and congestion: a comment. Socio-Econ Plann Sci 34(1):27–33

Färe R, Grosskopf S (2001) When can slacks be used to identify congestion? An answer to W. W. Cooper, L. Seiford and J. Zhu. Socio-Econ Plann Sci 35(3):217–221

Färe R, Grosskopf S, Logan J (1983) The relative efficiency of Illinois electric utilities. Resour Energy 5(4):349–367

Färe R, Grosskopf S, Lovell C (1985) The measurement of efficiency of production. Kluwer Academic Publishers, Boston

Färe R, Grosskopf S, Kokkelenberg E (1989) Measuring plant capacity, utilization and technical change: a non-parametric approach. Int Econ Rev 30(3):655–666

Färe R, Grosskopf S, Lee H (1990) A nonparametric approach to expenditure constrained profit maximization. Am J Agri Econ 72(3):574–581

Färe R, Grosskopf S, Lovell C (1994) Production frontiers. Cambridge University Press, Cambridge
Färe R, Grosskopf S, Norris M, Zhang Z (1994) Productivity growth, technical progress, and efficiency change in industrialized countries. Am Econ Rev 84(1):66–83
Färe R, Grosskopf S, Lee WF (2001) Productivity and technical change: the case of Taiwan. Appl Econ 33(15):1911–1925
Färe R, Grosskopf S, Hernandez-Sancho F (2004a) Environmental performance: an index number approach. Resour Energy Econ 26(4):343–352
Färe R, Grosskopf S, Weber W (2004b) The effect of risk-based capital requirements on profit efficiency in banking. Appl Econ 36(15):1–13
Farrell M (1957) The measurement of productive efficiency. J R Stat Soc Ser A (General) 120(3):253–290
Farrell M, Fieldhouse M (1962) Estimating efficient production functions under increasing returns to scale. J R Stat Soc Ser A (General) 125(2):252–267
Forsund F, Sarafoglou N (2002) The origins of data envelopment analysis. J Prod Anal 17(1):23–40
Gijbels I, Mammen E, Park B, Simar L (1999) On estimation of monotone and concave frontier functions. J Am Stat Assoc 94(445):220–228
Grosskopf S (1996) Statistical inference and nonparametric efficiency: a selective survey. J Prod Anal 7:161–176
Hoff A (2007) Second stage DEA: comparison of approaches for modelling the DEA score. Eur J Oper Res 181(1):425–435
Huang C, Fu TT (1999) An average derivative estimation of stochastic frontier. J Prod Anal 12:45–53
Huang MY, Juo JC, Fu TT (2015) Metafrontier cost Malmquist productivity index: an application to Taiwanese and Chinese commercial banks. J Prod Anal 44:321–335
Islam N, Xayavong V, Kingwell R (2014) Broadacre farm productivity and profitability in south-western Australia. Aust J Agri Resour Econ 58(2):147–170
Johnes J, Izzeldin M, Pappas V (2014) A comparison of performance of Islamic and conventional banks 2004–2009. J Econ Behav Organ 103(Supplement):S93–S107
Johnson A, Kuosmanen T (2011) One-stage estimation of the effects of operational conditions and practices on productive performance: asymptotically normal and efficient, root-n consistent StoNEZD method. J Prod Anal 36(2):219–230
Johnson A, Kuosmanen T (2012) One-stage and two-stage DEA estimation of the effects of contextual variables. Eur J Oper Res 220(2):559–570
Kerstens K, Vanden Eeckaut P (1999) Estimating returns to scale using non-parametric deterministic technologies: a new method based on goodness-of-fit. Eur J Oper Res 113(1):206–214
Kerstens K, O'Donnell C, Van de Woestyne I (2015) Frontier metatechnologies and convexity: a restatement. Document de travail du LEM 2015-08, Universit'e de Lille
Khan F, Salim R, Bloch H (2015) Nonparametric estimates of productivity and efficiency change in Australian broadacre agriculture. Aust J Agri Resour Econ 59(3):393–411
Kneip A, Park B, Simar L (1998) A note on the convergence of nonparametric DEA estimators for production efficiency scores. Econometric Theory 14(6):783–793
Kneip A, Simar L, Wilson P (2008) Asymptotics and consistent bootstraps for DEA estimators in nonparametric frontier models. Econometric Theory 24:1663–1697
Kneip A, Simar L, Wilson P (2011) A computationally efficient, consistent bootstrap for inference with non-parametric DEA estimators. Comput Econ 38(4):483–515
Kneip A, Simar L, Wilson P (2015) When bias kills the variance: central limit theorems for DEA and FDH efficiency scores. Econometric Theory 31(2):394–422
Korostelev A, Simar L, Tsybakov A (1995) Efficient estimation of monotone boundaries. Ann Stat 23(2):476–489
Koutsomanoli-Filippaki A, Margaritis D, Staikouras C (2012) Profit efficiency in the European Union banking industry: a directional technology distance function approach. J Prod Anal 37:277–293
Kumar S, Russell R (2002) Technological change, technological catch-up, and capital deepening: relative contributions to growth and convergence. Am Econ Rev 92(3):527–548

Kumbhakar S, Park B, Simar L, Tsionas E (2007) Nonparametric stochastic frontiers: a local maximum likelihood approach. J Econometrics 137(1):1–27

Kumtong R, Saosaovaphak A, Chaiboonsri C (2017) Measuring the total factor productivity for international seaport in South East Asia (ASEAN). J Adv Res Soc Sci Humanit 2(3):154–167

Kuosmanen T, Kortelainen M (2012) Stochastic non-smooth envelopment of data: semi-parametric frontier estimation subject to shape constraints. J Prod Anal 38(1):11–28

Kuosmanen T, Sipiläinen T (2009) Exact decomposition of the Fisher ideal total factor productivity index. J Prod Anal 31(3):137–150

Laurenceson J, O'Donnell CJ (2014) New estimates and a decomposition of provincial productivity change in China. China Econ Rev 30:86–97

Li Q (1996) Nonparametric testing of closeness between two unknown distribution functions. Econometric Rev 15(3):261–274

Li Q (1999) Nonparametric testing the similarity of two unknown density functions: local power and bootstrap analysis. J Nonparametric Stat 11:189–213

McDonald J (2009) Using least squares and tobit in second stage DEA efficiency analyses. Eur J Oper Res 197(2):792–798

Milner C, Weyman-Jones T (2003) Relative national efficiency and country size: evidence for developing countries. Rev Dev Econ 7(1):1–14

Mohammad A (2015) Analysis of total factor productivity change among Indian commercial banks using Fare-Primont index. Asian J Res Banking Finance 5(2):183–193

Mugera A, Langemeier M, Ojede A (2016) Contributions of productivity and relative price change to farm-level profitability change. Am J Agri Econ 98(4):1210–1229

Nguyen PA, Simioni M (2015) Productivity and efficiency of Vietnamese banking system: new evidence using Färe-Primont index analysis. Appl Econ 47(41):4395–4407

O'Donnell C (2010a) DPIN version 1.0: A program for decomposing productivity index numbers. Centre for efficiency and productivity analysis working papers WP01/2010, University of Queensland

O'Donnell C (2010b) Measuring and decomposing agricultural productivity and profitability change. Aust J Agri Resour Econ 54(4):527–560

O'Donnell C (2012) Nonparametric estimates of the components of productivity and profitability change in U.S. agriculture. Am J Agri Econ 94(4):873–890

O'Donnell C, Nguyen K (2013) An econometric approach to estimating support prices and measures of productivity change in public hospitals. J Prod Anal 40(3):323–335

O'Donnell C, Rao D, Battese G (2008) Metafrontier frameworks for the study of firm-level efficiencies and technology ratios. Empirical Econ 34(2):231–255

O'Donnell C, Fallah-Fini S, Triantis K (2017) Measuring and analysing productivity change in a metafrontier framework. J Prod Anal 47(2):117–128

Park B, Simar L, Weiner C (2000) The FDH estimator for productivity efficiency scores. Econometric Theory 16(6):855–877

Pastor J, Asmild M, Lovell C (2011) The biennial Malmquist productivity change index. Socio-Econ Plann Sci 45(1):10–15

Podinovski V (2004a) Production trade-offs and weight restrictions in data envelopment analysis. J Oper Res Soc 55(12):1311–1322

Podinovski V (2004b) Suitability and redundancy of non-homogeneous weight restrictions for measuring the relative efficiency in DEA. Eur J Oper Res 154:380–395

Podinovski V (2007) Computation of efficient targets in DEA models with production trade-offs and weight restrictions. Eur J Oper Res 181(2):586–591

Podinovski V, Bouzdine-Chameeva T (2013) Weight restrictions and free production in data envelopment analysis. Oper Res 61(2):426–437

Portela M, Thanassoulis E (2005) Profitability of a sample of Portuguese bank branches and its decomposition into technical and allocative components. Eur J Oper Res 162(3):850–866

Rahman S, Salim R (2013) Six decades of total factor productivity change and sources of growth in Bangladesh agriculture (1948–2008). J Agri Econ 64(2):275–294

Ray S (1988) Data envelopment analysis: nondiscretionary inputs and efficiency: an alternative interpretation. Socio-Econ Plann Sci 22(4):167–176

Seiford L, Thrall R (1990) Recent developments in DEA: the mathematical programming approach to frontier analysis. J Econometrics 46(1–2):7–38

Seitz W (1966) Efficiency measures for steam-electric generating plants. In: Thirty Ninth annual meeting of the Western farm economics association, pp 143–151

Shiu A, Zelenyuk V (2012) Production efficiency versus ownership. In: van Keilegom I, Wilson P (eds) Exploring research frontiers in contemporary statistics and econometrics. Springer, chap 2, pp 23–44

Simar L, Wilson P (1998) Sensitivity analysis of efficiency scores: how to bootstrap in nonparametric frontier models. Manag Sci 44(1):49–61

Simar L, Wilson P (2000) Statistical inference in nonparametric frontier models: the state of the art. J Prod Anal 13(1):49–78

Simar L, Wilson P (2007) Estimation and inference in two-stage, semi-parametric models of production processes. J Econometrics 136:31–64

Simar L, Wilson P (2011a) Inference by the m out of n bootstrap in nonparametric frontier models. J Prod Anal 36(1):33–53

Simar L, Wilson P (2011b) Two-stage DEA: Caveat emptor. J Prod Anal 36(2):205–218

Simar L, Wilson P (2013) Estimation and inference in nonparametric frontier models: recent developments and perspectives. Found Trends Econometrics 5(3–4):183–337

Simar L, Wilson P (2015) Statistical approaches for non-parametric frontier models: a guided tour. Int Stat Rev 83(1):77–110

Simar L, Zelenyuk V (2006) On testing equality of distributions of technical efficiency scores. Econometric Rev 25(4):497–522

Sitorus B (1966) Productive efficiency and redundant factors of production in traditional agriculture of underdeveloped countries. In: Thirty Ninth annual meeting of the Western farm economics association, pp 153–158

Suhariyanto K, Thirtle C (2001) Asian agricultural productivity and convergence. J Agri Econ 52(3):96–110

Temoso O, Villano R, Hadley D (2015) Agricultural productivity, efficiency and growth in a semi-arid country: a case study of Botswana. Afr J Agri Resour Econ 10(3):192–206

Tozer P, Villano R (2013) Decomposing productivity and efficiency among Western Australian grain producers. J Agri Resour Econ 38(3):312–326

Tulkens H, Vanden Eeckaut P (1995) Non-parametric efficiency, progress and regress measures for panel data: methodological aspects. Eur J Oper Res 80:474–499

Zelenyuk V (2009) Power of significance test of dummy variables in two-stage efficiency analysis model. Appl Econ Lett 16(15):1493–1495

Zhang N, Zhou P, Choi Y (2013) Energy efficiency, CO_2 emission performance and technology gaps in fossil fuel electricity generation in Korea: a meta-frontier non-radial directional distance function analysis. Energy Policy 56(May):653–662

Zhu J (2009) Quantitative models for performance evaluation and benchmarking: data envelopment analysis with spreadsheets, 2nd edn. Springer

Chapter 7
Deterministic Frontier Analysis

Production frontiers are often represented by distance, revenue, cost and/or profit functions. These functions can sometimes be written in the form of regression models in which the explanatory variables are deterministic (i.e., not random). This chapter explains how to estimate and draw inferences concerning the unknown parameters in so-called deterministic frontier models (DFMs). It then explains how the estimated parameters can be used to predict levels of efficiency and analyse productivity change. The focus is on least squares estimators and predictors. The idea behind least squares estimation of DFMs can be traced back to Winsten (1957).

7.1 Basic Models

DFMs are underpinned by the following assumptions:

DF1 production possibilities sets can be represented by distance, revenue, cost and/or profit functions;

DF2 all relevant quantities, prices and environmental variables are observed and measured without error; and

DF3 the functional forms of relevant functions are known.

If these assumptions are true, then production frontiers can be estimated using single-equation regression models with error terms representing inefficiency.

7.1.1 Output-Oriented Models

Output-oriented DFMs are mainly used to estimate the measure of OTE defined by (5.1). They can also be used to estimate the measures of OTME and OME defined by (5.2) and (5.3).

C. J. O'Donnell, *Productivity and Efficiency Analysis*,
https://doi.org/10.1007/978-981-13-2984-5_7

Estimating the measure of OTE defined by (5.1) involves estimating the output distance function. If they exist, then output distance functions are linearly homogeneous in outputs. This implies that $D_O^t(x_{it}, q_{it}, z_{it}) = q_{1it} D_O^t(x_{it}, q_{it}^*, z_{it})$ where $q_{it}^* \equiv q_{it}/q_{1it}$ denotes a vector of normalised outputs (the choice of the first output as the normalising output is arbitrary). Equivalently,

$$\ln q_{1it} = -\ln D_O^t(x_{it}, q_{it}^*, z_{it}) - u_{it} \tag{7.1}$$

where $u_{it} \equiv -\ln OTE^t(x_{it}, q_{it}, z_{it}) \geq 0$ denotes an output-oriented technical inefficiency effect. OTE is a relevant measure of managerial performance in situations where inputs and output mixes have been predetermined. If environmental variables have also been predetermined, then u_{it} is uncorrelated with x_{it}, q_{it}^* and z_{it}.

Assumption DF3 says the functional forms of output distance functions are known. In the efficiency literature, it is common[1] to assume they are either translog or double-log functions. If outputs and inputs are strongly disposable, then they cannot be translog functions.[2] If there is more than one output and output sets are bounded, then they cannot be double-log functions.[3] If outputs and inputs are strongly disposable and output sets are bounded, then the class of possible output distance functions includes (2.9). The output-oriented DFM associated with (2.9) is

$$\ln q_{1it} = \alpha(t) + \sum_{j=1}^{J} \delta_j \ln z_{jit} + \sum_{m=1}^{M} \beta_m \ln x_{mit} - \frac{1}{\tau} \ln \left(\sum_{n=1}^{N} \gamma_n q_{nit}^{*\tau} \right) - u_{it} \tag{7.2}$$

where $\alpha(t) \equiv \ln A(t)$. This model is nonlinear in the unknown parameters. However, if $\gamma_1, \ldots, \gamma_N$ and τ are known, then it can be rewritten as

$$\ln Q(q_{it}) = \alpha(t) + \sum_{j=1}^{J} \delta_j \ln z_{jit} + \sum_{m=1}^{M} \beta_m \ln x_{mit} - u_{it} \tag{7.3}$$

---

[1]See, for example, Greene (1980b, Eq. 1), Färe et al. (1993, Eq. 14), Grosskopf et al. (1995, Eq. 11), Coelli and Perelman (1999, Eq. 5), Ray (1998, Eq. 21), Fuentes et al. (2001, Eq. 3), Orea (2002, Eq. 5), Reig-Martinez et al. (2001, Eq. 13), O'Donnell and Coelli (2005, Eq. 5), Vardanyan and Noh (2006, Eq. 3.1), Ferrari (2006, Eq. 2), Zhang and Garvey (2008, Eq. 9) and Diewert and Fox (2010, p. 82).

[2]If outputs and inputs are strongly disposable, then the output distance function is nondecreasing in outputs and nonincreasing in inputs for all feasible input-output combinations. If the output distance function is a translog function, then it is possible to find feasible input-output combinations where these monotonicity properties do not hold. Ergo, the output distance function cannot be a translog function. If there is more than one output and the output distance function is a translog function, then there exists a feasible input-output combination where at least one shadow revenue share lies outside the unit interval.

[3]If there is more than one output and the output distance function is a double-log function, then output sets are unbounded (O'Donnell 2016, p. 330).

where $Q(q_{it}) = \left(\sum_{n=1}^{N} \gamma_n q_{nit}^{\tau}\right)^{1/\tau}$ is an aggregate output. This model is linear in the parameters. In this model, $\alpha(t)$ is an output-oriented measure of technical progress, δ_j is an unsigned elasticity that measures the percent change in the aggregate output due to a one percent increase in the j-th environmental variable, and β_m is a nonnegative elasticity that measures the percent increase in the aggregate output due to a one percent increase in the m-th input. If there is no technical progress, then $\alpha(t)$ does not, in fact, vary with t. If there are no environmental variables involved in the production process (i.e., if there is no environmental change), then the term involving the environmental variables can be deleted. If there is no technical progress and no environmental change, then (7.3) reduces to a DFM that has the same structure as the models of Richmond (1974, p. 517) and Schmidt (1976, Eq. 2). If there are only two inputs, then the Richmond and Schmidt models reduce to the model of Aigner and Chu (1968, Eqs. 3.4, 3.5).

Finally, output-oriented DFMs can also be used to estimate measures of OTME and OME. Whether this can be done analytically, rather than numerically, depends on the output aggregator function and the output distance function. If, for example, the output aggregator function is a linear function and the output distance function is given by (2.9), then measures of OTME and OME can be estimated using the analytical results presented in Sect. 5.1.4.

7.1.2 Input-Oriented Models

Input-oriented DFMs are mainly used to estimate the measure of ITE defined by (5.8). They can also be used to estimate the measures of ITME and IME defined by (5.9) and (5.10).

Estimating the measure of ITE defined by (5.8) involves estimating the input distance function. If they exist, then input distance functions are linearly homogeneous in inputs. This implies that $D_I^t(x_{it}, q_{it}, z_{it}) = x_{1it} D_I^t(x_{it}^*, q_{it}, z_{it})$ where $x_{it}^* \equiv x_{it}/x_{1it}$ denotes a vector of normalised inputs (the choice of the first input as the normalising input is arbitrary). Equivalently, after some simple algebra,

$$- \ln x_{1it} = \ln D_I^t(x_{it}^*, q_{it}, z_{it}) - u_{it} \tag{7.4}$$

where, in a slight abuse of notation, $u_{it} \equiv - \ln ITE^t(x_{it}, q_{it}, z_{it}) \geq 0$ now denotes an input-oriented technical inefficiency effect. ITE is a relevant measure of managerial performance in situations where outputs and input mixes have been predetermined. If environmental variables have also been predetermined, then u_{it} is uncorrelated with x_{it}^*, q_{it} and z_{it}.

Again, assumption DF3 says the functional forms of input distance functions are known. Again, it is common[4] to assume they are either translog or double-log

[4]See, for example, Diewert (1980, p. 462), Deprins et al. (1984, p. 292), Althin et al. (1996, Eq. 2.1), Coelli and Perelman (1999, Eq. 10), Coelli et al. (2003, p. 44), Tsekouras et al. (2004, p. 98),

functions. If outputs and inputs are strongly disposable, then they cannot be translog functions.[5] If there is more than one output and output sets are bounded, then they cannot be double-log functions.[6] If outputs and inputs are strongly disposable and output sets are bounded, then the class of possible input distance functions includes (2.13). The input-oriented DFM associated with (2.13) is

$$-\ln x_{1it} = \xi(t) + \sum_{j=1}^{J} \kappa_j \ln z_{jit} + \sum_{m=1}^{M} \lambda_m \ln x^*_{mit} - \frac{1}{\tau\eta} \ln\left(\sum_{n=1}^{N} \gamma_n q^{\tau}_{nit}\right) - u_{it} \quad (7.5)$$

where $\xi(t) \equiv \ln B(t)$. This model is nonlinear in the unknown parameters. However, if $\gamma_1, \ldots, \gamma_N$ and τ are known, then it can be rewritten as

$$-\ln x_{1it} = \xi(t) + \sum_{j=1}^{J} \kappa_j \ln z_{jit} + \sum_{m=2}^{M} \lambda_m \ln x^*_{mit} - \psi \ln Q(q_{it}) - u_{it} \quad (7.6)$$

where $Q(q_{it}) = \left(\sum_{n=1}^{N} \gamma_n q^{\tau}_{nit}\right)^{1/\tau}$ is an aggregate output and $\psi \equiv 1/\eta$ is the reciprocal of the elasticity of scale. This model is linear in the parameters. In this model, $\xi(t)$ is an input-oriented measure of technical progress, κ_j is an unsigned elasticity that measures the percent change in all inputs due to a one percent increase in the j-th environmental variable, and λ_m is a shadow cost share that lies in the closed unit interval. If there is no technical progress, then $\xi(t)$ is time-invariant. If there is no environmental change, then the term involving the environmental variables can be deleted.

Finally, input-oriented DFMs can also be used to estimate measures of ITME and IME. Whether this can be done analytically, rather than numerically, depends on the input distance function and the input aggregator function. If, for example, the input distance function is given by (2.13) and the input aggregator function is a linear function with positive weights, then measures of ITME and IME can be estimated using the analytical results presented in Sect. 5.2.4.

Hajargasht et al. (2008, Eq. 9), Stern (2010, p. 351), Das and Kumbhakar (2012, p. 211) and Coelli et al. (2013, Eq. 3).

[5]If outputs and inputs are strongly disposable, then the input distance function is nonincreasing in outputs and nondecreasing in inputs for all feasible input-output combinations. If the input distance function is a translog function, then it is possible to find feasible input-output combinations where these monotonicity properties do not hold. Ergo, the input distance function cannot be a translog function. If there is more than one input and the input distance function is a translog function, then there exists a feasible input-output combination where at least one shadow cost share lies outside the unit interval.

[6]If the input distance function is a double-log function, then the output distance function is also a double-log function. If there is more than one output and the output distance function is a double-log function, then output sets are unbounded (O'Donnell 2016, p. 330).

7.1.3 Revenue-Oriented Models

Revenue-oriented DFMs are mainly used to estimate the measure of RE defined by (5.15). This involves estimating the revenue function. The particular revenue function in (5.15) is linearly homogeneous in prices. This implies that $R^t(x_{it}, p_{it}, z_{it}) = p_{1it}R^t(x_{it}, p^*_{it}, z_{it})$ where $p^*_{it} \equiv p_{it}/p_{1it}$ denotes a vector of normalised output prices (the choice of the first price as the normalising price is arbitrary). Equivalently, after some simple algebra,

$$\ln(R_{it}/p_{1it}) = \ln R^t(x_{it}, p^*_{it}, z_{it}) - u_{it} \tag{7.7}$$

where $u_{it} \equiv -\ln RE^t(x_{it}, p_{it}, q_{it}, z_{it}) \geq 0$ now denotes a revenue inefficiency effect. The measure of RE defined by (5.15) is a relevant measure of managerial performance in situations where firms are price takers in output markets and inputs have been predetermined. If environmental variables have also been predetermined, then u_{it} is uncorrelated with x_{it}, p^*_{it} and z_{it}.

Again, assumption DF3 says the functional forms of revenue functions are known. Again, it is common[7] to assume they are either translog or double-log functions. If firms are price takers in output markets, then they cannot be translog functions.[8] If (a) firms are price takers in output markets, (b) there is more than one output, and (c) output sets are bounded, then they cannot be double-log functions.[9] If firms are price takers in output markets and output sets are bounded, then the class of possible revenue functions includes (2.17). The revenue-oriented DFM associated with (2.17) is

$$\begin{aligned} \ln(R_{it}/p_{1it}) = \alpha(t) &+ \sum_{j=1}^{J} \delta_j \ln z_{jit} + \sum_{m=1}^{M} \beta_m \ln x_{mit} \\ &+ \frac{1}{1-\sigma} \ln\left(\sum_{n=1}^{N} \gamma_n^{\sigma} p_{nit}^{*1-\sigma}\right) - u_{it} \end{aligned} \tag{7.8}$$

where $\alpha(t) \equiv \ln A(t)$. This model is nonlinear in the unknown parameters. However, if $\gamma_1, \ldots, \gamma_N$ and σ are known, then it can be rewritten as

[7] See, for example, Banker et al. (2003, Eq. 5).

[8] If firms are price takers in output markets, then the revenue function is nondecreasing in p for all nonnegative x. If the revenue function is a translog function, then there exists a nonnegative p and a nonnegative x where this monotonicity property does not hold. Ergo, the revenue function cannot be a translog function. If (a) firms are price takers in output markets, (b) there is more than one output, and (c) the revenue function is a translog function, then there exists a nonnegative p and a nonnegative x where at least one revenue-maximising revenue share lies outside the unit interval.

[9] If firms are price takers in output markets and the revenue function is a double-log function, then the output distance function is also a double-log function. If there is more than one output and the output distance function is a double-log function, then output sets are unbounded (O'Donnell 2016, p. 330).

$$\ln(R_{it}/P(p_{it})) = \alpha(t) + \sum_{j=1}^{J} \delta_j \ln z_{jit} + \sum_{m=1}^{M} \beta_m \ln x_{mit} - u_{it} \tag{7.9}$$

where $P(p_{it}) = \left(\sum_{n=1}^{N} \gamma_n^{\sigma} p_{nit}^{1-\sigma}\right)^{1/(1-\sigma)}$ is an aggregate output price. This model is linear in the parameters. In this model, $\alpha(t)$ is a revenue-oriented measure of technical progress, δ_j is an unsigned elasticity that measures the percent change in normalised revenue due to a one percent increase in the j-th environmental variable, and β_m is a nonnegative elasticity that measures the percent increase in normalised revenue due to a one percent increase in the m-th input. If there is no technical progress, then $\alpha(t)$ is time-invariant. If there is no environmental change, then the term involving the environmental variables can be deleted.

7.1.4 Cost-Oriented Models

Cost-oriented DFMs are mainly used to estimate the measure of CE defined by (5.20). This involves estimating the cost function. The particular cost function in (5.20) is linearly homogeneous in prices. This implies that $C^t(w_{it}, q_{it}, z_{it}) = w_{1it} C^t(w_{it}^*, q_{it}, z_{it})$ where $w_{it}^* \equiv w_{it}/w_{1it}$ denotes a vector of normalised input prices (the choice of the first price as the normalising price is arbitrary). Equivalently, after some simple algebra,

$$-\ln(C_{it}/w_{1it}) = -\ln C^t(w_{it}^*, q_{it}, z_{it}) - u_{it} \tag{7.10}$$

where $u_{it} \equiv -\ln CE^t(w_{it}, x_{it}, q_{it}, z_{it}) \geq 0$ now denotes a cost inefficiency effect. The measure of CE defined by (5.20) is a relevant measure of managerial performance in situations where firms are price takers in input markets and outputs have been predetermined. If environmental variables have also been predetermined, then u_{it} is uncorrelated with w_{it}^*, q_{it} and z_{it}.

Again, assumption DF3 says the functional forms of cost functions are known. Again, it is common[10] to assume they are either translog or double-log functions. If firms are price takers in input markets, then they cannot be translog functions.[11] If (a) firms are price takers in input markets, (b) there is more than one output, and

[10]See, for example, Greene (1980b, Eq. 3), Kopp and Diewert (1982, p. 328), Banker et al. (1986, Eq. 1), Baltagi and Griffin (1988, Eq. 4), Kumbhakar (1997, Eq. 11), Nadiri and Nandi (1999, p. 489), Kumbhakar and Lovell (2000, Eq. 4.2.27) and Zheng and Bloch (2014, p. 207).

[11]If firms are price takers in input markets, then the cost function is nondecreasing in w for all producible q. If the cost function is a translog function, then there exists a nonnegative w and a producible q where this monotonicity property does not hold. Ergo, the cost function cannot be a translog function. If (a) firms are price takers in input markets, (b) there is more than one input, and (c) the cost function is a translog function, then there exists a nonnegative w and a producible q where at least one cost-minimising cost share lies outside the unit interval.

(c) output sets are bounded, then they cannot be double-log functions.[12] If firms are price takers in input markets and output sets are bounded, then the class of possible cost functions includes (2.22). The cost-oriented DFM associated with (2.22) is

$$-\ln(C_{it}/w_{1it}) = \theta(t) + \sum_{j=1}^{J} \kappa_j \ln z_{jit} - \sum_{m=1}^{M} \lambda_m \ln w^*_{mit} - \frac{1}{\tau\eta} \ln\left(\sum_{n=1}^{N} \gamma_n q^{\tau}_{nit}\right) - u_{it} \tag{7.11}$$

where $\theta(t) \equiv \ln B(t) + \sum_m \lambda_m \ln \lambda_m$. This model is nonlinear in the unknown parameters. However, if $\gamma_1, \ldots, \gamma_N$ and τ are known, then it can be rewritten as

$$-\ln(C_{it}/w_{1it}) = \theta(t) + \sum_{j=1}^{J} \kappa_j \ln z_{jit} - \sum_{m=1}^{M} \lambda_m \ln w^*_{mit} - \psi \ln Q(q_{it}) - u_{it} \tag{7.12}$$

where $Q(q_{it}) = \left(\sum_{n=1}^{N} \gamma_n q^{\tau}_{nit}\right)^{1/\tau}$ is an aggregate output and $\psi \equiv 1/\eta$ is the reciprocal of the elasticity of scale. This model is linear in the parameters. In this model, $\theta(t)$ can be interpreted as a cost-oriented measure of technical progress, κ_j is an unsigned elasticity that measures the percent change in normalised cost due to a one percent increase in the j-th environmental variable, and λ_m is a nonnegative elasticity that measures the percent increase in normalised cost due to a one percent increase in the m-th normalised input price. If there is no technical progress, then $\theta(t)$ is time-invariant. If there is no environmental change, then the term involving the environmental variables can be deleted.

7.1.5 Profit-Oriented Models

Profit-oriented DFMs are mainly used to estimate the measure of PE defined by (5.27). This involves estimating the profit function. The particular profit function in (5.27) is linearly homogeneous in prices. This implies that $\Pi^t(w_{it}, p_{it}, z_{it}) = p_{1it}\Pi^t(w^*_{it}, p^*_{it}, z_{it})$ where $w^*_{it} \equiv w_{it}/p_{1it}$ denotes a vector of normalised input prices and $p^*_{it} \equiv p_{it}/p_{1it}$ denotes a vector of normalised output prices (the choice of the first output price as the normalising price is arbitrary). If firms make positive profits, then, after some simple algebra, this relationship can be rewritten as

$$\ln(\Pi_{it}/p_{1it}) = \ln \Pi^t(w^*_{it}, p^*_{it}, z_{it}) - u_{it} \tag{7.13}$$

---

[12]If firms are price takers in input markets and the cost function is a double-log function, then the output distance function is also a double-log function. If there is more than one output and the output distance function is a double-log function, then output sets are unbounded (O'Donnell 2016, p. 330).

where $u_{it} \equiv -\ln PE^t(w_{it}, x_{it}, p_{it}, q_{it}, z_{it}) \geq 0$ now denotes a profit inefficiency effect. The measure of PE defined by (5.27) is a relevant measure of managerial performance in situations where firms are price takers in output and input markets. If firms are price takers in output and input markets and environmental variables have been predetermined, then u_{it} is uncorrelated with w^*_{it}, p^*_{it} and z_{it}.

Again, DF3 says the functional forms of profit functions are known. Again, it is common[13] to assume that profit functions are either translog or double-log functions. If firms are price takers in output and input markets, then they cannot be translog functions.[14] In these cases, the class of possible profit functions includes (2.27). The profit-oriented DFM associated with (2.27) is

$$\ln(\Pi_{it}/p_{1it}) = \phi(t) + \frac{1}{(1-\eta)}\left(\sum_{j=1}^{J}\delta_j \ln z_{jit} - \sum_{m=1}^{M}\beta_m \ln w^*_{mit}\right) + \frac{1}{(1-\sigma)(1-\eta)}\ln\left(\sum_{n=1}^{N}\gamma_n^{\sigma}(p^*_{nit})^{1-\sigma}\right) - u_{it} \quad (7.14)$$

where $\phi(t) \equiv \ln(1-\eta) + (\ln A(t) + \sum_m \beta_m \ln \beta_m)/(1-\eta)$. This model is nonlinear in the unknown parameters. However, if $\gamma_1, \ldots, \gamma_N$ and σ are known, then it can be rewritten as

$$\ln(\Pi_{it}/p_{1it}) = \phi(t) + \sum_{j=1}^{J}\delta^*_j \ln z_{jit} - \sum_{m=1}^{M}\beta^*_m \ln w^*_{mit} + \psi^* \ln P(p^*_{it}) - u_{it} \quad (7.15)$$

where $P(p^*_{it}) = \left(\sum_{n=1}^{N}\gamma_n^{\sigma}(p^*_{nit})^{1-\sigma}\right)^{1/(1-\sigma)}$ is a normalised aggregate output price, $\delta^*_j \equiv \delta_j/(1-\eta)$ is an unsigned elasticity that measures the percent change in normalised profit due to a one percent increase in the j-th environmental variable, $\beta^*_m \equiv \beta_m/(1-\eta)$ is a nonnegative elasticity that measures the percent decrease in normalised profit due to a one percent increase in the m-th normalised input price, and $\psi^* \equiv 1/(1-\eta)$ is a nonnegative elasticity that measures the percent increase in normalised profit due to a one percent increase in the normalised aggregate output price. This model is linear in the parameters. In this model, $\phi(t)$ can be viewed as a profit-oriented measure of technical progress. If there is no technical progress, then $\phi(t)$ is time-invariant. If there is no environmental change, then the term involving the environmental variables can be deleted.

---

[13] See, for example, Diewert (1980, Eq. 8), Kumbhakar and Bhattacharyya (1992, Eq. 8), Chaudhary et al. (1999, Eq. 1), Kumbhakar (2001, Eqs. 7, 8) and Kumbhakar (2006, p. 254).

[14] If firms are price takers in output and input markets, then profit functions are nondecreasing in p for all nonnegative w. If the profit function is a translog function, then there exists a nonnegative w where this monotonicity property does not hold. Ergo, the profit function cannot be a translog function. If (a) firms are price takers in output and input markets, (b) there is more than one output, and (c) the profit function is a translog function, then there exists a nonnegative w where at least one profit-maximising revenue share lies outside the unit interval.

7.2 Growth Accounting Estimation

Growth accounting (GA) 'estimation' typically involves making enough restrictive assumptions about production technologies and managerial behaviour to allow most of the unknown parameters in DFMs to be identified. The basic idea can be traced back at least as far as Solow (1957).

7.2.1 Assumptions

It is common[15] to assume that

GA1 output and input sets are homothetic,
GA2 technical change is Hicks-neutral,
GA3 production frontiers exhibit constant returns to scale,
GA4 inputs are strongly disposable,
GA5 firms are price takers in input markets,
GA6 input prices are strictly positive, and
GA7 firm managers successfully minimise cost.

If these assumptions are true, then the slope parameters in production functions can usually be estimated using differential calculus. The associated estimates/predictions of technical and cost efficiency are equal to one.

7.2.2 Estimation

If DF1 to DF3 and GA1 to GA4 are true, then $Q(q_{it}) = A^t(z_{it})F(x_{it})D_O^t(x_{it}, q_{it}, z_{it})$ where $Q(q_{it})$ can be viewed as an aggregate output, $A^t(z_{it})$ can be viewed as a measure of technical and environmental change, $F(x_{it})$ can be viewed as an aggregate input, and $D_O^t(x_{it}, q_{it}, z_{it})$ is a measure of technical efficiency.[16] If GA5 to GA7 are also true, then $D_O^t(x_{it}, q_{it}, z_{it}) = 1$.[17] Thus, DF1 to DF3 and GA1 to GA7 together imply that

$$Q(q_{it}) = A^t(z_{it})F(x_{it}). \tag{7.16}$$

[15]Some authors make these assumptions implicitly. For example, Hsieh and Klenow (2009, Eq. 4) assume that production functions are double-log functions with observation-invariant slope coefficients that are positive and sum to one. This implies GA1 to GA4.

[16]GA1 to GA3 imply that $Q(q_{it}) = A^t(z_{it})F(x_{it})D_O^t(x_{it}, q_{it}, z_{it})$ where $F(.)$ is a nonnegative,, linearly-homogenous, scalar-valued function (see Proposition 17 in Appendix A.1). GA4 implies that $F(.)$ is also nondecreasing. Thus, it can be viewed as an aggregate input.

[17]GA5 to GA7 imply that $D_I^t(x_{it}, q_{it}, z_{it}) = 1$ (see Sect. 4.4.2). GA3 implies that $D_O^t(x_{it}, q_{it}, z_{it}) = 1/D_I^t(x_{it}, q_{it}, z_{it})$ (see the discussion of O10 and DO10 in Sects. 2.1.1 and 2.4.1).

If there is no environmental change, then z_{it} can be deleted. In this case, (7.16) reduces to a DFM that has the same basic structure, but not necessarily the same interpretation,[18] as the 'production function' of Solow (1957, Eq. 1a). In practice, our ability to estimate the components on the right-hand side of (7.16) depends on the (known) functional form of the output distance function. If the output distance function is given by (2.9), for example, then

$$Q(q_{it}) = A^t(z_{it}) \prod_{m=1}^{M} x_{mit}^{\beta_m} \tag{7.17}$$

where $\sum_m \beta_m = 1$. In this case, differential calculus can be used to show that $\beta_m = s_m$ where s_m is the m-th cost-minimising cost share. Assumption GA7 implies that observed cost shares are equal to cost-minimising cost shares. This means that the input component in (7.17) can be computed as a GY input index that compares x_{it} with a vector of ones. If the aggregate output is observed, then the technical and environmental change component can be computed as a residual. Measures of technical and environmental change that have been computed in this way are often referred to as 'Solow residuals'. If DF1 to DF3 and GA1 to GA7 are all true, then Solow residuals can be viewed as measures of TFP. If any input cost shares are firm- or time-varying, then DF1 to DF3 and GA1 to GA7 cannot all be true.

7.2.3 *Toy Example*

Reconsider the toy input quantity and price data reported earlier in Tables 1.1 and 1.5. Associated input cost shares are reported in Table 7.1. The fact that these shares vary across firms and over time implies that DF1 to DF3 and GA1 to GA7 cannot all be true. Thus, these data cannot be properly analysed in a GA framework.

7.3 Least Squares Estimation

Least squares (LS) estimation of DFMs involves choosing the unknown parameters to minimise the sum of squared inefficiency effects. The idea can be traced back at least as far as Winsten (1957). For simplicity, this section considers estimation of the following output-oriented model:

---

[18]If there is no environmental change, then $A^t(z_{it})$ reduces to a measure of technical change only. In this book, the term 'technical change' refers to the discovery of new technologies. In contrast, Solow (1957) uses the term 'technical change' "as a shorthand expression for *any kind of shift* in the production function. Thus, slowdowns, speedups, improvements in the education of the labor force, and all sorts of things will appear as [technical change]" (p. 312).

Table 7.1 Input cost shares

Row	Firm	Period	s_1	s_2
A	1	1	0.128	0.872
B	2	1	0.275	0.725
C	3	1	0.128	0.872
D	4	1	0.369	0.631
E	5	1	0.093	0.907
F	1	2	0.723	0.277
G	2	2	0.729	0.271
H	3	2	0.012	0.988
I	4	2	0.997	0.003
J	5	2	0.999	0.001
K	1	3	0.128	0.872
L	2	3	0.273	0.727
M	3	3	0.226	0.774
N	4	3	0.177	0.823
O	5	3	0.615	0.385
P	1	4	0.369	0.631
R	2	4	0.421	0.579
S	3	4	0.677	0.323
T	4	4	0.395	0.605
U	5	4	0.489	0.511
V	1	5	0.271	0.729
W	2	5	0.325	0.675
X	3	5	0.822	0.178
Y	4	5	0.250	0.750
Z	5	5	0.679	0.321

$$y_{it} = \alpha + \lambda t + \sum_{j=1}^{J} \delta_j \ln z_{jit} + \sum_{m=1}^{M} \beta_m \ln x_{mit} - u_{it} \tag{7.18}$$

where y_{it} denotes the logarithm of an aggregate output and u_{it} denotes an output-oriented technical inefficiency effect. This equation can be viewed as a special case of (7.3) corresponding to $\alpha(t) = \alpha + \lambda t$. To estimate the unknown parameters, we need to make some assumptions about the inefficiency effects.

7.3.1 Assumptions

It is common to assume that u_{it} is a random variable with the following properties:

LS1 $E(u_{it}) = \mu \geq 0$ for all i and t,
LS2 $var(u_{it}) \propto \sigma_u^2$ for all i and t,
LS3 $cov(u_{it}, u_{ks}) = 0$ if $i \neq k$ or $t \neq s$, and
LS4 u_{it} is uncorrelated with the explanatory variables.

LS1 says the inefficiency effects have the same mean. LS2 says they are homoskedastic. LS3 says they are serially and spatially uncorrelated. LS4 is self-explanatory.

7.3.2 Estimation

If LS1 is true, then (7.18) can be rewritten as

$$y_{it} = \alpha^* + \lambda t + \sum_{j=1}^{J} \delta_j \ln z_{jit} + \sum_{m=1}^{M} \beta_m \ln x_{mit} + e_{it} \tag{7.19}$$

where $\alpha^* = \alpha - \mu$ is a fixed parameter and $e_{it} = \mu - u_{it}$ is a random variable with a mean of zero. This equation has the same basic structure as the multiple regression model discussed in introductory econometrics textbooks. If LS1 to LS4 are true, then the ordinary least squares (OLS) estimators for α^* and the slope parameters are unbiased and consistent. A consistent estimator for α is $\hat{\alpha} = \hat{\alpha}^* + \hat{\mu}$ where $\hat{\alpha}^*$ denotes the OLS estimator for α^* and $\hat{\mu}$ denotes the maximum of the OLS residuals. In this book, $\hat{\alpha}$ and the OLS estimators for the slope parameters are collectively referred to as corrected ordinary least squares (COLS) estimators.[19] The idea behind COLS estimation is illustrated in Fig. 7.1. The dots in this figure represent the logarithms of a set of simulated input-output combinations. The dotted line is the OLS line of best fit; it passes through the centre of the scatterplot. The solid line is the COLS estimate of the production frontier; by design, it runs parallel to the OLS line of best fit and envelops all the points in the scatterplot.

It is common to impose linear equality restrictions on the parameters in models such as (7.18). If the restrictions (and LS1 to LS4) are true, then restricted least squares (RLS) estimators for the slope parameters are consistent. Again, a consistent estimator for the intercept can be obtained by adjusting (or correcting) the RLS estimator

---

[19]Elsewhere in the deterministic frontier literature, the term 'COLS' is often used to refer to slightly different estimators. These alternative estimators involve adjusting α^* upwards by an amount that depends on the probability distributions of the inefficiency effects. In this book, these alternative estimators are referred to as modified ordinary least squares (MOLS) estimators. The idea behind MOLS estimation of DFMs can be traced back at least as far as Richmond (1974). A problem with MOLS estimators is that some observations may lie above the estimated frontier. For more details, see Førsund et al. (1980, p. 12).

Fig. 7.1 COLS estimation

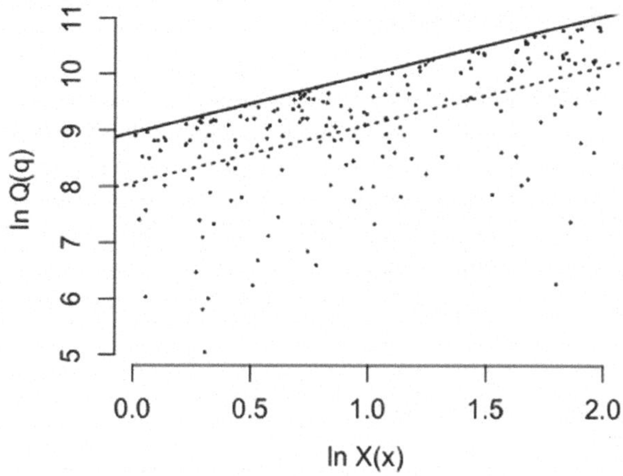

for the intercept by an amount equal to the maximum of the RLS residuals. In this book, the associated estimators are collectively referred to as corrected restricted least squares (CRLS) estimators.

Finally, Eq. (7.18) is linear in the unknown parameters. Some DFMs are *nonlinear* in the unknown parameters. If such a model contains an intercept term and LS1 to LS4 are true, then nonlinear least squares (NLS) estimators for the slope parameters are consistent.[20] Again, a consistent estimator for the intercept can be obtained by adjusting the NLS estimator for the intercept by an amount equal to the maximum of the NLS residuals. In this book, the associated estimators are collectively referred to as corrected nonlinear least squares (CNLS) estimators.

7.3.3 Prediction

We have been using u_{it} to denote the inefficiency of firm i in period t. The associated measure of efficiency is $\exp(-u_{it})$. A common predictor for u_{it} is $\hat{u}_{it} = \hat{\mu} - \hat{e}_{it}$ where $\hat{e}_{it}$ is the it-th OLS residual. The associated predictor for $\exp(-u_{it})$ is $\exp(-\hat{u}_{it})$. Amsler et al. (2013) show that if u_{it} is an independent exponential random variable, then it is possible to conduct exact finite-sample inference concerning u_{it} and $\exp(-u_{it})$. If the distribution of u_{it} is unknown, then it may still be possible to conduct asymptotically-valid inference using subsampling.

[20]For more details concerning the properties of NLS estimators, see, for example, Hill et al. (2011, p. 362).

7.3.4 Hypothesis Tests

It is common to test hypotheses about characteristics of production technologies by testing hypotheses about the parameters in DFMs. It is also common to test some or all of assumptions LS1 to LS4; tests of these assumptions are tests for fixed effects, heteroskedasticity, autocorrelation and endogeneity (respectively). If the data are time-series or panel data, then it is advisable to test whether any of the explanatory variables in the model are difference-stationary. If so, then it is advisable to test whether the dependent and explanatory variables are cointegrated.

7.3.4.1 Parameters

Suppose, for example, that we use a sample of size N to estimate the K intercept and slope parameters in (7.19). If LS1 to LS4 are true, then t and F tests concerning these parameters are asymptotically valid. If, for example, we want to conduct a t test of the null hypothesis that $\beta_m = c$, then we must compute the following statistic:

$$t = \frac{b_m - c}{se(b_m)} \tag{7.20}$$

where b_m denotes the LS estimator for β_m and $se(b_m)$ denotes its standard error. If the null hypothesis is true, then this statistic is asymptotically distributed as a standard normal random variable. The decision rule depends on the form of the alternative hypothesis: if the alternative hypothesis is $\beta_m \neq c$, for example, then we should reject the null hypothesis at the α level of significance if N is large and $|t| > z_{(1-\alpha/2)}$.

To conduct an F test of the null hypothesis that J independent equality restrictions concerning the parameters are true against the alternative that at least one restriction is not true, we must compute the following statistic:

$$F = \frac{(SSE_R - SSE_U)/J}{SSE_U/(N-K)} \tag{7.21}$$

where SSE_R denotes the restricted sum of squared errors (obtained by estimating the parameters subject to the restrictions specified under the null hypothesis) and SSE_U denotes the unrestricted sum of squared errors (obtained by estimating the parameters without any restrictions). If the null hypothesis is true, then this statistic is asymptotically distributed as a chi-squared random variable with J degrees of freedom. Thus, we should reject the null hypothesis at the α level of significance if N is large and $F > \chi^2_{(1-\alpha,J)}$.

7.3.4.2 Fixed Effects

Assumption LS1 says that the inefficiency effects have the same mean. Different tests of this assumption are distinguished by the form of the alternative hypothesis. A common alternative hypothesis is that, for all i, $E(u_{it}) = \mu_i \geq 0$ for all t. If this is true, then (7.18) can be rewritten as

$$y_{it} = \alpha_i^* + \lambda t + \sum_{j=1}^{J} \delta_j \ln z_{jit} + \sum_{m=1}^{M} \beta_m \ln x_{mit} + e_{it} \tag{7.22}$$

where $\alpha_i^* = \alpha - \mu_i$ is a firm-specific fixed effect and $e_{it} = \mu_i - u_{it}$ is a random variable with a mean of zero. This equation has the same basic structure as the standard fixed effects model discussed in introductory econometrics textbooks; see, for example, Hill et al. (2011, Eq. 15.8). If there are I firms in the dataset, then the unknown parameters in (7.22) can be estimated by replacing α^* in (7.19) with I firm-specific dummy variables. A test of the null hypothesis that all the dummy variable coefficients are equal to each other is equivalent to a test of the null hypothesis that LS1 is true. If LS2 to LS4 are true, then an F test of this hypothesis is asymptotically valid.

7.3.4.3 Heteroskedasticity

Assumption LS2 says that the inefficiency effects have the same variance. If LS2 is not true then the inefficiency effects are heteroskedastic. In this case, the COLS estimators are inefficient and their variances are not given by the usual OLS formulas. Again, different tests of LS2 are distinguished by the form of the alternative hypothesis (i.e., the form of heteroskedasticity). The type of heteroskedasticity that is typically discussed in econometrics textbooks is one in which the error terms have the same mean but different variances. There are not many ways in which this type of heteroskedasticity can arise in a DFM.[21] Tests that can be used in these rare cases include well-known tests developed by Glesjer (1969), Goldfeld and Quandt (1972), Godfrey (1978b), Breusch and Pagan (1979) (hereafter BP) and White (1980). Most of these tests involve regressing even functions[22] of LS residuals on transformations of the regressors. Koenker and Bassett (1982) find that these tests perform poorly under certain departures from normality. They propose an alternative test that rejects the null hypothesis of homokedasticity if estimates of the slope coefficients differ significantly at different percentiles. A similar test has been proposed by Newey and Powell (1987). The idea behind these percentile-based tests is illustrated in Fig. 7.2.

---

[21] This type of heteroskedasticity can arise when the inefficiency effects are gamma random variables and the scale parameters are the reciprocals of the shape parameters. It is also possible to imagine some types of group heteroskedasticity where the inefficiency effects have the same mean.

[22] A function $f(.)$ is even if $f(x) = f(-x)$ for all x and $-x$ in the domain of $f(.)$. Examples include $f(x) = |x|$ and $f(x) = x^2$.

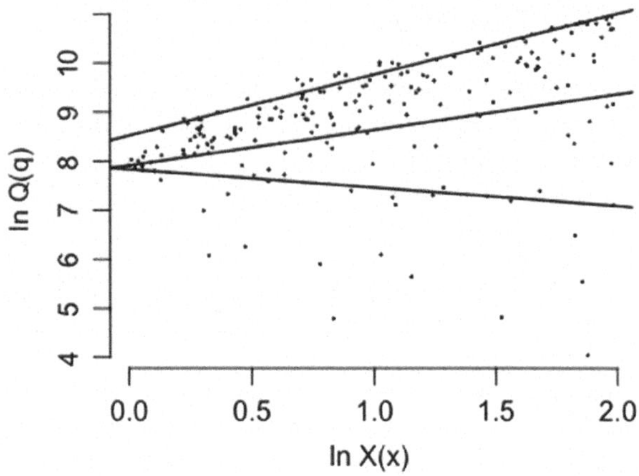

Fig. 7.2 Using quantile regression to detect heteroskedasticity

The dots in this figure represent the logarithms of a set of simulated input-output combinations. The three lines are quantile regression (QR) estimates of the frontier at the 10-th, 25-th and 90-th percentiles. The fanlike pattern in this figure is an indication that the inefficiency effects are heteroskedastic. In practice, very few efficiency researchers test for heteroskedasticity; the modern approach is to use the COLS estimators and simply compute robust (i.e., heteroskedasticity-consistent) standard errors.

7.3.4.4 Autocorrelation

Assumption LS3 says that the inefficiency effects are serially and spatially uncorrelated. If LS3 is not true, then the inefficiency effects are said to be autocorrelated. In this case, the COLS estimators are again inefficient and their variances are not given by the usual OLS formulas. Again, different tests of LS3 are distinguished by the form of the alternative hypothesis. Well-known tests for serial correlation in time-series models include tests developed by Durbin and Watson (1950, 1951) (hereafter DW), Breusch (1978), Breusch and Pagan (1980) and Godfrey (1978a). A DW-type test for serial correlation in panel data models has been developed by Bhargava et al. (1982). Tests for cross-section dependence in panel data models have been developed by Pesaran (2004). Again, in practice, very few efficiency researchers test for autocorrelation; the modern approach is to use the COLS estimators and simply compute robust (i.e., autocorrelation-consistent) standard errors.

7.3.4.5 Endogeneity

Assumption LS4 says that the inefficiency effects are uncorrelated with the explanatory variables. If this assumption is not true, then the explanatory variables are said to be endogenous. If the explanatory variables are endogenous, then, unless the dependent and explanatory variables in the model are cointegrated, the COLS estimators are biased and inconsistent.

If we suspect that B explanatory variables in the model are endogenous, then we should try and find at least B variables that (a) do not have a direct effect on the dependent variable, (b) are correlated with the B suspicious explanatory variables, and (c) are not correlated with the inefficiency effects. Such variables are called instrumental variables (or simply 'instruments'). If we can find enough instruments, then we can conduct a Hausman test for endogeneity. The idea behind a Hausman test is to find an estimator for the slope parameters that is consistent under the null hypothesis but not under the alternative (e.g., OLS), and a second estimator that is consistent under both the null and the alternative (e.g., the IV/TSLS estimator discussed immediately below). If the two estimators yield very different estimates of the slope parameters, then the null hypothesis is likely to be false. In the present context, an easy way to conduct a Hausman test is to complete the following steps:

1. Use OLS to regress each endogenous explanatory variable on all available instruments and exogenous explanatory variables. Save the residuals from each regression.
2. Add the residuals from step 1 to the original model and estimate the resulting artificial model by OLS.
3. Use an F test to test the null hypothesis that the coefficients of the residuals in the artificial model are all zero (against the alternative that at least one of them is not zero).

The test in step 3 is equivalent to a test of LS4. If we reject LS4, then one approach to estimating the parameters is to repeat step 1 and save the *predictions* from each regression. We can then replace the endogenous variables in the original model with the predictions and estimate the new model using OLS. This two-stage estimation procedure is known as an instrumental variables (IV) or two-stage least squares (TSLS) estimation. If the instruments are not correlated with the inefficiency effects (and LS1 to LS3 are true), then the IV/TSLS estimators for the parameters in (7.19) are consistent. The variances of the IV/TSLS estimators are messy nonincreasing functions of the squared correlations between the instruments and the endogenous variables. In practice, the estimated variances and standard errors are best computed using purpose-built IV/TSLS commands in econometrics software packages.

Two other hypothesis tests are relevant in this context. First, if the instruments are not correlated with the inefficiency effects, then they are said to be valid. A test of the null hypothesis that all available instruments are valid (against the alternative that at least one of them is not) is known as a test for overidentifying restrictions. If there are L available instruments and N observations in the dataset, then we can conduct the test using the following steps:

1. Use the IV/TSLS estimator (and all L instruments) to estimate the model and save the residuals.
2. Regress the residuals on the L instruments (only) and use the R^2 from this regression to compute $LM = N \times R^2$.

3. Reject the null hypothesis at the α level of significance if $LM > \chi^2_{(1-\alpha,L-B)}$.

Second, if the instruments are strongly (resp. weakly) correlated with the endogenous variables, then they are said to be strong (resp. weak). If there is only one endogenous variable in the model, then we can assess the strength of the available instruments using the following steps:

1. Use OLS to regress the endogenous explanatory variable on all available instruments and exogenous explanatory variables (this is the same regression we would run if we were completing step 1 of a Hausman test).
2. Use an F test to test the null hypothesis that the coefficients of the instruments are zero (against the alternative that at least one of them is not zero).

The test in step 2 is equivalent to a test of the null hypothesis that all available instruments are weak (against the alternative that at least one of them is strong). With one endogenous variable, we only need one strong instrument. With this in mind, it is common to use a low level of significance ($\Rightarrow$ a high critical value); a common[23] rule of thumb is to reject the null hypothesis if the F statistic takes a value greater than 10. If there is more than one endogenous variable in the model, then this F test is no longer valid. In this case, we can assess the strength of the available instruments using a test proposed by Cragg and Donald (1993). For more details on tests for weak instruments, see, for example, Hill et al. (2011, pp. 434ff).

7.3.4.6 Stationarity

The concept of stationarity is only meaningful in a time-series or panel data context. A time series is said to be stationary if the mean, variance and covariances of the series are all finite and do not depend on t. If the time series are long enough, then evidence of nonstationarity can usually be seen in time-series plots. A nonstationary process is said to be trend-stationary if it can be made stationary by detrending. A nonstationary process is said to be difference-stationary if it can be made stationary by differencing but cannot be made stationary by detrending. Difference-stationary processes are also known as unit root processes.

If a model contains a linear trend and all the remaining explanatory variables are either stationary or trend-stationary, then the OLS estimators for the slope parameters are consistent. However, if any explanatory variables are difference-stationary, then, unless the dependent and explanatory variables are cointegrated, the properties of the OLS estimators are unknown. Moreover, t and F statistics do not have well-defined distributions, well-known measures of goodness-of-fit are totally unreliable, and the DW statistic tends to zero. The associated regression is known as a *spurious regression*.

If there is evidence that a process is nonstationary, then we can test the null hypothesis that it is difference-stationary using a unit root test. Well-known unit root tests include Dickey-Fuller (DF), augmented Dickey-Fuller (ADF), Phillips-Perron

[23] See, for example, Hill et al. (2011, p. 414).

(PP) and Kwaitkowski-Phillips-Schmidt-Shin (KPSS) tests. For details concerning these and related tests, see Enders (2004, Chap. 4). If there is evidence that a process is nonstationary and we reject the null hypothesis that it is difference-stationary, then we should conclude that it is trend-stationary and include a time trend in the model. If we do not reject the null hypothesis, then we should test whether the dependent and explanatory variables in the model are cointegrated.

7.3.4.7 Cointegration

If a difference-stationary process can be made stationary by differencing only once, then it is said to be integrated of order one, or I(1). Stationary series are said to be integrated of order zero, or I(0). Linear combinations of I(1) variables are usually also I(1). However, sometimes linear combinations of I(1) variables are I(0). In such cases, the variables are said to be cointegrated. If the dependent and explanatory variables in a DFM are cointegrated, then the OLS estimators for the slope coefficients are consistent,[24] even if the explanatory variables are endogenous. Engle and Granger (1987) describe a simple test for cointegration in time-series models. The so-called Engle-Granger methodology involves estimating the model using OLS, then using a DF test to determine whether the OLS residuals are I(0). Because this test is based on residuals, the critical values for the test should be taken from Table 2 in Engle and Yoo (1987, p. 157). If any explanatory variables in a DFM are difference-stationary and we reject the null hypothesis that the dependent and explanatory variables are cointegrated, then we should estimate the model in either first-difference or error-correction form. For more details, see Enders (2004, Ch. 6).

7.3.5 Toy Example

Reconsider the toy data reported earlier in Tables 1.1 and 1.2. These data have been used to obtain COLS and CRLS estimates of the parameters in (7.18). The estimates are reported in Table 7.2. Both sets of estimates were obtained under assumptions LS1 to LS4. The CRLS estimates were obtained by restricting $\lambda \geq 0$ ($\Rightarrow$ there is no technical regress). Both sets of estimates have been used to predict levels of output-oriented technical efficiency (OTE). The predictions are reported in Table 7.3.

The restricted model has been used to conduct several hypothesis tests. The results are summarised in Table 7.4. All tests were conducted at the 5% level of significance. The CRS test was a test of the null hypothesis that $\beta_1 + \beta_2 = 1$. The test of LS1 was a test for time-invariant fixed effects (i.e., the alternative hypothesis was that the mean of the inefficiency effects varied across firms but not over time). The test of LS2 was a BP test; the variance function used to implement this test was

[24] They are, in fact, super-consistent. This means that, as the sample size increases, the distributions of the OLS estimators collapse around the true parameter values even faster than usual.

Table 7.2 LS parameter estimates

Parameter	COLS			CRLS		
	Est.	St. err.	t	Est.	St. err.	t
α	1.348	0.253	5.326***	1.174	0.129	9.088***
λ	−0.040	0.071	−0.564	0.000	0.000	NaN
δ_1	−0.151	0.314	−0.481	−0.182	0.304	−0.598
β_1	0.281	0.107	2.628***	0.274	0.105	2.621***
β_2	0.043	0.066	0.645	0.034	0.063	0.533

***, ** and * indicate significance at the 1, 5 and 10% levels

Table 7.3 LS predictions of OTE

Row	Firm	Period	COLS	CRLS
A	1	1	0.270	0.309
B	2	1	0.326	0.370
C	3	1	0.641	0.733
D	4	1	0.571	0.651
E	5	1	0.743	0.847
F	1	2	0.329	0.365
G	2	2	0.767	0.859
H	3	2	0.881	0.929
I	4	2	0.700	0.762
J	5	2	0.804	0.839
K	1	3	0.911	0.961
L	2	3	0.809	0.853
M	3	3	0.547	0.578
N	4	3	0.303	0.312
O	5	3	0.651	0.701
P	1	4	0.354	0.356
R	2	4	0.620	0.628
S	3	4	0.297	0.305
T	4	4	0.966	1
U	5	4	0.321	0.322
V	1	5	1	0.974
W	2	5	0.725	0.720
X	3	5	0.338	0.333
Y	4	5	0.350	0.339
Z	5	5	0.697	0.684
Geometric mean			0.547	0.577

Table 7.4 Hypothesis tests

Null hypothesis	Test statistic	Critical value(s)	Decision
CRS	$F = 25.27$	$\chi^2_{(0.95,1)} = 3.841$	Reject
LS1 (no fixed effects)	$F = 0.255$	$\chi^2_{(0.95,4)} = 9.488$	Do not reject
LS2 (homoskedasticity)	$BP = 1.720$	$\chi^2_{(0.95,3)} = 7.815$	Do not reject
LS3 (no autocorelation)	$CD = -0.426$	$\pm z_{(0.95)} = \pm 1.96$	Do not reject
LS4 (no endogeneity)	$H = 0.589$	$\chi^2_{(0.95,2)} = 5.991$	Do not reject

$\sigma^2_{uit} \propto h(\alpha_1 + \alpha_2 \ln z_{it} + \alpha_3 \ln x_{1it} + \alpha_4 \ln x_{2it})$. The test of LS3 was the Pesaran CD test for spatial correlation in panels. The test of LS4 was a Hausman test of the null hypothesis that the inefficiency effects are uncorrelated with the log-inputs; the two instruments used to implement this test were the logarithms of the input prices reported earlier in Table 1.5. Unfortunately, the number of observations in the toy dataset is not large enough for any of these tests to be considered valid.

7.4 Maximum Likelihood Estimation

Maximum likelihood (ML) estimation of DFMs involves choosing the unknown parameters to maximise the joint density (or 'likelihood') of the observed data. The idea can be traced back at least as far as Afriat (1972, Sect. 3). For simplicity, this section considers estimation of the following output-oriented model:

$$y_{it} = \ln F^t(x_{it}, z_{it}) - u_{it} \tag{7.23}$$

where y_{it} denotes the logarithm of an aggregate output, $F^t(.)$ can be viewed as a production function, and u_{it} denotes an output-oriented technical inefficiency effect. To estimate the unknown parameters in $F^t(.)$, we once again need to make some assumptions about the inefficiency effects.

7.4.1 Assumptions

It is common to assume that either

ML1 u_{it} is an independent $N^+(0, \sigma_u^2)$ random variable, or
ML2 u_{it} is an independent $G(P, \sigma_u)$ random variable.

In this context, the term 'independent' means that the inefficiency effects are neither with each other nor correlated with the explanatory variables (i.e., the inefficiency effects and the explanatory variables are mutually independent). ML1 says that u_{it}

is an independent half-normal random variable obtained by lower-truncating the $N(0, \sigma_u^2)$ distribution at zero; this assumption can be traced back to Schmidt (1976). ML2 says that u_{it} is an independent gamma random variable with shape parameter P and scale parameter σ_u; this assumption can be traced back to Afriat (1972, p. 581). If $P = 1$, then the gamma distribution collapses to an exponential distribution; this assumption can be traced back to Schmidt (1976). If ML2 is true and $P > 2$, then the associated ML estimators for the model parameters are consistent, asymptotically efficient and asymptotically normal (Greene 1980a). In all other cases (i.e., half-normal, or gamma with $P \leq 2$), the properties of the ML estimators are unknown.

7.4.2 Estimation

The likelihood function is a function that expresses the joint density of the observed data as a function of the unknown parameters. Finding the parameter values that maximise the likelihood function is equivalent to finding the parameter values that maximise the *logarithm* of the likelihood function. If, for example, ML2 is true, then the so-called log-likelihood function is

$$\begin{aligned}\ln L(y|X, \theta) = &-NP \ln \sigma_u + (P-1) \sum_{t=1}^{T} \sum_{i=1}^{I_t} \ln[\ln F^t(x_{it}, z_{it}) - y_{it}] \\ &- \sigma_u^{-1} \sum_{t=1}^{T} \sum_{i=1}^{I_t} [\ln F^t(x_{it}, z_{it}) - y_{it}] - N \ln \Gamma(P) \end{aligned} \tag{7.24}$$

where I_t denotes the number of firms in the dataset in period t, $N \equiv \sum_t I_t$ denotes the total number of observations in the dataset, y denotes a vector containing all the observations on y_{it}, X denotes a matrix containing all the observations on x_{it} and z_{it}, and θ is a vector containing P, σ_u and all the unknown parameters in $F^t(.)$. In practice, ML estimates of the parameters are invariably obtained by maximising the log-likelihood function numerically. This involves systematically evaluating the log-likelihood function at different values of the parameters until the maximum value is found. For details on numerical maximisation algorithms, see, for example, Greene (2008, Appendix E). Following estimation, ML estimates of $E(u_{it})$ and $E(\exp[-u_{it}])$ can be obtained by using the ML estimates of P and σ_u to evaluate

$$E(u_{it}) = P\sigma_u \tag{7.25}$$

$$\text{and} \quad E(\exp[-u_{it}]) = (1 + \sigma_u)^{-P}. \tag{7.26}$$

7.4.3 Prediction

The ML predictor for u_{it} is $\tilde{u}_{it} = \ln \tilde{F}^t(x_{it}, z_{it}) - y_{it}$ where $\tilde{F}^t(.)$ is obtained by replacing the unknown parameters in $F^t(.)$ with their ML estimators. The associated predictor for $\exp(-u_{it})$ is $\exp(-\tilde{u}_{it})$. If ML2 is true and $P > 2$, then these predictors are consistent. In all other cases, their properties are unknown.

7.4.4 Hypothesis Tests

It is advisable to test the null hypothesis that ML2 is true. A well-known test that can be used for this purpose is the Kolmogorov-Smirnov (KS) test. Alternatives include tests proposed by Bickel and Rosenblatt (1973), Rosenblatt (1975) and Fan (1994). For more details, see Pagan and Ullah (1999, Sect. 2.9.1).

If ML2 is true and $P > 2$, then t and F tests concerning the parameters in $F^t(.)$ are asymptotically valid. Standard likelihood ratio (LR) tests concerning these parameters are also asymptotically valid. To conduct an LR test of the null hypothesis that J independent equality restrictions concerning the parameters in $F^t(.)$ are true against the alternative that at least one restriction is not true, we must compute the following statistic:

$$LR = 2(LLF_U - LLF_R) \tag{7.27}$$

where LLF_R denotes the value of the restricted log-likelihood function (obtained by estimating the parameters subject to the restrictions specified under the null hypothesis) and LLF_U denotes the value of the unrestricted log-likelihood function (obtained by estimating the parameters without any restrictions). If the null hypothesis is true, then this statistic is asymptotically distributed as a chi-square random variable with J degrees of freedom. Thus, we should reject the null hypothesis at the α level of significance if the sample size is large and $LR > \chi^2_{(1-\alpha,J)}$.

7.4.5 Toy Example

Reconsider the toy data reported earlier in Tables 1.1 and 1.2. These data have been used to obtain ML and restricted ML (RML) estimates of the parameters in (7.18). The estimates are reported in Table 7.5. Both sets of estimates were obtained under assumption ML2. The RML estimates were obtained by restricting $\lambda \geq 0$ and $P \geq 2.001$. Both sets of estimates have been used to predict levels of output-oriented technical efficiency (OTE). The predictions are reported in Table 7.6. The restricted model was used to conduct a Kolmogorov-Smirnov (KS) test of the null hypothesis that ML2 is true. The null hypothesis was not rejected at the 5% level of significance (the KS test statistic was $D = 0.2086$; the two-sided p-value was 0.1967).

Table 7.5 ML parameter estimates

Parameter	ML			RML		
	Est.	St. err.	t	Est.	St. err.	t
α	1.340	n.a.	n.a.	1.182	21.75	0.054
λ	−0.039	n.a.	n.a.	0.017	75.001	0.000
δ_1	−0.199	n.a.	n.a.	−0.153	8.782	−0.017
β_1	0.279	n.a.	n.a.	0.251	22.321	0.011
β_2	0.044	n.a.	n.a.	0.035	42.723	0.001
σ_u	0.649	n.a.	n.a.	0.307	23.023	0.013
P	0.909	n.a.	n.a.	2.001	4.014	0.498

n.a. = not available (or useful)

Table 7.6 ML predictions of OTE

Row	Firm	Period	ML	RML
A	1	1	0.272	0.302
B	2	1	0.328	0.356
C	3	1	0.645	0.715
D	4	1	0.575	0.636
E	5	1	0.748	0.828
F	1	2	0.342	0.344
G	2	2	0.798	0.815
H	3	2	0.876	0.814
I	4	2	0.733	0.745
J	5	2	0.816	0.838
K	1	3	0.914	0.907
L	2	3	0.811	0.805
M	3	3	0.549	0.549
N	4	3	0.304	0.288
O	5	3	0.675	0.649
P	1	4	0.355	0.327
R	2	4	0.621	0.583
S	3	4	0.308	0.282
T	4	4	1	0.910
U	5	4	0.322	0.299
V	1	5	1.000	0.889
W	2	5	0.749	0.643
X	3	5	0.350	0.301
Y	4	5	0.350	0.308
Z	5	5	0.698	0.635
Geometric mean			0.555	0.541

7.5 Productivity Analysis

Productivity analysis involves both measuring and explaining changes in productivity. For purposes of comparison with Sect. 6.5, this section again focuses on measuring and explaining changes in TFP. Again, methods for measuring and explaining changes in MFP and PFP can be handled as special cases in which one or more inputs are assigned a weight of zero.

7.5.1 Measuring Changes in TFP

DFMs can be used to compute additive, multiplicative, primal and dual TFPI numbers. Again, additive TFPI numbers can be computed by using average estimated normalised shadow prices as weights in Eq. (3.41). These index numbers ultimately depend on the output and input distance functions. If the output distance function is given by (2.9), for example, then the input distance function is given by (2.13). In this case, the n-th normalised shadow output price and the m-th normalised shadow input price are

$$p_n^t(x_{it}, q_{it}, z_{it}) = \gamma_n q_{nit}^{\tau-1} \left(\sum_{k=1}^{N} \gamma_k q_{kit}^{\tau} \right)^{-1} D_O^t(x_{it}, q_{it}, z_{it}) \tag{7.28}$$

$$\text{and} \quad w_m^t(x_{it}, q_{it}, z_{it}) = \lambda_m D_I^t(x_{it}, q_{it}, z_{it})/x_{mit}. \tag{7.29}$$

Multiplicative TFPI numbers can be computed by using average estimated shadow value shares as weights in equation (3.42). If the output and input distance functions are given by (2.9) and (2.13), then the n-th shadow revenue share and the m-th shadow cost share are

$$r_n(q_{it}) = \gamma_n q_{nit}^{\tau} \left(\sum_{k=1}^{N} \gamma_k q_{kit}^{\tau} \right)^{-1} \tag{7.30}$$

$$\text{and} \quad s_m = \lambda_m. \tag{7.31}$$

Primal and dual TFPI numbers can be computed by evaluating (3.44) and (3.46). If the output and input distance functions are given by (2.9) and (2.13), then the primal and dual TFPIs are both given by (3.45). Estimates of the unknown parameters in (3.45) [and (7.28) to (7.31)] can be obtained using the LS and ML estimators described in Sects. 7.3 and 7.4.

For a numerical illustration, reconsider the toy data reported in Table 1.1. These data have been used to obtain CRLS estimates of the parameters in (7.2). The estimates were reported earlier in Table 1.11. Associated estimates of normalised shadow prices and shadow value shares are now reported in Table 7.7. These estimates were

Table 7.7 CRLS estimates of normalised shadow prices and shadow value shares[a,b]

Row	Firm	Period	$p_1^t(.)$	$p_2^t(.)$	$w_1^t(.)$	$w_2^t(.)$	$r_1(.)$	$r_2(.)$	s_1	s_2
A	1	1	0.227	0.087	62.651	0	0.724	0.276	1	0
B	2	1	0.267	0.102	62.651	0	0.724	0.276	1	0
C	3	1	0.227	0.087	2.877	0	0.724	0.276	1	0
D	4	1	0.224	0.085	4.357	0	0.724	0.276	1	0
E	5	1	0.224	0.085	3.156	0	0.568	0.432	1	0
F	1	2	0.236	0.090	54.561	0	0.724	0.276	1	0
G	2	2	0.212	0.081	3.001	0	0.571	0.429	1	0
H	3	2	0.711	0.271	73.988	0	0.728	0.272	1	0
I	4	2	0.155	0.059	0.321	0	1	0	1	0
J	5	2	0.150	0.057	0.225	0	1	0	1	0
K	1	3	0.227	0.087	3.175	0	0.434	0.566	1	0
L	2	3	0.227	0.087	8.686	0	0.236	0.764	1	0
M	3	3	0.209	0.080	13.049	0	0.467	0.533	1	0
N	4	3	0.310	0.118	223.849	0	0.724	0.276	1	0
O	5	3	0.236	0.090	4.594	0	0.724	0.276	1	0
P	1	4	0.256	0.097	62.651	0	0.724	0.276	1	0
R	2	4	0.227	0.087	13.049	0	0.467	0.533	1	0
S	3	4	0.196	0.075	54.561	0	0.724	0.276	1	0
T	4	4	0.236	0.090	2.323	0	0.576	0.424	1	0
U	5	4	0.227	0.087	62.651	0	0.724	0.276	1	0
V	1	5	0.227	0.087	4.078	0	0.337	0.663	1	0
W	2	5	0.242	0.092	4.594	0	0.724	0.276	1	0
X	3	5	0.212	0.081	54.561	0	0.724	0.276	1	0
Y	4	5	0.247	0.094	62.651	0	0.724	0.276	1	0
Z	5	5	0.185	0.070	3.156	0	0.568	0.432	1	0
Arithmetic mean			0.244	0.093	33.817	0	0.655	0.345	1	0

[a] $p_n^t(.) = n$-th estimated normalised shadow output price; $w_m^t(.) = m$-th estimated normalised shadow input price; $r_n(.) = n$-th estimated shadow revenue share; $s_m = m$-th estimated shadow cost share
[b] Numbers reported to less than three decimal places are exact; see the footnote to Table 1.2 on p. 8

obtained by using the CRLS estimates to evaluate (7.28)–(7.31). Associated additive, multiplicative and primal TFPI numbers are reported in Table 7.8. The additive and multiplicative numbers were obtained by using the arithmetic averages reported at the bottom of Table 7.7 as weights in Eqs. (3.41) and (3.42). The primal index numbers were obtained by evaluating (3.45). All of the index numbers in Table 7.8 are proper in the sense that they have been obtained by dividing proper output index numbers by proper input index numbers. They are also consistent with measurement theory. Observe, for example, that (a) the output vector in row Z is the same as the

Table 7.8 Additive, multiplicative and primal TFP index numbers[a,b]

Row	Firm	Period	q_1	q_2	x_1	x_2	A	M	P
A	1	1	1	1	1	1	1	1	1
B	2	1	1	1	0.56	0.56	1.786	1.786	1.786
C	3	1	2.37	2.37	1	1	2.37	2.37	2.37
D	4	1	2.11	2.11	1.05	0.7	2.010	2.010	2.010
E	5	1	1.81	3.62	1.05	0.7	2.199	2.190	2.199
F	1	2	1	1	0.996	0.316	1.004	1.004	1.004
G	2	2	1.777	3.503	1.472	0.546	1.531	1.526	1.531
H	3	2	0.96	0.94	0.017	0.346	56.146	56.061	56.146
I	4	2	5.82	0.001	4.545	0.01	0.927	0.064	0.927
J	5	2	6.685	0.001	4.45	0.001	1.088	0.072	1.088
K	1	3	1.381	4.732	1	1	2.306	2.113	2.306
L	2	3	0.566	4.818	1	1	1.739	1.186	1.739
M	3	3	1	3	1.354	1	1.146	1.080	1.146
N	4	3	0.7	0.7	0.33	0.16	2.121	2.121	2.121
O	5	3	2	2	1	1	2	2	2
P	1	4	1	1	0.657	0.479	1.522	1.522	1.522
R	2	4	1	3	1	1	1.552	1.462	1.552
S	3	4	1	1	1.933	0.283	0.517	0.517	0.517
T	4	4	1.925	3.722	1	1	2.421	2.417	2.421
U	5	4	1	1	1	0.31	1.000	1.000	1.000
V	1	5	1	5.166	1	1	2.149	1.764	2.149
W	2	5	2	2	0.919	0.919	2.176	2.176	2.176
X	3	5	1	1	1.464	0.215	0.683	0.683	0.683
Y	4	5	1	1	0.74	0.74	1.351	1.351	1.351
Z	5	5	1.81	3.62	2.1	1.4	1.100	1.095	1.100

[a] A = additive index obtained using averages of CRLS estimates of normalised shadow prices as weights; M = multiplicative index obtained using averages of CRLS estimates of shadow value shares as weights; P = primal index numbers obtained using CRLS estimates of the parameters of output and input distance functions. Some index numbers may be incoherent at the third decimal place due to rounding (e.g., the number in row Z of column A is not exactly half as big as the number in row E of column A due to rounding)

[b] Numbers reported to less than three decimal places are exact; see the footnote to Table 1.2 on p. 8

output vector in row E, (b) the input vector in row Z is twice as big as the input vector in row A, and (c) the TFPI numbers in row Z are half as big as the numbers in row E. Also observe that the TFPI numbers in rows A, B, C, O, W and Y are the same as the TFPI numbers reported in the corresponding rows of Tables 3.5 and 6.15.

7.5.2 Explaining Changes in TFP

Explaining changes in TFP generally involves decomposing proper TFPI numbers into measures of environmental change, technical change, and efficiency change. This section focuses on output- and input-oriented decompositions.

7.5.2.1 Output-Oriented Decompositions

Output-oriented decompositions of TFPI numbers tend to be most relevant in situations where managers have placed nonnegative values on outputs, and where inputs have been predetermined (i.e., situations where output-oriented measures of efficiency are most relevant). In these situations, a relatively easy way to proceed is to write $TFP(x_{it}, q_{it}) = TFP(x_{it}, q_{it}) \exp(-u_{it})/D_O^t(x_{it}, q_{it}, z_{it})$ where u_{it} denotes the output-oriented technical inefficiency effect in (7.1). A similar equation holds for firm k in period s. Substituting these equations into (3.40) yields

$$TFPI(x_{ks}, q_{ks}, x_{it}, q_{it}) = \left[TFPI(x_{ks}, q_{ks}, x_{it}, q_{it}) \frac{D_O^s(x_{ks}, q_{ks}, z_{ks})}{D_O^t(x_{it}, q_{it}, z_{it})} \right] \times \left[\frac{\exp(-u_{it})}{\exp(-u_{ks})} \right]. \tag{7.32}$$

The first term on the right-hand side is as an output-oriented environment, technology, and scale and mix efficiency index (OETSMEI). The second term is an output-oriented technical efficiency index (OTEI).

Whether a finer decomposition is possible (and economically meaningful) depends on both the output distance function and the TFPI. If, for example, the output distance function is given by (2.9), then (7.32) takes the following form:

$$\begin{aligned} TFPI(x_{ks}, q_{ks}, x_{it}, q_{it}) &= \left[\frac{A(t)}{A(s)} \right] \left[\prod_{j=1}^{J} \left(\frac{z_{jit}}{z_{jks}} \right)^{\delta_j} \right] \\ &\times \left[TFPI(x_{ks}, q_{ks}, x_{it}, q_{it}) \prod_{m=1}^{M} \left(\frac{x_{mit}}{x_{mks}} \right)^{\beta_m} \left(\frac{\sum_n \gamma_n q_{nks}^{\tau}}{\sum_n \gamma_n q_{nit}^{\tau}} \right)^{1/\tau} \right] \\ &\times \left[\frac{\exp(-u_{it})}{\exp(-u_{ks})} \right]. \end{aligned} \tag{7.33}$$

The first term on the right-hand side is an output-oriented technology index (OTI) (i.e., a measure of technical change). The second term is an output-oriented environment index (OEI) (i.e., a measure of environmental change). The third term is an output-oriented scale and mix efficiency index (OSMEI). The last term is the OTEI in (7.32). If $\tau > 1$ and the TFPI is the additive index defined by (3.41), then Eq. (5.6) can be used to decompose the OSMEI into the product of an output-oriented mix efficiency index (OMEI) and a residual output-oriented scale efficiency index (ROSEI); the algebra is left as an exercise for the reader. If the TFPI is the primal index defined by (3.45), then there is no mix inefficiency and the OSMEI is, in fact, an output-oriented scale efficiency index (OSEI). If production frontiers exhibit CRS and the TFPI is the primal index defined by (3.45), then the OSMEI vanishes. If $A(t) \propto \exp(\lambda t)$ and the TFPI is the primal index defined by (3.45), then (7.33) reduces to Eq. (6) in O'Donnell (2016).

For a numerical example, reconsider the GY TFPI numbers reported earlier in Table 3.5. An output-oriented decomposition of these numbers is now reported in Table 7.9. The OTI, OEI, and OSMEI numbers in this table were obtained by using the CRLS estimates reported in Table 1.11 to evaluate the relevant terms in (7.33). The OTEI numbers were obtained as residuals (i.e., OTEI = TFPI/(OTI × OEI × OSMEI)). The OTI, OEI and OTEI numbers in Table 7.9 are the same as the OTI, OEI and OTE numbers reported earlier in Table 1.13.

7.5.2.2 Input-Oriented Decompositions

Input-oriented decompositions of TFPI numbers tend to be most relevant in situations where managers have placed nonnegative values on inputs, and where outputs have been predetermined (i.e., situations where input-oriented measures of efficiency are most relevant). In these situations, a relatively easy way to proceed is to write $TFP(x_{it}, q_{it}) = TFP(x_{it}, q_{it})D_I^t(x_{it}, q_{it}, z_{it}) \exp(-u_{it})$ where u_{it} now denotes the input-oriented technical inefficiency effect in (7.4). A similar equation holds for firm k in period s. Substituting these equations into (3.40) yields

$$TFPI(x_{ks}, q_{ks}, x_{it}, q_{it}) = \left[TFPI(x_{ks}, q_{ks}, x_{it}, q_{it}) \frac{D_I^t(x_{it}, q_{it}, z_{it})}{D_I^s(x_{ks}, q_{ks}, z_{ks})} \right] \times \left[\frac{\exp(-u_{it})}{\exp(-u_{ks})} \right]. \tag{7.34}$$

The first term on the right-hand side is an input-oriented environment, technology, and scale and mix efficiency index (IETSMEI). The other term is an input-oriented technical efficiency index (ITEI).

Again, whether a finer decomposition is possible (and economically meaningful) depends on both the distance function and the TFPI. If, for example, the input distance function is given by (2.13), then (7.34) takes the following form:

$$\begin{aligned} TFPI(x_{ks}, q_{ks}, x_{it}, q_{it}) = & \left[\frac{B(t)}{B(s)} \right] \left[\prod_{j=1}^{J} \left(\frac{z_{jit}}{z_{jks}} \right)^{\kappa_j} \right] \\ & \times \left[TFPI(x_{ks}, q_{ks}, x_{it}, q_{it}) \prod_{m=1}^{M} \left(\frac{x_{mit}}{x_{mks}} \right)^{\lambda_m} \left(\frac{\sum_n \gamma_n q_{nks}^{\tau}}{\sum_n \gamma_n q_{nit}^{\tau}} \right)^{1/(\tau\eta)} \right] \\ & \times \left[\frac{\exp(-u_{it})}{\exp(-u_{ks})} \right]. \end{aligned} \tag{7.35}$$

Table 7.9 An output-oriented decomposition of GY TFPI numbers using CRLS[a,b]

Row	Firm	Period	TFPI	OTI	OEI	OTEI	OSMEI
A	1	1	1	1	1	1	1
B	2	1	1.786	1	1	1.176	1.518
C	3	1	2.37	1	1	2.37	1
D	4	1	2.539	1	1	2.081	1.220
E	5	1	3.133	1	1	2.278	1.375
F	1	2	1.948	1	0.962	1.041	1.945
G	2	2	3.054	1	0.962	2.102	1.511
H	3	2	9.811	1	1	2.988	3.283
I	4	2	0.464	1	0.962	2.867	0.168
J	5	2	1.890	1	1	3.186	0.593
K	1	3	2.634	1	1	2.306	1.143
L	2	3	1.740	1	1	1.739	1.000
M	3	3	1.565	1	1	1.426	1.098
N	4	3	3.221	1	1	0.955	3.373
O	5	3	2	1	0.962	2.079	1.000
P	1	4	1.827	1	1	1.125	1.624
R	2	4	1.779	1	1	1.552	1.146
S	3	4	1.568	1	0.962	0.864	1.886
T	4	4	2.720	1	0.962	2.516	1.124
U	5	4	1.966	1	1	1	1.966
V	1	5	2.366	1	1	2.149	1.101
W	2	5	2.176	1	0.962	2.129	1.063
X	3	5	2.067	1	0.962	0.934	2.300
Y	4	5	1.351	1	1	1.088	1.242
Z	5	5	1.567	1	1	1.876	0.835
Geometric mean			2.030	1	0.988	1.655	1.242

[a]TFPI = OTI × OEI × OTEI × OSMEI. Some index numbers may be incoherent at the third decimal place due to rounding (e.g., in any given row, the product of the OTI, OEI, OTEI and OSMEI numbers may not be exactly equal to the TFPI numbers due to rounding)
[b]Numbers reported to less than three decimal places are exact; see the footnote to Table 1.2 on p. 8

The first term on the right-hand side is an input-oriented technology index (ITI). The second term is an input-oriented environment index (IEI). The third term is an input-oriented scale and mix efficiency index (ISMEI). The last term is the ITEI in (7.34). If the TFPI is the additive index defined by (3.41), then Eq. (5.13) can be used to decompose the ISMEI into the product of an input-oriented mix efficiency index (IMEI) and a residual input-oriented scale efficiency index (RISEI); again, the algebra is left as an exercise for the reader. If the TFPI is the primal index defined by (3.45), then there is no mix inefficiency and the ISMEI is an input-oriented scale efficiency index (ISEI). If production frontiers exhibit CRS and the TFPI is the primal index defined by (3.45), then the ISMEI vanishes.

For a numerical example, reconsider the GY TFPI numbers reported earlier in Table 3.5. An input-oriented decomposition of these numbers is now reported in Table 7.10. The ITI, IEI, and ISMEI numbers in this table were obtained by using the CRLS estimates reported in Table 1.11 to evaluate the relevant terms in (7.35). The ITEI numbers were obtained as residuals (i.e., ITEI = TFPI/(ITI×IEI×ISMEI)). The ITI, IEI and ITEI numbers in Table 7.10 are the same as the ITI, IEI and ITEI numbers reported earlier in Table 1.13.

Table 7.10 An input-oriented decomposition of GY TFPI numbers using CRLS[a,b]

Row	Firm	Period	TFPI	ITI	IEI	ITEI	ISMEI
A	1	1	1	1	1	1	1
B	2	1	1.786	1	1	1.786	1
C	3	1	2.37	1	1	21.773	0.109
D	4	1	2.539	1	1	13.695	0.185
E	5	1	3.133	1	1	18.905	0.166
F	1	2	1.948	1	0.871	1.153	1.940
G	2	2	3.054	1	0.871	14.181	0.247
H	3	2	9.811	1	1	49.810	0.197
I	4	2	0.464	1	0.871	42.949	0.012
J	5	2	1.890	1	1	62.651	0.030
K	1	3	2.634	1	1	19.734	0.133
L	2	3	1.740	1	1	7.213	0.241
M	3	3	1.565	1	1	3.546	0.441
N	4	3	3.221	1	1	0.848	3.798
O	5	3	2	1	0.871	13.639	0.168
P	1	4	1.827	1	1	1.522	1.200
R	2	4	1.779	1	1	4.801	0.371
S	3	4	1.568	1	0.871	0.594	3.031
T	4	4	2.720	1	0.871	26.969	0.116
U	5	4	1.966	1	1	1	1.966
V	1	5	2.366	1	1	15.363	0.154
W	2	5	2.176	1	0.871	14.841	0.168
X	3	5	2.067	1	0.871	0.784	3.026
Y	4	5	1.351	1	1	1.351	1
Z	5	5	1.567	1	1	9.453	0.166
Geometric mean			2.030	1	0.957	6.046	0.351

[a]TFPI = ITI × IEI × ITEI × ISMEI. Some index numbers may be incoherent at the third decimal place due to rounding (e.g., in any given row, the product of the ITI, IEI, ITEI and ISMEI numbers may not be exactly equal to the TFPI numbers due to rounding)

[b]Numbers reported to less than three decimal places are exact; see the footnote to Table 1.2 on p. 8

7.5.2.3 Other Decompositions

There are many TFPI numbers that are not proper in the sense that they cannot generally be written as proper output index numbers divided by proper input index numbers. As we saw in Sect. 6.5.2.4, one way of decomposing such numbers to first write them as the product of proper TFPI numbers and statistical noise index (SNI) numbers. Subsequently, the proper TFPI numbers can be decomposed into measures of technical change, environmental change and various measures of efficiency change.

For a numerical example, reconsider the CCD TFPI numbers reported earlier in Table 3.6. Two decompositions of these numbers are reported in Table 7.11. CCD TFPI numbers are closely related to GY TFPI numbers (if observed revenue and cost shares are firm- and time-invariant, then they are equal). Output- and input-oriented decompositions of the GY TFPI numbers were presented earlier in Tables 7.9 and 7.10. The OTI, OEI, OTEI, OSMEI, ITI, OEI, ITEI and ISMEI numbers in those tables are now reported in Table 7.11. The numbers in the SNI columns in Table 7.11 were obtained by dividing the CCD TFPI numbers by the GY TFPI numbers. In this context, the SNI can be viewed as a revenue share index divided by a cost share index; if revenue and cost shares had been firm- and time-invariant, then all the SNI numbers would have been equal one.

7.6 Other Models

Other DFMs include various systems of equations. This section discusses systems of equations that can be used to explain variations in metafrontiers, output supplies and input demands.

7.6.1 Metafrontier Models

Metafrontier models are used in situations where firm managers can be classified into two or more groups, and where managers in different groups choose input-output combinations from potentially different production possibilities sets. For purposes of comparison with Sect. 6.6.1, this section considers situations where firm managers can be classified into two or more groups according to the technologies they use. Again, attention is restricted to the estimation of output-oriented metafrontier models; the estimation of input-, revenue-, cost-, and profit-oriented metafrontier models is analogous to the estimation of output-oriented models.

If we observe the technologies used by firm managers, then output-oriented metafrontier models can be used to predict the output-oriented metatechnology ratio (OMR) defined by (5.47), the measure of output-oriented technical efficiency (OTE) defined by (5.1), and the measure of residual output-oriented technical efficiency

Table 7.11 Output- and input-oriented decompositions of CCD TFPI numbers using CRLS[a,b]

Row	Firm	Period	TFPI	OTI	OEI	OTEI	OSMEI	SNI	ITI	IEI	ITEI	ISMEI	SNI
A	1	1	1	1	1	1	1	1	1	1	1	1	1
B	2	1	1.922*	1	1	1.176	1.518	1.076	1	1	1.786	1	1.076
C	3	1	2.37	1	1	2.37	1	1	1	1	21.773	0.109	1
D	4	1	2.870	1	1	2.081	1.220	1.130	1	1	13.695	0.185	1.130
E	5	1	3.600*	1	1	2.278	1.375	1.149	1	1	18.905	0.166	1.149
F	1	2	2.157	1	0.962	1.041	1.945	1.108	1	0.871	1.153	1.940	1.108
G	2	2	3.697	1	0.962	2.102	1.511	1.210	1	0.871	14.181	0.247	1.210
H	3	2	5.072	1	1	2.988	3.283	0.517	1	1	49.81	0.197	0.517
I	4	2	1.056	1	0.962	2.867	0.168	2.274	1	0.871	42.949	0.012	2.274
J	5	2	2.292	1	1	3.186	0.593	1.213	1	1	62.651	0.030	1.213
K	1	3	3.090	1	1	2.306	1.143	1.173	1	1	19.734	0.133	1.173
L	2	3	3.044	1	1	1.739	1	1.749	1	1	7.213	0.241	1.749
M	3	3	1.973	1	1	1.426	1.098	1.261	1	1	3.546	0.441	1.261
N	4	3	3.535	1	1	0.955	3.373	1.097	1	1	0.848	3.798	1.097
O	5	3	2.421*	1	0.962	2.079	1	1.211	1	0.871	13.639	0.168	1.211
P	1	4	2.113	1	1	1.125	1.624	1.157	1	1	1.522	1.200	1.157
R	2	4	2.366	1	1	1.552	1.146	1.330	1	1	4.801	0.371	1.330
S	3	4	1.549	1	0.962	0.864	1.886	0.988	1	0.871	0.594	3.031	0.988
T	4	4	3.104	1	0.962	2.516	1.124	1.141	1	0.871	26.969	0.116	1.141

(continued)

Table 7.11 (continued)

Row	Firm	Period	TFPI	OTI	OEI	OTEI	OSMEI	SNI	ITI	IEI	ITEI	ISMEI	SNI
U	5	4	2.324	1	1	1	1.966	1.182	1	1	1	1.966	1.182
V	1	5	2.418	1	1	2.149	1.101	1.022	1	1	15.363	0.154	1.022
W	2	5	2.332*	1	0.962	2.129	1.063	1.071	1	0.871	14.841	0.168	1.071
X	3	5	1.951	1	0.962	0.934	2.300	0.944	1	0.871	0.784	3.026	0.944
Y	4	5	1.482*	1	1	1.088	1.242	1.096	1	1	1.351	1	1.096
Z	5	5	2.154*	1	1	1.876	0.835	1.375	1	1	9.453	0.166	1.375
Geometric mean			2.324	1	0.988	1.655	1.242	1.145	1	0.957	6.046	0.351	1.145

[a]TFPI = OTI × OEI × OTEI × OSMEI × SNI = ITI × IEI × ITEI × ISMEI × SNI. Some index numbers may be incoherent at the third decimal place due to rounding (e.g., in any given row, the product of the ITI, IEI, ITEI, ISMEI and SNI numbers may not be exactly equal to the TFPI number due to rounding)

[b]Numbers reported to less than three decimal places are exact; see the footnote to Table 1.2 on p. 8

*Incoherent (not because of rounding)

(ROTE) defined by (5.48). This involves estimating a system of technology-and-environment-specific output distance functions. These functions are linearly homogeneous in outputs. This implies that $d_O^g(x_{it}, q_{it}, z_{it}) = q_{1it} d_O^g(x_{it}, q_{it}^*, z_{it})$ where $q_{it}^* = q_{it}/q_{1it}$ denotes a vector of normalised outputs. If there are T time periods represented in the dataset, then the associated metafrontier system can be written as

$$\ln q_{1it} = -\ln d_O^g(x_{it}, q_{it}^*, z_{it}) - u_{it}^g \quad \text{for all } g \in G_T, \tag{7.36}$$

where $u_{it}^g \equiv -\ln d_O^g(x_{it}, q_{it}, z_{it})$ denotes a residual output-oriented technical inefficiency effect and G_T denotes the set of technologies that existed in period T.

Let g_{it} denote the technology used by manager i in period t. The ROTE of the manager is $\exp(-u_{it}^{g_{it}})$. The OTE of the manager is $\exp(-u_{it})$ where $u_{it} = \max_{g \in G_t} u_{it}^g$. The OMR of the manager is $\exp(-m_{it}^{g_{it}})$ where $m_{it}^{g_{it}} = u_{it} - u_{it}^{g_{it}}$. The first step in predicting these quantities is to estimate the parameters in the system defined by (7.36). The second step is to use these parameter estimates to predict $\exp(-u_{it}^{g_{it}})$, $\exp(-u_{it})$ and $\exp(-m_{it}^{g_{it}})$.

To estimate the parameters in the system defined by (7.36), we need to make some assumptions about the inefficiency effects. If there are no cross-equation restrictions involving the parameters and the inefficiency effects are independent random variables with means and variances that only vary by group, then the g-th equation in (7.36) can be estimated separately, using all (and only) observations on firms that used technology g. The g-th equation in (7.36) has the same basic structure as (7.1). This implies that the unknown parameters can be estimated using the LS and ML estimators discussed in Sects. 7.3 and 7.4.

Let $\tilde{d}_O^g(x_{it}, q_{it}^*, z_{it})$ denote a consistent estimator for $d_O^g(x_{it}, q_{it}^*, z_{it})$. An associated predictor for u_{it}^g is $\tilde{u}_{it}^g = -\ln \tilde{d}_O^g(x_{it}, q_{it}^*, z_{it}) - \ln q_{1it}$. Associated predictors for the ROTE, OTE and OMR of manager i in period t are

$$\tilde{ROTE}^{g_{it}}(x_{it}, q_{it}, z_{it}) = \exp(-\tilde{u}_{it}^{g_{it}}), \tag{7.37}$$

$$\tilde{OTE}^{t}(x_{it}, q_{it}, z_{it}) = \exp(-\tilde{u}_{it}) \tag{7.38}$$

$$\text{and} \quad \tilde{OMR}^{g_{it}t}(x_{it}, q_{it}, z_{it}) = \exp(-\tilde{m}_{it}^{g_{it}}) \tag{7.39}$$

where $\tilde{u}_{it} = \max_{g \in G_t} \tilde{u}_{it}^g$ and $\tilde{m}_{it}^{g_{it}} = \tilde{u}_{it} - \tilde{u}_{it}^{g_{it}}$.

For a numerical example, reconsider the toy data reported in Table 1.1. For purposes of comparison with the results reported in Table 6.20, suppose that (a) technologies 1 and 2 existed in each period, (b) no other technologies existed in any period, (c) the managers of firms 1, 2 and 3 always used technology 1, and (d) the managers of firms 4 and 5 always used technology 2. Also suppose that the g-th technology-and-environment-specific output distance function is given by (2.40). In this case, the system defined by (7.36) can be written as

Table 7.12 CRLS parameter estimates

Parameter	Est.	St. err.	t
$\alpha_1 \equiv \ln a(1)$	0.975	0.230	4.235***
$\alpha_2 \equiv \ln a(2)$	1.296	0.220	5.895***
δ_1	0.034	0.324	0.106
β_1	0.250	0.112	2.239**
β_2	0	0.147	0
γ_1	0.794	0.302	2.632***
γ_2	0.206	0.302	0.682
τ	1	1.716	0.583

*** and ** indicate significance at the 1 and 5% levels

$$\ln q_{1it} = \sum_{g \in G_t} \alpha_g d_{git} + \sum_{j=1}^{J} \delta_j \ln z_{jit} + \sum_{m=1}^{M} \beta_m \ln x_{mit} - \frac{1}{\tau} \ln\left(\sum_{n=1}^{N} \gamma_n q_{nit}^{*\tau}\right) - \sum_{g \in G_t} d_{git} u_{it}^{g} \tag{7.40}$$

where $\alpha_g \equiv \ln a(g)$ and $d_{git} = I(g_{it} = g)$ is a dummy variable that takes the value 1 if manager i used technology g in period t (and 0 otherwise). CRLS estimates of the unknown parameters in this model are presented in Table 7.12. These estimates were obtained by restricting $\beta = (\beta_1, \ldots, \beta_M)' \geq 0$ and $\tau \geq 1$. Associated predictions of OTE, ROTE and the OMRs are reported in Table 7.13. If we observe the technologies used by firm managers, then the predictions of OTE reported in Table 7.13 are more reliable than the CRLS predictions reported earlier in Table 7.3. Among other things, the predictions reported in Table 7.13 indicate that the manager of firm 5 chose the right technology in each period but only used it properly in period 2 (i.e., he/she 'chose the right book' but only 'followed the instructions' in period 2).

7.6.2 Output Supply Systems

It is often possible to write profit- and revenue-maximising output supply functions as systems of equations in which the explanatory variables are deterministic. For any given firm, the exact form of the system depends on the exact form of the manager's optimisation problem. For example, if firm i is a price taker in output markets and all inputs and environmental variables have been predetermined, then the manager's period-t optimisation problem is given by (4.12). In this case, the logarithms of the N observed outputs can be written as

$$\ln q_{nit} = \ln \ddot{q}_n^t(x_{it}, p_{it}, z_{it}) + u_{nit} \quad \text{for } n = 1, \ldots, N, \tag{7.41}$$

Table 7.13 CRLS predictions of OTE, ROTE and OMRs[a,b]

Row	Firm	Period	OTE	OMR	ROTE
A	1	1	0.274	0.725	0.377
B	2	1	0.316	0.725	0.436
C	3	1	0.649	0.725	0.894
D	4	1	0.570	1	0.570
E	5	1	0.590	1	0.590
F	1	2	0.267	0.725	0.369
G	2	2	0.517	0.725	0.713
H	3	2	0.725	0.725	1
I	4	2	0.846	1	0.846
J	5	2	1	1	1
K	1	3	0.566	0.725	0.781
L	2	3	0.394	0.725	0.544
M	3	3	0.358	0.725	0.494
N	4	3	0.253	1	0.253
O	5	3	0.534	1	0.534
P	1	4	0.304	0.725	0.419
R	2	4	0.386	0.725	0.533
S	3	4	0.227	0.725	0.312
T	4	4	0.613	1	0.613
U	5	4	0.274	1	0.274
V	1	5	0.508	0.725	0.701
W	2	5	0.546	0.725	0.753
X	3	5	0.243	0.725	0.335
Y	4	5	0.295	1	0.295
Z	5	5	0.496	1	0.496
Geometric mean			0.432	0.825	0.524

[a] OTE = OMR × ROTE. Some predictions may be incoherent at the third decimal place due to rounding (e.g., in any given row, the product of the OMR and ROTE predictions may not be exactly equal to the OTE prediction due to rounding)

[b] Numbers reported to less than three decimal places are exact; see the footnote to Table 1.2 on p. 8

where $\ddot{q}^t_n(x_{it}, p_{it}, z_{it})$ denotes the n-th revenue-maximising output supply function and $u_{nit} \equiv \ln q_{nit} - \ln \ddot{q}^t_n(x_{it}, p_{it}, z_{it})$ is an unsigned variable that captures technical, scale and allocative inefficiency. The exact form of this system depends largely on the output distance function. For example, if output prices are positive and the output distance function is given by (2.9) with $\tau > 1$, then the n-th revenue-maximising output supply function is given by (4.13). In this case, the n-th equation in the system defined by (7.41) can be written as

$$\ln q_{nit} = \alpha_n(t) + \sum_{j=1}^{J} \delta_j \ln z_{jit} + \sum_{m=1}^{M} \beta_m \ln x_{mit} + \frac{\sigma}{1-\sigma} \ln\left(\sum_{k=1}^{N} \gamma_k^{\sigma} p_{kit}^{1-\sigma}\right) - \sigma \ln p_{nit} + u_{nit} \tag{7.42}$$

where $\alpha_n(t) \equiv \ln A(t) + \sigma \ln \gamma_n$. This equation is nonlinear in the unknown parameters. However, if $\gamma_1, \ldots, \gamma_N$ and σ are known, then it can be rewritten as

$$\ln q_{nit} = \alpha_n(t) + \sum_{j=1}^{J} \delta_j \ln z_{jit} + \sum_{m=1}^{M} \beta_m \ln x_{mit} + \sigma \left[\ln P(p_{it}) - \ln p_{nit}\right] + u_{nit} \tag{7.43}$$

where $P(p_{it}) = \left(\sum_{k=1}^{N} \gamma_k^{\sigma} p_{kit}^{1-\sigma}\right)^{1/(1-\sigma)}$ is an aggregate output price. This equation is linear in the parameters. In this equation, $\alpha_n(t)$ can be viewed as an output-specific measure of technical progress, δ_j is an unsigned elasticity that measures the percent change in output n due to a one percent increase in environmental variable j, β_m is a nonnegative elasticity that measures the percent increase in output n due to a one percent increase in input m, and σ is the elasticity of transformation between any two outputs. If there is no technical progress, then $\alpha_n(t)$ is time-invariant. If there is no environmental change, then the term involving the environmental variables can be deleted.

Equation (7.41) represents a system of N seemingly unrelated regression (SUR) equations in which each u_{nit} is uncorrelated with x_{it}, p_{it} and z_{it}. The unknown parameters in such systems can be estimated using feasible generalised least squares (FGLS) estimators. If the output mix is predetermined, then an alternative SUR system is

$$\ln q_{1it} = -\ln D_O^t(x_{it}, q_{it}^*, z_{it}) - u_{it} \tag{7.1}$$

and $$\ln q_{nit} = \ln \ddot{q}_n^t(x_{it}, p_{it}, z_{it}) + u_{nit} \quad \text{for } n = 2, \ldots, N, \tag{7.44}$$

where $u_{it} \equiv -\ln OTE^t(x_{it}, q_{it}, z_{it}) \geq 0$ denotes an output-oriented technical inefficiency effect. If the output mix is *not* predetermined, then (7.1) and (7.44) represent a system of N simultaneous equations. The unknown parameters in such systems can be estimated using corrected two-stage least squares (CTSLS) estimators.

7.6.3 Input Demand Systems

It is often possible to write profit-maximising and cost-minimising input demand functions as systems of equations in which the explanatory variables are deterministic. Again, for any given firm, the exact form of the system depends on the exact form of the manager's optimisation problem. For example, if firm i is a price taker in input markets and all outputs and environmental variables have been predetermined, then the manager's period-t optimisation problem is given by (4.17). In this case, the logarithms of the M observed inputs can be written as

$$\ln x_{mit} = \ln \ddot{x}_m^t(w_{it}, q_{it}, z_{it}) + u_{mit} \quad \text{for } m = 1, \ldots, M, \tag{7.45}$$

where $\ddot{x}_m^t(w_{it}, q_{it}, z_{it})$ denotes the m-th cost-minimising input demand function and $u_{mit} \equiv \ln x_{mit} - \ln \ddot{x}_m^t(w_{it}, q_{it}, z_{it})$ is an unsigned error that captures technical, scale and allocative inefficiency. The exact form of this system depends largely on the input distance function. For example, if input prices are positive and the input distance function is given by (2.13), then the m-th cost-minimising input demand function is given by (4.18). In this case, the m-th equation in the system defined by (7.45) can be written as

$$\begin{aligned}\ln x_{mit} = \theta_m(t) - \sum_{j=1}^{J} \kappa_j \ln z_{jit} + \sum_{k=1}^{M} \lambda_k \ln(w_{kit}/w_{mit}) \\ + \frac{1}{\tau\eta} \ln\left(\sum_{n=1}^{N} \gamma_n q_{nit}^{\tau}\right) + u_{mit}\end{aligned} \tag{7.46}$$

where $\theta_m(t) \equiv \ln \lambda_m - \ln B(t) - \sum_k \lambda_k \ln \lambda_k$. This equation is nonlinear in the unknown parameters. However, if $\gamma_1, \ldots, \gamma_N$ and τ are known, then it can be rewritten as

$$\ln x_{mit} = \theta_m(t) - \sum_{j=1}^{J} \kappa_j \ln z_{jit} + \sum_{k=1}^{M} \lambda_k \ln(w_{kit}/w_{mit}) + \psi \ln Q(q_{it}) + u_{mit} \tag{7.47}$$

where $Q(q_{it}) = \left(\sum_{n=1}^{N} \gamma_n q_{nit}^{\tau}\right)^{1/\tau}$ is an aggregate output and $\psi \equiv 1/\eta$ is the reciprocal of the elasticity of scale. This equation is linear in the parameters. In this equation, $\theta_m(t)$ can be viewed as an input-specific measure of technical progress, κ_j is an unsigned elasticity that measures the percent change in demand for input m due to a one percent increase in environmental variable j, and λ_k is a nonnegative elasticity that measures the percent increase in demand for input m due to a one percent increase in the the price of input k. If there is no technical progress, then $\theta_m(t)$ is time-invariant. If there is no environmental change, then the term involving the environmental variables can be deleted.

Equation (7.45) represents a system of SUR equations in which each u_{mit} is uncorrelated with w_{it}, q_{it} and z_{it}. Again, the unknown parameters in such systems can be estimated using FGLS estimators. If the input mix is predetermined, then an alternative SUR system is

$$-\ln x_{1it} = \ln D_I^t(x_{it}^*, q_{it}, z_{it}) - u_{it} \tag{7.4}$$

$$\text{and} \qquad \ln x_{mit} = \ln \ddot{x}_m^t(w_{it}, q_{it}, z_{it}) + u_{mit} \quad \text{for } m = 2, \ldots, M, \tag{7.48}$$

where $u_{it} \equiv -\ln ITE^t(x_{it}, q_{it}, z_{it}) \geq 0$ denotes an input-oriented technical inefficiency effect. If the input mix is *not* predetermined, then (7.4) and (7.48) represent a system of M simultaneous equations. Again, the unknown parameters in such systems can be estimated using CTSLS estimators.

7.7 Summary and Further Reading

Deterministic frontier models (DFMs) are underpinned by three assumptions: assumption DF1 says that production possibilities sets can be represented by distance, revenue, cost and/or profit functions; assumption DF2 says that all relevant quantities, prices and environmental variables are observed and measured without error; and assumption DF3 says the functional forms of relevant functions are known. If these assumptions are true, then production frontiers can be estimated using single-equation regression models with error terms representing inefficiency. The explanatory variables in these models are often assumed to be deterministic. The unknown parameters in so-called DFMs can be estimated using growth accounting (GA), least squares (LS) and maximum likelihood (ML) methods.

Most GA 'estimators' are underpinned by seven assumptions: assumption GA1 says that output and input sets are homothetic; assumption GA2 says that technical change is Hicks-neutral; assumption GA3 says that production frontiers exhibit constant returns to scale; assumption GA4 says that inputs are strongly disposable; assumption GA5 says that firms are price takers in input markets; assumption GA6 says that input prices are strictly positive; and assumption GA7 says that firm managers successfully minimise cost. If these assumptions are true, then the slope parameters in production functions can usually be estimated using differential calculus. The associated estimates/predictions of technical and cost efficiency are equal to one. If observed cost shares are firm- and/or time-varying, then DF1 to DF3 and GA1 to GA7 cannot all be true. The fact that all of these assumptions are rarely true has not diminished the popularity of the GA approach: Solow (1957) has used the approach to estimate a production frontier for the U.S. economy; Caselli and Coleman (2006) have used the approach to estimate a world production frontier; Hsieh and Klenow (2009) have used the approach to study resource misallocation in China, India and the U.S.; and O'Mahony and Timmer (2009) have used the approach to estimate the parameters of industry-level frontiers in Europe, the U.S. and Japan.

LS estimation of DFMs involves choosing the unknown parameters to minimise the sum of squared inefficiency effects. Most models are assumed to be linear in the unknown parameters, and the inefficiency effects are usually assumed to be independent random variables with a common mean and a common variance. If these assumptions are true, then the ordinary least squares (OLS) estimators for the slope parameters in the model are unbiased and consistent. However, the OLS estimator for the intercept must be adjusted (or corrected) to ensure that the estimated frontier envelops all the observations in the dataset. The associated estimators are commonly referred to as corrected ordinary least squares (COLS) estimators. The idea behind COLS estimation can be traced back at least as far as Winsten (1957, p. 283). For an empirical application, see Tsekouras et al. (2004).

ML estimation of DFMs involves choosing the unknown parameters to maximise the joint density (or 'likelihood') of the observed data. Different estimators are distinguished by different assumptions concerning the distributions of the inefficiency effects. Schmidt (1976) assumes they are either independent exponential or independent half-normal random variables. The associated ML estimators are equivalent to the linear programming and quadratic programming estimators of Aigner and Chu (1968). Afriat (1972, Sect. 3) assumes the inefficiency effects are independent gamma random variables. If the inefficiency effects are independent and identically distributed gamma random variables with shape parameter greater than two, then the associated ML estimators for the model parameters are consistent, asymptotically efficient and asymptotically normal. In all other cases (i.e., half-normal, or gamma with shape parameter less than or equal to two), the properties of the ML estimators are unknown. For more details, see Schmidt (1976, p. 239) and Greene (1980a, Sect. 3.2).

DFMs can be used to both measure and explain changes in TFP. *Measuring* changes in TFP involves computing proper TFP index (TFPI) numbers. DFMs can be used to compute additive, multiplicative, primal and dual TFPI numbers. *Explaining* changes in TFP generally involves decomposing proper TFPI numbers into measures of environmental change, technical change, and efficiency change. Both output- and input-oriented decompositions are available. Whether or not it is possible to separately identify all the components of TFP change depends on the both the TFPI and the output and input distance functions.

There are many TFPI numbers that are not proper in the sense that they cannot generally be written as proper output index numbers divided by proper input index numbers. One way of decomposing such numbers is to first write them as the product of proper TFPI numbers and statistical noise index (SNI) numbers. Subsequently, determinitic frontier models can be used to decompose the proper TFPI numbers into measures of technical change, environmental change and efficiency change. For an alternative decomposition methodology that involves a DFM but does not explicitly involve SNI numbers, see Tsekouras et al. (2004).

Other DFMs that are discussed in this chapter include metafrontier models and systems of output supply and input demand equations. Metafrontier models are used in situations where firm managers can be classified into two or more groups, and where managers in different groups choose input-output combinations from potentially different production possibilities sets.

References

Afriat S (1972) Efficiency estimation of production functions. Int Econ Rev 13(3):568–598

Aigner D, Chu S (1968) On estimating the industry production function. Am Econ Rev 58(4):826–839

Althin R, Fare R, Grosskopf S (1996) Profitability and productivity changes: an application to Swedish pharmacies. Ann Oper Res 66:219–230

Amsler C, Leonard M, Schmidt P (2013) Estimation and inference in parametric deterministic frontier models. J Prod Anal 40(3):293–305

Baltagi B, Griffin J (1988) A general index of technical change. J Polit Econ 96(1):20–41

Banker R, Conrad R, Strauss R (1986) A comparative application of data envelopment analysis and translog methods: an illustrative study of hospital production. Manage Sci 32(1):30–44

Banker R, Chang H, Cunningham R (2003) The public accounting industry production function. J Acc Econ 35(2):255–281

Bhargava A, Franzini L, Narendranathan W (1982) Serial correlation in the fixed effects model. Rev Econ Stud 49(4):533–549

Bickel P, Rosenblatt M (1973) On some global measures of the deviations of density function estimates. Ann Stat 1:1071–1095

Breusch T (1978) Testing for autocorrelation in dynamic linear models. Aust Econ Papers 17:334–355

Breusch T, Pagan A (1979) A simple test for heteroskedasticity and random coefficient variation. Econometrica 47:1287–1294

Breusch T, Pagan A (1980) The Lagrange multiplier test and its applications to model specification in econometrics. Rev Econ Stud 47:239–253

Caselli F, Coleman W (2006) The world technology frontier. Am Econ Rev 93(3):499–522

Chaudhary M, Khan M, Naqvi K, Ahmad M (1999) Estimates of farm output supply and input demand elasticities: the translog profit function approach [with comments]. Pak Dev Rev 37(4):1031–1050

Coelli T, Perelman S (1999) A comparison of parametric and non-parametric distance functions: with application to European railways. Eur J Oper Res 117(2):326–339

Coelli T, Estache A, Perelman S, Trujillo L (2003) A primer on efficiency measurement for utilities and transport regulators. WBI Development Studies, The World Bank

Coelli T, Gautier A, Perelman S, Saplacan-Pop R (2013) Estimating the cost of improving quality in electricity distribution: a parametric distance function approach. Energy Policy 53:287–297

Cragg J, Donald S (1993) Testing identifiability and specification in instrumental variable models. Econometric Theory 9:222–240

Das A, Kumbhakar S (2012) Productivity and efficiency dynamics in Indian banking: an input distance function approach incorporating quality of inputs and outputs. J Appl Econometrics 27(2):205–234

Deprins D, Simar L, Tulkens H (1984) Measuring labor efficiency in post offices. In: Marchand M, Pestieau P, Tulkens H (eds) The performance of public enterprises: concepts and measurements. North Holland Publishing Company, Amsterdam

Diewert W (1980) Aggregation problems in the measurement of capital. In: Usher D (ed) The measurement of capital. University of Chicago Press

Diewert W, Fox K (2010) Malmquist and Törnqvist productivity indexes: returns to scale and technical progress with imperfect competition. J Econ 101(1):73–95

Durbin J, Watson G (1950) Testing for serial correlation in least squares regression. I. Biometrika 37(3–4):409–428

Durbin J, Watson G (1951) Testing for serial correlation in least squares regression. II. Biometrika 38(1–2):159–179

Enders W (2004) Applied econometric time series, 2nd edn. Wiley, New Jersey

Engle R, Granger C (1987) Cointegration and error-correction: representation, estimation and testing. Econometrica 55:251–276

Engle R, Yoo B (1987) Forecasting and testing in co-integrated systems. J Econometrics 35(1):143–159

Fan Y (1994) Testing the goodness of fit of a parametric density function by Kernel method. Econometric Theory 10(2):316–356

Färe R, Grosskopf S, Lovell C, Yaisawarng S (1993) Derivation of shadow prices for undesirable outputs: a distance function approach. Rev Econ Stat 75(2):374–380

Ferrari A (2006) The internal market and hospital efficiency: a stochastic distance function approach. Appl Econ 38(18):2121–2130

Førsund F, Lovell C, Schmidt P (1980) A survey of frontier production functions and of their relationship to efficiency measurement. J Econometrics 13(1):5–25

Fuentes H, Grifell-Tatjé E, Sergio P (2001) A parametric distance function approach for Malmquist productivity index estimation. J Prod Anal 15(2001):79–94

Glesjer H (1969) A new test for heteroskedasticity. J Am Stat Assoc 64:316–323

Godfrey L (1978a) Testing against general autoregressive and moving average error models when the regressors include lagged dependent variables. Econometrica 46(6):1293–1301

Godfrey L (1978b) Testing for multiplicative heteroskedasticity. J Econometrics 8:227–236

Goldfeld S, Quandt R (1972) Nonlinear methods in econometrics. North-Holland, Amsterdam

Greene W (1980a) Maximum likelihood estimation of econometric frontier functions. J Econometrics 13(1):27–56

Greene W (1980b) On the estimation of a flexible frontier production model. J Econometrics 13(1):101–115

Greene W (2008) Econometric analysis, 6th edn. Prentice-Hall, Englewood Cliffs

Grosskopf S, Margaritis D, Valdmanis V (1995) Estimating output substitutability of hospital services: a distance function approach. Eur J Oper Res 80(1995):575–587

Hajargasht G, Coelli T, Rao D (2008) A dual measure of economies of scope. Econ Lett 100(2):185–188

Hill R, Griffiths W, Lim G (2011) Principles of econometrics, 4th edn. Wiley, New Jersey

Hsieh CT, Klenow P (2009) Misallocation and manufacturing TFP in China and India. Q J Econ 124(4):1403–1448

Koenker R, Bassett G (1982) Robust tests for heteroscedasticity based on regression quantiles. Econometrica 50(1):43–61

Kopp R, Diewert W (1982) The decomposition of frontier cost function deviations into measures of technical and allocative efficiency. J Econometrics 19(2–3):319–331

Kumbhakar S (1997) Modeling allocative inefficiency in a translog cost function and cost share equations: an exact relationship. J Econometrics 76(1–2):351–356

Kumbhakar S (2001) Estimation of profit functions when profit is not maximum. Am J Agri Econ 83(1):1–19

Kumbhakar S (2006) Specification and estimation of nonstandard profit functions. Empirical Econ 31(1):243–260

Kumbhakar S, Bhattacharyya A (1992) Price distortions and resource-use efficiency in Indian agriculture: a restricted profit function approach. Rev Econ Stat 74(2):231–239

Kumbhakar S, Lovell C (2000) Stochastic frontier analysis. Cambridge University Press

Nadiri M, Nandi B (1999) Technical change, markup, divestiture, and productivity growth in the U.S. telecommunications industry. Rev Econ Stat 81(3):488–498

Newey W, Powell J (1987) Asymmetric least squares estimation and testing. Econometrica 55(4):819–847

O'Donnell C (2016) Using information about technologies, markets and firm behaviour to decompose a proper productivity index. J Econometrics 190(2):328–340

O'Donnell C, Coelli T (2005) A Bayesian approach to imposing curvature on distance functions. J Econometrics 126(2):493–523

O'Mahony M, Timmer M (2009) Output, input and productivity measures at the industry level: the EU KLEMS database. Econ J 119(538):F374–F403

Orea L (2002) Parametric decomposition of a generalized Malmquist productivity index. J Prod Anal 18:5–22

Pagan A, Ullah A (1999) Nonparametric econometrics. Cambridge University Press, Cambridge, UK

Pesaran H (2004) General diagnostic tests for cross section dependence in panels. CESifo working paper 1229, Ifo Institute, Center for Economic Studies

Ray S (1998) Measuring scale efficiency from a translog production function. J Prod Anal 11(2):183–194

Reig-Martinez E, Picazo-Tadeo A, Hernandez-Sancho F (2001) The calculation of shadow prices for industrial wastes using distance functions: an analysis for Spanish ceramic pavements firms. Int J Prod Econ 69(2001):277–285

Richmond J (1974) Estimating the efficiency of production. Int Econ Rev 15(2):515–521

Rosenblatt M (1975) A quadratic measure of deviation of two-dimensional density estimates and a test of independence. Ann Stat 3:1–14

Schmidt P (1976) On the statistical estimation of parametric frontier production functions. Rev Econ Stat 58(2):238–239

Solow R (1957) Technical change and the aggregate production function. Rev Econ Stat 39(3):312–320

Stern D (2010) Derivation of the Hicks, or direct, elasticity of substitution using the input distance function. Econ Lett 108(3):349–351

Tsekouras K, Pantzios CJ, Karagiannis G (2004) Malmquist productivity index estimation with zero-value variables: the case of Greek prefectural training councils. Int J Prod Econ 89(1):95–106

Vardanyan M, Noh DW (2006) Approximating pollution abatement costs via alternative specifications of a multi-output production technology: a case of the US electric utility industry. J Environ Manage 80(2)

White H (1980) A heteroskedasticity-consistent covariance matrix estimator and a direct test for heteroskedasticity. Econometrica 48:817–838

Winsten C (1957) Discussion on Mr. Farrell's paper. J R Stat Soc Ser A (General) 120(3):282–84

Zhang T, Garvey E (2008) A comparative analysis of multi-output frontier models. J Zhejiang Univ Sci A 9(10):1426–1436

Zheng S, Bloch H (2014) Australia's mining productivity decline: implications for MFP measurement. J Prod Anal 41(2):201–212

Chapter 8
Stochastic Frontier Analysis

Distance, revenue, cost and profit functions can always be written in the form of regression models with unobserved error terms representing statistical noise and different types of inefficiency. In practice, the noise components are almost always assumed to be random variables (i.e., stochastic). The associated frontiers are known as stochastic frontiers. This chapter explains how to estimate and draw inferences concerning the unknown parameters in so-called stochastic frontier models (SFMs). It then explains how the estimated parameters can be used to predict levels of efficiency and analyse productivity change. The focus is on maximum likelihood estimators and predictors. Maximum likelihood estimation of SFMs dates back to Aigner et al. (1977) and Meeusen and van den Broeck (1977).

8.1 Basic Models

SFMs are underpinned by only one assumption, namely that production possibilities sets can be represented by distance, revenue, cost and/or profit functions. Each of these functions can be written as a single-equation regression model with two error terms, one representing statistical noise and the other representing inefficiency.

8.1.1 Output-Oriented Models

Output-oriented SFMs are mainly used to estimate the measure of OTE defined by (5.1). This involves estimating the output distance function. If the functional form of this function is known, then the relationship between inputs, outputs and environmental variables can be written in the form of (7.1). If the functional form of the output distance function is *not* known, then we can instead write

C. J. O'Donnell, *Productivity and Efficiency Analysis*,
https://doi.org/10.1007/978-981-13-2984-5_8

$$\ln q_{1it} = f^t(x_{it}, q^*_{it}, z_{it}) + v_{it} - u_{it} \tag{8.1}$$

where $q^*_{it} \equiv q_{it}/q_{1it}$ denotes a vector of normalised outputs, $f^t(.)$ is an approximating function chosen by the researcher, $v_{it} = -\ln D^t_O(x_{it}, q^*_{it}, z_{it}) - f^t(x_{it}, q^*_{it}, z_{it})$ represents statistical noise, and $u_{it} \equiv -\ln OTE^t(x_{it}, q_{it}, z_{it}) \geq 0$ denotes an output-oriented technical inefficiency effect. If statistical noise is stochastic, then frontier outputs are generally also stochastic (hence the term 'stochastic frontier'). If there is no statistical noise, then (8.1) reduces to (7.1).

In this book, statistical noise is viewed as a combination of functional form errors, measurement errors, omitted variable errors and included variable errors. In any given output-oriented SFM, the precise nature of statistical noise depends on both the approximating function and the output distance function. Suppose, for example, that the approximating function is

$$f^t(x_{it}, q^*_{it}, z_{it}) = \alpha + \lambda t + \sum_{j=1}^{J} \delta_j \ln z_{jit} + \sum_{m=1}^{M} \beta_m \ln x_{mit} - \ln Q(q^*_{it}) \tag{8.2}$$

where $Q(.)$ is a known, nonnegative, nondecreasing, linearly-homogenous function. In this case, Eq. (8.1) can be written as

$$\ln Q(q_{it}) = \alpha + \lambda t + \sum_{j=1}^{J} \delta_j \ln z_{jit} + \sum_{m=1}^{M} \beta_m \ln x_{mit} + v_{it} - u_{it} \tag{8.3}$$

where $Q(q_{it})$ is an aggregate output. This model has the same basic structure, but not necessarily the same interpretation,[1] as the models of Meeusen and van den Broeck (1977, p. 436), Aigner et al. (1977, Eq. 7) and Battese and Corra (1977, Eq. 1). If the output distance function is given by (2.9), for example, then

$$v_{it} = [\ln A(t) - \alpha - \lambda t] + \left[\ln Q(q_{it}) - \frac{1}{\tau} \ln \left(\sum_{n=1}^{N} \gamma_n q^{\tau}_{nit} \right) \right]. \tag{8.4}$$

The first term in square brackets can be viewed as a possible functional form error. The second term can be viewed as a possible measurement error. Importantly, the presence of statistical noise means we cannot generally interpret the parameters in (8.3) in the same way we interpreted the parameters in (7.3). For example, unless we know (or assume) that v_{it} is not a function of x_{mit}, we cannot interpret β_m as an elasticity that measures the percent change in the aggregate output due to a one percent change in the m-th input.

[1]The dependent variable in the Aigner et al. (1977) model is an output, not the logarithm of an output. The dependent variable in the Battese and Corra (1977) model is a value, not the logarithm of a quantity. If there is no statistical noise and the dependent variable is either an output or a value, then u_{it} can no longer be interpreted as an output-oriented technical inefficiency effect.

8.1.2 Input-Oriented Models

Input-oriented SFMs are mainly used to estimate the measure of ITE defined by (5.8). This involves estimating the input distance function. If the functional form of this function is known, then the relationship between inputs, outputs and environmental variables can be written in the form of (7.4). If the functional form of the input distance function is *not* known, then we can instead write

$$-\ln x_{1it} = f^t(x^*_{it}, q_{it}, z_{it}) + v_{it} - u_{it} \tag{8.5}$$

where $x^*_{it} \equiv x_{it}/x_{1it}$ denotes a vector of normalised inputs, $f^t(.)$ is an approximating function chosen by the researcher, $v_{it} = \ln D^t_I(x^*_{it}, q_{it}, z_{it}) - f^t(x^*_{it}, q_{it}, z_{it})$ represents statistical noise, and $u_{it} \equiv ITE^t(x_{it}, q_{it}, z_{it}) \geq 0$ now denotes an input-oriented technical inefficiency effect. If statistical noise is stochastic, then, frontier inputs are generally also stochastic. If there is no statistical noise, then (8.5) reduces to (7.4).

In any given input-oriented SFM, the precise nature of statistical noise depends on both the approximating function and the input distance function. Suppose, for example, that the approximating function is

$$f^t(x^*_{it}, q_{it}, z_{it}) = \xi + \sum_{j=1}^{J} \kappa_j \ln z_{jit} + \ln X(x^*_{it}) - \sum_{n=1}^{N} \alpha_n \ln q_{nit} \tag{8.6}$$

where $X(.)$ is a known, nonnegative, nondecreasing, linearly-homogenous function. In this case, Eq. (8.5) can be written as

$$-\ln X(x_{it}) = \xi + \sum_{j=1}^{J} \kappa_j \ln z_{jit} - \sum_{n=1}^{N} \alpha_n \ln q_{nit} + v_{it} - u_{it} \tag{8.7}$$

where $X(x_{it})$ is an aggregate input. This model has the same basic structure as the input-oriented SFM of O'Donnell and Nguyen (2013, Eq. 21). If the input distance function is given by (2.13), for example, then

$$\begin{aligned} v_{it} = [\xi(t) - \xi] &+ \left[\sum_{m=1}^{M} \lambda_m \ln x_{mit} - \ln X(x_{it})\right] \\ &+ \left[\sum_{n=1}^{N} \alpha_n \ln q_{nit} - \frac{1}{\tau\eta} \ln\left(\sum_{n=1}^{N} \gamma_n q^{\tau}_{nit}\right)\right] \end{aligned} \tag{8.8}$$

where $\xi(t) \equiv \ln B(t)$. The first term in square brackets can be viewed as an omitted dummy variable error. The second term is a possible measurement error. The last term is a functional form error. Again, the presence of statistical noise means we cannot generally interpret the parameters in (8.7) in the same way we interpreted the parameters in (7.6). For example, unless we know (or assume) that v_{it} is not a function of z_{jit}, we cannot interpret κ_j as an elasticity that measures the percent change in the aggregate input due to a one percent change in the j-th environmental variable. The presence of statistical noise also means it is not generally possible to establish relationships between the parameters in (8.7) and the parameters in other SFMs. For example, unless we know (or assume) the precise nature of statistical noise, we cannot establish the relationship between κ_j in (8.7) and δ_j in (8.3).

8.1.3 Revenue-Oriented Models

Revenue-oriented SFMs are mainly used to estimate the measure of RE defined by (5.15). This involves estimating the revenue function. If the functional form of the revenue function is known, then the relationship between total revenue, input quantities, output prices and environmental variables can be written in the form of (7.7). If the functional form of the revenue function is *not* known, then we can instead write

$$\ln(R_{it}/p_{1it}) = f^t(x_{it}, p^*_{it}, z_{it}) + v_{it} - u_{it} \tag{8.9}$$

where $p^*_{it} \equiv p_{it}/p_{1it}$ denotes a vector of normalised output prices, $f^t(.)$ is an approximating function chosen by the researcher, $v_{it} = \ln R^t(x_{it}, p^*_{it}, z_{it}) - f^t(x_{it}, p^*_{it}, z_{it})$ represents statistical noise, and $u_{it} \equiv -\ln RE^t(x_{it}, p_{it}, q_{it}, z_{it}) \geq 0$ denotes a revenue inefficiency effect. If statistical noise is stochastic, then maximum normalised revenue is generally also stochastic. If there is no statistical noise, then (8.9) reduces to (7.7).

In any given revenue-oriented SFM, the precise nature of statistical noise depends on both the approximating function and the revenue function. Suppose, for example, the approximating function is

$$\begin{aligned} f^t(x_{it}, p^*_{it}, z_{it}) = \alpha &+ \sum_{m=1}^{M} \beta_m \ln x_{mit} + \sum_{m=1}^{M}\sum_{h=m}^{M} \beta_{mh} \ln x_{mit} \ln x_{hit} \\ &+ \sum_{n=1}^{N} \alpha_n \ln p^*_{nit} + \sum_{n=1}^{N}\sum_{h=n}^{N} \alpha_{nh} \ln p^*_{nit} \ln p^*_{hit} \\ &+ \sum_{m=1}^{M}\sum_{n=1}^{N} \theta_{mn} \ln x_{mit} \ln p^*_{nit} \end{aligned} \tag{8.10}$$

In this case, Eq. (8.9) takes the form

$$\begin{aligned}\ln(R_{it}/p_{1it}) &= \alpha + \sum_{m=1}^{M} \beta_m \ln x_{mit} + \sum_{m=1}^{M}\sum_{h=m}^{M} \beta_{mh} \ln x_{mit} \ln x_{hit} \\ &+ \sum_{n=1}^{N} \alpha_n \ln p^*_{nit} + \sum_{n=1}^{N}\sum_{h=n}^{N} \alpha_{nh} \ln p^*_{nit} \ln p^*_{hit} \\ &+ \sum_{m=1}^{M}\sum_{n=1}^{N} \theta_{mn} \ln x_{mit} \ln p^*_{nit} + v_{it} - u_{it}. \qquad (8.11)\end{aligned}$$

This model has the same basic structure as the revenue-oriented SFM of Byma and Tauer (2007, Eq. 18). If the revenue function is given by (2.17), for example, then,

$$\begin{aligned}v_{it} &= [\ln A(t) - \alpha] + \left[\sum_{j=1}^{J} \delta_j \ln z_{jit}\right] - \left[\sum_{m=1}^{M}\sum_{h=m}^{M} \beta_{mh} \ln x_{mit} \ln x_{hit}\right. \\ &\left. + \sum_{n=1}^{N}\sum_{h=n}^{N} \alpha_{nh} \ln p^*_{nit} \ln p^*_{hit} + \sum_{m=1}^{M}\sum_{n=1}^{N} \theta_{mn} \ln x_{mit} \ln p^*_{nit}\right] \\ &+ \left[\frac{1}{1-\sigma} \ln\left(\sum_{n=1}^{N} \gamma_n^{\sigma} p_{nit}^{*1-\sigma}\right) - \sum_{n=1}^{N} \alpha_n \ln p^*_{nit}\right]. \qquad (8.12)\end{aligned}$$

The first term in square brackets can be viewed as an omitted dummy variable error. The second term is an omitted environmental variable error. The third term can be viewed as an included variable error. The last term is a functional form error. Again, the presence of statistical noise means we cannot generally interpret the parameters in (8.11) in the same way we interpreted the parameters in (7.9). For example, unless we know (or assume) that v_{it} is not a function of x_{mit}, we cannot simply differentiate (8.11) and interpret $\partial \ln(R_{it}/p_{1it})/\partial \ln x_{mit}$ as an elasticity that measures the percent increase in normalised revenue due to a one percent increase in the m-th input. Again, the presence of statistical noise also means it is not generally possible to establish relationships between the parameters in (8.11) and the parameters in other SFMs.

8.1.4 Cost-Oriented Models

Cost-oriented SFMs are mainly used to estimate the measure of CE defined by (5.20). This involves estimating the cost function. If the functional form of the cost function is known, then the relationship between total cost, input prices, output quantities and environmental variables can be written in the form of (7.10). If the functional form of the cost function is *not* known, then we can instead write

$$-\ln(C_{it}/w_{1it}) = f^t(w_{it}^*, q_{it}, z_{it}) + v_{it} - u_{it} \tag{8.13}$$

where $w_{it}^* \equiv w_{it}/w_{1it}$ denotes a vector of normalised input prices, $f^t(.)$ is an approximating function chosen by the researcher, $v_{it} = -\ln C^t(w_{it}^*, q_{it}, z_{it}) - f^t(w_{it}^*, q_{it}, z_{it})$ represents statistical noise, and $u_{it} \equiv -\ln CE^t(w_{it}, x_{it}, q_{it}, z_{it}) \geq 0$ denotes a cost inefficiency effect. If statistical noise is stochastic, then minimum normalised cost is generally also stochastic. If there is no statistical noise, then (8.13) reduces to (7.10).

In any given cost-oriented SFM, the precise nature of statistical noise depends on both the approximating function and the cost function. Suppose, for example, the approximating function is

$$f^t(w_{it}^*, q_{it}, z_{it}) = \theta - \sum_{m=1}^{M} \lambda_m \ln w_{mit}^* - \psi \ln Q(q_{it})$$

where $Q(.)$ is a known, nonnegative, nondecreasing, linearly-homogenous function. In this case, Eq. (8.13) takes the form

$$-\ln(C_{it}/w_{1it}) = \theta - \sum_{m=1}^{M} \lambda_m \ln w_{mit}^* - \psi \ln Q(q_{it}) + v_{it} - u_{it} \tag{8.14}$$

where $Q(q_{it})$ is an aggregate output. This model has the same basic structure as the cost-oriented SFM of Herr (2008, Eq. 2). If the cost function is given by (2.22), for example, then,

$$v_{it} = [\theta(t) - \theta] + \left[\sum_{j=1}^{J} \kappa_j \ln z_{jit}\right] + \left[\psi \ln Q(q_{it}) - \frac{1}{\tau\eta} \ln\left(\sum_{n=1}^{N} \gamma_n q_{nit}^{\tau}\right)\right] \tag{8.15}$$

where $\theta(t) \equiv \ln B(t) + \sum_m \lambda_m \ln \lambda_m$. The first term in square brackets can be viewed as an omitted dummy variable error. The second term is an omitted environmental variable error. The last term is a possible measurement error. Again, the presence of statistical noise means we cannot generally interpret the parameters in (8.14) in the same way we interpreted the parameters in (7.12). For example, unless we know (or assume) that v_{it} is not a function of w_{mit}^*, we cannot interpret λ_m as an elasticity that measures the percent increase in normalised cost due to a one percent increase in the m-th normalised input price. Again, the presence of statistical noise also means it is not generally possible to establish relationships between the parameters in (8.14) and the parameters in other SFMs.

8.1.5 Profit-Oriented Models

Profit-oriented SFMs are mainly used to estimate the measure of PE defined by (5.27). This involves estimating the profit function. If the functional form of the profit function is known, then the relationship between total profit, prices and environmental variables can be written in the form of (7.13). If the functional form of the profit function is *not* known, then we can instead write

$$\ln(\Pi_{it}/p_{1it}) = f^t(w^*_{it}, p^*_{it}, z_{it}) + v_{it} - u_{it} \tag{8.16}$$

where $w^*_{it} \equiv w_{it}/p_{1it}$ denotes a vector of normalised input prices, $p^*_{it} \equiv p_{it}/p_{1it}$ denotes a vector of normalised output prices, $f^t(.)$ is an approximating function chosen by the researcher, $v_{it} = \ln \Pi^t(w^*_{it}, p^*_{it}, z_{it}) - f^t(w^*_{it}, p^*_{it}, z_{it})$ represents statistical noise, and $u_{it} \equiv -\ln PE^t(w_{it}, x_{it}, p_{it}, q_{it}, z_{it}) \geq 0$ denotes a profit inefficiency effect. If statistical noise is stochastic, then maximum normalised profit is generally also stochastic. If there is no statistical noise, then (8.16) reduces to (7.13).

In any given profit-oriented SFM, the precise nature of statistical noise depends on both the approximating function and the profit function. Suppose, for example, the approximating function is

$$f^t(w^*_{it}, p^*_{it}, z_{it}) = \phi + \sum_{j=1}^{J} \delta^*_j \ln z_{jit} - \sum_{m=1}^{M} \beta^*_m \ln w^*_{mit} + \sum_{n=1}^{N} \alpha_n \ln p^*_{nit}$$

In this case, Eq. (8.16) takes the form

$$\ln(\Pi_{it}/p_{1it}) = \phi + \sum_{j=1}^{J} \delta^*_j \ln z_{jit} - \sum_{m=1}^{M} \beta^*_m \ln w^*_{mit} + \sum_{n=1}^{N} \alpha_n \ln p^*_{nit} + v_{it} - u_{it}. \tag{8.17}$$

If the profit function is given by (2.27), for example, then

$$v_{it} = [\phi(t) - \phi] + \left[\frac{1}{(1-\sigma)(1-\eta)} \ln\left(\sum_{n=1}^{N} \gamma_n^{\sigma} p^{*1-\sigma}_{nit}\right) - \sum_{n=1}^{N} \alpha_n \ln p^*_{nit}\right] \tag{8.18}$$

where $\phi(t) \equiv \ln(1-\eta) + (\ln A(t) + \sum_m \beta_m \ln \beta_m)/(1-\eta)$. The first term in square brackets can be viewed as an omitted dummy variable error. The second term can be viewed as a functional form error. Again, the presence of statistical noise means we cannot generally interpret the parameters in (8.17) in the same way we interpreted the parameters in (7.15). For example, unless we know (or assume) that v_{it} is not a function of w^*_{mit}, we cannot interpret β^*_m as an elasticity that measures the percent decrease in normalised profit due to a one percent increase in the m-th normalised input price. Again, the presence of statistical noise also means it is not generally possible to establish relationships between the parameters in (8.17) and the parameters in other SFMs.

8.2 Least Squares Estimation

Least squares (LS) estimation of SFMs involves choosing the unknown parameters to minimise the sum of squared noise and inefficiency effects. For simplicity, this section considers estimation of the output-oriented model defined by (8.3). This model can be written more compactly as

$$y_{it} = \alpha + \lambda t + \sum_{j=1}^{J} \delta_j \ln z_{jit} + \sum_{m=1}^{M} \beta_m \ln x_{mit} + \varepsilon_{it} \tag{8.19}$$

where $y_{it} = \ln Q(q_{it})$ is the logarithm of the aggregate output and $\varepsilon_{it} \equiv v_{it} - u_{it}$ is a composite error representing statistical noise and output-oriented technical inefficiency. To estimate the unknown parameters, we need to make some assumptions about this composite error.

8.2.1 Assumptions

It is common to assume that ε_{it} is a random variable with the following properties:

LS5 $E(\varepsilon_{it}) = -\mu \leq 0$ for all i and t,
LS6 $var(\varepsilon_{it}) = \sigma_{\varepsilon}^2$ for all i and t,
LS7 $cov(\varepsilon_{it}, \varepsilon_{ks}) = 0$ if $i \neq k$ or $t \neq s$, and
LS8 ε_{it} is uncorrelated with the explanatory variables.

LS5 says that the composite errors have the same mean. LS6 says they are homoskedastic. LS7 says they are serially and spatially uncorrelated. LS8 is self-explanatory.

8.2.2 Estimation

If LS5 is true, then (8.19) can be rewritten as

$$y_{it} = \alpha^* + \lambda t + \sum_{j=1}^{J} \delta_j \ln z_{jit} + \sum_{m=1}^{M} \beta_m \ln x_{mit} + e_{it} \tag{8.20}$$

where $\alpha^* \equiv \alpha - \mu$ is a fixed parameter and $e_{it} \equiv v_{it} - u_{it} + \mu$ is a random variable with a mean of zero. This equation has the same structure, but not the same interpretation,[2] as (7.19). If LS5 and LS8 are true, then the ordinary least squares (OLS) estimators for α^* and the slope parameters are unbiased and consistent. Consistent estimators for μ and α are also available, but only by making additional assumptions concerning the noise and inefficiency effects. In the efficiency literature, it is common to assume that v_{it} is a normal random variable and u_{it} is a half-normal random variable. In this case, a consistent estimator for μ is $\hat{\mu} = [2s_3/(\pi - 4)]^{1/3}$ where s_3 denotes the third moment of the OLS residuals.[3] The associated estimator for α is $\hat{\alpha} = \hat{\alpha}^* + \hat{\mu}$ where $\hat{\alpha}^*$ denotes the OLS estimator for α^*. In this book,[4] $\hat{\alpha}$ and the OLS estimators for the slope parameters are collectively referred to as modified ordinary least squares (MOLS) estimators. MOLS estimators are rarely used in practice because they are less efficient than maximum likelihood (ML) estimators.

It is common to impose linear equality restrictions on the parameters in models such as (8.20). If the restrictions (and LS5 and LS8) are true, then restricted least squares (RLS) estimators for the slope parameters are consistent. Again, a consistent estimator for the intercept can be obtained by modifying the RLS estimator for the intercept by an amount that depends on the distributions of the noise and inefficiency effects. In this book, the associated estimators are collectively referred to as modified restricted least squares (MRLS) estimators. Again, MRLS estimators are rarely used in practice because they are less efficient than ML estimators.

Finally, Eq. (8.20) is linear in the unknown parameters. Some SFMs are *nonlinear* in the unknown parameters. If such a model contains an intercept term and LS5 and LS8 are true, then nonlinear least squares (NLS) estimators for the slope parameters are consistent; for details, see Meesters (2013). Again, a consistent estimator for the intercept can be obtained by modifying the NLS estimator for the intercept by an amount that depends on the distributions of the noise and inefficiency effects. In this book, the associated estimators are collectively referred to as modified nonlinear least squares (MNLS) estimators. Again, MNLS estimators are rarely used in practice because they are less efficient than ML estimators.

8.2.3 Prediction

We have been using u_{it} to denote the inefficiency of firm i in period t. The associated measure of efficiency is $\exp(-u_{it})$. LS predictors for these variables are available, but only under stronger assumptions than LS5 to LS8. In the efficiency literature, it

---

[2]The error term in (7.19) is a mean-corrected inefficiency effect, whereas the error term in (8.20) is a mean-corrected noise and inefficiency effect.

[3]The n-th moment of the OLS residuals is $s_n = \sum_t^T \sum_i^{I_t} \hat{e}_{it}^n / \sum_t^T I_t$ where $\hat{e}_{it}$ denotes the it-th residual and I_t is the number of firms in the dataset in period t.

[4]Elsewhere, these estimators are sometimes referred to as corrected ordinary least squares (COLS) estimators; see, for example, Horrace and Schmidt (1996, p. 260). In this book, the term COLS is reserved for LS estimators for the parameters in deterministic frontier models.

is common to assume that v_{it} is an independent $N(0, \sigma_v^2)$ random variable and u_{it} is an independent $N^+(0, \sigma_u^2)$ random variable. If these assumptions are true, then LS predictors for u_{it} and $\exp(-u_{it})$ can be obtained by substituting the LS estimators into the following:

$$E(u_{it}|\varepsilon_{it}) = \mu_{it}^* + \sigma_* \left(\frac{\phi(\mu_{it}^*/\sigma_*)}{\Phi(\mu_{it}^*/\sigma_*)} \right) \tag{8.21}$$

$$\text{and} \quad E(\exp(-u_{it})|\varepsilon_{it}) = \exp\left(\sigma_*^2/2 - \mu_{it}^*\right) \left(\frac{\Phi(\mu_{it}^*/\sigma_* - \sigma_*)}{\Phi(\mu_{it}^*/\sigma_*)} \right) \tag{8.22}$$

where $\mu_{it}^* \equiv (-\varepsilon_{it}\sigma_u^2)/(\sigma_v^2 + \sigma_u^2)$ and $\sigma_*^2 \equiv \sigma_v^2\sigma_u^2/(\sigma_v^2 + \sigma_u^2)$. These predictors are rarely used in practice, for three main reasons. First, the LS estimator for σ_u^2 is

$$\hat{\sigma}_u^2 = \left(\frac{\pi}{2}\right)^{1/3} \left(\frac{\pi s_3}{\pi - 4}\right)^{2/3}$$

where s_3 is the third moment of the LS residuals. If $s_3 > 0$, then $\hat{\sigma}_u^2$ is not mathematically well-defined. In such cases, it is common[5] to set $\sigma_u^2 = 0$ and estimate a standard multiple regression model. Second, the LS estimator for σ_v^2 is

$$\hat{\sigma}_v^2 = s_2 - \left(\frac{\pi - 2}{\pi}\right) \hat{\sigma}_u^2$$

where s_2 is the second moment of the LS residuals. If $\hat{\sigma}_u^2$ is sufficiently large, then $\hat{\sigma}_v^2 < 0$. This is theoretically implausible (variances cannot be negative). In such cases, it would be reasonable to set $\sigma_v^2 = 0$ and estimate a deterministic frontier model. Finally, if the probability distributions of the noise and inefficiency effects are known, then LS predictors are less efficient than ML predictors.

8.2.4 Hypothesis Tests

Even though they cannot generally be given an economic interpretation, it is common to test hypotheses concerning the slope parameters in SFMs. It is also common to test some or all of assumptions LS5 to LS8; tests of these assumptions are tests for fixed effects, heteroskedasticity, autocorrelation and endogeneity (respectively). If the data are time-series or panel data, then it is advisable to test whether any of the explanatory variables in the model are difference-stationary. If so, then it is advisable to test whether the dependent and explanatory variables are cointegrated. All of these tests can be conducted using LS residuals and the testing procedures described in

[5]See, for example, Coelli (1995, p. 250).

Sect. 7.3.4. Other hypothesis tests that can be conducted using LS residuals include tests for skewness and tests for random effects.

8.2.4.1 Skewness

If the distribution of v_{it} is symmetric and $u_{it} > 0$, then the distribution of $\varepsilon_{it} \equiv v_{it} - u_{it}$ is left-skewed ($\Rightarrow$ it has a relatively long left-hand tail and the mean is less than the mode). A test of the null hypothesis that the distribution of ε_{it} is symmetric against the alternative that it is left-skewed (or 'negatively-skewed') can be viewed as a test of the null hypothesis that there are no inefficiency effects. Tests for skewness can be found in Schmidt and Lin (1984, p. 351),[6] Coelli (1995, p. 253), Kuosmanen and Fosgerau (2009) and Henderson and Parmeter (2015).

8.2.4.2 Random Effects

When using panel data, it is common to test for firm- and/or time-invariant random effects. To illustrate the main idea, suppose that $v_{it} = v_{it}^* + w_i$ where v_{it}^* is a random variable with a mean of zero and w_i is an independent random variable with a mean of zero and a variance of σ_w^2. If this is true, and if LS5 is also true, then (8.20) can be rewritten as

$$y_{it} = \alpha^* + w_i + \lambda t + \sum_{j=1}^{J} \delta_j \ln z_{jit} + \sum_{m=1}^{M} \beta_m \ln x_{mit} + e_{it}^* \tag{8.23}$$

where $\alpha^* \equiv \alpha - \mu$ is a fixed parameter and $e_{it}^* \equiv v_{it}^* - u_{it} + \mu$ is a random variable with a mean of zero. If $\sigma_w^2 = 0$, then $w_i = 0$ and (8.23) reduces to (8.20). Equation (8.23) has the same basic structure as the standard random effects model discussed in introductory econometrics textbooks; see, for example, Hill et al. (2011, Sect. 15.4). In the efficiency literature, it is commonly referred to as a 'true' random effects (TRE) model; this terminology can be traced back to Greene (2005, p. 11). A test of the null hypothesis that $\sigma_w^2 = 0$ against the alternative that $\sigma_w^2 > 0$ is known as a test for (time-invariant) random effects. A Lagrange multiplier test of this null against this alternative can be found in Hill et al. (2011, p. 554).

8.2.5 *Toy Example*

Reconsider the toy data reported earlier in Tables 1.1 and 1.2. These data have been used to obtain MOLS and MRLS estimates of the parameters in (8.3). The estimates

---

[6] Schmidt and Lin (1984) describe their test as a 'test of the existence of a frontier'.

Table 8.1 LS parameter estimates

	MOLS			MRLS		
Parameter	Est.	St. err.	t	Est.	St. err.	t
α	1.130	0.253	4.464***	1.026	0.129	7.941***
λ	−0.040	0.071	−0.564	0.000	0.000	NaN
δ_1	−0.151	0.314	−0.481	−0.182	0.304	−0.598
β_1	0.281	0.107	2.628***	0.274	0.105	2.621***
β_2	0.043	0.066	0.645	0.034	0.063	0.533

***, ** and * indicate significance at the 1, 5 and 10% levels

Table 8.2 LS predictions of OTE

Row	Firm	Period	MOLS	MRLS
A	1	1	0.482	0.489
B	2	1	0.547	0.553
C	3	1	0.769	0.784
D	4	1	0.738	0.752
E	5	1	0.804	0.817
F	1	2	0.549	0.549
G	2	2	0.810	0.820
H	3	2	0.836	0.835
I	4	2	0.791	0.793
J	5	2	0.820	0.815
K	1	3	0.842	0.841
L	2	3	0.821	0.818
M	3	3	0.724	0.715
N	4	3	0.521	0.492
O	5	3	0.773	0.773
P	1	4	0.576	0.539
R	2	4	0.760	0.741
S	3	4	0.514	0.485
T	4	4	0.851	0.847
U	5	4	0.541	0.503
V	1	5	0.856	0.843
W	2	5	0.798	0.779
X	3	5	0.559	0.515
Y	4	5	0.572	0.522
Z	5	5	0.789	0.766
Geometric mean			0.693	0.680

are reported in Table 8.1. Both sets of estimates were obtained under the assumption that v_{it} is an independent $N(0, \sigma_v^2)$ random variable and u_{it} is an independent $N^+(0, \sigma_u^2)$ random variable. The MRLS estimates were obtained by imposing the restriction that $\lambda \geq 0$. Both sets of estimates have been used to predict levels of output-oriented technical efficiency (OTE). The predictions are reported in Table 8.2. The presence of statistical noise means it is not possible to use the parameter estimates reported in Table 8.1 to predict levels of input-oriented technical efficiency (ITE).

8.3 Maximum Likelihood Estimation

Maximum likelihood (ML) estimation of SFMs involves choosing the unknown parameters to maximise the joint density (or 'likelihood') of the observed data. For simplicity, this section considers estimation of the following output-oriented model:

$$y_{it} = \alpha + f^t(x_{it}, z_{it}) + v_{it} - u_{it} \tag{8.24}$$

where y_{it} denotes the logarithm of an aggregate output, $f^t(.)$ is a known approximating function, v_{it} represents statistical noise, and u_{it} denotes an output-oriented technical inefficiency effect. The joint density of the observed data depends on the assumed probability distributions of the noise and inefficiency effects.

8.3.1 Assumptions

It is common[7] to assume that

ML3 v_{it} is an independent $N(0, \sigma_v^2)$ random variable, and
ML4 u_{it} is an independent $N^+(\mu, \sigma_u^2)$ random variable.

In this context, the term 'independent' means that the noise and inefficiency effects are neither correlated with each other nor correlated with the explanatory variables (i.e., all these variables are mutually independent). ML3 says that v_{it} is an independent normal random variable. ML4 says that u_{it} is an independent truncated-normal random variable obtained by lower-truncating the $N(\mu, \sigma_u^2)$ distribution at zero. So-called normal-truncated-normal models can be traced back at least as far as Stevenson (1980). If $\mu = 0$, then the truncated-normal distribution collapses to a half-normal distribution. So-called normal-half-normal models can be traced back to Aigner et al. (1977). If ML3 and ML4 are true, then ML estimators for the model parameters are consistent, asymptotically efficient and asymptotically normal.

---

[7] See, for example, Stevenson (1980), Battese and Coelli (1995) and Salas-Velasco (2018).

8.3.2 Estimation

Finding the parameter values that maximise the likelihood function is equivalent to finding the parameter values that maximise the *logarithm* of the likelihood function. If, for example, ML3 and ML4 are true, then the so-called log-likelihood function is

$$\ln L(y|X,\theta) = N \ln\left(\frac{2}{\sqrt{2\pi\sigma^2}}\right) - \frac{1}{2}\sum_{t=1}^{T}\sum_{i=1}^{I_t}\left(\frac{\varepsilon_{it}+\mu}{\sigma}\right)^2 + \sum_{t=1}^{T}\sum_{i=1}^{I_t}\ln \Phi\left(\frac{\mu}{\sigma\lambda} - \frac{\lambda\varepsilon_{it}}{\sigma}\right) \tag{8.25}$$

where I_t denotes the number of firms in the dataset in period t, $N \equiv \sum_t I_t$ denotes the total number of observations in the dataset, $\varepsilon_{it} \equiv y_{it} - \alpha - f^t(x_{it}, z_{it})$ can be viewed a composite error representing statistical noise and inefficiency, y denotes a vector containing all the observations on y_{it}, X denotes a matrix containing all the observations on x_{it} and z_{it}, $\Phi(.)$ denotes the standard normal cumulative distribution function (CDF), and θ denotes a vector containing α, μ, $\sigma^2 \equiv \sigma_u^2 + \sigma_v^2$, $\lambda \equiv \sigma_u/\sigma_v$, and all the unknown parameters in $f^t(.)$. In practice, ML estimates of the unknown parameters are invariably obtained by maximising the log-likelihood function numerically. Following estimation, ML estimates of $E(u_{it})$ and $E(\exp[-u_{it}])$ can be obtained by using the ML estimates of μ and σ_u to evaluate the following:

$$E(u_{it}) = \mu + \sigma_u\left(\frac{\phi(\mu/\sigma_u)}{\Phi(\mu/\sigma_u)}\right) \tag{8.26}$$

$$\text{and} \quad E(\exp[-u_{it}]) = \exp\left(\sigma_u^2/2 - \mu\right)\left(\frac{\Phi(\mu/\sigma_u - \sigma_u)}{\Phi(\mu/\sigma_u)}\right) \tag{8.27}$$

where $\phi(.)$ denotes the standard normal probability density function (PDF). If $\mu = 0$, then $E(u_{it}) = \sigma_u\sqrt{2/\pi} \approx 0.79788\sigma_u$ and $E(\exp[-u_{it}]) = 2\Phi(-\sigma_u)\exp(\sigma_u^2/2)$.

8.3.3 Prediction

Let $\mu_{it}^* \equiv (\mu\sigma_v^2 - \varepsilon_{it}\sigma_u^2)/(\sigma_v^2 + \sigma_u^2)$ and $\sigma_*^2 \equiv \sigma_v^2\sigma_u^2/(\sigma_v^2 + \sigma_u^2)$. If ML3 and ML4 are true, then the conditional distribution of u_{it} given ε_{it} is that of an $N^+(\mu_{it}^*, \sigma_*^2)$ random variable (Battese and Coelli 1993, Eq. A.9). It follows that[8]

[8]These equations follow from (A.48) and (A.51) in Appendix A.7. If the data are cross-section data and $\mu = 0$, then (8.28) reduces to equation (2) in Jondrow et al. (1982).

$$E(u_{it}|\varepsilon_{it}) = \mu_{it}^* + \sigma_* \left(\frac{\phi(\mu_{it}^*/\sigma_*)}{\Phi(\mu_{it}^*/\sigma_*)} \right) \tag{8.28}$$

and $$E(\exp(-u_{it})|\varepsilon_{it}) = \exp\left(\sigma_*^2/2 - \mu_{it}^*\right) \left(\frac{\Phi(\mu_{it}^*/\sigma_* - \sigma_*)}{\Phi(\mu_{it}^*/\sigma_*)} \right). \tag{8.29}$$

ML predictions of u_{it} and $\exp(-u_{it})$ are usually obtained by using the ML parameter estimates to evaluate these two equations. Jondrow et al. (1982, p. 235) observe that the variance of u_{it} conditional on ε_{it} does not go to zero as the sample size becomes infinitely large. Consequently, these ML predictors are inconsistent.

8.3.4 Hypothesis Tests

Even though they cannot generally be given an economic interpretation, it is common to test hypotheses concerning the parameters in SFMs. It is also common to test for fixed effects, heteroskedasticity, autocorrelation, endogeneity, unit roots, cointegration, skewness and various random effects. As we have seen, all of these tests can be conducted using LS residuals. If distributional assumptions like ML3 and ML4 are true, then many of them can also be conducted using likelihood ratio (LR) tests.

8.3.4.1 Parameters

Let θ denote a vector containing all the unknown parameters in the SFM, and let $g(\theta)$ be a vector of J independent functions of θ. To conduct an LR test of the null hypothesis that $g(\theta) = 0$ against the alternative that $g(\theta) \neq 0$, we must compute the following statistic:

$$LR = 2(LLF_U - LLF_R) \tag{8.30}$$

where LLF_R denotes the value of the restricted log-likelihood function (obtained by estimating the parameters subject to the restrictions specified under the null hypothesis) and LLF_U denotes the value of the unrestricted log-likelihood function (obtained by estimating the parameters without any restrictions). If the null hypothesis is true, then this statistic is asymptotically distributed as a chi-square random variable with J degrees of freedom. Thus, we should reject the null hypothesis at the α level of significance if the sample size is large and $LR > \chi^2_{(1-\alpha,J)}$.

The two-sided alternative hypotheses $g(\theta) \neq 0$ is not generally relevant when testing restrictions concerning variances (variances cannot be negative). To test the null hypothesis that a variance parameter is equal to zero against the alternative that it is nonnegative, we can still compute the LR statistic given by (8.30). However, according to Coelli (1995, p. 252),[9] the asymptotic distribution of this statistic is now a mixture of chi-squared distributions. In this case, we should reject the null hypothesis at the α level of significance if the sample size is large and $LR > \chi^2_{(1-2\alpha,1)}$.

8.3.4.2 Fixed Effects

Assumption ML3 implies that the noise effects have a mean of zero. Different tests of this assumption are distinguished by the form of the alternative hypothesis. Several alternative hypotheses have been considered in the literature. A relatively flexible alternative hypothesis is that, for all i and t, $E(v_{it}) = \delta_i + \lambda_t$. If this is true, then (8.24) can be rewritten as

$$y_{it} = \alpha_i + \lambda_t + f^t(x_{it}, z_{it}) + v_{it}^* - u_{it} \tag{8.31}$$

where $\alpha_i = \alpha + \delta_i$ is a firm-specific fixed effect, λ_t is a period-specific fixed effect, and $v_{it}^* = v_{it} - \delta_i - \lambda_t$ is a random variable with a mean of zero. This equation has the same basic structure as the SFM of Kumbhakar (1991, Eqs. 1, 2). If $\lambda_t = 0$ for all t, then it reduces to a model that has the same basic structure as the true fixed effects (TFE) model of Greene (2004, p. 277; 2005, p. 11). If the dataset contains observations on I firms over T periods, then the unknown parameters in (8.31) can be estimated by replacing α in (8.24) with $I + T - 1$ firm- and period-specific dummy variables. A test of the null hypothesis that all the dummy variable coefficients are equal to each other can be viewed as a test of the null hypothesis that the noise effects have a mean of zero. If standard regularity conditions hold, then a likelihood ratio test of this hypothesis is asymptotically valid.

8.3.4.3 Heteroskedasticity

Assumptions ML3 and ML4 imply that the noise and inefficiency effects are homoskedastic. Again, different tests of this assumption are distinguished by the form of the alternative hypothesis. Again, several alternative hypotheses have been considered in the literature. For example, Caudill and Ford (1993) consider a normal-half-normal cross-section data model in which the pre-truncation variance of the inefficiency effects is a nonlinear function of inputs. This assumption implies that mean inefficiency also varies with inputs. This form of heteroskedasticity is quite unlike the type of heteroskedasticity that is typically discussed in econometric textbooks (i.e., error terms with the same mean but different variances). A form of heteroskedasticity where the composite error terms have the same mean but different variances could be accommodated by assuming the noise effects are heteroskedastic and the inefficiency effects are homoskedastic.

---

[9]Coelli (1995) attributes this result to Gouriéroux et al. (1982). Those authors derive their results in the context of a linear regression model with a normally distributed error term. It is not obvious that their results carry over to the case of a (composite) error term that is not normally distributed.

8.3.4.4 Autocorrelation

Assumptions ML3 and ML4 imply that the noise and inefficiency effects are serially and spatially uncorrelated. Again, different tests of these assumptions are distinguished by the form of the alternative hypothesis. A limited number of alternative hypotheses have been considered in the literature. Recently, Huang et al. (2018) consider a panel data model with firm-specific random effects and a normal-half-normal composite error term that is assumed to follow an autoregressive moving average (ARMA) process. Lai and Kumbhakar (2018) consider a normal-half-normal panel data model in which the inefficiency effects are assumed to follow an autoregressive (AR) process of order one.

8.3.4.5 Random Effects

Suppose that $v_{it} = v_{it}^* + w_i$ where v_{it}^* is a random variable with a mean of zero and w_i is an independent random variable with a mean of zero and a variance of σ_w^2. If this is true, and if ML4 is also true, then (8.24) can be rewritten as

$$y_{it} = \alpha^* + w_i + f^t(x_{it}, z_{it}) + e_{it}^* \tag{8.32}$$

where $\alpha^* \equiv \alpha - \mu$ is a fixed parameter and $e_{it}^* \equiv v_{it}^* - u_{it} + \mu$ is a random variable with a mean of zero. This equation has the same basic structure as the TRE model defined by (8.23). Again, a test of the null hypothesis that $\sigma_w^2 = 0$ against the alternative that $\sigma_w^2 > 0$ is known as a test for (time-invariant) random effects. Again, if standard regularity conditions hold, then a likelihood ratio test of this hypothesis is asymptotically valid.

8.3.5 *Toy Example*

Reconsider the toy data reported earlier in Tables 1.1 and 1.2. These data have been used to obtain ML and restricted ML (RML) estimates of the parameters in (8.19). The estimates are reported in Table 8.3. Both sets of estimates were obtained under assumptions ML3 and ML4. The RML estimates were obtained by restricting $\lambda = 0$. Both sets of estimates have been used to predict levels of OTE. The predictions are reported in Table 8.4.

The presence of statistical noise means it is not possible to use the parameter estimates reported in Table 8.3 to predict levels of input-oriented technical efficiency (ITE). To predict levels of ITE, we must estimate an input-oriented SFM. The toy data in Tables 1.1 and 1.2 have been used to obtain ML and RML estimates of the parameters in the input-oriented model defined by (8.7). The estimates are reported in Table 8.5. Again, both sets of estimates were obtained under assumptions ML3 and ML4. The RML estimates were obtained by restricting $\alpha_1 + \alpha_2 = 1$. Both sets

Table 8.3 ML parameter estimates

	ML			RML		
Parameter	Est.	St. err.	t	Est.	St. err.	t
α	1.040	0.756	1.376	1.165	0.497	2.345*
λ	0.035	0.146	0.242	0	0	NaN
δ_1	−0.184	0.274	−0.671	−0.182	0.860	−0.212
β_1	0.145	0.230	0.631	0.244	0.812	0.301
β_2	0.019	0.118	0.163	0.041	0.532	0.078
$\sigma^2 \equiv \sigma_u^2 + \sigma_v^2$	0.501	0.332	1.508	0.475	1.000	0.475
$\gamma \equiv \sigma_u^2/\sigma^2$	1.000	1.0E−7	6.8E+3***	0.998	0.267	3.733***
μ	−0.080	0.492	−0.162	0.000	0.999	0.000

***, ** and * indicate significance at the 1, 5 and 10% levels

Table 8.4 ML predictions of OTE

Row	Firm	Period	ML	RML
A	1	1	0.341	0.313
B	2	1	0.376	0.369
C	3	1	0.809	0.740
D	4	1	0.720	0.661
E	5	1	0.936	0.859
F	1	2	0.383	0.372
G	2	2	0.955	0.882
H	3	2	0.577	0.837
I	4	2	0.925	0.834
J	5	2	0.980	0.933
K	1	3	0.989	0.963
L	2	3	0.878	0.861
M	3	3	0.619	0.589
N	4	3	0.271	0.309
O	5	3	0.723	0.709
P	1	4	0.331	0.357
R	2	4	0.624	0.635
S	3	4	0.325	0.318
T	4	4	0.995	0.980
U	5	4	0.314	0.328
V	1	5	0.934	0.970
W	2	5	0.683	0.726
X	3	5	0.328	0.344
Y	4	5	0.312	0.341
Z	5	5	0.726	0.705
Geometric mean			0.583	0.585

Table 8.5 ML parameter estimates

	ML			RML		
Parameter	Est.	St. err.	t	Est.	St. err.	t
ξ	0.504	0.777	0.649	0.549	1.661	0.331
κ_1	0.154	0.233	0.662	0.196	0.219	0.895
α_1	0.688	0.176	3.909***	0.846	0.029	29.396***
α_2	0.121	0.045	2.698***	0.154	0.029	5.344***
$\sigma^2 \equiv \sigma_u^2 + \sigma_v^2$	0.128	0.055	2.319**	0.133	0.123	1.075
$\gamma \equiv \sigma_u^2/\sigma^2$	0.005	0.431	0.011	0.004	0.923	0.005
μ	−0.050	1.186	−0.042	−0.049	1.893	−0.026

***, ** and * indicate significance at the 1, 5 and 10% levels

of estimates have been used to predict levels of ITE. The predictions are reported in Table 8.6.

8.4 Bayesian Estimation

Bayesian estimation of SFMs involves summarising sample and non-sample information about the unknown parameters in terms of a posterior probability density function (PDF). One of the advantages of the Bayesian approach is that it provides a formal mechanism for incorporating almost any type of non-sample information into the estimation process; this mechanism comes in the form of Bayes's theorem. Another advantage of the approach is that it is possible to draw exact finite-sample inferences concerning nonlinear functions of the unknown model parameters (e.g., measures of efficiency). For simplicity, this section considers estimation of the following output-oriented model:

$$y_{it} = x_{it}'\beta + v_{it} - u_{it} \tag{8.33}$$

where y_{it} denotes the logarithm of an aggregate output, x_{it} denotes a $K \times 1$ vector of nonstochastic explanatory variables, $\beta = (\beta_1, \ldots, \beta_K)'$ is an associated vector of unknown parameters, v_{it} represents statistical noise, and u_{it} denotes an output-oriented technical inefficiency effect. If the dataset contains N observations, then it is convenient to write

$$y = X'\beta + v - u \tag{8.34}$$

where y denotes an $N \times 1$ vector containing all the observations on y_{it}, X is an $N \times K$ design matrix containing all the observations on x_{it}, v denotes an $N \times 1$ vector of noise components, and u denotes an $N \times 1$ vector of inefficiency effects.

Table 8.6 ML predictions of ITE

Row	Firm	Period	ML	RML
A	1	1	0.990	0.991
B	2	1	0.991	0.991
C	3	1	0.991	0.991
D	4	1	0.991	0.991
E	5	1	0.991	0.991
F	1	2	0.991	0.991
G	2	2	0.991	0.991
H	3	2	0.991	0.991
I	4	2	0.991	0.991
J	5	2	0.991	0.991
K	1	3	0.991	0.991
L	2	3	0.990	0.991
M	3	3	0.990	0.991
N	4	3	0.991	0.991
O	5	3	0.991	0.991
P	1	4	0.991	0.991
R	2	4	0.991	0.991
S	3	4	0.991	0.991
T	4	4	0.991	0.991
U	5	4	0.991	0.991
V	1	5	0.991	0.991
W	2	5	0.991	0.991
X	3	5	0.991	0.991
Y	4	5	0.991	0.991
Z	5	5	0.990	0.991
Geometric mean			0.991	0.991

8.4.1 Bayes's Theorem

Let θ denote a vector of unknown model parameters. Bayes's theorem says that[10]

$$p(\theta|y) = \frac{p(y|\theta)p(\theta)}{p(y)}. \tag{8.35}$$

The term $p(\theta)$ is known as the prior PDF; it summarises what we know about the unknown parameters *before* we observe the data. The term $p(y|\theta)$ is the usual likeli-

[10]In the present context, Bayes's theorem actually says that $p(\theta|X, y) = p(y|X, \theta)p(\theta|X)/p(y|X)$. However, it is notationally convenient, and common practice, to suppress the X.

hood function. The term $p(\theta|y)$ is known as the posterior PDF; it summarises what we know about the unknown parameters *after* we observe the data. The term $p(y)$ is known as the marginal likelihood. Since the data are observed, the marginal likelihood is a constant that can generally be ignored (it merely ensures that the posterior PDF integrates to one). Indeed, Bayes's theorem is often stated as

$$p(\theta|y) \propto p(y|\theta)p(\theta). \tag{8.36}$$

This says "the posterior is proportional to the likelihood times the prior". Bayes's theorem can be viewed as an updating rule that tells us how to use data to update our prior views about the unknown parameters. To use Bayes's theorem, we must specify both the likelihood function and the prior PDF.

8.4.2 The Likelihood Function

Consider the model given by (8.34). As usual, the form of the likelihood function depends on our assumptions concerning the noise and inefficiency effects. It is common to assume that the noise effects are independent $N(0, h^{-1})$ random variables. In the Bayesian stochastic frontier literature, it is also common to treat the inefficiency effects as unknown parameters. In this case, the likelihood function is given by

$$p(y|\beta, h, u) = f_N(y|X'\beta - u, h^{-1}I_N) \tag{8.37}$$

where I_N denotes an $N \times N$ identity matrix.

8.4.3 The Prior PDF

Prior PDFs can take any form. A noninformative (or diffuse or vague) prior is one that conveys no information about any of the unknown parameters. An informative prior conveys information about at least one parameter (e.g., that a slope parameter is nonnegative). A proper prior is one that integrates to one over the admissible range of the unknown parameters. An improper prior is one that does not integrate to one (noninformative priors are often improper). Fernandez et al. (1997) show that proper priors on the unknown parameters of SFMs are generally needed to ensure the existence of the posterior PDF. In the stochastic frontier literature, it is common to use a proper prior of the form

$$p(\beta, h, u) = p(\beta)p(h)p(u|\lambda)p(\lambda) \tag{8.38}$$

where each of the component priors is proper. For example, it is common to use

$$p(\beta) \propto f_N(\beta|a, B)I(\beta \in R), \tag{8.39}$$

$$p(h) = f_G(h|1, k), \tag{8.40}$$

$$p(u|\lambda) = \prod_{i=1}^{I}\prod_{t=1}^{T} f_G(u_{it}|1, \lambda) \tag{8.41}$$

and $$p(\lambda) = f_G(\lambda|1, -\ln\tau) \tag{8.42}$$

where $I(.)$ is an indicator function that takes the value one if the argument is true (and 0 otherwise), R denotes the admissible range of β, and a, B, k and τ are prior hyperparameters chosen by the researcher. In practice, it is common to set B and k to large values ($\Rightarrow$ the priors for β and h are relatively noninformative) and set τ equal to a prior estimate of the average level of efficiency.

Equation (8.41) implies that u_{it} is an independent exponential random variable with rate (or inverse scale) parameter λ. Several alternative assumptions concerning the inefficiency effects can be found in the Bayesian stochastic frontier literature. For example, Tsionas (2007) assumes the inefficiency effects are Weibull random variables. Tsionas (2006) considers a panel data model in which the logarithm of inefficiency is assumed to follow a first-order autoregressive (AR) process. Emvalomatis (2012) considers a panel data model in which a log-odds-type function of efficiency is assumed to follow an AR process. Assaf et al. (2014) consider a panel data model in which the logarithm of inefficiency and a variable representing price distortions are assumed to follow a vector autoregressive (VAR) scheme.

8.4.4 Marginal Posterior PDFs

Combining (8.37) and (8.38) yields the following joint posterior PDF:

$$p(\beta, h, u|y) \propto p(y|\beta, h, u)p(\beta, h, u). \tag{8.43}$$

In practice, interest usually centres on *marginal* posterior PDFs. Finding the marginal posterior PDF for any subset of parameters involves integration. For example, the marginal posterior PDFs for β, h and u are given by

$$p(\beta|y) = \int\int p(\beta, h, u|y)\, dh\, du \tag{8.44}$$

$$p(h|y) = \int\int p(\beta, h, u|y)\, d\beta\, du \tag{8.45}$$

and $$p(u|y) = \int\int p(\beta, h, u|y)\, d\beta\, dh. \tag{8.46}$$

These marginal PDFs are averages. For example, the marginal PDF defined by (8.44) is an average of $p(\beta, h, u|y)$ over all possible values of h and u. Further averaging/integration of $p(\beta|y)$ and $p(u|y)$ can be used to obtain marginal posterior PDFs for particular elements of β and u. For example, the marginal posterior PDF for β_1 is given by

$$p(\beta_1|y) = \int \ldots \int p(\beta|y)\, d\beta_2 \ldots d\beta_K. \tag{8.47}$$

8.4.5 *Point Estimation*

Bayesian point estimators are chosen based on their ability to minimise expected loss. For a simple example, let b_k denote an estimator for β_k. A loss function is a function that measures the loss associated with an estimation error: a quadratic loss function takes the form $L(b_k, \beta_k) = (b_k - \beta_k)^2$; an absolute loss function takes the form $L(b_k, \beta_k) = |b_k - \beta_k|$; a zero-one loss function takes the form $L(b_k, \beta_k) = I(b_k \neq \beta_k)$. The estimators that minimise the (posterior) expected values of these three loss functions are the mean, median and mode of the marginal posterior PDF of β_k (respectively).

8.4.6 *Interval Estimation*

The marginal posterior PDF for a given parameter can be used to calculate the posterior probability that the parameter lies in a given interval. More commonly, Bayesians like to specify the interval in which "most of the distribution lies". Such an interval, known as a highest posterior density interval (HPDI), is the Bayesian counterpart to a confidence interval. A $100(1-\alpha)\%$ HPDI is the interval of shortest length that contains $100(1-\alpha)\%$ of the area under the marginal posterior PDF.

8.4.7 *Assessing Alternative Hypotheses*

Bayesians assess alternative hypotheses by calculating odds ratios. For a simple example, consider the hypotheses $H_0 : \beta \in R_0$ and $H_1 : \beta \in R_1$ where R_0 and R_1 are mutually exclusive, but not necessarily exhaustive, regions of the parameter space. Let $p(H_j)$ denote the prior probability assigned to hypothesis j. The prior odds ratio is $P_{01} = p(H_0)/p(H_1)$. If $P_{01} > 1$, then H_0 is a priori more likely than H_1. The posterior probability of hypothesis j is

$$p(H_j|y) = \int_{R_j} p(\beta|y)\, d\beta. \tag{8.48}$$

The posterior odds ratio is $K_{01} = p(H_0|y)/p(H_1|y)$. If $K_{01} > 1$, then we should favour H_0 over H_1. The ratio of the posterior odds to the prior odds is $B_{01} = K_{01}/P_{01}$. This ratio is known as the Bayes factor. It can be interpreted as the odds in favour of H_0 that are implied by the data. The Bayes factor may not be well defined unless the prior PDF is proper.

8.4.8 Simulation

In the present context, most of the quantities an analyst would want to estimate can be written in the following form[11]:

$$E\{g(\theta)|y\} = \int g(\theta)p(\theta|y)\, d\theta \tag{8.49}$$

where $\theta = (\beta, h, u)'$ and $g(.)$ is some function of interest: to estimate the mean of $p(h|y)$, for example, we would set $g(.) = h$; to estimate the posterior probability that β_k is nonnegative, we would set $g(.) = I(\beta_k \geq 0)$. Except in restrictive special cases, the integral on the right-hand side of (8.49) cannot be evaluated analytically. In practice, it is usually evaluated by drawing random samples (or 'simulating') from $p(\theta|y)$. Let $\theta^1, \ldots, \theta^S$ denote S random draws from $p(\theta|y)$. The associated estimator for $E\{g(\theta)|y\}$ is

$$\hat{g}(\theta) = S^{-1} \sum_{s=1}^{S} g(\theta^s). \tag{8.50}$$

It can be shown that this estimator converges to $E\{g(\theta)|y\}$ as $S \to \infty$. Because it involves random sampling, and because random sampling is closely associated with the casinos of Monte Carlo, this approach to evaluating integrals is known as Monte Carlo integration. Several Monte Carlo integration algorithms (i.e., sampling schemes) are available. Some generate correlated chains of draws that have the properties of Markov processes. These algorithms are known as Markov Chain Monte Carlo (MCMC) algorithms. Two of the most widely-used MCMC algorithms are the Gibbs sampler and the Metropolis-Hastings algorithm. For more details concerning these algorithms, see Casella and George (1992), Tierney (1994) and Robert and Casella (2004).

8.4.9 Toy Example

Reconsider the toy data reported earlier in Tables 1.1 and 1.2. These data have been used to obtain unrestricted and restricted estimates of the parameters in (8.19). Both

[11]One exception is the marginal likelihood given by $p(y) = \int p(y|\theta)p(\theta)\, d\theta$.

Table 8.7 Bayesian parameter estimates

	Unrestricted				Restricted			
Parameter	Mean	SD	2.5%	97.5%	Mean	SD	2.5%	97.5%
α	1.069	0.118	0.886	1.343	1.052	0.104	0.889	1.243
λ	0.039	0.035	−0.032	0.115	0.041	0.028	0.002	0.102
δ_1	−0.120	0.150	−0.373	0.233	−0.145	0.130	−0.380	0.153
β_1	0.191	0.092	−0.038	0.298	0.231	0.046	0.131	0.298
β_2	0.001	0.044	−0.106	0.061	0.028	0.017	0.002	0.063

sets of estimates were obtained under the assumption that the noise effects are independent $N(0, h^{-1})$ random variables. Equations (8.38) to (8.42) were used as a prior. The hyperparameters were chosen so that the prior was relatively noninformative. The unrestricted estimates were obtained by allowing the parameters in (8.19) to take any values; the restricted estimates were obtained by restricting all the parameters in (8.19) except α and δ_1 to be nonnegative. The MCMC chains were of length $S = 50{,}000$. The parameter estimates are reported in Table 8.7. Predictions of OTE are reported in Table 8.8. These tables report the means and standard deviations of the relevant MCMC chains. They also report estimated 95% HPDI limits. Estimated restricted posterior PDFs for the slope parameters and the OTE of firms 1 and 2 in period 1 are presented in Fig. 8.1.

8.5 Productivity Analysis

Productivity analysis involves both measuring and explaining changes in productivity. For purposes of comparison with Sects. 6.5 and 7.5, this section again focuses on measuring and explaining changes in TFP. Again, methods for measuring and explaining changes in MFP and PFP can be handled as special cases in which one or more inputs are assigned a weight of zero.

8.5.1 Measuring Changes in TFP

Measuring changes in TFP involves computing proper TFP index (TFPI) numbers. Except in restrictive special cases (e.g., there is no statistical noise), SFMs cannot be used to compute primal or dual TFPI numbers.[12] However, they can be used to

[12]Primal and dual indices are computed using distance, revenue and cost functions. SFMs are underpinned by the assumption that these functions exist. However, their functional forms are generally unknown. Moreover, the variables in these functions are often unobserved and/or measured with error.

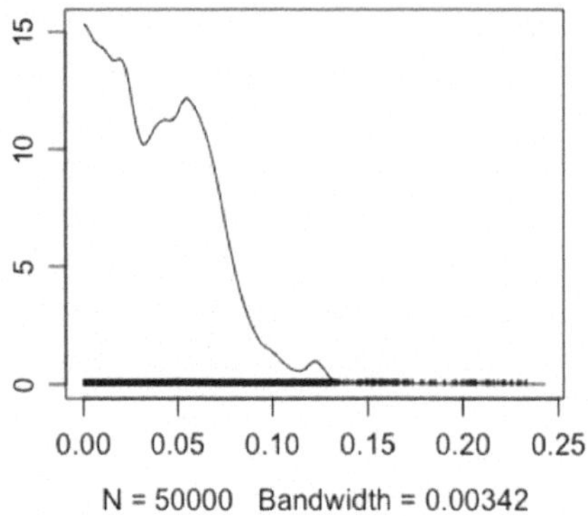

(a) λ

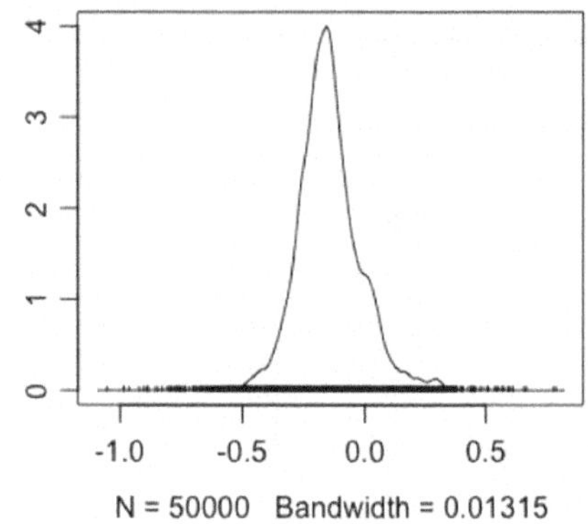

(b) δ_1

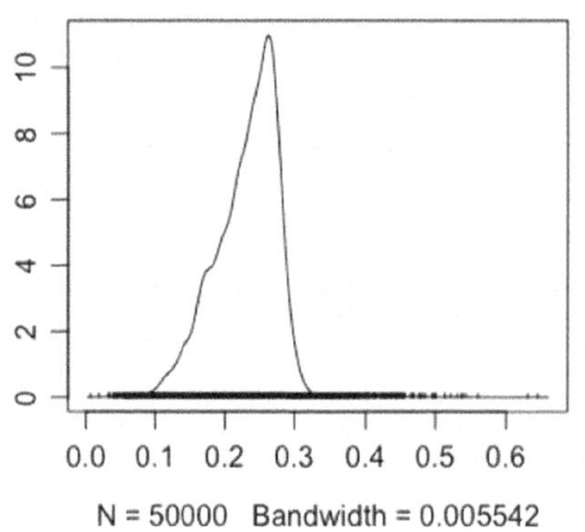

(a) β_1

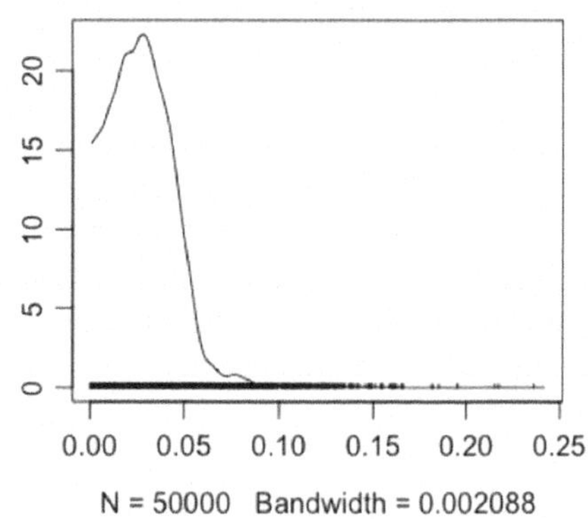

(b) β_2

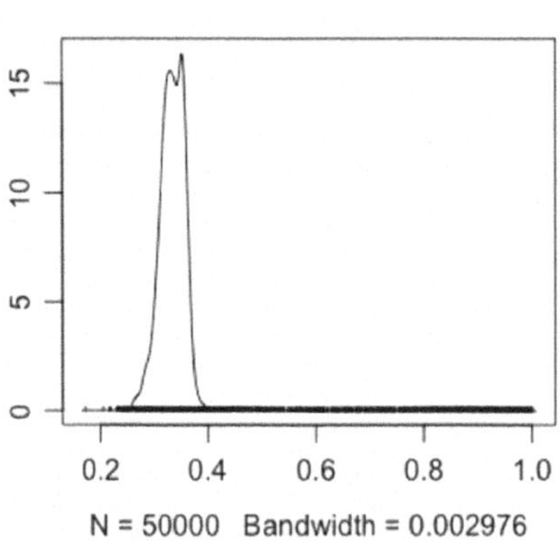

(a) OTE of Firm 1 in Period 1

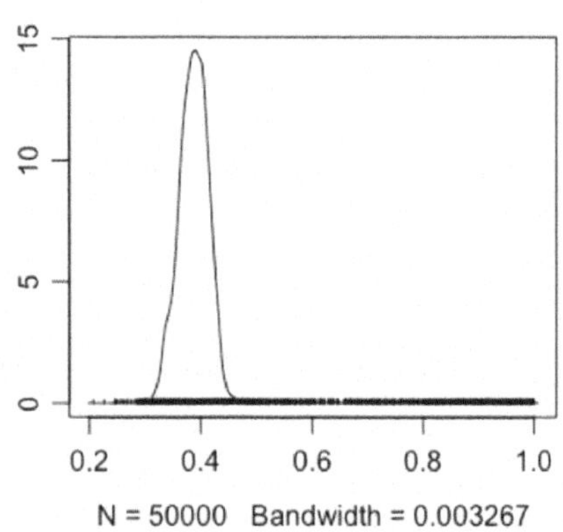

(b) OTE of Firm 2 in Period 1

Fig. 8.1 Estimated restricted posterior PDFs

Table 8.8 Bayesian predictions of OTE

			Unrestricted				Restricted			
Row	Firm	Period	Mean	SD	2.5%	97.5%	Mean	SD	2.5%	97.5%
A	1	1	0.332	0.030	0.269	0.378	0.342	0.071	0.284	0.388
B	2	1	0.371	0.037	0.284	0.431	0.396	0.068	0.335	0.452
C	3	1	0.786	0.067	0.638	0.894	0.794	0.058	0.672	0.898
D	4	1	0.694	0.056	0.566	0.780	0.707	0.056	0.602	0.807
E	5	1	0.899	0.069	0.734	0.995	0.912	0.059	0.781	0.996
F	1	2	0.349	0.041	0.270	0.413	0.375	0.071	0.299	0.436
G	2	2	0.859	0.087	0.670	0.989	0.879	0.073	0.713	0.992
H	3	2	0.701	0.219	0.237	0.989	0.811	0.131	0.528	0.993
I	4	2	0.743	0.125	0.486	0.950	0.803	0.085	0.627	0.958
J	5	2	0.798	0.167	0.409	0.995	0.887	0.082	0.711	0.997
K	1	3	0.946	0.047	0.838	0.999	0.950	0.045	0.835	0.999
L	2	3	0.844	0.047	0.744	0.920	0.849	0.046	0.742	0.930
M	3	3	0.588	0.041	0.511	0.662	0.589	0.054	0.506	0.662
N	4	3	0.269	0.043	0.185	0.327	0.301	0.075	0.251	0.340
O	5	3	0.667	0.062	0.524	0.762	0.685	0.060	0.556	0.781
P	1	4	0.321	0.034	0.259	0.368	0.341	0.071	0.286	0.381
R	2	4	0.599	0.042	0.505	0.661	0.606	0.055	0.509	0.682
S	3	4	0.284	0.033	0.220	0.332	0.300	0.075	0.235	0.342
T	4	4	0.909	0.076	0.718	0.998	0.927	0.066	0.755	0.998
U	5	4	0.296	0.030	0.235	0.336	0.314	0.072	0.260	0.351
V	1	5	0.890	0.074	0.709	0.995	0.893	0.069	0.721	0.993
W	2	5	0.628	0.065	0.484	0.735	0.647	0.066	0.514	0.754
X	3	5	0.289	0.040	0.212	0.349	0.309	0.075	0.239	0.358
Y	4	5	0.302	0.035	0.234	0.350	0.316	0.074	0.249	0.361
Z	5	5	0.678	0.082	0.531	0.864	0.656	0.068	0.521	0.774
Geometric mean			0.549	0.057	0.412	0.639	0.572	0.067	0.466	0.648

compute additive and multiplicative TFPI numbers. Additive TFPI numbers can be computed by using any nonnegative parameter estimates as weights in Eq. (3.41). If, for example, estimates of the γ_n (resp. β_m) parameters in (1.32) are all nonnegative, then they can be used as output (resp. input) weights. Multiplicative TFPI numbers can be computed by normalising any nonnegative parameter estimates to sum to one, then using these normalised estimates as weights in Eq. (3.42). If, for example, estimates of the γ_n (resp. β_m) parameters in (1.32) are all nonnegative, then they can be normalised to sum to one and used as output (resp. input) weights.

To illustrate, reconsider the toy data reported earlier in Table 1.1. These data have been used to obtain RML estimates of the parameters in (1.32). The estimates were reported earlier in Table 1.14. These parameter estimates have been used to compute

Table 8.9 Additive and multiplicative TFPI numbers[a,b]

Row	Firm	Period	q_1	q_2	x_1	x_2	A	M
A	1	1	1	1	1	1	1	1
B	2	1	1	1	0.56	0.56	1.786	1.786
C	3	1	2.37	2.37	1	1	2.37	2.37
D	4	1	2.11	2.11	1.05	0.7	2.690	2.734
E	5	1	1.81	3.62	1.05	0.7	3.055	2.935
F	1	2	1	1	0.996	0.316	2.084	2.400
G	2	2	1.777	3.503	1.472	0.546	3.037	3.193
H	3	2	0.96	0.94	0.017	0.346	3.575	5.696
I	4	2	5.82	0.001	4.545	0.01	3.568	8.034
J	5	2	6.685	0.001	4.45	0.001	4.212	50.916
K	1	3	1.381	4.732	1	1	2.466	2.058
L	2	3	0.566	4.818	1	1	1.943	1.133
M	3	3	1	3	1.354	1	1.518	1.327
N	4	3	0.7	0.7	0.33	0.16	3.483	3.675
O	5	3	2	2	1	1	2	2
P	1	4	1	1	0.657	0.479	1.916	1.935
R	2	4	1	3	1	1	1.648	1.427
S	3	4	1	1	1.933	0.283	1.469	2.224
T	4	4	1.925	3.722	1	1	2.507	2.383
U	5	4	1	1	1	0.31	2.100	2.433
V	1	5	1	5.166	1	1	2.349	1.702
W	2	5	2	2	0.919	0.919	2.176	2.176
X	3	5	1	1	1.464	0.215	1.938	2.929
Y	4	5	1	1	0.74	0.74	1.351	1.351
Z	5	5	1.81	3.62	2.1	1.4	1.528	1.468

[a] *A* additive index with RML parameter estimates used as weights; *M* multiplicative index with normalised RML parameter estimates used as weights. Some index numbers may be incoherent at the third decimal place due to rounding (e.g., the number in row Z of column A is not exactly half as big as the number in row E of column A due to rounding)
[b] Numbers reported to less than three decimal places are exact; see the footnote to Table 1.2 on p. 8

the additive and multiplicative TFPI numbers reported in Table 8.9. These index numbers are proper in the sense that they have been obtained by dividing proper output index numbers by proper input index numbers. They are also consistent with measurement theory. Observe, for example, that (a) the output vector in row O is twice as big as the output vector in row A, (b) the input vector in row O is the same as the input vector in row A, and (c) the index numbers in row O are twice as big as the numbers in row A. Also observe that the TFPI numbers in rows A, B, C, O, W and Y are the same as the TFPI numbers reported in the corresponding rows of Tables 3.5, 6.15 and 7.8.

8.5.2 *Explaining Changes in TFP*

SFMs can be used to decompose proper TFPI numbers into measures of environmental change, technical change, efficiency change and changes in statistical noise. This section focuses on output- and input-oriented decompositions.

8.5.2.1 Output-Oriented Decompositions

Output-oriented decompositions of TFPI numbers tend to be most relevant in situations where managers have placed nonnegative values on outputs, and where inputs have been predetermined (i.e., situations where output-oriented measures of efficiency are most relevant). In these situations, a relatively easy way to proceed is to rewrite (8.1) as

$$1 = q_{1it}^{-1} \exp\left(f^t(x_{it}, q_{it}^*, z_{it})\right) \exp(-u_{it}) \exp(v_{it}). \tag{8.51}$$

Multiplying both sides of this equation by $TFP(x_{it}, q_{it})$ yields

$$TFP(x_{it}, q_{it}) = \left[TFP(x_{it}, q_{it}) q_{1it}^{-1} \exp\left(f^t(x_{it}, q_{it}^*, z_{it})\right)\right] \exp(-u_{it}) \exp(v_{it}). \tag{8.52}$$

A similar equation holds for firm k in period s. Substituting these equations into (3.40) yields

$$\begin{aligned} TFPI(x_{ks}, q_{ks}, x_{it}, q_{it}) = & \left[TFPI(x_{ks}, q_{ks}, x_{it}, q_{it}) \left(\frac{q_{1ks}}{q_{1it}}\right) \frac{\exp\left(f^t(x_{it}, q_{it}^*, z_{it})\right)}{\exp\left(f^s(x_{ks}, q_{ks}^*, z_{ks})\right)} \right] \\ & \times \left[\frac{\exp(-u_{it})}{\exp(-u_{ks})}\right] \left[\frac{\exp(v_{it})}{\exp(v_{ks})}\right]. \end{aligned} \tag{8.53}$$

In theory, the presence of statistical noise means we cannot interpret the first term in this equation in the same way we interpreted the first term in (7.32). However, in practice, this term would normally be viewed as an output-oriented environment, technology, and scale and mix efficiency index (OETSMEI). In both theory and practice, the second term is an output-oriented technical efficiency index (OTEI), and the last term is a statistical noise index (SNI). If there is no statistical noise, then (8.53) reduces to (7.32).

Whether a finer decomposition is possible (and meaningful) depends on both the approximating function and the TFPI. If the approximating function is given by (8.2), for example, then (8.53) takes the following form:

$$
\begin{aligned}
TFPI(x_{ks}, q_{ks}, x_{it}, q_{it}) = & \left[\frac{\exp(\lambda t)}{\exp(\lambda s)}\right]\left[\prod_{j=1}^{J}\left(\frac{z_{jit}}{z_{jks}}\right)^{\delta_j}\right] \\
& \times \left[TFPI(x_{ks}, q_{ks}, x_{it}, q_{it}) \prod_{m=1}^{M}\left(\frac{x_{mit}}{x_{mks}}\right)^{\beta_m}\frac{Q(q_{ks})}{Q(q_{it})}\right] \\
& \times \left[\frac{\exp(-u_{it})}{\exp(-u_{ks})}\right]\left[\frac{\exp(v_{it})}{\exp(v_{ks})}\right]. \qquad (8.54)
\end{aligned}
$$

In practice, the first term on the right-hand side would normally be viewed as an output-oriented technology index (OTI). The second term would normally be viewed as an output-oriented environment index (OEI). The third term would normally be viewed as an output-oriented scale and mix efficiency index (OSMEI). The last two terms are the OTEI and SNI in (8.53). If $Q(q_{it}) \propto \prod_n q_{nit}^{\gamma_n}$, then (8.54) reduces to (1.40). If the TFPI is a geometric Young (GY) index, then (1.40) reduces to equation (16) in O'Donnell (2016).

For a numerical example, reconsider the GY TFPI numbers reported earlier in Table 3.5. An output-oriented decomposition of these numbers is now reported in Table 8.10. The OTI and OEI numbers in this table were obtained by using the RML estimates of λ and δ_1 reported in Table 8.3 to evaluate the first two terms in (8.54). The OSMEI numbers were obtained by using the GY TFPI numbers, the RML estimates of β_1 and β_2, and the aggregate outputs in Table 1.2 to evaluate the third term in (8.54). The OTEI numbers were obtained by taking ratios of the RML predictions reported in Table 8.4. The SNI numbers were obtained as residuals (i.e., SNI = TFPI/(OTI×OEI×OTEI×OSMEI)).

8.5.2.2 Input-Oriented Decompositions

Input-oriented decompositions of TFPI numbers tend to be most relevant in situations where managers have placed nonnegative values on inputs, and where outputs have been predetermined (i.e., situations where input-oriented measures of efficiency are most relevant). In these situations, a relatively easy way to proceed is to rewrite (8.5) as

$$
1 = x_{1it} \exp\left(f^t(x_{it}^*, q_{it}, z_{it})\right) \exp(-u_{it}) \exp(v_{it}). \qquad (8.55)
$$

Multiplying both sides of this equation by $TFP(x_{it}, q_{it})$ yields

$$
TFP(x_{it}, q_{it}) = \left[TFP(x_{it}, q_{it}) x_{1it} \exp\left(f^t(x_{it}^*, q_{it}, z_{it})\right)\right] \exp(-u_{it}) \exp(v_{it}). \qquad (8.56)
$$

A similar equation holds for firm k in period s. Substituting these equations into (3.40) yields

Table 8.10 An output-oriented decomposition of GY TFPI numbers using RML[a,b]

Row	Firm	Period	TFPI	OTI	OEI	OTEI	OSMEI	SNI
A	1	1	1	1	1	1	1	1
B	2	1	1.786	1	1	1.179	1.514	1.000
C	3	1	2.37	1	1	2.366	1.000	1.002
D	4	1	2.539	1	1	2.113	1.200	1.001
E	5	1	3.133	1	1	2.747	1.139	1.002
F	1	2	1.948	1	0.881	1.191	1.855	1.000
G	2	2	3.054	1	0.881	2.819	1.227	1.002
H	3	2	9.811	1	1	2.676	3.660	1.002
I	4	2	0.464	1	0.881	2.668	0.197	1.002
J	5	2	1.890	1	1	2.982	0.632	1.003
K	1	3	2.634	1	1	3.079	0.847	1.010
L	2	3	1.740	1	1	2.755	0.630	1.002
M	3	3	1.565	1	1	1.885	0.829	1.001
N	4	3	3.221	1	1	0.989	3.256	1.000
O	5	3	2	1	0.881	2.266	1.000	1.001
P	1	4	1.827	1	1	1.142	1.599	1.000
R	2	4	1.779	1	1	2.029	0.876	1.001
S	3	4	1.568	1	0.881	1.018	1.748	1.000
T	4	4	2.720	1	0.881	3.135	0.954	1.032
U	5	4	1.966	1	1	1.049	1.873	1.000
V	1	5	2.366	1	1	3.102	0.751	1.015
W	2	5	2.176	1	0.881	2.322	1.062	1.001
X	3	5	2.067	1	0.881	1.102	2.129	1.000
Y	4	5	1.351	1	1	1.090	1.240	1.000
Z	5	5	1.567	1	1	2.255	0.694	1.001
Geometric mean			2.030	1	0.960	1.870	1.127	1.003

[a]TFPI = OTI × OEI × OTEI × OSMEI × SNI. Some index numbers may be incoherent at the third decimal place due to rounding (e.g., in any given row, the product of the OTI, OEI, OTEI, OSMEI and SNI numbers may not be exactly equal to the TFPI number due to rounding)
[b]Numbers reported to less than three decimal places are exact; see the footnote to Table 1.2 on p. 8

$$TFPI(x_{ks}, q_{ks}, x_{it}, q_{it}) = \left[TFPI(x_{ks}, q_{ks}, x_{it}, q_{it}) \left(\frac{x_{1it}}{x_{1ks}} \right) \frac{\exp\left(f^t(x^*_{it}, q_{it}, z_{it})\right)}{\exp\left(f^s(x^*_{ks}, q_{ks}, z_{ks})\right)} \right] \times \left[\frac{\exp(-u_{it})}{\exp(-u_{ks})} \right] \left[\frac{\exp(v_{it})}{\exp(v_{ks})} \right]. \tag{8.57}$$

Again, in theory, the presence of statistical noise means we cannot interpret the first term in this equation in the same way we interpreted the first term in (7.34). However, in practice, this term would normally be viewed as an input-oriented environment, technology, and scale and mix efficiency index (IETSMEI). In both theory and practice, the second term is an input-oriented technical efficiency index (ITEI), and the last term is a statistical noise index (SNI). If there is no statistical noise, then (8.57) reduces to (7.34).

Again, whether a finer decomposition is possible (and meaningful) depends on both the approximating function and the TFPI. If the approximating function is given by (8.6), for example, then (8.57) takes the following form:

$$\begin{aligned} TFPI(x_{ks}, q_{ks}, x_{it}, q_{it}) = & \left[\prod_{j=1}^{J} \left(\frac{z_{jit}}{z_{jks}} \right)^{\kappa_j} \right] \\ & \times \left[TFPI(x_{ks}, q_{ks}, x_{it}, q_{it}) \prod_{n=1}^{N} \left(\frac{q_{nks}}{q_{nit}} \right)^{\alpha_n} \frac{X(x_{it})}{X(x_{ks})} \right] \\ & \times \left[\frac{\exp(-u_{it})}{\exp(-u_{ks})} \right] \left[\frac{\exp(v_{it})}{\exp(v_{ks})} \right]. \end{aligned} \quad (8.58)$$

In practice, the first term on the right-hand side would normally be viewed as an input-oriented environment index (IEI). The second term would normally be viewed as an input-oriented scale and mix efficiency index (ISMEI). The last two terms are the ITEI and SNI in (8.57).

For a numerical example, reconsider the GY TFPI numbers reported earlier in Table 3.5. An input-oriented decomposition of these numbers is now reported in Table 8.11. The IEI numbers in this table were obtained by using the RML estimate of κ_1 reported in Table 8.5 to evaluate the first term in (8.58). The ISMEI numbers were obtained by using the GY TFPI numbers, the RML estimates of α_1 and α_2 reported in Table 8.5, and the aggregate inputs in Table 1.2 to evaluate the second term in (8.58). The ITEI numbers were obtained by taking ratios of the RML predictions reported in Table 8.6. The SNI numbers were obtained as residuals (i.e., SNI = TFPI/(IEI×ITEI×ISMEI)).

8.5.2.3 Other Decompositions

There are many TFPI numbers that are not proper in the sense that they cannot generally be written as proper output index numbers divided by proper input index numbers. One way of decomposing such numbers to first write them as the product of proper TFPI numbers and SNI numbers. Subsequently, the proper TFPI numbers can be decomposed into technology index numbers, environment index numbers, efficiency index numbers and (more) SNI numbers.

For a numerical example, reconsider the CCD TFPI numbers reported earlier in Table 3.6. An output-oriented decomposition of these numbers is now reported in Table 8.12. CCD TFPI numbers are closely related to GY TFPI numbers (if observed

Table 8.11 An input-oriented decomposition of GY TFPI numbers using RML[a,b]

Row	Firm	Period	TFPI	IEI	ITEI	ISMEI	SNI
A	1	1	1	1	1	1	1
B	2	1	1.786	1	1.000	1.000	1.785
C	3	1	2.37	1	1.000	1.000	2.369
D	4	1	2.539	1	1.001	0.939	2.702
E	5	1	3.133	1	1.000	1.214	2.579
F	1	2	1.948	1.145	1.000	0.920	1.847
G	2	2	3.054	1.145	1.000	1.175	2.268
H	3	2	9.811	1	1.001	2.772	3.537
I	4	2	0.464	1.145	1.000	0.319	1.272
J	5	2	1.890	1	1.000	1.123	1.683
K	1	3	2.634	1	1.000	1.578	1.669
L	2	3	1.740	1	1.000	2.211	0.787
M	3	3	1.565	1	1.000	1.429	1.095
N	4	3	3.221	1	1.001	0.916	3.514
O	5	3	2	1.145	1.000	1.000	1.746
P	1	4	1.827	1	1.000	0.950	1.923
R	2	4	1.779	1	1.000	1.502	1.184
S	3	4	1.568	1.145	1.000	1.039	1.318
T	4	4	2.720	1.145	1.000	1.277	1.859
U	5	4	1.966	1	1.000	0.921	2.133
V	1	5	2.366	1	1.000	1.838	1.287
W	2	5	2.176	1.145	1.000	1.000	1.899
X	3	5	2.067	1.145	1.000	1.038	1.738
Y	4	5	1.351	1	1.000	1.000	1.351
Z	5	5	1.567	1	1.000	1.214	1.29
Geometric mean			2.030	1.044	1.000	1.133	1.716

[a]TFPI = IEI × ITEI × ISMEI × SNI. Some index numbers may be incoherent at the third decimal place due to rounding (e.g., in any given row, the product of the IEI, ITEI, ISMEI and SNI numbers may not be exactly equal to the TFPI number due to rounding)
[b]Numbers reported to less than three decimal places are exact; see the footnote to Table 1.2 on p. 8

revenue and cost shares are firm- and time-invariant, then they are equal). An output-oriented decomposition of the GY TFPI numbers was presented earlier in Table 8.10. The OTI, OEI, OTEI and OSMEI numbers in that table are now reported in Table 8.12. The numbers in the SNI column in Table 8.12 were obtained as residuals (i.e., SNI = TFPI/(OTI×OEI×OTEI×OSMEI)).

Table 8.12 An output-oriented decomposition of CCD TFPI numbers using RML[a,b]

Row	Firm	Period	TFPI	OTI	OEI	OTEI	OSMEI	SNI
A	1	1	1	1	1	1	1	1
B	2	1	1.922*	1	1	1.179	1.514	1.076
C	3	1	2.37	1	1	2.366	1.000	1.002
D	4	1	2.870	1	1	2.113	1.200	1.132
E	5	1	3.600*	1	1	2.747	1.139	1.151
F	1	2	2.157	1	0.881	1.191	1.855	1.108
G	2	2	3.697	1	0.881	2.819	1.227	1.213
H	3	2	5.072	1	1	2.676	3.660	0.518
I	4	2	1.056	1	0.881	2.668	0.197	2.278
J	5	2	2.292	1	1	2.982	0.632	1.216
K	1	3	3.090	1	1	3.079	0.847	1.185
L	2	3	3.044	1	1	2.755	0.630	1.753
M	3	3	1.973	1	1	1.885	0.829	1.262
N	4	3	3.535	1	1	0.989	3.256	1.097
O	5	3	2.421*	1	0.881	2.266	1.000	1.212
P	1	4	2.113	1	1	1.142	1.599	1.157
R	2	4	2.366	1	1	2.029	0.876	1.332
S	3	4	1.549	1	0.881	1.018	1.748	0.988
T	4	4	3.104	1	0.881	3.135	0.954	1.178
U	5	4	2.324	1	1	1.049	1.873	1.182
V	1	5	2.418	1	1	3.102	0.751	1.038
W	2	5	2.332*	1	0.881	2.322	1.062	1.073
X	3	5	1.951	1	0.881	1.102	2.129	0.944
Y	4	5	1.482*	1	1	1.090	1.240	1.096
Z	5	5	2.154*	1	1	2.255	0.694	1.377
Geometric mean			2.324	1	0.960	1.870	1.127	1.148

[a]TFPI = OTI × OEI × OTEI × OSMEI × SNI. Some index numbers may be incoherent at the third decimal place due to rounding (e.g., in any given row, the product of the OTI, OEI, OTEI, OSMEI and SNI numbers may not be exactly equal to the TFPI number due to rounding)
[b]Numbers reported to less than three decimal places are exact; see the footnote to Table 1.2 on p. 8
*Incoherent (not because of rounding)

8.6 Other Models

Other SFMs include various systems of equations. This section discusses systems of equations that can be used to explain variations in metafrontiers, output supplies, input demands, and inefficiency.

8.6.1 Metafrontier Models

Metafrontier models are used in situations where firm managers can be classified into two or more groups, and where managers in different groups choose input-output combinations from potentially different production possibilities sets. For purposes of comparison with Sects. 6.6.1 and 7.6.1, this section considers situations where firm managers can be classified into two or more groups according to the technologies they use. Again, attention is restricted to the estimation of output-oriented metafrontier models; the estimation of input-, revenue-, cost-, and profit-oriented metafrontier models is analogous to the estimation of output-oriented models.

If we observe the technologies used by firm managers, then output-oriented metafrontier models can be used to predict the output-oriented metatechnology ratio (OMR) defined by (5.47), the measure of output-oriented technical efficiency (OTE) defined by (5.1), and the measure of residual output-oriented technical efficiency (ROTE) defined by (5.48). This involves estimating a system of technology-and-environment-specific output distance functions. If there are T time periods in the dataset and the functional forms of the output distance functions are known, then the system can be written in the form of (7.36). If the functional forms of the output distance functions are *not* known, then we can instead write

$$\ln q_{1it} = f^g(x_{it}, q^*_{it}, z_{it}) + v^g_{it} - u^g_{it} \quad \text{for all } g \in G_T, \tag{8.59}$$

where G_T denotes the set of technologies that existed in period T, $q^*_{it} = q_{it}/q_{1it}$ denotes a vector of normalised outputs, $f^g(.)$ is an approximating function chosen by the researcher, $v^g_{it} = -\ln d^g_O(x_{it}, q^*_{it}, z_{it}) - f^g(x_{it}, q^*_{it}, z_{it})$ represents statistical noise, and $u^g_{it} \equiv -\ln d^g_O(x_{it}, q_{it}, z_{it})$ denotes a residual output-oriented technical inefficiency effect. If there is no statistical noise, then (8.59) reduces to (7.36).

Let g_{it} denote the technology used by manager i in period t. The ROTE of the manager is $\exp(-u^{g_{it}}_{it})$. The OTE of the manager is $\exp(-u_{it})$ where $u_{it} = \max_{g \in G_t} u^g_{it}$. The OMR of the manager is $\exp(-m^{g_{it}}_{it})$ where $m^{g_{it}}_{it} = u_{it} - u^{g_{it}}_{it}$. Coherent predictions of these quantities can be obtained using a method developed by Amsler et al. (2017). The first step is to obtain ML estimates of the parameters in the system defined by (8.59). The second step is to use these parameter estimates to draw random samples of observations on v^g_{it} and u^g_{it} for all $g \in G_t$. The final step is to use these random samples to predict $\exp(-u^{g_{it}}_{it})$, $\exp(-u_{it})$ and $\exp(-m^{g_{it}}_{it})$.

To obtain ML estimates of the parameters in the system defined by (8.59), we need to make some assumptions about the probability distributions of the noise and inefficiency effects. Amsler et al. (2017) assume that

MF1 u^g_{it} is an independent $N^+(0, \sigma^2_{ug})$ random variable, and
MF2 v^g_{it} is an independent $N(0, \sigma^2_{vg})$ random variable.

In this context, the term 'independent' means that the noise and inefficiency effects are neither correlated with each other nor correlated with the explanatory variables (i.e., all these variables are mutually independent). If there are no cross-equation restrictions involving the parameters and MF1 and MF2 are true, then the g-th equation in (8.59) can be estimated separately, using all (and only) observations on firms that used technology g.

Let $\tilde{f}^g(.)$, $\tilde{\sigma}^2_{vg}$ and $\tilde{\sigma}^2_{ug}$ denote the ML estimators for $f^g(.)$, σ^2_{vg} and σ^2_{ug}. The Amsler et al. (2017) algorithm for drawing B random samples of observations on the noise and inefficiency effects can be summarised as follows:

1. Compute $\tilde{\varepsilon}^{g_{it}}_{it} = \ln q_{1it} - \tilde{f}^{g_{it}}(x_{it}, q^*_{it}, z_{it})$, $\tilde{\mu}_{it} = \tilde{\varepsilon}^{g_{it}}_{it}\tilde{\sigma}^2_{vg_{it}}/(\tilde{\sigma}^2_{vg_{it}} + \tilde{\sigma}^2_{ug_{it}})$ and $\tilde{\sigma}^2_{it} = \tilde{\sigma}^2_{vg_{it}}\tilde{\sigma}^2_{ug_{it}}/(\tilde{\sigma}^2_{vg_{it}} + \tilde{\sigma}^2_{ug_{it}})$. Set $b = 1$.
2. For all $g \in G_t$, draw $v^g_{it}(b)$ from an $N(0, \tilde{\sigma}^2_{vg})$ distribution.
3. Redraw $v^{g_{it}}_{it}(b)$ from an $N(\tilde{\mu}_{it}, \tilde{\sigma}^2_{it})$ distribution truncated on the left at $\tilde{\varepsilon}^{g_{it}}_{it}$.
4. For all $g \in G_t$, compute $u^g_{it}(b) = \tilde{f}^g(x_{it}, q^*_{it}, z_{it}) + v^g_{it}(b) - \ln q_{1it}$.
5. Compute $u_{it}(b) = \max_{g \in G_t} u^g_{it}(b)$ and $m^{g_{it}}_{it}(b) = u_{it}(b) - u^{g_{it}}_{it}(b)$.
6. If $b < B$, then set $b = b + 1$ and return to step 2. Else stop.

After implementing this algorithm, the following equations can be used to predict the ROTE, OTE and OMR of manager i in period t:

$$\widetilde{ROTE}^{g_{it}}(x_{it}, q_{it}, z_{it}) = B^{-1}\sum_{b=1}^{B} \exp[-u^{g_{it}}_{it}(b)], \tag{8.60}$$

$$\widetilde{OTE}^{t}(x_{it}, q_{it}, z_{it}) = B^{-1}\sum_{b=1}^{B} \exp[-u_{it}(b)] \tag{8.61}$$

and

$$\widetilde{OMR}^{g_{it}t}(x_{it}, q_{it}, z_{it}) = B^{-1}\sum_{b=1}^{B} \exp[-m^{g_{it}}_{it}(b)]. \tag{8.62}$$

For a numerical example, reconsider the toy data reported in Table 1.1. For purposes of comparison with the results reported in Tables 6.20 and 7.13, suppose that (a) technologies 1 and 2 existed in each period, (b) no other technologies existed in any period, (c) the managers of firms 1, 2 and 3 always used technology 1, and (d) the managers of firms 4 and 5 always used technology 2. Also suppose that the g-th equation in the system defined by (8.59) takes the form

$$\ln q_{1it} = \alpha_g + \sum_{m=1}^{M} \beta_{mg} \ln x_{mit} - \sum_{n=1}^{N} \gamma_{ng} \ln q^*_{nit} + v^g_{it} - u^g_{it}. \tag{8.63}$$

ML estimates of the unknown parameters in the system are presented in Table 8.13. These estimates were obtained under assumptions MF1 and MF2. Associated predictions of OTE, ROTE and the OMRs are reported in Table 8.14. These predictions were obtained using $B = 5000$ samples. Among other things, the predictions reported in Table 8.14 indicate that the manager of firm 5 chose the right technology in period 5 but did not use it properly (i.e., he/she 'chose the right book' but did not 'follow the instructions').

Table 8.13 ML parameter estimates

	$g = 1$			$g = 2$		
Parameter	Est.	St. Err.	t	Est.	St. Err.	t
α_g	0.499	1.314	0.380	0.773	0.637	1.214
β_{1g}	0.060	0.064	0.943	0.583	0.991	0.588
β_{2g}	0.365	0.151	2.412**	0.068	0.792	0.086
γ_{2g}	0.364	0.115	3.159***	0.086	0.561	0.154
$\sigma_g^2 \equiv \sigma_{ug}^2 + \sigma_{vg}^2$	0.068	0.025	2.676***	0.130	0.972	0.133
$\gamma_g \equiv \sigma_{ug}^2/\sigma_g^2$	0.000	0.068	0.000	1.000	0.853	1.172

***, ** and * indicate significance at the 1, 5 and 10% levels

Table 8.14 ML predictions of OTE, ROTE and OMRs[a,b]

Row	Firm	Period	OTE	OMR	ROTE
A	1	1	0.462	0.462	0.999
B	2	1	0.673	0.674	0.999
C	3	1	0.999	1	0.999
D	4	1	0.964	0.994	0.970
E	5	1	0.882	0.999	0.883
F	1	2	0.500	0.501	0.999
G	2	2	0.723	0.724	0.999
H	3	2	0.999	1	0.999
I	4	2	0.662	0.919	0.720
J	5	2	0.967	1.000	0.968
K	1	3	0.709	0.710	0.999
L	2	3	0.314	0.315	0.999
M	3	3	0.425	0.426	0.999
N	4	3	0.683	0.978	0.699
O	5	3	0.907	0.982	0.923
P	1	4	0.620	0.621	0.999
R	2	4	0.507	0.508	0.999
S	3	4	0.343	0.343	0.999
T	4	4	0.938	0.997	0.941
U	5	4	0.500	0.999	0.500
V	1	5	0.532	0.532	0.999
W	2	5	0.975	0.976	0.999
X	3	5	0.410	0.411	0.999
Y	4	5	0.546	0.971	0.562
Z	5	5	0.562	1	0.562
Geometric mean			0.635	0.713	0.891

[a]OTE = OMR × ROTE. Some predictions may be incoherent at the third decimal place due to rounding (e.g., in any given row, the product of the OMR and ROTE predictions may not be exactly equal to the OTE prediction due to rounding)

[b]Numbers reported to less than three decimal places are exact; see the footnote to Table 1.2 on p. 8

8.6.2 Output Supply Systems

Output supply functions can always be written as systems of equations with unobserved error terms representing statistical noise and different types of inefficiency. For any given firm, the exact form of the system depends on the exact form of the manager's optimisation problem. For example, if firm i is a price taker in output markets and all inputs and environmental variables have been predetermined, then the manager's period-t optimisation problem is given by (4.12). In this case, the relevant system of equations is a system of revenue-maximising output supply functions. If the functional forms of these supply functions are known, then the system can be written in the form of (7.41). If the functional forms of the supply functions are *not* known, then we can instead write

$$\ln q_{nit} = f_n^t(x_{it}, p_{it}, z_{it}) + v_{nit} + u_{nit} \quad \text{for } n = 1, \ldots, N, \tag{8.64}$$

where $f_n^t(.)$ is a known approximating function chosen by the researcher, $v_{nit} = \ln \ddot{q}_n^t(x_{it}, p_{it}, z_{it}) - f_n^t(x_{it}, p_{it}, z_{it})$ is an unobserved variable representing statistical noise, and $u_{nit} \equiv \ln q_{nit} - \ln \ddot{q}_n^t(x_{it}, p_{it}, z_{it})$ denotes an unsigned error that captures technical, scale and allocative inefficiency. In any given equation, the precise nature of the statistical noise component depends on both the approximating function and unknown revenue-maximising output supply function. Suppose, for example, that the n-th approximating function is

$$f_n^t(x_{it}, p_{it}, z_{it}) = \alpha_n + \lambda t + \sum_{j=1}^{J} \delta_j \ln z_{jit} + \sum_{m=1}^{M} \beta_m \ln x_{mit} - \sigma \ln p_{nit}. \tag{8.65}$$

In this case, the n-th equation in (8.64) is

$$\ln q_{nit} = \alpha_n + \lambda t + \sum_{j=1}^{J} \delta_j \ln z_{jit} + \sum_{m=1}^{M} \beta_m \ln x_{mit} - \sigma \ln p_{nit} + v_{nit} + u_{nit}. \tag{8.66}$$

If the n-th revenue-maximising output supply function is given by (4.13), for example, then

$$v_{nit} = [\alpha_n(t) - \alpha_n - \lambda t] + \frac{\sigma}{1-\sigma} \ln \left(\sum_{k=1}^{N} \gamma_k^{\sigma} p_{kit}^{1-\sigma} \right). \tag{8.67}$$

The first term in square brackets can be viewed as a possible functional form error. The second term is an omitted variable error. Again, the presence of statistical noise means we cannot generally interpret the parameters in (8.66) in the same way we interpreted the parameters in (7.43). For example, unless we know (or assume) that

v_{nit} is not a function of z_{jit}, we cannot interpret δ_j as an elasticity that measures the percent change in output n due to a one percent increase in environmental variable j.

Equation (8.64) represents a system of N seemingly unrelated regression (SUR) equations in which each u_{nit} is uncorrelated with x_{it}, p_{it} and z_{it}. If the output mix is predetermined, then an alternative SUR system is

$$\ln q_{1it} = f^t(x_{it}, q^*_{it}, z_{it}) + v_{it} - u_{it} \quad (8.1)$$

and

$$\ln q_{nit} = f^t_n(x_{it}, p_{it}, z_{it}) + v_{nit} + u_{nit} \quad \text{for } n = 2, \ldots, N, \quad (8.68)$$

where $q^*_{it} \equiv q_{it}/q_{1it}$ denotes a vector of normalised outputs, $f^t(.)$ is an approximating function chosen by the researcher, v_{it} represents statistical noise, and $u_{it} \geq 0$ denotes an output-oriented technical inefficiency effect. If the output mix is *not* predetermined, then (8.1) and (8.68) represent a system of N simultaneous equations.

8.6.3 Input Demand Systems

Input demand functions can also be written as systems of equations with unobserved error terms representing statistical noise and different types of inefficiency. Again, for any given firm, the exact form of the system depends on the exact form of the manager's optimisation problem. For example, if firm i is a price taker in input markets and all outputs and environmental variables have been predetermined, then the manager's period-t optimisation problem is given by (4.17). In this case, the relevant system of equations is a system of cost-minimising input demand functions. If the functional forms of these demand functions are known, then the system can be written in the form of (7.45). If the functional forms of the demand functions are *not* known, then we can instead write

$$\ln x_{mit} = f^t_m(w_{it}, q_{it}, z_{it}) + v_{mit} + u_{mit} \quad \text{for } m = 1, \ldots, M, \quad (8.69)$$

where $f^t_m(.)$ is a known approximating function chosen by the researcher, $v_{mit} = \ln \ddot{x}^t_m(w_{it}, q_{it}, z_{it}) - f^t_m(w_{it}, q_{it}, z_{it})$ is an unobserved variable representing statistical noise, and $u_{mit} \equiv \ln x_{mit} - \ln \ddot{x}^t_m(w_{it}, q_{it}, z_{it})$ denotes an unsigned error that captures technical, scale and allocative inefficiency. In any given equation, the precise nature of the statistical noise component depends on both the approximating function and unknown cost-minimising input demand function. Suppose, for example, that the m-th approximating function is

$$f^t_m(w_{it}, q_{it}, z_{it}) = \theta_m(t) + \sum_{k=1}^{M} \lambda_k \ln(w_{kit}/w_{mit}) + \psi \ln Q(q_{it}) \quad (8.70)$$

where $Q(.)$ is a known, nonnegative, nondecreasing, linearly-homogenous function. In this case, the m-th equation in (8.69) is

$$\ln x_{mit} = \theta_m(t) + \sum_{k=1}^{M} \lambda_k \ln(w_{kit}/w_{mit}) + \psi \ln Q(q_{it}) + v_{mit} + u_{mit} \tag{8.71}$$

where $Q(q_{it})$ is an aggregate output. If the m-th cost-minimising input demand function is given by (4.18), for example, then

$$v_{mit} = \left[\frac{1}{\tau\eta} \ln\left(\sum_{n=1}^{N} \gamma_n q_{nit}^{\tau}\right) - \psi \ln Q(q_{it})\right] - \sum_{j=1}^{J} \kappa_j \ln z_{jit}. \tag{8.72}$$

The first term can be viewed as a possible measurement error. The second term can be viewed as an omitted variable error. Observe that neither of these terms vary with m. Again, the presence of statistical noise means we cannot generally interpret the parameters in (8.71) in the same way we interpreted the parameters in (7.47). For example, unless we know (or assume) that v_{mit} is not a function of input prices, we cannot interpret λ_k as an elasticity that measures the percent increase in the demand for input m due to a one percent increase in the price of input k.

Equation (8.69) represents a system of M seemingly unrelated regression (SUR) equations in which each u_{mit} is uncorrelated with w_{it}, q_{it} and z_{it}. If the input mix is predetermined, then an alternative SUR system is

$$-\ln x_{1it} = f^t(x_{it}^*, q_{it}, z_{it}) + v_{it} - u_{it} \tag{8.5}$$

and $$\ln x_{mit} = f_m^t(w_{it}, q_{it}, z_{it}) + v_{mit} + u_{mit} \quad \text{for } m = 2, \ldots, M, \tag{8.73}$$

where $x_{it}^* \equiv x_{it}/x_{1it}$ denotes a vector of normalised inputs, $f^t(.)$ is an approximating function chosen by the researcher, v_{it} represents statistical noise, and $u_{it} \geq 0$ denotes an input-oriented technical inefficiency effect. If the input mix is *not* predetermined, then (8.5) and (8.73) represent a system of M simultaneous equations.

In the productivity literature, some of the most widely-used systems of input demand functions are underpinned by much more imaginative, but not necessarily realistic, assumptions concerning production technologies and managerial behaviour. For example, Olley and Pakes (1996) assume, among other things,[13] that (a) there is only one output, (b) all inputs can be classified as either labour or capital goods, (c) the production function depends on the age of the firm, and (d) the manager makes his/her labour and capital investment decisions to maximise the expected discounted value of future net returns. Solving the manager's optimisation problem yields time-varying input demand functions for labour and capital goods. The capital goods function, for example, expresses the demand for capital goods in period t as a function of (a) the productivity of the manager in period t, (b) the age of the firm in period t, and (c) the capital stock at the beginning of period t (Olley and Pakes 1996, Eq. 5). Levinsohn and Petrin (2003) modify the Olley and Pakes (1996) model by assuming that all inputs can be classified as either labour, capital or intermediate goods. For simplicity, they ignore the age of the firm. They find that the demand for

[13]For a more complete list of assumptions, see Sect. 4.7.5.

intermediate goods in period t is a time-varying function of (a) the productivity of the manager in period t, and (b) the capital stock at the beginning of period t (Levinsohn and Petrin 2003, p. 322). For a related system, see Ackerberg et al. (2015).

8.6.4 Inefficiency Models

Measures of efficiency can be viewed as measures of how well firm managers have solved different optimisation problems. Theories of bounded rationality tell us that managers make optimisation errors due to a lack of knowledge, training and/or experience (see Sect. 4.7.6). Let a_{it} denote a vector of predetermined personal attributes (e.g., years of education, training and/or experience) that affect the optimisation errors that manager i makes in period t. The relationship between these attributes and the inefficiency of the manager, u_{it}, can be written as

$$u_{it} = g^t(a_{it}) + w_{it} \tag{8.74}$$

where $g^t(.)$ is an approximating function chosen by the researcher and w_{it} denotes a measure of statistical noise. The fact that u_{it} is nonnegative implies that $w_{it} \geq -g^t(a_{it})$. The superscript t in (8.74) accounts the fact that technical progress (i.e., the discovery of new 'books of instructions') increases the scope for inefficiency (i.e., the scope for 'choosing the wrong book' and/or 'failing to follow the instructions'). If there is no technical progress, then this superscript can be deleted. If the data are cross-section data, then *all* references to period t can be deleted and (8.74) takes the form of equation (8) in Reifschneider and Stevenson (1991). If $g^t(a_{it}) = a_{it}'\delta$, then it takes the form of equation (2) in Battese and Coelli (1995).

Equation (8.74) can be combined with any one of the single-equation SFMs described in Sect. 8.1 to form a system of two simultaneous equations. It is common to estimate the unknown parameters in such systems using the method of maximum likelihood. An empirical example is presented in Step 8 of Sect. 9.3. If either equation in such a system is misspecified, then associated estimators and predictors are likely to be biased and inconsistent.

For a classic example of a misspecified system, suppose that output sets are homothetic and technical change is implicit Hicks output neutral. In this case, the relationship between outputs, inputs and environmental variables can be written as $y_{it} = \ln F^t(x_{it}, z_{it}) - u_{it}$ where y_{it} denotes the logarithm of an aggregate output, $F^t(.)$ can be viewed as a production function, and $u_{it} \geq 0$ denotes an output-oriented technical inefficiency effect (this follows from properties DO11 and DO12 in Sect. 2.4.1). If the functional form of the production function is unknown, then we can write

$$y_{it} = f^t(x_{it}) - g^t(z_{it}) + v_{it} - u_{it} \tag{8.75}$$

where $f^t(.)$ and $g^t(.)$ are arbitrary approximating functions and $v_{it} = \ln F^t(x_{it}, z_{it}) - f^t(x_{it}) + g^t(z_{it})$ represents a functional form error. If the functional form of the production function is unknown *and we do not observe any environmental variables*, then we can instead write

$$y_{it} = f^t(x_{it}) + v_{it} - u_{it} \tag{8.76}$$

where $v_{it} = \ln F^t(x_{it}, z_{it}) - f^t(x_{it})$ now represent a functional form error and omitted environmental variables. On the other hand, if the functional form of the production function is unknown *and we do not observe any outputs or inputs*, then we can instead write

$$u_{it} = g^t(z_{it}) + w_{it} \tag{8.77}$$

where $w_{it} = \ln F^t(x_{it}, z_{it}) - g^t(z_{it}) - y_{it}$ represents functional form errors and omitted outputs and inputs. Equations (8.76) and (8.77) have the same basic structure as equations (1) and (2) in Battese and Coelli (1995). If we do, in fact, observe environmental variables, then failure to include them in (8.76) is an omitted variable error. If we do, in fact, observe outputs and inputs, then failure to include them in (8.77) is another omitted variable error. If we observe outputs, inputs and environmental variables, then, to avoid omitted variable errors, we should estimate (8.75). Estimating the misspecified system of equations defined by (8.76) and (8.77) is not equivalent to estimating (8.75). To see this, note that if we substitute (8.77) into (8.76), then we obtain the following reduced form equation:

$$y_{it} = f^t(x_{it}) - g^t(z_{it}) + v_{it} - w_{it}. \tag{8.78}$$

This equation appears to have the same structure as (8.75). However, u_{it} in (8.75) satisfies $u_{it} \geq 0$, whereas w_{it} in (8.78) satisfies $w_{it} \geq -g^t(z_{it})$. Unless there are no environmental variables involved in the production process, the system defined by (8.76) and (8.77) is misspecified.

Several other inefficiency models can be found in the stochastic frontier literature. Most of these models do not allow for omitted variable errors or other sources of statistical noise. For this reason, they are best described as expedient: they are statistically convenient and practical, but they are possibly improper insofar as they have no obvious connections to economic theory. For example, Pitt and Lee (1981, pp. 46, 47) assume that $u_{it} = u_i$. Battese and Coelli (1992) assume that $u_{it} = \exp[\eta(T - t)]u_i$ where T denotes the last period in the sample. Again, any one of these equations can be combined with any one of the single-equation SFMs described in Sect. 8.1 to form a system of two simultaneous equations. Again, if either equation in such a system is misspecified, then our estimators and predictors are likely to be biased and inconsistent.

8.7 Summary and Further Reading

Stochastic frontier models (SFMs) are underpinned by only one assumption, namely that production possibilities sets can be represented by distance, revenue, cost and/or profit functions. Each of these functions can be written as a single-equation regression model with two error terms, one representing statistical noise and the other representing inefficiency. Schmidt and Lovell (1979, p. 346), Kumbhakar (1987, p. 336), Kumbhakar and Lovell (2000, pp. 3, 4) and Kumbhakar et al. (2015, p. 55) assume that the noise component captures random variables that are outside the control of the firm (i.e., random environmental variables). Hill et al. (2011, p. 48) assume it also "captures any approximation error that arises because the ...functional form we have assumed may only be an approximation to reality". Carta and Steel (2012, p. 3757) write that the noise effect "is usually assumed to be a symmetric measurement error". Asteriou and Hall (2015, p. 180) write that "one of the most common specification errors is to estimate an equation that omits one or more influential explanatory variables, or an equation that contains explanatory variables that do not belong to the 'true' specification". In this book, statistical noise is viewed as a combination of all these factors: omitted variable errors (e.g., omitted environmental variables), functional form errors (e.g., assuming the cost function is a translog function), measurement errors (e.g., when changes in quantities are measured using indices that are not compatible with measurement theory) and included variable errors (e.g., when output prices are included in a cost function).

The unknown parameters in SFMs can be estimated using least squares (LS), maximum likelihood (ML) or Bayesian methods. LS estimation of SFMs involves choosing the unknown parameters to minimise the sum of squared noise and inefficiency effects. Most models are assumed to be linear in the unknown parameters, and composite errors representing the noise and inefficiency effects are usually assumed to be independent random variables with a common mean and a common variance. If these assumptions are true, then the ordinary least squares (OLS) estimators for the slope parameters in the model are unbiased and consistent. In the efficiency literature, it is common to make additional assumptions concerning the probability distributions of the noise and inefficiency effects (e.g., that the noise effects are normal random variables and the inefficiency effects are half-normal random variables). The OLS estimator for the intercept can then be adjusted (or 'modified') to account for the fact that the inefficiency effects have a nonnegative mean. In this book,[14] the associated estimators are referred to as modified ordinary least squares (MOLS) estimators. The idea behind MOLS estimation of SFMs can traced back at least as far as Olson et al. (1980). MOLS estimators are rarely used in practice because they are less efficient than ML estimators.

ML estimation of SFMs involves choosing the unknown parameters to maximise the joint density (or 'likelihood') of the observed data. Under weak regularity con-

[14] Olson et al. (1980) refer to these estimators as corrected ordinary least squares (COLS) estimators. In this book, the term COLS is reserved for LS estimators for the parameters in deterministic frontier models.

ditions, ML estimators are consistent, asymptotically normal and asymptotically efficient. The exact form of the likelihood function depends on the probability distributions of the noise and inefficiency effects. It is common to assume that the noise effects are independent normal random variables and that the inefficiency effects are independent truncated-normal random variables. The so-called normal-truncated-normal model can be traced back at least as far as Stevenson (1980). Several other assumptions concerning the inefficiency effects can be found in the literature. For example, Aigner et al. (1977) and Meeusen and van den Broeck (1977) consider the case where the inefficiency effects are exponential random variables, Stevenson (1980) and Greene (1990) consider the case where they are gamma random variables, Li (1996) assumes they are uniform random variables, Hajargasht (2015) assumes they are Rayleigh random variables, and Almanidis et al. (2014) assume they are doubly-truncated normal random variables. The Almanidis et al. (2014) assumption rules out the possibility that inputs can be used to produce zero output (i.e., it rules out assumption A1 from Sect. 1.2). Ondrich and Ruggiero (2001) show that standard ML predictors for the inefficiency effects are monotonic in the composite error if the probability density function (PDF) of the noise component is log-concave; an interesting implication of this result is that, irrespective of the assumed distribution of the inefficiency effects, if the noise effects are independent normal random variables, then the rankings of the inefficiency effects are the same as the rankings of the composite errors. Horrace and Parmeter (2018) assume the noise and inefficiency effects are Laplace and truncated-Laplace random variables respectively; an interesting feature of this model is that the conditional distribution of the inefficiency effects is constant (resp. variable) for positive (resp. negative) values of the composite error. Several authors assume the noise effects are correlated with the inefficiency effects: Smith (2008) models the correlation structure using copulas, Pal and Sengupta (1999) and Bandyopadhyay and Das (2006) assume the two effects are distributed as truncated-bivariate-normal random variables, while Gómez-Déniz and Pérez-Rodríguez (2015) assume they are distributed as bivariate-Sarmanov random variables. Empirical applications of these models can be found in almost every area of business and economics: for example, Lee and Tyler (1978) use a normal-half-normal model to estimate the average output-oriented technical efficiency of industrial firms in Brazil; Burns and Weyman-Jones (1996) use a normal-half-normal model to predict the cost efficiency of electricity distributors in England and Wales; and Ali and Flinn (1989) use a normal-half-normal model to predict the profit efficiency of rice producers in Pakistan.

Bayesian estimation of SFMs involves summarising sample and non-sample information about the unknown model parameters in terms of a posterior PDF. One of the advantages of the Bayesian approach is that it provides a formal mechanism for incorporating almost any type of non-sample information into the estimation process (e.g., inequality constraints concerning the model parameters). Another advantage is that it is possible to draw exact finite-sample inferences concerning nonlinear functions of the model parameters (e.g., measures of efficiency). Bayesian estimation of SFMs can be traced back at least as far as van den Broeck et al. (1994).

SFMs can be used to both measure and explain changes in TFP. *Measuring* changes in TFP involves computing proper TFP index (TFPI) numbers. SFMs can be used to compute additive and multiplicative TFPI numbers. However, they cannot generally be used to compute primal or dual TFPI numbers. *Explaining* changes in TFP involves breaking proper TFPI numbers into various components. SFMs can be used to decompose proper TFPI numbers into measures of environmental change, technical change, efficiency change *and changes in statistical noise*. Both output- and input-oriented decompositions are available. Whether or not it is possible to separately identify all the components of TFP change depends on the both the TFPI and the SFM.

There are many TFPI numbers that are not proper in the sense that they cannot generally be written as proper output index numbers divided by proper input index numbers. Examples include Fisher, Törnqvist, Hicks-Moorsteen, Malmquist, EKS and CCD TFPI numbers. If decision makers view measures of productivity change as measures of output quantity change divided by measures of input quantity change, then it is not clear why they would be interested in TFPI numbers of this type. Putting this issue to one side, one way of decomposing such numbers is to first write them as the product of proper TFPI numbers and statistical noise index (SNI) numbers. Subsequently, the proper TFPI numbers can be decomposed into technology index numbers, environment index numbers, efficiency index numbers and (more) SNI numbers.

Other SFMs that are discussed in this chapter include various systems of equations. These systems can be used to explain variations in metafrontiers, output supplies, input demands, and inefficiency. SFMs that are *not* discussed in this book include various semiparametric and nonparametric models. For details concerning these models, see, for example, Park and Simar (1994), Fan et al. (1996), Kneip and Simar (1996), Park et al. (1998), Henderson and Simar (2005), Kumbhakar et al. (2007), Kuosmanen and Kortelainen (2012), Simar and Zelenyuk (2011), Martins-Filho et al. (2015), Parmeter et al. (2017) and Simar et al. (2017).

References

Ackerberg D, Caves K, Frazer G (2015) Identification properties of recent production function estimators. Econometrica 83(6):2411–2451

Aigner D, Lovell C, Schmidt P (1977) Formulation and estimation of stochastic frontier production function models. J Econ 6:21–37

Ali M, Flinn J (1989) Profit efficiency among basmati rice producers in Pakistan Punjab. Am J Agric Econ 71(2):303–310

Almanidis P, Qian J, Sickles R (2014) Stochastic frontier models with bounded inefficiency. In: Sickles R (ed) Festschrift in Honor of Peter Schmidt: econometric methods and applications. Springer, Berlin

Amsler C, O'Donnell C, Schmidt P (2017) Stochastic metafrontiers. Econ Rev 36(6–9):1007–1020

Assaf A, Gillen G, Tsionas E (2014) Understanding relative efficiency among airports: a general dynamic model for distinguishing technical and allocative efficiency. Transp Res Part B 70:18–34

Asteriou D, Hall S (2015) Applied econometrics. Palgrave Macmillan, New York

Bandyopadhyay D, Das A (2006) On measures of technical inefficiency and production uncertainty in stochastic frontier production model with correlated error components. J Prod Anal 26(2):165–180
Battese G, Coelli T (1992) Frontier production functions, technical efficiency and panel data: with application to paddy farmers in India. J Prod Anal 3(1–2):153–169
Battese G, Coelli T (1993) A stochastic frontier production function incorporating a model for technical inefficiency effects. Working Papers in Econometrics and Applied Statistics 69, University of New England
Battese G, Coelli T (1995) A model for technical inefficiency effects in a stochastic frontier production function for panel data. Empirical Econ 20:325–332
Battese G, Corra G (1977) Estimation of a production frontier model: with application to the pastoral zone of Eastern Australia. Aust J Agric Econ 21(3):169–179
Burns P, Weyman-Jones T (1996) Cost functions and cost efficiency in electricity distribution: a stochastic frontier approach. Bull Econ Res 48(1):44–64
Byma J, Tauer L (2007) Exploring the role of managerial ability in determining firm efficiency. Selected paper prepared for presentation at the American Agricultural Economics Association Annual Meeting, Portland, Oregon, 30–31 June
Carta A, Steel M (2012) Modelling multi-output stochastic frontiers using copulas. Comput Stat Data Anal 56(11):3757–3773
Casella G, George E (1992) Explaining the Gibbs sampler. Am Stat 46(3):167–174
Caudill S, Ford J (1993) Biases in frontier estimation due to heteroskedasticity. Econ Lett 41:17–20
Coelli T (1995) Estimators and hypothesis tests for a stochastic frontier function: a Monte Carlo analysis. J Prod Anal 6:247–268
Emvalomatis G (2012) Adjustment and unobserved heterogeneity in dynamic stochastic frontier models. J Prod Anal 37(1):7–16
Fan Y, Li Q, Weersink A (1996) Semiparametric estimation of stochastic production frontier models. J Bus Econ Stat 14(4):460–468
Fernandez C, Osiewalski J, Steel M (1997) On the use of panel data in stochastic frontier models with improper priors. J Econ 79(1):169–93
Gómez-Déniz E, Pérez-Rodríguez J (2015) Closed-form solution for a bivariate distribution in stochastic frontier models with dependent errors. J Prod Anal 43(2):215–223
Gouriéroux C, Holly A, Monfort A (1982) Likelihood ratio test, Wald test, and Kuhn-Tucker test in linear models with inequality constraints on the regression parameters. Econometrica 50(1):63–80
Greene W (1990) A Gamma-distributed stochastic frontier model. J Econ 46(1–2):141–163
Greene W (2004) Reconsidering heterogeneity in panel data estimators of the stochastic frontier model. J Econ 126(2005):269–303
Greene W (2005) Fixed and random effects in stochastic frontier models. J Prod Anal 23(1):7–32
Hajargasht G (2015) Stochastic frontiers with a Rayleigh distribution. J Prod Anal 44(2):199–208
Henderson D, Simar L (2005) A fully nonparametric stochastic frontier model for panel data. Department of Economics Working Paper 0519, State University of New York at Binghamton
Henderson DJ, Parmeter CF (2015) A consistent bootstrap procedure for nonparametric symmetry tests. Econ Lett 131(C):78–82, https://doi.org/10.1016/j.econlet.2015.03, https://ideas.repec.org/a/eee/ecolet/v131y2015icp78-82.html
Herr A (2008) Cost and technical efficiency of German hospitals: Does ownership matter? Health Econ 17(9):1057–1071
Hill R, Griffiths W, Lim G (2011) Principles of econometrics, 4th edn. Wiley, Hoboken
Horrace W, Parmeter C (2018) A laplace stochastic frontier model. Econ Rev 37(3):260–280
Horrace W, Schmidt P (1996) Confidence statements for efficiency estimates from stochastic frontier models. J Prod Anal 7(2–3):257–282
Huang YF, Luo S, Wang HJ (2018) Flexible panel stochastic frontier model with serially correlated error. Econ Lett 163:55–58
Jondrow J, Lovell C, Materov I, Schmidt P (1982) On the estimation of technical inefficiency in the stochastic frontier production function model. J Econ 19(2–3):233–238

Kneip A, Simar L (1996) A general framework for frontier estimation with panel data. J Prod Anal 7(2–3):187–212
Kumbhakar S (1987) The specification of technical and allocative inefficiency in stochastic production and profit frontiers. J Econ 34(3):335–348
Kumbhakar S (1991) Estimation of technical inefficiency in panel data models with firm- and time-specific effects. Econ Lett 36(1):43–48
Kumbhakar S, Lovell C (2000) Stochastic frontier analysis. Cambridge University Press, Cambridge
Kumbhakar S, Park B, Simar L, Tsionas E (2007) Nonparametric stochastic frontiers: a local maximum likelihood approach. J Econ 137(1):1–27
Kumbhakar S, Wang HJ, Horncastle A (2015) A practitioner's guide to stochastic frontier analysis using stata. Cambridge University Press, New York
Kuosmanen T, Fosgerau M (2009) Neoclassical versus frontier production models? Testing for the skewness of regression residuals. Scand J Econ 111(2):351–367
Kuosmanen T, Kortelainen M (2012) Stochastic non-smooth envelopment of data: semi-parametric frontier estimation subject to shape constraints. J Prod Anal 38(1):11–28
Lai HP, Kumbhakar S (2018) Estimation of dynamic stochastic frontier model using likelihood-based approaches. MPRA Paper 87830, Munich Personal RePEc Archive
Lee L, Tyler W (1978) The stochastic frontier production function and average efficiency. J Econ 7(1978):385–389
Levinsohn J, Petrin A (2003) Estimating production functions using inputs to control for unobservables. Rev Econ Stud 70(2):317–341
Li Q (1996) Estimating a stochastic production frontier when the adjusted error is symmetric. Econ Lett 52(3):221–228
Martins-Filho C, Yao F, Torero M (2015) Higher-order conditional quantile estimation based on nonparametric models of regression. Econ Rev 34(6–10):907–958
Meesters A (2013) A non-linear stochastic frontier model. Technical report, available at SSRN https://ssrn.com/abstract=2199540 or https://doi.org/10.2139/ssrn.2199540
Meeusen W, van den Broeck J (1977) Efficiency estimation from Cobb-Douglas production functions with composed error. Int Econ Rev 18(2):435–444
O'Donnell C (2016) Using information about technologies, markets and firm behaviour to decompose a proper productivity index. J Econ 190(2):328–340
O'Donnell C, Nguyen K (2013) An econometric approach to estimating support prices and measures of productivity change in public hospitals. J Prod Anal 40(3):323–335
Olley G, Pakes A (1996) The dynamics of productivity in the telecommunications equipment industry. Econometrica 64(6):1263–1297
Olson J, Schmidt P, Waldman D (1980) A Monte Carlo study of estimators of stochastic frontier production functions. J Econ 13(1):67–82
Ondrich J, Ruggiero J (2001) Efficiency measurement in the stochastic frontier model. Eur Jo Oper Res 129(2):434–442
Pal M, Sengupta A (1999) A model of FPF with correlated error componenets: an application to Indian agriculture. Sankhya: Indian J Stat Series B 61(2):337–350
Park B, Simar L (1994) Efficient semiparametric estimation in a stochastic frontier model. J Am Stat Assoc 89(427):929–936
Park B, Sickles R, Simar L (1998) Stochastic panel frontiers: a semiparametric approach. J Econ 84(2):273–301
Parmeter CF, Wang HJ, Kumbhakar SC (2017) Nonparametric estimation of the determinants of inefficiency. J Prod Anal 47(3):205–221
Pitt M, Lee LF (1981) The measurement and sources of technical inefficiency in the Indonesian weaving industry. J Dev Econ 9(1):43–64
Reifschneider D, Stevenson R (1991) Systematic departures from the frontier: a framework for the analysis of firm inefficiency. Int Econ Rev 32(3):715–723
Robert C, Casella G (2004) Monte Carlo statistical methods, 2nd edn. Springer texts in statistics, Springer, New York

Salas-Velasco M (2018) Production efficiency measurement and its determinants across OECD countries: the role of business sophistication and innovation. Econ Anal Policy 57:60–73
Schmidt P, Lin TF (1984) Simple tests of alternative specifications in stochastic frontier models. J Econ 24:349–361
Schmidt P, Lovell C (1979) Estimating technical and allocative inefficiency relative to stochastic production and cost frontiers. J Econ 9(3):343–366
Simar L, Zelenyuk V (2011) Stochastic FDH/DEA estimators for frontier analysis. J Prod Anal 36(1):1–20
Simar L, van Keilegom I, Zelenyuk V (2017) Nonparametric least squares methods for stochastic frontier models. J Prod Anal 47(3):189–204
Smith M (2008) Stochastic frontier models with dependent error components. Econ J 11(1):172–192
Stevenson R (1980) Likelihood functions for generalized stochastic frontier estimation. J Econ 13(1):57–66
Tierney L (1994) Markov chains for exploring posterior distributions. Ann Stat 22(4):1701–1728
Tsionas E (2006) Inference in dynamic stochastic frontier models. J Appl Econ 21(5):669–676
Tsionas E (2007) Efficiency measurement with the Weibull stochastic frontier. Oxford Bull Econ Stat 69(5):693–706
van den Broeck J, Koop G, Osiewalski J, Steel M (1994) Stochastic frontier models: a Bayesian perspective. J Econ 61:273–303

Chapter 9
Practical Considerations

This chapter considers some of the steps involved in conducting a policy-oriented analysis of managerial performance. It also considers government policies that can be used to target the main drivers of performance. In this book, the term 'government' refers to a group of people with the authority to control any variables that are not controlled by firm managers.

9.1 The Main Steps

Policy-oriented performance analysis involves a number of steps that are best completed in a prescribed order or sequence. The main steps are the following (immediate predecessor steps are in parentheses):

1. Identify the manager(s).
2. Classify the variables that are physically involved in the production process (1).
3. Identify relevant measures of comparative performance (2).
4. Make assumptions about production technologies (2).
5. Assemble relevant data (3).
6. Select one or more functions to represent production possibilities sets (4, 5).
7. Choose an estimator (6).
8. Estimate the model and test the model assumptions (6, 7).
9. Check if the main results are robust to the assumptions and choices made in Steps 4, 6 and 7 (8).

Researchers with little interest in policy often complete these steps in a different order. For example, academic researchers who are primarily interested in getting their work published often start at Step 7 (i.e., they choose the estimation approach first).

C. J. O'Donnell, *Productivity and Efficiency Analysis*,
https://doi.org/10.1007/978-981-13-2984-5_9

Step 1. Identifying the Manager(s)

The first step in analysing managerial performance is to identify the manager(s). A manager is a person or other accountable body responsible for controlling (or administering) a firm. It is generally only meaningful to compare the performance of managers of the same type. For example, it is generally only meaningful to compare the performance of rice farmers with the performance of other rice farmers, not cattle producers.

Step 2. Classifying the Variables

In this book, all of the possibly millions of variables that are physically involved in production processes are classified into those that are controlled by firm managers and those that are not. Those that are controlled managers are then further classified into inputs and outputs. Those that are *never* controlled by managers are referred to as environmental variables. Here, the term 'environmental variable' refers to a characteristic of a *production* environment. When classifying variables, it is important to distinguish between characteristics of production environments (e.g., the road network in trucking) and characteristics of market and institutional environments (e.g., the degree of competition in output markets; regulations that govern business opening hours; intellectual property regulations). It is also advisable to have a specific manager, or group of managers, in mind. This is because a variable that is classified one way when measuring the performance of one manager might be classified differently when measuring the performance of another manager (e.g., a tractor would be classified as an output when measuring the performance of a tractor manufacturer, but would be classified as an input when measuring the performance of a farmer; a school building would be classified as an environmental variable when measuring the performance of a classroom teacher, but would normally be classified as an input when measuring the performance of an education minister).

Step 3. Identifying Relevant Measures of Comparative Performance

Arguably the simplest measures of comparative performance are index numbers. Indices that are widely used to compare managerial performance include output, input, revenue, cost, profit and productivity indices. Other measures of comparative performance include measures of efficiency. The measures of efficiency discussed in this book include measures of technical, revenue, cost, profit, scale, mix and allocative efficiency. Most of these measures can be viewed as total factor productivity indices (TFPIs). For example, measures of output-oriented technical efficiency can be viewed as indices that compare observed levels of TFP with the maximum levels of TFP that are possible when inputs and output mixes have been predetermined.

For any group of managers, the most relevant measures of comparative performance depend on their optimisation problems. In turn, the optimisation problems faced by managers depend on what they value, and on what they can and cannot choose. If, for example, a firm manager places nonnegative values on outputs (not necessarily market values) and all other variables involved in the production process have been predetermined (i.e., determined in a previous period), then (s)he will generally aim to maximise a measure of total output. In these situations, the most relevant measures of performance are output indices and output-oriented measures of technical and mix efficiency. In practice, it is common, but often unrealistic, to assume that all managers face the same type of optimisation problem (e.g., that they all minimise the cost of producing predetermined outputs).

Matters are slightly different from a government perspective. For a government, the most relevant measure of comparative performance depends on what *the government* values. If, for example, a government places nonnegative values on outputs and inputs (again, not necessarily market values), then the most relevant measures of performance include measures of net output and productivity. In a government context, these measures can be viewed as measures of social welfare.

Step 4. Making Assumptions About Production Technologies

It is possible to compute many measures of comparative performance (e.g., most index numbers) without knowing anything about production technologies. However, to compute others (e.g., most, if not all, measures of efficiency), we need to make some assumptions about the things that can and cannot be produced using different production technologies. In this book, a production technology (or simply 'technology') is defined as a technique, method or system for transforming inputs into outputs. For most practical purposes, it is convenient to think of a technology as a book of instructions.

We can often identify the things that can and cannot be produced using different technologies by thinking about the relevant science. For example, our knowledge of agricultural science tells us that there is a limit to how much rice can be produced with a given amount of land, labour, machinery and seed ($\Rightarrow$ output sets are bounded), and our knowledge of physics and chemistry tells us that it is not possible to use coal to produce electricity without also producing greenhouse gases ($\Rightarrow$ outputs are not strongly disposable). It is sometimes possible to get information about what can and cannot be produced using different technologies by 'reading the instructions' (e.g., reading a patent, or an article in the American Journal of Experimental Agriculture).

In most empirical contexts, it is reasonable to assume that output sets are bounded and both outputs and inputs are weakly disposable. If these weak assumptions are true, then production possibilities sets can be represented by distance, revenue and cost functions. Stronger assumptions (e.g., assumptions about returns to scale) imply restrictions on the parameters of these functions. If the restrictions are true, then restricted estimators of the parameters will be more efficient than unrestricted estimators. However, if the restrictions are not true, then restricted estimators will be biased. For this reason, we should generally avoid making unnecessary and/or empirically-untestable assumptions about technologies.

Step 5. Assembling the Data

The type of data required to analyse managerial performance depends largely on the measures of comparative performance identified in Step 3. For example, to compute productivity index numbers, we only require data on output and input quantities; to estimate levels of technical, scale and mix efficiency, we also need data on environmental variables; and to estimate levels of revenue efficiency, we generally need data on output prices, input quantities, environmental variables and revenues.

In practice, many of the variables we require are measured with error. To minimise measurement errors, we must (a) recognise the difference between a quantity, a price and a value, (b) recognise that products of different quality are, in fact, different products (e.g., 570 horsepower tractors and 620 horsepower tractors are different products), and (c) use proper indices to measure changes in quantities across time and/or space. One of the most common and easily-avoidable errors made in contemporary performance analysis is to use quantity indices that are not compatible with measurement theory (and therefore not proper).

In practice, data should be 'cleaned'. Data cleaning involves identifying, and subsequently correcting or removing, inaccurate or unreliable records in a dataset. Such records can often be identified by examining scatter plots, box plots and/or time-series plots of (a) variables and ratios of variables (e.g., measures of capital; capital-to-labour ratios; productivity index numbers), (b) efficiency estimates obtained from piecewise frontier models, and (c) residuals obtained from linear regression models. For other methods, see, for example, Hodge and Austin (2004) and Banker and Chang (2006).

Step 6. Selecting Functions to Represent Production Possibilities Sets

A production possibilities set is a set containing all input-output combinations that are physically possible. If enough assumptions are made in Step 4, then production possibilities sets can be represented by distance, revenue, cost and profit functions. They can also be represented by input demand and output supply functions. Whether we need to estimate the parameters of such functions depends on the measures of comparative performance identified in Step 3. Whether it is *possible* to estimate the parameters depends on the data that were assembled in Step 5. For example, if data on inputs, outputs and environmental variables are available, then we are in a position to estimate distance functions; these are the functions that should be selected if the relevant measures of comparative performance are measures of technical efficiency. As another example, if data on output and input prices, environmental variables and profits are available, then we are in a position to estimate profit functions; these are the functions that should be selected if the relevant measures of comparative performance are measures of profit efficiency.

Step 7. Choosing an Estimator

Three main types of estimator can be used to estimate the parameters of the function(s) identified in Step 6: piecewise frontier estimators, deterministic frontier estimators and stochastic frontier estimators. The choice of estimator depends on the measures of comparative performance identified in Step 3, the assumptions made in Step 4, and the data assembled in Step 5. Figure 9.1 presents a decision tree that can be used to guide the choice of estimator.

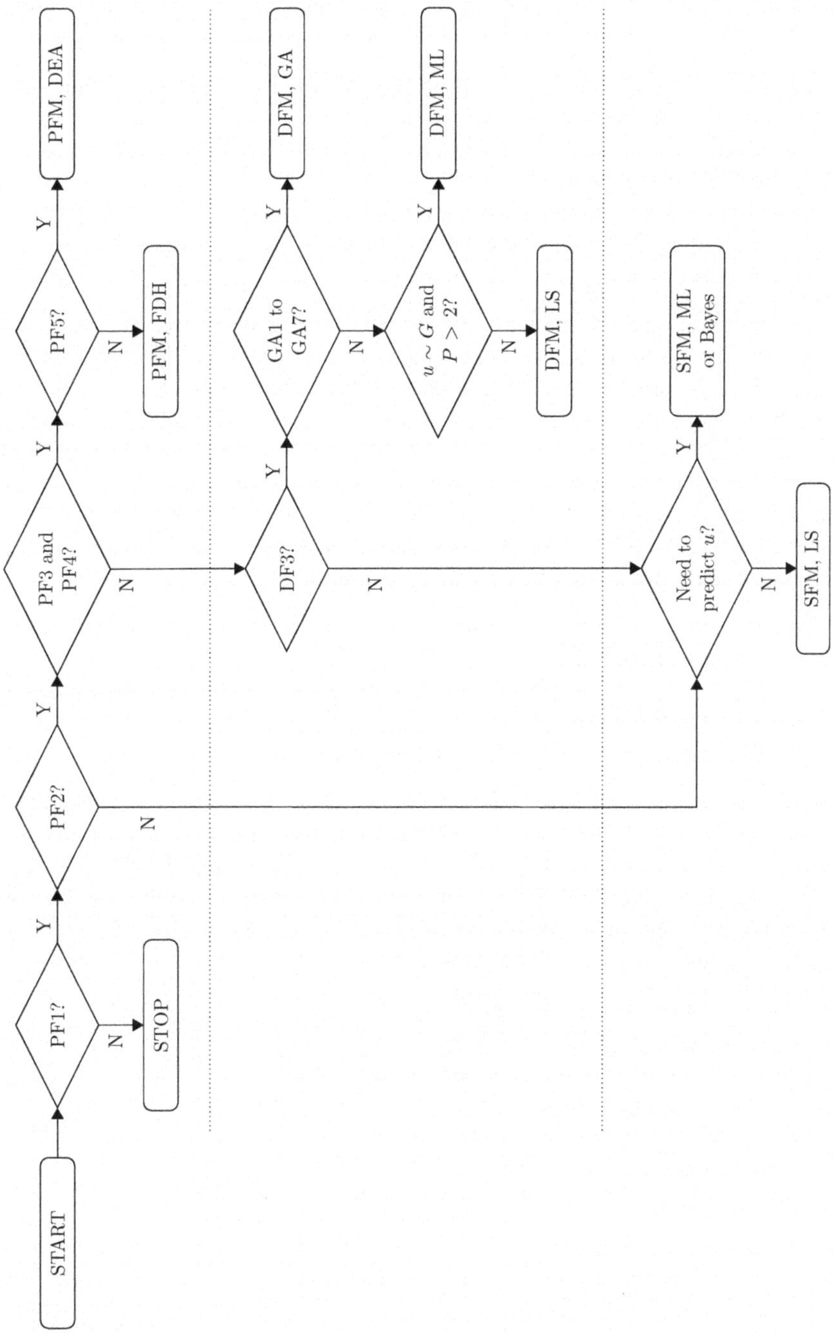

Fig. 9.1 A decision tree that can be used to guide the choice of frontier model and estimator

The top section of Fig. 9.1 focuses on piecewise frontier estimators. The most widely-used piecewise frontier estimators are underpinned by the following assumptions:

PF1 production possibilities sets can be represented by distance, revenue, cost and/or profit functions;
PF2 all relevant quantities, prices and environmental variables are observed and measured without error;
PF3 production frontiers are locally (or piecewise) linear;
PF4 inputs, outputs and environmental variables are strongly disposable; and
PF5 production possibilities sets are convex.

If these assumptions are true, then production frontiers can be estimated using linear programming (LP). The associated models are known as data envelopment analysis (DEA) models. In practice, it is common to relax assumption PF5. The models obtained by relaxing this assumption are known as free disposal hull (FDH) models. If the assumptions underpinning DEA and FDH models are true, then, under weak regularity conditions concerning the probability density functions (PDFs) of the inefficiency effects, associated estimators for (in)efficiency are consistent.

The middle section of Fig. 9.1 focuses deterministic frontier estimators. These estimators are underpinned by the following assumptions:

DF1 production possibilities sets can be represented by distance, revenue, cost and/or profit functions;
DF2 all relevant quantities, prices and environmental variables are observed and measured without error; and
DF3 the functional forms of relevant functions are known.

Observe that assumption DF1 (resp. DF2) is the same as assumption PF1 (resp. PF2). If assumptions DF1 to DF3 are true, then production frontiers can be estimated using single-equation regression models with error terms representing inefficiency. This book discusses three deterministic frontier estimators: growth accounting (GA), least squares (LS), and maximum likelihood (ML) estimators. Most GA estimators are underpinned by the following assumptions:

GA1 output and input sets are homothetic,
GA2 technical change is Hicks-neutral,
GA3 production frontiers exhibit constant returns to scale,
GA4 inputs are strongly disposable,
GA5 firms are price takers in input markets,
GA6 input prices are strictly positive, and
GA7 firm managers successfully minimise cost.

If these assumptions are true, then many of the parameters in production functions can be estimated using differential calculus. The associated estimates/predictions of technical and cost efficiency are equal to one. Let u_{it} denote the inefficiency of manager i in period t. The most widely-used LS estimators are underpinned by the assumption that u_{it} is a random variable with the following properties:

LS1 $E(u_{it}) = \mu \geq 0$ for all i and t,
LS2 $var(u_{it}) \propto \sigma_u^2$ for all i and t,
LS3 $cov(u_{it}, u_{ks}) = 0$ if $i \neq k$ or $t \neq s$, and
LS4 u_{it} is uncorrelated with the explanatory variables.

If these assumptions are true, then corrected ordinary least squares (COLS) estimators for the parameters in deterministic frontier models are consistent. The most widely-used ML estimators are underpinned by the assumption that either

ML1 u_{it} is an independent $N^+(0, \sigma_u^2)$ random variable, or
ML2 u_{it} is an independent $G(P, \sigma_u)$ random variable.

If ML2 is true and $P > 2$, then the associated ML estimators for the model parameters are consistent. If ML2 is not true, or if it is true but $P \leq 2$, then the properties of the ML estimators are unknown.

The bottom section of Fig. 9.1 focuses on stochastic frontier estimators. These estimators are underpinned by only one assumption, namely that production possibilities sets can be represented by distance, revenue, cost and/or profit functions (i.e., PF1, which is the same as DF1). Each of these functions can be written as a single-equation regression model with two error terms, one representing statistical noise and the other representing inefficiency. This book discusses three stochastic frontier estimators: least squares (LS), maximum likelihood (ML) and Bayesian estimators. If we do not need to predict levels of inefficiency (e.g., because we are only interested in decomposing a productivity index, and we are not interested in separating efficiency change from the change in statistical noise), then the estimators that require the weakest assumptions are LS estimators. Let $\epsilon_{it} \equiv v_{it} - u_{it}$ where v_{it} represents statistical noise and u_{it} denotes a measure of inefficiency. The most widely-used LS estimators are underpinned by the assumption that ϵ_{it} is a random variable with the following properties:

LS5 $E(\epsilon_{it}) = -\mu \leq 0$ for all i and t,
LS6 $var(\epsilon_{it}) = \sigma_\epsilon^2$ for all i and t,
LS7 $cov(\epsilon_{it}, \epsilon_{ks}) = 0$ if $i \neq k$ or $t \neq s$, and
LS8 ϵ_{it} is uncorrelated with the explanatory variables.

If these assumptions are true, and if the stochastic frontier model contains an intercept, then OLS estimators for the slope parameters are unbiased and consistent. However, consistent estimators for the intercept and the mean level of inefficiency are only available if additional assumptions are made about the noise and inefficiency effects. ML estimators are typically underpinned by the following additional assumptions:

ML3 v_{it} is an independent $N(0, \sigma_v^2)$ random variable, and
ML4 u_{it} is an independent $N^+(\mu, \sigma_u^2)$ random variable.

If these assumptions are true, then ML estimators for the model parameters are consistent, asymptotically efficient and asymptotically normal. Bayesian estimators are effectively underpinned by the same assumptions as ML estimators. They are particularly useful for incorporating certain types of prior information (e.g., inequality constraints) into the estimation process. ML estimators can be viewed as special cases of Bayesian estimators corresponding to noninformative prior information.

In practice, stochastic frontier analysis involves minimising functional form errors and other sources of statistical noise. To minimise functional form errors, we should select approximating functions that are compatible with the assumptions made in Step 4. For example, if outputs are strongly disposable, then we should approximate output distance functions using functions that are globally nondecreasing in outputs, and if output sets are convex, then we should approximate revenue functions using functions that are globally concave in inputs. Some common functions are presented in Table 9.1. The *linear* function is both concave and convex in x ($\Rightarrow$ it is also quasiconcave and quasiconvex in x); if $\alpha \geq 0$ and $\beta_k \geq 0$ for all k, then it is nonnegative for all $x \geq 0$; if $\beta_k \geq 0$ for all k, then it is nondecreasing in x; and if $\alpha = 0$, then it is linearly homogeneous in x. The *constant elasticity of substitution* (CES) function can be traced back at least as far as Arrow et al. (1961, p. 230). This function is homogeneous of degree r in x; if $\beta_k \geq 0$ for all k, then it is nonnegative for all $x \geq 0$; if $\beta_k \geq 0$ for all k, then it is nondecreasing in x; if $\tau \leq 1$ and $\beta_k \geq 0$ for all k, then it is quasiconcave in x; and if $\tau \geq 1$ and $\beta_k \geq 0$ for all k, then it is quasiconvex in x. The *double-log* function (often referred to as a Cobb-Douglas function) is nonnegative and homogeneous of degree $\sum_k \beta_k$ in x; if $\beta_k \geq 0$ for all k, then it is nondecreasing and quasiconcave in x; if $\beta_k \leq 0$ for all k, then it is quasiconvex in x; if $\beta_k \geq 0$ for all k and $\sum_k \beta_k \leq 1$, then it is concave in x. The *generalised linear* function is linearly homogeneous; if $\beta_{jk} \geq 0$ for all j and k, then it is nonnegative for all $x \geq 0$; if $\beta_{jk} \geq 0$ for all j and k, then it is nondecreasing and concave ($\Rightarrow$ it is also quasiconcave) in x; and if $\beta_{jk} \leq 0$ for all j and k, then it is convex ($\Rightarrow$ it is also quasiconvex) in x. The *translog* function can be traced back to Heady and Dillon (1961, Eq. 6.16). This function is nonnegative; if $\beta_k \geq 0$ and $\beta_{jk} = 0$ for all j and k, then it is nondecreasing in x (in this case, it collapses to a double-log function); if $\sum_k \beta_k = r$ and $\sum_k \beta_{jk} = 0$ for all j, then it is homogeneous of degree r in x; if $\beta_k \leq 0$ and $\beta_{jk} = 0$ for all j and k, then it is quasiconvex in x (in this case, it collapses to a double-log function); and if $\beta_k \geq 0$ for all k, $\sum_k \beta_k \leq 1$ and $\beta_{jk} = 0$ for all j and k, then it is concave ($\Rightarrow$ it is also quasiconcave) in x (in this case, it again collapses to a double-log function). Finally, if $\alpha \geq 0$, $\beta_k \geq 0$ for all k and $\beta_{jk} \geq 0$ for all j and k, then the *quadratic* function is nonnegative for all $x \geq 0$; if $\beta_k \geq 0$ for all k and $\beta_{jk} \geq 0$ for all j and k, then it is nondecreasing in x; if $\alpha = 0$ and $\beta_{jk} = 0$ for all j and k, then it is linearly homogeneous in x (in this case, it collapses to a linear function); and if $\beta_{jk} = 0$ for all j and k, then it is concave and convex ($\Rightarrow$ it is also quasiconcave and quasiconvex) in x (in this case, it again collapses to a linear function). For more details on functional forms and their properties, see, for example, Chambers (1988, Chap. 5) and Griffin et al. (1987).

Step 8. Estimation and Testing

Piecewise frontier estimators can be used to test hypotheses concerning technologies (e.g., no technical change; constant returns to scale; inputs strongly disposable; production possibilities sets convex) and inefficiency (e.g., that average levels of inefficiency are the same across groups). This often involves bootstrapping.

Table 9.1 Common functions

Function	Formula	Restrictions
Linear	$f(x) = \alpha + \sum_k \beta_k x_k$	
CES	$f(x) = \left(\sum_k \beta_k x_k^\tau\right)^{r/\tau}$	$\tau > 0,\ r > 0$
Double-log	$f(x) = \exp\left(\alpha + \sum_k \beta_k \ln x_k\right)$	
Generalised linear	$f(x) = \sum_j \sum_k \beta_{jk}(x_j x_k)^{1/2}$	$\beta_{jk} = \beta_{kj}$
Translog	$f(x) = \exp\left(\alpha + \sum_k \beta_k \ln x_k + \sum_j \sum_k \beta_{jk} \ln x_j \ln x_k\right)$	$x > 0,\ \beta_{jk} = \beta_{kj}$
Quadratic	$f(x) = \alpha + \sum_k \beta_k x_k + \sum_j \sum_k \beta_{jk} x_j x_k$	$\beta_{jk} = \beta_{kj}$

Deterministic frontier estimators can also be used to test hypotheses concerning technologies and inefficiency. Tests concerning inefficiency include standard econometric tests for fixed effects, heteroskedasticity, autocorrelation and endogeneity.

Stochastic frontier estimators can be used to test hypotheses concerning composite error terms representing a combination of statistical noise and inefficiency. Again, these hypothesis tests include tests for fixed effects, heteroskedasticity, autocorrelation and endogeneity. The presence of the noise component means it is not generally possible to interpret the parameters of stochastic frontier models in the same way we can interpret the parameters of deterministic frontier models. Consequently, it is not generally possible to use stochastic frontier estimators to test hypotheses concerning production technologies.

Step 9. Conducting Robustness Checks

It is good practice to examine and report information on the sensitivity of the main results to the assumptions and choices made in Steps 4, 6 and 7. For a brief discussion of this 'methodology cross-checking' principle, see Charnes (1988, p. 2) and Ferrier and Lovell (1990, p. 230)

9.2 Government Policies

Changes in most measures of managerial performance can be attributed to four main factors: (a) technical progress, (b) environmental change, (c) technical efficiency change, and (d) scale, mix and/or allocative efficiency change. Different government policies affect, and can therefore be used to target, these different components.

(a) Technical Progress

In this book, the term 'technical progress' refers to the discovery of new technologies (i.e., new techniques, methods and systems for transforming inputs into outputs). Investigative activities aimed at discovering new technologies are referred to as 'research and development' (R&D) activities. Governments can often increase rates of technical progress by, for example, (a) conducting their own R&D (e.g., the Australian government conducts its own R&D through the Commonwealth Scientific and Industrial Research Organisation), (b) directly funding others to conduct R&D (e.g., the U.S. government funds research through the National Science Foundation grants), and (c) providing incentives for others to conduct more R&D (e.g., Article 33s of the 1994 WTO TRIPs Agreement encourages so-called 'private' R&D by strengthening intellectual property rights).[1]

(b) Environmental Change

In this book, the term 'environmental change' refers to changes in variables that are physically involved in production processes but never controlled by firm managers. Examples of so-called environmental variables include rainfall in crop production and the road network in trucking. Governments can often change production environments by, for example, (a) regulating (or failing to regulate) the impact of production processes on the natural environment (e.g., making it unlawful to discharge pollutants from industrial plants into waterways), and (b) providing and/or decommissioning different types of public infrastructure (e.g. building ports, railroads, bridges and electricity distribution networks).

(c) Technical Efficiency Change

For most practical purposes, it is useful to think of a production technology as a book of instructions, or recipe. Measures of technical efficiency can be viewed as measures of how well production technologies are chosen and used (i.e., how well managers 'choose books/recipes from the library' and 'follow the instructions'). Governments can raise levels of technical efficiency by, for example, (a) removing barriers to the adoption of particular technologies (e.g., removing financial constraints that prevent managers from purchasing expensive 'ingredients'; removing patent protections), (b) providing education and training services to advise managers about the existence and proper use of new technologies (e.g., agricultural extension programs), and (c) ensuring that output markets are competitive (e.g., by removing barriers to entry) or pseudo-competitive (e.g., by regulating output prices).

(d) Scale, Mix and/or Allocative Efficiency Change

Measures of scale, mix and/or allocative efficiency can be viewed as measures of how well managers have captured economies of scale and substitution (i.e., the benefits obtained by changing the scale of operations, the output mix, and the input mix). Governments can often raise levels of scale and mix efficiency by changing the key variables that drive managerial behaviour. If, for example, firm i is a price taker in output and input markets, then the manager's period-t profit-maximisation problem can be written as

---

[1] Article 33s of the agreement provides that the term of a patent (i.e., the maximum period during which it can be enforced) shall not be less than twenty years from the patent filing date.

$$\max_{q,x}\{p'_{it}q - w'_{it}x : D^t_O(x, q, z_{it}) \leq 1\}.$$

The key variables in this problem are environmental variables and relative prices. In this case, governments may be able to increase scale and mix efficiency by, for example, (a) changing the production environment, (b) changing relative output and input prices (e.g., by changing minimum wages, interest rates, taxes and/or subsidies), and (c) placing (or removing) legal restrictions on output and input choices (e.g., prohibiting the use of child labour; legalising the use of medicinal cannabis).

9.3 Rice Example

To illustrate the main steps involved in managerial performance analysis, this section analyses the performance of a group of smallholder rice farmers in the Tarlac municipality of the Philippines.

Step 1. The Manager(s)

The managers are a group of smallholder farmers. Each farmer typically grows rice, maize, mungbeans and/or vegetables. Most farmers also engage in off-farm employment. In this empirical example, we are only concerned with how well each farmer manages the rice production process (not the maize, mungbeans or vegetable production process, nor other aspects of running the farm household).

Step 2. Classifying the Variables

The rice production system in the Tarlac municipality is a rainfed system. All fields are planted to rice in the rainy season and either left fallow or planted to other crops in the dry season. Outputs include different varieties of rice (e.g., traditional; IR60; IR64). Inputs include land, different types of labour (e.g., family labour; hired labour; specialist labour for land preparation, transplanting, harvesting and threshing), capital (e.g., tractors; buffalos), seed (e.g., traditional; IR60; IR64), fertilisers (e.g., nitrogen; phosphorus; potassium), insecticides and herbicides. The production environment is characterised by variations in altitude (e.g., upland, lowland) and weather (e.g., temperature; rainfall).

Step 3. Identifying Relevant Measures of Comparative Performance

The farmers in the study group are price-takers in output and input markets. At the beginning of each production period, they choose inputs and planned outputs to maximise expected profits in the face of uncertainty about output prices and weather variables. During the production period, they may be able to adjust some inputs (e.g., insecticides, labour for harvesting and threshing) as weather variables and outcomes of earlier production stages are realised. In these situations, arguably the most relevant measures of comparative performance are measures of partial factor productivity (PFP), total factor productivity (TFP) and output-oriented technical efficiency (OTE).

Step 4. Making Assumptions About Production Technologies

Technologies for planting, growing and harvesting rice in the Philippines are described in, for example, IRRI (2015). With these technologies,

A1 it is possible to produce no rice (i.e., inactivity is possible);
A2 there is a limit to how much rice can be produced using a finite amount of land, labour, seed and other inputs (i.e., output sets are bounded);
A3 positive amounts of land, labour and seed are needed in order to produce a positive amount rice (i.e., most inputs are weakly essential; there is 'no free lunch');
A6s if particular inputs can be used to produce a given amount of rice, then they can also be used to produce less rice (i.e., outputs are strongly disposable); and
A7 if a particular amount of rice can be produced using a given input vector, then it can also be produced using a scalar magnification of that input vector (i.e., inputs are weakly disposable).

The science suggests that there is a point at which increases in labour per hectare will cause yield losses through overcrowding/congestion. Furthermore, according to IRRI (2015, pp. 15, 19), high rates of fertiliser application may cause yield losses through lodging (i.e., bending over of stems near ground level) and/or increased susceptibility to pests and diseases (esp. with nitrogen fertilisers). This implies that labour and fertiliser inputs are not strongly disposable.

Step 5. Assembling the Data

The data were originally assembled by the International Rice Research Institute (IRRI). A data file containing observations on key variables was made publicly available by Coelli et al. (2005). This file[2] contains observations on forty-three farmers over the eight years from 1990 to 1997. Table 9.2 provides a brief description of the variables. Some descriptive statistics are presented in Table 9.3. In this data file, outputs of different rice varieties have been aggregated into a single measure of rice output; different types of labour have been aggregated into a single measure of the labour input; inputs of nitrogen, phosphorus and potassium have been aggregated into a single measure of the fertiliser input; and inputs of seeds, tractors, buffalos, insecticides and herbicides have been aggregated into a single measure of other inputs. The data file contains information on two farmer attributes, two (irrelevant) household-related variables and one environmental variable (altitude). The data file contains no information on weather variables. More details concerning the data can be accessed from Pandey et al. (1999) and Coelli et al. (2005).

---

[2]The file can be accessed from http://www.uq.edu.au/economics/cepa/crob2005/software/CROB2005.zip. The file is contained in the folder for Chap. 9.

Table 9.2 Variables in the rice dataset

Variable	Description
t = YEARDUM	Year index (1990 = 1)
i = FMERCODE	Farmer code
q = PROD	Output (tonnes of freshly threshed rice)
x_1 = AREA	Area planted (hectares)
x_2 = LABOR	Labour (man-days of family and hired labour)
x_3 = NPK	Fertiliser (kg of active ingredients)
x_4 = OTHER	Other inputs (Laspeyres index = 100 for Firm 17 in 1991)
p = PRICE	Output price (pesos per kg)
w_1 = AREAP	Rental price of land (pesos per hectare)
w_2 = LABORP	Labour price (pesos per hired man-day)
w_3 = NPKP	Fertiliser price (pesos per kg of active ingredient)
w_4 = OTHERP	Price of other inputs (implicit price index)
a_1 = AGE	Age of household head (years)
a_2 = EDYRS	Education of household head (years)
h_1 = HHSIZE	Household size
h_2 = NADULT	Number of adults in household
z = BANRAT	Percentage of area classified as upland fields

Table 9.3 Descriptive statistics for selected variables

Variable	Mean	Std. dev.	Minimum	Maximum
q = PROD	6.540	5.107	0.09	31.10
x_1 = AREA	2.144	1.458	0.20	7.00
x_2 = LABOR	108.342	77.191	8	437
x_3 = NPK	189.235	169.803	10.0	1030.9
x_4 = OTHER	125.345	158.24	1.459	1083.4
a_1 = AGE	49.445	11.022	25	81
a_2 = EDYRS	7.244	1.910	6	14
z = BANRAT	0.734	0.293	0	1

Step 6. Selecting Functions to Represent Production Possibilities Sets

The measures of comparative performance identified in Step 3 were PFP, TFP and OTE. To compute measures of PFP and TFP, we only need data on outputs and inputs. These data are available. We made enough assumptions in Step 4 for production possibilities sets to be represented by distance, revenue and cost functions. To estimate/predict OTE, we need to estimate the output distance function. This means we need data on outputs, inputs and environmental variables. Unfortunately, data on some environmental variables (e.g., temperature, rainfall) are unavailable.

Step 7. Choosing an Estimator

The assumptions made in Step 4 ensure that production possibilities sets can be represented by distance, revenue and cost functions ($\Rightarrow$ PF1 is true). However, many environmental variables are unobserved, and many inputs are measured with error ($\Rightarrow$ PF2 is not true). In this situation, Fig. 9.1 leads us to estimate the parameters of a stochastic frontier model (SFM). The measures of comparative performance identified in Step 3 include OTE. To predict OTE, we need to use ML or Bayesian estimators.

Step 8. Estimation and Testing

A theoretically-plausible SFM that involves most of the variables in the dataset (i.e., utilises most of the available sample information) is the following system of simultaneous equations:

$$\ln q_{it} = \alpha_i + \lambda t + \delta z_{it} + \sum_{m=1}^{M} \beta_m \ln x_{mit} + v_{it}^* - u_{it} \tag{9.1}$$

and

$$u_{it} = \phi_0 + \phi_1 a_{1it} + \phi_2 a_{2it} + w_{it} \tag{9.2}$$

where $u_{it} \equiv -\ln OTE^t(x_{it}, q_{it}, z_{it}) \geq 0$ denotes an output-oriented technical inefficiency effect and v_{it}^* and w_{it} represent different measures of statistical noise. Equation (9.1) can be viewed as a special case of (8.31) corresponding to $f^t(x_{it}, z_{it}) = \lambda t + \delta z_{it} + \sum_m \beta_m \ln x_{mit}$ and $\lambda_t = 0$. Equation (9.2) is a special case of the inefficiency effects model defined by (8.74). ML estimates of the unknown parameters in this system are reported in Table 9.4. These estimates were obtained under the assumption that v_{it}^* is an independent $N(0, \sigma_v^2)$ random variable and w_{it} is an independent random variable obtained by lower-truncating the $N(0, \sigma_w^2)$ distribution at $L_{it} = -\phi_0 - \phi_1 a_{1it} - \phi_2 a_{2it}$. Separate likelihood ratio tests were used to test $H_0 : \alpha_i = \alpha$ for all i and $H_0 : \phi_1 = \phi_2 = 0$. Both hypotheses were rejected at the 1% level of significance.

The estimate of γ reported in Table 9.4 indicates that $v_{it}^* = 0$. The estimate of λ indicates that the rate of technical progress was 1.7% per annum. The estimate of β_1 indicates that, *ceterus paribus*, a one-percent increase in land area gives rise to a 0.45% increase in rice output. The estimate of ϕ_1 indicates that technical efficiency increases with age; this supports the hypothesis that managers 'learn by doing'. The estimated elasticity of scale is 0.894, indicating that the production frontier exhibits decreasing returns to scale; this could help explain why farm sizes are relatively small.

The measures of comparative performance identified in Step 3 include measures of PFP and TFP. Selected PFP and TFP index numbers are reported in Table 9.5. The numbers reported in the column labelled LND (resp. LAB) are land (resp. labour) productivity index numbers that compare the output per unit of land (resp. labour) on each farm in each period with the output per unit of land (resp. labour) on farm 1 in

Table 9.4 ML parameter estimates

Parameter	Est.	St. err.	t
α_1	−0.611	0.153	−3.984***
α_2	−0.279	0.167	−1.669*
α_3	−0.553	0.153	−3.602***
α_4	−0.181	0.129	−1.400
⋮	⋮	⋮	⋮
α_{43}	−0.360	0.140	−2.568***
λ	0.017	0.005	3.547***
δ	0.004	0.032	0.126
β_1	0.450	0.028	15.793***
β_2	0.264	0.032	8.272***
β_3	0.136	0.030	4.590***
β_4	0.045	0.015	2.978***
ϕ_0	0.260	0.336	0.773
ϕ_1	−0.014	0.005	−2.745***
ϕ_2	−0.012	0.028	−0.444
$\sigma^2 \equiv \sigma_u^2 + \sigma_v^2$	0.357	0.029	12.345***
$\gamma \equiv \sigma_u^2/\sigma^2$	1.000	1.0E−7	6.5E+5***

***, ** and * indicate significance at the 1, 5 and 10% levels

period 1. The LND (resp. LAB) index numbers should be used by decision makers who regard land (resp. labour) as the only input of value. The numbers reported in the columns labelled L, GY and BOD are Lowe, geometric Young and benefit-of-the-doubt index numbers that compare the TFP of each farm(er) in each period with the TFP of farm(er) 1 in period 1. The L (resp. GY) index numbers should be used by decision makers who regard input prices (resp. cost shares) as appropriate measures of relative value. The BOD index numbers should be used by decision makers who believe measures of relative value should vary from one input comparison to the next.

Equation (9.1) can be used to decompose any PFP or TFP index into measures of technical progress, environmental change and efficiency change. Equation (9.2) can be used to further decompose measures of OTE change into age and education effects. For example, Eq. (9.1) can be used to write any TFP index as

$$
\begin{aligned}
TFPI(x_{ks}, q_{ks}, x_{it}, q_{it}) = &\left[\frac{\exp(\lambda t)}{\exp(\lambda s)}\right]\left[\frac{\exp(\delta z_{it})}{\exp(\delta z_{ks})}\right] \\
&\times \left[TFPI(x_{ks}, q_{ks}, x_{it}, q_{it}) \prod_{m=1}^{M}\left(\frac{x_{mit}}{x_{mks}}\right)^{\beta_m}\left(\frac{q_{ks}}{q_{it}}\right)\right] \\
&\times \left[\frac{\exp(-u_{it})}{\exp(-u_{ks})}\right]\left[\frac{\exp(v_{it}^* + \alpha_i)}{\exp(v_{ks}^* + \alpha_k)}\right].
\end{aligned}
\tag{9.3}
$$

Table 9.5 Selected PFP and TFP index numbers

Firm	Period	LND	LAB	L	GY	BOD
1	1	1	1	1	1	1
1	2	0.912	1.064	0.919	0.898	1.013
1	3	1.133	1.303	0.910	0.578	1.135
1	4	0.929	1.178	0.772	0.493	0.973
1	5	0.958	1.064	0.785	0.507	0.952
1	6	0.573	0.750	0.488	0.305	0.618
1	7	0.617	0.721	0.466	0.294	0.613
1	8	1.074	1.709	0.952	0.643	1.230
:	:	:	:	:	:	:
43	1	0.379	0.421	0.394	0.409	0.468
43	2	0.371	0.398	0.380	0.424	0.389
43	3	0.861	0.840	0.856	1.083	0.975
43	4	0.526	1.011	0.737	1.243	1.205
43	5	0.891	1.195	0.863	0.629	1.248
43	6	1.412	1.641	1.380	1.147	1.497
43	7	0.672	2.163	0.975	1.345	1.944
43	8	1.228	1.952	1.520	1.892	1.876
Minimum		0.114	0.230	0.112	0.159	0.142
Geo. mean		0.918	1.176	0.913	0.923	1.193
Maximum		2.416	3.366	2.102	5.175	3.406

The first term on the right-hand side can be viewed as an output-oriented technology index (OTI). The second term can be viewed as an output-oriented environment index (OEI). The third term can be viewed as an output-oriented scale and mix efficiency index (OSMEI). The last two terms are an output-oriented technical efficiency index (OTEI) and a statistical noise index (SNI). Equation (9.2) can be used to write the OTEI as

$$\left[\frac{\exp(-u_{it})}{\exp(-u_{ks})}\right] = \left[\frac{\exp(-\phi_1 a_{1it})}{\exp(-\phi_1 a_{1ks})}\right]\left[\frac{\exp(-\phi_2 a_{2it})}{\exp(-\phi_2 a_{2ks})}\right]\left[\frac{\exp(-w_{it})}{\exp(-w_{ks})}\right]. \tag{9.4}$$

In the present context, the first term on the right-hand side is an age index (AGEI). The second term is an education index (EDUCI). The last term is (another) statistical noise index (SNI). To illustrate, Table 9.6 reports two decompositions of the Lowe TFPI numbers in Table 9.5. The OTI, OEI, OSMEI, AGEI and EDUCI numbers in Table 9.6 were obtained by using the ML estimates reported in Table 9.4 to evaluate the relevant components in (9.3) and (9.4). The OTEI numbers were obtained by taking ratios of ML predictions of OTE. The SNI numbers were obtained as residuals.

Table 9.6 ML decompositions of Lowe TFPI numbers[a,b]

Firm	Period	TFPI	OTI	OEI	OSMEI	OTEI	SNI	OTI	OEI	OSMEI	AGEI	EDUCI	SNI
1	1	1	1	1	1	1	1	1	1	1	1	1	1
1	2	0.919	1.017	1	1.017	0.887	1	1.017	1	1.017	1.014	1	0.875
1	3	0.910	1.035	1	0.895	0.986	0.996	1.035	1	0.895	1.029	1	0.955
1	4	0.772	1.053	1	0.895	0.819	1	1.053	1	0.895	1.043	1	0.786
1	5	0.785	1.071	1	0.909	0.806	1	1.071	1	0.909	1.058	1	0.762
1	6	0.488	1.090	1	0.856	0.523	0.999	1.090	1	0.856	1.073	1	0.487
1	7	0.466	1.109	1	0.863	0.487	0.999	1.109	1	0.863	1.088	1	0.447
1	8	0.952	1.128	1	0.884	0.955	1	1.128	1	0.884	1.104	1	0.865
:	:	:	:	:	:	:	:	:	:	:	:	:	:
43	1	0.394	1	0.998	1.044	0.293	1.288	1	0.998	1.044	1.029	0.951	0.386
43	2	0.380	1.017	0.998	1.058	0.276	1.283	1.017	0.998	1.058	1.043	0.951	0.356
43	3	0.856	1.035	0.998	1.086	0.592	1.288	1.035	0.998	1.086	1.058	0.951	0.758
43	4	0.737	1.053	0.998	1.018	0.535	1.288	1.053	0.998	1.018	1.073	0.951	0.674
43	5	0.863	1.071	0.998	0.904	0.694	1.286	1.071	0.998	0.904	1.088	0.951	0.862
43	6	1.380	1.090	0.998	1.000	0.985	1.287	1.090	0.998	1.000	1.104	0.951	1.208
43	7	0.975	1.109	0.998	1.046	0.655	1.286	1.109	0.998	1.046	1.119	0.951	0.791
43	8	1.520	1.128	0.998	1.053	0.997	1.285	1.128	0.998	1.053	1.135	0.951	1.187
Geo. mean		0.913	1.062	0.999	0.988	0.726	1.200	1.062	0.999	0.988	1.192	0.966	0.756

[a]TFPI = OTI × OEI × OSMEI × OTEI × SNI = OTI × OEI × OSMEI × AGEI × EDUCI × SNI. Some index numbers may be incoherent at the third decimal place due to rounding (e.g., in any given row, the product of the OTI, OEI, OSMEI, OTEI and SNI numbers may not be exactly equal to the TFPI number due to rounding)

[b]Numbers reported to less than three decimal places are exact; see the footnote to Table 1.2 on p. 8

Step 9. Conducting Robustness Checks

Robustness checking involves checking the sensitivity of the main results to the assumptions and choices made in Steps 4, 6 and 7. In any given empirical analysis, the main results typically concern the measures of comparative performance identified in Step 3. In the present case, these are measures of PFP, TFP and OTE. The measures of PFP and TFP reported in Table 9.5 do not depend on any of the assumptions or choices made in Steps 4, 6 and 7; the only results that are affected by those choices/assumptions are the predictions of OTE.

Table 9.7 reports three sets of estimates/predictions of OTE. The estimates reported in the column labelled PFM were obtained using a modified version of DEA problem (6.4); the modification involved replacing the inequality signs in the labour, fertiliser and environmental variable constraints with strict equality signs (this reflects the assumption that these variables are not strongly disposable). The predictions reported in the column labelled DFM were obtained using COLS estimates of the parameters in a noiseless version of Eq. (9.1). The predictions reported in the column labelled SFM are the ML predictions obtained by estimating the parameters in (9.1) and (9.2); ratios of these predictions were used earlier to compute the OTEI numbers in Table 9.6. The estimates reported in Table 9.7 indicate that the OTE results are sensitive to the choice of estimation framework.

Table 9.7 Estimates/predictions of OTE[a]

Firm	Period	PFM	DFM	SFM
1	1	1	0.555	0.994
1	2	1	0.489	0.883
1	3	0.818	0.556	0.981
1	4	0.617	0.468	0.815
1	5	0.561	0.464	0.801
1	6	0.404	0.309	0.520
1	7	0.380	0.288	0.484
1	8	0.796	0.576	0.949
⋮	⋮	⋮	⋮	⋮
43	1	0.308	0.229	0.292
43	2	0.282	0.213	0.274
43	3	0.630	0.488	0.589
43	4	0.740	0.408	0.532
43	5	0.702	0.554	0.690
43	6	1	0.786	0.980
43	7	1	0.512	0.652
43	8	1	0.777	0.992
Geo. Mean		0.825	0.450	0.722

[a]Numbers reported to less than three decimal places are exact; see the footnote to Table 1.2 on p. 8

References

Arrow K, Chenery H, Minhas B, Solow R (1961) Capital-labor substitution and economic efficiency. Rev Econ Stat 43(3):225–250

Banker R, Chang H (2006) The super-efficiency procedure for outlier identification, not for ranking efficient units. Eur J Oper Res 175(2):1311–1321

Chambers R (1988) Applied production analysis. Cambridge University Press, New York

Charnes A, Cooper W, Sueyoshi T (1988) A goal programming/constrained regression view of the Bell system breakup. Manage Sci 34:1–26

Coelli T, Rao D, O'Donnell C, Battese G (2005) An introduction to efficiency and productivity analysis, 2nd edn. Springer, New York

Ferrier G, Lovell C (1990) Measuring cost efficiency in banking: econometric and linear programming evidence. J Econ 46(1–2):229–245

Griffin R, Montgomery J, Rister M (1987) Selecting functional form in production function analysis. West J Agric Econ 12(2):216–227

Heady E, Dillon J (1961) Agricultural production functions. Iowa State University Press, Ames, Iowa

Hodge V, Austin J (2004) A survey of outlier detection methodologies. Artifiical Intell Rev 22(2):85–126

IRRI (2015) Steps to successful rice production. International Rice Research Institute, Los Baños (Philippines). http://knowledgebank.irri.org/images/docs/12-Steps-Required-for-Successful-Rice-Production.pdf

Pandey S, Masicat P, Velasco L, Villano R (1999) Risk analysis of rainfed rice production system in Tarlac. Central Luzon. Philippines. Exp Agric 35(2):225–237

Appendix A

A.1 Propositions

Proposition 1 *If output sets are homothetic, then* $D_O^t(x, q, z) = D_O^t(\iota, q, z)/G^t(x, z)$.

Proof Let $\kappa \equiv G^t(x, z)$. If output sets are homothetic, then $P^t(x, z) = \kappa P^t(\iota, z) \Rightarrow D_O^t(x, q, z) = \inf\{\rho > 0 : q/\rho \in P^t(x, z)\} = \inf\{\rho > 0 : q/\rho \in \kappa P^t(\iota, z)\} = \inf\{\rho > 0 : q/(\rho\kappa) \in P^t(\iota, z)\} = \inf\{(\rho\kappa)/\kappa > 0 : q/(\rho\kappa) \in P^t(\iota, z)\} = (1/\kappa)\inf\{(\rho\kappa) > 0 : q/(\rho\kappa) \in P^t(\iota, z)\} = D_O^t(\iota, q, z)/\kappa = D_O^t(\iota, q, z)/G^t(x, z)$. □

Proposition 2 *If output sets are homothetic, then* $R^t(x, p, z) = G^t(x, z)R^t(\iota, p, z)$.

Proof Let $\kappa \equiv G^t(x, z)$. If output sets are homothetic, then, by Proposition 1, $D_O^t(x, q, z) = D_O^t(\iota, q, z)/\kappa \Rightarrow R^t(x, p, z) = \max_q\{p'q : D_O^t(x, q, z) \leq 1\} = \max_q \{p'q : D_O^t(\iota, q, z)/\kappa \leq 1\} = \max_q\{p'q : D_O^t(\iota, q/\kappa, z) \leq 1\} = \max_q\{\kappa p'(q/\kappa) : D_O^t (\iota, q/\kappa, z) \leq 1\} = \kappa \max_{q/\kappa}\{p'(q/\kappa) : D_O^t(\iota, q/\kappa, z) \leq 1\} = \kappa R^t(\iota, p, z) = G^t(x, z) R^t(\iota, p, z)$. □

Proposition 3 *If technical change is IHON, then* $D_O^t(x, q, z) = D_O^1(x, q, \iota)/E^t(x, z)$.

Proof Let $\kappa \equiv E^t(x, z)$. If technical change is IHON, then $P^t(x, z) = E^t(x, z)P^1(x, \iota) \Rightarrow D_O^t(x, q, z) = \inf\{\rho > 0 : q/\rho \in P^t(x, z)\} = \inf\{\rho > 0 : q/\rho \in \kappa P^1(x, \iota)\} = \inf \{\rho > 0 : q/(\rho\kappa) \in P^1(x, \iota)\} = \inf\{(\rho\kappa)/\kappa > 0 : q/(\rho\kappa) \in P^1(x, \iota)\} = (1/\kappa)\inf \{(\rho\kappa) > 0 : q/(\rho\kappa) \in P^1(x, \iota)\} = D_O^1(x, q, \iota)/\kappa = D_O^1(x, q, \iota)/E^t(x, z)$. □

Proposition 4 *If technical change is IHON, then* $R^t(x, p, z) = E^t(x, z)R^1(x, p, \iota)$.

Proof Let $\kappa \equiv E^t(x, z)$. If technical change is IHON, then, by Proposition 3, $D_O^t(x, q, z) = D_O^1(x, q, \iota)/\kappa \Rightarrow R^t(x, p, z) = \max_q\{p'q : D_O^t(x, q, z) \leq 1\} = \max_q \{p'q : D_O^1(x, q, \iota)/\kappa \leq 1\} = \max_q\{p'q : D_O^1(x, q/\kappa, \iota) \leq 1\} = \max_q\{\kappa p'(q/\kappa) : D_O^1 (x, q/\kappa, \iota) \leq 1\} = \kappa \max_{q/\kappa}\{p'(q/\kappa) : D_O^1(x, q/\kappa, \iota) \leq 1\} = \kappa R^1(x, p, \iota) = E^t(x, z) R^1(x, p, \iota)$. □

Proposition 5 *If output sets are homothetic and technical change is IHON, then* $D_O^t(x, q, z) = Q(q)/F^t(x, z)$ *where* $Q(q) = D_O^1(\iota, q, \iota)$ *and* $F^t(x, z) = E^t(\iota, z) G^t(x, z)$.

C. J. O'Donnell, *Productivity and Efficiency Analysis*,
https://doi.org/10.1007/978-981-13-2984-5

Proof If output sets are homothetic, then, by Proposition 1, $D^t_O(x,q,z) = D^t_O(\iota,q,z)/G^t(x,z)$ (A). If technical change is IHON, then, by Proposition 3, $D^t_O(x,q,z) = D^1_O(x,q,\iota)/E^t(x,z) \Rightarrow D^t_O(\iota,q,z) = D^1_O(\iota,q,\iota)/E^t(\iota,z)$ (B). Substituting (B) into (A), $D^t_O(x,q,z) = Q(q)/F^t(x,z)$ where $Q(q) = D^1_O(\iota,q,\iota)$ and $F^t(x,z) = E^t(\iota,z)G^t(x,z)$. □

Proposition 6 *If output sets are homothetic and technical change is IHON, then* $R^t(x,p,z) = P(p)F^t(x,z)$ *where* $P(p) = R^1(\iota,p,\iota)$ *and* $F^t(x,z) = E^t(\iota,z)G^t(x,z)$.

Proof If output sets are homothetic, then, by Proposition 2, $R^t(x,p,z) = G^t(x,z)R^t(\iota,p,z)$ (A). If technical change is IHON, then, by Proposition 4, $R^t(x,p,z) = E^t(x,z)R^1(x,p,\iota) \Rightarrow R^t(\iota,p,z) = E^t(\iota,z)R^1(\iota,p,\iota)$ (B). Substituting (B) into (A), $R^t(x,p,z) = P(p)F^t(x,z)$ where $P(p) = R^1(\iota,p,\iota)$ and $F^t(x,z) = E^t(\iota,z)G^t(x,z)$. □

Proposition 7 *If output sets are homothetic and technical change is IHON, then* $QI^P(q_{ks},q_{it}) = D^1_O(\iota,q_{it},\iota)/D^1_O(\iota,q_{ks},\iota)$.

Proof If output sets are homothetic and technical change is IHON, then, by Proposition 5, $D^{\bar t}_O(\bar x,q_{it},\bar z) = D^1_O(\iota,q_{it},\iota)/F^{\bar t}(\bar x,\bar z)$ and $D^{\bar t}_O(\bar x,q_{ks},\bar z) = D^1_O(\iota,q_{ks},\iota)/F^{\bar t}(\bar x,\bar z)$ $\Rightarrow QI^P(q_{ks},q_{it}) \equiv D^{\bar t}_O(\bar x,q_{it},\bar z)/D^{\bar t}_O(\bar x,q_{ks},\bar z) = D^1_O(\iota,q_{it},\iota)/D^1_O(\iota,q_{ks},\iota)$. □

Proposition 8 *If output sets are homothetic and technical change is IHON, then* $PI^D(p_{ks},p_{it}) = R^1(\iota,p_{it},\iota)/R^1(\iota,p_{ks},\iota)$.

Proof If output sets are homothetic and technical change is IHON, then, by Proposition 6, $R^{\bar t}(\bar x,p_{it},\bar z) = R^1(\iota,p_{it},\iota)/F^{\bar t}(\bar x,\bar z)$ and $R^{\bar t}(\bar x,p_{ks},\bar z) = R^1(\iota,p_{ks},\iota)/F^{\bar t}(\bar x,\bar z) \Rightarrow$ $PI^D(p_{ks},p_{it}) \equiv R^{\bar t}(\bar x,p_{it},\bar z)/R^{\bar t}(\bar x,p_{ks},\bar z) = R^1(\iota,p_{it},\iota)/R^1(\iota,p_{ks},\iota)$. □

Proposition 9 *If input sets are homothetic, then* $D^t_I(x,q,z) = D^t_I(x,\iota,z)/K^t(q,z)$.

Proof Let $\kappa \equiv K^t(q,z)$. If input sets are homothetic, then $L^t(q,z) = \kappa L^t(\iota,z) \Rightarrow$ $D^t_I(x,q,z) = \sup\{\theta > 0 : x/\theta \in L^t(q,z)\} = \sup\{\theta > 0 : x/\theta \in \kappa L^t(\iota,z)\} = \sup\{\theta > 0 : x/(\kappa\theta) \in L^t(\iota,z)\} = \sup\{(\kappa\theta)/\kappa > 0 : x/(\kappa\theta) \in L^t(\iota,z)\} = (1/\kappa)\sup\{(\kappa\theta) > 0 : x/(\kappa\theta) \in L^t(\iota,z)\} = D^t_I(x,\iota,z)/\kappa = D^t_I(x,\iota,z)/K^t(q,z)$. □

Proposition 10 *If input sets are homothetic, then* $C^t(w,q,z) = K^t(q,z)C^t(w,\iota,z)$.

Proof Let $\kappa \equiv K^t(q,z)$. If input sets are homothetic, then, by Proposition 9, $D^t_I(x,q,z) = D^t_I(x,\iota,z)/\kappa \Rightarrow C^t(w,q,z) = \min_x\{w'x : D^t_I(x,q,z) \geq 1\} = \min_x\{w'x : D^t_I(x,\iota,z)/\kappa \geq 1\} = \min_x\{w'x : D^t_I(x/\kappa,\iota,z) \geq 1\} = \min_x\{\kappa w'(x/\kappa) : D^t_I(x/\kappa,\iota,z) \geq 1\} = \kappa \min_{x/\kappa}\{w'(x/\kappa) : D^t_I(x/\kappa,\iota,z) \geq 1\} = \kappa C^t(w,\iota,z) = K^t(q,z)C^t(w,\iota,z)$. □

Proposition 11 *If technical change is IHIN, then* $D^t_I(x,q,z) = D^1_I(x,q,\iota)/J^t(q,z)$.

Proof Let $\kappa \equiv J^t(q,z)$. If technical change is IHIN, then $L^t(q,z) = \kappa L^1(q,\iota) \Rightarrow$ $D^t_I(x,q,z) \equiv \sup\{\theta > 0 : x/\theta \in L^t(q,z)\} = \sup\{\theta > 0 : x/\theta \in \kappa L^1(q,\iota)\} = \sup\{\theta > 0 : x/(\kappa\theta) \in L^1(q,\iota)\} = \sup\{(\kappa\theta)/\kappa > 0 : x/(\kappa\theta) \in L^1(q,\iota)\} = (1/\kappa)\sup\{(\kappa\theta) > 0 : x/(\kappa\theta) \in L^1(q,\iota)\} = D^1_I(x,q,\iota)/\kappa = D^1_I(x,q,\iota)/J^t(q,z)$. □

Proposition 12 *If technical change is IHIN, then* $C^t(w, q, z) = J^t(q, z)C^1(w, q, \iota)$.

Proof Let $\kappa \equiv J^t(q, z)$. If technical change is IHIN, then, by Proposition 11, $D_I^t(x, q, z) = D_I^1(x, q, \iota)/\kappa \Rightarrow C^t(w, q, z) = \min_x\{w'x : D_I^t(x, q, z) \geq 1\} = \min_x \{w'x : D_I^1(x, q, \iota)/\kappa \geq 1\} = \min_x\{w'x : D_I^1(x/\kappa, q, \iota)/ \geq 1\} = \min_x\{\kappa w'(x/\kappa) : D_I^1 (x/\kappa, q, \iota) \geq 1\} = \kappa \min_{x/\kappa}\{w'(x/\kappa) : D_I^1(x/\kappa, q, \iota) \geq 1\} = \kappa C^1(w, q, \iota) = J^t(q, z) C^1(w, q, \iota)$. □

Proposition 13 *If input sets are homothetic and technical change is IHIN, then* $D_I^t(x, q, z) = X(x)/H^t(q, z)$ *where* $X(x) = D_I^1(x, \iota, \iota)$ *and* $H^t(q, z) = J^t(\iota, z) K^t(q, z)$.

Proof If input sets are homothetic, then, by Proposition 9, $D_I^t(x, q, z) = D_I^t(x, \iota, z)/K^t (q, z)$ (A). If technical change is IHIN, then, by Proposition 11, $D_I^t(x, q, z) = D_I^1(x, q, \iota)/J^t(q, z) \Rightarrow D_I^t(x, \iota, z) = D_I^1(x, \iota, \iota)/J^t(\iota, z)$ (B). Substituting (B) into (A), $D_I^t(x, q, z) = X(x)/H^t(q, z)$ where $X(x) = D_I^1(x, \iota, \iota)$ and $H^t(q, z) = J^t(\iota, z) K^t(q, z)$. □

Proposition 14 *If input sets are homothetic and technical change is IHIN, then* $C^t(w, q, z) = W(w)H^t(q, z)$ *where* $W(w) = C^1(w, \iota, \iota)$ *and* $H^t(q, z) = J^t(\iota, z)K^t (q, z)$.

Proof If input sets are homothetic, then, by Proposition 10, $C^t(w, q, z) = K^t(q, z)C^t (w, \iota, z)$ (A). If technical change is IHIN, then, by Proposition 12, $\Rightarrow C^t(w, q, z) = J^t(q, z)C^1(w, q, \iota) \Rightarrow C^t(w, \iota, z) = J^t(\iota, z)C^1(w, \iota, \iota)$ (B). Substituting (B) into (A), $C^t(w, q, z) = W(w)H^t(q, z)$ where $W(w) = C^1(w, \iota, \iota)$ and $H^t(q, z) = J^t(\iota, z)K^t (q, z)$. □

Proposition 15 *If input sets are homothetic and technical change is IHIN, then* $XI^P(x_{ks}, x_{it}) = D_I^1(x_{it}, \iota, \iota)/D_I^1(x_{ks}, \iota, \iota)$.

Proof If input sets are homothetic and technical change is IHIN, then, by Proposition 13, $D_I^{\bar{t}}(x_{it}, \bar{q}, \bar{z}) = D_I^1(x_{it}, \iota, \iota)/H^{\bar{t}}(\bar{q}, \bar{z})$ and $D_I^{\bar{t}}(x_{ks}, \bar{q}, \bar{z}) = D_I^1(x_{ks}, \iota, \iota)/H^{\bar{t}}(\bar{q}, \bar{z}) \Rightarrow XI^P(x_{ks}, x_{it}) \equiv D_I^{\bar{t}}(x_{it}, \bar{q}, \bar{z})/D_I^{\bar{t}}(x_{ks}, \bar{q}, \bar{z}) = D_I^1(x_{it}, \iota, \iota)/D_I^1(x_{ks}, \iota, \iota)$. □

Proposition 16 *If input sets are homothetic and technical change is IHIN, then* $WI^D(w_{ks}, w_{it}) = C^1(w_{it}, \iota, \iota)/C^1(w_{ks}, \iota, \iota)$.

Proof If input sets are homothetic and technical change is IHIN, then, by Proposition 14, $C^{\bar{t}}(w_{it}, \bar{q}, \bar{z}) = C^1(w_{it}, \iota, \iota)H^{\bar{t}}(\bar{q}, \bar{z})$ and $C^{\bar{t}}(w_{ks}, \bar{q}, \bar{z}) = C^1(w_{ks}, \iota, \iota)H^{\bar{t}}(\bar{q}, \bar{z}) \Rightarrow WI^D(w_{ks}, w_{it}) \equiv C^{\bar{t}}(w_{it}, \bar{q}, \bar{z})/C^{\bar{t}}(w_{ks}, \bar{q}, \bar{z}) = C^1(w_{it}, \iota, \iota)/C^1(w_{ks}, \iota, \iota)$. □

Proposition 17 *If (a) output and input sets are homothetic, (b) technical change is HN, and (c) production frontiers exhibit CRS, then* $D_O^t(x, q, z) = Q(q)/[A^t(z)F(x)]$ *where* $Q(q) = D_O^1(\iota, q, \iota)$, $A^t(z) = E^t(\iota, z)$ *and* $F(x) = D_I^1(x, \iota, \iota)/D_I^1(\iota, \iota, \iota)$.

Proof If technical change is HN, then it is both IHON and IHIN. If output sets are homothetic and technical change is IHON, then, by Proposition 5, $D_O^t(x,q,z) = Q(q)/F^t(x,z)$ where $Q(q) = D_O^1(\iota,q,\iota)$ and $F^t(x,z) = E^t(\iota,z)G^t(x,z)$. If output sets are homothetic, then, by Proposition 1, $D_O^t(x,q,z) = D_O^t(\iota,q,z)/G^t(x,z) \Rightarrow G^t(x,z) = D_O^t(\iota,q,z)/D_O^t(x,q,z) \Rightarrow F^t(x,z) = E^t(\iota,z)D_O^t(\iota,q,z)/D_O^t(x,q,z)$. If production frontiers exhibit CRS, then we have that $D_O^t(x,q,z) = 1/D_I^t(x,q,z) \Rightarrow F^t(x,z) = E^t(\iota,z)D_I^t(x,q,z)/D_I^t(\iota,q,z)$. If input sets are homothetic and technical change is IHIN, then, by Proposition 13, $D_I^t(x,q,z) = D_I^1(x,\iota,\iota)/H^t(q,z) \Rightarrow D_I^t(\iota,q,z) = D_I^1(\iota,\iota,\iota)/H^t(q,z) \Rightarrow D_I^t(x,q,z)/D_I^t(\iota,q,z) = D_I^1(x,\iota,\iota)/D_I^1(\iota,\iota,\iota) \Rightarrow F^t(x,z) = E^t(\iota,z)D_I^1(x,\iota,\iota)/D_I^1(\iota,\iota,\iota) = A^t(z)F(x)$ where $A^t(z) = E^t(\iota,z)$ and $F(x) = D_I^1(x,\iota,\iota)/D_I^1(\iota,\iota,\iota)$. □

Proposition 18 *If (a) output and input sets are homothetic, (b) technical change is HN, and (c) production frontiers exhibit CRS, then* $D_I^t(x,q,z) = B^t(z)X(x)/H(q)$ *where* $B^t(z) = J^t(\iota,z)$, $X(x) = D_I^1(x,\iota,\iota)$ *and* $H(q) = D_O^1(\iota,q,\iota)/D_O^1(\iota,\iota,\iota)$.

Proof If technical change is HN, then it is both IHON and IHIN. If input sets are homothetic and technical change is IHIN, then, by Proposition 13, $D_I^t(x,q,z) = X(x)/H^t(q,z)$ where $X(x) = D_I^1(x,\iota,\iota)$ and $H^t(q,z) = J^t(\iota,z)K^t(q,z)$. If input sets are homothetic, then, by Proposition 9, $D_I^t(x,q,z) = D_I^t(x,\iota,z)/K^t(q,z) \Rightarrow K^t(q,z) = D_I^t(x,\iota,z)/D_I^t(x,q,z) \Rightarrow H^t(q,z) = J^t(\iota,z)D_I^t(x,\iota,z)/D_I^t(x,q,z)$. If production frontiers exhibit CRS, then $D_I^t(x,q,z) = 1/D_O^t(x,q,z) \Rightarrow H^t(q,z) = J^t(\iota,z)D_O^t(x,q,z)/D_O^t(x,\iota,z)$. If output sets are homothetic and technical change is IHON, then, by Proposition 5, $D_O^t(x,q,z) = D_O^1(\iota,q,\iota)/F^t(x,z) \Rightarrow D_O^t(x,\iota,z) = D_O^1(\iota,\iota,\iota)/F^t(x,z) \Rightarrow D_O^t(x,q,z)/D_O^t(x,\iota,z) = D_O^1(\iota,q,\iota)/D_O^1(\iota,\iota,\iota) \Rightarrow H^t(q,z) = J^t(\iota,z)D_O^1(\iota,q,\iota)/D_O^1(\iota,\iota,\iota) = B^t(z)H(q)$ where $B^t(z) = J^t(\iota,z)$ and $H(q) = D_O^1(\iota,q,\iota)/D_O^1(\iota,\iota,\iota)$. □

Proposition 19 *If (a) firms are price takers in output markets, (b) output sets are homothetic, (c) technical change is IHON, and (d) the OAE of firm k in period s is equal to the OAE of firm i in period t, then* $QI^{ID}(q_{ks},q_{it},\ldots) = QI^P(q_{ks},q_{it})$.

Proof If output sets are homothetic and technical change is IHON, then, by Propositions 8 and 7, $PI^D(p_{ks},p_{it}) = R^1(\iota,p_{it},\iota)/R^1(\iota,p_{ks},\iota)$ and $QI^P(q_{ks},q_{it}) = D_O^1(\iota,q_{it},\iota)/D_O^1(\iota,q_{ks},\iota)$ (A). If firm i is a price taker in output markets, then the OAE of firm i in period t is $OAE^t(x_{it},p_{it},q_{it},z_{it}) = RE^t(x_{it},p_{it},q_{it},z_{it})/OTE^t(x_{it},q_{it},z_{it})$ where $RE^t(x_{it},p_{it},q_{it},z_{it}) = R_{it}/R^t(x_{it},p_{it},z_{it}) \Rightarrow OAE^t(x_{it},p_{it},q_{it},z_{it}) = R_{it}/[R^t(x_{it},p_{it},z_{it})\ OTE^t(x_{it},q_{it},z_{it})]$ (B). If output sets are homothetic and technical change is IHON, then, by Propositions 6 and 5, $R^t(x_{it},p_{it},z_{it}) = R^1(\iota,p_{it},\iota)F^t(x_{it},z_{it})$ and $OTE^t(x_{it},q_{it},z_{it}) = D_O^1(\iota,q_{it},\iota)/F^t(x_{it},z_{it}) \Rightarrow R^t(x_{it},p_{it},z_{it})OTE^t(x_{it},q_{it},z_{it}) = R^1(\iota,p_{it},\iota)D_O^1(\iota,q_{it},\iota)$ (C). Substituting (C) into (B), the OAE of firm i in period t is $OAE^t(x_{it},p_{it},q_{it},z_{it}) = R_{it}/[R^1(\iota,p_{it},\iota)D_O^1(\iota,q_{it},\iota)] \Rightarrow D_O^1(\iota,q_{it},\iota) = R_{it}/[R^1(\iota,p_{it},\iota)OAE^t(x_{it},p_{it},q_{it},z_{it})]$ (D). Substituting (D) into (A) yields $QI^P(q_{ks},q_{it}) = RI(p_{ks},q_{ks},p_{it},q_{it})/[PI^D(p_{ks},p_{it})\quad OAE^t(x_{it},p_{it},q_{it},z_{it})/OAE^s(x_{ks},p_{ks},q_{ks},z_{ks})]$ where $RI(p_{ks},q_{ks},p_{it},q_{it}) = R_{it}/R_{ks}$. If $OAE^t(x_{it},p_{it},q_{it},z_{it}) = OAE^s(x_{ks},p_{ks},q_{ks},z_{ks})$, then $QI^P(q_{ks},q_{it}) = RI(p_{ks},q_{ks},p_{it},q_{it})\ /PI^D(p_{ks},p_{it}) = QI^{ID}(q_{ks},q_{it},\ldots)$. □

Proposition 20 *If (a) firms are price takers in input markets, (b) input sets are homothetic, (c) technical change is IHIN, and (d) the IAE of firm k in period s is equal to the IAE of firm i in period t, then* $XI^{ID}(x_{ks}, x_{it}, \ldots) = XI^P(x_{ks}, x_{it})$.

Proof If input sets are homothetic and technical change is IHIN, then, by Propositions 16 and 15, $WI^D(w_{ks}, w_{it}) = C^1(w_{it}, \iota, \iota)/C^1(w_{ks}, \iota, \iota)$ and $XI^P(x_{ks}, x_{it}) = D_I^1(x_{it}, \iota, \iota)/D_I^1(x_{ks}, \iota, \iota)$ (A). If firm i is a price taker in input markets, then the IAE of firm i in period t is $IAE^t(w_{it}, x_{it}, q_{it}, z_{it}) = CE^t(w_{it}, x_{it}, q_{it}, z_{it})/ITE^t(x_{it}, q_{it}, z_{it})$ where $CE^t(w_{it}, x_{it}, q_{it}, z_{it}) = C^t(w_{it}, q_{it}, z_{it})/C_{it} \Rightarrow IAE^t(w_{it}, x_{it}, q_{it}, z_{it}) = C^t(w_{it}, q_{it}, z_{it}) / [C_{it} ITE^t(x_{it}, q_{it}, z_{it})]$ (B). If input sets are homothetic and technical change is IHIN, then, by Propositions 14 and 13, $C^t(w_{it}, q_{it}, z_{it}) = C^1(w_{it}, \iota, \iota)H^t(q_{it}, z_{it})$ and $ITE^t(x_{it}, q_{it}, z_{it}) = H^t(q_{it}, z_{it})/D_I^1(x_{it}, \iota, \iota) \Rightarrow C^t(w_{it}, q_{it}, z_{it})/ITE^t(x_{it}, q_{it}, z_{it}) = C^1(w_{it}, \iota, \iota)D_I^1(x_{it}, \iota, \iota)$ (C). Substituting (C) into (B) yields $IAE^t(x_{it}, p_{it}, q_{it}, z_{it}) = C^1(w_{it}, \iota, \iota)D_I^1(x_{it}, \iota, \iota)/C_{it} \Rightarrow D_I^1(x_{it}, \iota, \iota) = C_{it} IAE^t(x_{it}, p_{it}, q_{it}, z_{it})/C^1(w_{it}, \iota, \iota)$ (D). Substituting (D) into (A) yields $XI^P(x_{ks}, x_{it}) = CI(w_{ks}, x_{ks}, w_{it}, x_{it}) IAE^t(w_{it}, x_{it}, q_{it}, z_{it}) / [IAE^s(w_{ks}, x_{ks}, q_{ks}, z_{ks}) WI^D(w_{ks}, w_{it})]$ where $CI(w_{ks}, x_{ks}, w_{it}, x_{it}) = C_{it}/C_{ks}$. Finally, if $IAE^t(w_{it}, x_{it}, q_{it}, z_{it}) = IAE^s(w_{ks}, x_{ks}, q_{ks}, z_{ks})$, then $XI^P(x_{ks}, x_{it}) = CI(w_{ks}, x_{ks}, w_{it}, x_{it}) / WI^D(w_{ks}, w_{it}) = XI^{ID}(x_{ks}, x_{it}, \ldots)$. □

Proposition 21 *If (a) firms are price takers in output and input markets, (b) output and input sets are homothetic, (c) technical change is HN, and (d) the OAE and IAE of firm k in period s are equal to the OAE and IAE of firm i in period t, then* $TFPI^{ID}(x_{ks}, q_{ks}, x_{it}, q_{it}, \ldots) = TFPI^P(x_{ks}, q_{ks}, x_{it}, q_{it})$.

Proof If firms are price takers in output markets, output sets are homothetic, technical change is IHON, and the OAE of firm k in period s is equal to the OAE of firm i in period t, then, by Proposition 19, $QI^{ID}(q_{ks}, q_{it}, \ldots) = QI^P(q_{ks}, q_{it})$. If firms are price takers in input markets, input sets are homothetic, technical change is IHIN, and the IAE of firm k in period s is equal to the IAE of firm i in period t, then, by Proposition 20, $XI^{ID}(x_{ks}, x_{it}, \ldots) = XI^P(x_{ks}, x_{it})$. It follows that $TFPI^{ID}(x_{ks}, q_{ks}, x_{it}, q_{it}, \ldots) \equiv QI^{ID}(q_{ks}, q_{it}, \ldots)/XI^{ID}(x_{ks}, x_{it}, \ldots) = QI^P(q_{ks}, q_{it}) / XI^P(x_{ks}, x_{it}) = TFPI^P(x_{ks}, q_{ks}, x_{it}, q_{it})$. □

A.2 Rates of Growth

Define $z_{jt} \equiv z_j(t)$ where $z_j(.)$ is a differentiable function and t denotes time. Also define $Z_t \equiv Z(z_t)$ where $z_t = (z_{1t}, \ldots, z_{Jt})'$ is a $J \times 1$ vector and $Z(.)$ is a differentiable function. The rate of growth in z_{jt} per unit of time is $\dot{z}_{jt} \equiv dz_{jt}/dt$. The *percentage* rate of growth in z_{jt} per unit of time is $\dot{z}_{jt}/z_{jt} = d \ln z_{jt}/dt$. The rate of growth in Z_t per unit of time is $\dot{Z}_t \equiv dZ_t/dt = \sum_j a_{jt}\dot{z}_{jt}$ where $a_{jt} \equiv \partial Z(z_t)/\partial z_{jt}$. Thus, the rate of growth in Z_t per unit of time is a weighted sum of the rates of growth in $z_{1t}, \ldots, z_{Jt}$. If $\sum_j a_{jt} = 1$, then $\dot{Z}_t$ is an *average* rate of growth. The *percentage* rate of growth in Z_t per unit of time is $\dot{Z}_t/Z_t = d \ln Z_t/dt = \sum_j b_{jt}(\dot{z}_{jt}/z_{jt})$ where $b_{jt} \equiv \partial \ln Z(z_t)/\partial \ln z_{jt}$. Thus, the percentage rate of growth in Z_t per unit of time is a weighted sum of the percentage rates of growth in $z_{1t}, \ldots, z_{Jt}$. If $Z(.)$ is homogeneous of degree one, then $\sum_j b_{jt} = 1$ and $\dot{Z}_t/Z_t$ is an *average percentage* rate of growth.

The fact that most economic variables are measured at discrete points in time means that the smallest measurable change[1] in t is $\Delta t = 1$. The associated change in $\ln z_{jt}$, for example, is

$$\left.\frac{\Delta \ln z_{jt}}{\Delta t}\right|_{\Delta t=1} = \Delta \ln z_{jt} = \ln z_{jt} - \ln z_{j,t-1}. \tag{A.1}$$

Moreover, the percentage rate of growth in z_{jt} per unit of time is

$$\frac{d \ln z_{jt}}{dt} = \lim_{\Delta t \to 0} \frac{\Delta \ln z_{jt}}{\Delta t} = \frac{\Delta \ln z_{jt}}{\Delta t} + e(\Delta t)$$

where $e(\Delta t)$ is an error that goes to zero as fast as Δt goes to zero.[2] In practice, it is common to ignore this error.

Researchers are often interested in measuring growth over several periods. Let $ZI_{st} \equiv Z_t/Z_s$ denote the index that compares Z_t with Z_s. If the rate of growth in Z_s is a constant g percent per period, then the *percentage* rate of growth in Z_s per period is $g = ZI_{st}^{1/(t-s)} - 1$. If the percentage rate of growth in Z_s per period is *not* a constant, then the *average percentage* rate of growth in Z_s per period can be measured as

$$\bar{g} = \frac{1}{(t-s)} \sum_{k=1}^{t} \left(\frac{Z_{s+k} - Z_{s+k-1}}{Z_{s+k-1}} \right). \tag{A.2}$$

A.3 Exponential Random Variables

An exponential random variable is a gamma random variable with shape parameter $P = 1$ (see Sect. A.4). If X is an exponential random variable with *scale* parameter $\sigma > 0$, then we write $X \sim EXP(\sigma)$. The *probability density function* (PDF) of X is (e.g., Larson 1982, p. 195):

$$f_G(x|1, \sigma^{-1}) = \sigma^{-1} e^{-x/\sigma} I(x > 0) \tag{A.3}$$

[1] In econometrics, Δ usually denotes the first backward difference operator (e.g., Abadir and Magnus 2002). Thus, $\Delta z_{jt} = z_{jt} - z_{j,t-1}$. In this book, ∇ denotes the first forward difference operator. Thus, $\nabla z_{jt} = z_{j,t+1} - z_{jt}$. In mathematics more generally, the opposite is usually the case: Δ usually denotes the forward operator and ∇ usually denotes the backward operator.

[2] Formally, $e(\Delta t) = O(\Delta t)$ as $\Delta t \to 0$. In mathematics, $e(h) = O(h)$ as $h \to 0$ if and only if there exist positive numbers δ and M such that $|E(h)| \leq M|h|$ for $|h| < \delta$.

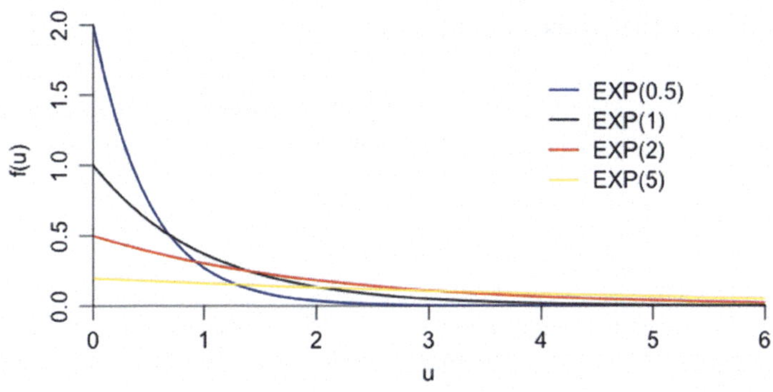

Fig. A.1 Selected exponential PDFs

where $I(.)$ is the indicator function. Several exponential PDFs are depicted in Fig. A.1. The mean, mode, variance, *moment generating function* (MGF) and *cumulative distribution function* (CDF) of X are (e.g., Larson 1982, pp. 195–196):

$$E(X) = \sigma, \tag{A.4}$$

$$M(X) = 0, \tag{A.5}$$

$$Var(X) = \sigma^2, \tag{A.6}$$

$$E(e^{tX}) = 1/(1 - \sigma t) \tag{A.7}$$

and

$$P(X \leq x) = (1 - e^{-x/\sigma})I(x > 0). \tag{A.8}$$

The joint density (likelihood) of a sample of T independent exponential random variables, $x_1, \ldots, x_T$, is

$$L = \prod_{t=1}^{T} \sigma^{-1} \exp(-x_t/\sigma) = \sigma^{-T} \exp\left(-\sigma^{-1} \sum_{t=1}^{T} x_t\right) = \sigma^{-T} \exp(-T\bar{x}/\sigma) \tag{A.9}$$

where $\bar{x} \equiv (1/T) \sum_t x_t$. It is common to parameterise the exponential distribution in terms of the *rate* (or *inverse scale*) parameter $\lambda \equiv \sigma^{-1}$. With this parameterisation,

$$f_G(x|1, \lambda) = \lambda e^{-\lambda x} I(x > 0), \tag{A.10}$$

$$E(X) = 1/\lambda, \tag{A.11}$$

$$Var(X) = 1/\lambda^2, \tag{A.12}$$

$$E(e^{tX}) = \lambda/(\lambda - t), \tag{A.13}$$

$$P(X \leq x) = (1 - e^{-\lambda x})I(x > 0) \tag{A.14}$$

and

$$L = \lambda^T \exp(-T\lambda\bar{x}). \tag{A.15}$$

A.4 Gamma Random Variables

If X is a gamma random random variable with *shape* parameter P and *scale* parameter $\sigma > 0$, then we write $X \sim G(P, \sigma)$. The PDF of X is (e.g., Larson 1982, p. 200):

$$f_G(x|P, \sigma^{-1}) = \frac{x^{P-1}}{\sigma^P \Gamma(P)} e^{-x/\sigma} I(x > 0) \tag{A.16}$$

where $I(.)$ is the indicator function and $\Gamma(.)$ is the *gamma function*.[3] Several gamma PDFs are depicted in Fig. A.2. The mean, mode, variance, MGF and CDF of X are (e.g., Larson 1982, p. 200):

$$E(X) = P\sigma, \tag{A.17}$$

$$M(X) = (P-1)\sigma \quad \text{for } P \geq 1, \tag{A.18}$$

$$Var(X) = P\sigma^2, \tag{A.19}$$

$$E(e^{tX}) = (1 - \sigma t)^{-P} \tag{A.20}$$

$$\text{and} \qquad P(X \leq x) = \frac{\gamma(P, x/\sigma)}{\Gamma(P)} I(x > 0) \tag{A.21}$$

where $\gamma(.)$ is the *lower incomplete gamma function*.[4] If P is a positive integer, then the gamma distribution is an *Erlang* distribution and (e.g., Larson 1982, p. 198):

$$P(X \leq x) = \left(1 - \sum_{i=0}^{P-1} \frac{(x/\sigma)^i}{i!} e^{-x/\sigma}\right) I(x > 0). \tag{A.22}$$

It is common to parameterise the gamma distribution in terms of the *rate* (or *inverse scale*) parameter $\lambda \equiv \sigma^{-1}$. With this parameterisation:

$$f_G(x|P, \lambda) = \frac{\lambda^P x^{P-1}}{\Gamma(P)} e^{-\lambda x} I(x > 0), \tag{A.23}$$

$$E(X) = P/\lambda, \tag{A.24}$$

$$M(X) = (P-1)/\lambda \quad \text{for } P \geq 1, \tag{A.25}$$

$$Var(X) = P/\lambda^2, \tag{A.26}$$

$$E(e^{tX}) = [\lambda/(\lambda - t)]^P \tag{A.27}$$

$$\text{and} \qquad P(X \leq x) = \frac{\gamma(P, \lambda x)}{\Gamma(P)} I(x > 0). \tag{A.28}$$

---

[3] The gamma function is defined as $\Gamma(a) = \int_0^\infty t^{a-1} e^{-t} dt$. Among other things, $\Gamma(a) = (a-1)\Gamma(a-1)$ for any positive real number, $\Gamma(a) = (a-1)!$ if a is a positive integer, and $\Gamma(1/2) = \pi^{1/2}$ (e.g., Larson 1982, p. 199).

[4] Mathematically, $\gamma(a, b) = \int_0^b t^{a-1} e^{-t} dt$. A special case is $\gamma(1, b) = 1 - e^{-b}$.

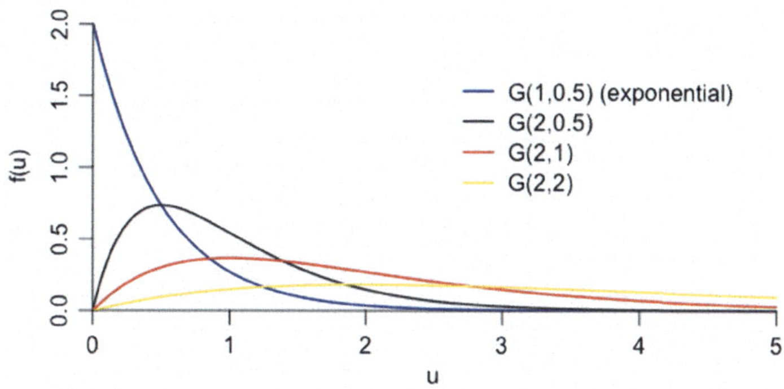

Fig. A.2 Selected gamma PDFs

If P is a positive integer, then

$$P(X \le x) = \left(1 - \sum_{i=0}^{P-1} \frac{(\lambda x)^i}{i!} e^{-\lambda x}\right) I(x > 0). \tag{A.29}$$

If $P = 1$ then, the gamma distribution is an exponential distribution.

A.5 Normal Random Variables

If X is a normal random variable with mean μ and variance σ^2, then we write $X \sim N(\mu, \sigma^2)$. The PDF of X is

$$f_N(x|\mu, \sigma^2) = \frac{1}{\sqrt{2\pi\sigma^2}} \exp\left(-\frac{(x-\mu)^2}{2\sigma^2}\right). \tag{A.30}$$

Several normal PDFs are depicted in Fig. A.3. The mode, MGF and CDF of X are

$$M(X) = \mu, \tag{A.31}$$

$$E(e^{tX}) = \exp(\mu t + \sigma^2 t^2/2) \tag{A.32}$$

and $$P(X \le x) = \frac{1}{\sqrt{2\pi}} \int_{-\infty}^{(x-\mu)/\sigma} \exp(-t^2/2) dt. \tag{A.33}$$

The standard normal distribution is a normal distribution with $\mu = 0$ and $\sigma^2 = 1$. If $X \sim N(0, 1)$, then the PDF and CDF are usually denoted $\phi(x)$ and $\Phi(x)$ respectively. The standard normal PDF has the property $\phi(x) = \phi(-x)$. The first- and second-derivatives of the standard normal PDF are $\phi'(x) = -x\phi(x)$ and $\phi''(x) = (x^2 - 1)\phi(x)$. The complement of the standard normal CDF is $Q(x) = 1 - \Phi(x) =$

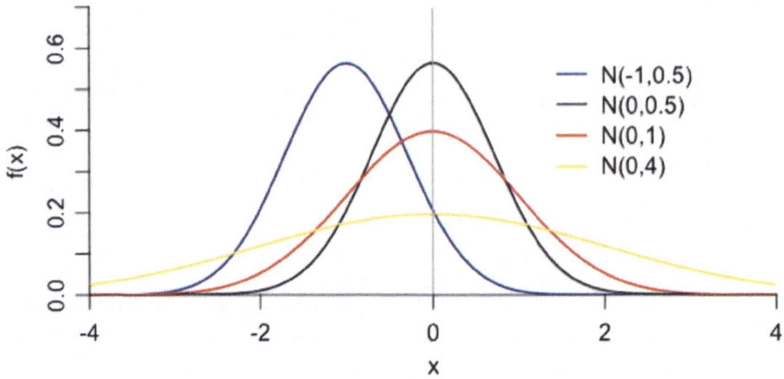

Fig. A.3 Selected normal PDFs

$\Phi(-x)$ (sometimes known as the *Q-function*). Finally, if X is a $K \times 1$ vector of normal random variables with mean vector μ and covariance matrix Σ, then we write $X \sim N(\mu, \Sigma)$. In this multivariate case, the PDF of X is

$$f_N(x|\mu, \Sigma) = (2\pi)^{-K/2}|\Sigma|^{-1/2} \exp\left[-(1/2)(x-\mu)'\Sigma^{-1}(x-\mu)\right]. \quad \text{(A.34)}$$

A.6 Half-Normal Random Variables

If X is a random variable obtained by lower-truncating the $N(0, \sigma^2)$ distribution at zero, then X is a half-normal random variable. In this case, we write either $X \sim N^+(0, \sigma^2)$ or $X \sim N(0, \sigma^2, 0, \infty)$. The PDF of X is

$$f_N(x|\sigma^2, 0, \infty) = \frac{2}{\sigma}\phi(x/\sigma)I(x \geq 0) \quad \text{(A.35)}$$

where $I(.)$ is the indicator function and $\phi(.)$ is the standard normal PDF. Several half-normal PDFs are depicted in Fig. A.4. The mean, mode, variance, MGF and CDF of X are

$$E(X) = \sigma\sqrt{2/\pi} \approx 0.79788\sigma, \quad \text{(A.36)}$$

$$M(X) = 0, \quad \text{(A.37)}$$

$$Var(X) = \sigma^2([\pi - 2]/\pi) \approx 0.36338\sigma^2, \quad \text{(A.38)}$$

$$E(e^{tX}) = 2\Phi(\sigma t)\exp(\sigma^2 t^2/2) \quad \text{(A.39)}$$

$$\text{and} \quad P(X \leq x) = [2\Phi(x/\sigma) - 1]I(x \geq 0) \quad \text{(A.40)}$$

where $\Phi(.)$ is the standard normal CDF.

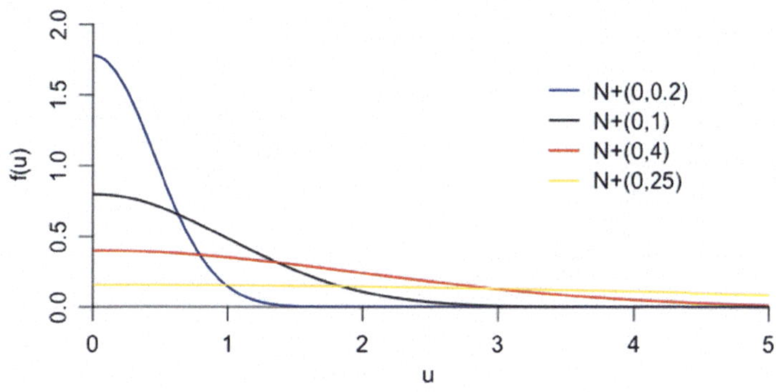

Fig. A.4 Selected half-normal PDFs

A.7 Truncated-Normal Random Variables

If X is a random variable obtained by truncating the $N(\mu, \sigma^2)$ distribution to lie in the interval (a, b), then X is a truncated normal normal random variable and we write $X \sim N(\mu, \sigma^2, a, b)$. The PDF of X is

$$f_N(x|\mu, \sigma^2, a, b) = \frac{1}{\sigma}\left(\frac{\phi(z)}{\Phi(b^*) - \Phi(a^*)}\right) I(a \leq x \leq b) \tag{A.41}$$

where $z \equiv (x - \mu)/\sigma$, $a^* \equiv (a - \mu)/\sigma$, $b^* \equiv (b - \mu)/\sigma$ and $I(.)$ is the indicator function. Several truncated-normal PDFs are depicted in Fig. A.5. The mean, mode, variance, MGF and CDF of X are

$$E(X) = \mu + \sigma\left(\frac{\phi(a^*) - \phi(b^*)}{\Phi(b^*) - \Phi(a^*)}\right), \tag{A.42}$$

$$M(X) = \begin{cases} a \text{ if } \mu < a, \\ \mu \text{ if } a \leq \mu \leq b, \\ b \text{ if } \mu > b, \end{cases} \tag{A.43}$$

$$Var(X) = \sigma^2\left[1 + \frac{a^*\phi(a^*) - b^*\phi(b^*)}{\Phi(b^*) - \Phi(a^*)} - \left(\frac{\phi(a^*) - \phi(b^*)}{\Phi(b^*) - \Phi(a^*)}\right)^2\right], \tag{A.44}$$

$$E(e^{tX}) = \exp\left(\mu t + \frac{\sigma^2 t^2}{2}\right)\left(\frac{\Phi(b^* - \sigma t) - \Phi(a^* - \sigma t)}{\Phi(b^*) - \Phi(a^*)}\right) \tag{A.45}$$

and $$P(X \leq x) = \left(\frac{\Phi(z) - \Phi(a^*)}{\Phi(b^*) - \Phi(a^*)}\right) I(x \geq a). \tag{A.46}$$

If $Y = cX$, then $Y \sim N(c\mu, c^2\sigma^2, ca, cb)$. If $b = \infty$ (no upper truncation) and $a = 0$ (lower truncation at zero), then $\phi(a^*) = \phi(\mu/\sigma)$, $\phi(b^*) = 0$, $\Phi(a^*) = 1 - \Phi(\mu/\sigma)$,

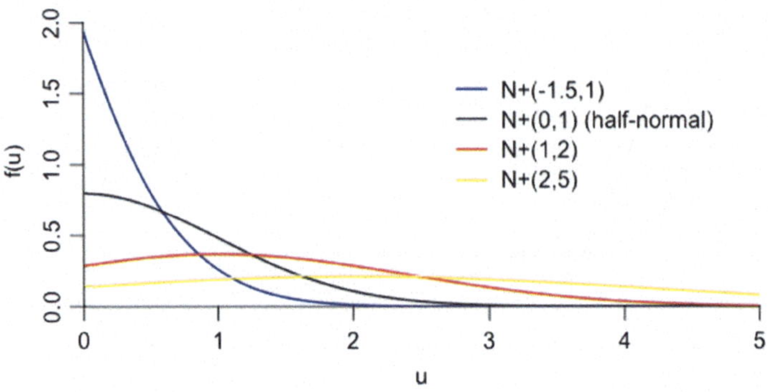

Fig. A.5 Selected truncated-normal PDFs

$(a^* - \sigma t) = -[(\mu/\sigma) + \sigma t]$, $\Phi(b^*) = \Phi(b^* - \sigma t) = 1$,

$$f_N(x|\mu, \sigma^2, 0, \infty) = \frac{1}{\sigma}\frac{\phi(z)}{\Phi(\mu/\sigma)}I(x \geq 0), \tag{A.47}$$

$$E(X) = \mu + \sigma\left(\frac{\phi(\mu/\sigma)}{\Phi(\mu/\sigma)}\right), \tag{A.48}$$

$$M(X) = \begin{cases} 0 \text{ if } \mu < 0, \\ \mu \text{ otherwise }, \end{cases} \tag{A.49}$$

$$Var(X) = \sigma^2\left[1 - \frac{\mu}{\sigma}\frac{\phi(\mu/\sigma)}{\Phi(\mu/\sigma)} - \left(\frac{\phi(\mu/\sigma)}{\Phi(\mu/\sigma)}\right)^2\right], \tag{A.50}$$

$$E(e^{tX}) = \exp\left(\mu t + \frac{\sigma^2 t^2}{2}\right)\left(\frac{\Phi[(\mu/\sigma) + \sigma t]}{\Phi(\mu/\sigma)}\right) \tag{A.51}$$

$$\text{and} \quad P(X \leq x) = \left(\frac{\Phi(z) - 1}{\Phi(\mu/\sigma)} + 1\right)I(x \geq 0). \tag{A.52}$$

If $a = 0, b = \infty$ and $\mu = 0$ (half-normal), then $\phi(\mu/\sigma) = 1/\sqrt{2\pi}$, $\Phi(\mu/\sigma) = 0.5$, and the PDF, mean, mode, variance, MGF and CDF of X are given by (A.35)–(A.40).

A.8 The Maximum of Bivariate-Normal Random Variables

Let $X_{\max} = \max\{X_1, X_2\}$ where X_1 and X_2 are bivariate-normal random variables with means μ_1 and μ_2, variances σ_1^2 and σ_2^2, and correlation coefficient ρ. If $|\rho| < 1$, then the mean and variance of $X_{\max}$ are (Kella 1986, p. 3271):

$$E(X_{\max}) = \mu_1\Phi(\mu/\sigma) + \mu_2\Phi(-\mu/\sigma) + \sigma\phi(\mu/\sigma) \tag{A.53}$$

and

$$\begin{aligned} Var(X_{\max}) &= \sigma_1^2\Phi(\mu/\sigma) + \sigma_2^2\Phi(-\mu/\sigma) \\ &\quad + [\mu\Phi(\mu/\sigma) + \sigma\phi(\mu/\sigma)][\mu\Phi(-\mu/\sigma) - \sigma\phi(\mu/\sigma)] \end{aligned} \tag{A.54}$$

where $\mu \equiv \mu_1 - \mu_2$ and $\sigma^2 \equiv \sigma_1^2 - 2\rho\sigma_1\sigma_2 + \sigma_2^2$. Finally, $P(X_1 \geq X_2) = \Phi(\mu/\sigma)$ (Kella 1986, p. 3271).

A.9 The Maximum of Independent Normal Random Variables

Let $X_{\max} = \max\{X_1, \ldots, X_S\}$ where $X_s \sim N(\mu, \sigma_s^2)$ for $s = \{1, \ldots, S\}$. If the X_s are independent, then the CDF and PDF of $X_{\max}$ are[5]

$$P(X_{\max} \leq x) = \prod_{s=1}^{S} P(X_s \leq x) = \prod_{s=1}^{S} \Phi(z_s) \tag{A.55}$$

and

$$p(x) = \left[\sum_{s=1}^{S}\left(\frac{1}{\sigma_s}\frac{\phi(z_s)}{\Phi(z_s)}\right)\right]\left[\prod_{s=1}^{S}\Phi(z_s)\right] \tag{A.56}$$

where $z_s \equiv (x - \mu)/\sigma_s$. Closed form expressions for characteristics (e.g., means and variances) of this distribution are not generally available. However, if $S = 2$, then the mean and variance are special cases of (A.53) and (A.54) corresponding to $\rho = 0$.

References

Abadir K, Magnus J (2002) Notation in econometrics: a proposal for a standard. Econometrics J 5(1):76–90

David H, Nagaraja H (2003) Order statistics, 3rd edn. Wiley, New York

Kella O (1986) On the distribution of the maximum of bivariate normal random variables with general means and variances. Commun Stat Theory Methods 15(11):3265–3276

Larson H (1982) Introduction to probability theory and statistical inference. Wiley, Singapore

Simon M (2002) Probability distributions involving Gaussian random variables: a handbook for engineers and scientists. Springer, New York

[5]The PDF is obtained by differentiating (A.55) with respect to x. Equation (A.56) agrees with David and Nagaraja (2003, p. 26, Ex. 2.3.2(a)). Both (A.55) and (A.56) agree with Simon (2002, p. 80) for the case where $S = 2$.

Author Index

C. J. O'Donnell, *Productivity and Efficiency Analysis*,
https://doi.org/10.1007/978-981-13-2984-5

Subject Index

C. J. O'Donnell, *Productivity and Efficiency Analysis*,
https://doi.org/10.1007/978-981-13-2984-5

The manufacturer's authorised representative in the EU is Springer Nature Customer Service Centre GmbH, Europaplatz 3, 69115 Heidelberg, Germany. If you have any concerns regarding our products, please contact ProductSafety@springernature.com

Printed and bound by CPI Group (UK) Ltd, Croydon, CR0 4YY
25/09/2026
02222884-0007